Food Preparation FOR THE Professional

Food Preparation FOR THE Professional

second edition

David A. Mizer

Mary Porter

Beth Sonnier
EL CENTRO COLLEGE

JOHN WILEY & SONS
New York   Chichester
Brisbane   Toronto   Singapore

Cover and interior design: Dawn L. Stanley
Production supervision: Cindy Funkhouser
Test illustration: Marilyn MacGregor
Cover photo: Marjory Dressler

Library of Congress Cataloging in Publication Data:

Mizer, David A.
  Food preparation for the professional.

  (Wiley service management series)
  Bibliography: p.
  Includes index.
  1. Quantity cookery.   I. Porter, Mary.   II. Sonnier, Beth.   III. Title.   IV. Series.

TX820.M55   1987   641.5'7   86-24630
ISBN 0-471-88303-4

Printed in the United States of America

10 9 8 7 6 5

CHAPTER-OPENING PHOTOS

Chapter 1	Farrell Grehan/Photo Researchers
Chapter 2	Fred Anderson/Black Star
Chapter 3	Courtesy W. Atlee Burpee Company
Chapter 4	Monique Manceau/Photo Researchers
Chapter 5	Dan Brinzac/Peter Arnold
Chapter 6	Courtesy Revere Copper and Brass, Inc.
Chapter 7	Courtesy Borden, Inc.
Chapter 8	Courtesy Revere Copper and Brass, Inc.
Chapter 9	Courtesy Borden, Inc.
Chapter 10	Courtesy Mazola Corn Oil
Chapter 11	Courtesy The Rice Council
Chapter 12	Courtesy National Live Stock and Meat Board
Chapter 13	Courtesy American Egg Board
Chapter 14	Courtesy Mazola Corn Oil
Chapter 15	Michael Stuckey/Comstock
Chapter 16	Courtesy Borden, Inc.
Chapter 17	Courtesy National Restaurant Association
Chapter 18	Courtesy National Restaurant Association

Printed and bound by the Arcata Graphics Company

THIS BOOK IS DEDICATED TO
RIETA, FRANK, JOHN
AND EVANGELINE

THIS new edition of our basic "book for the cook" adds several new features that give depth and clarity to the original text. It provides many new recipes, each carefully chosen to illustrate a cooking principle or process or technique. It contains two new chapters—on baking and desserts—to round out the story of kitchen production. It includes metric measures for those who are ready to use them. It adds learning and teaching aids in each chapter—objectives, a summary, a cook's vocabulary, and discussion questions.

In addition to these new features, several chapters are reorganized and combined to provide a smoothly developing story of basic food preparation. The text is updated, simple nutrition information is introduced, and some new trends in cuisine are briefly explored.

Yet this is still the same book—a complete text providing the basics of food preparation in concise, compact form, geared to the beginning student and written in a clear, informal, readable style. It has the same focus, the same objectives and philosophy, and the same scope as the first edition.

Focus

This book comes straight out of today's food-service kitchens. Its focus is on *doing*—what to do, how to do it, and why. It is designed to train beginning students in the principles, techniques, and skills needed to prepare food for production. Whatever the student's future role in the industry, this kind of firsthand knowledge is essential to success.

The text centers its teaching around the actual preparation of different kinds of foods. Not only does it give specific instructions for basic dishes; it also explains clearly, in everyday terms, what is going on in the pot or the oven or the mixing bowl as raw foods are turned into finished menu items. Thus the student can absorb the principles of cooking in terms of real food products and actual cooking processes. Step-by-step instructions and illustrations explain techniques essential to the dish being prepared. The student's learning

Preface

experiences, repeated and reinforced as the chapters unfold, build into a real-world body of knowledge and understanding.

Objectives and philosphy

Our aim is to provide the student with the following essentials:

1. *A thorough grasp of basic cooking principles and techniques.* We want the student to gain a real understanding of cooking. The industry needs people who not only can follow a recipe but also know how the recipe works and why. By reducing cooking to its simplest terms—basic recipes, basic ratios or proportions, basic cooking principles—we can show how ingredients in a given dish function to produce that dish. Then it becomes easy to understand not only that dish but others made the same way. Cooking becomes not a bewildering succession of individual recipes but a fascinating series of elaborations on a few simple themes.

2. *A vocabulary of cooking, processing, and menu terms, with precise definitions and pronunciations.* We want to equip the student with the tools for quick communication and easy understanding, which are often missing in the interchange between supervisors and workers in food-service kitchens. Well-defined terms, correctly used, will smooth both communications and relationships—up, down, and sideways.

3. *A working knowledge of the foods, equipment, and methods of preparation in common use in today's kitchens.* We want students not only to be familiar with this basic core of information but also to know how to put foods and equipment and methods to use, how to work with them, how to choose between them. It is useless to know *what* if you do not also know *how, when, where* and *why.*

4. *A feeling for the real world of food preparation and for the practical application of classroom learning.* We want students to absorb information as it relates to the working world rather than to see it as rules and facts coming from the printed page. We use realistic problems and settings and give specific detail—how to deal with a sauce that is too thick or too thin, how a broiler cook sets up for cooking steaks to order. We talk about many kinds of operations and about different responses to differing conditions—different styles of cooking and service, different clienteles, different menus and cuisines.

5. *Knowledge of quality standards and a sense of pride and pleasure in producing good food efficiently and presenting it attractively.* We want students to know what excellence is and to set their sights high, even though they won't achieve perfection on the first try or even on the tenth. Though time, costs, and other on-the-job realities often require compromises, the goal is always quality, the best quality circumstances will allow. To set standards of mediocrity in a textbook would surely turn out students who did not meet even these standards, and inferior food has no potential for sale or profit. So we teach students tastes and textures and eye appeal and mise en place, along with such practicalities as batch cooking and portion control and converting recipes. Along the way we hope to convey some of the fascination of food and cooking and the challenge of creating good things to eat.

Scope

The text covers all phases of food preparation—the raw products, processing, cooking, and the safe handling, holding, and storing of each major category of food; the building of flavor, body, and texture; quality measures for finished dishes; visual presentation; planning and setting up; on-job production; menu planning. There are special discussions on many subjects not normally found in depth in other food texts—mise en place, metrics, prepreparation, flavoring and seasoning, presentation, convenience foods, kitchen communication and paperwork. There is a brief history of kitchens, cooking, and cuisine, and anecdotes from the past are interspersed throughout, to create awareness of our rich culinary heritage. For the serious culinarian there are glimpses into advanced cooking skills—special soups and sauces, special baking techniques, buffet presentation—showing how special skills follow logically from basic principles and techniques.

The text explains the scientific side of cooking in the simplest terms. These explanations are highlighted at points where a principle becomes relevant to a cooking process—emulsion along with butter sauces, gelatinization with the making of roux. This enables the student not only to understand the why of a process but also to use the knowledge in making other dishes. Principles illustrated in this simple, relevant way build a practical foundation for students going on to food-theory courses.

Though the book's point of view is the cook's point of view and its scope is deliberately limited to the cook's sphere, it teaches principles of good management from the bottom up—quality in raw and finished products, good planning and production techniques, sanitation, service to the customer, and the faithful carrying out of management policies. There is also a wealth of detailed information on foods and cooking that every manager should know. The book's content thus builds a good foundation for future supervisors and managers as well as beginning Escoffiers.

Learning and teaching aids

In addition to the chapter objectives, summaries, vocabulary, and questions, the book includes many features designed to help the learning–teaching process:

Recipes—prototypes of the most important kinds of dishes—provide the basis for text discussion. A repeating T format is used to show how ingredients function together to produce a dish. Additional mini-recipes show how the pattern of a basic dish can be applied and reapplied to provide endless menu versatility.

Pictures—more than 300 of them—illustrate things words alone cannot convey—techniques, equipment, sequence of steps, specific foods, food cuts, plate layouts, temperatures, proportions, and so on. Always functional, they are integral parts of the text, amplifying and reinforcing its teachings.

How-to-do-it features—often text-and-picture combinations—show how to cut with a french knife, how to use a pastry bag, how to shuck an oyster, saddleback a lobster tail, truss a bird, flip eggs, make an omelet, how to do a score of other things.

Tables and charts, designed specifically for this text, present valuable reference information in easy-to-use form.

Terminology is highlighted. Terms of the trade, in boldface, are precisely defined and phonetically pronounced at their first appearance. Key concepts are fully discussed for greater understanding.

A *glossary* gathers all the text terms together for ready reference and adds others the student is likely to encounter in reading or on the job.

A *bibliography,* organized by subject, suggests additional resources for teaching, research, and reading pleasure.

An *instructor's manual* outlines points of emphasis for teaching each chapter. It also suggests lab exercises and enrichment activities to further the student's gradual progression toward insight, understanding, and mastery of techniques and skills. The manual also supplies test questions and answers for each chapter as well as transparency masters for key figures from the text.

ACKNOWLEDGMENTS

We have been lucky to have the input of many people in this endeavor. We were especially fortunate in having the expert assistance of Jo Marie Powers of the University of Guelph in providing the appropriate metric measures in our recipes and text. We have been equally lucky in tapping into the expertise of Richard Lavallee, baking instructor at El Centro College and long-time pastry chef, who reviewed the two baking chapters. And we are indebted to another expert, Dr. Frances Hitt, R.D., of El Centro College for advice and counsel on matters relating to dietitians, dietetics, and hospital kitchens.

We wish to express our thanks to our reviewers for their many suggestions of both substance and detail: George Dragisity, University of Houston, Houston, Texas; John Farris, Lansing Community College, Lansing, Michigan; John D. Hedley, Los Angeles Trade & Technical College; Marian E. Jardine, R.D., State University College, Oneonta, New York; Richard Lavallee, El Centro College, Dallas, Texas; Geoffrey R. Lough, George Brown College, Toronto, Ontario; Terry Panella, Cerritos College, Norwalk, Connecticut; Jo Marie Powers, University of Guelph, Guelph, Ontario;

Jean D. Schwab of Szabo Food Service Company, Dallas, Texas; Edward Sherwin, Essex Community College, Baltimore County, Maryland; Carol Wohlleben, Kirkwood Community College, Cedar Rapids, Iowa.

We of course remain responsible for any errors remaining in the text as well as for the book's philosophy and point of view.

We wish to thank the many people in the industry who helped us develop our thumbnail sketches of different kinds of kitchens. We are also indebted to colleagues at El Centro who offered general support and to the students who tested the recipes. And we thank Jeane Pursur and Yvonne Donaldson for hours and hours and hours of typing under deadline pressures.

Finally we want to express our thanks to our Wiley editor, Judy Joseph, for taking on this project and for her guidance and support in helping us bring it to fruition.

David Mizer
Mary Porter
Beth Sonnier

Contents

15 THE BAKESHOP 377

16 DESSERTS 409

17 OUT OF THE LAB AND INTO PRODUCTION 445

Food Preparation FOR THE Professional

The Kitchen

"**THERE'S** a romance to it—and maybe something a little bit crazy. . . ." This is the owner–manager of a restaurant talking about the food-service industry. His face, his voice, the sparkle in his eyes tell you that he is a man who loves what he is doing, that all the unpredictables and problems and demands on his time ("*unreal,* sometimes!") are worth it—maybe even part of the romance. "It's a whole new world every day," he says, with a mixture of frustration and relish. "And of course there's a profit to be made."

"There is a fascination about hospital food service—at least for me," says a dietitian who is tops in her profession. "I get involved in other aspects of dietetics—teaching, research—but I'm always being drawn back to hospital kitchens in some way—designing them, placing students, getting involved in day-to-day operations."

"It's the creativity you have," says a sous-chef in a large hotel, "taking some plain thing like a chicken or a piece of sole or beef and preparing an elegant meal, and the satisfaction you get when somebody tells you, 'Hey, that was delicious!' I've always been fascinated with it. I started when I was 14."

"Food service is an industry where people can really make a difference." The woman speaking manages an in-plant feeding unit serving a thousand meals a day. "I can make a difference, the cook can, the cashier can—we make the difference in whether this restaurant is good or bad. I think that's why I like it, why other people like it. We have an effect on what we're doing, and we can see it happen."

Whatever the lure of food service as a career, whatever your own special career goals, it is important to understand cooking and to learn basic food preparation techniques. Even if you are headed for a management career and never expect to cook professionally, a knowledge of cooking will be very important to you. You can't write a job description for a cook, or hire one intelligently, unless you understand the skills needed and how to judge them. You need to know how a product should look and taste when it comes from a new cook

1

you have just hired, and what to do about it if it isn't right. You should be able to fill in for the cook in an emergency. (One manager in such a situation discovered she didn't even know how to turn on the gas ovens.) You ought to have done some cooking yourself in order to plan a day's production, so that you know how long things take and what you are asking of your employees. ("When they give me the story they don't have enough time," says the in-plant feeding manager, " 'Okay,' I say, 'I can do it in half the time—watch me!' And they know that I can.")

"Dietitians need training in cooking as well as in food science, in the presentation of food and the taste of it," the hospital dietitian says. "We get engrossed in the scientific aspects— the sodium in a piece of meat or potassium in milk—and we may produce something that is totally antiseptic and sanitized and it may not be fit to eat. We need the cooking knowledge as well as the science."

If your goal is culinary skill, if you aspire to master all the arts of cooking, a good understanding of basic principles will help you on your way. It will enable you to make more sense of each of the many jobs you will have as you acquire the experience necessary for true mastery. You will know what to look for as you observe skilled cooks, and you can ask intelligent questions to get the most out of your education on the job.

After completing this chapter you should be able to

- Discuss the basic features of kitchen organization in today's food-service facilities.
- Compare and contrast kitchens in different types of facilities.
- Describe the duties and responsibilities usually associated with typical kitchen positions.
- Trace the development of quantity cooking methods, equipment, traditions, and cuisines from early times to the present.

CHARACTERISTIC FEATURES OF FOOD-SERVICE KITCHENS

There are many different types of food-service establishments. Most common are the commercial restaurant, the hospital kitchen, the fast-food service, the coffee shop, the school cafeteria, airline catering, banquet catering, in-plant feeding, and the large hotel, which may include several kinds of service. There are also many food services that do not fit into any category.

Although there are many types of kitchens and every kitchen is different in some way, the tasks performed in these kitchens are similar. The differences arise from the kinds of meals served, the numbers served, the menus, and the production and service goals. But kitchens are all doing the same thing—preparing food for service—so all are alike in certain basic ways.

Consider the following:

- The kitchen is divided into **stations,** or preparation areas, according to the types of food prepared.
- There is equipment appropriate to the menu and to the number of meals to be served.
- There is a staff structure or hierarchy with clearly defined lines of authority and responsibility.
- Each job requires a certain set of skills.

Let us look more closely at some of these features of food-service kitchens.

Kitchen stations

Most kitchens, even small ones, have at least two stations, one for hot food and one for cold. Large operations may have more, the number and type depending on the menu and the volume of production. There are no formulas governing the number of stations or the way they are divided. It depends on what is most efficient for each operation.

Each station typically has its own equipment, its own storage areas, its own **station head,** or supervisor, and its own staff. In effect each station is a little production department that is semi-independent within the larger kitchen structure.

Equipment

Each station of the kitchen has the equipment it needs to process, cook, and hold the menu items assigned to it in the volume needed. Again there is no formula for what equipment is found at any given station. It depends not only on the menu and the volume of production but also on whether the kitchen makes everything from scratch or buys preprepared convenience foods. A kitchen buying processed potatoes, for example, would have no need for an electric potato peeler.

At times the same piece of equipment may be shared by more than one station. This will depend on such factors as menu, volume, number of workers, schedule, and sometimes even health and sanitation regulations.

Staff structure

Each kitchen staff is organized in terms of who has responsibility for what and who reports to whom. Many kitchens have this structure of relationships plotted out in a formal organization chart such as those in Figures 1-1 to 1-6. There may be as many variations in staff structure as there are kitchens. But there is always structure, and the lines of responsibility and authority must be clearly understood on all sides if the kitchen is to function properly.

At this point let us look at some real kitchens in different kinds of food-service establishments. You will see how they are similar and how and why they differ. Then we will come back to the staff and examine the different positions and the skills and experience they require.

SOME TYPICAL KITCHENS

A fast-food operation

Let us begin our tour with the most familiar kind of operation—a fast-food service. We're visiting an actual facility at the lunch hour. Busy and crowded as it is, we are greeted quickly and cordially and our order is taken and delivered in minutes. Fast food is a good name for it.

The kitchen in this facility is a shiny display of tile and stainless steel projecting an image of sanitation in silver. A large grill, a deep fryer, and a furniture-sized toaster are the only pieces of cooking equipment. A whole crew of workers moves in synchronized fashion to cook, assemble, and serve the orders, each person carrying out one small step of the task. Behind them all is the manager, keeping everyone supplied, shifting people about as needed, solving problems as they arise. The result is speed, high volume, and happy customers.

How do they do it? The secret is simple. Everything is premeasured, precut, preportioned, preprocessed, electronically controlled, precisely timed. Custom equipment does the cooking. It is practically person-proof, requiring only that things be put in it or on it and taken out or off again in response to electronic signals. Substituting precision for creative cooking, the system turns out the standardized products its customers love.

A fast-food operation, whether it is burgers or barbecue or chicken or pizza or sandwiches or fish or whatever, is food preparation reduced to its simplest terms. It typically has a limited menu requiring a minimum of cooking equipment and cooking skills. Precut and preportioned raw products reduce labor to a minimum. Production is divided into a series of small tasks anyone can be trained to do.

A fast-food operation is typically one unit of a chain, all alike in menu, equipment, operation, product, quality, and image. The parent corporation provides the facility and the product, sets the standards, and trains both managers and crew. In some cases unit managers report to corporate management; in others the units are franchises whose managers function as independent owners.

Staff structure in each unit is simple: a unit manager, an assistant manager, and a crew reporting directly to the manager (Figure 1-1). All are thoroughly trained in every procedure of cooking and service and are interchangeable on the job. Thus during rush periods any crew member can shift from one task to another without missing a beat. After the rush the crew will drop to a handful, doubling up on duties and taking care of cleanup as well.

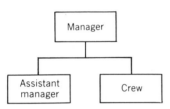

FIGURE 1-1. Organization chart for a fast-food unit.

A hotel food service

Now let us move to the other extreme in size and complexity and visit the kitchens of a large hotel in a big city. This hotel (also an actual operation) has a huge main kitchen that prepares all the food for a high-volume banquet service. Satellite kitchens serving various restaurant areas supplement the main-kitchen production.

The minute you step into the main kitchen you are in a special world. Big as it is, it is crowded with people and food and movement and clatter. Sizes and quantities boggle the mind of the uninitiated visitor: 2500 servings of broccoli . . . steaks by the hundreds . . . a 20-gallon pot of soup . . . 40 liters of mayonnaise, one day's supply. The sights, scents, and sizzle of steaks, soups, and sauces seduce the senses and quicken the appetite. How can there be so many thin people among all these cooks?

A bank of ranges, ovens, fryers, grills, and broilers identifies the area, or station, where the hot foods are prepared—roasts, braised meats, steaks, chops, fried chicken, fish, eggs, sauces. In any full-service kitchen this is the backbone of the operation, its main production station. It has its own supervisor, or station head, and its own team of station cooks and helpers as well as its own special equipment and storage areas. The sauce cook, or **saucier** (so-see-ay), is the station head in this hotel. In other hotel kitchens the head of this station may have a different specialty and a different title.

On either side of the range area are two more large production areas, the soup and vegetable station and the cold-food station. They too are separate departments, each with its own equipment, storage areas, station head, and staff. In this kitchen the cold-food station is called the **garde manger** (gard mon-zhay) **department**. It produces all the cold food except pastries and ices—the salads and salad dressings, fruits for breakfast and dessert, cold meats and cheeses, canapés and cold hors d'oeuvre, buffet platters, decorated molds, fat sculptures, ice carvings, display foods. The head of this department is called the **chef garde manger,** the classical title for this culinary specialty. It represents a high level of skill in preparing elaborate cold foods and food displays. In a smaller operation offering simpler foods, this area might be called the **salad station** or the **pantry.**

Room service has a station to itself—a complete kitchen-within-a-kitchen laid out for the use of one cook. Another station belongs to the hotel butcher—something of a rarity these days. He breaks down (cuts up) wholesale meat cuts into the special cuts required by the hotel menu. He also bones chickens, skins and fillets fish, opens oysters, watches over live lobsters, turns meat scraps into cocktail meatballs. But he is one of the last of his kind. Pretrimmed and preportioned meats are rapidly making the hotel butcher obsolete.

Another unusual department of this kitchen is the **pastry shop** (most hotels and restaurants buy their baked goods ready-made). The holding areas for this station are like scenes from a dream: a five-tiered and pillared wedding cake decked with the most delicate flowers and intricate scrollwork . . . a huge bar-mitzvah cake with the young man's name and tomorrow's date iced in thin tall lettering as distinctive as an artist's signature . . . cakes in various stages: ready for layering, ready for icing, ready for decorating, ready to be topped with ice cream and meringue for baked alaska.

In the satellite kitchen for the hotel's expensive dinner restaurant is a set of production stations of a different kind. Here each menu dish is prepared to the diner's order just before it is served. This is known as **a la carte cookery,** and these are a la carte production stations.

Each station has its own cook, highly skilled, highly specialized—a broiler cook, a fish cook, a vegetable cook, a saucier, a garde manger, a soufflé cook. Each station has its own equipment, appropriate to the dishes its cook prepares. In a single evening some of them cook for as many as 500 diners, one or a few portions at a time. The action is fast, the tension is high, the timing is critical. Perfect coordination with serving personnel is absolutely essential to get each dish to the diner at its peak of quality—worthy of its price tag. To the onlooker it seems impossible, but they do it every night.

All the food production for the hotel—banquet service, restaurants, employee cafeteria—is the responsibility of one person, the **executive chef** (*chef exécutif* or *directeur des cuisines*). This is entirely a management role, complete with a private office, a secretary, and a handsome salary. But this chef came up through the kitchens and knows every station firsthand. Such intimate knowledge of food and cooking pays off every day in a hundred ways. Where so many different things are going on, where every day is different (maybe 500 meals on a really slow day and 5000 in one day a week later), where needs change

from hour to hour and the unpredictable happens frequently, only someone who knows cooking, cooks, and kitchens inside out is capable of running the show.

The executive chef reports to the food and beverage director, who has final responsibility not only for the food side of this food-service operation but for the service side and the beverage side as well.

Below the executive chef is the **sous-chef** (French for under-chef, pronounced soo-shef), who is production supervisor for the entire operation. The sous-chef is also a skilled cook and manager. Below the sous-chef are the **banquet chef,** the station heads, the chef supervisors for the restaurant kitchens, and the cafeteria head.

An organization chart for this kitchen is given in Figure 1-2. Though it is for a specific kitchen, it is fairly typical of a hotel doing this volume of business. Station divisions may vary from one hotel to another; titles may vary; but the organizational structure is similar. Smaller hotel kitchen staffs may be simpler versions of the same pattern.

A hospital kitchen

Let us now visit a different type of large, complex operation—a hospital kitchen serving about 3000 meals a day.

One is immediately struck by its antiseptic cleanliness (again this is a real operation). Not only does it look and feel clean, but clues to the importance of sanitation are everywhere. The storeroom is filled with supplies of paper dishes: using them avoids the handling of china and glass, with all its possibilities for contamination. An entire room is devoted to hosing down and sanitizing the carts on which dirty trays have been stacked. The aides who dish out the food wear plastic gloves.

This kitchen is in many ways a simpler version of the hotel kitchen. There are three production stations—hot foods, salads, and baking—each having its own special equipment and storage areas and its own staff. Much of the equipment is like the hotel's, and

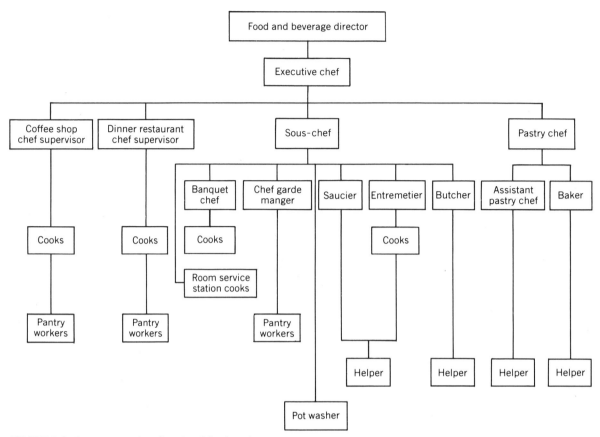

FIGURE 1-2. Organization chart for a hotel food service.

so is the staff organization—at least on the production level. The two kitchens even have some of the same problems to solve: both, for example, must deliver hot and cold foods to distant serving places.

Most of the differences in the two kitchens come from a single important element that shapes every food-service operation: the clientele. In the hospital the food is prepared primarily for people who are ill. In the hotel it is prepared primarily for out-of-town visitors with money to spend or for people celebrating a special occasion. The difference means two very different kinds of menus.

In the hospital kitchen nutrition and diet therapy are primary concerns. Meals are carefully planned to provide a balanced diet. In addition there are several versions of the patient menu to fit special needs—a liquid diet, a low-fat diet, a low-sodium diet, a children's diet, and so on. Since the right food is part of making the patient well, the kitchen works closely with the medical staff. Standardized recipes are scrupulously followed. Doctors' orders are carried out to the letter.

Since patients in a hospital eat all their meals there day after day, the menu changes daily. Contrast this with the hotel menu, where the offerings are the same every day. The hospital cook's assignments will change daily; the hotel cook will generally make the same things every day.

The organization chart for this hospital kitchen is shown in Figure 1-3. On the produc-

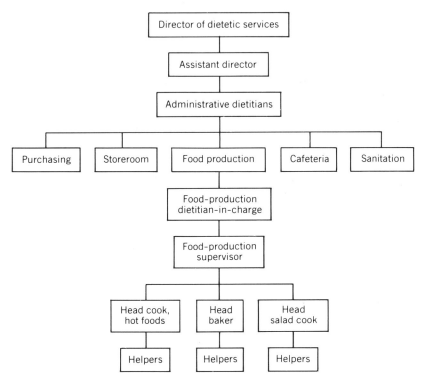

FIGURE 1-3. Organization chart for a hospital food service.

tion level it is similar to that of the hotel kitchen. There is a production supervisor, and skilled cooks head the stations, assisted by workers with varying degrees of skill. The skills required of the station heads include the ability to follow a standardized recipe to produce a quality product and the capacity to supervise the workers on the station.

You'll notice a number of dietitians on the organization chart. These positions require extensive training tailored to the special requirements of feeding the sick and the special problems of hospital administration.

At the top of the organization is the director. This position is comparable in kitchen authority to the hotel's food and beverage director. It includes such additional responsibilities as purchasing and sanitation.

One senses calm and order in this kitchen. Perhaps it comes from the high degree of or-

ganization. Perhaps it is due to the nature of the operation—after all, demand is steady and predictable for the most part, and most problems are foreseeable. Perhaps it reflects the administrative skills of its top people. Perhaps it is all these things.

A specialty restaurant

Next let us look at a specialty restaurant. This is a broad term applying to almost any commercial restaurant that features a special menu. It might be a steakhouse, a seafood restaurant, or one serving continental cuisine, or the best barbecue in town, or home-style cooking. It usually has table service and an atmosphere that goes with the type of food. The fast-food operation is in a way a specialty restaurant. But its stripped-down service, simplified production, and limited menu place it in a category of its own.

The small specialty restaurant we have chosen (another real place) features extra-good food at modest prices in an atmosphere a local columnist described as "casual class." It has 130 seats and serves an average of 250 meals a day.

The kitchen would fit into one corner of one station of the big hotel or hospital kitchen. Its equipment is a mixture of old reliable and shiny new. It has two stations, cold and hot, and two cooks, one in charge of each station. A third staff member works as a prep person under the hot-food cook during prepreparation time and doubles as dish and pot washer during the service period. On weekends a part-time cook backs up both cooks during the serving period.

We have timed our visit for the dinner hour. In spite of the small staff the tiny kitchen seems full of people. What with a dishwasher and pot sink fitted in along one wall, and waiters coming in and going out, there are few square inches of space unused. But the layout has been well planned, the traffic patterns carefully calculated. The kitchen works.

Everything is ready that can be prepared ahead. A steam table holds hot foods ready for service. The few items cooked to order are done quickly with a minimum of motion. Though the pace is fast, things move smoothly. These cooks are skilled, with several years of experience and training behind them. They have to be experts to keep up with the orders.

In this small operation there is no separate production supervisor. The kitchen staff reports directly to the restaurant manager. The manager knows cooks and cooking firsthand, though she plays no part in the kitchen operations other than to schedule the day's production. She also does the purchasing, plans the menu specials, and supervises the service personnel. Figure 1-4 shows the organization of this operation.

Every specialty restaurant is different in staff and equipment, because its menu is different. Its volume makes a difference too. But

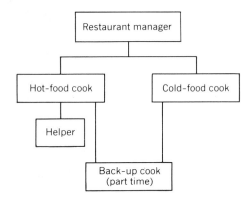

FIGURE 1-4. Organization chart for a specialty restaurant.

its organization will not vary greatly from the pattern of this small restaurant, though there may be more cooks, more helpers, more stations.

An airline-catering kitchen

The airline-catering kitchen we have chosen to visit works right around the clock seven days a week, preparing some 25,000 meals a day for an airline that averages 150 flights a day. It is one of a chain of 28 kitchens at airports across the country, serving some 50 airlines in all.

Each outgoing plane must have on board the correct number and types of meals for all the passengers, packed in special holding or cooking equipment that fits into each aircraft galley (there are seven different types). Every plane *must* depart on time: it has a departure slot in the air traffic control pattern and a landing slot in another city at a specific time. For the kitchen, this turns each day into a series of 150 inflexible deadlines.

The huge stainless-steel and tile kitchen contains two food-production areas—hot food and cold food—each with production and storage equipment similar to what we have seen in other high-volume operations. But in this kitchen, when people talk about equipment, they are usually referring to the equipment that travels on the planes—the holding and heating and cooking equipment they must custom-load for each flight, the small square plates they must pack the meals in, and the trays they must set up for each passenger. Equipment is the focal point of this kitchen, and the Equipment and Sanitation department (E&S) is the heartbeat of the operation, controlling the vital flow.

E&S personnel unload the carts from the incoming planes, wash and sanitize the dishes and carts, and put everything in readiness to be packed and sent out again, usually within hours. It is up to this department to see that the equipment that must go out has come in and that there is enough of the right kind of everything to service each scheduled flight. The food department packs the equipment with its products. The Ramp and Dispatch department transports and installs the equipment on the outbound planes and brings back the used equipment to repeat the cycle.

The cold-food production area seems full of people—almost more people than food. Each worker performs one small step—washing lettuce, destemming strawberries, slicing roast beef, breaking parsley into sprigs of a specified size. For assembly, a moving belt carries the dishes for a menu item past assemblers, each of whom places one ingredient in its specified position on the dish. The moving belt is the caterer's version of plating or dishout, which is usually done in other kitchens by the cook. At the end of the line each dish is checked, wrapped, loaded into a waiting cart, and rolled off to a cooler to await departure.

The hot-food area is much smaller, since only the entrées for the first-class passengers are made from scratch. They are prepared in 100-portion batches, assembled and chillpacked in individual portions, and held in refrigerators until use. Entrées for coach passengers are bought frozen, prepared by vendors to airline specifications.

Two to three hours before flight time, the exact number and kinds of meals for each plane are moved from the refrigerator to the ramp area. Here another moving belt is activated, carrying the trays that will be served to the passengers. Assemblers position each tray mat, napkin, cup, salad, dressing, dessert, roll, butter—everything but the hot entrée, which will be added to the tray when it is served. These trays are then packed in dry ice and loaded into the equipment that fits into the plane's galley.

The hot entrées are also packed into equipment that fits the plane for which they are headed. If that equipment can heat or cook, the food is packed cold; otherwise it is heated, packed hot, and kept hot until service two to five hours later. Both hot and cold equipment are then loaded onto the waiting truck that will service that particular flight.

Delivery to the plane completes the caterer's service goal. The caterer serves the airline rather than the individual customer. In fact, each airline it serves plans its own menus, develops its own recipes, and sets the quality standards and the budget. The caterer simply meets the airline's specifications.

Figure 1-5 shows how this huge food-service operation is organized. The food manager is comparable to a sous-chef or production manager. The ramp and dispatch manager and the equipment and sanitation manager have comparable responsibility in their own spheres. The sanitation side of the E&S is as important as the equipment responsibility because of the many problems of handling and holding such large amounts of food safely under potentially hazardous conditions. The operations manager at the top of the chart would correspond to the food and beverage director. The food-production supervisors are comparable to a sous-chef in a hotel kitchen, but unless there is an emergency they seldom do any food preparation.

Part of the challenge of everyone's job is the need to adjust to the unexpected. A situation can change dramatically minutes before flight time if a canceled flight from another airline adds an extra 200 passengers. The weather in airports 3000 miles away can play havoc with schedules, force changes in the type of plane, and turn the best-laid plans into a game of musical chairs.

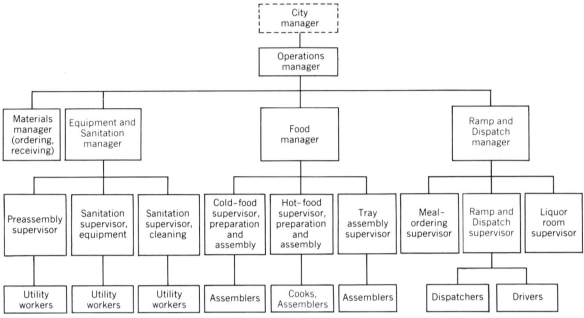

FIGURE 1-5. Organization chart for an airline-catering service.

Overall, this is an intricate, complex, sophisticated operation. Everything is systematized and prescribed to the last detail and the airline calls the tune. Yet system alone cannot do the job, and the caterer must remain flexible and sensitive if the operation is to meet the service goal.

A cruise ship's kitchen

The cruise ship we are visiting makes its way from one warm-weather port to another on cruises of three to seven days. It carries 1000 passengers. Food—really good food— is part of its tourist package and a major feature of its entertainment and shipboard activities. Deck luncheons, midnight buffets, morning snacks, afternoon snacks, bouillon, teas, parading and singing waiters, and of course breakfast, lunch, and a six-course dinner all happen every day. Of its crew of 500, a full 200 are food-service personnel—80 in production, 80 in service, and 40 in sanitation.

The kitchen is busy from morning till morning: cleanup after the 1 A.M. buffet is fin-

ished only a few hours before breakfast prep begins. At noon and at dinnertime the kitchen is a wall-to-wall buzz of activity as 1000 people are served in two sittings with a choice of six or seven entrées prepared to order. It is like serving two banquets back to back twice a day, but with the guests selecting the food.

A tour through the kitchen reveals the same banks of ovens, banks of ranges, steam tables, and full array of equipment found in any other kitchen. Since all baking is done aboard ship (no ready-made bread or pastries), there is a full complement of baking ovens. A separate kitchen prepares three meals a day for the crew and serves as a training kitchen.

Some unusual features of this type of food service may not be apparent to the casual eye: they have to do with the high priority given to sanitation. Since all food for passengers and crew originates in the same production and storage areas, a single instance of food-borne disease could affect everyone aboard. Consequently standards are high and are continu-

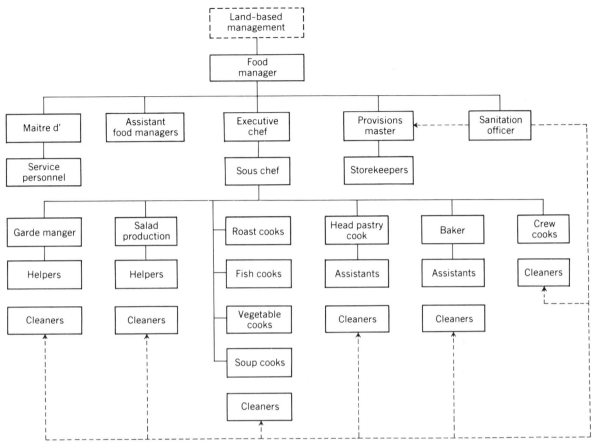

FIGURE 1-6. Organization chart for a cruise-ship food service.

ously enforced. To reduce the spread of bacteria from one food to another, production stations are more strictly separated than those in land-based operations, and separation of foods in storage is stricter. There are more hand sinks—one within 20 feet of every kitchen worker. Everything is scrubbed and sanitized from top to bottom after every meal—walls, floors, refrigerators, equipment, even the racks in the ovens. Leftovers are forbidden.

A sanitation officer ranks high on this organization chart (Figure 1-6). Through a large staff committed solely to sanitation, this manager's control and influence pervade the pro-

duction and storage areas. The person in this job also has charge of chlorinating the drinking water, since there is no reliable source.

Most of the staff structure is similar to that of many land-based operations. The position of food manager is like that of a food and beverage director without the beverage responsibility. The assistant managers relieve the executive chef and sous-chef of responsibilities they would have in other kitchens. They are responsible for the smooth flow of production from storage areas to kitchen and from kitchen to dining room, and they see that all activities begin and end as they should. Perhaps the most challenging of their duties is the role of expediter—getting the a la carte entrées from the cooks to the servers at the height of the luncheon and dinner service.

The station cooks are all fully trained. The luxury of an ample labor force offers opportunity to prepare classical dishes found only at great price in the best hotels, or to experiment with new dishes and new production techniques.

Everybody works 12 hours a day or more, seven days a week, except when the ship is in port. The work is difficult and the hours are long, but the ship's vacation atmosphere is stimulating, and when the passengers are off the ship sightseeing and shopping there are chances to take a few free hours and explore ports in foreign lands.

Why kitchens differ

Once you have examined several kitchens you can begin to see that the menu and the service goal are the two most important factors dictating the physical organization, the equipment, the staff, and the structure of the organization chart. In the cruise ship's kitchen, for example, you have special stations for dish-out in order to feed large numbers of people simultaneously. In the airline-catering kitchen, on the other hand, you have a transportation department because the meals must be transported to aircraft for service at a later time. Hotel and hospital kitchens are also concerned with delivering foods at different times and places.

KITCHEN STAFF

The jobs and duties of staff members also vary from kitchen to kitchen, and so do the titles attached to the jobs. But certain positions and titles do recur throughout the industry. Here are some of the most common positions, with a general definition for each and a place in the typical kitchen hierarchy.

An **executive chef** (*chef exécutif*) is a person in charge of the administration of the kitchens of a large food service such as that of a hotel. In the hierarchy of the kitchen the executive chef is typically one level above the sous-chef or production manager, though sometimes the executive chef and the production manager are the same person. On the other hand, larger operations often have an executive sous-chef along with several other sous-chefs.

The position of executive chef carries overall responsibility for all aspects of production, for the quality of the products served, for hiring and managing the kitchen staff, for controlling costs and meeting budgets, and for coordinating with departments not directly involved in food production. Duties may also include creating new menus, purchasing, costing, and scheduling of employees. This is a position requiring extensive training and experience, both as a cook and as a manager.

A **working chef** (*chef de cuisine*) is a person in charge of a kitchen who spends part of the time managing but most of the time actually working at production tasks. This position would typically be found in a small kitchen having a small staff.

The **food-production manager** is the person responsible for all levels of food handling, production, and often service of food. The exact amount of control depends on the size of the operation. This is the key position in any kitchen operation. Other typical titles are kitchen manager, food services manager, food manager, production supervisor, kitchen supervisor, to name a few. In a large kitchen having an executive chef the sous-chef would be the production manager.

Below these positions in the kitchen hierarchy are the station heads—the *chefs de partie* (shef de par-tee), as they are called in classical terminology. Each is in charge of a particular area of production. In the classical kitchen team (*brigade de cuisine*—bree-gahd de kwee-zeen) you might have the following positions.

- **Sauce chef** (*saucier*—so-see-ay), responsible for sauces and sauce-related dishes.

The saucier may also be the sous-chef, especially in smaller establishments.

- **Fish cook** (*poissonnier*—pwa-sawn-yay), responsible for all fish dishes.
- **Vegetable cook** (*entremetier*—on-tra-met-yay), responsible for the preparation of vegetables.
- **Soup cook** (*potager*—poh-ta-zhay), responsible for the preparation of soups and stocks.
- **Roast cook** (*rôtisseur*—ro-tee-sur), responsible for roasted and braised meats and meat dishes.
- **Broiler cook** (*grillardin*—gree-yar-dan), responsible for grilled and broiled meats, seafood, and poultry.
- **Pantry chef** (*chef garde manger*—gard mon-zhay), responsible for the preparation of all cold foods.
- **Pastry chef** (*pâtissier*—pa-tees-yay), responsible for the preparation of pastries, desserts, and other baked goods such as breads, rolls, and muffins.
- **Relief cook** (*tournant*—toor-non), also called **swing cook** or **rounds cook,** a cook with all-round skills and constantly changing duties who relieves any of the other positions in the kitchen.

These positions are defined here in a classical sense. In the real world they are combined, altered, and adapted to fit the specific goals of the individual operation. Typical examples combine two or more positions—soup and fish cook, vegetable and soup cook, and so on.

The station head, or **chef de partie,** typically has charge of all production and all staff of the department. That staff may be one person (himself or herself), or it may consist of station cooks and helpers of varying degrees of skill. Each station head must be fully skilled in the preparation of every dish made by the station. Station heads must also have administrative skills. Each must be able to plan and carry out production schedules for the station, supervise the workers, and train each worker in the skills required.

Farther down the ladder, a **chef** is a person in charge of either a production task or a production station. The term has a broad variety of applications, and there is little consistency in the meaning attached to it. It depends on the particular operation and on the rest of the title—pastry chef, executive chef, chef de partie, and so on. Often a kitchen having only one cook will refer to that person as "the chef."

A **cook** is any person responsible for the preparation of food. This title has broad application: it may refer to persons who are accomplished and well paid, or to those who simply turn hamburgers on a grill, or to anyone in between.

An **apprentice** is an individual who is receiving formal training for a career in food service. Apprentices rotate among kitchen stations and may be assigned according to their level of skill.

A **helper** is a person in training or one lacking the skills necessary to merit the title of cook. This is an entry-level job at the first rung of the kitchen ladder.

Now let us look at some positions on the staff of a hospital kitchen. Above the production staff in Figure 1-3 is a superstructure of dietitians. A **dietitian** has a B.S. degree in foods and nutrition or institutional management, has met the educational and training requirements of the American Dietetic Association (ADA), and has passed an ADA registration examination giving that person the right to use the initials R.D. (Registered Dietitian). These initials are required for professional-level jobs in the dietetic field. Many states now require a licensing examination granting dietitians who qualify the right to use the initials L.D. Both sets of initials may soon be required everywhere for practicing dietitians.

In a hospital kitchen the counterpart of the executive chef is the **administrative dietitian.** This position may require an advanced degree and typically requires years of experience in addition to the formal training. Like the executive chef, the head of a hospital food service is responsible for production; control of quality, quantity, and cost; staffing and supervision of personnel; and coordination with other departments. In addition he or she is responsible for seeing that patients' dietary needs are being met. For this there may be a staff of several dietitians in specialized roles, working with doctors, patients, and cooks.

Dietitians are also being used more and more by hotels, chain restaurant headquarters, and even food brokers, distributors, and food equipment companies. They also act as consultants to many corporations serving the food industry. You will find them wherever they can apply their specialized knowledge of food science and nutrition to menu planning, product development, sales, and marketing.

The position of **dietetic technician** is common in today's hospital kitchens. It requires an A.A. or A.S. degree in foods and nutrition. The technician, having less training than the dietitian, is involved at the production level and generally reports to an administrative dietitian.

An **aide** is a helper in a hospital kitchen. This is an entry-level job corresponding to helper in a hotel or restaurant kitchen.

Given the variety of kitchens and kinds of operations today, there is no way to attach specific duties or rank to a title, job, or station. Each operation has its own staff structure, and every well-organized kitchen has a written description of each job and the duties and skills it requires. Table 1-1 will give you some idea of the vast spread of opportunities available in the industry. Experience and education are requirements for positions of skill, but seldom does a given job require a specific level of either one.

A SHORT HISTORY OF QUANTITY COOKERY

Now let us travel quickly through history to see how kitchens came to be the way they are, and how styles of cooking, called **cuisines** (kweezeens), developed over the centuries.

The early empires

Quantity cooking is at least as old as the feasts of the kings and emperors of ancient Egypt, Assyria, Persia, and Israel. Banquet guests in those days often numbered a thousand or more, and sometimes whole herds of cattle were slaughtered for a single feast. Large households consumed food in quantity every day. King Solomon's 700 wives, 300 concubines, and numerous retainers required a daily food supply of "thirty measures of fine flour, and threescore measures of meal, ten fat oxen, and twenty oxen out of the pastures, and an hundred sheep, beside harts, and roebucks, and fallowdeer, and fatted fowl," according to the Bible.

When the Romans built their empire, they helped themselves to the foods, the cooks, and the culinary splendors of the peoples they vanquished. The emperor Julius Caesar set a new record for quantity food service when he celebrated one of his military triumphs with a feast for 260,000 people that lasted for several days.

The Roman cook was typically a male slave brought from conquered Greece, where cooking skills and cuisine were highly developed. Cooks were in great demand in Rome, and cooking was considered an art. A good cook became a status symbol for his master. Often he was given money and presents and became rich enough to buy his freedom.

Cooking in the Roman kitchen was done with a wood or charcoal fire built on a raised stone or brick hearth. Foods were cooked over the fire in pots or cauldrons. Meats were roasted on spits above the fire or placed on grills on glowing embers. Breads and cakes—including cheesecake—were baked in ovens. The oven was heated by burning a fire inside it; then the ashes were scraped out and the food was put in. Having no chimneys, kitchens were smoky.

Even in those days the kitchen was organized for production by dividing the work into specialized tasks. The head cook supervised from a platform where he could see what was

TABLE 1-1 Kitchen Positions: Requirements and Opportunities

	Four-Year Degree Required	Four-Year Degree Helpful	Two-Year Degree Required	Two-Year Degree Helpful	Years Experience to Full Position	Fast Food	Hotel Kitchen	Small Restaurant	Large Restaurant	Airline Catering	Cruise Ship	School, Hospital
									Opportunities in			
Executive chef		X		X	5–10	(X)*	X	X	X	X	X	X
Working chef		X		X	5–10		X	X	X	X	X	X
Sous-chef		X		X	3–5		X	X	X	X	X	X
Sauce cook				X	2–5		X	X	X	X	X	X
Chef garde manger				X	2–5		X		X	X	X	
Pastry cook				X	2–5		X	X	X	X	X	X
Fish cook				X	2–5	X	X	X	X	X	X	X
Fry cook				X	1–3	X	X	X	X	X	X	X
Production manager		X		X	5–10	X	X	X	X	X	X	X
Sanitarian	X				2–5	(X)	X			X	X	X
Dietitian	X				5–7		X			(X)	X	X
Dietetic technician			X	X	2–5	X	X					X
Pantry cook				X	1–3	X	X	X	X	X	X	X

* (X) indicates corporate headquarters only.

15

going on. There were slaves to keep the fires going, turn the spits, crush things in huge mortars with huge pestles, fetch and carry.

Roman cuisine was long on meats, fish, and birds, specially bred and fattened for the tables of the rich. Some were cooked in their own juices, and the juices were used to make sauces, as we do with some dishes today. The Roman menu included most of the foods we use today in the way of vegetables, fruits, dairy products, grains, and spices, but olive oil was used for cooking and honey for sweetening. Though they searched the known world for rare and unusual foods, the Romans' cuisine was not delicate and refined but highly spiced and heavy.

Medieval Europe

After the barbarians overran the Roman Empire, the well-organized Roman kitchen and the elaborate Roman cuisine all but disappeared. Life in most of Europe was reduced to mere survival. People lived clustered in and about the noble's manor or the monastery and ate what was provided by the nobles or the monks. Quantity cooking, far from dying out, was more important than ever.

The food was cooked outdoors, or over fires built in the middle of a great hall with a hole in the roof. Many a manor hall was dining room, living room, and bedroom for everyone. The food was boiled in cauldrons or roasted on hand-turned spits. It was served on slabs of hard bread, called trenchers, and eaten with the fingers. Kitchen workers were serfs, the medieval equivalent of slaves, so the labor supply was plentiful.

Food supplies were scanty—whatever could be grown in the fields with primitive plows, raised in the barnyard, or caught in the streams and forests. All in all, the early Middle Ages did not offer the cook much chance for fame and fortune.

After several hundred years times began to improve. Trade revived, new techniques of

farming were developed, kings and nobles and monasteries grew richer. The later Middle Ages were a time of pomp and pageantry, and the great halls of the manor houses and castles were scenes of lavish feasting. In fact, eating and drinking were the chief forms of entertainment. Often there would be music and dancing between courses. It was the day of the juggler, the jester, and the wandering minstrel.

Kitchens by this time were separate rooms or separate buildings. They had fireplaces with chimneys, ovens for baking, high vaulted ceilings for carrying away the smoke. But the spit and the cauldron at the open fire were still the means of food production, and the knife and the mortar and pestle were the primary processing tools. A cauldron for quantity production is illustrated in Figure 1-7.

The cook now had more and better raw materials to work with. Spices from the Far East were now available, along with raisins, currants, almonds, and sugar from the Near East. The cook still struggled, however, with problems of taste and texture. The salt taste of winter meats was moderated by soaking and boiling, by stewing meat with bland starchy foods or with honey or wine, or by masking the taste with spices or sauces. Tough meats—and most were tough—were minced or pounded. Fresh meats, poultry, and game were spit-roasted and brought whole to the serving table. There they were carved into small pieces (forks had not yet made their appearance) and tasted for poison before being served to the king or noble.

Chefs in royal households were now persons of importance, respected and well paid. The most famous chef of the period, head chef to King Charles VI of France, was in fact made a knight. His coat of arms, still to be seen on his tombstone, bears three cooking pots and six roses. Taillevent, as he called himself, wrote one of the earliest cookbooks, called *Le Viandier* (The Meat Cook). In it he describes many new cooking techniques and dishes of his day, such as sauces thickened with bread crumbs and various kinds of stews.

FIGURE 1-7. Cooking with an open fire. A kettle of fish or a pot of stew for a large household required strength as well as cooking skill. (From Bartolomeo Scappi, *Dell arte dell cucinare* [On the Arts of Cooking], 1643. Courtesy Rare Books and Manuscripts Division, The New York Public Library, Astor, Lenox and Tilden Foundations.)

New foods and a new cuisine

The sixteenth century brought new foods from across the seas following the voyages of Columbus and other explorers—turkey, potatoes, corn, red and green peppers, tomatoes, coffee, and chocolate. It also brought Italian cuisine to France when two 14-year-olds were married—Catherine de' Medici of Florence and the heir to the French throne, the future Henry II. Catherine brought with her to Paris a complete staff of Italian cooks. In Italy some of the old Roman ways with food had survived, and a cuisine of considerable elegance had developed, enriched with foods and cooking techniques from other parts of the Mediterranean world.

Now the French court learned to eat veal, artichokes, truffles, melons, macaroons, quenelles, ice cream, frangipane tarts. They also adopted the more elegant Italian manners. Catherine even introduced the table fork, although she herself ate with her fingers. It took another century for the fork to catch on in France and England.

French cooks were quick to learn the new cuisine, and over the next several generations they built upon this foundation to develop the classical French cuisine we still enjoy today.

The heavy, highly spiced medieval fare gave way to lighter foods more delicate in taste and texture. Vegetables and fruits and even flowers were added to the diet.

Fine food and fine cooking became favorite pastimes of the French nobility. Not only did they dine well; they learned to cook. Louis XV, who ruled France for much of the eighteenth century, was both an avid eater and an amateur cook, and he demanded the same of those around him. It became important to be a good cook, and especially to invent a new dish, if you wanted to succeed at the French court. So arose the multiplication of sauces and garnitures—the basic dish served with a certain sauce or a certain garnish or a certain set of vegetables. Many a garniture or sauce, however, was invented not by the person it was named for but by the chef.

It was the heyday of French chefs. They were honored and well paid. Their fame spread throughout Europe. Nobles from other countries sent their chefs to France for training or imported French chefs to head their kitchens.

But the chef's work was not easy. A dinner might require the preparation of a hundred or

FIGURE 1-8. Carême's kitchen. Here is the kitchen in which Carême produced elaborate dinner parties for the prince regent of England. Notice the spits for roasting on the right, the rows of copper cookware along the rear wall, the high ceiling with windows at the top for carrying off the smoke and heat and fumes from the charcoal. Below the hood on the left wall are ranges. Under the clock, a cook is using a waist-high mortar and pestle for grinding or puréeing. On the center table are silver serving dishes ready for the prince's table. The chef directs his brigade of assistants, cook's knife tucked in his belt. (Aquatint by John Nash, 1821, from his *Views of the Royal Pavilion at Brighton*, 1826. Photo courtesy Royal Pavilion, Art Gallery and Museums, Brighton.)

more different dishes. It is true that the kitchen had improved. Pots and pans were better. There were charcoal braziers—small burners containing live coals—and by the eighteenth century there were stoves with 12 or 20 grates. This equipment made it possible to sauté and to season and to manipulate the food in the pan, which could not be done near the roaring fires of the Middle Ages. But the cook still lacked clean and steady heat sources and power-driven equipment. Fortunately for the chef and for French cuisine, there still were plenty of helpers for the menial tasks.

This grand era of French cookery ended in 1793 with the stroke of the guillotine by which Louis XVI lost his head. The French nobility fled to other countries or lost their fortunes or their heads as the French Revolution turned society upside down. Many fine chefs, finding themselves without jobs, opened their own eating places in Paris. So began the restaurant industry. Within 20 years there were some five hundred restaurants in Paris.

Carême

During the period of upheaval a young nobody named Marie-Antoine Carême worked his way into kitchens that served some of the surviving aristocrats. By working under one great chef and then another, he mastered all branches of cooking—pastry, sauces, cold foods, hot foods. He quickly became the most sought-after chef in Europe. Among his employers were the czar of Russia, the future king of England, and the French foreign minister Talleyrand. It is said that Talleyrand's dinner table was responsible for settling the peace of Europe after the Napoleonic Wars.

But Carême was also busy writing books, often working all day in the kitchen, then staying up most of the night to study and write. He considered it his life's work to pass on to the world his intimate knowledge of every phase of the chef's art and of classical cuisine. A passage from one of his books conveys a strong impression of his intensity and dedication, as well as a vivid picture of Talleyrand's kitchen:

Imagine yourself in a large kitchen such as that of the Foreign Minister at the moment of a great dinner. There one sees twenty chefs at their urgent occupations, coming, going, moving with speed in this cauldron of heat. Look at the great mass of live charcoal, a cubic metre for the cooking of the entrées, and another mass on the ovens for the cooking of the soups, the sauces, the ragoûts, the frying and the bains-marie.

Add to that a heap of burning wood in front of which four spits are turning, one of which bears a sirloin weighing from 45 to 60 lb., another a piece of veal weighing 35 to 45 lb., the other two for fowl and game.

In this furnace everyone moves with tremendous speed; not a sound is heard; only the chef has the right to make himself heard, and at the sound of his voice, everyone obeys. Finally, to put the lid on our sufferings, for about half an hour the doors and windows are closed so that the air does not cool the dishes as they are being dished up. And in this way we pass the best days of our lives.

But honour commands. We must obey even though physical strength fails. But it is the burning charcoal which kills us!*

Carême's kitchen in England (Figure 1-8) was much better. It had everything an extravagant prince could buy—spits turned ingeniously by fans powered by the heat of the fire itself, a wall-length bank of ovens and ranges, a mortar and pestle standing waist-high and two feet across, shelves upon shelves of gleaming copper utensils. Windows at the top of the high ceiling helped to cope with the heat and fumes.

Classical cuisine

The classical cuisine detailed in Carême's books was made up of hundreds of different dishes, each defined right down to the shape of the potato and the arrangement on the plate. In contrast to the heavy, spicy fare of medieval times, classical cuisine was light and

*Reprinted from Larousse Gastronomique by Prosper Montagné. Copyright © 1961 by Crown Publishers, Inc. Used by permission of Crown Publishers, Inc.

delicate. The goals of the cook were to build flavor with the flavors of the foods themselves, to create, smooth, rich textures, to achieve an effect of luxury and elegance as pleasing to the eye as to the palate.

To distill the essence of the flavor of a meat might require days of cooking. The refinement of a sauce's texture might require several cooks for the straining and puréeing. The number of dishes served at a meal (a Carême menu for 40 guests lists 144 separate dishes) might require a very large kitchen staff.

It was a cuisine difficult to produce unless there was plenty of money for staffing the kitchen and buying foods that were often scarce and expensive. The chefs who opened restaurants in Paris after the revolution had a hard time of it. They either modified their menus or went out of business. There were still plenty of rich people, however, especially among the new and powerful middle class. Eating was still the pleasure of the rich, and French cuisine continued to flourish and to develop still further. New dishes were invented reflecting the times—prepared *à la financière* and *à la bourgeoise*. The common touch became popular too in dishes *à la meunière, à la bonne femme, à la paysanne* (in the style of the miller, the housewife, the peasant). What we call classical cuisine today is this French cuisine of the nineteenth century, which in turn is an expanded, refined, and codified version of classical eighteenth-century cuisine.

Now cooks got their training by working in kitchens of successful restaurants and in the big hotels being built to cater to the rich. The skilled French chef who made it to the top was more than ever in demand.

Escoffier

Georges Auguste Escoffier was the most famous chef of his day. He is also the master chef best known to our generation. Escoffier was a superb and imaginative cook. But more important to his profession, he radically changed methods of food service and kitchen organization during his years of managing the kitchens of the Savoy and Carlton hotels in turn-of-the-century London.

Escoffier fathered the modern menu by serving a carefully planned sequence of courses. He constructed it as though it were a symphony of contrasting movements; the soup, he said, should be like an overture suggesting the theme. This system of planning and serving the food replaced the old system of serving 20 to 40 different dishes at once, elaborately arranged on the table to overwhelm the diners. The dishes would grow cold before they could be eaten, and diners had to eat only what they could reach. Escoffier's system of courses—one or two dishes per course, served to each person—ensured that diners received their food quickly at its proper temperature and its peak of quality, a primary goal of any food service today.

Escoffier also reorganized the work of the different kitchen stations, eliminating duplication and improving efficiency. He had the same purpose in mind—to speed the food to the waiting customer. More than anyone else, he pointed the developing restaurant industry toward success by catering to the customer's needs and desires.

The modern kitchen and cuisine

In one respect Escoffier was very old-fashioned. He refused to cook with gas or electricity, though both were available by the 1890s. He felt that only coal and charcoal could produce perfection of flavor in roasting and grilling. Spit roasting gave way to oven roasting only in the twentieth century.

The last hundred years have seen more change in kitchens and cooking than all the thousands of years preceding. Among the most revolutionary changes are the use of gas and electricity for cooking, cooling, and freezing; thermostatic controls for cooking and cooling; power-driven machines to perform the endless tasks of the apprentice and the slave; the discovery of bacteria and ways to cope with them; improvements in raw materials through agriculture, stock breeding, food processing, and refrigerated transportation; and the development of convenience foods. Not the least important is the invention of the automobile, which has strung food-service facilities along every highway in America and made it easy and pleasant to travel miles for a single meal.

Today's cuisine is changing too. The innovative **nouvelle cuisine** is a fresh approach to food, adapting techniques of classical cuisine to newly invented dishes. It emphasizes the flavors and textures of fresh ingredients, unusual flavor combinations, and artistic arrangements on the plate. An offshoot of nouvelle cuisine, **cuisine minceur,** eliminates the use of high-calorie and high-fat items such as oil, butter, cream, flour, and sugar. The rise to prominence of American-born chefs has contributed to the emergence of distinctive regional American cuisines, again using classical techniques but with fresh foods native to the area.

We have also added dishes from all over the world to our menus. But our cuisine has changed less than our kitchens. Much of it still stems from European cooking. And we still eat the same basic foods the Romans ate two thousand years ago.

SUMMING UP

The kitchen of every food-service facility is different—uniquely adapted to its own needs. These needs are determined by the nature and purpose of the operation, its menu, the volume of production, the clientele, the type of service, and such other factors as special dietary and sanitation requirements.

Yet all food-service kitchens have certain things in common. They are typically divided into production stations. Each station prepares certain kinds of food and each has its own production area, equipment, storage, and staff. All kitchens have a staff structure—a network or ladder of relationships by which authority and responsibility are assigned. All kitchens have specific job categories, and each job requires a certain set of skills.

Job titles and the skills and experience required vary widely from one operation to another. Opportunities exist everywhere, and now is the time for you to begin looking at kitchens in action with a critical eye toward planning your own training and experience and setting your career goals.

The modern food-service facility is so well equipped and so many convenience products are available that we sometimes hear it said that the cook's job is not to cook but to produce food. It is a point of view that would soon reduce the food-service industry to homoge-

nized mediocrity—the only difference between one operation and another would be that one had a live band and another had a live girl swinging from the ceiling. The fact is that good cooking is still essential to producing good food, and good food is the basis of every successful operation, whether it is a gourmet restaurant or a hospital, a school cafeteria or a cruise ship.

There is no reason why food produced on a large scale should not be good food—very good food. And there is no reason why intelligent cooking should cost more than mindless production. Many food services today are proving the point.

Whether your own goal is kitchen stardom or a management career, understanding good cooking from the inside out is essential to your success.

THE COOK'S VOCABULARY

kitchen station

station head, *chef de partie*

garde manger department, salad station, pantry

pastry shop

a la carte cookery, a la carte production

executive chef, *chef exécutif, directeur des cuisines*

sous-chef

banquet chef

food-production manager, kitchen manager

working chef, *chef de cuisine*

brigade de cuisine

sauce cook, *saucier*

fish cook, *poissonnier*

vegetable cook, *entremetier*

soup cook, *potager*

roast cook, *rôtisseur*

broiler cook, *grillardin*

pantry chef, *chef garde manger*

pastry chef, *pâtissier*

relief cook, swing cook, rounds cook, *tournant*

chef

cook

apprentice

helper, aide

dietitian, administrative dietitian

dietetic technician

cuisine, classical cuisine, nouvelle cuisine, cuisine minceur

QUESTIONS FOR DISCUSSION

1. How do you account for the differences in a hotel kitchen and a hospital kitchen?

2. Explain how the menu of an operation will affect its kitchen organization, equipment, and staff. Give examples.

3. After learning something about job opportunities and requirements, which jobs look most interesting to you? Why?

4. Compare a modern food-service kitchen with one of Roman times, the Middle Ages, or the time of Carême in terms of the food prepared, the equipment, and the labor force. What is simpler today than it was in those days, and what problems does a modern operation have that were unknown in that earlier era?

FIRST things first. Before you become absorbed in foods and cooking, let us focus on the kitchen as a work environment and open your eyes to its hazards. If you know how to practice sanitation and safety, the kitchen can be a safe, clean, tidy, and healthful place to work. But if you are negligent, you may cause accidents to yourself or your coworkers, or you may bring suffering to victims of food-borne disease and disaster to the establishment where you work.

Sanitation means taking measures to keep food free of anything that might cause disease. Numerous health organizations—state, local, and federal—check the health standards and practices of food establishments. But the fact that these agencies exist and enforce regulations is not the real reason for paying special attention to sanitation and safety. For the true professional it is a matter of personal pride and integrity as well as legal and economic good sense. When you consider how many people's lives may be affected by the way you practice sanitation day in and day out, your own professional standards are going to be the same as the goals of the health agencies.

In a single chapter we can give you only a bare-bones discussion on sanitation and safety, but it should be enough to open your eyes and launch you safely as a cook. After completing this chapter you should be able to

- Name four bacteria that are likely to contaminate foods and explain how they produce disease in people.
- Explain how to keep bacteria out of the kitchen and how to prevent their spread from one food to another.
- Understand the role of temperature in preventing food-borne disease, and keep foods at safe temperatures during preparation, holding, and storage.
- Appreciate the importance of "successful cleaning," and clean equipment, utensils, and work surfaces properly.

2

Sanitation and Safety

- Avoid food spoilage, nonfood poisons, and foreign substances in foods.
- Work safely, avoiding cuts, burns, falls, and back injuries.

BACTERIA THAT CAUSE FOOD-BORNE DISEASE

Most food-borne disease is caused by **bacteria.** Only a small amount comes from chemicals, parasites, or poisons. So sanitation is first of all a constant war against disease-producing organisms.

Some bacteria are beneficial. If it were not for bacteria we would not have such foods as cheese, yogurt, buttermilk, sour cream, wine, aged meats. It is not the beneficial bacteria we fight but the harmful bacteria. Some of these create poisonous substances, or **toxins,** in foods, which make people sick if they are eaten. Other harmful bacteria attack the body directly.

Toxin-producing bacteria

There are two very important toxin-producing bacteria. *Staphylococcus aureus* (staff-uh-luh-cock'-us or'-ee-us), generally referred to as **staph,** is the most common of all the toxin-producing bacteria. Staph bacteria produce their toxin in many foods—especially dairy products, foods containing eggs, sauces, and moist high-protein foods. They produce their toxins at temperatures of 44–115°F (7–46°C), temperatures characteristic of preparation and holding of foods. It is very important to realize that these toxins are not killed by subsequent cooking or storage: neither high temperatures nor low temperatures destroy them. The only way to fight these toxins is prevention—by keeping foods above or below toxin-producing temperatures.

Staph bacteria enter the kitchen most often on people. They are commonly found in the throat and nose, and on the hands and skin, especially in infected areas such as cuts, boils, pimples, and abrasions. People who have such infections should not be handling food at all. But even such precautions cannot eliminate staph bacteria: a cough or sneeze even from a healthy person may send staph bacteria toward food being prepared.

A second type of toxin-producing bacteria is *Clostridium botulinus* (klos-trid'-ee-um botch-a-lee'-nus). These bacteria produce the toxin causing *botulism* (botch'-a-lism), a deadly poisoning that kills more than half its victims and can be fatal after a single bite. Botulinus bacteria produce their toxin in low-acid foods in the absence of air—in canned foods, for example, or in tightly covered cooked foods stored too long.

Botulism toxins can be destroyed by high temperatures. Commercial food processors are under strict regulations to subject canned foods to very high temperatures for long periods of time, and for the most part commercially canned foods are free of this dread toxin. But errors do occur. You should always examine cans for dents, swelling, and rust or corrosion. Never use contents that look foamy or smell bad. Be alert to announcements of recall of certain lot numbers of canned goods. In addition to watching what you have purchased, keep track of what you have cooked, and throw out leftover foods that are not used within a day or two of preparation.

Bacteria that attack the body

Many kinds of bacteria attack the body directly. Two of them are common kitchen offenders, entering the body by way of contaminated food.

Salmonella (sal-mun-ell'a) is probably the most common family of bacteria: there are more than 400 kinds, including typhoid. They are present in the intestines of all forms of animal life. They are spread by contact—to eggshells in hens, for example, and to almost anything in the kitchen that touches them. These bacteria can multiply in any environment containing moisture, oxygen, and favorable temperatures. It is almost impossible to keep them out of the kitchen. Your chief concern is to keep the numbers down.

Clostridium perfringens (klos-trid'-ee-um per-frin'-junz) bacteria, though far less common than salmonella, are especially dangerous in that they do not need oxygen to reproduce, only moisture and warmth, and they often survive cooking. Thus they cause problems in cooked meats and other cooked foods that are held at room temperatures before being served or left to cool before being stored. Leftover cooked foods should be stored *immediately*.

Since you as a cook cannot tell what bacteria or toxins are present in foods, your only course of action is to take every precaution you can. There are four basics of good sanitation that keep bacteria from reaching harmful levels:

- Limiting their entry
- Stopping their spread
- Preventing their growth
- Killing them

KEEPING BACTERIA OUT

Bacteria enter the kitchen in a number of ways: with people, foods, flies, roaches, rats, and mice. Controlling all these sources of entry is an important way of keeping undesirable bacteria out of food-preparation areas.

People as carriers

People who handle food are a great threat to good sanitation. The places people go, the things they do, and the sanitation and personal hygiene habits they practice make it easy for them to harbor and transport bacteria. Many states still require health examinations and periodic follow-up exams for workers in food establishments. But the small piece of paper certifying freedom from disease tends to create a false sense of security. The only value of such an exam is to certify that the person did not have an infection at the time of the examination. You could contract an infectious disease between the examination and your first day of work.

You should be constantly aware of your health and that of those around you. If you are concerned about your health, have it checked; if you are concerned about the health of those around you, report it to management.

Even when you are in perfect health you have bacteria on your skin and in your mouth, nose, throat, and all parts of your body. Everyone does. Cleanliness of person and how to maintain that cleanliness are getting more and more attention from health agencies, and what it means to be clean becomes a necessary part of learning to be a cook.

First things first again: when you start working you should never wear the same clothes in a food-preparation area that you wear outside. Most operations today provide clean, sanitary uniforms or clothing for working in food-preparation areas. If you are not provided with uniforms, it is your responsibility to have clean uniforms that you change at your workplace to limit the transportation of bacteria from outside.

Second, you should put a clean person into a clean uniform. You should wash regularly, especially those parts of you that harbor bacteria readily—your hair, hands, fingernails, and so on. You must wash your hands almost every time you change activities or places.

Today's public health regulations require numerous hand sinks in kitchens, placed so that they are available to each station. In ship kitchens the U.S. Public Health Service is so strict that it requires a hand sink with soap and towels within 20 feet (6 meters) of each worker at all times. It can be assumed with some accuracy that an accessible hand sink will be used more often than one that is difficult to get to, but it is up to *you* to use it.

Third, covering certain parts of your body is a must. Hair, no matter how long or short, should be covered to keep hairs from getting into food or onto food preparation surfaces. Long hair should be put up and netted to keep it restrained. Your hands should be covered with sanitary gloves whenever you handle foods ready to be served or foods that will not be heated to 140°F (60°C) or higher. Remember, however, that gloves can transmit bacteria as easily as hands can. Your gloves should be as clean as your hands should be.

Foods as carriers

Foods are the second carrier of bacteria from outside. All foods and their containers entering the kitchen can bring bacteria with them. Yet too often the task of handling incoming foods is given little attention, and many bacteria enter and multiply before anyone is aware of the danger.

You cannot keep all bacteria out, but there are several ways to keep their numbers down. Store all foods properly and quickly. Be sure frozen foods are received frozen from refrigerated vehicles and show no signs of thawing. Carefully inspect all foods you receive to be sure they are not spoiled or contaminated. Look on the products for stamps of inspection and wholesomeness. Get *all* products from reputable suppliers. Examine canned products for dents, swelling, unlabeled cans, and dirty or rusted cans.

If you have any doubt about the quality, freshness, or safety of any item, don't use it. *Don't even taste it.*

Pests as carriers

Roaches, rodents, and flies are the third common source of bacteria from outside. They are all notorious carriers and must be controlled and exterminated regularly. This is a job for professionals. Pesticides are poisons and are not to be handled by food handlers. These poisons could find their way into the food.

There are a number of things you can do to help prevent the harboring of pests. Cover all refuse containers. Keep all paper containers in which foods are received out of the kitchen. Cover all foods whenever production allows, and always cover them in storage. Keep your work area clean and free from anything that would attract pests.

The ways bacteria get into kitchens are be-

yond imagining. No one simple rule will keep them out; it takes constant awareness in key areas. *Think clean, work clean,* and *clean!*

STOPPING BACTERIAL SPREAD

Bacteria do not move on their own but are moved from one food to another. The transfer of bacteria in this way is called **cross-contamination.** It is most often the food handler—you—who transmits bacteria from one food to another via the dirty knife, towel, counter, sink, dish, cutting board, or your own two hands. It is particularly dangerous because you are probably unaware of it.

To a great degree you can control this transfer of bacteria; it is one of the most important things you can do to maintain a sanitary kitchen. The first thing is to become aware of how it happens.

Product to product

All foods carry bacteria, just as all people do. But some are more likely than others to bring bacteria into the kitchen and to transmit them to other foods. Raw poultry, fish, meats, and eggs are the most likely carriers. Along with milk products they are also the most susceptible to contamination from other foods as well as to bacteria brought in by people. Any food product can pass along bacteria to these more susceptible foods, or to any other food, via work surfaces, utensils, and hands.

To prevent product-to-product contamination, everything must be kept scrupulously clean. After you prepare one product on a work surface, you must **sanitize** that surface— clean it with a special chemical solution—before you prepare another product on it. Even when it is another batch of the same product, if there is a gap of more than 15 or 20 minutes between preparations, you must clean and sanitize that surface. And, as pointed out earlier, you must wash your hands whenever you are shifting from one preparation to another.

Once a piece of equipment, either large or small, has been used, it must be considered contaminated. Knives, tongs, serving utensils, even portion scales must not be overlooked. Can openers are a common offender: the cutting blade accumulates food, grows bacteria, and passes them on to the food in the next can. You can see the danger point in Figure 2-1. Contamination by large equipment—slicers, meat grinders, mixers, and cooking equipment—is just as likely to happen. The meat slicer is a frequent offender; it should be taken apart and cleaned hourly when used over a period of time. The same rule applies to everything, of whatever size: clean and sanitize it between uses to prevent cross-contamination.

Splashing and dripping

Cross-contamination can also occur through splashing and dripping. Splashing can happen between stations, sending bacteria from one to another. Splashing can also happen when you wash your hands. Today's kitchens are installing splash guards on preparation tables and hand sinks to prevent this kind of cross-contamination. Splashing is also a cleaning hazard, especially in mopping and scrubbing: dirty water may splash onto a clean surface or equipment or even onto food.

Dripping may occur when moisture from above, such as condensation from cooking, drops onto food products or preparation surfaces below. Often these overhead surfaces are neglected in cleaning and can harbor bacteria, which drip with the condensation into food being prepared.

The most serious dripping hazard is one raw product dripping on another raw or cooked product. Raw meats, poultry, and fish are products that may drip. In storage they should be placed on the lower refrigerator shelves so that they do not drip on any other food product. This is especially true of fish that have been iced to keep them fresh.

Improper storage

Improper storage is an open invitation to cross-contamination. To avoid it, store raw

FIGURE 2-1. The can opener's cutting blade is a frequent cross-contaminator. (Photo courtesy Edlund Company.)

and cooked foods separately. Divide them into three categories:

- Raw, processed or unprocessed
- Processed ready-to-serve
- Cooked on premises

Though this sounds simple, it isn't always easy to tell which processed products are raw and which are cooked because foods come into the kitchen in so many different forms.

"Raw processed" includes bacon, breaded shrimp, frozen vegetables, frozen dough—any products that have had some processing but must be cooked to be edible.

"Processed ready-to-serve" includes such items as frozen cooked shrimp, smoked fish and meat products, franks, cold cuts, cheeses.

Any processed product that does not need further processing to be edible falls into this category.

"Cooked-on-premises" foods are such items as roasts and cooked dishes that are being held for later use. These foods should be stored separately from the other two categories. This does not mean that they cannot be stored in the same refrigerator or freezer. It means that they must be stored in separate sections, on racks or shelves that are clearly marked to indicate what is to be stored there.

There are other important storage rules for avoiding the spread of bacteria.

- Cover all foods. Label and date them.
- Store foods in properly sanitized containers.
- Store all products off the floor.
- Do not store decorative items (fat sculptures, ice carvings, flowers) with items to be consumed.

To avoid cross-contamination, proper storage is every bit as important as proper cleaning and handling.

When you carry foods from storage to preparation areas, do not bring them in the unsanitary boxes and bags in which they arrived. Transfer them to sanitary containers such as clean plastic carrying boxes or kitchen utensils such as pans or bowls. If you must use the original containers—egg cartons, for example—never put them on food-preparation surfaces. This is especially important when you are preparing foods that will be served without being cooked.

PREVENTING BACTERIAL GROWTH

Preventing bacterial growth is primarily a matter of temperatures. It requires knowing safe and unsafe temperatures; controlling cooking, holding, and storage temperatures; and limiting the time foods are exposed to unsafe temperatures. Let us explore this a bit further.

Bacteria can multiply with fantastic speed by dividing—each into two, then those two into two each, and so on until you have thousands in a matter of hours. A single organism, dividing every 20 minutes under ideal growth conditions, will produce more than 4000 bacteria in 4 hours and billions in 10 to 12 hours. The susceptible foods you have met before—milk and milk products, eggs, meats, poultry, seafood—are the foods most likely to provide favorable conditions for rapid multiplication.

Danger-zone temperatures

To multiply, bacteria need food, moisture, and above all warmth. The key temperatures for bacterial growth are from *40 to 140°F (4–60°C)*. This is known as the **bacterial growth range** or the **danger zone.** Below 40°F (4°C) there is little or no growth. From 40 to 60°F (4–15°C) they grow slowly. From 60 to 120°F (15–50°C), growth is rapid and toxins may be formed. Between 120 and 140°F (50–60°C) growth slows down but may continue. Figure 2-2 tells the temperature story graphically.

The safe zones

Temperatures above 140°F (60°C) are in the **upper safe zone,** or the zone of normal cooking temperatures. Temperatures below 40°F (4°C) are in the **lower safe zone,** or the zone of normal refrigeration and freezer temperatures.

Above 140°F (60°C) bacteria may survive but do not multiply. Above 165°F (74°C) most bacteria are killed. Below 32°F (0°C) bacteria do not grow, but many survive.

The secret of preventing multiplication, then, is to keep foods in either the upper safe zone or the lower safe zone. It is when foods are not in either of these temperature zones that we must give them the greatest attention. Foods must never be allowed to stand at room temperature. Body temperature, 98.6°F (37°C), is the ideal growth temperature for bacteria, and many areas in a kitchen are at or near body temperature.

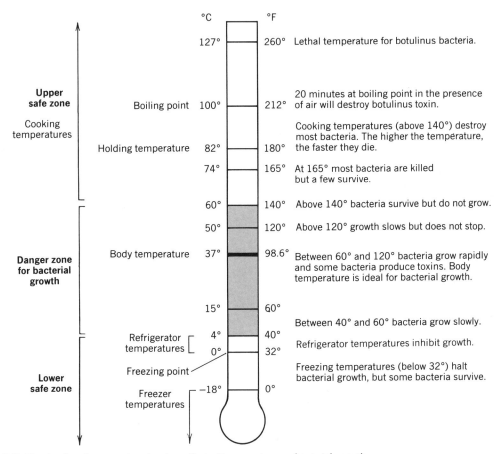

°C		°F	
127°		260°	Lethal temperature for botulinus bacteria.

Upper safe zone

Cooking temperatures

Boiling point 100° / 212° — 20 minutes at boiling point in the presence of air will destroy botulinus toxin.

Holding temperature 82° / 180° — Cooking temperatures (above 140°) destroy most bacteria. The higher the temperature, the faster they die.

74° / 165° — At 165° most bacteria are killed but a few survive.

60° / 140° — Above 140° bacteria survive but do not grow.

50° / 120° — Above 120° growth slows but does not stop.

Danger zone for bacterial growth

Body temperature 37° / 98.6° — Between 60° and 120° bacteria grow rapidly and some bacteria produce toxins. Body temperature is ideal for bacterial growth.

15° / 60° — Between 40° and 60° bacteria grow slowly.

Refrigerator temperatures 4° / 40° — Refrigerator temperatures inhibit growth.

0° / 32° — Freezing point

Freezing temperatures (below 32°) halt bacterial growth, but some bacteria survive.

Lower safe zone

Freezer temperatures −18° / 0°

FIGURE 2-2. Food safety thermometer showing effect of temperature on bacterial growth.

How to keep foods in the safe zones

Here are some simple hints for keeping foods from remaining in the danger zone longer than *absolutely necessary:*

- Anything at room temperature more than 15 to 20 minutes cannot be considered in process and should be returned to heat or refrigeration.
- Cool foods as quickly as possible. Small amounts may be refrigerated immediately using broad shallow pans with the food no more than 4 inches deep. Large amounts may be cooled by surrounding the container with ice or cold running water, stirring every few minutes. (This technique is illustrated in Figure 6-4.) Refrigerate when cool.
- Heat refrigerated foods to be served hot as quickly as possible, bringing them to a safe *internal* temperature. Never put food from the refrigerator into the steam table or other holding equipment without first bringing it into the upper safe zone.
- Thaw frozen foods in the refrigerator. Do not let them sit thawing at room temperature; the outside will move into the danger zone while the inside is still thawing.

- Check interior temperatures of hot foods frequently to see that they are above 140°F (60°C). Check the food itself, not the holding unit. A testing thermometer is illustrated in Figure 2-3a.
- Check refrigerator temperatures frequently to see that they are well below 40°F (4°C)—comfortably in the lower safe zone. (Figure 2-3b shows a typical refrigerator thermometer.)
- Open refrigerator doors as little as possible to avoid a rise in temperature.

a.

b.

FIGURE 2-3. Temperature measures. *a.* A testing thermometer. *b.* A refrigerator thermometer. (Photos courtesy Taylor Scientific Instruments.)

In short, avoid the hazardous temperature zone with all foods, especially susceptible foods such as eggs, raw poultry, raw meats (especially pork), cooked meats and poultry, milk, and combinations containing any of these products, such as stocks, sauces, puddings, and creams.

Above all, remember that it is the temperature of the food itself that counts. Even though food is on a steam table or in a heating cabinet or a refrigerator, it must be *maintained in a safe zone.* This introduces two more temperatures you must always keep in mind. Hot-food holding equipment must *maintain* 180°F (82°C) to hold foods at 140°F (60°C). Cold-food holding equipment must be at 35°F (2°C) to keep cold foods below 40°F (4°C). The checking of these temperatures is your responsibility.

KILLING DISEASE-CAUSING ORGANISMS

Killing by cooking

Ordinary cooking of foods destroys many disease-causing organisms. Others can survive low-temperature cooking (low crock or oven temperatures or low-temperature frying). It is important to realize that it is not the temperature of the oven or the fry pan but the internal temperature of the food that must reach lethal levels.

Lethal temperatures vary widely depending on the kind of food, the kind of bacteria, and the length of time the food remains at a given temperature. It takes 3 to 10 minutes to destroy salmonella bacteria in whole egg at 138°F (59°C) but less than a minute at 150°F (66°C). Most bacteria and other disease-producing organisms cannot survive a temperature of 165°F (74°C). This includes the parasite **trichina** (trick-eye´-na), sometimes found in fresh pork, which causes **trichinosis** in humans.

On the other hand, though a temperature of 165°F (74°C) will kill staph bacteria, it will not destroy toxin they may have already produced in foods at danger-zone temperatures, and it is the toxin that makes the diner ill. Some special forms of bacterial life called spores can also outlive high temperatures and grow into active disease-causing organisms later on. (*Clostridium perfringens* is one example.) So it is a mistake to think of cooking as a cure-all for food-borne disease.

Cleaning and sanitizing

Bacteria surviving on equipment and utensils can be killed by high temperatures or chemical solutions. The temperature of the rinse water in the automatic dishwasher must be kept at 180°F (82°C) for 10 seconds to kill bacteria and sanitize the dishes. Where such hot temperatures cannot be maintained, as in washing utensils by hand and in cleaning counters, floors, and large equipment, a chlorine or iodine solution is used in the final rinse to kill bacteria. State and local laws specify what chemical may be used in what quantity, and it is your responsibility to follow these guidelines carefully.

Here is a general procedure used for washing equipment and tools by hand in a three-compartment sink. Temperatures given are those required by federal standards. To follow them you will need long rubber gloves and long-handled brushes.

- On the drainboard, scrape and prerinse with a spray in order to keep the wash water as clean as possible.

- In the first sink, wash with detergent in 140–150°F (60–66°C) water, removing all food particles and traces of grease. If necessary for utensils with baked-on foods, soak in detergent and scrape and prerinse again.

- In the second sink, rinse in clean warm water at 150–160°F (66–71°C). Change the water frequently, or use a sink with an overflow drain and keep the water running.

- In the last sink, sanitize, using either an approved chemical disinfectant at the proper concentration or water at 180°F (82°C) for 10 seconds.

- Drain and allow to air-dry. Wiping with a towel might recontaminate sanitized surfaces.

The same steps are followed using a dish or pot machine, except that the machine does the washing and rinsing and sanitizes with 180°F (82°C) water instead of a chemical solution.

The three steps of washing, rinsing, and sanitizing also apply to cleaning work surfaces and stationary equipment. Use clean cloths, sponges, and brushes that have been held in a chemical disinfectant and are used only for this purpose. Always unplug machinery with cutting blades before disassembling. Never place knives, sharp-edged tools, or cutting blades in a soapy sink: immediately wash, rinse, and sanitize them and allow to air-dry.

Clean and sanitize cutting boards, processing machines, can openers, and scales after each use. Clean and sanitize regularly and frequently everything that has contact with foods—refrigerators, mobile carts, worktables, deep fryers, steamers, ranges, ovens.

Good food and good business demand a clean kitchen. The dangers of bacterial growth and cross-contamination demand as much emphasis on successful cleaning as on the production of quality foods. Successful cleaning means producing sanitary surfaces. A piece of equipment that is *clean* not only looks clean and feels clean but has no invisible residue such as might be left by wiping with a dirty towel. A piece of equipment that is *sanitary* not only is clean but has had bacteria reduced to a safe level.

OTHER FOOD-BORNE TROUBLEMAKERS

Food spoilage

Spoilage comes from the action of bacteria, yeasts, and molds on foods and from chemical changes within the food. The spoiled food, if eaten, is likely to cause illness. Spoilage can be prevented by storing foods at or below 40°F (4°C) and using them promptly, or storing them for longer periods at 0°F (−18°C) or below. Freezing slows down chemical change and inhibits bacterial growth, but it does not kill all bacteria.

Never use food that shows signs of spoilage—off color, off flavor, off odor, off feel (slimy or mushy). Don't use any food that has simply been kept too long either: often spoilage does not signal its presence. *When in doubt throw it out.*

Chemical and metal hazards

Chemical and metal residues in foods can also cause illness. Chemicals may be brought into the kitchen in the form of cleaning compounds: chlorine, iodine, cyanide, acids, and caustics are common poisons in cleaning supplies. Pesticides are also used in kitchens to exterminate insects and control rodents. These poisons can kill not only pests but also people.

Keep all these products away from food and food preparation surfaces and equipment. Store them in clearly labeled containers in a separate storage area away from food supplies. Never put any such products into an empty food or drink container; keep them in their original containers where they will not be mistaken for another product.

Another source of pesticide poisoning is the chemicals sprayed on fruits and vegetables before harvest. These are easily disposed of by thoroughly washing all produce before use.

Metal residues in foods usually come from defective cooking utensils. A number of poisonous metals are used in making pots and pans—*zinc,* used in galvanizing; *cadmium,* a common plating used in gray enamelware; *lead,* used in soldering; and *copper,* used in pots, pans, bowls, and molds. High-acid foods such as fruits, fruit juices, and tomatoes can interact with such metals and cause poisoning.

If you find such utensils in your kitchen, check to be sure that galvanized utensils are not chipped, that copper does not have direct contact with food, and that all plated surfaces are not scratched or damaged. Today most commercial cookware has eliminated these hazards, except for copperware. Copper cookware and molds are usually lined with tin to prevent metal poisoning. But tin is a soft metal and melts at a fairly low temperature. It can be scratched by scouring, and it can be ruined by leaving an empty pan on a burner, which may cause the pan to buckle and the lining to separate from the copper. Anything that exposes the copper is a food hazard, because copper interacts chemically with the moisture in the air, with acid, with salt, and with nearly everything else.

It is, however, safe to beat egg whites in a polished copper bowl, a technique important to the professional baker. The time it takes is not long enough to allow any interaction between egg and metal.

Foreign substances

Foreign substances in food can sometimes cause trouble—not disease but injury. A can opener with a dull blade can produce metal shavings that may drop into the can's contents. The remedy is to throw out the contaminated food and replace the blade of the opener. Glasses can be broken by scooping up ice cubes in them; the pieces may not be found and may turn up in someone's glass of iced tea or bloody mary. The preventive is to use an ice scoop—*always.* Ingested glass or bits of metal can cause serious injury.

KITCHEN SAFETY

The kitchen abounds in potential safety hazards. You can keep them just potential if you recognize them and take appropriate precautions. The well-run kitchen has its own safety rules and first-aid procedures and supplies. Learn how to use them and follow the rules.

The most frequent kitchen accidents fall into four main categories: burns, cuts, strains, and falls.

Burns

In the kitchen you are surrounded by hot things—hot range tops and grills, hot fat in the fryer, hot pans, hot foods, steam under pressure. Not only are things hot; they are large-scale—whole kettles of fat, multi-gallon pots of stew—so spills, if they occur, can be catastrophic. Some things are superhot: hot fat can be twice as hot as boiling water; broilers can heat up to 1200°F (650°C).

We could give you a long list of don'ts, but if your eyes are open to the dangers you won't need someone else's rules. You will work with caution and common sense. You will handle hot pans with dry towels (a wet towel will give you a steam burn). You will keep pan handles out of aisles so that no one can bump into them and upend the hot contents. You will remove covers from pots by tipping them away from you to send the steam in the other direction. You will not try to carry a heavy pot of hot food across a room alone. You will work with an awareness of those around you so that you don't create hazards for others.

The most important safety precaution is to know your cooking equipment and use it with respect. Every piece of equipment you use in cooking has an operator's manual furnished by the manufacturer. Study this manual. Learn how to operate the equipment correctly, what its safety hazards are, how to deal with them, how to clean and maintain the equipment, and how to turn off the power supply. In particular, learn how to work with steam and gas. Ask for help with any unfamiliar equipment before you use it.

Second, learn what to do in case of fire. Know the precautions, equipment, and routines of your facility. Learn where the fire extinguishers are kept and how to operate them. In addition you should know these things about fires:

- There are three common types of fires: Class A, an ordinary fire, such as burning wood, paper, cloth; Class B, a grease or oil fire; Class C, an electrical fire.
- All types need oxygen to burn. If you can smother a fire, cutting off the oxygen supply, you can put it out—a lid on a kettle of

burning fat, a blanket wrapped around burning clothing, carbon dioxide or foam on an electrical fire.
- Water will work only on an ordinary fire. It will make a grease or electrical fire worse.

Fire prevention is the best treatment. Work carefully. Keep equipment grease-free, including hoods and vents. And don't smoke in the kitchen. If a fire does start, call the fire department unless you can put it out immediately.

Cuts
Possibly the worst type of kitchen accident comes from careless handling of power-driven mixing and cutting machines. To classify such injuries as cuts is really the height of understatement.

As with cooking equipment, before you ever use a machine study the operator's manual and attend a demonstration on its use. Learn how to operate the machine correctly, how to clean and maintain it, what its safety hazards are, and how to deal with them. In addition follow these general precautions:

- *Never* touch food in a machine, even with a utensil, when the machine is in motion. If you must scrape, remove, or rearrange something, turn the machine off before you do it.
- Set the safety switch or pull the plug before cleaning a machine, changing an attachment, or handling a cutting part.

Cuts from hand tools seem minor in comparison with machine accidents, but they can be painful and incapacitating. They seldom occur when the tool is being used correctly for its appointed task. The trouble comes when you misuse a tool for another purpose, such as prying off a bottle cap with a knife point, or when your mind is on something else. Don't gesture or turn around suddenly with a knife in your hand. If you must carry a knife across the room, point it down and carry it slightly behind you. Don't put it in your hip pocket; you could

FIGURE 2-4. Lifting and carrying.

RIGHT   WRONG

a. To lift a load from the floor, squat with one foot flat on the floor and lift with your leg muscles. Keep your knees bent and your back rounded. To set it down, slowly resume the original position.

b. To carry a heavy load, keep your knees bent and your back rounded, with your load at waist level or below.

c. You can safely carry a heavy load on your back. You will automatically round your lower back to balance the load.

The wrong ways of lifting and carrying will make you arch your lower back and your neck. This pushes vertebrae together, pressing on disks and nerves.

sit on it. To wash and dry a knife wipe both sides at once with the sharp edge away from your hand and the towel.

Strains and back injuries

Quantity food preparation can require a lot of lifting and carrying of heavy things. There are ways of lifting and carrying that minimize the chance of strained muscles and back injuries.

Figure 2-4 shows right and wrong ways to lift and carry. The secret is to use your leg and stomach muscles instead of your back muscles. Keep your back rounded, so that your vertebrae do not pinch the cushioning disks between them or the nerves that run through them. Such injuries can be serious and do permanent damage. You can also strain muscles if you do not lift correctly.

To avoid carrying heavy things long distances, use a dolly or a cart, or ask someone to help you.

Falls

Falls are among the most common of kitchen accidents. They often happen because workers are unaware of the hazards. Most falls come from spills of food or grease. The simplest precaution is to wipe up a spill as soon as it happens, and wipe it up *clean.* Another precaution is to watch your step in any working area, since workers are not always aware of spills they have created. A fall can be compounded if the person falling is carrying something hot; then burns can be added to injuries.

You can see that cleanliness is as important to safety as it is to sanitation. If you keep your work area clean and use your tools and equipment properly, you can cook in safety and confidence. But be wary of overconfidence. If you begin to get the feeling that you'll never get hurt and you start to relax your caution, that's just when it will happen to you! Work seriously and professionally. Clowning and fooling around are invitations to accident.

SUMMING UP

The practice of sanitation is just as important to the food-service operation as the production of quality food. The hazards of food-borne disease are everywhere all the time.

The major enemy is the ever-present bacteria. Some types of bacteria produce toxins in food, notably staph, which is common, and botulinus, which is rare but deadly. Others attack the body directly. Of these, salmonella is common, and *C. perfringens* is noteworthy for surviving cooking.

Bacteria can multiply with unbelievable speed. We can never get rid of them entirely, but we can keep their numbers at safe levels in several ways. We can keep them from entering the kitchen along with people, foods, and pests. We can prevent their spread from one food to another by sanitary work habits, proper storage, and constant cleaning of tools, work surfaces, and hands. We can stop them from multiplying by keeping foods out of danger-zone temperatures of 40–140°F (4–60°C). We can kill them by cooking foods and sanitizing equipment touched by foods. We must *think clean, work clean, and clean;* we must make sanitation a habit.

Other hazards to which foods are susceptible are spoilage, contamination by chemicals from pesticides and cleaning supplies, metal residues from certain kinds of cooking utensils, and foreign substances such as broken glass or metal shavings.

The kitchen is full of safety hazards. Common accidents are burns, cuts, strains, back injuries, and falls. The best way to prevent them is to work with awareness, caution, and common sense. Handle all tools and equipment properly. Handle your body properly when lifting and carrying. Avoid spills, and clean them up immediately if they happen. Know how to prevent fires and how to put them out. Think safety as you think sanitation, and never take it for granted.

THE COOK'S VOCABULARY

sanitation

bacteria

food-borne disease

toxin

Staphylococcus aureus, staph

Clostridium botulinus, botulism

salmonella

Clostridium perfringens

cross-contamination

bacterial growth range, danger zone, 40–140°F (4–60°C)

upper safe zone, lower safe zone

trichina, trichinosis

sanitize

spoilage

fires: class A, class B, class C

QUESTIONS FOR DISCUSSION

1. Of the many sanitation practices discussed in this chapter, which do you consider most important, and why?

2. Of the four strategies for keeping bacteria at safe levels, which do you think is most important? From your own experience, which is the most commonly ignored?

3. What role does personal hygiene play in food service? How, specifically, can it affect sanitation?

4. In your opinion what is the most serious kitchen safety hazard? How will you avoid it at work?

5. Cite instances you have seen in which cross-contamination could or did occur. How could they have been avoided?

GO into the Yacht Club kitchen any mid-afternoon in summer. It hums with noise and action. Pans and trays clatter on counters; knives rap out staccato rhythms on cutting boards. A cook's mallet thumps veal down to scallopini thinness. Water gushes from taps as vegetables are scrubbed. A rush of steam hisses from the cabinet steamer. Five prime ribs are sizzling gently in the convection oven. Pans sputter to themselves on the range. The mixer motor is purring hoarsely. The exhaust fans are droning. "Hot stuff coming through!" shouts a cook. "Somebody's burning the butter!" yells another.

All the cooks are intently busy. There is a formidable sense of bustle and hustle. Yet serving time is several hours away, and except for soup, prime rib, baked potatoes, and rice, every menu item will be finished in the few minutes before it is served. So what is everyone doing?

The blanket term for all this activity is **prepreparation.** In the hours before serving time not only the cooks but numbers of other persons from the executive chef to the kitchen helpers and potwashers are engaged in numberless tasks that add up to precooking readiness.

As the serving hour draws near, a great crescendo of noise and activity crests and then suddenly subsides. Everything comes into sync. Quiet descends, and the cooks wait, relaxed and confident, for the first orders of the evening.

At such a moment the old-school continental chef used to sit down to his glass of pernod to savor the interlude of readiness that formed the threshold of triumphs to follow. Today it is a coffee break, or a split between shifts, or time out for the employee meal. In continuous-service operations there is no such moment; prepreparation and preparation go on simultaneously all the time.

In this chapter we will look at some of the many tasks and techniques of prepreparation. This is an area neglected by most books on cookery, and yet it can make or break a dish,

3

Prepreparation

or a meal, or a restaurant. After completing this chapter you should be able to

- Understand the importance of prepreparation and the meaning and importance of mise en place.
- Clean fresh produce properly.
- Use and care for knives and cutting machines correctly, and choose the appropriate tool or machine for the task.
- Identify and produce standard food cuts.
- Define and carry out basic processing techniques.
- Hold and store foods properly for sanitation and product quality.
- Organize a production task or station efficiently.

THE MEANING
OF PREPREPARATION

The tasks involved in turning raw products into menu dishes are separated into two groups: those that can be done ahead and those that are completed at or just before serving time. The terms used to describe this division of tasks are prepreparation (oftened shortened in kitchen jargon to preprep) and final preparation, or **finish cooking.**

If you were to make a casserole of chicken tetrazzini, for example, you would cook the spaghetti and the chicken ahead of time. You would dice the chicken, sauté the mushrooms, make the sauce, and grate the cheese ahead of time, and you would assemble the dish in the casserole. All this is prepreparation. The only steps left for final preparation are to heat the dish and glaze it.

In food production everything it is possible to do ahead is done ahead—preprepared. This is partly because there is a great deal left that cannot be done ahead, partly because it is more efficient to spread the tasks throughout the time available, and partly because some things *must* be done before other things *can*

be done in making many products. One of the most important aspects of food preparation is efficient organizing of prepreparation tasks.

There is a term used with pride throughout the profession—**mise en place** (meez on plass). Freely translated from the French, it means "everything in its proper place." A simpler English version is "a good setup." It means that the precooking procedures have been carried out with understanding and good organization, and everything is ready to go. As you pursue your career in the food-service industry, you will be evaluated on your mise en place more than you can probably conceive at this point.

In this chapter you will meet many other terms that are new to you, and you will meet everyday words with new meanings. How do you *fold* egg whites, for example? What about *dice*—is that something you roll at coffee break? Like every other trade or profession, food preparation has its own vocabulary.

There are several reasons for learning the specialized meanings of terms—learning them so thoroughly that they become part of your everyday vocabulary. They enable you to communicate with those around you and to understand what is going on. They help you to follow what you read, whether it is a recipe, a textbook, or a cookery dictionary. The right term is an excellent tool for finding information, both from people and from books. Many terms are interesting for their own sake. Much of the language of the kitchen goes back to classical times and earlier, and it carries pleasant overtones of banquets served to royalty and the culinary triumphs of such great chefs as Carême and Escoffier.

But there are problems. Some people use terms incorrectly. Some products are called by different names in different parts of the country. Some terms have different meanings in different operations. Some terms even the experts do not agree on. Many terms have changed in meaning over the years.

We need definitions to work with. "Define your terms," said Socrates, setting forth the first requirement for any fruitful discussion. We will go on defining terms throughout this book.

The definitions we will give you are as precise and yet as broadly applicable as we can make them. If they do not always agree exactly with those you find elsewhere, or with your own experience, perhaps they will intrigue you into working out better definitions of your own. Meantime, master ours as we explore prepreparation in more detail.

CLEANING

In many kitchens the workday starts with the cleaning of the produce to be used that day. Kitchen slang for this phase of food preparation is **rough prep** or **prepping.** Many other kitchens, particularly large-volume operations, buy their produce already cleaned. But seldom is every cleaning need solved by purchasing, so it is important for you to know all the proper techniques.

The term cleaning, as applied to vegetables and other food products, can have multiple meanings. Many items have portions that are discarded as part of the cleaning. With lettuce and cabbage, for example, the discolored outer leaves are discarded, and usually the core. Tough parts, such as spinach stems and the bottoms of fresh asparagus and fresh broccoli stalks, are cut away; so are blemishes. Many fruits and vegetables are peeled; this can vary with the dish for which they are intended.

The other aspect of cleaning is washing. Most fruits and vegetables arrive at your door in anything but a clean condition. Some products are dirtier than others by virtue of the way they grow. Root vegetables such as carrots and beets have a lot of surface dirt. Lettuce, leeks, and other vegetables that grow in the earth or close to it may have a great deal of dirt in the leaves of the plant.

Cleaning such foods properly means washing them thoroughly, and "thoroughly" means getting them as clean and dirt-free as possible. Cleanliness is of vital importance for a number of reasons. Insecticides, sprays,

powders, and dirt are certainly not things that can be banished with sauces and seasonings. A gritty salad or vegetable is quite unpleasant and may be a health hazard.

Different vegetables are cleaned in different ways. The way a vegetable is cleaned is determined by its type and texture:

- Hard vegetables such as potatoes and carrots with skins should be scrubbed with a vegetable brush under cold running water. If they are to be peeled they need not be scrubbed, but they should still be washed. You don't want to pass along dirt, sprays, or contamination to cut surfaces as you peel.
- Soft or fragile vegetables—such as tomatoes, asparagus, okra, and corn—and most fruits should be washed thoroughly in cold running water but not scrubbed.
- Leafy vegetables should be broken apart and washed thoroughly under cold running water to remove dirt from inside.

For large volume it is sometimes necessary to clean vegetables by submerging them in water. This is not totally wrong, but using cold running water is certainly more desirable. Washing vegetables by submerging them means that you are washing the second item in the dirty water from the first.

When the submersion method is used, the vegetables are placed on large draining racks, which are then submerged in a sinkful of water. Leafy vegetables are plunged up and down to force water between the leaves. A raised screen placed on the bottom of the sink allows the dirt to settle. The water is changed frequently. After washing, the racks are removed from the sink and the produce is allowed to drain before storage.

Cold water is used for washing because it keeps vegetables crisp. Warm water wilts them.

Both vegetables and fruits should be washed as close to use time as possible. They are then at their cleanest when used. In addition, some raw products begin to deteriorate after washing—mushrooms and berries, for example. Cleaned fresh fruits and vegetables are stored in the cooler, covered, until use.

CUTTING

Cutting terminology

Here are the basic cutting terms defined. You will meet others shortly.

- **Cut** To divide into pieces or to shape using a knife.
- **Chop** To cut into pieces of no specified shape.
- **Mince** To chop very fine.
- **Dice** To cut into small uniform cubes.
- **Slice** To cut into uniform slices, usually across the grain.

Cutting, of course, is the general term that includes all the others. Chopping and mincing involve the same action but refer to different sizes of products—an important distinction. Dicing and slicing create specific kinds of cuts. Notice the word "uniform" in both definitions.

You may also meet some French cutting terms—*concasser, émincer*. **Concasser** (kon-kass-ay) is similar to chop; it means to cut rough-shaped but even-sized pieces. **Émincer** (ay-man-say) means to mince; it also means to slice thinly or cut into thin uniform strips.

Cutting is probably the most basic skill a cook must have—the ability to handle a knife quickly and efficiently to cut the exact size and shape of product needed. Although cutting machines often save time and labor, no machine can cut with the versatility and judgment of a good cook with a good knife. "He (or she)

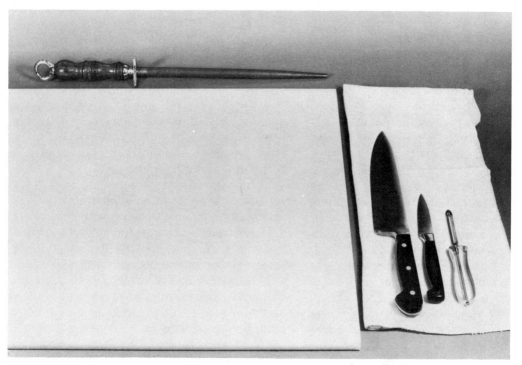

FIGURE 3-1. Station setup for cutting. This heavy plastic **cutting board** is flanked on the right with the cook's most-used cutting tools—the **french knife**, the **paring knife**, and the **peeler**—placed on a clean towel. Above the board is the **steel**. Left-handed cooks will reverse the arrangement. The board rests on a damp cloth so that it will not slip. (Photo by Patricia Roberts.)

42 / **Prepreparation**

is a good hand with a knife" is high praise in the industry and an entry into almost any kitchen.

The knife

The knife in question is the **french knife**— a fairly thick, rigid, wide-bladed knife with a distinctive triangular profile. It is illustrated in Figure 3-1, which shows a typical station setup for cutting. This knife is designed for heavy-duty cutting and chopping. Its sturdy blade is strong enough to withstand the constant beating it takes against the cutting board. The blade extends well below the knife handle, allowing the fingers to come all the way around under the handle without hitting the board (see Figure 3-3).

If you could have only one knife it would probably be this one. The french knife is the cook's right hand.

Most professional cooks have their own french knives and perhaps other hand tools as well. You can do your best work with a knife whose length, weight, balance, and handle grip suit you—a knife that feels good in your hand. It should be made of high-quality stainless steel that contains a high percentage of carbon steel, which helps the knife retain its sharpness. The **tang**—the extension of the blade into the handle—should run the entire handle length.

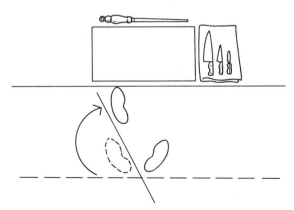

FIGURE 3-2. How to position yourself for cutting. The diagonal line shows the angle of your body as you work.

Using the knife

The french knife is used for many things, such as cutting, mincing, and puréeing. There are machines for doing such tasks. Then why use the knife? You will use it in the following situations:

- Whenever precise, uniform cuts are called for, such as cubes or slices, and you do not have a machine that makes these cuts. (The chopper chops; it does not and cannot make crisp, even cuts.)

- Whenever the knife takes less time than the machine. Cleaning a machine is time-consuming, and unless you must cut a large quantity it is not worthwhile to use the machine.

- To cut foods whose texture would be spoiled by machine cutting, such as parsley or onions, which become crushed and juicy in a machine.

For a comfortable position while working, first stand at arm's length from the work surface with your heels together at a 45-degree angle. Then take a short step forward—with your left foot if you are right-handed and your right foot if left-handed. Your body is now automatically placed at a 45-degree angle to the cutting board (Figure 3-2). This position allows you a natural movement with your shoulder, arm, and hand in line with each other. It will reduce fatigue, especially when you are working long periods of time.

To learn how to cut with a french knife, first watch a demonstration and then try it yourself under supervision. Begin by holding the knife correctly. Figure 3-3 shows you how. Hold the base of the blade with your thumb and forefinger. Relax the remaining fingers loosely around the handle. This gives you good control. Many beginners hold the knife far back on the handle and push down with a forefinger along the top of the blade. The right grip takes far less effort and gives far more control. The knife is in balance. A simple wrist motion makes the weight of the knife itself do a good bit of the work.

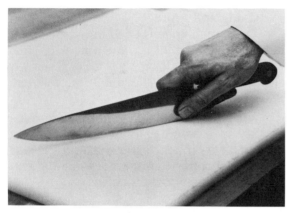

FIGURE 3-3. How to hold a french knife. (Photo by Patricia Roberts.)

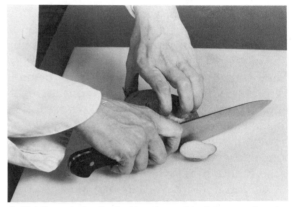

b. Cut through the food with a forward and downward stroke. The knife does the work.

Now move your hand into position to guide the next cut. Bring the knife back to its starting position and repeat the stroke. The forward part of the blade does the cutting.

FIGURE 3-4. How to cut with a french knife.
a. Place your other hand on top of the food you are going to cut, with your fingers curled. Your hand is relaxed. It holds the food lightly. Cut a thin piece off one side of a round food to make a flat place for it to rest on.

With the food resting on the flat place you have cut, place the knife tip on the food with its blade against your knuckles. Your knuckles should guide the blade, telling it where to cut. You can sight along them to see that they are in position to produce the thickness of slice you want.

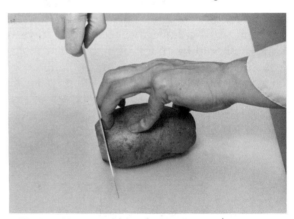

c. The knuckles guide the knife. Keep your hands relaxed, your knuckles in the guiding position. You can either move the action backward slice by slice or push the food under the knife with your guiding hand. In cutting thin foods, keep the tip of the knife on the cutting board and let it glide back and forth as you cut. (Photos by Patricia Roberts.)

Now study carefully the photos and instructions in Figure 3-4. Then try them out yourself.

Work very slowly until you have established a comfortable rhythm. Be sure the food is positioned for the knife, not the other way around.

Next, concentrate on making even cuts—pieces all the same thickness. Keep your knife straight. Do not try to get up speed until you have mastered the motions and the evenness. It takes weeks and months of concentrated practice for real proficiency.

Using the french knife to mince foods takes a slightly different technique. Figure 3-5 shows you how it is done. Minced parsley is often referred to in recipes as "chopped parsley."

A few foods don't lend themselves to straightforward cutting techniques. The onion is a special case because it is layered and the layers will separate. If you work with the layers rather than against them, you can cut the onion quickly and uniformly. Figure 3-6 shows you how. Minced shallots and garlic are also cut this way rather than using the mincing technique in Figure 3-5.

Puréeing is still another knife technique. To **purée** (pew-ray) is to mash a food to a fine pulp. It is usually done by forcing it through a sieve or putting it into a blender, but a small amount can be done with the blade of the french knife. Figure 3-7 shows you the technique.

Sharpening the knife

Two tools will keep your knives sharp: the **stone** (short for **whetstone**) and the **steel.** The stone is for sharpening the knife initially; the steel is for keeping it sharp. The steel should accompany your knife at all times. If you use the steel frequently as you work, you will seldom have to use the stone.

Figure 3-8 shows how to use the steel. Watch a demonstration before you try this yourself; then try it under supervision.

To sharpen a dull knife you must use a whetstone. Figure 3-9 shows how this is done. Watch a demonstration before you try it. The stone is often moistened with a special cutting oil before use.

When your knife is sharp, finish with several strokes on the steel. This is called **trueing**

FIGURE 3-5. How to mince.
a. Cut the food coarsely, using the technique described in Figure 3-4. Then, with your cutting hand in its usual position, hold the knife tip in one place on the board with your other hand.

b. Rock the knife up and down in short strokes while moving the handle end in an arc that crosses the pile of food. Repeat, moving the arc backward and forward over the food until it reaches the desired fineness. After a number of passes across the food, you can scrape the pieces into a pile and go at it from a slightly different direction.   (Photos by Patricia Roberts.)

FIGURE 3-6. How to dice onions.

a. Cut an onion in half lengthwise.

b. Place one half down on the cutting board and make an even series of lengthwise cuts as shown, leaving the segments attached at one end.

c. Holding the segments together, make a similar series of cuts parallel to the board, at right angles to the first series. Your hand is above the knife, well out of its way.

d. Now make a series of cross cuts, and you have your diced onion.   (Photos by Patricia Roberts.)

FIGURE 3-7. How to purée with a knife. After mincing a food as shown in Figure 3-5 or 3-6, place the flat of the knife blade over it at a 20-degree angle, sharp edge flat on the cutting board. With your other hand, press down on the blade while you draw the flat of the blade hard across the food—in this case, garlic. Repeat until you have the fineness of purée desired.   (Photo by Patricia Roberts.)

FIGURE 3-8. How to use the steel.

a. Hold the knife handle in your cutting hand. Hold your steel in front of you in your other hand. Place the base of your knife blade just below the tip of the steel, with the sharp edge of the blade resting on the steel at an angle of 15 or 20 degrees.

b. Maintaining this angle, use a wrist motion to bring the blade across the length of the steel in one long stroke that ends with the tip of the knife near the base of the steel.

c. and **d.** Repeat this stroke with the other side of the sharp edge on the other side of the steel.

Use this pair of strokes 10 or 12 times, always alternating sides of the blade edge.   (Photos by Patricia Roberts.)

FIGURE 3-9. How to use the stone.

a. Place the tip of your knife blade on one end of the flat stone. Use the fingers of your other hand to apply a light, even pressure.

b. Move your knife slowly across the stone in a slow, even stroke from blade tip to blade base.

Repeat for the other side. Repeat the pair of strokes several times, until your knife is sharp. You can test it on your thumbnail.   (Photos by Patricia Roberts.)

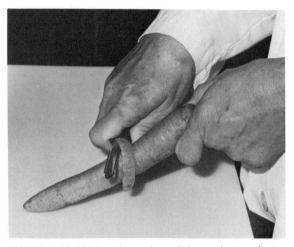

FIGURE 3-10. Holding the peeler and the product as shown, push the peeler away from you in a sweeping stroke the length of the product.   (Photo by James C. Goering.)

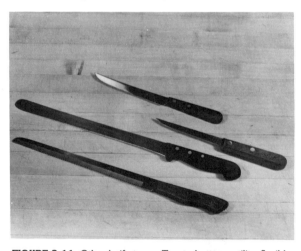

FIGURE 3-11. Other knife types. Top to bottom: utility, flexible boning, slicer, serrated.   (Photo by Patricia Roberts.)

the blade: it removes burrs from the knife edge. Then wipe the blade to remove any steel dust. You will not need the whetstone again if you use your steel often enough.

Do not use an electric sharpener or a sharpening wheel on a good knife. It will not do an even job, and it wears away the blade. Do not oversharpen your knife. It does not need to do the work of a razor. But don't be afraid to use a sharp knife. It is much safer than a dull one because it will do a good job and is less likely to slip out of position.

Other knives and cutting tools

Two more indispensable cutting tools are pictured in Figure 3-1: the **peeler** and the **paring knife.** Figure 3-10 demonstrates how to use the peeler. Figure 3-11 shows other types of knives. Figure 13-12 illustrates still other specialized hand tools for cutting. If there is a special cutting task of any sort, there is bound to be a special cutting tool to do it (see, for example, the **router** in Figure 3-14c).

Figure 3-13 shows the paring knife in action. It is used here for cutting the oval

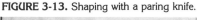

FIGURE 3-13. Shaping with a paring knife.

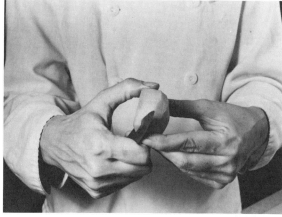

a. Curl your four fingers around the knife handle and part of the blade with the sharp edge toward you. You want your firm grip on the knife to be as close to the action as possible. Brace your thumb on the product. Hold the product firmly in your other hand.

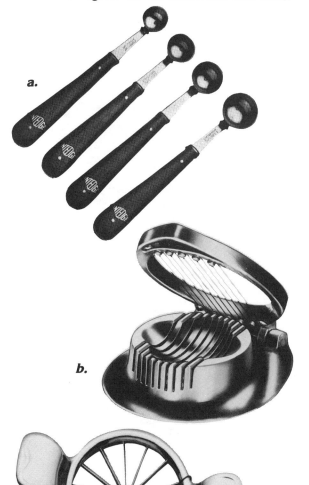

FIGURE 3-12. Some specialized cutting tools. **a. Ball cutters.** (Photo courtesy Intedge Industries, Inc.) **b. Egg slicer.** (Photo courtesy Bloomfield Industries.) **c. Appler corer/cutter.** (Photo courtesy Intedge Industries, Inc.)

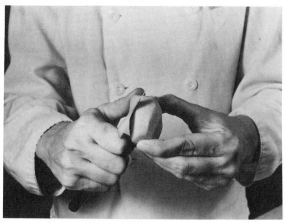

b. Pull the knife slowly toward you. Make sure the blade bites firmly into the food. The thumb of your cutting hand steadies everything. (Photos by Patricia Roberts.)

shape called **tourné** used in some classical dishes. The paring knife is also used for any cutting task requiring a short, sharp knife, such as making fancy garnishes (Figure 3-14). You can also use the paring knife as you do the french knife for cutting on the board.

Treat knives with tender loving care. Do not put them in the dishwasher, and never use them on a metal surface.

Clean the cutting board and knife after each use. Their surfaces can become unnoticed cross-contaminators, especially if used for cutting poultry, fish, or meat.

Precision cutting

The importance of careful cutting of vegetables cannot be overstated. For any one vegetable, pieces of the same size cook at the same rate, and pieces of different sizes cook at different rates. If, for example, two different-

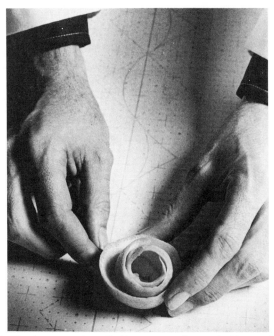

b. The orange peel is rolled into a rose, skewered with a toothpick.

FIGURE 3-14. Using the paring knife to make garnishes.

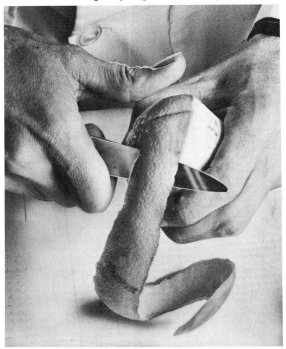

a. The rhythmic turning of the two hands in opposite directions yields a single long strip of orange peel.

c. The cucumber is scored with a **router** . . .

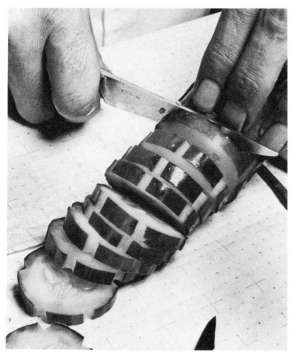

d. . . . then sliced . . .

e. . . . and becomes part of a bouquet. (Photos courtesy *The Dallas Times Herald*/Jay Dickman.)

size cuts of potato are boiled in the same pot, the larger of the two will be undercooked when the smaller one is done, and the smaller one will be overcooked when the larger one is done.

Many different cuts of foods are used in the many dishes you will be making. Each cut has a special name that communicates specific information about shape or size or both. Figure 3-15 shows some common cuts. You may recognize some of them already. As you pursue cooking they will all become familiar. The range of sizes given for some of the cuts means simply that these are the sizes to which the term applies. It does not mean that a batch of french fries, for example, can vary in size from 3/8 to 1/2 inch (3/4 to 1 cm). They must all be the same.

The essence of good cutting is to make smooth, clean cuts of food, with all pieces equal in size and shape for even cooking. A clean cut is one that is crisply cut, with a sharp knife and good cutting technique. Clean and even cutting is the foundation of good vegetable preparation.

What is true of vegetables is true also of meats and fruits. Cubes of meat for a stew or slices of apple for pies should be cut with the same care and precision as the vegetables that are to be served at the table. These foods too must cook evenly, to the same degree of doneness.

Machine cutting

Certain types of cutting are often best done by machine, especially if large quantities are needed. Machines are monsters and should be treated with suitable respect and dread. An accident with a machine is always serious. Before you attempt to use any machine you must do three things:

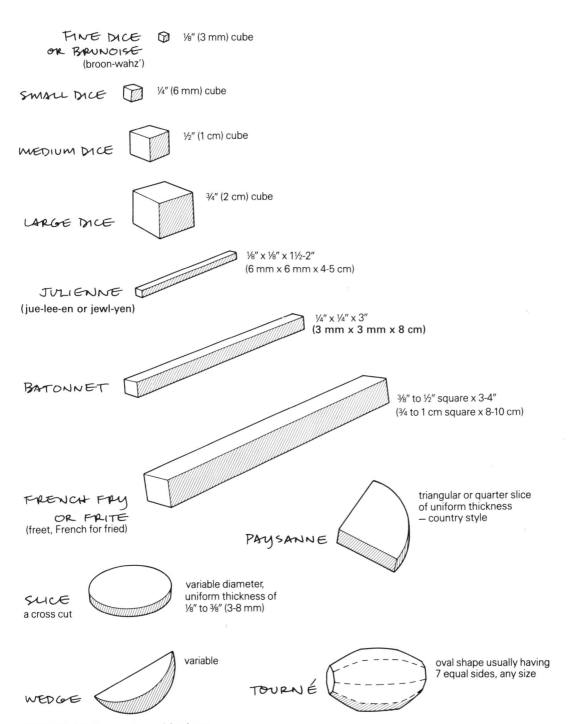

FINE DICE OR BRUNOISE (broon-wahz') ⅛" (3 mm) cube

SMALL DICE ¼" (6 mm) cube

MEDIUM DICE ½" (1 cm) cube

LARGE DICE ¾" (2 cm) cube

JULIENNE (jue-lee-en or jewl-yen) ⅛" x ⅛" x 1½-2" (6 mm x 6 mm x 4-5 cm)

BATONNET ¼" x ¼" x 3" (3 mm x 3 mm x 8 cm)

FRENCH FRY OR FRITE (freet, French for fried) ⅜" to ½" square x 3-4" (¾ to 1 cm square x 8-10 cm)

PAYSANNE triangular or quarter slice of uniform thickness — country style

SLICE a cross cut variable diameter, uniform thickness of ⅛" to ⅜" (3-8 mm)

WEDGE variable

TOURNÉ oval shape usually having 7 equal sides, any size

FIGURE 3-15. Commonly used food cuts.

- Attend a demonstration and lecture on its use.
- Study the manufacturer's instructions thoroughly.
- Use the machine only under supervision until your instructor or supervisor is satisfied that you know what you are doing.

For slicing, the **food slicer** is superior to hand cutting in many instances. It is used most frequently for slicing meats, cheese, and vegetables in quantity. It gives you slices of uniform thickness and is therefore very useful in producing a standardized portion. You can set the machine to produce the thickness of slice you want. A typical slicer is illustrated in Figure 3-16a.

The **food chopper,** usually called the **buffalo chopper,** uses revolving knives to cut things up. The degree of fineness is determined by the number of times the ingredients go under the knife blades. It is shown in Figure 3-16b.

Another type of chopper, the **vertical cutter/mixer,** or **VCM** (Figure 3-16c), uses whirling knives in an enclosed bowl. It is super high-speed. It can cut up your salad greens in 5 seconds and will reduce them to soup if you run it a few seconds too long. As the name implies, this machine can also be used as a mixer for such things as dough and mayonnaise.

Choppers can process such items as meats, nuts, vegetables, and bread crumbs with great speed. Manufacturer's instructions must be followed, and hands and hand tools must be kept away from whirling knives. They make no distinction between an onion and a human hand.

The **grinder** (Figure 3-16d) is used most often for meats, seafood, and poultry. The food is put into a hopper and pushed into a revolving screw that forces it through one or more cutting plates. The size of the pieces is determined by the size of the holes in the plates.

PROCESSING

Processing includes all the things done to get foods ready for cooking and serving. In some kitchens more time and labor may be spent in processing than in the cooking itself.

Cleaning and cutting, of course, are major processing activities. In addition there are many specific processes and techniques that figure in the prepreparation of many different kinds of foods.

Putting things together

Let us look first at some processing terms and techniques that have to do with putting ingredients together.

- **Mix**   To combine ingredients in such a way that the parts of each ingredient are evenly dispersed in the total product.
- **Blend**   To mix two or more ingredients so completely that they lose their separate identities.
- **Bind**   To cause a mixture of two or more ingredients to cohere as a homogeneous product, usually by adding a binding agent.
- **Beat**   To move an implement back and forth to blend ingredients together or to achieve a smooth texture (Figure 3-17a).
- **Whip**   To beat with a rapid lifting motion to incorporate air into a food (Figure 3-17b).
- **Fold**   To mix a whipped ingredient lightly with another ingredient or mixture by gently turning one over and over the other with a flat implement (Figure 3-17c).

The first of these terms, *mix,* is a general term that includes the other five, which refer to specialized kinds or ways of mixing. Mixing also includes less specialized processes of combining, such as stirring together chicken, celery, and mayonnaise to make a chicken salad.

FIGURE 3-16. Cutting equipment.

a. The typical **slicer** has a sharp blade that whirls at high speed. The food to be sliced is placed on the carriage, which moves across the rotating blade and back again. You must use the end weight—not your hand—to feed the food. The whirling blade is quite capable of amputating a finger.

c. The **vertical cutter/mixer** is a large-quantity, high-speed giant blender.

b. In the **food chopper** the knives are set vertically under the hood, and the bowl revolves to carry ingredients under the knives. It feeds in the foods automatically and needs no assistance from hands or implements.

d. The **grinder** cuts up foods by forcing them through holes in cutting plates. (Photos courtesy Hobart Corporation.)

FIGURE 3-17. Beat, whip, fold.

a. BEAT

a. Beating uses a back-and-forth motion of the utensil to mix or smooth out a product.

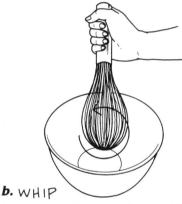

b. WHIP

b. Whipping uses a rapid beating stroke with a lift to it to incorporate air. The back-and-forth motion becomes circular.

c. FOLD

c. Folding uses a continuous slow circular stroke that scoops up the product from the bottom and spreads it gently over the top.

Blending is a specific kind of mixing in which ingredients are indistinguishably merged. Milk and ice cream are blended to make a milk shake. The yolks and whites of eggs are blended to make an omelet.

Binding is a process that gives permanence to a blend. Blending is a mechanical mixing, and some blends may not stay blended. To make them cohere, or stick together, as a homogeneous product—one that is the same throughout—you can add a binding agent to hold them together. The binding agent usually changes the texture, too, by thickening the product. Some binding agents, such as starches, require cooking the blend together with the binding agent. Others, such as gelatin, simply require mixing and chilling.

Beating is a particular way of mixing. Beating may also be a way of getting lumps out of a product. Getting rid of lumps in this way is actually another aspect of mixing, since what you are doing is breaking up the lumps and blending their contents into the product.

Whipping is a particular way of beating in which you mix air into a food so evenly that it stays there as part of the product. When you "beat" egg whites for a meringue you are really whipping them.

Folding is a special technique for handling a whipped product so as to retain the air you have whipped into it. You would fold whipped egg whites into a mixture to make a soufflé, or dry ingredients into a sponge cake batter, for example, or whipped cream into a gelatin mixture to make a bavarian cream.

Figure 3-18 illustrates some of the hand tools used in putting things together. Bowls are indispensable all-purpose utensils; stainless steel is the material of choice since it is light in weight and impervious to acid. Whips are used to beat, whip, and blend liquids and semiliquids; a mixture that is too thick will become enmeshed in the wires. Rubber spatulas are often used in folding, and they are invaluable in scraping out the contents of containers.

Mixing is also done by machine; the power

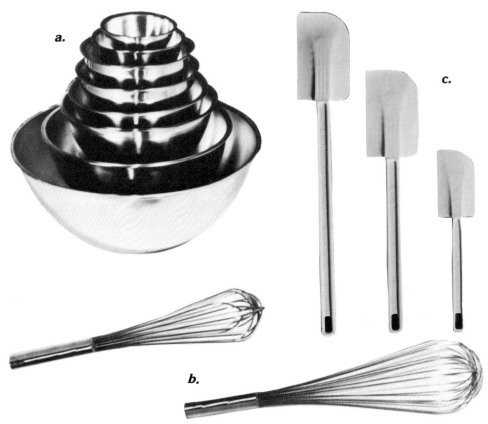

FIGURE 3-18. Mixing tools and utensils. **a. Round-bottom stainless-steel bowls.** (Photo courtesy Bloomfield Industries.) **b. Wire whips.** (Photos courtesy Intedge Industries, Inc.) **c. Rubber scraper/spatula.** (Photo courtesy Rubbermaid Commercial Products.)

mixer is one of the major workhorses of the quantity kitchen. Mixers come in various sizes, from 5 quarts (5 liters) to 140. They perform many tasks, using whips, hooks, and paddles. Figure 3-19 shows a typical mixer with attachments.

For efficiency, and above all for safety, follow the manufacturer's instructions carefully. Use the right attachment for the job, the right-size bowl, and the right motor speed for the task. Stop the motor while you are scraping the bowl or handling the product. Don't leave the machine running unattended.

The vertical cutter/mixer is also a mixer, as noted earlier. Similar safety warnings apply. In addition, do not uncover the bowl until the knives have stopped spinning.

Coating

The term **coating** refers to covering a food with a layer of crumbs, meal, flour, or other fine substance before cooking it. There are several different ways of coating a food, notably dredging, breading, and battering. Let us examine these one at a time.

Dredging means passing a food through a fine dry or powdery substance in order to coat it. A number of different substances can be used—flour, cornmeal, almonds, and others. The key to dredging is not the substance used

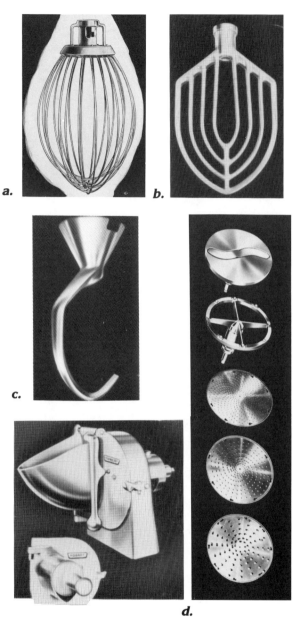

FIGURE 3-19. The mixer. This 60-quart (56-liter) **mixer** stands on the floor. It uses a wire whip (**a**) to whip eggs, make salad dressings, and whip cream. It uses a paddle (**b**) for heavier tasks such as cake and cookie batters and mashed potatoes. A special dough hook (**c**) mixes bread doughs. Special attachments will (**d**) grate and slice, (**e**) grind, and (**f**) dice. (Photos courtesy Hobart Corporation.)

a.

b.

c.

d.

(Figure continues on page 58.)

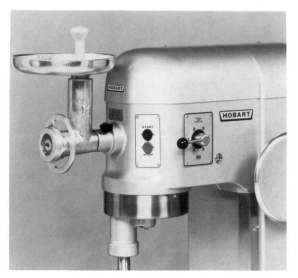

e.

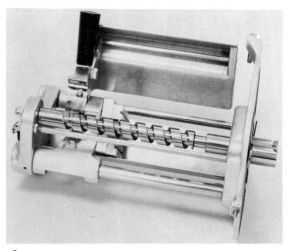

f.

to coat but the way it is applied. Another term used commonly to describe this technique is **rolling.** A recipe may read, "Roll in flour," or in cornmeal, and so on. After rolling, the excess is shaken off, to produce an even coat.

Dredging is often used to prepare meats and fish for sautéing. The coating adds color to the finished product and is sometimes used for flavor, as with almonds or cornmeal. Often it is seasoned. A dredged food cannot be held but must be cooked at once or the dry coating will become moist and soggy.

Dredging is often confused with **dusting**— a totally different process. Outside the kitchen, dusting is lightly removing particles from a surface. In the kitchen it is just the opposite: it is lightly adding particles to a surface by sprinkling them on gently. In baking we dust a worktable with flour to prevent a dough from sticking. And we dust corn fritters, french toast, waffles, and soufflés with powdered sugar, mostly for appearance and for taste.

Dredging is also confused sometimes with breading. It is, in fact, the first step of the breading process.

Breading is a three-step process of coating a food with crumbs or meal. It is applied to many kinds of foods—meats, vegetables, fish, poultry, croquettes. Breaded items are usually deep-fried; occasionally they are pan-fried.

The coat of breading around a food does a number of things. It transmits heat from the fat to the food. It keeps the food from absorbing the fat. It helps the food to retain its moisture. It forms a shield that allows the food to be seasoned without harm to the fat. It produces a crisp and crunchy texture that contrasts pleasantly with the softness of the food. Properly cooked, the breading adds its own pleasant taste to complement the taste of the product.

The food to be breaded is seasoned before breading begins, since there is no way to season it afterward. Seasoning and flavoring are sometimes added to the breading, but they will season or flavor only the breading and not the food itself. In addition, the seasonings may be harmful to the cooking fat, causing it to break down.

The three steps of the **standard breading procedure** are shown in Figure 3-20. The seasoned product is first dredged in flour, then dipped in **egg wash** (a mixture of eggs and liquid), and then in crumbs. It is then set on a pan or rack to await final cooking. The breaded product is fried to a golden brown and served as soon as possible.

This may all sound simple. But problems can arise in cooking if the breading is not done right.

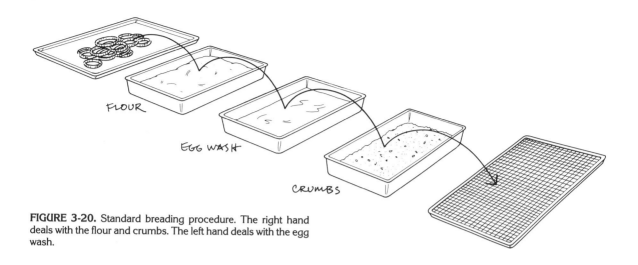

FIGURE 3-20. Standard breading procedure. The right hand deals with the flour and crumbs. The left hand deals with the egg wash.

FLOUR

EGG WASH

CRUMBS

PROBLEM: The breading may not stick to the food.

SOLUTION: To be sure the breading will stick, always follow these steps carefully:

1. Dry the excess moisture from the food so the flour will stick to it readily.

2. Pass it through the flour, making sure it is completely covered; then shake off the excess. This gives a dry, even coat for the wash to stick to.

3. Dip it in egg wash. Again make sure it is completely covered; then drain off the excess. This gives a wet, even coat for the crumbs or meal to adhere to.

4. Put the food in the crumbs, coat it completely, and shake off the excess.

A product carefully breaded in this fashion will not shed its coat in cooking.

PROBLEM: The breading may cook golden brown before the product inside is cooked.

SOLUTION: If the product is one that requires more than a short cooking time, precook it prior to breading. Meat in croquettes, for example, should be precooked before breading.

PROBLEM: The breading may break during frying.

SOLUTION: The breading will indeed crack if eggs alone are used. An egg wash, however, is not just beaten eggs; it is the eggs plus a liquid, usually in a ratio of 2 parts egg to 1 part liquid by volume. The milk or water that is added to the eggs will eliminate cracking.

PROBLEM: The finished product may have a ragged appearance or have dark spots marring its golden coat.

SOLUTION: You can achieve a uniformly good appearance by always using dried crumbs that are very fine. They will adhere evenly and cook evenly. Toasting or drying bread, crushing it, and running it through a screen (Figure 3-21 *a*) makes fine crumbs.

The first time you attempt to bread something you may find that your hands are getting as fully breaded as the product, and that you are getting egg wash in the crumbs and crumbs in the flour, and that your temperature is rising. The secret of successful technique is to keep one hand dry for the flour and crumbs,

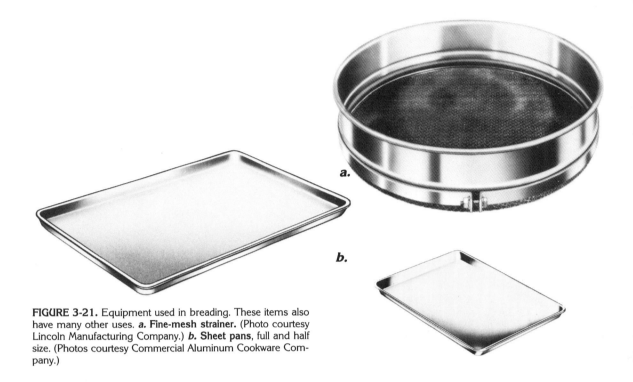

FIGURE 3-21. Equipment used in breading. These items also have many other uses. **a. Fine-mesh strainer.** (Photo courtesy Lincoln Manufacturing Company.) **b. Sheet pans**, full and half size. (Photos courtesy Commercial Aluminum Cookware Company.)

and to use the other hand only for the egg wash. If you are working from left to right keep your right hand dry. If you go from right to left use your left hand for the flouring and crumbing and your right for the wash.

In spite of good technique your flour, egg wash, and crumbs may invade the wrong containers after a time. Then you can sift the flour, strain the wash, and sift the crumbs to restore them. Otherwise your breading may lump.

Place your breaded items neatly on a sheet pan (Figure 3-21 b) or rack in a single layer, so that they do not sweat or become soggy or stick to one another. If you must stack breaded items put wax paper between the layers.

Breaded items may be prepared in advance of cooking and held in the cooler or frozen for future use. They should not be held at room temperature because, as raw-egg products, they are likely places for bacterial growth.

A third way of coating a food to be cooked is dipping it in batter, or **battering.** A **batter** is a semiliquid—too stiff to be called a liquid and too fluid to be called a solid. It is often used with chicken, fish, and vegetables.

A batter usually consists of an egg-and-liquid mixture thickened with flour to achieve a smooth, rich consistency. Cornstarch is often added to batter to give a crisp and shiny finish coat. A recipe is given in Chapter 15.

The food to be cooked is battered by dipping it in the batter just before cooking. For good results it is often dredged in flour first to give the batter a dry surface to adhere to.

Here is another term that is often confused with breading. Battering is used for the same kinds of foods as breading and performs the same functions, but the tastes and textures are different. Battered products cannot be held; they must be cooked immediately.

Precooking and partial cooking

Processing often includes cooking. Depending on the food and the dish in which it is to be used, the cooking can be either total or partial.

In many instances a food must be totally cooked before it is used in a dish—for example, the chicken for a chicken salad, the macaroni for macaroni and cheese, the hard-cooked egg in a thousand island dressing. Precooking may be carried out by any cooking process appropriate to the food.

Partial cooking refers to any cooking process that is stopped before the product reaches doneness. There are two methods of partial cooking that every cook must understand and master: parboiling and blanching.

- **Blanch**   To plunge into boiling liquid and cook 10 to 20 percent of doneness.
- **Parboil**   To simmer until 50 percent done.

Stock or water is typically used in both methods.

There is no way to measure these degrees of doneness. You have to build your experience of these things, product by product. By feeling, tasting, seeing, experimenting, you will develop your own methods of judging degrees of doneness.

A special means of blanching and parboiling is cooking in the deep fryer. Potatoes are often partially cooked this way, usually for a style of potato that will be finished by either sautéing or deep-frying.

Partial cooking is done for several reasons. It may be necessary in order to allow additional things to be done to a food. It may be a way of bringing a food to an equality with others, such as partially cooking a carrot that is going to share a soup with quicker-cooking celery and tomatoes. It may be a technique of preparing a food somewhat short of doneness in order to hold it for finish-cooking. This is often done to save time during the serving period, when partially cooked foods may be finish-cooked quickly in batches as needed.

Partial cooking is also done to extend the shelf life of many items. Potatoes, for example, when peeled, deteriorate rapidly. Partial cook-

ing slows deterioration and enables them to be stored in the cooler or freezer to prevent loss.

Marinating

Another prepreparation process, marinating, has produced some of the most famous dishes in the world—sauerbraten from Germany, chicken tandoori from India, beef teriyaki from the Far East, shish kebab from the Near East. **Marinating** is soaking a food in a marinade to add flavor or to tenderize it or both. A **marinade** is any liquid made up for the purpose of marinating.

Marinades are made from many ingredients, ranging from sour cream to peach brandy, depending on the particular flavor the cook wants to add to the dish. Vegetables, fruits, and meats are marinated with an infinite number of flavor combinations. The cook's choice will be guided by the preferences of the clientele.

Meats are usually marinated for both flavor and tenderization. A typical formula for a meat marinade would be made up of oil, flavor builders, and acid. Each of these ingredients has a specific purpose.

The oil is a vegetable oil, used to help hold natural juices in the meat to avoid loss of the meat's own flavor.

Flavor builders are such tastemakers as onion, garlic, spices, and herbs. The choice depends on the specific flavors desired.

Acid is used to tenderize by breaking down connective tissue. There is some controversy over how much of this an acid can do. Evidence shows that unless meat is marinated for a considerable length of time, little tenderizing takes place. Nevertheless cooks go on marinating less tender cuts of meat with apparent success. Perhaps the meat *seems* tenderer because of the added flavor.

Marinating can be a matter of minutes or it can take several days. It depends on the purpose and on the nature and size of the product. Cubes of meat for shish kebab need not be marinated as long as a pot roast. Game might be marinated a day or more because it lacks tenderness. Sauerbraten is sometimes marinated a week or longer. Whatever the length of time, it must be taken into account in planning for precooking readiness.

Marinating must be done in a container that is impervious to acid, such as stainless steel, glass, or crockery. Foods being marinated must be kept refrigerated at proper temperatures.

HOLDING AND STORAGE

Now what do you do with all the foods you have cleaned, cut up, breaded, partially cooked, precooked, marinated, and otherwise preprepared while you are prepreparing other products? You hold or store them.

The terms **holding** and **storage** are often used interchangeably, but they actually have distinct meanings. Both refer to the keeping of food products, but the keeping is for different lengths of time and different purposes. **Holding** is the keeping of a food product for a short period before its intended use at a specific time. **Storage** is the keeping of a food product for future use for an unspecified period of time.

Holding

Holding usually applies to a food that has been partly or fully processed. For most foods it is a matter of hours or minutes, though it may extend 24 hours or longer for such items as gelatin salads and hard-cooked eggs. Most foods are held right in the kitchen in equipment designed for this specific purpose. Foods may be held either cold or hot, a major difference between holding and storage.

Foods that are held cold may be fully prepared dishes ready for service, such as salads or cold hors d'oeuvre. Or they may be partially processed items awaiting further processing or cooking, such as peeled vegetables and fruits or breaded items or partially cooked foods awaiting finish cooking, or almost anything in process of preparation. Such products are held in the refrigerator or in special cold-food holding boxes, such as the airline caterer uses to deliver cold food to the plane. Cold-food holding equipment must maintain a temperature of 35°F (2°C) to keep foods below 40°F (4°C). The careful cook will check the temperature of holding equipment whenever placing something in it.

Processed foods to be held should be well covered or wrapped to prevent their absorbing odors and flavors from other foods. They should be held either above or below danger-zone temperatures. As you know, sanitary codes require cooked foods in refrigerators to be covered and separated from raw foods to avoid cross-contamination.

How long you can hold a processed food depends on the product and the processing. Good production planning will help you keep holding time to a minimum.

Peeled vegetables and fruits present special holding problems unless they are partially cooked. Most of them discolor rapidly when exposed to air. Potatoes are a familiar example. Eggplant probably holds the record for quick color change: the first slice of an eggplant can discolor before you cut the last one. Apples, peaches, pears, bananas, and avocados are among the fruits that behave this way.

Two things can be done to prevent discoloring.

- Rinse with an ascorbic acid solution or citrus fruit juice (for fruits only) before holding. A tablespoon of lemon juice to a quart of water will do the trick.

- Hold in water, immersing completely.

The best way to eliminate problems with peeled products is to schedule production carefully. Do not peel items far in advance of further processing or use. Refrigerate until used.

Fully prepared foods to be served hot must be held either below or above danger-zone temperatures—that is, either in the refrigerator if serving time is hours away or in special hot-food holding equipment if serving time is approaching.

FIGURE 3-22. Steam table and **pans.** Hot foods are kept hot with steam from below. Pans of various sizes and depths fit the openings in the table exactly. An unused opening is covered, so that the heating temperature is maintained below the food. (Photo courtesy The Vollrath Company.)

Several types of equipment keep foods hot for service. The **steam table** (Figure 3-22) is probably the most familiar. It forms the hot-food part of a cafeteria serving line. In the kitchen it is typically the heart of the serving area. Some operations use a dry service counter that heats electrically.

Another holding device is the **bain-marie** (ban-ma-ree). This hot-water bath is kept at a thermostatically controlled 180°F (82°C) to keep pots of sauce, soup, or stew above the bacterial growth range but not hot enough to cook them further and cause evaporation. A bain-marie in use is pictured in Figure 8-5. Typical bain-marie pots are illustrated in Figure 3-23.

Today's kitchens also have all types of enclosed holding containers for hot foods. They are like ovens set at low heat (180–200°F or 90–100°C). As you will remember from Chapter 2, hot-food holding equipment must maintain a temperature of 180°F (82°C) to sustain an internal temperature of 140°F (60°C) and keep foods in the upper safe zone.

There are many types of hot-food cabinets, designed for special needs. Other devices such as the **chafing dish** and the **overhead heat lamp** keep hot foods hot on the buffet and on the kitchen serving line (Figure 3-24). Special kitchen equipment heats dishes so that hot foods will stay hot all the way to the table. Using the right equipment keeps foods both safe and appetizing.

Most hot foods hold well on the steam table and in chafing dishes if treated properly. This means that moist foods must be kept

FIGURE 3-23. Bain-marie pots.   (Photo courtesy The Vollrath Company.)

FIGURE 3-24. Hot-food buffet service.
a. A **chafing dish** with a hot-water inset and a cover keeps moist foods hot. Mini-burners maintain temperature.
(Photo courtesy Legion Utensils Company.)

b. **Overhead heat lamps** on this buffet server supplement heat from below. (Photo courtesy Crescent Metal Products.)

moist and crisp foods crisp. To hold rice on a steam table, for example, put a thin layer of butter in the bottom of the pan before you put the rice in. This keeps the rice from drying out. Any moist food should have a source of continuing moisture or fat during its stay in a chafing dish.

Crisp foods, on the other hand, must be protected from moisture. Never cover a pan of fried chicken or any deep-fried food; it will quickly lose its crunch and become soggy.

Storage

Storage—keeping foods for future use for unspecified periods of time—may apply to products of any kind, raw, processed, or fully cooked.

The three main kitchen storage areas are the dry storage area, the refrigerator, and the freezer. The latter two are spoken of together as **cold storage.**

The **dry storage area** is typically a clean, cool, dry, shelf-lined place near the receiving area. It is kept at 60–70°F (15–20°C) with humidity below 60 percent. Types of foods requiring this kind of storage include

- Rice, dried beans and peas
- Flour, cereals, and other grains
- Sugar, salt, dried herbs and spices
- Breads
- Oils and shortenings
- Unopened canned and bottled goods

Dry foods should be stored off the floor. Containers should be clean and closed or tightly covered to prevent contamination from dust, insects, and rodents. New products are always placed either behind or under existing supplies of the same product to ensure that the oldest will be used first. This is called **rotating the stock** and is standard practice in all storage. *First in, first out* is the universal rule. Dating stock as it is shelved aids in efficient rotation and use.

The storage methods for raw foods and processed foods are refrigeration and freezing. A refrigerator, known in everyday terms as a **cooler,** holds and stores foods at temperatures of 35 to 40°F (2–4°C). There are many forms—*walk-in,* often referred to simply as "the walk-in," *reach-in, pass-through*—and many sizes.

The purpose of keeping foods in a cooler is to prevent bacterial growth and to maintain the texture, size, and weight of foods until use. Three factors in addition to temperature play a part: humidity, air circulation, and cleanliness. Since texture, size, and weight of foods are greatly affected by their water content, the relative humidity in a cooler is usually 80 to 85 percent to keep the foods from drying out. Air circulation, provided by fans in all but smaller coolers, maintains even temperature and humidity throughout. Cleanliness is essential to prevent spoilage.

Ideal storage temperatures vary depending on the product. Meat and dairy products should be stored at 34–36°F (1–2°C). Fresh produce does better at a slightly warmer 36–38°F (2–3°C) so that there is no chance of freezing. Large operations, such as the airline caterer described in Chapter 1, will have separate refrigerators to maintain appropriate temperatures for different products.

Produce that has had no processing goes into the cooler for storage. Fruits and vegetables normally arrive cooled, packed in cartons or crates. These should be emptied promptly and the produce repacked into perforated plastic containers. Such containers assure good air circulation, which prolongs freshness. The repacking allows you to check product quality right down to the bottom of the crate or carton.

Store produce off the floor, covered, and do not store it in the same area with processed foods. Put it behind or under existing supplies, and label and date it.

Meats, seafood, and poultry, both processed and unprocessed, should be covered or wrapped well to prevent drying. Store processed and unprocessed products separately (see Chapter 2). Label with name, date, and quantity, and rotate the stock.

Storage of meats may play an important role in the cook's day-to-day food handling, not because of any special requirements but because of the high cost of meat. Losses from improper handling or storage are prohibitively expensive.

Cooked-on-premises foods of any kind must be stored separately from raw foods or commercially processed foods. Foods being held during prepreparation follow the same rules: refrigerate covered and store separately.

It is important to keep the cooler door closed at all times—to keep the temperature constant, the air humid, and the circulation effective. For similar reasons do not put large amounts of hot foods in a cooler but cool them *quickly* to room temperature first. Check temperatures when placing anything in the cooler and report variations to your supervisor.

The freezer is a special refrigerator kept at 0°F (−18°C) or below. The typical freezer is primarily for storing foods already frozen, not for freezing from scratch. Freezing large quantities of foods takes special equipment and techniques.

Sometimes partially cooked and otherwise processed foods are frozen to prepare for large banquets or to prevent high loss from spoilage. Most foods that have had some processing have a limited **shelf life** (safe keeping time) in the cooler—hours or days at most. The freezer can extend shelf life by weeks or months.

But using the freezer to extend shelf life is something you should do only if you must. Though the typical kitchen freezer will freeze foods, they do not keep as well as commercially frozen foods. Furthermore, freezing makes demands on the equipment that may affect its performance.

To freeze products properly you must cover them tightly or, preferably, wrap them in plastic or foil to prevent **freezer burn**—white spots having off flavors and a pulpy texture that comes from loss of moisture. Label each item with name of product, date, and quantity. Package meat to be frozen in sensible units. Thawing a 50-pound pack of ground beef in a hurry can be frustrating. Avoid the necessity of freezing meats by good production planning.

Open the freezer door only when you must, and never leave it open. It is essential to maintain a constant freezer temperature in order to preserve product quality. *Never* use the freezer to cool down a large pot quickly. Check the temperature whenever you put something in or take something out, and report to your supervisor any reading varying from the 0 to −10°F range (−18 to −23°C).

Keeping foods successfully

We will have more to say about holding, storage, and shelf life in the chapters on specific kinds of foods. Meantime let us summarize the keys to successful holding and storage in the following rules.

- Know the product and its shelf life.
- Store and hold at safe temperatures—below 40°F or above 140°F (below 4° or above 60°C).
- Cover or wrap all foods.
- Store and hold in clean, odor-free areas.
- Store raw, processed, and cooked foods separately.
- Label stored foods with name, date, and quantity.
- Rotate stock.
- Plan production carefully to minimize holding.

ORGANIZING FOR PRODUCTION

The overall task of planning the day's production is carried out by management. For their place in the scheme of things cooks rely on the plans management has formulated. A production worksheet developed by the manager or supervisor becomes the tool of communication. Such worksheets contain assignments for each cook. We will have a look at a typical production worksheet in Chapter 17.

The worker's responsibility

Even though worksheets may be supplied, each worker's setup—mise en place—is an individual responsibility. So is organizing one's own time in order to complete assignments and meet deadlines. The cook's part in precooking readiness, then, means setting up for maximum efficiency. Only if you spend time getting ready for a job can you do the job effectively.

To set yourself up properly to prepare anything in the kitchen, you must answer several basic questions.

- What is the job?
- What is the product?
- How is the product prepared?
- How much is needed?
- When is it needed?
- What equipment is needed?
- What is the style of service?

Each one of your answers can affect your course of action in preparing the product. The first task in readiness is to answer the questions and take steps to satisfy them. Let's look at these questions one at a time.

To answer the first question—*What is the job?*—you could simply say the job is one of production: producing the assigned product. But the complete answer can be given only after all the other questions have been answered and a plan of action has been formulated.

What is the product? The answer to this question can narrow your course of action considerably. Each class of products—meat, vegetable, egg, soup, and so on—has certain preparation techniques that work well for all products within that class. Each dish within the class may impose more specific requirements.

How is the product prepared? The method of preparation will determine the ingredients needed, the equipment to be used, the techniques of preparation, the length of time required for preparation, and the order in which the various steps are taken. A recipe may provide these answers. A good setup will include assembling the ingredients needed and understanding how they are all going together.

How much is needed? The answer to this question will affect the amounts of ingredients to be prepared, the length of time required to prepare them, what kind of equipment should be set up to complete the job, and whether the entire quantity can be prepared at one time with the equipment available or must be done in several batches. This in turn may require handling and storage.

When is it needed? This is a basic question. The answer to it will determine not only the end point of the preparation timetable but also what prepreparation steps must be taken. When a product is needed, along with how much is needed, will be major determinants in any plan of action.

What equipment is needed? The important thing is to have the equipment ready for the job before the job is started. This includes both large and small equipment. Large equipment will normally be ready for use, but don't take it for granted; check it out and allow for warm-up time. Check temperatures too: they may be set higher or lower than the temperatures you need. Check availability: planning is very important if one piece of equipment is to be involved in the production of two or more items. Assemble all small equipment ready to go.

What is the style of service? Service style can alter some routes to completion of the job. Whether the product or meal is to be a la carte, banquet, or buffet can drastically affect what equipment is needed and even at times what methods of cookery are best.

Setting up

Some of the answers to these basic questions will be given on the production worksheet. Others will be left to you. The production supervisor is not going to tell you, for example, what tools you need, or how you should set up your station, or what you should do first. The supervisor assumes you know how to go about your work. If you don't, there are ways of looking up information and figuring out answers. Recipes, diagrams of plate layouts, even menus—all these are your raw materials. If a piece of information is still missing, ask.

As you were reading about the basic questions, it must have occurred to you that each answer affects the others and they must all be worked out as a whole. This is the secret of good organization—figuring out each factor in relation to the others and then planning out the entire production process for your particular task. This kind of good beginning increases the potential for a good ending. Not only does it ensure a quality product; it also increases your efficiency as a cook and hence your ability to produce profitably—a very important ingredient of career success.

Find your answers. Plan your course of action. Calculate your timetable. Check your large equipment. Lay out your tools efficiently. Assemble your ingredients. Are you ready? How is your mise en place?

SUMMING UP

Prepreparation means preparing everything ahead that can be done ahead, so that the final cooking at service time can be done without delay. Everything ready and in place—mise en place—is the goal.

The many tasks of prepreparation revolve around the cleaning, cutting, and processing of raw products. They require skill with the knife and careful operation of the kitchen's powerful machines as well as the ability to choose the right tool for the task. They also require knowing the precise meanings of kitchen terms and learning the techniques of blending, beating, whipping, folding, dredging, dusting, breading, battering, marinating, blanching, parboiling, and many more.

Holding and storage of preprepared foods constitute a critical stage of preparation for reasons of both sanitation and product quality. Successful holding of preprepared products requires the correct use of holding equipment and above all the maintenance of safe temperatures.

The key to carrying out production tasks successfully is careful organization—finding out exactly what is needed, planning it carefully, and setting up your own mise en place. Not only do really skillful cooks know how to produce a quality product; they can do it with a minimum expenditure of time, motion, materials, and energy because they know how to organize their work. Some of the greatest achievements of great chefs and managers have stemmed from their ability to organize well prior to cooking. *This is the essence of precooking readiness.*

THE COOK'S VOCABULARY

prepreparation, preprep

final preparation, finish cooking

mise en place

rough prep, prepping

cut, chop, mince, dice, slice, purée

concasser, émincer

french knife, tang

stone, whetstone, steel, trueing the blade

fine dice, brunoise, medium dice, large dice

julienne, batonnet, french fry cut

slice, paysanne, wedge, tourné

mix, blend, bind, beat, whip, fold

coat, dredge, dust, roll, bread, batter

standard breading procedure

egg wash

blanch, parboil

marinate, marinade

hold, store, dry storage, cold storage, shelf life

bain-marie

freezer burn

rotating the stock

QUESTIONS FOR DISCUSSION

1. Discuss the meaning and importance of mise en place and describe how you would apply it in preparing a specific recipe.

2. How do cleaning procedures differ in preparing leafy vegetables, soft or fragile vegetables, and hard vegetables? Explain why.

3. Discuss proper techniques in using the french knife and in sharpening and trueing knives.

4. Name the basic cuts with their dimensions and discuss the importance of careful, precise cutting.

5. Describe the standard breading procedure and explain the differences between it and other coating procedures.

COOKING is one of those everyday marvels like television and flying and the weather that are so commonplace no one thinks twice about how remarkable they are. Cooking makes all sorts of interesting transformations in raw foods to whet the appetite, delight the taste buds, and nourish the body. It softens some foods—the celery stalk, the potato, the grain of rice. It makes others firm—the egg, the cake batter, the meringue. It enlarges some things, such as popcorn, popovers, and soufflés; deflates some (spinach, for one); and makes others disappear altogether, like a liquid left forgotten on a hot burner or the alcohol in cherries jubilee.

Cooking changes colors—turns the brown lobster red and the red meat brown—and the green vegetable too if you cook it too long—and it changes butter from yellow to brown to black. It can bind foods together, as it does in sauces and cream soups and croquettes. It can break foods down—curdled milk, overheated hollandaise. It tenderizes flesh or toughens it, depending on how it is done. It can thin gelatin and thicken broth, liquefy fat and crystallize maple syrup. It makes some foods more nourishing by making their nutrients more available to the body, yet it can destroy other nutrients, such as vitamins. It can make foods safer to eat by killing disease-producing organisms. It does remarkable things with taste—blends and mellows flavors, heightens them, sometimes transforms them entirely, sometimes ruins them by burning, scorching, or just plain cooking too long.

How do such things happen? This chapter will lay the foundations for understanding at least some of them. After completing it you should be able to

- Define cooking and describe the three ways in which heat is transferred to a product.

- Explain how heat affects such food substances as proteins, carbohydrates, fats, vitamins, minerals, and water.

4

Cooking

71

- Name and describe the various moist-heat and dry-heat cooking methods.
- Identify the major pieces of cooking equipment and their uses.
- Take proper care of fat for the deep fryer.

THE COOKING PROCESS

Cooking defined

The changes just mentioned all come about through a single process—applying heat over a period of time. That is what **cooking** is: bringing about a change in a food product by the application of heat over a period of time. The overall purpose of cooking is to make the food more edible. Speaking in the language of the kitchen, we say we are increasing its **palatability.**

Notice that two things are necessary in cooking to bring about change: heat and time. You will find that many specific cooking techniques have to do with the interplay of these two factors: the length of time and the degree of hotness, or the temperature.

When we talk about cooking temperature we are usually talking about the temperature of the cooking medium—the fat in the fry kettle, the air in the oven, the water in the pot. The real purpose, of course, is to raise the temperature of the food itself to the point where the desired change will take place. This is what takes time. The lower the temperature of the cooking medium, the longer it takes to bring about change.

How heat affects food substances

In addition to temperature and time, the makeup of the food itself is a determining factor in the changes cooking brings about. Foods are made up of varying combinations of the following substances:

- Proteins
- Carbohydrates
- Fats and oils
- Vitamins and minerals
- Water

Nutritionally these substances, taken together, provide energy (measured in calories); they build and maintain bones, body tissues, and blood cells; and they keep everything in working order. In a well-balanced diet, protein should provide 10 to 15 percent of the calories, carbohydrates 55 to 58 percent, and fats and oils not more than 30 percent. Vitamins, minerals, and water contribute no calories but are essential to growth and health. One of the goals of good cooking is to conserve the nutrient values of foods.

These different components of foods react in certain distinctive ways to the heat of cooking. If you understand these reactions, you can control the changes and obtain the results you want.

Proteins. Foods high in protein are the flesh foods (meats, poultry, fish), milk products, eggs, nuts, and certain vegetables. Nutritionally, proteins are the major building and maintenance materials of the body. On the menu, foods high in protein are the entrées, the backbone of the meal.

In cooking, heat causes proteins to **coagulate**—that is, to become firm, join together, cohere. You can see this happen before your eyes if you fry an egg over low heat: the transparent liquid becomes white and opaque as the heat reaches it. If you cook it too long or at too high a temperature, it toughens—becomes too firm. The same thing happens in flesh cookery: as the temperature of the product increases, the protein firms. Overcooking will make the flesh tough.

If you heat milk too rapidly or too long, its protein will coagulate into curds and separate from the liquid whey, and we say it has **curdled.** This will spoil your soup, sauce, or custard. Cheese, which is made from milk curd, reacts to high or prolonged heat by quickly becoming tough, stringy, and unmanageable.

Connective tissue in meats is formed of certain kinds of protein that are naturally tough. The type known as **collagen** can be broken down and changed into gelatin by cooking at low temperatures with moisture. Acids can also soften meat fibers to some extent, as in marinating (Chapter 3). On the other hand, acid can reinforce the coagulation process. Adding vinegar to the water in which eggs are poached makes a firmer, more compact and shapely product.

Carbohydrates. Carbohydrates include *starches, sugars,* and *cellulose,* or *fiber.* They are found mainly in plant foods such as cereal grains, vegetables, and fruits; in products made from cereal grains such as flours and cornstarch; in milk; and in refined sugar products such as granulated sugar and sugar syrups.

Nutritionally, starches and sugars are the body's main sources of energy. Those from grains, rice, fruits, and vegetables are the most useful to the body, while refined sugar is often said to contribute "empty calories." On the menu, starches and sugar are served in bread and rolls, desserts, rice, pasta, cereal, potatoes and some other vegetables, and many soups and sauces.

In cooking, heat affects the three types of carbohydrates in different ways. With starches, the most important change that heat brings is **gelatinization.** This is the process by which dry starch granules (flour, cornstarch, and so on) absorb moisture in the presence of heat, thickening and binding the food with which they are mixed. This is an important part of making soups and sauces, and it also plays a role in baking. You will understand gelatinization better when we deal with these products. Acid can affect this process too: adding lemon juice, tomato, or wine can result in a thinner product unless it is added at the end after gelatinization is complete.

The most important change heat brings to sugar is **caramelization.** High temperatures will cause chemical changes in sugars that alter their flavor and color, turning them brown. The heat must be dry: if water is present the sugars will dissolve, and because they are then limited by the boiling point of water they can-not reach high enough temperatures to caramelize until most of the water has evaporated.

Sugar can be caramelized by itself, or the sugar contained in a food product can be caramelized, as in the browning of baked goods and the caramelization of sugar in browned onions and in hash-browned potatoes. Similar browning occurs in meats seared or sautéed at high temperatures.

Cellulose, or fiber, is the substance that gives structure and texture to fruits, vegetables, and grains. The effect of heat on fiber in the presence of moisture is to soften it. This will make it more palatable, up to a point. However, a certain firmness of texture is often desirable. One of the marks of the skilled cook is the ability to produce the exact texture desired in cooked fruits, vegetables, and such starchy foods as pasta and rice.

Fats and oils. Fats and oils are characteristic components of meats, poultry, some fish, many dairy products, nuts, egg yolks, and certain vegetables. As nutrients they provide energy to the body and play an essential role in its functioning. But fats can also be health hazards. Too much fat in the diet, especially saturated fat (animal fats, butter, shortenings) and a fat-related substance called cholesterol, may cause heart disease and cancer.

In addition to fats found in menu foods, fats and oils are used as ingredients in recipes and as the cooking medium in frying. Some, such as butter, lard, and shortenings (hydrogenated oils), are solids at room temperature and go from solid to liquid as heat is applied. Oils are liquid at room temperature; they are generally extracted from vegetables such as soybeans, corn, olives, and nuts. As temperatures increase, fats will eventually **break down**—undergo chemical change. This change becomes visible when they begin to smoke. Breakdown and **smoke point** differ for different kinds of fats.

Most fats can reach much higher temperatures than water can. The fat in the fry kettle often cooks at 375°F (190°C), whereas water does not go above its boiling point of 212°F (100°C).

In meats and poultry, fats contribute much of the flavor. The flavor of a fat used in cooking is often added to the food cooked. The flavor of broken-down fat can spoil the palatability of a food that has been cooked in it.

Minerals and vitamins. Minerals and vitamins are minute components in foods that are important to nutrition. Vitamins found in vegetables are easily lost in cooking. Some are water-soluble and may be thrown out with the cooking liquid. Others are sensitive to high or prolonged heat. Cooking with minimum nutrient loss is among the most challenging of cooking problems.

Heat also brings about chemical changes that affect both color and flavor in foods. This becomes a problem particularly in cooking vegetables. Good cooking techniques can help to retain the natural colors and flavors in foods, as we shall see later.

Water. Water—or moisture, as we often refer to it—is the major ingredient in most foods. Fresh raw meats, fruits, and vegetables are at least 70 percent water; some fruits are as much as 96 to 98 percent. The water in a food contains much of its flavor and many of its nutrients.

The effect of heat on the water in foods is very important in cooking them and in the finished product. The water in a food does a good deal of the cooking by conveying heat throughout the product. Moisture also helps to soften certain tough connective tissues in meat, as noted earlier.

On the other hand, the heat of cooking causes the product to lose moisture, and with it can go flavor, nutrients, and the moist, tender texture that makes food palatable.

We will examine all these effects of heat on foods as we discuss the preparation of various food items in later chapters.

Applying heat in cooking

How does the cook apply heat to a food to raise its temperature and bring about change? Heat can be transferred to food in three ways: by conduction, by convection, and by radiation.

Conduction is the transfer of heat from something hot to something touching it that is cooler. For example, heat from the fire passes to a pot; the pot conducts heat to liquid contained in it; the heated liquid conducts heat to any food submerged in it—a vegetable, an egg, a lobster.

Conduction also takes place within food: the eggshell in the hot liquid conducts heat to the egg; the outer portions of the egg—or of any food—conduct heat to adjacent portions, so that heat is transferred continuously within it. The fat in the fryer conducts heat to the breading, which conducts heat to the breaded food. The larger the product, the longer it takes for heat to be transferred to the center.

Convection is the spread of heat by a flow of hot air or steam or liquid. This flow may be either natural or mechanical. In a pot of liquid, for example, the liquid at the bottom nearest the fire is heated first. As it is heated, it becomes lighter and rises to the top. The cooler, heavier liquid sinks down, becomes heated in turn, and rises. In this way a naturally circulating current of hot liquid is set up throughout the pot. The same kind of natural convection current occurs in the air of an oven or in the steam of a covered pan or steamer.

In mechanical convection the circulation of the heated air or steam or liquid is maintained mechanically. In a convection oven, for example, fans force the heated air to flow to and around the food, and vents carry off the cooler, moister air. When the term convection is used in the kitchen it usually refers to this type of convection. A convection oven is illustrated in Figure 4–8b.

Radiation is the transfer of heat through energy waves radiating directly from a heat source to the food, in the same way that your skin is sunburned by the sun's rays. In radiation the food to be cooked is exposed directly to the energy waves from the heat source—a steak on a grill, a fish under a broiler, a chicken on a spit.

The microwave oven also cooks by radiation. It converts electrical power into high-frequency energy waves. These waves penetrate the food placed in the oven, causing the water molecules in the food to vibrate. This creates heat and cooks the food without heating the oven itself.

Probably the most important consideration in applying heat in cooking is whether the heat is moist or dry. Cooking methods in which heat is provided by water-based liquids or steam are called **moist-heat methods.** The remaining methods are called **dry-heat methods** because water is not the vehicle providing the heat. The type of method used has a profound effect on what happens during cooking and how the product turns out.

In this chapter we will examine both groups of cooking methods and define precisely the term that is attached to each individual method. Only when you learn a term's exact meaning can you translate it into action properly.

MOIST-HEAT COOKING

All moist-heat cooking methods involve water or a water-based liquid as a vehicle of heat transfer. Among these methods are boiling, simmering, poaching, steaming, and braising.

Cooking in the pot

Several methods of cooking take place in a pot of liquid. They stem from the ancient practice of cooking over the open fire—in the primitive cook's clay pot, the earthen, bronze, and silver vessels of the Greeks and Romans, the medieval iron pot hung on a hook in the fireplace, the great cauldrons of manor and castle with legs to straddle the fire. Consider the following definitions:

- **Boil**   To cook food submerged in a boiling liquid or to cook the liquid itself at a boil. A boiling liquid is in turmoil, its surface agitated and rolling. "Seethe" was the word for it in medieval cookbooks. Water and most other cooking liquids, except liquid fat, boil at 212°F (100°C) at sea level.

- **Simmer**   To cook food submerged in liquid just below a boil, or to cook the liquid itself, at temperatures of 180°F (85°C) to just short of the boiling point. A simmering liquid has bubbles floating slowly from the bottom to the surface. There is some action in the liquid, but it is not agitated, as in a boil, and the surface is fairly quiet.

- **Poach**   To cook food submerged in liquid at a temperature of roughly 160–180°F (70–85°C). A liquid at this temperature will have bubbles on the bottom of the pot, but they will tend to stay there and not disturb the body of the liquid.

In all these methods the temperature range is the most important factor. You don't measure the temperature; you tell how hot it is by the way the liquid behaves. Figure 4-1 shows the characteristic behavior patterns.

Above sea level the temperature of water at the boiling point drops in proportion to the altitude, at a rate of 1°F for every 550 feet above sea level (1°C for every 300 meters). This means that it takes longer to cook something at a boil in the mountains than it does at a seaside resort. Poaching and simmering temperatures will also produce more action in the water at high altitudes than at sea level.

Turning up the heat does not make a boiling liquid any hotter at any altitude. The **boiling point** is the temperature at which the liquid turns to vapor, and boiling it harder simply makes it evaporate faster.

Boiling is seldom used as a cooking method. The lower temperatures and gentler action of simmering and poaching produce much better results and give the cook greater control. The boiling point, however, is very useful. It is customary in many instances to bring a liquid to a full rolling boil and then turn the heat down until the liquid reaches the desired degree of action. The rolling boil does two things: it brings the full pot to the same temperature throughout, and it provides a point of departure from which to turn the heat down to maintain a lower temperature. Some-

a. POACH **b.** SIMMER **c.** BOIL

FIGURE 4-1. Poach, simmer, boil. **a.** Bubbles on the bottom of a pot of liquid that is otherwise calm indicate a temperature suitable for poaching. **b.** Bubbles rising from the bottom, barely breaking the surface, indicate simmering temperatures. **c.** A liquid that is agitated throughout and has a vigorously bubbling or rolling surface is at the boiling temperature of 212°F (100°C).

times getting the right degree of action in the pot takes several adjustments. Adding a food to the liquid lowers the temperature and the action, and heavy pots and electric heating coils respond slowly to change.

Many foods are cooked at a simmer—vegetables, shellfish, stews, soups, sauces. Poaching is used for shelled eggs and the delicate flesh of fish, which cook quickly even at low temperatures and retain their shape better in a calm liquid. Boiling is used mainly for pastas; with this product the vigorous action of the liquid keeps the strands of pasta from sticking together.

Boiling and simmering are also used as processing techniques for partial cooking. The last chapter discussed two such techniques—blanching and parboiling. Both are done at a simmer. Though blanching begins at a boil, the entry of the food to be blanched reduces the temperature immediately. A food to be parboiled may be started in cold water and brought to a simmer or it too may be plunged into boiling water and the heat adjusted to maintain a simmer.

Still another technique that uses boiling or simmering is reducing:

• **Reduce** To boil or simmer a liquid down to a smaller volume.

In reducing, the simmering or boiling action causes some of the liquid to evaporate. The purpose may be to thicken the product or to concentrate the flavor, or to do both. A soup or sauce is often simmered for one or both reasons. A mixture of highly flavored ingredients such as wine or vinegar and spices may be boiled down to a few tablespoons of concentrated flavor to be added to a sauce—one of the few uses of boiling. The resulting product is called a **reduction.** In nouvelle cuisine sauces are often thickened by reducing rather than by thickening agents.

Equipment for cooking with liquids

To start with, let us look at ranges, since a great deal of moist-heat cooking takes place on them. The **range** has been called the jack-of-all-trades, the workhorse, the backbone of the kitchen. Here you can boil, simmer, poach, braise; you can make stocks, soups, sauces, stews. You can also cook by several dry-heat methods, and you can warm, heat, and hold foods already cooked.

Figure 4-2 shows common types of ranges. For moist-heat cooking you would use the open-top burners on either of the ranges pictured or the hot-top burners in Figure 4-2*b*.

Traditionally, turning on the ranges was the first thing done by the first person entering the kitchen. In these times of high utility cost this is not always done. But remember that the flat-top and the griddle need preheating before use.

The most important thing about cooking on a range is knowing your own equipment. This comes from operator's manuals and from experience.

Figure 4-3 illustrates typical pans for moist-heat cooking. You should learn to know each kind by name. But don't be inhibited by the name. Don't think, for example, that you have to have a brazier for braising, or that you can't do anything but braise in it. Use logic: select a cooking utensil according to what you are going to use it for. Choose a pan size appropriate to the amount of food you are going to put in it and to the cooking process you intend to use. Study the pictures and captions to see how pan shapes are suited to needs.

Most pots and pans for quantity cooking are made of heavy-duty aluminum. This

a.

b.

FIGURE 4-2. Ranges.
a. The **open-top range** has open burners, individually controlled. You put your pot or pan on the burner directly over the heat source and adjust cooking temperature by turning the heat up or down.   (Photo courtesy Vulcan-Hart Corporation.)
b. The **flat-top** (or **hot-top**) on the left side of this range has continuous metal plates that are heated from underneath. You put your pots and pans on the hot plates. Different parts of a flat-top range are usually set at different temperatures (low, moder-

ate, high). You adjust cooking temperature by moving what's cooking from one place to another.

On the right side, the **fry-top,** or **griddle,** often mistakenly called a grill, has a continuous smooth, slick surface on which such foods as eggs, pancakes, hot dogs, and hamburgers are fried directly (no pans)—a dry-heat method. The top must be kept oiled, or **seasoned.** Different parts of this range can also be set at different temperatures.   (Photo courtesy Garland Commercial Industries.)

FIGURE 4-3. Pots and pans for the range.

a. **Stockpots** are tall and narrow so that a large amount of simmering liquid will offer only a small surface for evaporation. (Photo courtesy Commercial Aluminum Cookware Company.)

b. Straight-sided pans (double-handled **saucepot,** long-handled **saucepans**) are easiest for mixing and blending, as in making sauces. (Saucepot and deep saucepan courtesy Commercial Aluminum Cookware Company; shallow saucepan courtesy Lincoln Manufacturing Company.)

c. The **brazier,** also called a **rondeau,** is designed for long, slow cooking on the back of the range or in the oven. (Photo courtesy Commercial Aluminum Cookware Company.)

d. The **double boiler** is used for cooking or holding foods at low temperatures. You put the food in the top part and boiling water in the bottom. (Photo courtesy Commercial Aluminum Cookware Company.)

heavy-duty metal prevents scorching and burning, resists warping and denting, and conducts heat well.

You'll notice that the two pans have long handles. These enable the cook to utilize all parts of the range with ease and keep a comfortable distance from its intense heat—up to 140°F (60°C) right beside it. To grasp a pan handle you will use a dry towel to keep from burning your hand.

Most pans have flat bottoms for even con-tact with the range surface. A few are made with slightly rounded bottoms designed to fit the contour of the open gas burner. It's important not to try to cook with a round-bottom pan on an electric burner or a flat-top range. You would get your direct contact with the heat in only one spot, and the food there would scorch or burn while the rest of it scarcely heated at all.

Figure 4-4 shows implements and uten-sils used with range-top cooking. The profes-

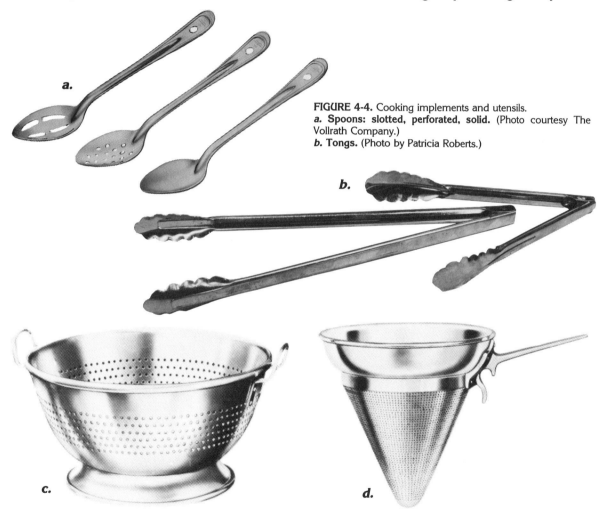

FIGURE 4-4. Cooking implements and utensils.
a. **Spoons: slotted, perforated, solid.** (Photo courtesy The Vollrath Company.)
b. **Tongs.** (Photo by Patricia Roberts.)

c. **Colander,** used to drain liquid from foods. (Photo courtesy Lincoln Manufacturing Company.)
d. **China cap,** or **chinois,** used to strain liquids into another container. (Photo courtesy Lincoln Manufacturing Company.)

sional cook uses fewer utensils in cooking than you might expect. To stir and to turn you often flip things by manipulating the pan. There are two reasons for this. One is time. The other is that metal on metal—spatulas and spoons on pans—can give food a metallic taste. If you must use an implement, stir with a wooden spoon and turn with tongs, which you can use without touching the pan. If you must use a wire whip, keep it brief. Continual whipping in an aluminum pan can turn a white sauce gray. To make a really white-looking sauce use a stainless-steel pan.

There is a limit to the amounts of food you can cook on a range and the numbers of dif-ferent things you can have going there at once. Two pieces of special equipment supplement the range and perform similar tasks, sometimes better than the range itself. These are illustrated in Figure 4-5.

The **tilting fry pan,** also called a **tilting skillet** or **tilting brazier,** is a large, shallow pan with a continuous heat source. It plays many roles. At a high temperature setting it is a great big fry pan. With lower heat and its cover down, you can convert it into a brazier. Or fill the uncovered pan with water, set the heat to maintain a simmer, and you have a perfect egg poacher. Its name comes from the fact that it tilts for emptying and draining.

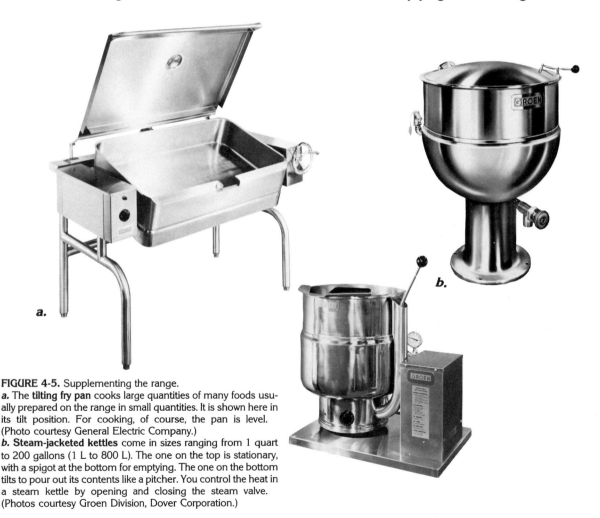

FIGURE 4-5. Supplementing the range.
a. The **tilting fry pan** cooks large quantities of many foods usually prepared on the range in small quantities. It is shown here in its tilt position. For cooking, of course, the pan is level. (Photo courtesy General Electric Company.)
b. **Steam-jacketed kettles** come in sizes ranging from 1 quart to 200 gallons (1 L to 800 L). The one on the top is stationary, with a spigot at the bottom for emptying. The one on the bottom tilts to pour out its contents like a pitcher. You control the heat in a steam kettle by opening and closing the steam valve. (Photos courtesy Groen Division, Dover Corporation.)

The **steam-jacketed kettle (steam kettle** for short) is just what the name implies. It is a kettle surrounded on the bottom and sides with a hollow jacket that fills with steam when turned on. Steam transfers heat to the bottom and sides of the kettle, which then heats the product inside more quickly and evenly than does a pot on a range, where the heat is only on the bottom. You can use the steam kettle for boiling, simmering, poaching, and braising, and for making such finished products as soups, sauces, stews, and puddings.

Anything using steam is a serious burn hazard if not used properly, so it is important for you to learn the correct operating and safety procedures. If your steam supply is in the kitchen, turn it on well ahead of time, so that it will be ready to go when you need it.

Steaming

The steam or vapor created by a boiling or superheated liquid captured in an enclosed space provides another moist-heat cooking method.

• **Steam**   To cook with steam, usually in a cabinet-type steamer with or without pressure.

In this method steam is the heat conductor. If it is under pressure, the temperature is hotter than a water-based liquid can ever be. Water will not get hotter than 212°F (100°C) no matter how hard you boil it. But steam under pressure of 5 psi (pounds per square inch) reaches 225°F (105°C) or more, and at 15 psi it will be 250°F (120°C). (Expressed in metric, steam under pressure of 35 kPa reaches 105°C or more, and at 100 kPa it will be 120°C.) Therefore steam cooking under pressure is considerably faster than cooking in liquid. A typical pressure steamer is illustrated in Figure 4-6.

The pressureless steamer is not as fast as the pressure steamer, but it is more easily controlled and is safer overall. It is becoming increasingly popular.

Steaming is a good method for cooking many vegetables; it helps them retain flavor, color, texture, and certain vitamins and minerals. You can also cook rice and pasta, fish and shellfish, meats, poultry, eggs, and steamed puddings in a steamer, and you can use it to defrost, moisten, and blanch. It robs some foods of flavor, notably meats and poultry.

Even more than the steam kettle, this piece of equipment is very hazardous if not used properly. Learn thoroughly all operating and safety procedures.

Food may also be steamed by its own moisture. Cooking a food with butter in a covered pot without added moisture is

FIGURE 4-6. Pressure steamer. This **cabinet (compartment) steamer** cooks foods at a pressure of 13 psi (90 kPa). Foods are spread in large shallow pans, and tiny jets of superhot steam are directed at them for extra-speedy cooking. Different kinds of steamers require different cooking times for the same product, so you must follow the manufacturer's instructions.   (Photo courtesy Garland Commercial Industries.)

called **poëler** (po-a-lay) or **étuver** (ay-too-vay). Steaming a food wrapped in foil or heavy paper is referred to as **en papillote** (on pap-ee-yote). Fish are sometimes steamed this way. A "baked" potato wrapped in foil is also steamed—cooked by its own moisture.

Braising

Still another kind of moist-heat cooking is braising.

- **Braise** (brayz) To cook food until tender with a small amount of liquid in a covered container over a low fire or in a low-heat oven.

Braising falls somewhere between simmering and steaming. Up to two-thirds of the food is immersed in liquid. The rest is bathed in hot, vapor-filled air inside the pot. Steam, condensation, hot air, and simmering liquid all play their part.

Braising is particularly appropriate for less tender cuts of meat because long cooking with moist heat can soften the texture of collagen, bringing many flavorful meats within the range of palatability. Stews, pot roasts, and sometimes vegetables are among the dishes prepared this way. Braising may be done in a covered container in the oven, on the range, or in a covered steam-jacketed kettle or tilting fry pan.

The many roles of liquids

In all the moist-heat methods of cooking, the moisture or liquid does a great deal more than simply conduct heat to a product. It interacts with the food being cooked in ways that can influence the final taste and texture. It softens not only the collagen of meats but the cellulose of vegetables. On the other hand, moist heat can have negative effects. It can rob vegetables of vitamins, flavor, and color unless carefully managed, and it can leach flavor from meats. If you cook a turkey wrapped in foil, it will be practically tasteless.

A cooking liquid can play an important part in the flavor of a dish. You often season vegetables by adding salt to the cooking water. You can enhance the flavor of a product by adding herbs and spices and wine to the cooking liquid, as in simmering shrimp and poaching fish and chicken. If the liquid is to become part of the finished dish, as it does in soups and sauces, you build in the flavor very carefully to produce the final taste you want.

Vegetables and meats will give up flavor to liquid in which they are cooked. You can often use the liquid as stock in making a sauce or a soup. Many dishes depend for their success on the right balance between liquid and product, the length of time they stay together, and the right temperature for bringing about a happy ending.

DRY-HEAT COOKING

Dry-heat cooking methods transfer heat without use of water or steam. They may rely on hot air, hot fat, radiation, or hot metal.

Cooking with hot air or radiant heat

Consider the following definitions.

- **Bake** To cook by heated air in an enclosed area called an oven. The term typically applies to pastries, cookies, breads, certain vegetables, and casseroles. It does not apply to braised dishes that are cooked in the oven in covered containers.
- **Roast** To cook by heated air, usually in an enclosed space such as an oven or barbecue pit (note the similarity to baking). The term also applies to cooking on a revolving spit before an open fire, hardly a common method in industry today but the way everything was roasted for several thousand years. Spit-roasting is a radiant-heat method.

The term roasting nearly always refers to meats. Some oven-cooked meats are said to be baked—ham, fish, meat loaf—though the cooking method is the same as roasting.

- **Barbecue** A special method of slow-roasting at low heat in or over a pit infused with smoke to flavor the product. Almost any kind of meat may be barbecued, right down to rattlesnake and armadillo, but it is most often beef, pork, or chicken.
- **Broil** To cook by direct heat from above, a radiant-heat process. The term broil is also commonly used to refer to grilling.
- **Grill** To cook on a grate with heat from below, also a radiant-heat process. Grilling is often called broiling. Figure 4-7 illustrates the difference between the two processes.

The term grill is also loosely used to mean cooking such items as hamburgers, bacon, or ham on the fry-top range, which is often called a grill (Figure 4-2*b*). This method of cooking is not grilling in the true sense.

- **Sear** To expose the surfaces of a piece of meat to extreme heat before cooking at a lower temperature. Searing (sometimes called **browning**) can be done in a hot pan in a little oil or in a hot oven (450–550°F or 230–290°C).

Searing, like blanching and parboiling, is a partial-cooking process rather than a cooking method. It is done to give color and sometimes to produce a distinctive flavor. It does not seal in the juices of a product, as many people think.

Dry-heat methods are used when some drying action is desired, as in baking, or when the effect of a moist environment is not needed or wanted, as in the cooking of tender, flavorful flesh. Large tender cuts of meat and tender whole birds are usually roasted. Steaks and chops are usually broiled; chicken and some kinds of fish also broil well. Broiling is often the method of choice for quick cooking of tender flesh of any kind containing fat.

Equipment for oven and broiler cooking

The major piece of equipment for roasting and baking is the **oven.** It is an enclosed space inside of which heated air does the cooking. The oven is another kitchen workhorse. In addition to roasting and baking, you can use an oven to sear, braise, stew, poach, simmer, melt, toast, defrost, warm, heat, hold. There are conventional ovens below the ranges in Figure 4-2; they have adjustable racks on which to set pans. Figure 4-8 shows two other kinds of ovens.

When you use an oven, there are a few simple things to remember.

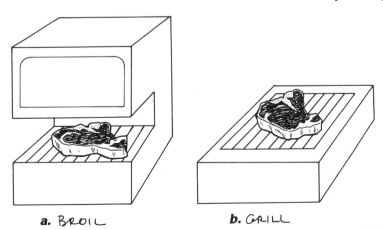

a. BROIL   **b.** GRILL

FIGURE 4-7. Broil, grill. **a.** Cooking by direct heat from above is broiling. **b.** Cooking by direct heat from below is grilling.

FIGURE 4-8. Ovens.

a. The **stack** (or **deck**) oven is an enclosed space 8 to 15 inches high, in which you put your pans directly on the oven bottom, or deck. The ovens are typically installed one on top of another in a stack.   (Photo courtesy Vulcan-Hart Corporation.)

b. In the **convection oven** a fan or blower forces heated air to circulate throughout the oven. The constant even distribution of hot air cooks foods at lower temperatures, often faster, and with less fuel than a conventional oven. Follow the operator's manual, not the recipe, for temperature settings and cooking times. (Photo courtesy Vulcan-Hart Corporation.)

- Preheat, allowing plenty of time.
- Keep the door closed. Every time you open it the temperature drops, and the longer it is open the more the oven cools. This can prolong cooking time, interrupt the cooking process, cause cakes to fail and soufflés to fall.
- Load ovens carefully with space between items for air circulation.

Figure 4-9 shows pans for oven use. Ovenware must be heavy-duty in order to withstand high oven temperatures without warping. Be careful not to substitute a lighter-weight utility pan for the roasting pan. They may be similar in shape and size, but a warped utility pan could produce a disaster in a hot oven. As with range-top pots and pans, choose a pan size appropriate to the amount of food to be roasted or baked.

Major equipment for broiling is illustrated in Figure 4-10. All broilers cook by radiant heat—that is, heat radiating directly from the heat source to the food.

You will use the grill mostly for steaks, chops, poultry, hamburgers—foods you place directly on the grate. You can use the overhead broiler for all these plus foods you would cook on pans, such as fish, vegetables, and foods to be browned.

A small overhead broiler known as a **salamander** is common in restaurant kitchens for quick glazing and browning of a product that is already cooked. The salamander is usually mounted over the range, as in Figure 4-2b.

In overhead broilers there are two ways to control the cooking temperature. You can move the cooking surface toward the fire or away from it, or you can turn the heat up or down. Broilers, like other cooking equipment, should be preheated before use.

Frying

The cooking methods generally called frying are classified as dry-heat methods. To **fry** is to cook food in hot fat. It includes the following methods.

FIGURE 4-9. Pans for the oven.

a. **Roasting pans** are shallow for even heat distribution, but deep enough to hold juices. Choose a pan slightly larger than the roast.　(Photos courtesy Lincoln Manufacturing Company.)
b. A **loaf pan** can cook a meat loaf or a loaf of bread with equal ease, as well as elegant foods like pâté en croûte.　(Photo courtesy Wear-Ever Aluminum Inc.)

- **Pan-fry**　To cook food in a small to moderate amount of fat in a pan over moderate heat.
- **Deep-fry**　To cook food submerged in hot fat.
- **Sauté** (so-tay)　To flip food quickly in a small amount of hot fat in a pan over high heat.

At first glance you might think that frying is a moist-heat method, since the medium that conducts heat to the food is a liquid. Fat, however, does not contain moisture. Moreover, it does not interact with the food in the way that liquids do in moist-heat cooking. Fat may become part of a finished product by being absorbed in the food's coating, but in good fat cookery the temperature is kept hot enough for the food to cook quickly with a minimum of fat absorption. A greasy product is never desirable.

Frying in all its forms is a quick cooking process suitable for small tender foods such as eggs, fish, chicken pieces, chops, and soft vegetables, or for foods partially cooked by some other method, such as deep-fried potatoes or croquettes made from cooked chicken. It is not a suitable method for large products or foods needing long, slow cooking.

Now let's look at the ways in which the various frying methods differ.

Deep-frying, pan-frying, and sautéing differ in the amount of fat used. In deep-frying, the food is totally surrounded by hot fat. In pan-frying, a small to moderate amount of fat is used. In sautéing, little fat is used.

In deep-frying, the food is exposed to heat on all sides at once and cooks quickly and evenly. In pan-frying and sautéing, it must be turned or flipped to expose all sides to the hot fat.

Pan-frying differs from sautéing in several ways. One is a time and temperature difference: sautéing is done quickly at high heat, while pan-frying uses moderate heat and slower, more deliberate cooking. Another difference is that pan-frying is generally used for

FIGURE 4-10. Broilers.

a. In the **overhead broiler** you put the food *under* the fire, either on a rack or in a pan. The handles at right control distance from the fire.　　(Photo courtesy Vulcan-Hart Corporation.)

a.

larger pieces of food such as fish fillets or chicken pieces, while sautéing cooks smaller, equal-sized pieces of food, such as thin slices of veal or beef or vegetables, in a smaller amount of fat.

Perhaps the most interesting difference is that pan-frying is a quiet process that takes little of the cook's attention, and sautéing is an active process demanding the cook's full participation. To pan-fry, the cook places the foods in the hot fat and they cook by themselves until they are ready to be turned. To sauté, the cook adds the foods to sizzling fat and then shakes the pan back and forth vigorously to keep them in motion. By using long strokes that send the food pieces to the far rim, the cook can flip them over with a slight upward movement. Figure 4-11 shows the difference in the two methods. (The French word *sauter* also means to leap, jump, hop, skip.)

Both sautéing and pan-frying are often used as partial-cooking processes. Meats are often seared in a small amount of hot fat be-

b. On the **grill** you set the food *over* the fire, directly on a grate. Different parts of the grill can be set to different temperatures: you can have one section hot for cooking rare steaks quickly and another section cool for steaks well done.　　(Photo courtesy Garland Commercial Industries.)

b.

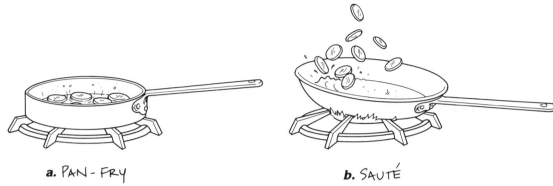

a. PAN-FRY   **b.** SAUTÉ

FIGURE 4-11. Pan-fry, sauté. **a.** Pan-fried foods are cooked quietly and fairly slowly in fat over moderate heat. **b.** Sautéed foods are flipped quickly in hot fat.

fore braising. This process falls somewhere between pan-frying and sautéing. If the pieces are small, such as those for making a stew, the sautéing technique may be used. Larger pieces of meat are turned once with tongs or a spatula; this would be a form of pan-frying, though the heat is higher than usual.

Another instance of partial cooking in fat is sweating. To **sweat** is to cook slowly in fat over low or moderate heat without browning, sometimes with a cover on the pan. Flavorful foods such as onions, celery, mushrooms, ham, and herbs are frequently sweated to bring out their flavors before they go into the making of a stock, soup, or sauce.

Another cooking method that resembles sautéing comes from the Orient and is called **stir-frying.** Bite-size ingredients are cooked over high heat in a small amount of oil, usually in a bowl-shaped pot called a wok, although any heavy skillet can be used. The food is tossed with utensils rather than being "jumped" and is cooked until crisp-tender.

Equipment for frying

Pan-frying and sautéing take place on the range, in the types of pans illustrated in Figure 4-12a and b. Certain products such as eggs, hamburgers, and pancakes can also be fried on the griddle (Figure 4-2b) with the help of the offset spatula (Figure 4-12c) to turn them.

Deep-frying requires special equipment.

FIGURE 4-12. Fry pans and utensils.

a. Sautoir, a straight-sided fry pan. Broad and shallow, it is used for browning, sautéing, and pan-frying.

FIGURE 4-12 (Continued)
b. **Sauteuse,** a slope-sided fry pan, used for flipping (jumping) foods without using a spatula. A 6-inch sauteuse is perfect for cooking eggs to order.

c. **Offset spatula,** used to turn foods in frying.   (Photos courtesy Lincoln Manufacturing Company.)

FIGURE 4-13. The deep fryer. This typical **deep fryer** has a compartment, or kettle, in which fat is heated. Wire baskets fit into the compartment and hold food in the hot fat while it cooks. They are then raised for draining.   (Photo courtesy Garland Commercial Industries.)

The **deep fryer,** also called the **fry kettle** or simply the **fryer,** has the single function of cooking food submerged in hot fat. It is used to cook many kinds of foods, from meat and potatoes to doughnuts and tarts. Figure 4-13 shows a typical fryer.

The deep fryer is found in almost every kind of kitchen. It is a piece of equipment you must learn to know well and treat with respect. Hot fat is highly flammable, and a grease fire is difficult to deal with.

Knowing how to use the deep fryer includes knowing how to take care of its fat, which is not discarded after use but can be reused with proper care. The box on page 89 is worth your close attention. Review it again when you start to cook.

Microwave cooking

Microwave cooking follows its own rules, which are radically different from those of other methods. The cook does not cook the foods; the equipment does the cooking. The cook simply uses the equipment correctly. Its uses are very specialized: defrosting, heating, cooking small individual portions of certain foods. It cannot deal with large amounts of food. In today's kitchens the microwave is playing an ever-increasing role as an accessory to other forms of cooking—melting butter and chocolate or heating milk without scorching, for example.

A microwave oven is illustrated in Figure 4-14.

FIGURE 4-14. A microwave oven. In the **microwave oven** electronic tubes produce microwaves that penetrate the food and generate heat inside the food itself. This high-speed oven is used mainly to defrost, reheat, or reconstitute previously prepared foods. (Photo courtesy Hobart Corporation.)

HOW TO CARE FOR FAT FOR THE FRYER

Keeping fat for the deep fryer ready for cooking takes a special kind of care that goes on before, during, and after cooking.

To begin with, you must use the right kind of fat. A suitable fat is one that is odorless and tasteless and can withstand the continuous high temperatures needed without smoking or breaking down—that is, changing in chemical structure. Animal fats (meats, fish, poultry, butter) and olive oil are unsuitable because they have distinctive tastes and they smoke at low temperatures. Most vegetables oils are not stable enough. The best fats are certain vegetable-oil products that have been specially processed to increase their stability. Such fats are **hydrogenated,** meaning that extra hydrogen has been added to their chemical structure to make them more stable.

Even a good fat is easily broken down by carelessness in use or storage. Breakdown can be caused by overheating, by exposure to copper, by salt, water, crumbs, and certain fatty foods. When fat breaks down it cooks poorly, tastes bad, and must be discarded. Have you ever tasted rancid or fishy-flavored fried foods at a fly-by-night snack shack or a roadside Greasy Spoon?

If you take good care of it, fat will stay fresh and can be used several times. Care pays off, since good cooking fat is very expensive. Here are some important rules of care.

- Heat fat very gradually to cooking temperature. Do not let the temperature go above 200°F (100°C) until the fat all around the heating element is liquid.

- Keep salt, water, and loose crumbs away from the fryer. Drain wet foods such as potatoes before frying. Bread products with care for a firm coat. Skim off crumbs that surface during cooking.

- Do not deep-fry fatty foods.

- Strain fat at least once a day, oftener if volume is heavy. Use a special fat strainer or several layers of cheesecloth or a paper filter in a china cap or strainer.

- Add fresh fat after each day's use—oftener if needed—to replace fat absorbed by foods during frying. The fresh fat helps to maintain the quality of the fat as a whole. Daily fat replacement should total 20 percent or more of the total amount. This continuing replacement is known as **fat turnover.** But . . .

- Do not add good fat to bad fat. It will not restore quality. Add fresh fat only to fat in good condition. Throw bad fat out.

- If fat breaks down, replace it entirely. Be alert to these signs of breakdown: off flavors (taste fat daily); smoking at cooking temperatures; yellow foam while cooking (good fat produces clear, distinct white bubbles).

- Remove the fat and clean the fryer after each day's use, oftener if needed.

- Store fats and oils, covered, in a cool, dark dry place.

SUMMING UP

Cooking is a way to change plain raw foods into delectable dishes that please the customer, supply the schoolchild with energy, and help to make the patient well. The way we bring about such changes is to apply heat to foods over a period of time. We can do this in a number of ways.

Heat is applied by being transferred from something that is hot to something that is not. There are three methods of heat transfer: conduction, convection, and radiation. Often more than one process is involved.

Heat brings about change in foods by affecting the various substances of which they are made—the proteins, carbohydrates, fats, water, and minute substances that provide their flavor and color. It can also determine whether the vitamins and minerals present in raw foods are passed on to the diner or lost along the way. You will understand better how all this works as you learn more about specific foods and how to cook them in chapters to come.

The many ways of transferring heat are divided into moist-heat and dry-heat methods, depending on whether or not moisture is the vehicle of heat transfer. Moist-heat methods include boiling, simmering, poaching, steaming, and braising. Dry-heat methods depend on hot air, radiation, or fat for heat transfer; they include baking, roasting, broiling, grilling, barbecuing, deep-frying, pan-frying, and sautéing.

This chapter has given you a big dose of terms and concepts that you may not fully understand as yet. But learn them well and use them precisely: they will help you to understand what you are doing as you cook, and why it works, and how to do it better.

Many times cooking terms defy precision and usage crisscrosses accuracy, as with broil for grilling and grill for cooking on a griddle. There is the backyard barbecue, a good American term for a process that is not truly barbecuing; it is either grilling over coals or roasting on a spit with a barbecue sauce brushed on the meat. If you have ever attended a corn roast you know that the corn and potatoes are not really roasted. If you've been to a real clambake you know the clams are not actually baked. You may work in kitchens that use terms in their own way and not as we have defined them.

To deal with such situations, follow this simple rule: "When in Rome, do as the Romans do." If you can't do that, it's time to head for Greece.

THE COOK'S VOCABULARY

cooking

palatability

coagulation, gelatinization, caramelization, curdling

collagen

conduction, convection, radiation

moist-heat cooking: boil, simmer, poach, steam, braise, poëler, étuver, en papillote

reduce, reduction

brazier, rondeau, china cap, chinois, sautoir, sauteuse, salamander

dry-heat cooking: bake, roast, barbecue, broil, grill, sear, brown

fry, pan-fry, deep-fry, sauté, sweat, stir-fry

fat breakdown, fat turnover, smoke point

QUESTIONS FOR DISCUSSION

1. Name the important substances of which foods are made, and discuss how cooking affects them.

2. Name and describe the three ways in which heat is transferred to a product, and give examples of each.

3. Discuss the differences between the two types of cooking methods, and give examples of each type. What methods would be suitable for cooking small tender cuts of meat? Vegetables? Cakes?

4. Discuss the need for caring for the fat used in the deep fryer, and cite several things you should and should not do to keep it fresh.

5. What equipment would you choose in preparing the following: pot roast, 50 pounds of broccoli, poached eggs, meat loaf, baked ham, hamburgers, french fries, pancakes? Explain why in each case.

A RECIPE is a communications tool. It is an abbreviated way of passing information from one person to another. It tells the cook what ingredients are needed to make a given dish and gives instructions about how to make it. It tells the person who buys the food what products must be on hand for each menu item the establishment serves. Recipes give the manager essential information for figuring food costs and keeping them from getting out of hand. The typical food-service kitchen revolves around recipes that have been standardized for its menu.

But one thing a recipe does not communicate very well is how to become a good cook. Some people think that following a recipe is all there is to cooking. Many cooks simply follow one recipe after another for all their cooking lives. If a recipe is mislaid, they can't make the dish. If they don't have all the ingredients on hand, they are lost. They do not really understand what they are doing.

Learning to cook by following one recipe after another is like learning English by reading the dictionary. You could memorize the meanings of all the words in the book but you would never know how to put them together to make meaningful sentences. In the same way you could know dozens of recipes by heart and make them over and over, and never understand how the ingredients function together to make a dish, or why a certain product turns out well one time and poorly the next.

This chapter will look at both sides of recipes—their indispensable roles in the kitchen and the pitfalls of trying to learn to cook from them. It will suggest a more meaningful approach to recipes than the one-ingredient-after-another point of view of most cookbooks. You will see how to look at ingredients in terms of what they do in a recipe and how they relate to one another. We will introduce you to the concept of cooking with your senses and your common sense. We will also give you some nuts-and-bolts information about weights, measures, and temperatures and explain how to convert recipes from one quantity to another.

5

Recipes and Measurement

After completing this chapter you should be able to

- Define a standardized recipe and cite reasons for its use.
- Understand the concepts of recipe structure and ingredient roles.
- Explain and demonstrate three ways of measuring ingredients.
- Convert a recipe to a larger or smaller yield or a different portion size.
- Cost a standardized recipe.
- Understand the relationship of Fahrenheit to Celsius temperatures.

RECIPES

A recipe is a bridge between someone who knows how to make a certain dish and someone who wants to make it. Ideally the teacher and the would-be cook would be in the same place at the same time, but that is not always possible. Since food preparation is ongoing and universal, a permanent, universal method of communication is needed. This is the written recipe—a set of directions for making a dish or product. The directions give the reader two things: the ingredients needed and instructions for combining them to make the finished product.

The standardized recipe

Written recipes are often developed for use in a particular operation to record the way in which that establishment makes the various dishes it serves. This kind of recipe is called a **standardized recipe.**

The typical standardized recipe lists the ingredients in order of use, states the amount of each ingredient required to make a certain number of servings of a certain size, and gives instructions for putting the ingredients together to make the dish. The number and size of servings are listed on the recipe as the **yield.**

The recipe is written for numbers of servings commonly used in the operation. Many establishments write recipes for 25 or 50 servings. In some the recipe may also be figured for larger yields, such as 100, 500, or 1000 servings. Often the serving dish, garnish, and plate layout are specified. Sometimes the card has a picture of the dish in color.

A standardized recipe applies only to one operation. Many people have the mistaken idea that a standardized recipe contains a foolproof set of ingredients, amounts, and instructions that will work every time in every kitchen for every cook. There is no such thing. If you transplant a recipe standardized for one kitchen to another kitchen and another set of cooks, it may work or it may not. If it works in the new kitchen after thorough testing of a small amount, it may be extended to larger yields and adopted as the operation's standardized recipe. If it doesn't work, that kitchen may make adjustments in the recipe to fit its equipment and its cooks and its clientele and to achieve the precise yield and quality standards required. When all the necessary adjustments are incorporated, it then becomes a standardized recipe for that operation.

The standardized recipe is useful in several ways. For one thing, it helps to assure that a product offered by the establishment is consistent from one cook to another. A customer who brings friends in to taste a well-remembered mushroom soup won't find the soup of memory gone and a new cook making a very different product. The new cook can refer to the standardized recipe, and it will indicate the special things that give that particular mushroom soup its character. Each establishment's standardized recipes are records of dishes that have proved to be successful for that operation.

Another function of standardized recipes is to provide a basis for cost analysis. Accurate costs per serving can be projected and analyzed from the precise data the recipes contain. Many standardized recipes have the cost data recorded on the recipe card. Some establishments keep their standardized recipes on a computer, where changes in ingredients and costs can easily be kept up to date. When cost problems occur—when food costs run higher than projected—the quantities and costs of items being used can be compared to quantities and costs that should have been used, in order to see what is wrong and how to correct it.

With microcomputers being used in increasing numbers, the standardized recipe is playing an ever more important role in making an inefficient industry more efficient. Good standardized recipes coupled with the computer enable management to control expenses or costs even before they are incurred. Current market prices, availability, and alternate ingredients can be programed into the computer so that costs can be determined instantly before food products are bought and used. Before the computer, figuring costs with a pencil or a calculator took hours and was seldom done. Thus the standardized recipe is one of management's most useful tools for achieving profitability, and profitability is the one essential in the commercial kitchen—something the cook must never forget.

Standardized recipes are also highly useful to the person who orders supplies or makes purchasing forecasts. A person planning a banquet can quickly figure what is needed to serve the expected number of diners because the items, quantities, and yields are right there in the recipe.

Standardized recipes are especially valuable in hospital kitchens, and their cooks must follow the recipes to the letter. The amount of salt or butter in a portion of food may be critical for a patient on a special diet. Bakers, too, use standardized recipes because a tiny variation in the ratios of ingredients can make the finished product a total failure. Operations requiring penny-by-penny cost control, such as many public-school food services, depend heavily on standardized recipes. And many large institutional food services find that standardized recipes carefully worded for the low-skill worker help to keep labor costs down yet still produce good, consistent results.

In an efficient operation each standardized recipe is checked periodically to ensure that it reflects current kitchen practice, or that current kitchen practice follows the recipe, whichever is more important. Changes in practice are noted on the card, so that it remains an accurate master record of that dish for that establishment.

Common problems with recipes

You can readily see that the standardized recipe is an essential industry tool. But learning to cook by following such a recipe one ingredient at a time is not the best way to do it. The standardized recipe was written as a record, not as a teaching tool. How good is a recipe—any recipe—at telling you how to make a dish you have never made before?

To answer this question let's examine a typical recipe for a classical cream soup (Figure 5-1). It is not a standardized recipe because it is not designed to be used in a particular operation. It is the kind of recipe you find in dozens of books. If you gave this recipe to 20 beginning cooks they might very well turn out 20 different soups.

How can this be? The recipe gives specific ingredients. It specifies exact quantities. It states exact cooking times. It spells out each step in the cooking process. How can anything go wrong?

The problem of variables

The fact is that, in cooking, there are many variables, and these variables practically guarantee a variety of results unless you understand how to deal with them. Many recipes give rigid instructions about things that vary from one kitchen to another, from product to product, from person to person.

For example, no two ranges perform in exactly the same fashion. No two heads of cauliflower are exactly alike. No two products of any kind are exactly alike, no two utensils, no two cooks. You yourself are not likely to turn the flame of the gas burner to exactly the same height two days in a row. Even the weather, the altitude, and the kitchen temperature can change things.

CREAM OF CAULIFLOWER SOUP

Yield: 20 6-ounce servings

Ingredients	Amounts	Method
butter	6 oz (175 g)	Cook vegetables, herbs, and spices in butter for 5 minutes.
cauliflower	1 head	Blend in flour and cook for 10 minutes over low heat.
celery, diced	2 ribs	Add stock and blend well. Cook over low heat for 20 minutes.
leek, diced	1	Blend in hot cream. Season with salt and pepper. Strain and serve.
onion, diced	1	
parsley, diced	few stems	
bay leaf	½	
clove	1	
garlic	½ clove	
rosemary	pinch	
thyme	pinch	
peppercorns, crushed	pinch	
flour	6 oz (175 g)	
stock	1 gal (4 L)	
cream	1 pt (500 mL)	
salt	1 Tb (15 mL)	
pepper	1 tsp (5 mL)	

FIGURE 5-1. A typical recipe.

The recipe, in trying to assure a standard result by specifying cooking times, actually guarantees a variety of results because of all the variables. Different pots of soup prepared by different people on different equipment do not cook in exactly the same length of time. One cook's soup will evaporate more than another's, so the two soups will not have the same taste and texture and will not need the same amount of salt.

Perhaps the most common and most serious variable is cooking time. The recipe in Figure 5-1 tells you to cook the vegetables and herbs in butter for 5 minutes and to blend in flour and cook for 10 minutes over low heat. The conscientious, unsuspecting recipe fol-

lower will go on cooking it for 10 minutes no matter what. But cooking times vary widely, and unless the cook understands what is supposed to be happening, disaster may follow.

Cooking with your senses

In this book the recipe instructions will seldom specify cooking times. They may give you a time range as a guideline, but they will hardly ever tell you to cook something for a specific number of minutes or hours. Instead they will give you observable checkpoints such as "when it thickens," or "when it begins to produce an aroma," or "it should feel firm to the touch," or "until no starch taste remains." These checkpoints will usually be more accurate and realistic than exact times, because they adapt to all the variables and avoid the difficulty of measurement.

Many professional cooks use guidelines like these. They don't time things, except in a general way. They know how something is supposed to look, feel, smell, taste as it develops into a dish, and they take action accordingly.

Admittedly, descriptive guidelines in a set of instructions, no matter how carefully worded, can be somewhat imprecise in communicating exactly what is going on. They may not mean much to you until you see something cooked and cook it yourself. Then you too will get the feel, the look, the taste, the smell of it, and you will really be cooking.

Using precise terminology

In order to cope with another variable— the meanings of words to the reader—the instructions in this book are built around the precise use of terms as they are defined in Chapters 3 and 4. Other terms, added as we go along, are incorporated into recipe instructions in the same way. Often such a term avoids a long, involved instruction giving directions on time, temperature, and method. The term sauté, for example, tells you to flip briefly, at a hot temperature, in a small amount of fat. The term communicates all this simply and precisely.

Structure and function in a dish

Most recipes do not give you any idea of why each ingredient is included in the recipe and how it relates to the others. The common practice of arranging ingredients in order of use makes them look like a meaningless shopping list. But if we rearrange them according to their function in the soup they begin to make sense.

What do we mean by "their function in the soup"?

Any dish created in the kitchen has certain qualities. It has a **major flavor**—beef, or mushroom, or asparagus, for example. It has a **body**—that is, it has substance and volume.

It has a **texture**—thin or thick, smooth or coarse, crunchy, creamy, chewy, and so on. To create these qualities in a dish you use certain ingredients.

In our soup the cauliflower provides the predominant flavor. That is its function in the dish. The liquids provide the body; that is their main function. The flour and butter, cooked together, thicken the soup to provide its characteristic texture; that is their function. These ingredients play the major roles in the dish; they are the stars of the show.

Then there is a cast of supporting characters in this soup: the celery, onion, leek, parsley, herbs, spices, seasonings. They assist the major ingredients but never upstage them. Their function is to build up, blend, enhance, enrich, or accent the flavor, body, and texture provided by the stars.

A diagram of our typical recipe, functionally rearranged, looks like Figure 5-2a. Ingredients appear on the two sides of a large T. Those that determine the character of the dish appear on the left-hand side of the T, and those that play supporting roles appear on the right. The ingredients are grouped according to the roles they play. You do not need them listed in order of use. The instructions tell you that. Figure 5-2b is a master diagram of a functional recipe format. It will give you a basic structure for making a dish and help you to see the role of each ingredient and understand how they all fit together. We will use this format in the recipes in this book.

Ratios and proportions

Another thing that the traditional recipe format does not communicate is the relationships between ingredients. The information is there but it is buried. Let us add quantities to our new format and see what emerges (Figure 5-2c).

Probably the first thing you notice is that there are large quantities of the major ingredients and very small quantities of the supporting ingredients. This is hardly surprising in view of their functions in the recipe.

FIGURE 5-2. A functional recipe format.

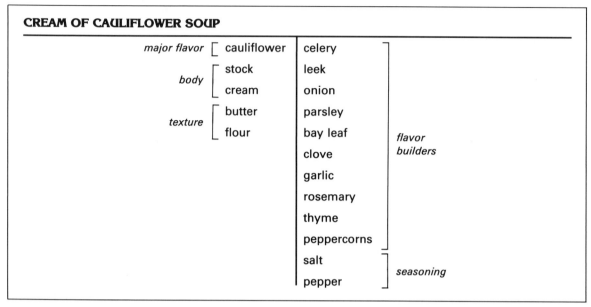

a. Diagram of Figure 5-1.

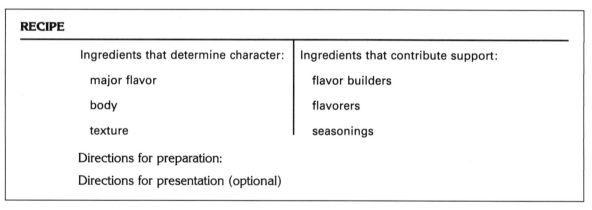

b. Functional T format.

If you look more closely at the left-hand side you can see some basic quantity relationships between the various major ingredients: 1 pound of cauliflower to 1 gallon of stock; ¾ pound of flour-butter thickener to 1 gallon of stock. (Or, in metric, 500 grams of cauliflower to 4 liters of stock to 350 grams of thickener makes 4 liters of soup.) If you examine the right-hand side you can see that there are specific relationships between the various supporting ingredients. There are further relationships between each supporting ingredient and the quantities of major ingredient and finished soup. Half a bay leaf to a pound of cauliflower to a gallon of soup. One onion. One clove.

These relationships are all present in the

CREAM OF CAULIFLOWER SOUP
Yield: 1 gallon (4 liters) = 20 6-oz portions

major flavor	1 lb	cauliflower	500 g	2	celery ribs		
body	1 gal	stock	4 L	1	leek		
	1 pt	cream	500 mL	1	onion		
texture	6 oz	butter	175 g	few	parsley stems		
	6 oz	flour	175 g	½	bay leaf		
				1	clove	*flavor builders*	
				½	garlic clove		
				pinch	rosemary		
				pinch	thyme		
				pinch	peppercorns, crushed		
					salt	*seasoning*	
					pepper		

c. Recipe in T format.

original recipe, but because of the grocery-list effect they don't become visible. When you group the ingredients according to function you see specific quantity relationships that give you a handle on the whole recipe. It is the proportions of ingredients to one another that make the dish what it is. If you lost the recipe but remembered these proportions you could still make cream of cauliflower soup.

This is the way many professionals approach their cooking. They think of ingredients in groups according to their functions and memorize the basic proportions. They refer to the recipe card for quantities and yields and the special variations practiced by the kitchen where they work.

Recipes as basic patterns

A recipe is what you make of it. As you study cooking, much of your success will depend on how you are able to use a recipe. If you follow it blindly step by step without understanding, you will be a slave to it. If you see it as a blueprint for the construction of a dish, it can open doors for you. When you understand its pattern, learn its basic proportions, and master the techniques required, you can make the dish in any quantity with or without a recipe. You can also apply the pattern and proportions to similar products. Thousands and thousands of recipes are really variations of a few basic patterns. It makes the whole world of cooking very simple.

After you have been cooking for a while with this functional recipe format, you will begin to be able to turn anybody's recipe around and rearrange its ingredients according to their function in the dish. Then, even though you have never seen the dish, you will be able to analyze what kind of product it is and what is supposed to happen in the making. You can then make a good product even from a poorly written recipe.

But these open doors are a long way down the road. Let's go back to some basic information you must master before you travel that road.

HOW QUANTITIES ARE MEASURED

Recipes may communicate quantities of ingredients in three different ways: by number (count), by volume, and by weight. These methods of communication represent three different systems of measurement. Number is measured by counting items. Volume is measured in utensils of the necessary sizes. Weight is measured with scales. Our soup recipe in Figure 5-1 uses all three systems.

Number

Ingredients that come in fairly uniform sizes are sometimes measured and expressed in numbers—6 apples, 3 eggs, 1 radish. In our recipe you see amounts of several ingredients expressed in numbers—2 celery ribs, ½ bay leaf, ½ garlic clove, and so on. Numbers are often used as measures of quantity where exact proportions are not of critical importance. It is quicker and easier to count than it is to weigh and measure.

Numbers are also used where units of food will remain identifiable in the end product. For example, a recipe for 50 stuffed avocado halves would specify 25 avocados.

Volume

On the other hand, a recipe for an avocado dip might call for a quart (liter) of mashed pulp rather than a certain number of avocados, since these fruits can vary greatly in size and yield. A quart or liter represents a way of measuring quantity by volume—that is, by the amount of space it occupies. Units of volume measurement are teaspoons, tablespoons, fluidounces (often called simply ounces), cups, pints, quarts, gallons. Common metric measures of volume are milliliters (mL) and liters (L). Figure 5-3 shows typical volume measures for large and small amounts.

Volume is used mainly to measure liquids, or fluids, since measuring a liquid is easier than weighing it. In our soup recipe the quantities of stock and cream are expressed in volume. The pinch of herb or spice is also an expression of volume, though it is not an exact unit of measurement and doesn't apply to liquids. The fluid equivalent of a pinch is a dash.

Volume is also used to measure portion sizes for serving finished items. For this purpose special utensils are used, such as those pictured in Figure 5-4. Portion scoops (Figure 5-4a) are used for such foods as meat and potato salads, cottage cheese, and sandwich fillings. Ladles (Figure 5-4b) measure out liquids such as soups, sauces, and salad dressings. Sizes of ladles and scoops are given in Tables 17-3 and 17-4.

FIGURE 5-3. Volume measures.

a. Liquid measures come in sizes from pint to gallon (500 mL to 4 L). Gradations are not labeled, so you have to know equivalents. (Photo courtesy Lincoln Manufacturing Company.)

b. Measuring spoons range from 1/4 tsp through 1 tablespoon (1 mL through 15 mL). They are used mostly for measuring herbs and spices. Fill them full, then level off with a straight edge. (Photo courtesy Foley Manufacturing Company.)

FIGURE 5-4. Portion measures.

a. Portion scoops are precisely sized for portion control. The number on each scoop indicates the number of scoops in a quart or liter.

b. Ladles are also used for portioning. They are sized in ounces or milliliters for serving liquids such as soups and sauces. (Photos courtesy Intedge Industries, Inc.)

Weight

Weight is usually used for solids, especially where exact quantities are of critical importance. Its units of measurement are pounds and ounces (grams, milligrams, and kilograms in metric). Weight is a much more precise measurement than number, because many products vary in size. Weight is also more precise than volume for solid ingredients. A cup of flour will vary in amount depending on whether it is sifted or unsifted. A cup of brown sugar will have more or less sugar according to how firmly it is packed. A quart of potatoes will be a variable amount according to how finely chopped the potatoes are. But a pound or a kilogram of any product is always the same amount of that product no matter how much space it occupies.

Where ratios or proportions of ingredients are of critical importance, quantities of solids are usually expressed entirely in weight. This is particularly true in baking. Even eggs and egg whites are listed in terms of pounds and ounces rather than numbers because eggs vary slightly in size.

Various kinds of scales are used to measure weight. Two spring scales are illustrated in Figure 5-5, and a baker's scale is pictured in the chapter on baking (Figure 15-2). If a container is used to hold the ingredient being weighed, the weight of the container must be subtracted from the total weight.

Equivalents

It is important, in working with recipes, to be thoroughly familiar with all the units of measurement. It is also important to know the equivalents of each unit in terms of the others. You will be using such information constantly.

A basic table of units of measure is given in Table 5-1. The information on volume is expanded in Table 5-2 to show the equivalent of each unit of volume in terms of all the others. If you want to turn one unit of measure into another—fluidounces into quarts, for example—read across the table from *1 fluidounce* to the figure below *Quarts.* To find out how many of one unit are contained in another—such as the number of tablespoons in a quart—read down the column headed *Tablespoons* to the figure in the *1 quart* line. The table will even tell you how many gallons there are in a teaspoon.

Abbreviations

It is also important to know the common abbreviations for each unit of measurement (Table 5-3). If you mix up tsp and Tb you may have a disaster. Some measures have more than one abbreviation. The ones we use in this text are given first in the table.

FIGURE 5-5. Spring scales.

a. A spring scale with 1/4-ounce markings.

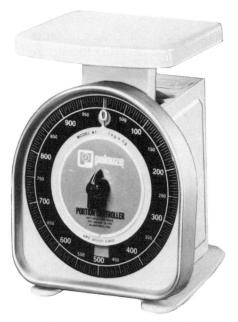

b. A spring scale with 5-gram markings.   (Photos courtesy Pelouze Scale Company.)

TABLE 5-1 **Units of Measure**
less than ⅛ teaspoon = pinch/dash
3 teaspoons = 1 tablespoon
2 tablespoons = 1 fluidounce
8 fluidounces = 1 cup
16 tablespoons = 1 cup
2 cups = 1 pint
2 pints = 1 quart
32 fluidounces = 1 quart
4 quarts = 1 gallon
8 pints = 1 gallon
16 ounces = 1 pound
1000 milliliters = 1 liter
1 pound = 454 grams
1000 grams = 1 kilogram

Although it is important to know the number of tsp in a Tb and the number of Tb in a C, these familiar household measures are used very little in industry. The amounts cooked make them impractical. It is best to begin thinking and cooking in terms of ounces and pounds and quarts and gallons (or grams and kilograms and liters and milliliters if you have converted to the metric system).

Two other abbreviations sometimes appear with an ingredient quantity in a recipe—**AP** and **EP**. AP stands for "as purchased" and EP stands for "edible portion." Thus if a recipe lists "5 lb potatoes AP," it means whole unpeeled potatoes. If it says "5 lb potatoes EP," it means peeled potatoes. You can readily see that an EP potato will weigh less than an AP potato.

CONVERTING RECIPES

Equivalents are indispensable when it comes to increasing or decreasing a recipe to produce a larger or smaller amount. This process usually involves translating some units into others, such as pounds to ounces or quarts to gallons, or vice versa.

TABLE 5-2 Volume Equivalents

		Teaspoons	Tablespoons	Fluidounces	Cups	Pints	Quarts	Gallons		Milliliters (rounded)
1 teaspoon	=	1	1/3	1/6	1/48	1/96	1/192	1/768	=	5
1 tablespoon	=	3	1	1/2	1/16	1/32	1/64	1/256	=	15
1 fluidounce	=	6	2	1	1/8	1/16	1/32	1/128	=	30
1 cup	=	48	16	8	1	1/2	1/4	1/16	=	250
1 pint	=	96	32	16	2	1	1/2	1/8	=	500
1 quart	=	192	64	32	4	2	1	1/4	=	1000 (1 liter)
1 gallon	=	768	256	128	16	8	4	1	=	4000 (4 liters)

TABLE 5-3 Abbreviations

teaspoon = tsp or t	milliliter = mL
tablespoon = Tb, Tbsp, or T	liter = L
cup = C or c	gram = g
fluidounce = fl oz	kilogram = kg
pint = pt	
quart = qt	
gallon = gal or G	
ounce = oz	
pound = lb	

To produce a different amount of the same product you must keep the proportions of ingredients the same or you will not get the same product. Figuring the amounts of ingredients in the correct proportions for a different number of servings is called **converting the recipe.**

Converting a recipe is really very simple. Everything stays in the correct proportions if you multiply every ingredient by the same number. To find what number to use, you divide the amount you want by the amount the recipe yields. The answer will be a number larger than 1 if you are increasing and smaller than 1 if you are decreasing.

To see how this works, let's take as an example our cauliflower soup recipe. Table 5-4 lists the ingredients in that recipe in Column 1. Column 2 lists the amount of each ingredient for 20 6-ounce portions (yield given). Suppose we want to make 100 6-ounce portions (yield desired, Column 3). (To keep this example simple, we have omitted the metric figures, but metrics work in exactly the same way.)

Step 1 is to find the multiplier. To do this you divide the number of portions desired (100) by the number of portions given:

$$\frac{100 \text{ portions desired}}{20 \text{ portions given}} = 100 \div 20 = 5 \text{ (multiplier)}$$

Step 2 is to multiply the amount of each ingredient by your multiplier—in this case 5—to give you the amount you need for 100 portions:

$$1 \text{ lb cauliflower} \times 5 = 5 \text{ lb}$$
$$1 \text{ gal stock} \times 5 = 5 \text{ gal}$$

and so on. Multiplying the amount of each ingredient in Column 2 by 5 gives you the amounts in Column 3.

Column 4 shows the same recipe converted to 10 servings. The multiplier is determined in the same way:

TABLE 5-4 Converting a Recipe

Ingredients	20 Servings (yield given)	× 5 =	100 Servings (yield desired)	or × 0.5 or ½ =	10 Servings (yield desired)
Cauliflower	1 lb		5 lb		½ lb
Stock	1 gal		5 gal		½ gal
Cream	1 pt		5 pt = 2½ qt		½ pt
Butter	6 oz		30 oz = 1 lb 14 oz		3 oz
Flour	6 oz		30 oz = 1 lb 14 oz		3 oz
Celery	2 ribs		10 ribs		1 rib
Leeks	1		5		½
Onions	1		5		½
Parsley stems	few		5 × few = handful		1–2
Bay leaf	½		2½		¼
Clove	1		5		½
Garlic	½ clove		2½ cloves		¼ clove
Rosemary	pinch		5 pinches		½ pinch
Thyme	pinch		5 pinches		½ pinch
Peppercorns	pinch		5 pinches		½ pinch
Salt	to taste		to taste		to taste
Pepper	to taste		to taste		to taste

$$\frac{10 \text{ portions desired}}{20 \text{ portions given}} = 10 \div 20 = 0.5 \text{ or } ½$$

Notice that, in Column 3, equivalents have been used to convert such amounts as 30 ounces and 5 pints to units of measurement you would use if you were actually going to make the dish. In practice you would also convert such amounts as 5 pinches to something more practical. You might guesstimate a quantity equal to 5 pinches. If you were going to make the larger quantity regularly, you might establish an exact amount by using a measured amount each time until you achieved a taste identical to that of the smaller recipe. You would record this tested and proved amount on your standardized recipe.

It is a good idea to look at your ingredient amounts when you have finished a conversion to see whether they make sense. It is easy when multiplying to slip in an extra digit by mistake. You might end up with 100 celery ribs instead of 10.

Another factor that is important in converting recipes is the way the yield is expressed. It may be in gallons or in 6-ounce servings and you may want 8-ounce servings. In such cases you must first use your equivalents to convert the yield desired and the yield given to the same unit (that is, a gallon or an 8-ounce serving) so that you can divide one by the other in order to find your multiplier.

For example: Your recipe yields 1 gallon. You want 80 8-ounce servings. You can choose an 8-ounce serving as your unit of measurement and convert 1 gallon into 8-ounce servings thus:

$$1 \text{ gal} = 128 \text{ oz}$$
$$128 \text{ oz} \div 8 \text{ oz per serving} = 16 \text{ servings}$$
$$\frac{80 \text{ servings desired}}{16 \text{ servings given}} = 5 \text{ (multiplier)}$$

Or you can convert 80 8-ounce servings into gallons:

$$80 \text{ 8-oz servings} = 640 \text{ oz}$$
$$640 \text{ oz} \div 128 \text{ oz per gal} = 5 \text{ gal}$$
$$\frac{5 \text{ gal desired}}{1 \text{ gal given}} = 5 \div 1 = 5 \text{ (multiplier)}$$

Or perhaps you have a yield of 20 6-ounce servings and you want 60 8-ounce servings. Here again you use equivalents to convert the yield to a common unit and then proceed as before:

$$60 \text{ servings} \times 8 \text{ oz} = 480 \text{ oz desired}$$
$$20 \text{ servings} \times 6 \text{ oz} = 120 \text{ oz given}$$
$$\frac{480 \text{ oz desired}}{120 \text{ oz given}} = 480 \div 120 = 4 \text{ (multiplier)}$$

Converting by multiplying seems simple and straightforward on paper, but in actual cooking problems do occur. Not all recipes increase and decrease well. Recipes that are converted by small amounts usually work all right. When a recipe is converted to very large numbers, problems can arise.

For example, a recipe for 4 people converted to 500 can run into trouble. Not all ingredients multiply well. Some problem items are eggs, thickening agents, and seasonings. Some foods, such as soufflés and some kinds of sauces, do not adapt well to large-quantity production because of mixing, cooking, and equipment limitations. You might have to make a smaller quantity several times.

Experienced cooks are aware of such problems and allow for them in preparation. They make adjustments by feel, and note them on standardized recipes for future use.

COSTING A RECIPE

Another set of calculations relating to recipes has to do with the cost of one portion. Many operations record these portion costs on their standardized recipe cards. Because raw food prices fluctuate constantly, these costs must be revised frequently to keep them current. In order to do this, you must **cost a recipe.** Figure 5-6 takes you step-by-step through the entire process. This is something every cook should know.

Cost figures are then used to determine whether menu prices need to be changed or whether portions and ingredients should be modified to meet budget requirements. Recipe costs are also used in developing new menu items.

THE METRIC SYSTEM

The units of weight and volume that we use in the United States are not used in other countries. Most of the world uses the **metric system.**

You may run into recipes using the metric system, perhaps in Canadian and European publications. Someday we will probably all be cooking in metric units. Meantime it is useful to know metric terms and equivalents and be able to translate them into the units of measurement for which our equipment is designed.

The metric system is simple and logical. It is based on the decimal system. You are familiar with this system through our money, in which units are decimal parts or multiples of a basic unit, the dollar. A penny is 0.01 dollar, a dime is 0.10 dollar, and so on.

The metric system of measurement applies the decimal system to weight, volume, and other systems of measurement such as

FIGURE 5-6. HOW TO COST A RECIPE.

1. Find the as-purchased (AP) cost of each ingredient.

2. Convert the recipe amount of the ingredient and the AP amount to the same unit of measure. Usually you would convert the AP unit of measure (e.g., gallons, below) to the recipe unit of measure (e.g., pints). Occasionally you would do it the other way around (e.g., numbers of eggs to dozens).

3. Find the cost of 1 unit by dividing the AP cost by the number of units.

4. Find the recipe cost of the ingredient by multiplying the cost of 1 unit by the number of units the recipe calls for.

5. Find the total cost of the recipe by adding up all the ingredient costs.

6. Find the cost per portion by dividing the total recipe cost by the number of portions (yield).

For example:

THOUSAND ISLAND DRESSING

Yield: 1 qt (1 L) or 32 1-oz (30-g) portions

Ingredients	Step 1 AP Cost	Step 2 Unit Conversion	Step 3 Unit Cost	Step 4 Recipe Cost
1½ pt mayonnaise	5.21 per gal	1 gal = 8 pt	$\frac{5.21}{8} = 0.651$	$0.651 \times 1.5 = 0.977$
¼ pt chili sauce	3.57 per #10 can	1 can = 6 pt	$\frac{3.57}{6} = 0.595$	$0.595 \times 0.25 = 0.149$
¼ pt catsup	3.29 per #10 can	1 can = 6 pt	$\frac{3.29}{6} = 0.548$	$0.548 \times 0.25 = 0.137$
6 eggs	0.91 per dozen	6 eggs = ½ doz	0.91	$0.91 \times 0.5 = 0.455$
2 oz onions	0.11 per lb	1 lb = 16 oz	$\frac{0.11}{16} = 0.007$	$0.007 \times 2 = 0.014$
2 oz dill pickles	0.99 per lb	1 lb = 16 oz	$\frac{0.99}{16} = 0.062$	$0.062 \times 2 = 0.124$

Step 5: TOTAL RECIPE COST: 1.856

Step 6: $\dfrac{\text{cost of recipe}}{\text{number of portions}}\quad \dfrac{1.856}{32} = 0.058$ COST PER PORTION

length, distance, and area. Units of measurement are decimal parts or multiples-by-10 of a basic unit:

milli- = 0.001 unit (1/1000)
centi- = 0.01 unit (1/100)
deci- = 0.1 unit (1/10)
basic unit

deca- = 10 units (10 × unit)
hecto- = 100 units (100 × unit)
kilo- = 1000 units (1000 × unit)

Metric weight

The basic unit of weight is the gram. In the kitchen the units of weight used are the gram (abbreviated g or gm) and the kilogram (abbreviated kg and pronounced kill-o-gram), sometimes shortened to kilo (pronounced kee'-loh). A kilogram is 1000 grams.

- A gram is 0.035 ounce.
- A kilogram is 2.2 pounds.

In translating a recipe from metric weight to U.S. weight, these are your multipliers. You multiply each ingredient as you do in converting a recipe from one quantity to another.

Here is a recipe in which metric measures are converted to pounds:

Ingredient	Metric	Multiplier	U.S.
Lima beans	15 kilograms	× 2.2	= 33.0 pounds
Mushrooms	4 kilograms	× 2.2	= 8.8 pounds
Shallots	500 grams (0.5 kilograms)	× 2.2	= 1.1 pounds
Butter	1 kilogram	× 2.2	= 2.2 pounds

If all quantities in a recipe are given in the same system of measurement, you can convert the recipe simply by using the proportions of ingredients. In the metric recipe all units are given by weight and can be converted to kilograms. You have 15 units of lima beans to 4 units of mushrooms to 1/2 unit of shallots to 1 unit of butter. Using these proportions you can substitute the pound as your unit:

Ingredient	Kilograms	Units	Pounds
Lima beans	15	15	15
Mushrooms	4	4	4
Shallots	0.5	0.5	0.5 = 8 oz
Butter	1	1	1

Using proportions will give you the same product but not the same yield. The yield of the pound recipe will be 5/11 (that is, 1/2.2) of the metric recipe yield—a little less than half as much.

The scales in Figure 5-5 show metric and U.S. measures of weight.

Metric volume

The basic unit of volume is the liter (abbreviated L and pronounced lee-ter). The liter is also the basic kitchen measure. You may also meet the deciliter (dL, pronounced dess-a-lee-ter) and the milliliter (mL—mill-a-lee-ter) in recipes. The deciliter is 1/10 liter and the milliliter is 1/1000 liter.

- A liter is 1.056 quarts.
- A deciliter is 0.106 quart or 3.379 fluid-ounces.
- A milliliter is 0.001 quart or 0.034 fluid-ounce.

If you wanted to convert a recipe from metric volume to U.S. volume, these would be your multipliers. Or you could use the proportion method if your recipe is all in volume. Since the liter and the quart are so close in size, your yield converted by proportions would be almost the same.

Converting to metric measure

To convert from U.S. measure to metric measure you use the same process as in converting from metric to U.S. measure.

- A pound is 0.454 kilogram.
- An ounce is 28.35 grams.
- A quart is 0.946 liter.
- A fluidounce is 29.57 milliliters or 0.3 deciliter.

You can use these as your multipliers, or you can convert with proportions if the recipe quantities are all given in the same system of measures.

In real life, you will seldom have to convert a recipe from one measuring system to another. The recipes in this book provide both

U.S. and metric quantities. You will have excellent results using either system. Do not use a mixture of the two systems, however: we have usually used rounded measures rather than exact conversions, so the quantities may be slightly different.

MEASURING TEMPERATURE

Another form of measure that has two standards is temperature, which expresses the intensity of heat. Again the United States uses one standard, the **Fahrenheit scale,** and the rest of the world uses another, the **Celsius scale,** also called the **centigrade scale.**

On the Fahrenheit scale the freezing point of pure distilled water is 32° and its boiling point is 212° at standard atmospheric pressure. On the Celsius scale the freezing point of pure distilled water is 0° and the boiling point is 100° at standard atmospheric pressure. One Celsius degree equals 1.8 Fahrenheit degrees. The thermometer in Figure 5-7 shows the relationships between the two scales.

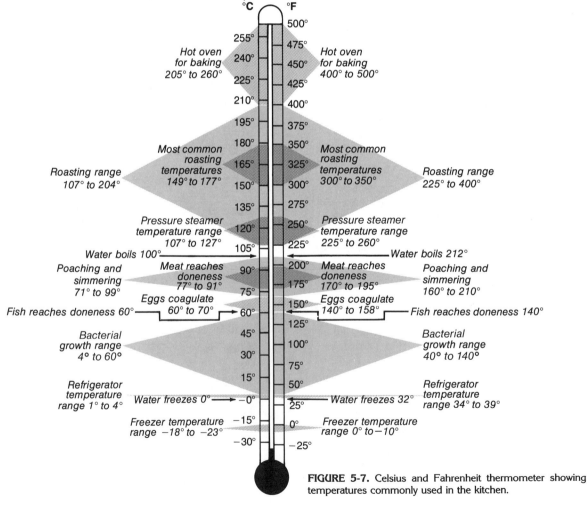

FIGURE 5-7. Celsius and Fahrenheit thermometer showing temperatures commonly used in the kitchen.

Temperatures can be converted from one scale to the other by using the following formulas:

$$C = 5/9 \ (F - 32)$$
$$F = 9/5 \ C + 32$$

In other words, to find degrees Celsius start with degrees Fahrenheit, subtract 32, and multiply by 5/9. To find degrees Fahrenheit start with degrees Celsius, multiply by 9/5, and add 32.

Suppose, for example, you want to find the Celsius equivalent of a simmering temperature of 185°F:

$$C = 5/9 \ (F - 32)$$
$$185 - 32 = 153$$
$$5/9 \times 153 = 85°C$$

Or suppose your room thermometer reads 25°C and you want to find the Fahrenheit equivalent:

$$F = 9/5 \ C + 32$$
$$9/5 \times 25 = 45$$
$$45 + 32 = 77°F$$

An alternate formula for converting from one system to the other is 1.8 (°C) = (°F − 32). It is another way of saying the same thing, and you might find it easier to use. Simply plug the known temperature into the formula and solve the equation algebraically for the unknown temperature.

Celsius temperatures are coming into common use, so it is wise to become familiar with them. Learning to think in Celsius terms is even better than translating from one system to the other.

Temperature, as you know, is measured with thermometers. A **thermometer** is an instrument that measures the intensity of heat and reads it out on a Fahrenheit or Celsius scale.

We use thermometers for many purposes. We can check the operation of thermostatic controls on our equipment: the thermometer in Figure 5-8a can be placed in a refrigerator or freezer to check the readings of the equipment's own gauges. Similarly, Figure 5-8b will check out the fat in the deep fryer.

Another very important type of thermometer indicates the internal temperature of foods being cooked or held. The meat thermometer in Figure 5-8c is an indispensable cooking tool: it measures the internal temperature of meats as they cook so that you know when they reach the right degree of doneness. With the testing thermometer (Figure 5-8d) you can determine the temperature of anything

FIGURE 5-8. Temperature measures.

a. A thermometer for indicating temperature in a refrigerator or freezer.

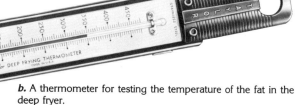

b. A thermometer for testing the temperature of the fat in the deep fryer.

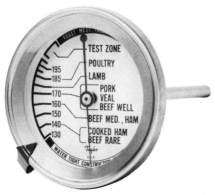

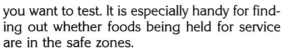

c. A meat thermometer tells you the internal temperature of meat.

d. A testing thermometer gives you an instant reading for any product, hot or cold, wet or dry.   (Photos courtesy Taylor Scientific Instruments.)

you want to test. It is especially handy for finding out whether foods being held for service are in the safe zones.

Thermometers are key features of the cook's domain. Learn how to interpret what they tell you, check them regularly on your equipment, and use them intelligently in cooking and holding foods.

SUMMING UP

A recipe is an abbreviated way of communicating the necessary information for making a dish. A standardized recipe is one written for use in a given operation specifying exactly how a given dish is made in that operation. The standardized recipe has many roles. It helps the cook to maintain consistency of product. It provides the data for cost analysis, thus helping to control costs and assure profitability. It provides essential data for purchasing and planning for future needs.

A standardized recipe applies to one operation only; it is not a universal key to making a given dish anywhere, any time, by anybody. Many uncontrollable variables complicate the picture: differences in equipment, differences in cooks, differences in products, differences in temperature, differences in understanding and communication. A written recipe cannot substitute for understanding the structure of a dish, the roles and relationships of its ingredients, and what is supposed to happen in the making.

In order to understand and follow recipes, you must know how ingredients are measured, the various quantity measures and their equivalents, and how to convert one yield to another. You should also be familiar with the two systems of measuring temperature and know how to convert from one to the other.

This chapter is basic to your understanding of everything that comes after. From here on you will be working with recipes—analyzing them, converting them, using them most of all in understanding what takes place when you put a group of ingredients together and cook them in a certain way. Learn to make recipes your tools, not your masters. Learn measures and equivalents; they too are indispensable kitchen tools.

Come back and reread this chapter after you have engaged in battle with some recipes in the kitchen, and you will discover new insights.

THE COOK'S VOCABULARY

recipe, standardized recipe, yield

major flavor, body, texture

flavor builder, flavorer, seasoning

number or count, volume, weight

AP, EP

converting a recipe

costing a recipe

metric system

Fahrenheit, centigrade, Celsius

QUESTIONS FOR DISCUSSION

1. Why doesn't the same recipe always produce the same product in any kitchen for any cook? Cite instances from your own experience in which a recipe produced different results. Can you think of still other factors that might affect the outcomes?

2. What is meant by *the structure of a dish?* If you can, give examples of two or more finished dishes that have the same basic structure.

3. Explain why it is helpful to know equivalents in converting recipes. Give examples from your own experience of mistakes in using equivalents and what happened as a result.

4. Discuss the three methods used in measuring ingredients. Give examples of types of foods appropriate to each method.

THERE are two different kinds of cooking. One is the cooking of foods that are so good in themselves that nothing need be added—the broiled steak, the baked potato, the poached egg. All you have to do to such a food is cook it properly.

The other kind of cooking is the blending together of several foods to make another kind of food—a soup, a sauce, many kinds of main dishes. This kind of cooking requires an understanding of how such foods are built.

The process is something like the building of a house. There is a plan. Raw materials are put together according to this plan. Because of the way everything is combined, the finished product is more than just the raw materials added together. It has its own identity. The house has its own shape, size, and style. The dish has its own flavor, body, and texture.

The raw materials the cook uses to build flavor in soups, sauces, and entrées are spices, herbs, vegetables, meat, and bones. For body you add a liquid. For texture you use another set of raw materials called thickening agents, which are mostly starches or starch-fat combinations.

In this chapter we'll see how the cook puts together raw materials to build flavor, body, and texture. We'll also take a close look at the whole subject of flavor, the ingredients used to season and flavor, and how to use seasonings to bring out the natural flavors of foods.

After completing this chapter you should be able to

- Understand and explain the concepts of building flavor, body, and texture in a dish.

- Describe or demonstrate how to prepare a sachet, an onion piqué, and basic, light, and dark mirepoix.

- Describe or demonstrate how to prepare good-quality light and dark stocks, and explain their uses and how they differ.

- Know how and when to use convenience products in making stocks.

- Explain how to build texture in a liquid using various types of thickening agents.

6

Building Flavor, Body, and Texture

113

- Explain the difference between seasoning, flavoring, and flavor-building.
- Use seasonings to bring out the natural flavors of foods.

BUILDING FLAVOR: FLAVOR BUILDERS

Flavor is the way a food tastes. A carrot has a carrot flavor, an onion has an onion flavor, chicken tastes like chicken, and a stew is a blend of meat and vegetable flavors. People who like to analyze flavor will point out that there are only four basic tastes: sweet, sour, bitter, and salt. These are perceived by the taste buds on various regions of the tongue—sweet at the tip, sour and salt along the sides, bitter at the back. When you eat, these tastes combine with the aromas perceived by your nose to produce the flavor of the food you are eating.

Cooks do not think in terms of flavor analysis. They are concerned with the totality of flavor perceived by the diner. They know how a dish is supposed to taste, and they build toward that taste each time they make that dish.

In building foods the cook works with two kinds of flavor, *predominant flavor* and *support flavor*. Just as a building has a major structural element, such as wood, concrete, or steel, a dish can have a major material in its construction, such as beef, onion, or asparagus. It may not be the major material in terms of volume (celery soup, for example, has far less celery than it has liquid), but it is the material that determines the character of the dish. This major material, or main ingredient, will contribute the predominant flavor—**major flavor**—of the dish.

Other ingredients may be added in the cooking to enhance the flavor of the main ingredient. We call these **flavor builders,** and the kind of flavor they provide is what we call support flavor. The flavor builders should never be allowed to overwhelm the predominant flavor. A good understanding of the relationships between predominant and support flavors is one of the most important keys to successful cooking.

The basic flavor builder in soups and sauces is a liquid known as stock. Stock itself has a predominant flavor that comes from bones, and it has support flavors that come from flavor builders.

Let us look at some of the flavor builders commonly used in making stocks, soups, and sauces. Several standard groupings are used in professional cooking: mirepoix, bouquet garni, sachet, onion piqué, and the group of herbs and spices used with a mirepoix in making stock.

The group of flavor builders known as a **mirepoix** (meer-pwah) is a combination of rough-cut vegetables—onion, carrot, celery, and sometimes leek. A standard flavor builder for stocks, it is also used in soups, sauces, and braised dishes, and it is often added to the pan liquids from roast meat if a sauce is to be made from them. Mirepoix was named for a French general. Though this custom of naming foods after the cook's master or the king's mistress can be confusing until you get used to it, it also lends color to the kitchen. "Mirepoix," once you've mastered it, is much more interesting than "cut-up vegetables."

Standard ratios of ingredients for a **basic mirepoix** are 50 percent onion (or part onion and part leek), 25 percent carrot, and 25 percent celery. These proportions will yield a balanced blend of flavors. Thus if a recipe specifies a pound (500 grams) of mirepoix you know it means

8 oz (250 g) onion (or onion/leek)

4 oz (125 g) carrot

4 oz (125 g) celery

This would be enough for 1 gallon (4 liters) of flavorful stock. It is important to maintain these ratios so that no one ingredient will become a predominant flavor and spoil the stock, soup, or sauce. Leeks, if they are available, will enhance the flavor blend.

Mirepoix ingredients are chosen not only for flavor but for color. Carrots and the skins of onions will lend their color to the liquid in which they are cooked. This can be an asset in most stocks and sauces, but it may spoil the appearance of a fish stock or a white sauce. So we have two variations of the basic mirepoix, light and dark.

For a **light mirepoix** you would use roughly 60 percent peeled onion/leek and 40 percent celery, or, for 1 gallon (4 liters) of stock,

5 oz (150 g) onion, peeled

5 oz (150 g) leek (white and light green)

5 oz (150 g) celery

For a **dark mirepoix** tomatoes are sometimes added for more color and flavor, in a ratio of 2 oz (60 g) to 1 lb (500 g) mirepoix. Thus you would have

8 oz (250 g) onion (or onion/leek)

4 oz (125 g) carrot

4 oz (125 g) celery

2 oz (60 g) tomato

Tomatoes have a very strong flavor that can easily take over if too much is used.

The size of the pieces will vary according to use. If you are going to cook them a long time, as in making a stock, you will cut them in 1- to 1½-inch (2½–3 cm) pieces so that their flavor will not be exhausted before the stock is finished. If the cooking will be brief, as in making a sauce from pan juices or a cream soup, you will cut them much finer—say small dice. This will expose more vegetable surface to the liquid and draw out more flavor in the allotted time. Whatever the size, the pieces should be roughly equal so that all the ingredients will cook at the same rate. The following guidelines will give you the most flavor and the best flavor from a mirepoix of any kind.

- Use only good-quality products.

- Thoroughly wash all products, especially the leek, which is usually very sandy. To clean it well, cut it in half lengthwise and rinse thoroughly under running water.

- Cut all vegetables the same size.

- Keep the ratios of ingredients carefully balanced.

- If the mirepoix is going to be cooked a long time, use low heat to avoid a bitter flavor.

But vegetables are only half the flavor-building story for stocks, soups, and sauces. Most of the time the mirepoix vegetables are accompanied by certain herbs and spices that enhance the flavor blend. Some cooks consider these to be part of the mirepoix and some don't, since they may vary with the product being made. To avoid confusion we will use the term mirepoix to refer to the vegetables alone.

For making stock the standard group of herbs and spices that goes with the mirepoix consists of bay leaf, thyme, parsley, clove, and peppercorns. In this book we refer to them as **stock herbs and spices.** Recipe 6-1 lists the amounts suitable for making a gallon (4 liters) of any kind of stock. In this recipe they appear alongside the standard mirepoix so that you can begin to think of these proportions as going together.

Another combination of herbs and vegetables is the **bouquet garni** (boo-kay gar-nee— literally, garnished bouquet). This term originally referred to sprigs of herbs—parsley, thyme, and bay leaf—tied together with a string which in turn was tied to the handle of the stockpot. When cooking was done, the herbs could easily be pulled out of the pot. Sometimes a celery rib, cut in half, was added to the bouquet. The herbs were placed in the trough of one half and covered with the other half, and the string was tied tightly around the celery, as in Figure 6-1a.

Today the term bouquet garni is used in several different ways. For some cooks it al-

6-1 BASIC MIREPOIX WITH STOCK HERBS AND SPICES

Yield: enough for 1 gallon (4 liters) stock

4 oz	onion	125 g	½	bay leaf	½
4 oz	leek	125 g	5–6	parsley stems	5–6
4 oz	carrot	125 g	1/2 tsp	thyme	2 mL
4 oz	celery	125 g	2	cloves	2
			5–6	peppercorns	5–6

1. Wash vegetables thoroughly. Trim if necessary. Concassé in 1–1½″ (2½–3 cm) pieces.
2. Use vegetables, herbs, and spices as directed in stock recipe.

FIGURE 6-1. Flavor builders.

c. An **onion piqué** is a peeled or unpeeled onion half with a bay leaf affixed to it with a clove.

a. A **bouquet garni** readied for the pot in classical fashion.

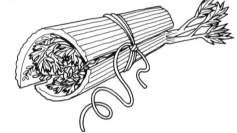

b. A **sachet** is a cheesecloth bag filled with herbs and spices.

ways means those three specific herbs—parsley, thyme, and bay leaf—used together but not necessarily tied together if the liquid they are enriching is to be strained. For other cooks a bouquet garni is any group of herbs and spices used together in making a stock, soup, or sauce. Still others use the term to include whole mirepoix vegetables tied together or floating free in the pot. Yet another usage of the term refers (incorrectly) to tying dried herbs and spices in cheesecloth. This is more properly called a sachet.

Because there are so many versions of the bouquet garni, we avoid this term in recipes in order to prevent confusion. If you run into the term as you pursue cooking, you will be wise to find out exactly what people mean when they use it.

A **sachet** (sa-shay—French for a small bag) is any mixture of herbs and spices tied in a square of cheesecloth. It is used in making soups and sauces when the product is not strained, as well as in braised dishes. The string that ties the sachet is usually tied to the handle of the stockpot so that it can easily be removed and discarded. Figure 6-1*b* illustrates the sachet.

An **onion piqué** (pee-kay) is another technique for adding certain flavor builders in making a stock or sauce. The flavor builders are onion, bay leaf, and clove. The technique is to attach the bay leaf to the onion by using the clove as a nail (Figure 6-1c). It is another way of keeping the flavor builders together for easy removal. Usually the onion is peeled, to be used in flavoring a light or white sauce without adding color. If color does not matter you can use the onion with the skin on.

An interesting way of using an onion to build flavor and color in a dark stock or sauce is to caramelize it. To understand how this works, you must understand the onion. Onion has a high sugar content. This contributes two good things: a pleasant sweet flavor and a tinge of caramel color. To coax these out of the onion, cut the onion in half crosswise and place the cut surface on a hot griddle. This will caramelize the sugar and fill the kitchen with a heavenly aroma. You then add the onion to the liquid, cut side down, and the caramelized sugar dissolves as the half onion floats around, adding flavor and especially color to the liquid.

BUILDING BODY: STOCKS

A **stock** is a flavored liquid that is used in making soups and sauces. Stock functions as the body of the finished soup or sauce and also as a flavor builder. The French call stocks *fonds de cuisine* (fawn da kwee-zeen), meaning bases of cooking, which describes their role exactly.

What do we mean by body? **Body** is two things—physical substance and strength of flavor.

A stock provides the physical body of a soup or sauce. The physical body of an entrée may be solid food such as meat or vegetables, or it may be a combination of solid food and sauce.

Body in the sense of strength of flavor is a less tangible quality. We speak of a light-bodied soup or a rich, hearty soup, a light wine or a full-bodied wine. If a liquid tastes watery or

tasteless, we say it is lacking in body. Body, then, refers to the amount of flavor—its strength or richness. Even a solid food can be said to lack body if its taste has been cooked away and its flavor is pallid.

The way to build body is to build flavor, as you can guess. The way to build a stock is to take water, a flavorless liquid, and give it body with a predominant flavor and support flavors. The predominant flavor of a stock will come from the major ingredient. There are several different predominant flavors for stocks: chicken, beef, veal, fish, and vegetable. Of these, the meat flavors come from bones. The support flavors for stocks come from a mirepoix coupled with stock herbs and spices.

How to make good stocks

In brief, stocks are made by simmering water, bones, and flavor builders together for hours (Figure 6-2). As they simmer, the flavor-producing substances are extracted from the bones and flavor builders and dissolve in the water. The resulting liquid product is the stock. Gelatin is also drawn from the bones, adding body to the liquid. Though it may be imperceptible in a hot stock, it will cause the stock to thicken or jell when chilled.

FIGURE 6-2. Making stock. This is a light stock simmering on the range. Notice the tall, narrow shape of the pot, the ratio of bones to water, the mirepoix floating on top, the quiet surface with bubbles rising, indicating that the temperature is just right.

Before examining stock-making in detail, let's consider some general points that apply to all stocks.

In building a good stock you need to know the nature of the product you are aiming for. Here are the principal measures of stock quality.

- A good stock is fat-free.
- A good stock is clear—translucent and free of solid matter.
- A good stock is pleasant to the senses of smell and taste.
- A good stock is flavorful, but the flavor is neutral. The flavor of the main ingredient, though predominant, is not overpowering. No one flavor builder is identifiable over the flavor of the main ingredient.

And here are some very important guidelines to observe in making stock.

- Use good raw bones—bones that are pleasant smelling and fresh. They should be cracked or cut up crosswise to expose the marrow. Shank and knuckle bones are preferred.
- Use fat-free bones. Fat will produce grease in the stock, spoiling its flavor and appearance.
- Do not wash the bones or you will wash away many water-soluble flavor-producing substances. Some chefs prefer to wash or blanch the bones, but this should not be necessary if they are fresh.
- Start with cold liquid. Some proteins in bones are soluble only in cold water. And a cold-water start will produce a clear stock, whereas starting with hot water will produce a cloudy one.
- Use a tall, narrow pot to minimize evaporation. A certain amount of flavor is lost in evaporation, and the rate of evaporation depends on the surface area of the liquid.
- **Skim** occasionally—that is, remove the impurities that rise to the surface, using a skimmer or ladle. Figure 6-3 illustrates the technique.
- Keep the cooking temperature below the boil. It takes long, slow simmering to extract the flavors you want from the bones

FIGURE 6-3. Skimming with a ladle. First move the underside of the ladle bowl rapidly around in a circle in the center of the surface. This will send the gray scummy particles toward the sides of the pot. Then, tipping the ladle toward the side of the pot, run the lip of the ladle under the scum as shown, taking as little as possible of the liquid underneath. Empty the ladle into the bowl that you have set next to the pot.   (Photo by Patricia Roberts.)

and flavor builders. Too high a temperature will increase evaporation and loss of desirable flavors. It will also break down vegetable textures, producing undesirable flavors and a cloudy stock.

- **Strain** the stock by passing it through a china cap lined with several thicknesses of dampened cheesecloth.

- Do not season the stock. It will be used in making other products, so keep it uncommitted in taste.

- **Degrease** the finished stock—that is, remove the fat from the surface. The most effective method is to chill the stock and remove the layer of fat that congeals on top. If you must use the stock immediately, you can skim the hot fat off the top with a ladle or blot it with a clean cloth containing ice cubes.

Classes of stocks

There are two classes of stocks: light and dark. The **light stocks** are light in color and are generally made from bones of light or white meats—veal, chicken, or fish—with beef bones substituting when veal bones are unavailable. **Dark stocks**—or **brown stocks,** as they are often called—are a rich dark brown in color and are generally made from the browned bones of beef and veal. Both classes of stock use a ratio of 5 lb (2.5 kg) bones, 5 qt (5 L) water, and 1 lb (500 g) mirepoix plus stock herbs and spices to produce 1 gallon (4 liters) of stock.

To understand the two classes of stock, let us examine them separately.

Light stocks

Here is a list of the most common light stocks and their ingredients. Their French names (in parentheses) are given because you may well encounter them in the kitchen or the cookbook. The pronunciations given are common in American kitchens; the true French pronunciations are untranslatable.

- *Veal stock (fond blanc*—fawn blahnk): veal shank bones, water, mirepoix, stock herbs and spices
- *Chicken stock (fond de volaille*—fawn da vol-eye′): chicken bones, water, mirepoix, stock herbs and spices
- *Fish stock (fond de poisson*—fawn da pwa-sone′): fish bones, heads, tails, water, light mirepoix, lemon, stock herbs and spices
- *Ordinary stockpot (petite marmite*—puh-teet mar-meet; *grande marmite*—grahnd mar-meet): veal, beef, or chicken bones, or combinations of bones, water, mirepoix, stock herbs and spices

In today's industry, when stock is made from scratch, the ordinary stockpot is the most common. Since much more beef than veal is eaten in America, beef bones are available more cheaply and in greater volume. To produce the best possible stock use as much veal shank bone as you can get. As a general rule shank of beef is the logical substitute when veal bones are not available.

Recipe 6-2 provides a formula that can be used to make any light stock (except fish stock) simply by changing the kind of bones. Light stocks made from this formula are the bases for many dishes in the kitchen. The dish you are going to serve will dictate the kind of stock you make. To make this recipe, follow the guidelines spelled out earlier.

The asterisk beside the cooking time given in the recipe indicates that this is a guideline only and that cooking time is variable. The stock is done when it has achieved full-bodied flavor and the color desired.

In our recipes we use two special symbols, which are explained in the box on page 121. Now is the time to study the box. Refer to it later as necessary until the symbols become second nature.

Fish stock has some special requirements, as you can see in recipe 6-3. It uses a light mirepoix, for color reasons, and it has a much shorter cooking time. Because of the short

6-2 LIGHT STOCK

Yield: 1 gallon (4 liters)

				Mirepoix:			
major flavor	5 lb	bones, cracked or cut	2.5 kg	4 oz	onion	125 g	
body	5 qt	cold water	5 L	4 oz	leek	125 g	
				4 oz	carrot	125 g	
				4 oz	celery	125 g	flavor builders
				5–6	parsley stems	5–6	
				½	bay leaf	½	
				2	cloves	2	
				½ tsp	thyme	2 mL	
				5–6	peppercorns, crushed	5–6	

Basic ratios: 5 lb bones / 5 qt water / 1 lb mirepoix
2.5 kg bones / 5 L water / 500 g mirepoix

1. Prepare flavor builders.
2. Put bones in a tall pot or steam kettle and cover with cold water.
3. Bring to a simmer and skim. Add flavor builders and return to a simmer.
4. Simmer *3 hours, skimming occasionally.
5. Strain and degrease.

cooking time, less liquid will evaporate, so you need less to begin with. You cut the mirepoix finely so that maximum flavor will be extracted in the short time the stock cooks. The parentheses used in the recipe indicate that the ingredients and the instructions are optional.

Some dishes may call for a strong stock. You can strengthen a stock in either of two ways: you can increase the usual ratio of solid ingredients to liquid at the start, or you can reduce the strained finished stock through further simmering. Both methods will give you a stronger flavor—more body, in other words.

Dark stocks

Dark or brown stocks make up the second class of stocks. Two types of dark stock are made today.

- *Brown stock* (*fond brun*—fawn brun): beef bones or beef and veal bones, basic mirepoix, stock herbs and spices, water or light stock
- *Ordinary brown stock* (*grand jus*—grahn zhue): bones—all kinds, with beef and veal predominant—basic mirepoix, vegetable trimmings, water or light stock

Today grand jus is the most commonly made of the dark stocks. Sometimes trimmings of meat are added and even, occasionally, the bones remaining from a prime rib roast. The idea of this stock is to put to work all the unused meat, bones, and good mirepoix-type vegetables in the kitchen. But products of dubious freshness must never be put in the stock. Its quality should be high even though it

HOW TO USE THE SYMBOLS IN RECIPES

* = Variable. The asterisk is used to indicate that the quantity of an ingredient will vary with circumstances and must be determined by the person doing the cooking.

When the asterisk is used by itself in place of an amount, a description of the amount needed (usually small) is given with the recipe and is identified with the same symbol. For example, in recipe 6-4 the amount of oil needed is described in the instructions as "*enough to coat the bottom of the pan." If we gave you a specific quantity, it might be too much for a small deep pan and too little for a large shallow one.

When the asterisk is used with a specific quantity—such as "4–8 oz*"—it indicates that the quantity is to be used only as a general guideline and may have to be modified by the cook. Again, the actual amount needed is described with the recipe so that you will know how to adjust it appropriately. Such an adjustment may often require changing amounts of other ingredients as well, to keep proportions the same.

The asterisk may also be used with specified cooking times to indicate that actual cooking times are variable. Such time guidelines are given to satisfy planning needs but should not be followed as indicators of doneness.

() = Optional. An ingredient placed in parentheses in a recipe is one that you can include or omit without changing the basic character of the recipe. Parentheses are also used for optional instructions, as in recipe 6-3, Step 1.

6-3 FISH STOCK

Yield: 1 gallon (4 liters)

major flavor	5 lb	bones, heads, and tails of dover sole or other flatfish	2.5 kg	1 lb	light mirepoix, brunoise	500 g		
body	3½ qt	cold water	3.5 L	½ tsp	thyme	2 mL		*flavor builders*
	1 pt	white wine	500 mL	½	bay leaf	½		
				5–6	parsley stems	5–6		
				½–1 Tb	lemon juice	10–15 mL		
				(½ pt	mushroom trimmings	250 mL)		

Basic ratio: 5 lb bones, etc. / 1 gal liquid / 1 lb mirepoix
2.5 kg bones, etc. / 4 L liquid / 500 g mirepoix

1. (Wash bones, heads, and tails.) Prepare flavor builders.
2. In stockpot or steam kettle, cover bones, heads, and tails with cold water.
3. Bring to a simmer and skim. Add flavor builders and wine and return to a simmer.
4. Simmer *30 minutes. Strain.

6-4 BROWN STOCK

Yield: 1 gallon (4 liters)

				Mirepoix:			
major flavor	5 lb	bones, cracked or cut	2.5 kg				
body	5 qt	cold liquid (water or light stock)	5 L	4 oz	onion	125 g	
				4 oz	leek	125 g	
				4 oz	carrot	125 g	
				4 oz	celery	125 g	flavor builders
				5–6	parsley stems	5–6	
				½	bay leaf	½	
				2	cloves	2	
				½ tsp	thyme	2 mL	
				5–6	peppercorns, crushed	5–6	
				*	oil	*	

Basic ratio: 5 lb bones / 5 qt liquid / 1 lb mirepoix
2.5 kg bones / 5 L liquid / 500 g mirepoix

1. Brown bones in a hot oven (400°F/200°C) with a small amount of oil—*enough to coat the bottom of the pan. Stir bones occasionally to ensure even browning.
2. When bones are golden brown, add mirepoix and brown.
3. When the onion or leek is brown and lightly caramelized and the bones are dark brown, remove from oven and pour off any oil remaining.
4. Add cold liquid (about ¼ of total) to deglaze pan.
5. Transfer everything to a stockpot and add the remaining cold liquid.
6. Bring to a boil and skim. Add remaining flavor builders.
7. Reduce to a simmer. Simmer for *3–6 hours, skimming occasionally.
8. Strain and degrease.

may not have the thoroughbred ancestry of other stocks.

Recipe 6-4 gives you a basic formula for any dark stock made from any type of bones. As you can see by reading the instructions, brown stocks are more complicated to make than light stocks, but the techniques are worth learning. Not only do they make good stocks; they are also important in other areas of cook-ing. The procedures of browning bones, adding flavor builders, and then simmering in a liquid are used in making many sauces and meat dishes.

The technique known as **deglazing**—adding cold liquid to the hot pan (Step 4)—is also used in making sauces and meat dishes. Any browned bits of food sticking to the pan are scraped up and added to the liquid.

Glazes

Glazes (*glaces,* pronounced glahss) are basic preparations in classical cookery and are the forerunners of today's convenience products. They are simply stocks reduced to a thick, gelatinous consistency. Meat glaze, or *glace de viande* (vee-ond), is made from brown stock. *Glace de volaille* is made from chicken stock, and *glace de poisson* is made from fish stock.

To prepare a glaze, you reduce stock over moderate heat, frequently skimming off the foam and impurities that rise to the top. When the stock has reduced by about half, strain it through cheesecloth into a smaller heavy pan. Place it over low heat and continue to reduce until the glaze will form an even coating on a spoon. Cool, cover, and refrigerate or freeze.

Glazes are used in producing many of the small sauces of classical cuisine. They can also be added to soups or stocks to improve and intensify flavor. However, they cannot be used to recreate the stock from which they were made; the flavor is not the same after the prolonged cooking at higher temperatures.

Vegetable stocks

Stocks made from vegetables do not have the same broad uses as stocks made from bones. A vegetable stock is usually made from a single vegetable for a single purpose, such as making a specific soup. For example, you might make an asparagus stock to use instead of a meat stock in an asparagus soup.

Vegetable stocks are usually made from trimmings that would otherwise be discarded, such as the tough portions of asparagus stalks. You simmer these in water until they are cooked through—no longer. Longer cooking will cause unwanted flavor changes and loss of good flavor through evaporation. Often in making vegetable stocks you do not use a mirepoix because your aim is not a flavor blend but a single intensified flavor.

Handling and storing stocks

The straining, cooling, and storage of stocks follow the same procedures for both classes—light and dark. The straining is relatively simple. Ideally the stockpot will have a spigot at the bottom. If it does, simply open the spigot and strain the liquid through a fine china cap and cheesecloth into a clean storage pot. If there is no spigot, carefully pour the liquid from the pot through the strainer—using proper safety precautions—or dip it out of the pot with a ladle.

It is easy to store stocks successfully if you observe sanitary practices. The most important of these is to cool the stock rapidly to room temperature and then transfer it to a cooler. Its time in the danger-zone temperatures of 40–140°F (4–60°C) must be kept to an absolute minimum—1 hour at the most. To cool quickly (Figure 6-4) place the pot of stock on a rack in the sink and surround it with ice water or cold running water, stirring occasionally. This will cool the stock evenly instead of leaving a warm core where bacteria can develop quickly. Cover the stock after it is cool but never while it is cooling. A cover will slow the cooling and increase the health hazard.

A stock's shelf life is no more than three to five days in the cooler. Stocks can be frozen without loss of quality. However, it is safest and most practical to make no more than you will use in a few days. The amounts and kinds of stock you make will be determined by the soups and sauces on your menu and the number of people you expect to serve.

Convenience bases and bouillons

Today's convenience-food industry has developed a number of products that are often used in lieu of stocks. These convenience products travel under many names—soup base, meat base, bouillon (bull'-yon) cubes, bouillon powder, and others. In view of the time and labor required in making stocks, convenience products are widely used in making soups and sauces, and the stockpot is seen in fewer and fewer kitchens.

The results vary widely, partly because of the bewildering variety of products on the market and partly because they are often misused.

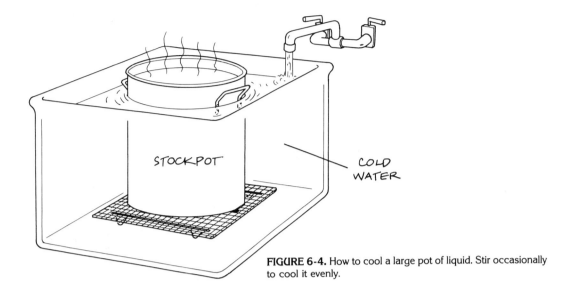

FIGURE 6-4. How to cool a large pot of liquid. Stir occasionally to cool it evenly.

Few of them can function as instant stocks. They must be used with great restraint and understanding. In making use of them you will find it very helpful to compare the different products to a stock made from scratch. Then use each product accordingly.

Bases, for instance, are stocks cooked down to thick gelatin concentrates, to which salt has been added as a preservative with probably other additives as well. Bases have a very respectable ancestry in the meat glazes of classical European cookery, which were added in small quantities to enrich a stock or soup or sauce that needed additional flavor and texture.

Today's soup bases and meat bases are widely used to make stocks, soups, and sauces. However, most of them do not make good substitutes for stock. They are more successful as flavor boosters. Compare the taste of a suitably diluted base with the taste of a stock made from scratch and you will see why. Many have a high salt content and other seasonings and preservatives. This gives them strong and definite tastes that are difficult to work with in building subtle flavors for soups and sauces. Among the many bases available, take care to choose the highest-quality products, though these are expensive. Look for those that list beef, chicken, or fish extract as the first ingredient. If you must use a base as a stock, try simmering with a mirepoix and stock herbs and spices to improve flavor. Strain before using in a recipe.

Bouillon cubes and powders are another type of convenience product often used in the role of a stock. They are completed bouillons that have been dehydrated, like instant coffee. Add water and you restore them to their finished state. Convenience bouillons do not undergo the extra cooking beyond doneness that the bases do, but they differ from stocks in that they are finished off by seasoning.

Bouillon cubes and powders can be substituted for bouillons made from fresh stock. But let there be no doubt that they will not substitute well because of their high salt content and inferior flavor. If you use bouillon cubes or powders you should again add a mirepoix with herbs and spices to the reconstituted bouillon and simmer it to mellow and enrich the flavor.

Cooking without fresh stock means using your head. There is no one all-purpose stock substitute. If a recipe calls for stock, you will have to analyze the role the stock is to play in that recipe and choose the type of convenience item accordingly. Use with caution, and taste the product as you go. Remember that salt is the major ingredient in nearly every base or bouillon cube, and adjust the amount of salt in your recipe. Follow the package instructions for the mechanics of using the convenience product and the proportion of water to be added; different brands and types have different requirements. Consider too that water alone can sometimes be a substitute body builder. Let your head, your taste buds, and your conscience be your guides.

You will understand all this a good deal better when you learn more about how stocks function in the making of soups and sauces. Then you will see why it is important to know how stock is made even if you never make it outside the laboratory. It will give you a basis for choosing the right convenience item for the right purpose and using it intelligently for optimum results. Convenience products are not foolproof substitutes. If anything they require more sophisticated cooking knowledge than cooking from scratch.

The importance of good stocks and good flavor builders cannot be overemphasized. If a good building is to be built, good building materials are a must.

BUILDING TEXTURE: THICKENING AGENTS

All food products have texture, a natural texture granted by mother nature. It may be thick or thin, rough or smooth, coarse or fine. The natural texture of a product may not be the most desirable serving texture for a finished dish, so the cook may create another texture. One measure of a cook's skill is the ability to create proper texture in such dishes as sauces and soups.

The creation of texture in cooking usually means making a thin food thicker. This is accomplished with a group of products known as **thickening agents.** Thickening agents increase the viscosity of a liquid, or, simply stated, make it harder to pour.

Many foods have been used in this role over the years. In medieval times, bread crumbs were added to meat juices to make them thick enough to eat with the fingers. (The French essayist Montaigne confessed to eating so fast he sometimes bit his fingers.) Almonds ground to a paste were added to thicken sauces. Blood, which coagulates, was sometimes used in classical dishes, along with puréed goose liver. In creole cooking, powdered sassafras leaves were borrowed from the Indians to make a dark-green spicy thickener known as filé (fil-lay' or fee-lay'). Eggs, arrowroot, gelatin, tapioca, cornstarch, flour, potatoes, and rice have all been used as thickeners.

Thickening can be achieved in two ways: naturally and by using a starch thickener. Natural thickening means using a high-starch food such as potato, rice, beans, or dried peas as an integral part of a dish. As these products cook, their starch content is released into the liquid surrounding them, causing it to thicken, while their flavor is added to the dish. Natural thickening is used mostly in soups, and the thickener is also the major flavor ingredient.

The second way to thicken means adding a starch product whose primary function is to thicken. The thickening power comes from the fact that starch granules, when heated with liquid, will absorb moisture, swell, and become jellylike. This process, known as gelatinization, was discussed in Chapter 4. For a smoothly thickened product the starch granules must be evenly dispersed in the liquid and evenly heated, so that the swelling will take place at an even rate and lumps will not form. These thickeners for hot foods fall into two groups: fat-and-flour combinations and starch-and-water combinations.

Roux

Of the fat-flour group, the single most important one for the beginning cook to master is **roux** (roo). Roux is a one-to-one ratio by weight of fat and flour blended and cooked over low heat. The definition is broad: any fat can be used to make a roux. Butter or margarine is the best choice whenever possible.

Many fats will impart their own distinct flavor to a product, thus limiting the versatility of the roux. Bacon drippings, for example. Think what they would do to a cream of asparagus soup!

There are several kinds of roux.

- **White roux** is cooked until the mixture is foamy and begins to have a chalky look.
- **Blond roux** is cooked somewhat longer, until the roux is blond in color.
- **Brown roux** is cooked until the color is brown and the taste is nutty.

To make a roux you melt the fat in a heavy-bottom pan over moderate heat and stir in the flour to make a smooth, lump-free paste. Once the roux is smooth, you lower the heat and cook the roux to the desired degree of doneness—white, blond, or brown. It takes only minutes. Simple.

Simple, that is, once you have mastered the technique. There are several tricky parts:

- One is smoothing out the roux when you add the flour to the fat. This takes good agitation with a whip and persistence. Eventually the lumps will go. They are tiny clumps of dry flour surrounded by granules that have begun to swell. Agitation breaks these lumps apart and releases the dry flour before the surrounding granules gelatinize.
- Another tricky point is recognizing the degree of doneness you want when you have reached it. This comes with experience. The neat trick here is to cook long enough without overcooking. Not only do color and flavor change with prolonged cooking, but the roux begins to lose its thickening power, and by the time you have reached the brown-roux stage the loss is considerable.
- On the other hand, undercooking has its hazards too. The roux must cook until the

flour is fully cooked and no starch taste remains. The flour is at least partly cooked by the time the roux reaches the foamy stage. It cooks further when added to a liquid. The mixture must come close to the boiling point before the flour reaches its full thickening power. To ensure complete cooking, test-taste the thickened liquid and simmer it until all raw-flour taste is gone.

- Be careful not to brown the roux if you don't want brown roux. The taste is permanent. You can brown it with too hot a fire as well as by cooking it too long.

Adding the roux to the product is tricky too. The easiest way is to remove your *hot* roux from the heat and add part of your liquid *cold,* once again stirring the lumps out vigorously until you have a smooth blend. Then you can add the remaining liquid *hot,* with no complications. The blend will be thin, but you cook it, stirring steadily, until it thickens again. No lumps, no bumps. Figure 6-5*a* shows the two steps.

It is also possible to add *cold* roux to a *hot* liquid over heat a little at a time, agitating vigorously with a whip so that the roux melts and softens easily without lumping (Figure 6-5*b*). But don't try to mix hot roux and hot liquid; this is likely to produce little hard lumps and bumps.

A good white roux is smooth and pleasant tasting but for the most part uncommitted in flavor—that is, it has no taste that will conflict with or modify the taste of another food with which it is combined. White roux is the most widely used of the three types. It creates texture for many soups, sauces, stews, soufflés, and other entrées.

Brown roux is strong in flavor and will carry a definite taste to the final dish. It has less thickening power than a light roux, so more must be used to produce the same texture. Brown roux is used for brown sauce and also in creole cooking; it is often baked for hours in the oven at low heat.

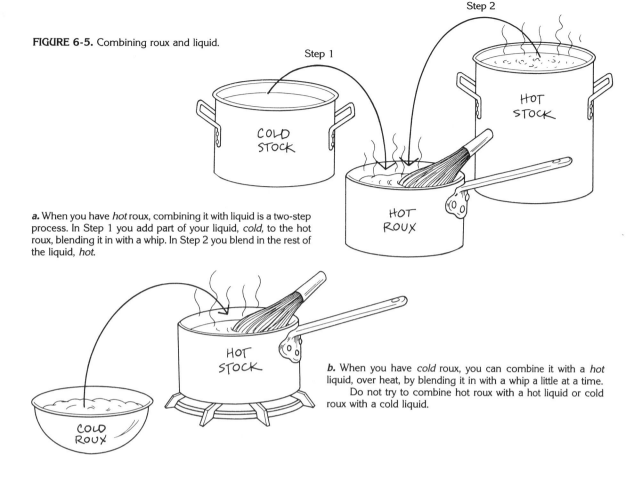

FIGURE 6-5. Combining roux and liquid.

a. When you have *hot* roux, combining it with liquid is a two-step process. In Step 1 you add part of your liquid, *cold,* to the hot roux, blending it in with a whip. In Step 2 you blend in the rest of the liquid, *hot.*

b. When you have *cold* roux, you can combine it with a *hot* liquid, over heat, by blending it in with a whip a little at a time.

Do not try to combine hot roux with a hot liquid or cold roux with a cold liquid.

Beurre manié

A thickening agent that is similar to roux is **beurre manié** (burr man-yay)—literally, worked butter. The ratio of fat to flour is the same, but the fat is butter and the method of preparation is different. The flour and soft butter are kneaded together to the consistency of paste, and the mixture is not cooked before use. Today margarine is often used in place of butter because of cost.

To use beurre manié to thicken, you pinch a small piece off, whip it into simmering liquid until it disappears, and keep repeating the process until the liquid reaches the consistency you want. Then you cook the thickened liquid a few minutes more until no raw flour taste remains. A day's supply of beurre manié may be made ahead, kept in the cooler, and used as needed.

Starch-and-water thickeners

The starch-and-water thickeners are simpler to understand and use than the starch-and-fat thickeners. You mix equal parts by volume of starch and cold water, stir until the starch is evenly dispersed, blend this mixture into a hot liquid, and bring it to a boil. When the liquid boils, the thickening is complete, though it may need further cooking to get rid of the taste of starch. You can adjust the texture by adding more starch mixture for a thicker product or more liquid to thin it down. Cornstarch, arrowroot, and many name-brand combination-starch products are among the available thickeners that can be used in this way.

Flour is another starch that can be dispersed in water and used to thicken, but it must be cooked longer than the other starch mixtures to get rid of its raw taste. The flour-water mixture is called a **slurry** or, sometimes, a **whitewash.** It is not a good substitute for roux for general use. Use it only in an emergency.

The liaison

Another product commonly referred to as a thickening agent is the **liaison** (lee-ay-zon). A liaison is a combination of egg yolks and cream used to give a velvety texture to soups and sauces. Although a liaison does tend to thicken, this is not its real purpose, and its thickening power is slight. It would take a ridiculous number of eggs to provide the same thickening power as a pound of roux. The real purpose of a liaison is to refine and smooth the texture of a thickened liquid by binding. It is added to liquids that have already been thickened by something else.

A liaison is made by blending together egg yolks and cream in a ratio of 2 parts cream to 1 part egg yolk by volume. The method of adding it to a soup or sauce is shown in Figure 6-6. First you add up to a third of the hot liquid to the liaison little by little, blending it in vigorously with a whip. This is known as **tempering.** Its purpose is to raise the temperature of the liaison (especially the egg) closer to the tem-

FIGURE 6-6. Tempering a liaison into a liquid.

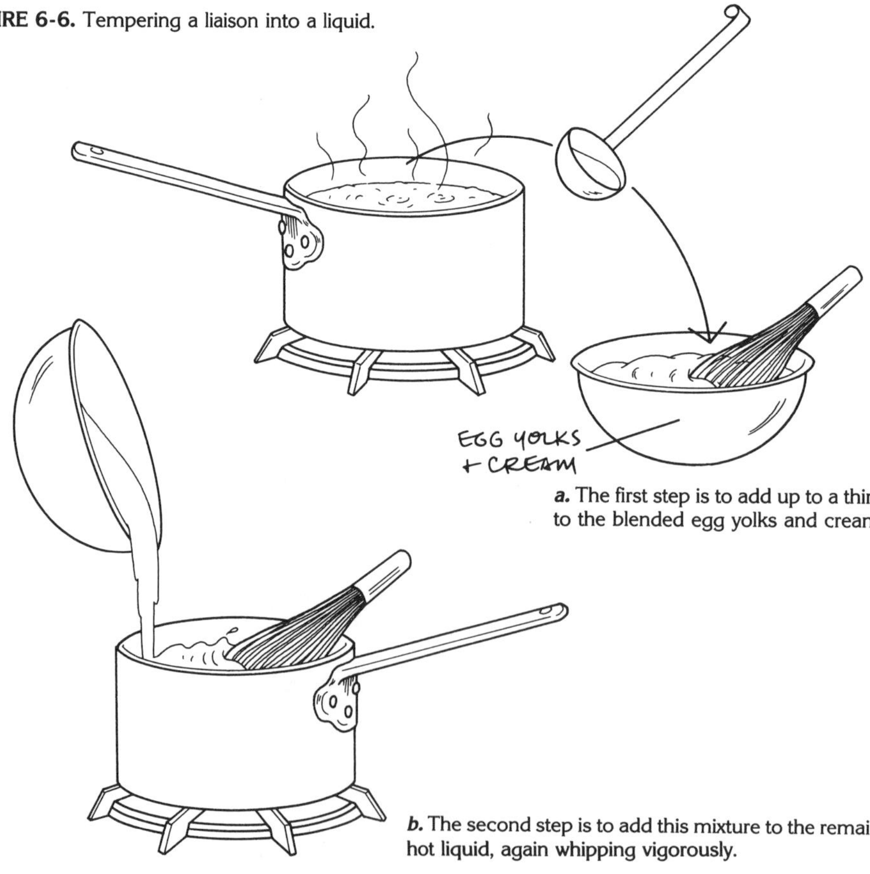

EGG YOLKS + CREAM

a. The first step is to add up to a third of the hot liquid gradually to the blended egg yolks and cream, whipping it in vigorously.

b. The second step is to add this mixture to the remainder of the hot liquid, again whipping vigorously.

perature of the hot liquid. If this were not done, the hot liquid would cause the egg yolk to coagulate, spoiling everything. The second step is to add the liaison mixture to the remainder of the hot liquid.

In contrast to the starchy thickeners, the liaison requires great care and patience. Egg yolks will coagulate at temperatures well below the boiling point. This creates problems in both preparation and holding of anything to which a liaison is added. For this reason the liaison is always added to the finished product shortly before use.

Although the liaison is not used as much today as it once was, tempering—the technique of combining eggs and hot liquids—applies in other areas of cooking, especially in the making of desserts.

SEASONINGS, FLAVORINGS, AND FLAVOR BUILDERS

Cooks have at their disposal a splendid array of food products that have pleasing and distinctive tastes and some that have the ability to enhance the tastes of other foods. Among these are wines and spirits, extracts and oils, condiments, spices, herbs, and seasonings. These are the secret ingredients in the secret recipes we are always hearing about.

There are three distinctly different ways of using these products: seasoning, flavoring, and flavor-building. Let us explore these concepts further.

Seasoning is the addition of substances that heighten the taste of a food without altering that taste or adding their own flavors. Such substances are called **seasonings.** They will bring out the rich flavors hidden in a bland, unseasoned stock or make a cream of chicken soup taste more like chicken. Whenever possible they are added at the end of the cooking, after the product is complete in every other respect. They are added earlier to such solid foods as meats and vegetables, however, to give the seasonings time to penetrate and bring out their flavor.

Flavoring, on the other hand, is the addition of a product for the purpose of adding its own distinctive flavor to the final dish. It is the blending of one flavor into another in such a way that the two complement each other but retain their own identity. A good example of flavoring is the addition of sherry wine to consommé. The basic consommé flavor then has a perceptible taste of sherry.

Flavoring and seasoning are often confused because both are usually end processes, or final steps in completing a dish. But flavoring makes a change in the taste of the dish by adding a new flavor, while seasoning brings out the flavor that is already there.

Flavor-building is different from both seasoning and flavoring in that it is an integral part of the cooking process. Flavor builders are cooked right into the dish, so that their separate flavors merge with the total flavor. This, for example, is what happens to the mirepoix when you make stock.

In flavor-building, the added flavor is not perceived separately, whereas in flavoring it is easily recognizable. In seasoning, the added product is not perceived at all.

With these differences in mind let's look more closely at each process in turn and at the kinds of products that function as seasonings, flavorings, and flavor builders.

Seasoning and seasonings

Seasoning is one of the most important processes in the entire field of cooking. Everything else you learn about cooking can be futile if you do not master seasoning. It is the finish work of cooking and, like finish work in any trade or profession, it is a measure of the cook's skill. Skill in seasoning is the ability to use seasonings to bring a food to its peak of flavor, its ultimate in taste.

What are these miracle workers that can make a food taste more like itself? They are three familiar everyday products. *Salt* and *pepper* are standard seasonings for all foods and all cooks. *Fresh lemon juice* may or may not be used, depending on the cook and the dish. The kind of pepper used may also vary from one cook to another. Some cooks also use a fourth substance, *MSG* (short for monosodium glutamate).

Seasonings are limited to these three or four because they alone enhance a food's flavor without altering it. Used in the right quantities, they do not add their own flavors to a food. If you can taste any one of them you have added too much of it.

Salt. A crystalline substance mined from the earth or extracted from brine, salt is cheap and plentiful. In other times and places it was often scarce and valuable and was sometimes used as money. It was used for centuries to preserve meats and fish, and the cook's chief concern with it was not how much to add but how to get rid of the taste.

Salt is essential to health, and the desire for it is said to be a natural instinct in both humans and animals. But the amount of salt essential to health is far less than we Americans habitually consume. In fact, excess salt in the diet contributes to high blood pressure and heart disease. The inevitable salt shaker on the dining table is a testament to its universal use. Fortunately, habits are beginning to change, and the trend is toward less use of salt and more interest in natural food flavors.

There is only one rule to follow in seasoning with salt: do not overuse it. Once a dish is too salty there is no way to correct it. It is far better to undersalt than to risk a salty flavor. For one thing, the heavy hand of an insensitive diner can spoil your finest creation. For another, customers who must watch their salt intake for health reasons will certainly not come back if they can taste the salt in your food.

Pepper. Like salt, pepper was scarce in other times and places and was used as money. Taxes, ransoms, dowries, and bribes were often paid in peppercorns. The barbarians who conquered Rome demanded, among other things, 3000 pounds of pepper as tribute. Pepper even changed the course of history: Columbus was looking for pepper when he sailed west to the East and discovered America instead.

Three kinds of pepper are commonly used as seasonings: white, black, and red. White and black pepper both come from the oriental pepper plant. Black pepper is the dried unripe berry; white pepper is the kernel of the ripe berry. Red pepper was discovered in America by Columbus's companions. It comes from dried pepper pods.

Black pepper comes in three forms: whole black peppercorns, crushed peppercorns, and table-ground pepper. Only the table-ground form is used for seasoning.

Whole pepper is used as a flavor builder during cooking, as in making stocks. It is a spice, never a seasoning. There is one overwhelming reason: whole peppercorns are difficult to chew.

Crushed black pepper is used in several ways. It can function as a flavor builder during cooking, as in making stocks. It can be added as flavoring to a finished dish; many Americans enjoy the flavor contrast of fresh crushed peppercorns straight from the pepper mill on a crisp green salad. It can be used in cooking meats in a combined role of flavor builder/ major flavor/flavoring, as in pepper steak. But crushed pepper, too, is not used as a seasoning. It simply cannot be used subtly.

Table-ground black pepper is pepper ground fine enough to be shaken from a shaker on the dining table. Some cooks use it as a seasoning, but its flavor has the sharpness of the unripe berry from which it comes, and it is difficult to use it without conveying this flavor to the food.

The table-ground-pepper flavor is characteristic of certain cuisines and certain parts of the country. Cooks catering to these clienteles are likely to add this flavor as they season the food. One way to be sure of pleasing everybody is to season for natural flavor and allow the guest to add the extra black-pepper flavor at the table.

As a seasoning, black pepper is used only in dark-colored foods; it spoils the appearance of light-colored foods. Light peppers—white and red—are used in both light and dark foods.

White pepper comes in two forms: whole peppercorns and ground white pepper. White peppercorns are used in the same ways as black. Ground white is seldom used as a table pepper. It is expensive and its flavor is breathtaking.

Ground white pepper is a good pepper for all-around seasoning. It blends imperceptibly into white dishes both in appearance and in flavor, and it has the strength necessary to season dark dishes. Very little is needed. Ground white pepper is chosen by most good cooks as the true seasoning pepper.

Red pepper is the most difficult of the peppers to use. It is quite hot and easily overdone. Two kinds are used as seasonings: *cayenne* and one called simply red pepper. Both are hot, but the flavor of cayenne has a great deal more to it than hotness. Used with restraint in soups and sauces, cayenne is one of the better seasoning peppers.

Fresh lemon juice. Lemon juice is seldom called a seasoning, and yet its use as a seasoning is not unusual. Many recipes call for small amounts of lemon juice, primarily with fish dishes. When it is used with restraint to spark the flavor of the dish itself and the lemon flavor cannot be perceived, lemon juice is a seasoning. Many chicken and veal dishes and cream soups such as asparagus, mushroom, cauliflower, and broccoli can be enhanced by seasoning with fresh lemon.

MSG. A crystalline substance made in the laboratory, MSG is also a natural ingredient in seaweed, soybeans, sugar beets, and mushrooms. Known and used for centuries in the Far East, it is an essential feature of contemporary oriental cuisines. It is also a popular additive in today's packaged foods.

MSG looks something like salt. But unlike salt and the other seasonings, it does not really bring out flavor in a dish. Instead, in some mysterious way it heightens the diner's perception of flavor, possibly by sensitizing the taste buds. Wide-awake taste buds can fool the taster about the food, which has not changed at all. An ordinary celery soup can taste like super celery.

As a seasoning MSG should be used with caution or not at all. It is easy to overuse it. Even a slight overuse can give a food an unusual flat taste, and the taste of MSG itself is far from pleasing. Used in great quantities it has been known to cause headache, chest pain, and numbness among susceptible diners, plus great embarrassment for offending restaurants.

If food is properly cooked using high-quality products, MSG should not be necessary. It should never be used as a salt substitute, a cover-up, or a crutch.

How to season. Seasonings must be added in suitable proportions in order to bring out the flavor of a food without adding their own. There are no rules for defining "suitable proportions" because every product is slightly different every time you make it. The process is one of trial and error, or, more accurately, trial and taste. Add, taste, adjust, taste, adjust, taste, until your product has reached its best possible flavor.

A standardized recipe will often give specific quantities of seasonings. These represent the carefully measured trial-and-taste process of the skilled cook who standardized the recipe. They are very useful as seasoning guidelines if used with caution. It is a good idea, if you are working with such a recipe, to start with amounts somewhat below those specified, and then taste, adjust, taste to refine the final flavor.

Figure 6-7 shows the equipment needed for seasoning a hot liquid: small plate, ladle, spoon, and seasonings. The plate is for cooling the hot liquid quickly. You ladle a small amount onto the plate and taste with the spoon. It is important not to put into the pot any implement that may be contaminated in the tasting process.

The basic rules for seasoning are the two you are already aware of.

1. Do not overseason. You should not be able to taste the seasoning itself.

2. Seasoning a liquid is an end cooking process.

FIGURE 6-7. Equipment for seasoning a liquid. Ladle a little liquid onto the plate for quick cooling. Taste from the plate.

The second rule has several corollaries.

- When a liquid product is to be reduced in volume, season after reduction, not before.
- When a liquid product is to act as a base for another, do not season it at all. Season the new product when it is finished.
- When a product cannot be seasoned after cooking, season before cooking. This applies to solid products such as meats, which will not absorb seasonings after cooking.

Some cooks misuse as seasonings products that change the taste of the food or intrude their own tastes. For this reason many potentially good dishes never reach their peak of flavor. Many potentially good cooks never quite make it for the same reason. Recipe books can add to the problem. "Season the sauce with sherry," a recipe will say, or "Season to taste with garlic salt and oregano." Here is a confusion of seasoning with flavoring, or of seasonings with flavor builders, or of one term with another, and more than likely a confusion of tastes in the products being seasoned.

It is important to use as seasonings only the products you know will do the job. Other products can be used to change taste but not to perfect taste that is already there. Let us therefore add a third basic rule of seasoning.

3. Season only with true seasonings—products that will heighten flavor without changing it or adding their own taste.

We noted earlier that true seasoning skill is the ability to use seasonings to bring a food to its ultimate in taste. The goal is the food's own flavor—the way a food "ought" to taste. The instrument you use to achieve this goal is your own sense of taste.

Your first step in mastering seasoning is to train your own sense of taste. You may be making many dishes you have never tasted before. You need to learn what each dish tastes like when made by a good cook. Then when you make the same product you will have an idea of what taste to aim for in seasoning.

In addition you can sharpen your own sensory awareness. Experiment with seasonings and become aware of their effects on flavor. Start working with very small amounts of seasonings until your product tastes good. Then try a little more. It may taste even better or it may be ruined. But you won't recognize its ultimate flavor until you've gone beyond it.

But, you may say, people's tastes differ. Indeed they do. This is why the word "ought" is in quotes. Who decides? Do you please the good cook whose product you first tasted, the customer, or yourself?

The answer is that you strive to please the customer. To do this you must learn to know the customer's taste in tastes. Every culture has preferences in food taste. Every area of the country has preferences. Southerners, for example, like heavily seasoned dishes. Parts of the Midwest and North prefer mild or subtly seasoned foods. You can learn to know your customers' tastes by watching their reactions to the foods you serve. Knowing customer tastes is one of the most important skills a cook can develop.

Then you must put aside your personal preferences and give the customers what they want, not what you want them to have. It is not easy to learn this—to use your own sense of taste to season to someone else's taste. It takes experience and practice.

Making a food taste the way a customer expects it to taste is seasoning at its indispensable minimum. Making that same food taste better than the customer's highest expectations is achieving the ultimate in taste. Foods with the ultimate in flavor are bound to have come-back appeal.

Flavoring and flavorings

Flavoring adds a complementary flavor to a dish at the end of its preparation. It creates a blend in which both the original flavor and the added flavor are identifiable, as in the addition of black pepper to a green salad.

Most flavorings are products with distinctive tastes, capable of holding their own in a dish. For example, wines, brandy, cognac, and other spirits are often added as flavorings at the end of cooking. Sherry is a popular American flavoring for sauces. Wine or brandy is often poured over a dish and flamed—set afire—at the time of service. This adds some flavor but is done more for show.

In such dishes as sauces, wines and spirits may be added during cooking to become part of the total flavor. They are then flavor builders rather than flavorings. The same product can play one role in one dish and another in another.

Another flavoring of distinctive taste is the anchovy (an-cho-vee), a small salted fish of pungent flavor that is used in very small quan-

tities in sauces, entrées, salads, and dressings. A caesar dressing for salads has the full force of the anchovy flavor. Anchovies come in cans as fillets or in tubes as a paste.

Capers add an interesting taste to cold sauces and dressings as well as to many warm sauces. They are flower buds of the caper bush, pickled in salt and vinegar.

Grated rind of fresh citrus fruits such as lemon and orange is often added to a sauce or used in baking. Only the colored outer portion, called the **zest,** is suitable; it contains flavorful oils. The white beneath it is acid and has a bitter taste.

Extracts and oils from aromatic plants are used in small quantities in the pastry shop—extracts of vanilla, lemon, and almond; oils such as peppermint and wintergreen.

Condiments are highly flavored bottled "sauces" that are added to a dish as flavorings after the cooking is complete, usually by the diner. Among these are catsup, soy sauce, chili sauce, prepared mustard, prepared horseradish, chutney, hot-pepper sauce, pickle relish, and worcestershire sauce (worcestershire is pronounced wuss'-ter-sheer; wuss rhymes with puss). Generally speaking, condiments are served at the table and are not used in the kitchen, but occasionally one is used in flavoring a cooked food or cold sauce. Girondin (zhee-ron-dan) sauce, for example, uses prepared mustard for its distinctive flavor, and several different sauces are made with prepared horseradish. Soy sauce is used particularly in oriental cooking, as both flavoring and flavor builder. Worcestershire sauce is used as a flavoring in gravies and salad dressings.

A few fresh herbs are used as flavorings: parsley, mint, chives, garlic, minced onion. With rare exceptions dried herbs and spices are not suitable as flavorings; they should be used only for flavor-building. It is true that dill weed can be a delicious complement to tomatoes; hungarian paprika (pa-pree'-ka) is used to flavor sauces; freshly grated nutmeg is indispensable to the holiday eggnog; black pepper is universally used as a flavoring. A few dried herbs such as tarragon and chervil can be used as flavorings when they are added to a liquid product such as soup or mayonnaise, which restores their moisture. But these dried herbs and spices are exceptions to the rule.

The rule in question is: Don't try to remedy lack of flavor in a dish by adding dried herbs and spices at the end of the cooking process. Think of their nature and you will see the reasons why. They are uncooked. They are demoisturized. They need cooking to mellow their raw taste and moisture to bring out their full flavor, and time for both things to happen. If you add them raw to a dish you are adding undesirable raw, dry flavors. Adding raw rosemary to a finished soup, for example, is like adding a mouthful of pine needles.

The real purpose of herbs and spices is not to rescue, remedy, flavor, or season, but to build. Spices and herbs are basically flavor builders. You have seen some of them in action in this role in making stocks. This is their proper use in cooking; they should be cooked with the dish as it is being made so that their flavors blend smoothly with the others in the dish. With rare exceptions they should never be added raw to a food at the moment of completion.

Spices and herbs

A closer look at spices and herbs will help you to understand and use them effectively.

Spices and herbs come from various parts of plants—bud, bark, bulb, fruit, root, seed, flower. **Spices** are the dried roots, bark, and seeds of tropical plants. **Herbs** are the leafy parts of plants.

In medieval Europe spices were among the most important ingredients in cookery. In a large household the grinding of spices was a full-time job performed by a person known as a powder beater. Pepper, cinnamon, ginger, and cloves were imported at great cost from the Far East and used to mask the taste of rancid or salty meats. Garden herbs like parsley, sage, rosemary, and thyme (pronounced time) were used for flavoring and also for the medicinal properties they were believed to have.

In today's kitchen spices and herbs are usually flavor builders. A few can be flavorings, and a few can also play the part of a major flavor, as hot peppers do in Mexican cuisine and curry powders do in many oriental dishes. When properly used they can help the cautious cook, and when misused they can hurt the careless cook. They must be used in small amounts and carefully coordinated with other ingredients, or their flavor will take over.

Spices and herbs usually arrive in the kitchen in the form of dried powders, seeds, or leaves. They come in tins of 1, 2 or 5 pounds (500 g, 1 kg, and 2.25 kg). As long as they are kept dry in tightly closed containers and stored in a cool, dry place, spoilage is not a problem.

One factor limits their shelf life: over a period of time they lose strength and thus their power to do the job. Most spices and herbs, once opened, hold well up to six months; they then lose flavor rapidly and by the time they have been open a year the loss is appreciable. As a rule of thumb, discard an opened tin more than a year old. It is a good idea to date the tin when you open it. It is also wise to buy a tin size you will empty within six months.

Learning to identify the innumerable different herbs and spices requires a keen sense of taste and smell. Simply looking at them is not enough. Taste them, smell them, feel them, use them. The key to most of them is their aroma, for in their aroma is about 60 percent of their flavor. The aromatic quality of a spice not only adds flavor to the food as it is eaten but heightens the anticipation of the diner as the food is being cooked and served.

There are many, many herbs and spices. Let's look at those most likely to be found in the kitchen. To help you understand them we'll sort them into groups.

You are already familiar with the first group, the five stock herbs and spices—parsley, bay leaf, clove, thyme, black pepper. Indispensable to any kitchen, they are used separately as well as together in many kinds of dishes.

Bay leaf is used as a flavor builder in dishes made with liquids: soups, sauces, stews, braised and poached entrées. It is generally used whole and removed before service, since it retains its tough, brittle texture even after long cooking. Bay leaf comes from the sweet bay or laurel tree, the same tree whose fresh leaves crowned the winners in the original Olympic games.

One or two *cloves* accompany a bay leaf in many a simmering pot. Cloves are also, in greater numbers, stuck into ham and pork as it cooks. A dried tree bud shaped like a nail, the clove gets its name from the French word for nail, *clou.* Ground cloves are used in baking and in sweet desserts.

Thyme has a strong and pungent flavor that calls for sparing use. Powdered thyme is an ingredient of many sauces and meat and poultry dishes.

Black pepper, garlic, and *parsley* play multiple roles. Black pepper is the only spice that can function in all three taste-making roles—seasoning, flavoring, and flavor-building. Parsley can be either a flavoring or a flavor builder in sauces, soups, and stews. Fresh parsley is, of course, the universal garnish. Dried parsley flakes are also available. They have a very different flavor and cannot substitute for fresh parsley in most recipes. Fresh *cilantro,* also called Italian flat-leaf or Chinese parsley, is another variety with a piquant flavor, often used in Mexican, Italian, and Chinese dishes. It is the plant from which coriander seeds derive.

Now let's look at nine spices that are used as often for their distinctive flavors as for general flavor enrichment. As a flavor builder each goes beyond the subtlety of the stock herbs and spices and gives a definitely different support flavor—even though you can't single it out from the flavor of the dish as a whole. Used in quantities large enough to taste, these spices become major flavors rather than flavor builders. Several of them can also be used as flavorings.

Three of these spices—basil, oregano, and tarragon—come in the form of crushed dried leaves and look somewhat alike. Their tastes, however, are very different.

Basil (bay-sul or baz-ul) has a warm, sweet flavor that is welcome in many soups, sauces, and entrées. It blends especially well with tomato. Like many other herbs it has a symbolism: in India it expresses reverence for the dead; in Italy it is a symbol of love.

Oregano (a-reg'-a-noh) belongs to the same herb family as basil, but it makes a very different contribution to a dish—a strong bittersweet taste and aroma you may have met in spaghetti sauce. Oregano comes in powder form as well as flakes.

Tarragon (tair'-a-gon) has a flavor that is somehow light and strong at the same time. It tastes something like licorice. Its flavor is most closely associated with tarragon vinegar and with béarnaise (bare-naze or bay-ar-nez) sauce.

Rosemary, like bay leaf, is used in dishes where a liquid is involved—soups, sauces, stews, poached foods. The leaf of an evergreen shrub of the mint family, it has a pungent flavor and fragrance. Dried, it looks and feels like pine needles. Rosemary is a traditional symbol of fidelity and remembrance.

Powdered *sage* comes from the dried leaves and stems of the sage plant. It is used to flavor sausage and stuffings for poultry, fish, and pork. Sage complements pork beautifully. The velvet-leaved plant was traditionally valued highly as a guarantor of good health. "Why should a man die whilst sage grows in his garden?" goes a medieval saying.

Two spices have flavors that will be very familiar to you: dill as in pickle and mustard as in hot dog. Dried *dill* leaves, often called dill weed, are used in soups, fish dishes, stews, and butters. *Dry mustard,* a powdered spice made from the seed of the mustard plant, comes in two varieties: white and brown. The brown has the sharper and more pungent flavor. Both kinds are used to flavor sauces and entrées. Prepared mustards are also made from both kinds. The mustard flavor is especially popular with ham.

Paprika is another powdered spice that comes in two flavors, mild and hot. Both kinds are made from dried pods of the same pepper family as red pepper and cayenne, and they look something like the seasoning peppers, but they do not do the work of seasonings. Hungarian paprika is the hot spicy one; spanish paprika has little flavor but its red color has lots of eye appeal. Paprikas are sensitive to heat and will turn brown if exposed to direct heat.

Still another branch of this same pepper-pod family gives us *chili peppers,* the crushed or dried pods of several kinds of Mexican peppers. Colors range from red to green and flavors from mild to hot. Chili peppers are used in Mexican cuisine and in the spice combination called chili powder.

Several spice blends are available. Two of them are standards in any kitchen. *Chili powder* is one, with a spice called *cumin* (coo-min) predominating. Other more familiar ingredients may be garlic, chili pepper, black pepper, oregano, and clove. Chili powder varies from mild to hot. It is used, of course, in chili, where it functions as a major flavor.

Curry powder is a blend of up to 20 oriental spices. In India, where it originated, cooks blend their own curry powders, which may vary considerably. In the United States curry powder comes premixed in various blends from mild to hot. Curry powders usually include cloves, black and red peppers, cumin, garlic, ginger, cinnamon, coriander, turmeric (which provides the characteristic yellow color), and sometimes other spices.

A group of powdered sweet aromatic spices from the tropics are used frequently in baking and in dessert cookery and occasionally in sauces, vegetables, and entrées. Among these are *cinnamon, nutmeg* and its counterpart *mace,* and *ginger.* Cinnamon comes from the dried bark of the cinnamon or cassia tree, nutmeg and mace from the seed of the nutmeg tree, and ginger from the dried root of the ginger plant.

In hot foods the nutmeg flavor goes well with potatoes and spinach and some kinds of veal dishes, and it gives the French béchamel

sauce its distinctive taste. Mace, a somewhat paler alternative to nutmeg, has a similar flavor. Cinnamon and ginger are used in oriental dishes.

Cinnamon is available also in sticks. They make good swizzlers for hot buttered rum or after-dinner coffee.

Mint is a sweet herb, with the familiar flavor you meet in toothpaste and chewing gum. In the kitchen it usually comes in the form of crushed leaves. The flavor of a mint sauce offers a refreshing complement to lamb. Fresh mint is sometimes available and makes a good flavoring and garnish for both fruit and iced tea.

In fact, many fresh herbs are available today, and their use is becoming more and more common, especially in nouvelle cuisine. When replacing dried herbs with fresh in a recipe, use three times as much. The dried herbs are three to four times as potent as fresh herbs because the aromatic oils have been concentrated in the drying. You should also add fresh herbs later in the cooking because they turn brown when cooked too long. Always taste carefully as you add, just as you do in seasoning.

Seeds of various herbs are used whole in baking and in salad dressings—the dark-brown, crescent-shaped caraway seed, the round, blond sesame seed, the blue-black seeds of the poppy flower. Seeds have the added advantage of textural interest as well as flavor.

This mini-catalog of herbs and spices is not meant to be memorized and then forgotten. Come back to it as a reference as you cook with flavor builders and flavorings, and again later as you begin to develop dishes on your own. Use it as a resource for experiment. Variety, as the old saying goes, is the spice of life.

The onion and its relatives
Onions and their cousins garlic, scallions, leeks, shallots, and chives are a special category of herbs that add strong and distinctive

flavors and aromas to both cooked and uncooked foods. These bulbous plants of the lily family arrive in the kitchen whole and fresh rather than dried and powdered, though some are available in dried forms. We use them in greater quantity, except for garlic, than the "pinch" or the "few" that is our limit on most herbs and spices. Figure 6-8 illustrates this herb family.

The *onion* is the scaly bulb of an herb used since ancient times and grown the world over, the commonest and most versatile flavor builder in the kitchen. You already know the onion well. Raw, it adds a pungent flavor to salads and cold sauces. Cooked, it has a sweet, mellow, come-on flavor that blends with almost anything. Cooked onions are also served as a vegetable. Dried onion powder, dried minced onions, and onion juice are also available. Although they are used extensively in the industry for cost and laborsaving reasons, they do not substitute well for fresh onions as tastemakers.

Garlic, the bulb of a plant of the same family, is available as cloves (bulblets), as a powder, or in juice form, with the fresh clove having by far the best flavor. Garlic is used as a flavor builder in stocks, stews, and sauces and as an uncooked flavoring in salads and salad dressings. It has been used for centuries not only for its pungent flavor but as a medicine and tonic.

FIGURE 6-8. The onion family (clockwise from top): leek, green onion, chives, shallot, red onion, yellow onion, white onion, garlic. (Photo by Patricia Roberts.)

Chives are another bulbous herb of the onion family, the only one whose leaves rather than bulb are eaten. Chives are usually used raw, since most of their flavor is lost if they are cooked. They are clipped from the plant and added, minced, to cold foods and sauces just before service. Minced chives are also marketed in fresh-cut, freeze-dried, and frozen form.

The *leek,* a mild-flavored relative of the onion, has a cylindrical bulb. It is the partner of the onion in the mirepoix. Leaves and all are used in stocks, but for soups most of the green is cut off because it seems to develop a bitterness. Boiled leeks are very popular as a vegetable in France, where they are known as the poor man's asparagus. The leek's triumph is the cold soup known as vichyssoise (vee-she-swahz), which was created in an American kitchen by the famous French chef Louis Diat.

The *scallion* is a young onion, also known as a green onion or spring onion. It has a mild flavor as onions go. Minced or sliced, it is added to salads, tops and all. It can pinch-hit in cooking for the full-grown onion, and its green top, minced, can substitute for chives in an emergency.

The *shallot* (shall'-et or sha-lot') is a cluster of brown-skinned bulblets similar to garlic. It is usually bought fresh; it is also available dehydrated and freeze-dried. It is somewhere between garlic and onion in both size and flavor but is milder and more delicate than either. If browned it acquires a bitter flavor. One thinks of shallots with wine cookery, with mushrooms in a marvelous stuffing called duxelles, and with special butters.

SUMMING UP

In Chapter 5 we talked about the structure of a dish—its flavor, body, and texture. This chapter has dealt with the materials and techniques for building each element of the structure.

To build flavor in stocks, the cook uses bones, mirepoix, herbs, and spices. The mirepoix is a standard combination of flavorful vegetables, which is usually used with a standard combination of herbs and spices to flavor stocks, soups, and sauces. Stocks in turn are used to build flavor in soups and sauces.

To build body for soups and sauces, the cook makes stocks from water, bones, mirepoix, herbs, and spices, building flavor at the same time. Two classes of stocks, light and dark, have their own special ingredients, techniques, and uses in soups and sauces. Stocks may be turned into glazes by reducing meat, chicken, or fish stocks to gelatin. These are used mainly to add flavor and texture to sauces. In today's kitchen convenience products often replace stock made from scratch, but they must be chosen with care and used with understanding.

To build texture the cook uses thickening agents. Natural thickeners are high-starch foods that often function as the major ingredient in a dish, providing flavor and character as well as thickening. Artificial thickeners are starch products whose primary function is to thicken. They include two fat-flour combinations—roux and beurre manié—and starch-water thickeners made with cornstarch, flour, arrowroot, or various name-brand starch combinations.

Another texture builder is the liaison, made of egg yolks and cream. It is not a thickener, though it has some thickening power. Its main function is to refine and smooth the texture of already thickened products.

In addition to a food's own taste, the cook has available many strong-flavored ingredients that are used in minute amounts in producing flavorful and distinctive dishes. These special ingredients are used in three ways: to season, to add a specific flavor accent, or to build a total flavor that supports or enriches a dish's major flavor.

In seasoning, the added products—salt, pepper, and fresh lemon juice—bring out the food's own flavor. The taste of a seasoning should not be perceived at all in the finished dish. The art of seasoning depends on the cook's sensory awareness, knowledge of tastes, and experience.

In flavoring, the product added brings its own distinctive flavor to complement the major flavor of the dish so that both are perceived separately. Flavorers commonly used are wines and spirits, extracts and oils, condiments, anchovies, capers, and zest.

In flavor-building, herbs and spices are cooked right into the dish so that their separate flavors merge with the major flavor. In stocks, and sometimes in soups, herbs and spices are used with a mirepoix to build flavor.

Flavor builders, stocks, and thickening agents are the building materials for endless numbers of menu items. The final dish can be only as good as the flavor, body, and texture built with these materials. As Escoffier said of one of them, "If one's stock is good, what remains of the work is easy; if, on the other hand, it is bad or merely mediocre, it is quite hopeless to expect anything approaching a satisfactory result."

THE COOK'S VOCABULARY

flavor, body, texture, major flavor, flavor builders

basic mirepoix, light mirepoix, dark mirepoix, stock herbs and spices

bouquet garni, sachet, onion piqué

stock, *fond de cuisine*

light stock, veal stock, chicken stock, fish stock, ordinary stockpot

dark stock, brown stock, grand jus

skim, strain, degrease, deglaze

glaze, glace

convenience base, convenience bouillon

thickening agent

roux, white roux, blond roux, brown roux

beurre manié

slurry, whitewash

liaison

temper

seasonings, flavorings

zest

condiment

spices, herbs

QUESTIONS FOR DISCUSSION

1. What role do a mirepoix, bouquet garni, sachet, and onion piqué play in producing flavor?

2. Discuss differences in the procedures for making light stocks and dark stocks.

3. Describe the techniques used when combining:
   a. Roux with liquid.
   b. Beurre manié with liquid.
   c. Starch thickeners with liquid.
   d. A liaison with liquid.

4. Describe the differences in seasonings, flavorings, and flavor builders. Name some ingredients that might be used in each role.

5. Suggest some guidelines for developing seasoning skill.

NOTHING begins a meal better than a cup of steaming-hot soup. Soup teases and yet soothes the appetite. The tempting aroma of broth and herbs makes the diner look forward with relish to a pleasant experience.

Soup may also be a main course, or it may be a pick-me-up between meals. In today's health-oriented society the coffee break has become a soup break for many people, and soup is a popular late-night snack. Soup-and-sandwich is a typical midday meal. Some people even like hot soup for breakfast.

What is soup? It is so familiar it is almost hard to define. Let us say that **soup** is a flavored, seasoned liquid, usually cooked, that is served as a dish in itself.

There are many, many different kinds of soup. To classify them according to flavor would be like measuring wealth in pennies—we would spend a great deal of time counting. But if we look at soup textures, and if we examine the methods of achieving different textures, we find that most soups group themselves naturally into three categories: unthickened, naturally thickened, and starch-thickened soups.

We are going to look at the different categories of soup and the ways they are made, and you will see how to make many different soups from a few basic formulas. We will also consider some well-known specialty soups, as well as some soups that are served cold. Soup cookery will introduce you to many different cooking techniques. Once you learn to cook all kinds of soup you will have mastered the basics of many other dishes.

After completing this chapter you should be able to

- Understand and explain the structure of clear soups, naturally thickened soups, and cream soups.
- Prepare each class of soup to meet specified quality standards.
- Use purées, roux, beurre manié, and liaisons successfully to produce specific soup textures.

7

Soups

- Identify well-known specialty soups.
- Prepare cold soups.
- Choose appropriate soup ingredients.
- Hold and store soups to maintain quality and avoid bacterial growth.

CLEAR SOUPS

Most unthickened soups are translucent; that is, they allow light to pass through. Because of this quality, they are known as **clear soups.**

To make the simplest possible clear soup, you take a good stock and season it. This is the cup of **bouillon** for the coffee break. Bouillon is also at home on the hospital tray, where its simplicity and good taste help to spark the listless appetite.

The kinds of clear soups you find on the typical menu add a great variety of ingredients to good stocks to make a great variety of good clear soups. Let us look at several of the most popular ones.

Onion soup

First we will look at a great favorite, onion soup, and see just how it is prepared. Figure 7-1 shows what it takes to make it, and recipe 7-1 shows its structure and the way you put it all together.

Here, by adding a flavor-determining ingredient and some supporting herbs and spices to the stock, we have created another soup. It is a simple soup because of the limited number of ingredients. Yet even the simplest soup requires a certain skill—to produce the flavor, texture, aroma, and appearance the diner expects.

As you can see from the recipe, the structure of the soup is simple. The onions provide the major flavor and the stock provides the body. Onions and stock together create an interesting texture that is thin yet has substance. The flavor-building herbs and spices enhance the major flavor without intruding their own tastes. You tie them in a piece of cheesecloth to make a sachet so that you can remove them before serving the soup.

To cut the onions julienne you cut the peeled onions in half lengthwise and slice them thin. As they cook, the layers will separate into individual strips. The onions should be cooked long enough to caramelize the sugar in them so that they are golden throughout, but there should be no dark-brown edges. Nor should they be overcooked in the simmering. They should be tender but still retain their shape. This may take anywhere from 45 seconds to 45 minutes depending on the quantity and other variables.

FIGURE 7-1. Onion soup. Onions, stock, and flavor builders make an easy, inexpensive, flavorful clear soup. The onions are cut julienne.

7-1 ONION SOUP

Yield: approximately 1 gallon (4 liters) = 16 8-oz (250 mL) portions

major flavor	2 lb	onions, julienne	1 kg	¼	bay leaf	¼	flavor builders in sachet
body	¾ gal	dark stock	3 L	½	clove	½	
				3–4	peppercorns	3–4	
				pinch	rosemary	pinch	
				pinch	thyme	pinch	
				*	seasonings	*	
				*	butter	*	

Basic ratio: 2 lb onions / ¾ gal stock
1 kg onions / 3 L stock

1. Melt *enough butter to cover the bottom of a pot to a depth of ⅛" (3 mm), and cook onions with sachet over moderate heat until onions are golden.

2. Add stock and simmer until onions have thoroughly flavored stock and are cooked through but still retain their shape.

3. Remove sachet and season soup *to taste.

7-1a FRENCH ONION SOUP

To recipe 7-1 add:

16	bread or roll slices, ¼–½" (½–1 cm) thick	16
4 oz	soft butter or margarine	125 g
3 oz	grated parmesan cheese	90 g

1. Blend butter and cheese to make a paste; spread on bread slices.
2. Bake at 350°F (180°C) until dry and brown, or brown lightly in salamander or broiler.
3. At service, float 1 crouton on each portion.

7-1b ONION AND ALMOND SOUP

To recipe 7-1 add:

4 oz	sliced blanched almonds	125 g
1 tsp*	ground cumin	*5 mL
16	croutons	16
⅓ C	sliced almonds, toasted	75 mL

1. In blender, grind almonds fine.
2. Gradually add 4 oz (125 mL) soup; process until smooth and milky. Add cumin *to produce a balance of flavors.
3. Add almond mixture to soup; heat to holding temperature.
4. At service, float 1 crouton topped with 1 tsp (5 mL) toasted almonds on each portion.

The seasonings should bring out the maximum flavor of the ingredients. A well-made onion soup is clear and flavorful with a rich, appetizing aroma.

You can turn this simple soup into another simple soup by topping it with a special **crouton**—a slice of bread with a butter-cheese spread baked or broiled until crisp and brown

(recipe 7-1a). Or you can turn the basic soup into a more sophisticated soup by adding special flavorings, as in recipe 7-1b. It gives you a good example of how flavorings function in a dish. The result is a balance in which the on-

7-2 VEGETABLE SOUP

Yield: 1 gallon (4 liters) = 16 8-oz (250 mL) portions

major flavor and body	2½ lb	vegetables, diced:	1.2 kg	¼	bay leaf	¼		
		1 part onions		½	clove	½		
		1 part celery		½	garlic clove	½	*flavor builders in sachet*	
		1 part carrots		pinch	rosemary	pinch		
		1 part potatoes		pinch	thyme	pinch		
		1 part tomatoes, peeled, seeded		3–4	peppercorns	3–4		
				*	seasonings	*		
body	¾ gal	dark stock	3 L	*	butter	*		

Basic ratio: 2½ lb vegetables / ¾ gal stock
1.2 kg vegetables / 3 L stock

1. Parboil carrots.
2. In stockpot, sweat onions, celery, and sachet of spices and herbs in *⅛″ (3 mm) butter over moderate heat until onions are translucent.
3. Add stock and simmer until celery is about half done.
4. Add potatoes and carrots.
5. Simmer until all vegetables are done—al dente.
6. Remove from fire and add tomatoes.
7. Remove sachet and season soup *to taste.

ion, almond, and cumin are individually perceptible while blending harmoniously. The asterisks accompanying cumin in the recipe indicate that the amounts given are guidelines rather than absolute amounts, since the strength of the cumin may vary. Let your taste buds be your guide.

Vegetable soups

Going back to stocks as our point of departure, we can take our soup-making one step farther and add to a stock not just one major vegetable flavor but several. Almost any number of vegetables can be combined with different-flavored stocks to create a great variety of clear vegetable soups.

Recipe 7-2 is one example. Examining it carefully, you will see that it is made with several vegetables having different textures and different cooking rates. Yet to make a good vegetable soup all the ingredients must be done—fully done but not overdone—and must reach doneness at the same time. This is why it is put together the way it is.

Notice that to produce the most flavor and the best texture for the ingredients, several different cooking processes are used. The herb and vegetable flavor builders are *sweated* to get a nice blend of flavors before the stock is added. The carrots are *parboiled* before being added to the soup, so they will reach doneness at the same time as the other vegetables. The soup is *simmered* to achieve doneness with a minimum of flavor loss through evaporation. The tomatoes are *poached* last in the hot liquid to avoid overcooking.

Here are the guidelines for combining different stocks and different vegetables successfully.

- Begin with a well-flavored stock.
- Know what flavors complement each other.
- Know the rates at which different foods cook.
- Do not overcook.

Although flavor and taste are to some extent a matter of opinion, certain flavor combinations seem to be universally pleasing—chicken and celery, for example, or beef and tomato. Certain spices and herbs blend well with certain stocks—chicken and clove, fish stock and lemon, beef and thyme.

Knowing the rates at which different foods cook comes best through experience. Feel their texture, cook them, taste them. Here are some general groupings.

7-3 MINESTRONE

Yield: 1 gallon (4 liters) = 16 8-oz (250 mL) portions

major flavor and body	3 lb	vegetables, diced:	1.5 kg	¼	bay leaf	¼	flavor builders in sachet
		1 part onions		½	clove	½	
		1 part celery		1½	garlic cloves, peeled	1½	
		1 part carrots					
		1 part potatoes		pinch	rosemary	pinch	
		1 part zucchini		pinch	thyme	pinch	
		1 part tomatoes		3–4	peppercorns	3–4	
	4 oz	cabbage or spinach, shredded	125 g	*	seasonings	*	
				*	olive oil	*	
	½ lb	white beans, cooked until tender, drained	250 g	½ tsp	chopped parsley or cilantro	2 mL	per portion
				1 tsp	grated parmesan cheese	5 mL	
	4 oz	spaghetti, cooked, drained	125 g				
body	¾ gal	light stock	3 L				

Basic ratio: 4 lb flavor ingredients / ¾ gal stock
2 kg flavor ingredients / 3 L stock

1. In stockpot, sweat first five vegetables with sachet in *⅛″ (3 mm) olive oil until onion is translucent. Do not brown.
2. Add stock and cabbage. (If using spinach, add in Step 3.) Simmer until vegetables are al dente.
3. Add beans, spaghetti, and tomatoes. Heat to a simmer, then remove from fire.
4. Season *to taste.
5. Add parsley and cheese to each portion when served.

- Hard vegetables such as carrots and raw green beans take longest to cook. They should be parboiled before being added to a soup-in-the-making.

- Soft vegetables such as tomatoes, lettuce, and canned vegetables take the shortest time, or no time at all, and should be added late in the cooking.

- In between are the medium vegetables, such as potatoes, celery, turnips, and frozen vegetables. They can be cooked right in the soup during the soup-making.

Do not overcook! "Done" for vegetables is firm to the bite, a texture known as **al dente.** Al dente vegetables will keep their separate flavors and their bright, attractive colors along with their pleasant texture.

There is a common and persistent belief that soup should be cooked for long periods of time to extract flavor from the ingredients. Although prolonged cooking does extract flavor, what is added to the soup is lost to the individual vegetables. Some vegetables change flavor as well as color when they are overcooked. And much flavor can be lost through evaporation.

A more logical approach than prolonged cooking is to simmer the soup just to doneness. Whether you hold it for service hot or cold, flavors will continue to blend and be released by the vegetables within. In the perfect vegetable soup you should be able to taste the individual flavors and at the same time the blended flavor of the soup as a whole.

Meat, rice, pasta, barley, and many other products can be added to a vegetable soup. Many such ingredients are cooked separately and added to the soup at the end of the cooking process. One reason for doing this is to maintain the soup's clarity. Starchy foods such as cereals and pastas will cloud the liquid in which they are cooked without contributing flavor in the process.

The minestrone soup in recipe 7-3 is a case in point: the spaghetti and beans are precooked and added at the end. This well-known Italian specialty is a hearty soup thick with ingredients, yet it is still a clear soup. The liquid has not been thickened and it is still translucent.

Consommé

Many clear soups use an enriched stock called **consommé** (con-sum-may) as the body liquid in preference to a simple stock. Consommé is also a clear soup in itself and a very important one. It has a rich color and a hearty flavor that give it top rank among clear soups.

Historically, the making of a perfect consommé was a measure of a cook's skill. A perfect consommé has two outstanding qualities: *clarity* and *strength of flavor.*

These two measures of quality are achieved through a single process known as **clarification**—the removing of particles in a stock by a special cooking process. At the same time that the stock is being cleared, flavor is being added to it to make the consommé. Consommé is thus defined as a double-strength clarified stock. It may be made from any kind of stock, though beef is the one most commonly used.

Making consommé is a long and exacting process. Recipe 7-4 gives you a modern version of the classical method.

In Step 1 you combine very lean ground meat with flavor builders and egg whites to make a mixture called **clearmeat.** This is what is going to clarify the stock. Chill it thoroughly.

In Step 2 you mix clearmeat with cold, flavorful stock. The cold liquid will dissolve proteins in the meat.

In Step 3 you heat and stir the mixture gently, keeping the clearmeat moving so it won't stick to the pan. As the stock approaches a boil, the clearmeat rises slowly. This is when clarification begins. The egg white and dissolved meat proteins begin to coagulate and gather up all the particles from the stock as they rise. The acid of the tomato helps in the coagulation process.

As soon as the pot approaches a boil, it is reduced to a simmer (Step 4). When the clearmeat reaches the top it forms a mass called a **raft.** At this point all stirring stops. These critical stages of clarification are shown in Figure 7-2.

As the soup simmers (Step 5), flavor is extracted from the raft to give the soup its double strength. It is literally being beefed up. At the same time, the stock is further clarified as convection currents in the simmering pot carry particles upward to cling to the bottom of the raft.

When the consommé has reached its full flavor and clarity (1 to 2 hours of simmering after the raft has formed), it is strained through a double thickness of dampened cheesecloth in a china cap (Step 6).

Here are the important guidelines for making consommé.

- Use cold stock.
- Use low heat throughout.
- Do not allow the clearmeat to stick to the bottom of the pot. Stir in the beginning.
- Keep the liquid quiet. Do not boil.
- Do not stir after the raft has formed.
- Do not disturb the raft.
- Measure cooking time from raft formation.
- Judge doneness by clarity and flavor.
- Strain carefully, keeping the raft intact.

Versatility in clear soups

Stocks, bouillons, and consommés are points of departure for countless clear soups. Following the basic patterns and methods of the soups we have examined, you can make hundreds of different soups by adding almost any ingredients that are compatible in flavor— vegetables, meats, cereal products, croutons, dumplings, stuffed pastas, and so on.

The amounts of ingredients and the size of the pieces depend on the cook's intent. You can use flavorful foods as major flavors, as we do in our onion and vegetable soups, cooking them right in the soup so that they enrich the liquid. Or you can use the same ingredients as a **garniture** to complement or contrast with the basic bouillon or consommé, enhancing its flavor and appearance rather than changing it. In this case you would use them in small amounts and cut them very fine.

A garniture is a specific way of transforming a single basic dish into many different dishes. It is a term often confused with garnish:

- **Garnish** Something edible added to a finished dish entirely for eye appeal, such as a sprig of mint or parsley beside a lamb chop or a cherry in the center of a grapefruit half. A garnish may be eaten but that is not its purpose.

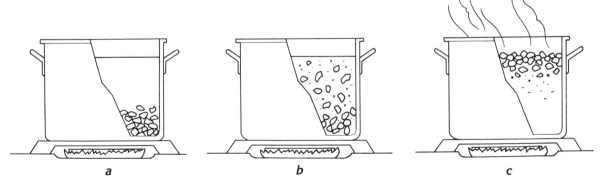

FIGURE 7-2. Clarifying stock to make consommé. **a.** Clearmeat is placed in the bottom of a stockpot, cold stock is added, and the pot is placed over a low fire. **b.** As the temperature approaches a simmer, bits of clearmeat move slowly toward the surface, absorbing particles from the stock as they rise—clarifying it. **c.** The clearmeat forms a raft at the surface. Simmering extracts its flavors, strengthening the stock to produce consommé.

7-4 BEEF CONSOMMÉ

Yield: 1 gallon (4 liters) = 16 8-oz (250 mL) portions

major flavor	1 lb	lean ground beef	500 g	**Clarifiers:**		
				8 oz	egg whites	250 mL
body	5 qt	beef stock, cold	5 L	8 oz	canned crushed tomatoes	250 mL
				Mirepoix:		
				8 oz	onions, small dice	250 g
				4 oz	celery, small dice	125 g
				4 oz	carrots, small dice	125 g
				6	parsley stems, finely chopped	6
				pinch	thyme	pinch
				½*	bay leaf	*½
				2*	cloves	*2
				½ tsp	crushed peppercorns	2 mL
				*	seasonings	*

flavor builders

Basic ratios: 1 lb beef + 1 lb mirepoix / 5 qt stock
500 g beef + 500 g mirepoix / 5 L stock

1. Mix thoroughly all ingredients except stock to make clearmeat. Chill.
2. Place clearmeat in stockpot and slowly add cold stock, stirring gently to combine.
3. Over low heat, bring to just below boiling point, gently moving clearmeat to keep it from sticking to bottom of pot.
4. Reduce at once to a low simmer.
5. After raft has formed on top, simmer slowly without stirring for *1 to 2 hours until full-flavored and clear.
6. Strain, degrease, and season *to taste.

• **Garniture** Something edible added to a finished dish for eye appeal, flavor, and often textural contrast, such as croutons added to a bowl of soup. A garniture becomes part of the dish and is eaten with it.

With a garniture you can turn a consommé, whether bought or made, into any number of classic clear soups. Add a garniture of vegetables brunoise for a consommé brunoise (7-4a). In the same way, add thinly sliced

7-4a CONSOMMÉ BRUNOISE

To 1 gal (4 L) finished consommé add:

    1 pt   vegetables brunoise   500 mL

Parboil vegetables separately in a little consommé. Add 2 Tb (25 mL) per portion when served.

7-4b CHICKEN CONSOMMÉ

In recipe 7-4 make the following changes:

    Add ½ lb (250 g) ground raw chicken.

    Substitute chicken stock for beef stock.

    Omit tomatoes.

    Add 1½ oz (50 mL) lemon juice.

Add ground chicken and lemon juice in Step 1. Proceed as in recipe 7-4.

crêpes to make consommé célestine. Julienne of fresh spinach turns it into consommé florentine.

In each case the flavor of the garniture is an essential part of the soup, and the name of the garniture becomes the name of the soup. In the world of cooking there are hundreds of special garnitures. Their names mean the same thing the world over, providing a universal language of cookery. *Florentine,* for example, always includes spinach, whatever the basic dish. *Printanière* is always diced spring vegetables.

The crouton that turns a simple onion soup into a French onion soup is also a garniture. So is the parmesan cheese added to the minestrone soup.

You can do other things with consommé besides adding garnitures. Enrich it with sherry just before service time for a consommé au sherry in which two complementary flavors are evident. Add gelatin to the consommé and serve it jellied and well chilled on a hot summer evening.

You can make a chicken consommé by making a few changes in the basic consommé recipe (7-4b). Add tomatoes to the chicken consommé to make consommé madrilène. These are all examples of how a single dish can be turned into dozens of others.

All the soups we have been discussing are clear soups, no matter what is added. The liquid has not been thickened and it is still translucent.

Whatever the ingredients and however they are used, the same few rules apply to all clear soups. Use flavor combinations that go well together, add raw ingredients in order of their cooking times, and do not overcook.

NATURALLY THICKENED SOUPS: POTAGES

The next step in our venture toward mastery of soupology is to learn how to create a heavier texture. The simplest way to do this is to purée the ingredients that give a particular soup its character and blend them back into the liquid. This gives us our second category of soups—naturally thickened soups, or **potages** (poh-tahzh—rhymes with garage). *Potage* is also a French word for several different kinds of soup and for the soup course on a menu.

The texture of the puréed potage is thick and slightly rough or coarse to the tongue, as compared with the clear soup and the cream soup. The potage may vary greatly in consistency depending on the intent of the cook, the taste of the diner, or the use to which it is put. A potage served as an appetizer may be no thicker than cold whipping cream, for example, but a meal-in-itself luncheon serving might be much thicker. Potages appeal to the hearty appetite and are likely to have more of a peasant quality than the consommés and creams, though vichyssoise does honor to the most elegant table.

Potages have a range of textures, from a smooth, glossy, and elegant purée to hearty and chunky soups in which the ingredients are left whole or only a portion of them is puréed.

7-5 POTATO-LEEK POTAGE

Yield: 1 gallon (4 liters) = 16 8-oz (250 mL) portions

major flavors, body, texture	2 lb	peeled potatoes, medium dice	1 kg	½	bay leaf	½	*flavor builders in sachet*	
	½ lb	leek (white and pale green only), ⅛″ (3 mm) slices	250 g	1	clove	1		
				4–5	peppercorns, crushed	4–5		
				*	seasonings	*		
	½ lb	onion, small dice	250 g	*	butter	*		
body	¾ gal	light stock	3 L					
	1 pt	cream, hot	500 mL					

1. In stockpot, melt butter to *⅛″ (3 mm) depth and sweat onion and leek with sachet until onions are translucent.
2. Add stock and potatoes.
3. Simmer until potatoes are done. Remove sachet.
4. Purée ingredients and blend them back into the liquid. Strain if necessary.
5. Add cream. If too thick, adjust texture with stock or additional cream. If too thin, reduce by simmering.
6. Season *to taste.

7-5a VICHYSSOISE

To recipe 7-5 add:

8 oz	minced fresh chives	250 g

1. Chill soup. Adjust seasoning when cold.
2. Serve in chilled cups. To each portion add a garniture of 1 Tb (15 mL) chives.

7-5b POTATO AND WATERCRESS SOUP

To recipe 7-5 add:

3 bunches watercress, concassé

Add watercress along with stock and potatoes in Step 2.

Usually such potages are made with starchy ingredients—beans or potatoes—and some of the starch is dispersed in the liquid during cooking, providing natural thickening even though the solid ingredients are not puréed.

How to make a potage

The making of potages is not very different from the making of clear soups, except for the puréeing process. Flavor is built with familiar flavor builders, using familiar techniques, and the cooking process is the same. But the requirements of thickening with a purée call for some special attention. Consider the recipe for potato-leek potage (7-5). Figure 7-3 shows the ingredients.

You can see at a glance that preparation of this typical potage is not at all complicated. The one critical step is Step 3. At this point a good soup is assured if you understand doneness. "Done" for this soup is when the potatoes have been cooked 100 percent but still retain their shape—slightly past al dente but not mushy. If they are not fully cooked, they will not thicken the soup properly. If they are overcooked, flavor is lost. Doneness is even more important for the potage than it was for the clear soup. The time range is broad, but it should take well under an hour.

Any thickened soup may need some adjustment of texture (Step 5) as one of the finishing touches. To thin, add an appropriate liquid—for this soup, light stock or extra cream. To thicken, simmer the soup until it reaches the consistency desired. Seasoning (Step 6) always follows as a last step because thinning and thickening will change the proportions of seasoning to liquid.

You can turn this delicious hot soup into vichyssoise by chilling it and adding a garniture of chives (7-5a). Or make another hot soup by adding another major flavor as in recipe 7-5b.

Many recipes for potages call for the ingredients to be cooked until they fall completely apart into the soup. But to do this would require the cook to choose one of two undesirable alternatives: to increase heat to cause boiling, or to cook for a much longer time. Both would increase evaporation of good food flavor and reduce the yield.

Not every vegetable makes a successful potage. Generally speaking, high-starch vegetables work best. Among the most common in addition to potato are the dried **legumes:** split peas, lentils, and the various beans—lima, red kidney, white or navy, pinto, black, and others. (It was a "pottage of lentiles" for which Esau of the Bible sold his birthright to his brother Jacob.) The cook is not limited to these vegetables, but they are starchy enough to be good natural thickeners.

Vegetables that don't work well as thickeners are those having little or no starch and

FIGURE 7-3. Potato-leek potage. Potatoes, leeks, and onions provide flavor and texture for a hearty potage.

7-6 NAVY BEAN SOUP

Yield: 1 gallon (4 liters) = 16 8-oz (250 mL) portions

major flavor	1 lb	dried navy beans	500 g	2 oz	bacon, diced	60 g	*flavor builders*
				Mirepoix:			
body	1 gal	light stock or water	4 L	4 oz	onions, small dice	125 g	
				2 oz	celery, small dice	60 g	
				2 oz	carrots, small dice	60 g	
				Sachet:			
				2	garlic cloves	2	
				1	bay leaf	1	
				pinch	thyme	pinch	
				pinch	crushed peppercorns	pinch	
				1	ham hock	1	*flavorers*
				1 pt	canned crushed tomatoes with juice	500 mL	
				*	seasonings	*	

Basic ratio: 1 lb dried beans / 1 gal liquid
500 g dried beans / 4 L liquid

1. Wash and pick over beans; soak overnight in water or stock.
2. Render fat from bacon in stockpot.
3. Add mirepoix and sachet to bacon fat and sweat until vegetables are almost tender.
4. Add stock, ham hock, and beans and simmer until beans are tender.
5. Add tomatoes and reheat to a simmer; remove from fire.
6. Remove ham hock and sachet.
(7. Purée one-third of soup; combine purée and remaining soup.)
8. Adjust to desired texture by adding stock or water.
9. If desired, dice meat from hock and return to soup.
10. Season *to taste.

7-6a SPLIT PEA SOUP

In recipe 7-6 make the following changes:

> Substitute split peas for navy beans.
>
> Omit tomatoes.

1. Follow instructions, omitting Step 5.
2. Simmer until peas are tender (*1 hour or less).
3. In Step 7, purée all ingredients.

7-6b POTAGE MONGOLE

Yield: 1 gallon (4 liters)

To 2 qt (2 L) split pea soup (recipe 7-6a) add:

1 qt	stock	1 L
1 qt	tomato purée	1 L
¾ pt	green peas, diced carrots, diced leeks, parboiled	400 mL

1. Blend stock with tomato purée. Stir into hot soup.
2. Reheat to serving temperature.
3. Serve each portion with 1½ Tb (25 mL) mixed vegetables.

those whose strong flavors create an undesirable taste when used in the volume necessary to thicken a soup. Examples of these are celery and onion. Such vegetables are often used as flavor builders in potages and puréed along with the main ingredient. Tomato makes a good purée but it has too strong and acid a flavor to be used alone as a thickener. It is usually combined with another purée or made into a cream soup. Watercress is combined with potatoes in recipe 7-5b, but it too would not do well alone because it has too little starch to provide a satisfactory texture.

The basic method of soup-making given for the potato-leek potage can be used for any starchy vegetable, with some modifications. One is that most dried vegetables need to be soaked several hours or overnight in water or stock. Use about a gallon of liquid to the pound of vegetables, and keep them in the cooler while they are soaking. Cook them in the same liquid, adding more if necessary to cover. A shortcut is to boil them for 2 minutes and then let them soak for an hour. You can cook split peas and lentils without soaking. You can even cook beans without soaking, but it will prolong the cooking time.

You can use a mirepoix for added flavor. Smoked meat is another welcome flavor builder. You can simmer a ham bone in the pot along with everything else. You can chop bits of the meat and blend them into the final soup along with the puréed vegetables, or you can sauté finely diced smoked meat and blend it in shortly before service.

Recipe 7-6 is an example of how it all goes together. To **render** the fat from the bacon in Step 2 means to heat the bacon until the fat separates from the connective tissue.

Dried vegetables may take longer to reach doneness than potatoes. Again the range is broad: soaked split peas will probably take less than an hour and navy beans may take three. The others fall somewhere in between. The test of doneness is the same—slightly past al dente but not mushy. Too thick a consistency can be adjusted by adding stock, water, or cream. If texture is too thin, adjust by simmering.

Versatility in potages

You can make many other potages from a simple one by adding different garnitures. This is how vichyssoise is made, as we've already observed. You can also make the potato-leek potage into new soups by adding potatoes cut in different shapes, or chopped parsley, or diced bacon. Combining garnitures will create still other soups, each with its own distinctive flavor. You can do the same thing with other potages.

You can make other soups from legumes by adapting the navy bean soup recipe as in 7-6a. You can also substitute any other dried bean for the navy bean and follow the recipe exactly.

Another way to create different potages is to combine purées. Potage mongole is made by combining purée of split peas with puréed tomatoes and stock (7-6b).

Any country-cousin potage can be given city sophistication by adding a liaison of egg yolks and cream just before serving. This imparts the finest texture possible by binding the ingredients together. Adding it to the humble potage is like transforming rabbit fur into mink. We will discuss the use of the liaison in detail when we talk about cream soups, where its use is much more common.

CREAM SOUPS

Of the three classes of soup, cream soups require the most effort and the greatest skill. Texture in the clear soups and potages was achieved naturally and simply. The smooth, creamy texture of cream soups is achieved through the use of thickening agents. A **cream soup,** then, is defined as a soup made with a thickening agent.

Cream or milk adds to the smoothness and flavor of a cream soup; it also adds a lot of confusion in classifying soups. It is not cream that makes a soup a cream soup; it is the creamy consistency produced by thickening with starch.

Cream soups consist of three main elements: liquid, one or more flavor-determining ingredients, and thickening agent. Flavor builders may also be used, and seasonings are added at the end of the cooking. Most cream soups are thickened with a flour-butter thickening agent, either roux or beurre manié.

There are two methods of making a good cream soup. In one method you start making the soup by making roux, introducing flavor-

FIGURE 7-4. Two ways of making a cream soup.

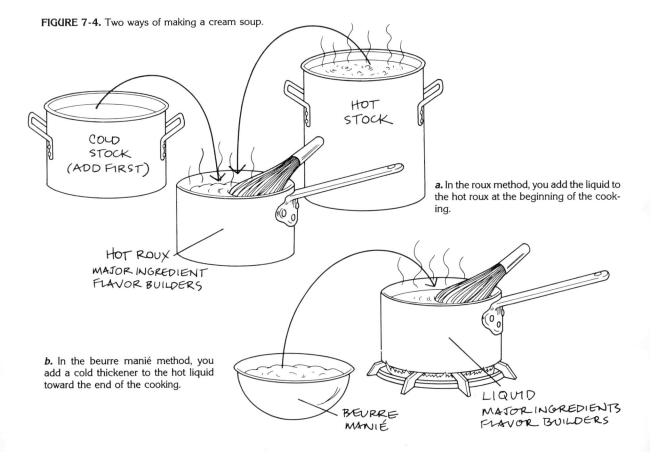

a. In the roux method, you add the liquid to the hot roux at the beginning of the cooking.

b. In the beurre manié method, you add a cold thickener to the hot liquid toward the end of the cooking.

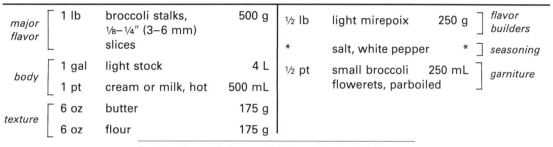

7-7 CREAM OF BROCCOLI SOUP (ROUX METHOD)

Yield: 1 gallon (4 liters) = 16 8-oz (250 mL) portions

major flavor	1 lb	broccoli stalks, ⅛–¼″ (3–6 mm) slices	500 g	½ lb	light mirepoix	250 g	*flavor builders*	
				*	salt, white pepper	*	*seasoning*	
body	1 gal	light stock	4 L	½ pt	small broccoli flowerets, parboiled	250 mL	*garniture*	
	1 pt	cream or milk, hot	500 mL					
texture	6 oz	butter	175 g					
	6 oz	flour	175 g					

Basic ratio: 1 lb broccoli / 1 gal stock / ¾ lb roux
500 g broccoli / 4 L stock / 350 g roux

1. Sweat mirepoix in total butter called for in recipe until flavors are blended and ingredients give off an aroma.
2. Reduce heat and add flour, blending to make roux.
3. Cook roux until light and foamy.
4. Remove from heat. Add *cold* stock (¼ total quantity) to dissolve roux.
5. Return to heat and add remaining stock, *hot,* and broccoli, stirring until thickened.
6. When thickened, blend in cream or milk. Simmer until done.
7. Strain. Adjust texture as necessary. Season *to taste.
8. Add 1–3 tsp (5–15 mL) broccoli flowerets to each portion when served.

determining ingredients and flavor builders into the roux-making process. Then you add the liquid and complete the cooking. We'll call this the roux method.

In the second method you start making the soup by cooking the flavor-determining ingredients and flavor builders in the liquid. You add a cold flour-butter thickener toward the end of the cooking. Beurre manié is the thickener most commonly used, so we'll call this the beurre manié method. Figure 7-4 illustrates the differences in the two methods.

A close examination of a soup made by the two methods will give you a better understanding of the methods and the special techniques involved in each.

The roux method

In recipe 7-7 you will see that the roux forms the base to which the liquid is added.

This is a traditional method of soup cookery going back perhaps two hundred years. It involves a number of critical matters of technique.

In Steps 2 and 3 the roux must be well blended so that all the flour is evenly dispersed, and the heat must be low so that the roux does not brown. If you get a brown-flour taste in a cream soup it is going to taste brown no matter what you do to it. At this point the roux should look like wallpaper paste with lumps of vegetables in it.

In Step 4 the abrupt temperature change "breaks" the roux, or stops the thickening action, and the roux dissolves readily in the cold stock with the help of some vigorous blending. It is at this point that the ultimate texture of the soup is determined. It is important to use cold liquid to dissolve the hot roux. If you add hot stock to hot roux, little balls of roux that won't dissolve are likely to form. Although you can strain these out of the final soup, their thickening power is lost and the soup will be thinner than it was supposed to be.

After a successful Step 4, Step 5 is no problem. The hot stock blends right in.

The thin liquid of Step 5 thickens as it nears the boiling point. After it has thickened, add the cream or milk (Step 6). If you add milk sooner, it may curdle.

Simmer the soup until done. "Done" is the point at which the soup reaches the taste and texture the cook is aiming for. The broccoli should be completely cooked and the liquid should have the desired broccoli taste. Cooking time will average 30 minutes. It may take more time or less, depending on quantity and other variables.

The texture of the liquid should be smooth, its consistency slightly thicker than that of ordinary whipping cream. The texture may be thinned by adding cream or stock in Step 7 after straining. It may be thickened by blending in beurre manié.

Does this all sound complicated? It is. But this is a technique you will use over and over, so learn it well.

The beurre manié method

The beurre manié method is simpler. In this method everything is added to the liquid, as shown in recipe 7-8. There are only a few points of possible difficulty.

- In Step 1, it is important to use heavy cream. Neither milk nor light cream nor half-and-half will stand up to the simmering.
- In Step 2 the beurre manié must be added a little at a time and blended in well each time with a whip until no lumps remain.
- After the final addition, the soup must continue to simmer a few minutes to cook the flour in the beurre manié (Step 3).

7-8 CREAM OF BROCCOLI SOUP (BEURRE MANIÉ METHOD)

Yield: 1 gallon (4 liters) = 16 8-oz (250 mL) portions

major flavor	1 lb	broccoli stalks, 1/8–1/4" (3–6 mm) slices	500 g	1/2	bay leaf	1/2	*flavor builders*	
				1	clove	1		
body	1 gal	light stock	4 L	*	salt, white pepper	*	*seasoning*	
	1 pt	heavy cream	500 mL	1/2 pt	small broccoli flowerets, parboiled	250 mL	*garniture*	
texture	3/4 lb*	beurre manié:	*350 g					
		1 part flour						
		1 part butter						

Basic ratio: 1 lb broccoli / 1 gal stock / 3/4 lb beurre manié
500 g broccoli / 4 L stock / 350 g beurre manié

1. Simmer broccoli and flavor builders in stock and cream until broccoli is al dente and liquid is full-flavored.
2. Thicken with beurre manié *to consistency desired.
3. Simmer until no starch taste remains.
4. Strain. Season *to taste.
5. Add 1–3 tsp (5–15 mL) broccoli flowerets to each portion when served.

- Final success depends on skillful seasoning to bring out the maximum flavor of the main ingredient (Step 4).

You can see that the beurre manié method is much simpler than the traditional method. With fewer ingredients and fewer steps, preparation time is shortened and less attention is needed during cooking.

The newer method with its few ingredients produces a singleness of flavor that makes a refreshingly distinctive soup. In the older method the blended flavor base created by the mirepoix makes a delicious soup but tends to give all cream soups a common flavor.

Both cream soup methods may be used with almost any vegetable as a main ingredient. The usual ratio is 1 pound (500 g) of vegetable to 1 gallon (4 liters) of stock. For a strong-flavored vegetable such as celery only half a pound (250 g) is needed. In making celery, carrot, or mushroom soup by the roux method, you can sweat the major vegetable along with the mirepoix for fuller flavor. If you make mushroom soup this way, you need more butter because the mushrooms soak it up, and you must add lemon juice to keep them from turning brown (7-7a). Compare this with the beurre manié method in 7-8a.

A few special cream soups are made with stock alone as the flavor-determining ingredient—cream of chicken, for example. Such a soup is made by either method, using an extra-rich stock and adding a garniture of chicken meat cut julienne or diced (7-7b and 7-8b).

A liaison may be added to any cream soup for the ultimate in texture, using the technique illustrated in Figure 6-6. But liaisons are tricky: they must be added to the hot soup without letting the egg cook in the process. After the liaison is added, the soup must not be allowed to reach the boiling point, nor does it hold well. A liaison must therefore be added just before serving time.

Success with a liaison is not as easy to measure as failure. If failure is the outcome, the soup will have scrambled egg yolks floating on top. Success will be a velvety texture known best to the educated palate of the diner in the very expensive a la carte restaurant. Because of holding problems with liaisons they are impractical for everyday use.

Quality measures for cream soups

Whatever the method, the finished cream soup should be smooth to the tongue and free from lumps, with a consistency no thinner than that of fresh, cold whipping cream. It may be somewhat thicker if desired, but it should pour readily in a smooth, free-flowing fashion.

A good cream soup looks very smooth. It has gloss and color, the latter deriving from the flavor-determining ingredient.

Its flavor is that of the major ingredient subtly enriched by the supporting flavors. The latter will modify the major flavor more in the soup made by the first method, but in either soup no supporting flavor should be identifiable. There should be no taste of roux or flour.

The soup should be seasoned to bring out the maximum flavor, but no taste of seasonings themselves should be detectable.

Cream soup versatility

Like the other kinds of soup, cream soups take readily to garnitures as a method of creating new varieties. A simple cream of chicken is transformed by a garniture of asparagus tips and diced chicken into a crème de la princesse. Add a garniture of cheese straws to a cream of chicken and it becomes crème monaco. The garniture is always added as close to serving time as possible so that it remains distinct from the body of the soup and retains its own texture.

Cream soups need not always be served as the smooth finished dish we have been describing. Instead of straining the vegetables out you may leave them in the liquid and serve a hearty soup more like a potage in spirit. This is often done with mushroom soup. In this version of a cream soup, if you make it by the beurre manié method, you would use a sachet for your flavor builders.

Roux method

7-7a CREAM OF MUSHROOM SOUP

1 lb	mushrooms, chopped	500 g
½ lb	light mirepoix	250 g
2 Tb	lemon juice	25 mL
1 gal	light stock	4 L
1 pt	cream or milk, hot	500 mL
8 oz	butter	250 g
6 oz	flour	175 g
*	salt, white pepper	*

Sweat mushrooms and lemon juice with mirepoix. Proceed as in recipe 7-7.

Beurre manié method

7-8a CREAM OF MUSHROOM SOUP

1 lb	mushrooms, chopped	500 g
1 gal	light stock	4 L
1 pt	heavy cream	500 mL
½	bay leaf	½
1	clove	1
¾ lb*	beurre manié	*350 g
*	salt, white pepper, lemon juice	*

Proceed as in recipe 7-8.

7-7b CREAM OF CHICKEN SOUP

1 gal	strong chicken stock	4 L
½ lb	light mirepoix	250 g
¾ lb	roux	350 g
1 pt	cream or milk, hot	500 mL
*	seasonings	*
4 oz	cooked chicken, julienne or small dice	125 g

1. Follow Steps 1–6 in recipe 7-7, simmering to desired flavor intensity.
2. Strain, adjust texture, and season *to taste.
3. Add chicken.

7-8b CREAM OF CHICKEN SOUP

1 gal	strong chicken stock	4 L
1 pt	heavy cream	500 mL
½	bay leaf	½
1	clove	1
¾ lb*	beurre manié	*350 g
*	seasonings	*
4 oz	cooked chicken, julienne or small dice	125 g

1. Simmer stock, cream, and flavor builders to desired flavor intensity.
2. Follow Steps 2–5 in recipe 7-8, adding chicken in Step 5.

Still another way to vary a cream soup is to purée the ingredients. Since this will thicken the soup, you will need to adjust the texture with cream or stock, seasoning to taste after the liquid is added.

SPECIALTY SOUPS

The many soups discussed thus far come mostly from classical European cuisine and are common throughout the world. They fall neatly into our three soup categories. Now we come to some exceptions that use many of the same techniques and methods, but they create their own categories. Each of these soups has a characteristic set of ingredients, or flavor, or texture, or method of cooking. Often they grew up outside the classical kitchen in some particular part of the world and became famous because they were so good. Usually they began as a meal in a pot using local ingredients. Most of them remain associated with their place of origin.

Bouillabaisse (boo-yah-bess) is a fish soup or stew in a class by itself and a meal in itself. One legend says that Venus, the goddess of love, invented the dish to put her husband into a sound sleep so that she could pursue her pleasures unhindered. Legend aside, bouillabaisse comes from Provence in southern France and originated as a simple Mediterranean fisherman's soup.

From the point of view of soup cookery, bouillabaisse is unique in that it does not use stock but creates the stock as the soup is made. Ideally, six or more kinds of fish and shellfish are cooked together in a tall pot with olive oil, flavor builders, water, and sometimes white wine. Leeks or onions, tomatoes, saffron, garlic, and some milder vegetables and herbs blend with the main ingredients to give this dish its distinctive flavor.

The fish in true French bouillabaisse are local Mediterranean fish most Americans have never heard of, such as rascasse, chapon, conger eel, red mullet. Each Mediterranean village has its own version of bouillabaisse, Paris has still another, and rivalry is intense. A similar dish can be made in this country with lobster and shrimp and various kinds of American fish.

Chowders are an American contribution to soup cookery, though they are said to have originated in the fishing villages of Brittany, where successful fishing expeditions were celebrated by cooking a huge communal cauldronful of fish and vegetables. Whatever their origin, the chowders we know today come from the East Coast, where fish and clams are plentiful.

There are thick chowders and thin chowders. They are characteristically hearty soups of fish or vegetables, with a large proportion of solid ingredients served in the liquid. They are made with rendered salt pork or bacon and usually have quite a bit of potato. Thick or thin, they typically use milk as the liquid. Manhattan clam chowder is an exception; it substitutes tomatoes for milk. There is much controversy between New Englanders and New Yorkers over which is the true clam chowder. A bill was once introduced in the Maine state legislature to make it illegal to put a tomato into clam chowder.

The New England clam chowder in recipe 7-9 is a roux-thickened soup. In the recipe you will recognize many techniques used for cream soups. Fat from salt pork substitutes for butter in the roux. The liquid is clam juice plus fish stock. The straining step for cream soups is eliminated, and the milk is added at the end. After the milk is added, the soup must not be allowed to boil or it may scorch or curdle.

Black pepper is traditional in this chowder—an exception to the rule of using white pepper in a light-colored dish.

Gumbos are another American specialty, native to Louisiana. Creole versions, developed in New Orleans, blended the culinary heritage of French and Spanish upper classes with local ingredients such as seafood and hot peppers and contributions from native Indians and slave cooks from Africa. New Orleans gumbos have a certain city sophistication. Another type of gumbo, made by the Cajuns of southwest Louisiana, is country food, stemming from the hearty meal-in-a-pot fare that French Acadian fishermen and farmers developed after fleeing British rule in Canada in the 1700s. Bringing with them a French peasant heritage, they too used local ingredients and borrowed from the Indians.

The typical gumbo is so crowded with meat or fish and vegetables that the liquid plays a minor role. Among its distinctive ingredients are brown roux, hot pepper, tomatoes (in New Orleans), okra, and filé—ground sassafras adopted from the Indians. Both okra and filé have a slight thickening effect. Creole cooks generally use okra but not filé, and Cajun cooks generally use filé but not okra.

A *bisque* (pronounced bisk) is a thick shellfish soup. The bisque made its appearance in nineteenth-century Europe and has

7-9 NEW ENGLAND CLAM CHOWDER

Yield: Approximately 1 gallon (4 liters) = 16 8-oz (250 mL) portions

major flavor, body, texture	1 qt	canned clams with juice	1 L	4–6 oz	salt pork, small dice	125–175 g		flavor builders
	1½ lb	potatoes, small dice	750 g	8 oz	onions, small dice	250 g		
body	2 qt	juice from clams plus fish stock or water	2 L	(¼ tsp*	thyme	*1 mL)		
				*	salt, black pepper	*		seasoning
	1 qt	milk, hot	1 L					
	½ pt	cream, hot	250 mL					
texture	4 oz	flour	125 g					

1. Drain clams, reserving clams and juice separately. Add fish stock or water to clam juice to total 2 qt (2 L).

2. Cook potatoes separately until al dente in additional fish stock or water to cover.

3. In stockpot, render salt pork. Add onions and sweat until translucent.

4. Add flour and make roux.

5. Add clam liquid/water (¼ cold, then ¾ hot) and thyme if used; simmer until thickened and no starch taste remains.

6. Stir in milk, cream, potatoes, and clams. Reheat to a simmer, then remove from fire. Do not boil.

7. Season *to taste.

been adopted as a regional specialty in parts of the United States where shellfish are plentiful. You'll find lobster bisque in New England and crayfish bisque in Louisiana. The bisque is a smooth, rich, hearty soup that is expensive to prepare. The traditional finished soup is thickened by two methods—puréeing the fish flesh and thickening with a roux. The bisque in recipe 7-10 is a somewhat simplified version: it does not purée the shrimp but leaves them coarsely chopped, providing a different texture.

Notice that the extra flavor contained in the shrimp shells is extracted in Step 2. This is similar to sweating the vegetables in Step 1: the higher heat of sautéing brings out the maximum flavor from the ingredients. The coarsely chopped shrimp are added at service time to avoid overcooking during holding.

Famous national soups

There are many individual soups associated with particular countries. *Borscht* (pronounced borsh) is a Russian or Polish soup, a thin soup made with beets and other ingredients in many versions. In addition to beets it usually contains cabbage and an acid ingredient such as vinegar, which keeps the beets from losing their red color. Sour cream is another typical ingredient, either blended into the soup or used as a garniture.

The best-known Italian soup is *minestrone,* an unthickened soup full of vegetables and pasta that can easily be a meal in itself. As

7-10 SHRIMP BISQUE

Yield: About 2 quarts (2 liters) = 10 6-oz (200 mL) portions

major flavor	1 lb	shrimp, raw in shell	500 g	4 oz	onion, brunoise	125 g			
				2 oz	carrot, brunoise	60 g			
body	1½ qt	water	1.5 L	2 oz	celery, brunoise	60 g	*flavor builders*		
	1 qt	milk, hot	1 L	1	bay leaf	1			
	1 pt	cream, hot	500 mL	2	cloves, whole	2			
texture	8 oz*	roux	*250 g	½	lemon, thin-sliced	½			
				2 oz	sherry or brandy	50 mL	*flavoring*		
				*	salt, white pepper	*	*seasoning*		
				*	butter	*			

1. In stockpot, sweat vegetables in *⅛″ (3 mm) butter. Add bay leaf, cloves, lemon, and water. Simmer 15 minutes.
2. In another pan, sauté shrimp until shells are lightly browned.
3. Deglaze pan with a little of the liquid and return to stockpot along with shrimp.
4. Simmer until shrimp flesh is pink and firm.
5. Strain, reserving liquid.
6. Peel and devein shrimp and chop coarsely. Reserve.
7. Add reserved liquid to roux. Blend in milk and cream. Simmer until lightly thickened and smooth and no flour taste remains. Adjust texture if necessary.
8. Add sherry. Season *to taste.
9. Add coarsely chopped shrimp at time of service.

NOTE: If deeper pink color is desired, add 1 tsp (5 mL) tomato paste or ½ tsp (2 mL) sweet paprika to roux.

we saw earlier (recipe 7-3), minestrone is made using familiar techniques such as sweating the flavor builders and adding ingredients according to their cooking times. Some of the ingredients that make this a typically Italian soup are the olive oil, garlic, zucchini, tomatoes, some type of beans, the pasta, and the parmesan cheese.

Mulligatawny is a famous soup that represents a culture of the past: it came from British India. It is a curry-flavored chicken soup, lightly thickened with roux, containing diced chicken meat, often rice, and sometimes tart apples. Some versions even include vegetables. It is

easily made using the roux method for cream soups.

Spain is famous for *olla podrida* (ah-la pa-dree'-da or ohl-ya pa-dree'-da) and *gazpacho* (gah-spah-cho). Olla podrida, often called the Spanish national soup, resembles an unthickened stew of meats and vegetables, always including Spanish sausage and chickpeas. In its full-scale version it is an entire feast.

Gazpacho, another Spanish soup, is better known in this country and far more easily made. It originated as a salad composed of marinated leftover vegetables. An exception to the usual concept of soup, it is an uncooked purée thickened with bread crumbs and served cold.

By looking at the ingredients in recipe 7-11, you can see clearly the salad origin of this soup. The bread crumbs not only thicken it slightly but help to bind the oil, which normally tends to separate from water-based liquids.

Cold soups

Cold soups can make a refreshing hot-weather meal or the first course of an elegant dinner or luncheon. Fruit soups are often served at breakfast in some European countries. Such soups make appropriate items for brunch, which combines two meals in one.

Cold soups may belong to any of the three classes of soups discussed so far, or they may take off in a new direction as gazpacho does. You have already seen how a hearty leek-and-potato potage can be transformed into an elegant vichyssoise (7-5a). The same thing can be done with cream soups by chilling and blending in a little cream. Or use a pound of peeled and seeded cucumbers in either cream soup formula, chill the finished soup, blend in cream or sour cream and a tablespoon of dill, and you have a delicate, refreshing summer soup. Mulligatawny is another cream soup sometimes served cold, with the chicken meat diced as a garniture.

Borscht can be served hot as a thin soup, or you can turn it into a naturally thickened cold soup. Purée it in a blender after cooking

---

7-11 GAZPACHO

Yield: 1 gallon (4 liters) = 16 8-oz (250 mL) portions

major flavors, body	2½ qt	canned tomatoes, chopped	2.5 L	3	garlic cloves, puréed	3		*flavorers*
				4 oz	red wine vinegar	125 mL		
	1½ lb	peeled cucumbers, chopped	750 g	5 oz	olive oil	150 mL		
	12 oz	onions, chopped fine	350 g	*	salt, pepper, lemon juice	*		*seasoning*
	6 oz	seeded green peppers, chopped fine	175 g	2 oz	onion, small dice	80 mL		
				2 oz	peeled and seeded cucumber, small dice	80 mL		*garniture*
body, texture	1 pt	tomato juice or cold water	500 mL					
	3 oz	fresh bread crumbs	100 g	2 oz	seeded green pepper, small dice	80 mL		

1. Purée in a blender all ingredients except seasonings and garniture. Or pass everything but olive oil, seasonings, and garniture through a food mill; gradually whip in oil.

2. Season *to taste; chill.

3. When served, add 1 Tb (15 mL) garniture to each portion.

---

and serve it chilled with a teaspoon of sour cream on each portion—a beautiful sight.

Some soups are only served cold and are not related to cooked soups at all. The fruit soup in recipe 7-12 is an example. It is cooked only to thicken it with cornstarch and then to blend the flavors. Cooking also helps the sugar to dissolve and plumps the raisins. The amount of lemon juice needed will depend on how sweet or tart the other flavors are. You might consider the lemon as a seasoning as well as a flavorer.

Avocado soup (7-13) is another soup that is always served cold. It too is unrelated to the traditional cooked soup. Like gazpacho, it is not cooked at all, does not use stock, and re-lies on different types of ingredients for its body. The buttermilk and sour cream provide not only body and texture but additional flavor.

Using the avocado soup format, you can make a cold cucumber soup by changing the avocado to grated cucumber and the parsley to dill. This soup is quickly made and delicious, with a subtle zing to its taste.

Cold soups often need extra seasoning. Taste buds do not pick up flavors as readily in chilled foods, and there is less aroma. So taste and season carefully.

Cold soups are always served ice cold in chilled cups. The soup cup may be embedded in a dish of crushed ice, a style of service known as suprême (soo-prem).

7-12 FRUIT SOUP

Yield: 1 gallon (4 liters) = 16 8-oz (250 mL) portions

major flavor, body, texture	8 oz	drained sweet pitted cherries	250 g	4 oz*	sugar	*125 g	flavorers
	8 oz	drained canned sliced peaches	250 g	3 oz*	lemon juice	*100 mL	
	11 oz	mandarin oranges with their syrup	325 mL				
	3 oz	seedless raisins	100 g				
body	1½ qt	cold water	1.5 L				
	1½ qt	orange juice	1.5 L				
texture	1½ oz*	cornstarch	*50 g				

1. Mix cornstarch with a small amount of the cold water.
2. In stockpot, bring orange juice and remaining water to boiling point. Blend in cornstarch mixture. Simmer until thickened. Adjust texture (texture will be somewhat thicker when cold).
3. Add all remaining ingredients and simmer until flavors are blended (5 minutes or so).
4. Adjust tartness *to taste with sugar or lemon juice.
5. Chill.

7-13 AVOCADO SOUP

Yield: 1 gallon (4 liters) = 16 8-oz (250 mL) portions

major flavor, texture	3 lb	avocado pulp	1.5 kg	3 oz	onions, small dice, blanched, drained	100 g		flavorers
body, texture	3 qt	buttermilk	3 L	1 Tb*	minced parsley	*15 mL		
	1½ pt	sour cream	750 mL	*	salt, white pepper, lemon juice	*		seasoning
				3 oz	sliced almonds, toasted	90 g		garniture
				3 oz	avocado, small dice	90 g		

1. Purée avocado with liquids until smooth.
2. Stir in flavorers.
3. Season *to taste.
4. Serve each portion with 1 tsp (5 mL) each of almonds and diced avocado.

NOTE: Hold avocado in ½ pt (250 mL) water with 1 tsp (5 mL) lemon juice.

SELECTING INGREDIENTS, HOLDING, AND STORING

Selecting the right stock

The choice of stocks open to the soup cook includes every stock in his or her repertoire. Many soups may be made using any of several different stocks, and using different stocks may be one way of making different soups from the same recipe. In other situations the use of different stocks may simply have a subtle effect on flavor and color.

How do you choose a stock for a given soup? You must always consider two qualities of the stock, *color* and *taste*, in relation to the color and taste of the soup you are going to make.

The color of the stock should harmonize with the color of the soup. Cream soups and potages whose major ingredients are light in color are made with light stocks. Darker cream soups and potages and even clear soups may use the darker stocks. A good example of a soup that uses dark stock is onion soup. Most American versions of onion soup are quite dark in color and have a strong beef flavor. Often beef and chicken stocks are used together for onion soup in a 1-to-1 ratio.

But you cannot choose a stock on the basis of color alone. Taste is equally important, and the taste must not compete with the soup's predominant flavor. Chicken stock is suitable in color for any light cream soup or potage, for instance, but it can create problems of flavor. A cream of mushroom soup made with chicken stock would taste more like a cream of chicken soup with mushrooms added for a garniture. A light stock made from veal bones or a vegetable stock made from mushroom pieces would be more appropriate. It goes without saying that a fish stock would not be used for any soup but fish.

Taste selection has its positive side also. You may want to use a specific stock flavor subtly as a flavor builder. As you become really expert at creating soups, you will begin to think in these terms.

Because the liquid or stock plays such an important role in a soup, it is important to use care and thought in its selection.

Now suppose your particular kitchen does not make stock, as is so often the case nowadays. What will you use for stock—for the body of the soup?

The kind of soup you make will determine the kind of stock you must create. If you need a meat-flavored stock you can make one using a powdered bouillon. Start making your soup with water in place of stock as the body ingredient, and add the powdered bouillon toward the end of the cooking, using taste as your guide. Canned beef and chicken bouillon, either full strength or diluted, are sometimes used as stock substitutes.

For a clear vegetable soup, when you want a stock for general flavor support rather than specific meat flavor, use a small amount of base. Add it by taste at the end of the cooking until you get the general support flavor you want, but stop before you can taste the base itself. Since every base and every bouillon powder is different, it is impossible to give proportions.

Selecting major ingredients

The ingredients used in soups should be fresh and high in quality. Some of them may be leftovers in the sense of trimmings from products used in preparing other dishes—bones, celery tops, mushroom stems and peelings, parsley stems—or products whose shape or size or color caused them to be rejected for some other use, or the remaining half of a package opened and half used. But they should not be warmed-over foods cooked for another purpose or another day. The flavor has already gone into another product, and everyone will know it.

Canned vegetables have similar drawbacks when used for soups. (Tomatoes and beets are exceptions.) Whatever happens to raw vegetables during cooking that puts flavor into the soup has already happened to the canned vegetable before the soup-making begins. In addition, the canned vegetable has already undergone the texture and flavor changes that come from the overcooking necessary to can foods safely. Frozen vegetables are often used and are somewhat better than canned since they are only partially cooked, but they are no substitute for fresh.

Holding and storing soups

Just as the ingredients should be fresh, so should the soup itself be freshly made. Each day's supply will usually be made in the morning for the entire day. It should be stored in the refrigerator and heated for service in small amounts as needed.

Soups awaiting service should be held in a bain-marie or steam table at an internal temperature of 180°F (60°C), well above the bacterial growth range but not hot enough to cook further. Heat additional amounts quickly on the range as needed. In this way you can avoid overcooking caused by prolonged holding.

Stir the soup occasionally. During lulls in service you should put a cover on the pot to prevent evaporation, which will affect not only the texture but also the yield. You can correct the texture with stock or cream if it becomes too thick. Check the seasoning if you add anything, and adjust it if necessary.

When storing a soup for later use, treat it as you would a stock: put it in the cooler at 40°F (4°C) or below. Do not cover it while it is cooling, but do keep it covered during storage. Clear soups can be stored for a day or two without problems, but cream soups need special care: cover them with plastic wrap right on the surface of the soup after they have cooled to refrigerator temperature.

SUMMING UP

Soup is an appetizing and relatively inexpensive way to open a meal or to make a meal. Soups fall naturally into three classes: clear or unthickened soups, naturally thickened soups (potages), and cream soups, thickened with starches. Nearly all of them are based on stocks and take off from there in all directions.

Of the unthickened soups, consommé is the star performer and is famous as the classical clear soup from which many other classical soups are made. Other familiar unthickened soups are vegetable soup and onion soup, each capable of many variations. Soup quality depends on the cook's skill in combining flavors and in cooking the ingredients to retain both form and texture.

Naturally thickened soups are made with such ingredients as potatoes and legumes, which lend their natural texture to thicken the soup. In smooth soups these ingredients are puréed and blended with the liquid. In some potages made from legumes, the vegetable is left whole or only a portion is puréed. These are hearty soups with a country or peasant quality.

Cream soups are made with artificial thickeners. The major flavor ingredients are simmered in stock either after thickening (the roux method) or before thickening (the beurre manié method). Often a liaison is added to perfect the texture.

The techniques of making these three types of soup are also used in making many special soups such as the regional and national soups that originated as meals in a pot. Among these are bouillabaisse, chowders, gumbos, and such national soups as borscht and olla podrida. Still another type is the cold soup of the summertime menu, which may be made as a thin soup, a purée, a cream soup, or something entirely different based on fruit juice or buttermilk.

Soup puts together in the kitchen all the things we have been discussing in previous chapters. Once you can make soups you have learned to use techniques and concepts that appear and reappear in other areas of the kitchen. You have met all kinds of thickeners—roux (white roux, brown roux), beurre manié, purées, cornstarch, liaisons, and bread crumbs. You have discovered a great deal about flavor building, texture, seasoning, doneness, cooking times and cooking methods, garnitures and garnishes, patience and the pleasures of success. You may also have learned more than you care to know about overcooking, undercooking, lumping, burning, too much celery, too much salt—the lessons of culinary disaster sometimes linger longer than the triumphs.

Soup-making offers possibilities often overlooked by restaurants. Not only does soup bring a good price on the menu; it can be made for a good price. Trimmings, scraps, and water, put together with tender loving care, can create an outstanding soup du jour (soup of the day) for pennies a portion.

"All it takes is a little barter, a little scavenging, a little kitchen thievery, if you will," says one exuberant soup-and-vegetable cook. "I beg ham bones from the garde manger, trade soup bases for fresh mushrooms from the saucier, pick over everybody's cooler for a little of this and that, and then I create!" No other dish can be made for so little and possess so much.

THE COOK'S VOCABULARY

soup, clear soup, potage, cream soup

bouillon

doneness, al dente

consommé, clarification, clearmeat, raft

garniture, garnish

crouton

legumes

render

QUESTIONS FOR DISCUSSION

1. Discuss the differences in procedures in making the three classes of soup. Which techniques provide the textures desired in each one?

2. What role does each of the following ingredients play in producing a consommé: egg whites, mirepoix, lean meat, tomato product, stock?

3. Using the description of mulligatawny soup, develop a recipe including ingredients and procedures using the T format.

4. What extra steps and ingredients would you add to a cream soup to serve it "en suprême"?

THE mystique surrounding sauce cookery has been cultivated for centuries by chefs of the European tradition. Only cooks with years of experience were allowed to learn the secrets hiding under enigmatic names having nothing to do with the nature of the sauces. Small wonder that sauce-making has not flourished in the home kitchen, and that for many people sauce is synonymous with catsup and worcestershire. It is time to tear away the veil and expose the real simplicity of sauce cookery.

A **sauce** is a thickened, seasoned liquid used to enhance a dish. The making of sauces has much in common with the making of soups and stocks. Historically sauces, like soups, originated in the pot in which meat or game or fowl was cooked over the open fire. The juices from the cooking were thickened in medieval times with bread crumbs or pounded almonds so they would stick to the meat or the sop of bread. Later, starch-thickened sauces were developed as part of the more delicate classical cuisine. Inventing a sauce became a fashionable way of inventing a new dish.

Today sauces are still made from the juices of the pot. It is more likely to be the stockpot than the pot in which meat is cooked, though sauces are made both ways.

After completing this chapter you should be able to

- Identify classical sauce families, describe or diagram their structure, and explain the relationship between basic and finished sauces.

- Describe or demonstrate how a reduction is used in sauce-making.

- Explain the nature of an emulsion and describe or demonstrate how to emulsify butter and egg yolks.

- Describe or demonstrate how to adjust sauce texture and how and when to season a sauce.

- Describe or demonstrate how to make compound butters.

8

Sauces

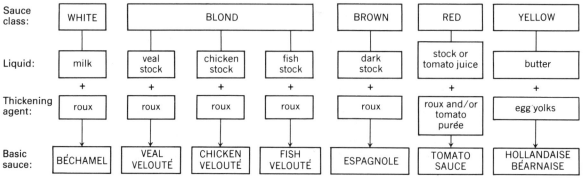

FIGURE 8-1. Basic sauce structure.

• Hold and store sauces to maintain quality and sanitation.

THE STRUCTURE OF SAUCES

The hundreds of sauces of classical cuisine all stem from a few basic sauces. Because of these relationships the basic sauces are often known as **mother sauces** or **leading sauces.** The sauces deriving from them are sometimes called **small sauces** or **secondary sauces.**

All these sauces fall naturally into five colorful groups—white, blond, brown, red, and yellow. Although each group is different from the others in important ways, they all have a common structure: they are all built from a liquid that is turned into a sauce by using a thickening agent. Figure 8-1 illustrates these similarities in structure.

The chart also gives you clues to some of the differences between the various groups. The basic white sauce—béchamel—is made from milk with roux as the thickening agent. The basic blond sauces—the veloutés—are made with light stocks thickened with roux. The basic brown sauces—espagnole and fond lié—are made from dark stocks thickened with brown roux or cornstarch. Tomato sauce, the basic red sauce, is made from light stock or tomato juice thickened with tomato

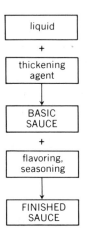

FIGURE 8-2. Finished sauce structure.

purée, or roux, or both. The basic yellow sauces, hollandaise and béarnaise, use melted butter as the liquid and egg yolks as the thickener.

A **basic sauce** is not a finished product. It is a base for a **finished sauce,** or for many different finished sauces. To make a finished sauce from a basic sauce, you add flavoring and seasoning, or seasoning alone, with perhaps a liaison for texture. That is all there is to the structure of a sauce. Figure 8-2 shows you the simple framework. Master sauce structure well, and you will have learned the first secret of sauce cookery.

In a large operation serving European cuisine the saucier, or sauce cook, makes up large batches of basic sauces at a time, according to menu needs. The stocks will have been made the day before, or several days before. Once the basic sauces have been prepared, the cook can make one, ten, or twenty different finished sauces from each basic sauce, in the quantities needed that day.

Now that you have seen what these sauces have in common, let's look at each sauce group separately. What gives each class of sauce its individuality, and how is it made?

THE WHITE SAUCES

The mother sauce for all the white sauces is **béchamel** (bay-sha-mel or besh-a-mel). The elegant name for this simple sauce comes from a French nobleman who was lord steward of the royal household for Louis XIV. He was not a cook but a financier; he did not invent the sauce; nor was it made then as it is now. It was probably seventeenth-century kitchen politics that immortalized Louis de Béchamel in this creamy sauce.

A glance at Figure 8-1 shows that most of the sauces use stock as the liquid. Béchamel is different: it uses milk—a good, rich, flavorful stock made by the cow with no effort on the cook's part.

Basic white sauce

Basic béchamel is the starting point for many small sauces. It is an easy sauce to make if you deal with the milk properly. In other contexts cooking with milk can pose problems. If milk by itself is overheated, the protein in it may scorch (burn) or the milk may curdle, separating into solid protein curds and a watery liquid called whey. However, you will not run into these problems in making béchamel if you make it properly—over low heat. Do not allow the milk to reach the boiling point until after you have incorporated it into the roux. The roux keeps it from separating. For extra security you can make the sauce in a double boiler or a steam-jacketed kettle.

Recipe 8-1 shows you how to make a basic béchamel. Do the instructions sound familiar? A basic white sauce is made using the traditional techniques of making cream soups.

As in the soups, there are several critical points.

- Make a good, well-blended white roux, cooked until it looks foamy and begins to lighten (Steps 1 and 2). Be careful not to brown it.
- Add *cold* milk to the *hot* roux and blend it well (Step 3).
- Simmering the sauce with the flavor builders (Step 6) will enrich the sauce and spark the general flavor without adding a specific taste. (Note that the onion is peeled so that it will not color the sauce.) If you do not use the flavor builders you must still simmer the sauce to get rid of the starch taste.
- Adjust texture with hot milk if the sauce has become too thick (Step 7). Checking the texture at this point and adjusting it as necessary should be an automatic part of making any sauce.
- Strain the sauce carefully (Step 8), using a china cap lined with dampened cheesecloth for a smooth, velvety texture. The extra refinement of texture can make the difference between an ordinary sauce and an extraordinary one.

Master the techniques of making a basic sauce with roux and you will have learned the second secret of sauce cookery. It should not be difficult after your experience with cream soups.

There is one major difference between a cream soup and a basic white sauce. The soup is a finished product; the basic sauce is not. You want the sauce's flavor to be uncommitted, so that you can go in any flavor direction you wish when you use it to make finished sauces. For this reason you do not use specific flavors in a basic sauce, as you do in a cream

8-1 BASIC BÉCHAMEL SAUCE

Yield: 1 gallon (4 liters)

					Onion piqué:			
major flavor, body	1 gal	milk	4 L		1	small peeled onion	1	
texture	8 oz	butter	250 g		½	bay leaf	½	flavor builders
	8 oz	flour	250 g		1	clove	1	
					pinch	nutmeg	pinch	
					(See note below.)			

Basic ratio: 1 lb roux / 1 gal milk
500 g roux / 4 L milk

1. Melt butter in heavy-bottom pan; add flour, blending to make roux.
2. Cook roux until light and foamy. Remove from heat.
3. Add *cold* milk (about ¼ of total amount); blend until smooth.
4. Return to heat and blend in remaining milk, *hot,* stirring constantly until thoroughly combined.
5. Cook over low heat, stirring occasionally with whip, until sauce is thickened.
6. Add onion piqué and nutmeg and simmer *30–45 minutes, stirring occasionally.
7. Adjust texture as necessary.
8. Strain.

NOTE: Some cooks omit the onion piqué and nutmeg, simmering the sauce only until no starch taste remains. This makes a bland, neutral basic sauce.

8-1a CREAM SAUCE

1 qt	basic béchamel from 8-1	1 L
4–8 oz*	cream, hot	*75–125 mL
*	salt, white pepper	*

1. Blend sauce and cream.
2. Simmer until flavors are blended.
3. For a finished sauce, season *to taste.

8-1b MORNAY SAUCE

1 qt	basic béchamel from 8-1	1 L
4 oz	swiss-style cheese, grated	125 g
2 oz	parmesan, grated	60 g
*	milk, hot	*
(2 oz	butter, softened	50 g)
*	seasonings	*

1. Over low heat, stir in cheeses just until melted.
2. Adjust texture with milk *as necessary.
(**2a.** Off heat, swirl in butter.)
3. Season *to taste.

soup. For the same reason you do not season a basic sauce. Seasoning belongs only to finished sauces.

Finished white sauces

The simplest finished sauce is made by seasoning the basic sauce. Looking back again at soups, you can see that this is like making bouillon from stock.

Structurally the sauce will look like this:

If you add another flavor or texture to the basic sauce, you get a new sauce. If you season the new sauce, you have a finished sauce. If you plan to add something more to the new sauce later, you leave it unseasoned.

Suppose you do these things to a basic béchamel. To one quantity of this sauce you add seasoning to taste, which gives you a finished béchamel. To a second quantity of sauce you add cream, which makes it cream sauce.

This cream sauce has a new flavor and texture but it is still uncommitted. If you want a finished cream sauce you season it. A diagram of all these béchamel sauces looks like this:

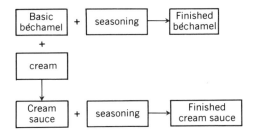

You can carry this process further. You can go in two directions.

- You can add to the basic béchamel: for example, add swiss and parmesan cheeses and seasonings to make a finished mornay sauce.
- You can add to the unseasoned cream sauce: for example, add horseradish, or-ange juice, and seasoning to make a finished warsaw sauce.

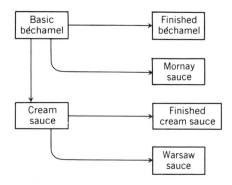

In the making of warsaw sauce the unseasoned cream sauce has played the role of a basic sauce. Since many other sauces are made from cream sauce, the cook may make up a large supply of unseasoned cream sauce and use it like a large supply of basic sauce.

In exactly the same way, many finished sauces—small sauces—are also made from the basic veloutés, brown sauces, tomato sauces, and butter sauces. This makes it simple to offer many sauces on a restaurant menu without creating utter confusion in the kitchen.

You can now appreciate one contemporary cook's definition of sauces: "Sauces are basic things you add to to make hundreds of."

Recipes 8-1a and 8-1b show two of the finished sauces that can be made from a basic béchamel. Recipe 8-1a is a finished cream sauce. The amount of cream you add depends on the taste and texture you want, which in turn will depend on the menu use. Cream sauce is often served with poached fish, poultry, eggs, and vegetables.

If you leave the cream sauce unseasoned, you can use it as a basic sauce for other sauces such as warsaw sauce, which is often served with such foods as broccoli, chicken, or game.

Recipe 8-1b is an example of a finished sauce from basic béchamel. This cheese sauce can be used in casseroles or to complement and add variety to vegetables. When cooking with cheese, keep the heat low and do not leave the sauce over heat any longer than necessary. Too much heat will cause the proteins in the cheese to become tough and stringy, and its butter fat may even separate out.

The technique of swirling butter into a sauce (8-1b) is called **monter au beurre.** The butter is added a little at a time and blended thoroughly into the sauce to give it an extra gloss and flavor. Other expressions for this practice are to **bring up** the sauce or to **finish** it. Wine and cream are among other flavorings added at the end to bring up or finish a sauce. Finishing is done only when the sauce is soon to be served, to keep the added ingredient from separating.

If you add a liaison to mornay sauce, you can use it as a glaze for a sauced dish. To **glaze** means to add a shiny coat to a dish. When a product is covered with this sauce and run briefly under the broiler or salamander, it will acquire a shiny golden-brown coat. The egg supplies the shine, and both egg and cheese provide the browning.

The liaison is the third secret of fine sauce cookery—a secret to be mastered by every serious cook. As you will discover, a number of classical sauces require a liaison, and it can add the ultimate in smoothness to any sauce.

But once you have added egg yolks, handling the sauce becomes a problem. It cannot be brought to the boiling point or anywhere near it, nor can it be held at the usual safety temperature of 180°F (82°C) without risking a breakdown. For this reason the cook finishes a sauce with a liaison in small batches just before serving it.

You will notice that in all these sauces the seasoning is the final step. Only at the end of making a finished sauce can you determine what and how much you need in order to bring out the full flavor. If you had seasoned the basic sauce, the seasonings would stay there no matter what you did in making a finished sauce. Simmering would reduce the sauce and increase the proportion of seasonings. Adding new flavors would totally change your needs. You want all your flavor and texture adjustments to be in place before you season.

Seasoning is the fourth secret of fine sauce cookery. Your choice of seasonings will be made from the basic three: salt, pepper (white or cayenne for a white sauce), and fresh lemon juice. Your purpose is, as always, to bring out the natural flavor, considering both the sauce itself and the dish it is to enhance.

Salt and pepper are commonly used in any sauce of any class. Lemon juice is nearly always used in any sauce that is to be served with fish. Lemon juice may be added to a béchamel even though lemon and milk do not normally mix successfully. The acid in lemon juice has the same effect on milk that heat does: it causes proteins to separate from the liquid, curdling the milk. But since the milk in béchamel is bound with roux, it is stable and will not curdle when lemon juice—or any other acid food such as wine—is added to the sauce. The French typically use fresh lemon juice in their béchamel and flavor it with a little bit of nutmeg.

Béchamel is used in almost every type of kitchen. It is as useful to the casserole cookery of the low-budget cafeteria as it is to the continental cuisine of the most expensive restaurant. Béchamel-based sauces usually accompany vegetables or eggs and occasionally meats. Heavier versions having a higher proportion of roux to milk (1½ lb or 750 g roux to 1 gal or 4 L milk) are used in making thickened cooked dishes such as mousses, soufflés, and croquettes.

Béchamel is also used to make cream soups. Sweated vegetables are combined with the basic sauce and simmered until done. The sauce is then thinned with hot milk and finished with cream. This was a classical way of making a cream soup, and a very logical one when you already had a pot of basic béchamel in the bain-marie.

The perfect sauce

The quality of a roux-based sauce is judged by its flavor, its strength, and its texture. Its strength derives from the quality of its basic stock. Its texture is determined by cooking technique—the skillful use of the thickening agent and the liaison, the careful straining and the final adjustment of sauce consistency. Its flavor comes from stock, flavor builders, and flavorings, and it is perfected by seasoning.

A good sauce is smooth and velvety in texture with no lumps. It has color and gloss and a fluid appearance: "it must seem vaguely in motion even after it has been poured," wrote the master chef Louis De Gouy. It is thin enough to pour easily but thick enough to stay with the food it accompanies. There is no sign of fat, no taste of fat or flour. It is warm and inviting, never cold, set, or solid. It has a subtle bouquet or aroma suggesting the pleasure to come. Its flavor enhances the flavor of the food with which it is served, complementing or contrasting but never dominating. Whether delicate or strong, it tastes very special.

THE BLOND SAUCES

The blond sauces are made with light stocks and roux, as shown in Figure 8-1. They are called blond sauces because in classical cuisine they were made with pale or blond roux. In the modern kitchen either a white or blond roux may be used. The stock also adds a touch of color. Yet both in structure and in method these sauces are so similar to béchamel that they are sometimes all lumped together as white sauces.

The mother sauces in this group are the three veloutés—veal, chicken, and fish. The name **velouté** (ve-loo-tay) is the French word meaning velvety, an apt characterization of a sauce that feels like velvet to the tongue and taste buds.

Basic veloutés

Making a basic velouté follows the same pattern as making a basic béchamel, as you can see by comparing recipe 8-2 with 8-1. The major difference is the use of stock rather than milk. A good flavorful stock is the key to a good velouté. The sauce does not need added flavor builders because the flavor is already in the stock. The longer the sauce is simmered the more flavor it develops. Evaporation concentrates the flavor, and when you adjust texture by adding more stock you add more flavor too.

Like basic béchamel, the veloutés remain unseasoned. Each is the mother sauce for several finished sauces.

Chicken, veal, and fish veloutés are all made by the same method. The only difference is the kind of stock used. The kinds of velouté the cook makes on any given day will be determined by the dishes the finished sauces are to accompany—veal velouté with veal, chicken with chicken, fish with fish. Small sauces made from veal and chicken veloutés may also be used with eggs and with other white meats such as pork.

Finished sauces from veloutés

Small sauces based on veloutés take off from the mother sauce in the same way the small white sauces do. They are made by adding flavoring, seasoning, or textural ingredients to a basic velouté. In each case the added ingredients determine the special character of the finished sauce.

Recipes 8-2a and 8-2b are examples of sauces derived from veloutés. Allemande (alla-mahnd) sauce (8-2a) is a veal or chicken velouté enriched with a liaison and a touch of lemon. It is often used as a basic sauce in the same way that cream sauce is. In this case seasonings are omitted. Raifort sauce, for instance, is simply allemande with the addition of horseradish, usually served to accompany roast or braised beef. Poulette sauce is allemande made with mushrooms.

8-2 BASIC VELOUTÉ SAUCE (veal, chicken, or fish)
Yield: 1 gallon (4 liters)

major flavor, body	1 gal	stock (veal, chicken, or fish)	4 L	
texture	8 oz	butter	250 g	
	8 oz	flour	250 g	

Basic ratio: 1 lb roux / 1 gal stock
500 g roux / 4 L stock

1. Melt butter in heavy-bottom pan; add flour, blending to make roux.
2. Cook roux until light and foamy. Remove from heat.
3. Add cold stock (about 1/4 of total amount); blend until smooth.
4. Return to heat and blend in remaining stock, *hot,* stirring constantly until thoroughly combined.
5. Cook over low heat, stirring with whip, until sauce is thickened.
6. Simmer *45–60 minutes, stirring occasionally.
7. Adjust texture as necessary.
8. Strain.

8-2a ALLEMANDE SAUCE

1 qt	basic velouté (veal or chicken) from recipe 8-2	1 L	
Liaison of:			
2	egg yolks	2	
4 oz	cream	125 mL	
1 Tb	lemon juice	15 mL	
*	salt, white pepper	*	

1. Simmer velouté to reduce it slightly.
2. Temper liaison into velouté.
3. Reheat to just below a simmer. Season and strain.

8-2b SUPRÊME SAUCE

1 qt	chicken velouté from recipe 8-2	1 L	
½ pt	heavy cream	250 mL	
1 oz	butter	25 g	
*	salt, white pepper, lemon juice	*	

1. Simmer velouté until reduced by one-fourth to 1½ pt (750 mL).
2. Temper cream into sauce; simmer until flavors are blended.
3. Off heat, swirl in butter. Season and strain.

Suprême sauce (8-2b) is chicken velouté enriched with cream. Like allemande, it is sometimes used as a basic sauce, as in ivory sauce, which has meat glaze added, and in aurora sauce, which adds tomato paste and is finished with butter. In these two small sauces, color as well as flavor is important. The meat glaze produces a beautiful ivory color, and the tomato is meant to create the color of a rosy dawn (French *aurore,* meaning dawn). Aurora can also be made from a basic velouté.

Note the tempering of the cream in making suprême sauce. This is the same technique as tempering a liaison: you stir up to a third of the hot sauce into the cream to bring it gradually to the sauce's temperature. If you shocked it by adding it cold to the hot sauce, it might curdle.

Notice also that in making suprême sauce you simmer the basic sauce to reduce it. This is to allow the cream to be added without making the sauce too thin. You reduce the sauce by one-fourth (half a pint—250 mL) because that is the amount of cream you are adding. In making allemande sauce you also reduce the basic sauce slightly for the same reason. You do this *before* adding the liaison because you cannot simmer it afterward.

Notice that you reduce first and season last. If the process were reversed you would have too much seasoning. Seasoning in sauce cookery, as with soups, is always an end process.

A white wine sauce (8-3), made from a basic fish velouté, presents a more complex technique of dealing with sauce texture by concentrating a great deal of flavor in a small volume. It uses a combination of flavor ingredients (Figure 8-3) cooked together to blend and concentrate their combined flavor. This is known in sauce-making as a **reduction.**

The reduction is the fifth fundamental se-

8-3 WHITE WINE SAUCE

Yield: 1 quart (1 liter)

flavor, body, texture				Reduction of:			
	1 qt	fish velouté	1 L				
	½ pt	cream	250 mL	4 oz	fish stock	125 mL	
				4 oz	dry white wine	125 mL	flavoring
				1 oz	mushrooms	25 g	
				2–3	peppercorns, crushed	2–3	
				*	seasonings	*	

Basic ratio: 4 parts sauce / 1 part reduction / 1 part cream

1. Combine stock, wine, mushrooms (scraps and peelings are fine), and peppercorns; simmer until volume is reduced by two-thirds or more to about 2½ oz (75 mL).
2. Add velouté to reduction in pan, blending well; blend in cream.
3. Simmer sauce to desired consistency.
4. Strain.
5. For a finished sauce, season *to taste.

FIGURE 8-3. Ingredients for white-wine-sauce reduction. These high-flavor ingredients are blended and concentrated by cooking them down to a fraction of their original volume. This reduction is then added to the basic sauce.

cret of sauce cookery. Examine the procedures in the recipe closely to see how it is done. In Step 1, ingredients of the reduction, chosen for their specific flavors, are cooked together to blend and concentrate these flavors. A maximum of total flavoring is thus added to the basic sauce with a minimum of liquid (Step 2). Step 3 is then an adjustment of texture, and Steps 4 and 5 finish off the sauce.

The reduction was a favorite technique of the classical French chef for concentrating a great deal of flavor in a small volume. "When the stock is reduced to a coating on the bottom of the pan—" reads a Carême recipe for a brown sauce.

There is a standard ratio of basic sauce to reduction to cream that will enable you to make enriched sauces without a written recipe once you know the ingredients. Use 4 parts sauce to 1 part reduction liquid (measured before reduction). If the reduction contains more than one liquid, use equal parts of each. To complete the formula add 1 part cream. Thus our white wine sauce recipe calls for 1 quart (1 liter) of basic sauce to ½ pint (250 mL) of reduction liquid composed of 4 ounces (125 mL) of fish stock and 4 ounces (125 mL) of wine, with ½ pint (250 mL) of cream to complete the formula. Figure 8-4 may help you to visualize the proportions.

When you put the sauce together and reduce it to the right consistency, you will end up with the same amount of sauce you started with before adding the reduction and cream.

The white wine sauce given here can play the role of a basic or mother sauce for many small sauces, or it can be a finished sauce in its own right. The cook will season it or not depending on its role.

Quality standards for finished velouté sauces are the same as those for other roux-based sauces. The quality of the stock is an important factor in both color and flavor. Salt and white pepper are standard seasonings, with lemon juice essential to any fish velouté.

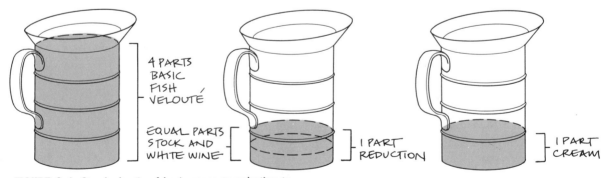

FIGURE 8-4. Standard ratio of basic sauce to reduction to cream.

Black pepper is sometimes used as a flavoring, as in our white wine sauce, but not as a seasoning.

THE BROWN SAUCES

Brown sauces use dark stock as their liquid base. They are thickened with brown roux or cornstarch. They use more ingredients than the white and blond sauces, they take more time, and they may seem more complicated, but they are probably less difficult to make.

Basic brown sauces

There are several ways of making a good basic brown sauce. One of these is the classical **espagnole,** whose formula is given in recipe 8-4.

8-4 BASIC ESPAGNOLE (ESPAGNOLE I)

Yield: 1 gallon (4 liters)

flavor	2½ lb	bones, beef or veal	1.25 kg	1 lb	basic mirepoix	500 g		
body	1 gal	dark stock, cold	4 L	2 oz	tomato	50 g		
texture	8 oz	flour	250 g	*Sachet of:*				
	*	oil	*	½	bay leaf	½		
				¼ tsp	thyme	1 mL	*flavor builders*	
				5–6	parsley stems	5–6		
				½	garlic clove	½		
				1–2	cloves	1–2		
				5–6	peppercorns, crushed	5–6		
				(4 oz	white wine	125 mL)		

Basic ratio: 2½ lb bones / 1 gal stock / 1 lb roux
1.25 kg bones / 4 L stock / 500 g roux

1. Place bones in heavy pan and toss with *enough oil to coat lightly.
2. Brown bones in hot oven, stirring several times with a paddle.
3. When bones are golden brown, add mirepoix and brown.
4. Shortly before bones and mirepoix have finished browning, sprinkle flour over them and mix everything with a paddle to make roux. Return to oven to cook roux.
5. When roux is a deep, rich brown and has a nutlike aroma, remove from oven and deglaze pan with part of the cold stock (or with wine).
6. Transfer everything to a stockpot or trunnion kettle and add remaining stock, tomato, and sachet.
7. Bring to a simmer; simmer until desired texture is reached (*3–4 hours).
8. Strain.

You will find the procedures familiar—you've been here before. This is the set of procedures for making dark stock, with one extra step—the addition of flour. There is one other difference in the formula: the liquid is dark stock instead of water.

As a matter of fact, what you are doing is enriching a stock by cooking it again with additional ingredients and turning it into a sauce at the same time by thickening it. It is a sauce that is rather light in texture but rich brown in color and hearty in flavor.

The handling of the flour may puzzle you. After you have learned to make roux so carefully in soups and white sauces, it may seem strange to sprinkle flour on bones to make roux. Actually, you spread the flour around carefully and evenly and mix everything well.

Since the bones are coated with oil, the flour adheres to this coating, and things tend to take care of themselves.

The watchwords for this sauce are the same as those for stocks.

- Don't burn the mirepoix.
- Deglaze with *cold* liquid.
- Don't boil—simmer.

Today few kitchens can afford the time and trouble to brown bones and simmer a sauce for hours. Many use a simpler version, spelled out in recipe 8-5. It is not strictly speaking an espagnole, but today this name is commonly used for any basic brown sauce. Its preparation is something like that of cream soups, except that the mirepoix and roux are

---

8-5 BASIC BROWN SAUCE (ESPAGNOLE II)

Yield: 1 gallon (4 liters)

flavor, body	6 qt	dark stock	6 L	1 lb	basic mirepoix, medium dice	500 g		
texture	8 oz	butter	250 g	8 oz	tomatoes or tomato purée	250 g		flavor builders
	8 oz	flour	250 g	Sachet of :				
				½	bay leaf	½		
				¼ tsp	thyme	1 mL		
				5–6	parsley stems	5–6		

Basic ratio: 6 qt stock / 1 lb roux / 1 lb mirepoix
6 L stock / 500 g roux / 500 g mirepoix

1. Melt butter in stockpot and cook mirepoix until it is golden brown and onions are caramelized.
2. Add flour and stir to make a roux. Cook until roux is dark brown with a nutty aroma.
3. Add stock (¼ cold, then ¾ hot) and tomato, stirring until sauce comes to a boil.
4. Reduce heat, add sachet, and simmer until sauce is reduced to 1 gallon (4 liters)—*1–1½ hours. Skim surface frequently.
5. Strain, pressing on mirepoix to extract juices.

8-5a DEMIGLACE

Yield: 1 gallon (4 liters)

1 gal	brown sauce	4 L
1 gal	dark stock	4 L

1. Combine sauce and stock in heavy stockpot.
2. Simmer, skimming frequently, until reduced to 1 gallon (4 liters).
3. Strain through china cap lined with cheesecloth.

8-5b ROBERT SAUCE

1 qt	basic brown sauce from 8-5 or demiglace from 8-5a	1 L
4 oz	minced shallots	125 g
½ pt	white wine	250 mL
1 tsp	dry mustard	5 mL
1 Tb	lemon juice	15 mL
*	seasonings	*
*	butter	*

1. Sweat shallots in butter until aroma is apparent.
2. Add white wine; reduce by two-thirds.
3. Add sauce; simmer until flavors are blended; strain.
4. Blend mustard with lemon juice and stir into sauce. Season *to taste.

8-5c MUSHROOM SAUCE

1 qt	basic brown sauce from 8-5 or demiglace from 8-5a	1 L
8 oz	sliced mushrooms	250 g
2 oz	minced shallots	50 g
2 oz	sherry	50 mL
*	seasonings	*
*	butter	*

1. Cook mushrooms and shallots in butter until golden.
2. Add sauce; simmer until flavors are blended.
3. Add sherry. Season *to taste.

8-5d MARCHAND DU VIN SAUCE

1 qt	basic brown sauce from 8-5 or demiglace from 8-5a	1 L
Reduction of:		
6 oz	red wine	175 mL
2 oz	minced shallots	50 g
*	seasonings	*

1. Boil reduction until reduced by two-thirds, to about 3 oz (75 mL).
2. Add sauce; simmer to desired texture; strain.
3. Season *to taste.

browned and the cooking time is longer. It may not have the richness of flavor that comes from browned bones and the long simmering of the classical espagnole, but it makes a very good sauce.

Another type of brown sauce, known as **fond lié** (fawn lee-ay), is made by thickening a dark stock with cornstarch. Sometimes it is made like the classical espagnole, with bones and flavor builders and long simmering, but is thickened with cornstarch at the end. Sometimes it is simply dark stock reduced by half and then thickened with cornstarch. Sometimes it is simply a dark stock thickened with cornstarch. It is a sauce with a beautiful sheen and an almost transparent quality. Fond lié is seldom made as a basic sauce, but it is made when pan juices from cooked meats are turned into finished sauces, as we will see in Chapters 11 and 12.

Often a basic brown sauce is enriched still further with additional stock before being used to make small or finished sauces. This makes another sauce known as **demiglace** (demi-glass or demi-glaze). As recipe 8-5a shows, it is half brown sauce and half dark stock, reduced by half. The procedure is simple though time-consuming. The sauce must be skimmed often as it reduces and strained through cheesecloth like other fine sauces. The result is a rich, robust sauce, one used so often to make small sauces that Escoffier called it a *"grande sauce de base."*

The brown sauces obviously have more strength and flavor built into them than the more delicate white sauces. Brown sauces go well with red meat and some kinds of game.

Basic brown sauces, however hearty, remain uncommitted as long as they are unseasoned. Any of them can be finished by seasoning or can be made ahead in quantity and used as the basic sauce for any number of different finished sauces.

Finished brown sauces

Most finished brown sauces have added flavor ingredients. They are typically used with entrées, and their flavors are chosen to produce a specific dish, such as duckling bigarade or steak bordelaise. Often they are used as a braising liquid, as you will see in Chapter 12.

Recipes 8-5b through 8-5d offer you some typical examples. Mushroom and marchand du vin (wine merchant) are typically served with beef. Robert (roh-bare) is *the* sauce for grilled pork chops or roast pork. If you add a julienne of sour pickles at serving time, you will turn it into a charcutière (pork butcher) sauce.

Notice the use of a flavor reduction in marchand du vin sauce and the reducing of the white wine in robert sauce. Notice also the technique of simmering a sauce to adjust texture as well as to blend and enhance flavors. There is an interesting variation of the usual pattern in robert sauce: the mustard and lemon are added *after* the sauce is strained. The slight graininess of the mustard accents the bite of its flavor, and you don't want to lose any of it. The finished mushroom sauce is not strained at all, and the mushrooms become part of the dish to which the sauce is added.

Quality standards for finished brown sauces are the same as those for the other roux-based sauces. The quality of the stock makes all the difference in a brown sauce. Sauce flavors should be hearty, color a rich brown, and aromas enticing. Salt and white pepper are standard seasonings, with other peppers used judiciously. Lemon juice is seldom used in a brown sauce. As always, seasoning is an end process.

THE RED SAUCES

The red sauces are tomato-based, and the stock (Figure 8-1) is really subordinate to the juices of the tomato in both the flavor and the body of the sauce. There are two types of red, or tomato, sauces: those that are roux-based and those made without roux. The latter depend for their thickening on careful reducing through simmering. The two types of sauce look and taste rather different. A roux-based sauce is creamier both in appearance and in the feel of the sauce on the tongue. The other type, known as Italian style, is more familiar, since most Americans eat their tomato sauce on spaghetti and other Italian dishes. Both types can be made as basic or mother sauces to which various flavor ingredients can be added to make a variety of finished sauces.

Recipe 8-6 is a roux-based tomato sauce. It is an easy sauce to make. It requires no new techniques, and you need only one word of caution: simmer very slowly over low heat (Step 5) to avoid burning the tomatoes. The secret ingredient in this sauce is a little sugar to cut the acid bitterness of the tomato. The onions also curb the acidity. The sauce may also be made using tomato juice or even water as a body liquid in place of stock.

Using this sauce as a mother sauce, you can add herbs, vegetables, and garlic to make other sauces, as in recipes 8-6a through 8-6c. Unlike the mother sauce, these sauces are not strained. The added ingredients give them a wholly different texture. In relation to the classically smooth mother sauce, they have a more peasant quality—rather like the potages in relation to the classical cream soups. These sauces are used for omelets and vegetables. Creole sauce is also used with shrimp and fish,

8-6 TOMATO SAUCE I

Yield: 1 gallon (4 liters)

flavor, body, texture	1 gal	tomato purée	4 L	4 oz	bacon scraps	125 g		
				1 lb	basic mirepoix	500 g		
flavor, body	1 qt	stock (usually grand jus)	1 L	½	bay leaf	½		
				5–6	parsley stems	5–6	flavor builders	
texture	5 oz	flour	150 g	pinch	thyme	pinch		
	4–5 oz	butter	125–150 g	1–2	cloves	1–2		
				5–6	peppercorns	5–6		
				½	garlic clove, peeled	½		
				*	sugar	*		
				*	seasonings	*		

1. Sauté flavor builders in butter.
2. Add flour and make roux; cook until foamy.
3. Remove from heat; blend in cold stock and tomato purée.
4. Return to heat; bring to boil; then reduce to simmer.
5. Simmer slowly until reduced about 20 percent (about 2 hours).
6. Strain and add sugar *to taste.
7. For a finished sauce, add seasonings *to taste.

8-6a SPANISH SAUCE

1 qt	basic tomato sauce I from 8-6	1 L
6 oz	onions, small dice	175 g
4 oz	green peppers, small dice	125 g
2	garlic cloves, puréed	2
4 oz	mushrooms, sliced	125 g

Sachet of:

1	bay leaf	1
pinch	thyme	pinch
pinch	crushed peppercorns	pinch
*	salt, pepper, hot pepper sauce	*
*	oil	*

1. Sweat onions and green pepper in oil.
2. Add garlic and mushrooms; cook until garlic aroma is evident.
3. Add tomato sauce and sachet; simmer until flavors are blended.
4. Remove sachet. Season *to taste.

8-6b CREOLE SAUCE

Add to spanish sauce recipe (8-6a):

4 oz	celery, small dice	125 g

Add celery to onions and green pepper in Step 1.

8-6c PORTUGAISE SAUCE

1 qt	unseasoned spanish sauce from 8-6a	1 L
1 lb	tomatoes, concassé	500 g
2–4 Tb	minced parsley	25–50 mL
*	seasonings	*

1. Combine sauce and tomatoes; simmer until reduced by one-third.
2. Stir in minced parsley. Season *to taste.

8-7 TOMATO SAUCE II

Approximate yield: 1 gallon (4 liters)

flavor, body, texture	6 lb	canned tomatoes (1 #10 can)	3 kg	2½ lb	onions, small dice	1.25 kg		flavor builders
	18 oz	tomato paste	550 mL	1 Tb	puréed garlic	15 mL		
	4 oz	olive oil	125 mL	½ pt	minced parsley	250 mL		
	(3 lb	bones, pork neck or fresh hocks	1.5 kg)	1–2 tsp	basil	5–10 mL		
				1–2 tsp	oregano	5–10 mL		
				½	bay leaf	½		
				*	sugar	*		
				*	salt and pepper	*		

1. In heavy pot, sweat onions, garlic, (bones), and parsley in oil until onions are translucent.
2. Coarsely purée tomatoes, blend in paste, and add to onion mixture.
3. Add remaining flavor builders. Cover pot and simmer 1–2 hours over *low* heat, or simmer, covered, in 350°F (180°C) oven to prevent scorching.
4. Strain through china cap. Add sugar *to taste. If too thick, adjust texture with white stock. If too thin, reduce by simmering uncovered.
5. For a finished sauce, add seasonings *to taste.

8-7a RED CLAM SAUCE

1 qt	tomato sauce II from 8-7	1 L
1 lb	canned baby clams, drained, chopped	500 g

Add clams to sauce; simmer until heated through and flavors are blended (*15 minutes).

8-7b MILANAISE SAUCE

1 qt	tomato sauce II from 8-7	1 L
5 oz	mushrooms, sliced	150 g
1 Tb*	butter	*15 mL
¾ lb	ground beef, cooked, drained	350 g
5 oz	cooked ham, julienne	150 g
5 oz	cooked tongue, julienne	150 g

1. Sauté mushrooms in butter until lightly golden.
2. Add beef, ham, and tongue. Stir in sauce and simmer until ingredients are heated through and flavors are blended (*45 minutes).

and portugaise is served with fish, poultry, ham, and braised beef.

Recipe 8-7 is an Italian-style tomato sauce, made without roux. It is thickened by its major flavor ingredients. It too can function as a mother sauce, as you see in recipes 8-7a and 8-7b. These sauces are typically served with pasta.

A good tomato sauce of any type should be full-bodied, full-flavored, and hearty. The mother sauces must be smooth and free of lumps, but they need not attain the velvet smoothness of the other classical sauces. Many of the small sauces, being unstrained, deliberately have a certain country quality in keeping with their origins and uses. All the tomato sauces should be free of sharp, bitter, or scorched flavors.

THE YELLOW SAUCES

Butter sauces constitute the fifth group of thickened sauces—the yellow sauces. Like the others, the butter sauces are a family, with dozens of sauces deriving from two mother sauces, **hollandaise** (hol-un-daze) and **béarnaise** (bare-naze or bay-er-nez). But the yellow sauces are different from the white, brown, and red sauces in two important ways.

First, the yellow sauces are unique in their structure. Whereas the white, brown, and red sauces depend on thickening agents for their texture, the creamy thick texture of the yellow sauces derives from an emulsion of butter and egg yolks. You can see these differences in structure clearly by referring back to Figure 8-1.

Second, the preparation techniques are very different. The sauces made with thickening agents depend heavily on the cooking process. The butter sauces are scarcely cooked at all, but what cooking there is is critically important. So is the technique of creating the emulsion—getting the ingredients to go together by beating them at a temperature falling within a narrow range.

The differences in techniques may be summed up by saying that the ingredients of the butter sauces are whipped together at a warm temperature, while those of the stock–thickening-agent sauces are simmered together at a higher temperature.

The making of butter sauces depends entirely on the unique characteristics of the two major ingredients, egg yolks and butter. The egg yolk plays the key role. You have met the egg yolk in the liaison, and you know that handling eggs with care does not always refer to keeping their shells from breaking. Two peculiarities of egg yolks are important in making butter sauces and require careful handling. One is the low coagulation temperature of the yolk; the other is the yolk's capacity as an emulsifier.

Coagulation, as you know, is the process of firming, solidifying, or coming together in a mass that takes place as the egg is heated. The coagulated egg is, in a word, cooked. Egg yolks coagulate somewhere between 144 and 158°F (62–70°C). If they are mixed with liquid food products, they include these products in the coagulation process, or bind them. This is a major purpose of the liaison, as we saw in Chapter 6.

Adding things to eggs raises the coagulation temperature somewhat, but at higher temperatures the egg yolk will break away from the other products, solidifying separately and losing its ability to bind. This is similar to the curdling of overheated milk. Thus the right temperature becomes very important in the making of a sauce in which the egg yolk is the vehicle. It must be hot enough to begin coagulation, to thicken or firm the egg yolk slightly, but not hot enough to harden it and shut out the butter.

The second characteristic of the egg yolk, its talent for **emulsifying,** or forming an emulsion, is what makes the butter sauces possible. The liquid yolk can hold tiny droplets of liquid butter in suspension: that is, once they are dispersed in the yolk it will keep them apart. The result is a thickened semiliquid of incredible smoothness.

This remarkable quality of the egg yolk is one that the cook must treat with tender loving care. The yolk can emulsify only a little oil at a time and that little bit must be evenly dispersed before the yolk can handle more. There is a limit, too, to its total capacity. Too much, too fast, too little beating, and the droplets of oil will coalesce—run together—and the emulsion will break.

The art of making a butter sauce, then, is being able to work with the unique qualities of the egg yolk to create a stable emulsion of yolk and liquid butter. The emulsion is the sixth secret of fine sauce cookery.

Butter is at least 80 percent fat, with a residue of milk solids, water, and salt. Since we do not want the residues in a butter sauce, we **clarify** the butter by melting it over low heat. When butter is melted it separates. All the pure butterfat rises, and all the water, salt, and solid residues settle to the bottom. Then we skim off the foam that floats on the melted butter and carefully pour off the liquid butterfat, leaving the water and solids behind. A pound of whole butter (454 g) will yield about 12 ounces (350 mL) of liquid butterfat, or **clarified butter.**

This clarified butter is what you use to make a butter sauce. Removing the solids raises the smoking point, so clarified butter does not burn as easily as whole butter. Without the water and milk solids the sauce will have a creamier texture.

Basic butter sauces

The two mother butter sauces, hollandaise and béarnaise, are both made the same way. There are two differences between them: the reductions are different, and the hollandaise is strained but the béarnaise is not. By closely examining the hollandaise recipe (8-8) you can grasp the basic principles of both sauces.

Each step in the making of a butter sauce is critical:

In Step 1, the reduction must be sufficiently reduced. If there is too much liquid the egg yolks will not foam or thicken properly in Step 5.

In Step 2, the reduction must be cooled. If it is hot it will cook the egg yolks in Step 4 and the sauce is lost then and there.

In Step 3, the clarified butter must be warm but not hot. If it is hot it will cook the egg in Step 7. If it is not warm enough it will tend to solidify and form larger droplets than the egg yolk can handle, and emulsification will not take place.

In Step 4, the round-bottom bowl (Figure

FIGURE 8-5. Thickening the egg yolks.

a. For a small amount of sauce, you can whip the yolks by hand in a round-bottom bowl over hot water.

b. For a large amount of sauce, whip the yolks in the mixer bowl in the hot water of the bain-marie.   (Photo by Patricia Roberts.)

8-8 BASIC HOLLANDAISE

Approximate yield: 1 pint (500 mL)

flavor, body, texture	12 oz	clarified butter	350 mL	1½ oz	liquid: 1 part lemon juice 1 part distilled vinegar (1 part white wine)	50 mL		flavor reduction
	4–5	egg yolks	4–5	1 Tb	shallots	15 mL		
				½	bay leaf	½		
				few	parsley stems	few		
				few	peppercorns	few		

Basic ratio: 4–5 egg yolks / 12 oz clarified butter / 1½ oz reduction
4–5 egg yolks / 350 mL clarified butter / 50 mL reduction

1. Cook the ingredients of the reduction together until liquid is reduced by 80 percent.
2. Cool the reduction.
3. Warm the butter.
4. Place the egg yolks in a round-bottom stainless-steel bowl and add the reduction, straining it into the bowl.
5. Heat the egg yolk–reduction mixture over hot water or in a bain-marie, whipping steadily, until the mixture is foamy and slightly thickened.
6. Remove the bowl from the hot water.
7. While whipping the egg yolk–reduction mixture constantly, slowly add the warm clarified butter.
8. When half the butter has been added, adjust texture with a few drops of warm water.
9. Continue slowly whipping in the remainder of the clarified butter.

8-5) is essential so that every bit of egg yolk can be picked up by the whip. The bowl must be stainless steel to avoid any reaction with the acid in the reduction. If you are making a large quantity you will use the bowl of the mixer. The reduction is strained at this point because it is much simpler to strain than the finished sauce.

Step 5 is one of the two most critical steps. You want the eggs to cook slightly and evenly. If you undercook them you are going to wind up with a watery sauce. If you overcook them you will have lumps of cooked egg in the sauce that won't form an emulsion with the butter. You must whip steadily so that the cooking is even. The mixture will have reached the right degree of thickness when it becomes foamy, lightens in color, increases in volume, and shows a slight but perceptible thickening.

Step 6 stops the cooking action at this very critical point. If you are using the mixer, put the bowl in place and begin whipping, using medium speed. If you are making the sauce by hand, move your bowl to a worktable. A damp cloth under it will help it to stay put as you beat, so that you don't need a third hand.

Step 7 is the other most critical step. It is at this point that the emulsion is created. The two essentials here are to keep the whipping constant and to add the warm butter slowly (Figure 8-6)—very, very slowly at first. After an emulsion is started—a smooth thickening process that is easy to recognize—the butter can be added a bit more quickly. Never add it faster than it can be absorbed.

FIGURE 8-6. Whipping in the butter. Add the clarified butter very, very slowly in a thin, steady stream while whipping on medium speed.   (Photo by Patricia Roberts.)

In Step 8, the few drops of water increase stability and improve texture.

Step 9 finishes the basic sauce.

If your butter has not cooled too much, the egg yolks will be able to handle all the butter with no problem. The yolk of a large egg will emulsify about 3 ounces (90 mL) of clarified butter. Smaller eggs will handle proportionately less. This is why the proportions in the recipe call for 4 or 5 yolks to 12 ounces (350 mL) of butter: the number you use will depend on their size.

If your emulsion begins to break during Step 7—that is, if the yolks and butter begin to separate—there are several kinds of first aid you can try:

• You can use more egg yolks in another bowl, and beat the broken sauce little by little into the fresh yolks. This is the best possibility.

• You can put an ice cube in the center of the bowl and keep beating in the same spot. The quick temperature change may cause things to happen: the sauce will either re-form or break completely.

Hollandaise is the sauce toward which most young culinarians feel the greatest awe. Actually, if the rules are followed carefully, it is not hard to make. Sometimes students who do not know that it is supposed to be a difficult sauce have no trouble at all, while some who have been bombarded with directives and cautions have problems. So relax as you work and enjoy seeing hollandaise happen before your very eyes.

Just don't neglect it. Once you have begun to make it you are committed to giving it your full attention. *There is no way you can make a butter sauce and do something else at the same time.*

Many of today's kitchens no longer bother with a reduction but use the simplified version given in recipe 8-9. It makes a good sauce, but it does not have the richness of flavor of the traditional formula. The same guidelines apply

8-9 HOLLANDAISE (modern version)

Approximate yield: 1 pint (500 mL)

1 lb	butter, clarified	500 g	1½ oz*	lemon juice	*50 mL
4–5	egg yolks	4–5	*	salt, cayenne	*
1 oz	cold water	25 mL			

1. Whip together egg yolks and water until thoroughly blended.
2. Over hot water, continue to whip until thick and creamy.
3. Off heat, whip in butter slowly and gradually. Add lemon juice *as necessary when mixture becomes too thick.
4. For a finished sauce, season *to taste with lemon juice and other seasonings.

when heating the egg yolks and incorporating the butter.

In comparing the two hollandaise recipes you may notice that the butter in 8-8 is given as "clarified butter" and the butter in 8-9 is given as "butter, clarified." These terms make an important point. "Clarified butter" is butter measured after clarifying. "Butter, clarified" is butter measured before clarifying, which will of course be a larger amount than you will have left to blend with the egg yolks.

Béarnaise sauce is made in exactly the same way as hollandaise except that the reduction is somewhat different. The béarnaise reduction is heavily flavored with tarragon, and the ingredients are finely minced or crushed since it is not strained. This makes it look quite different from hollandaise, whose creamy appearance is unbroken by any speck of herb or spice. Compare the reduction in the béarnaise recipe (8-10) with the hollandaise reduction in 8-8.

Béarnaise sauce is often made by simply adding tarragon to hollandaise. This is not, however, a true béarnaise, for the tarragon does not cook together with the other flavor builders, and as a result the sauce has a raw taste. Nor do the other herbs appear in person in the final sauce, as they do in a true béarnaise.

8-9a MOUSSELINE SAUCE

To recipe for hollandaise (8-9) add:

6 oz	cream, whipped	175 mL

Carefully fold whipped cream into sauce until thoroughly combined. Season *to taste.

8-9b DIVINE SAUCE

5 oz	hollandaise from recipe 8-9	150 mL
5 oz	chicken velouté	150 mL
5 oz	cream, stiffly whipped	150 mL
*	seasonings	*

1. Blend velouté and hollandaise.
2. Fold in whipped cream. Season *to taste.

Finished butter sauces

Béarnaise and hollandaise are, as we have noted, mother sauces, and the formula we have given for hollandaise is for a basic sauce. Making finished sauces from a basic butter sauce is similar to making a finished sauce from any other basic sauce. You can make a finished hollandaise by seasoning it. Or you can make another sauce by adding something else—another flavor-building reduction, a special ingredient for flavor or texture, a garniture.

Mousseline (moos-a-leen) sauce, for example, is hollandaise combined with whipped cream and seasoned (8-9a). Maltaise (moltez) sauce is hollandaise flavored with orange juice and grated orange rind. Girondin (zhee-ron-dan) sauce is hollandaise with prepared mustard; powdered mustard would make it aegir (ay-zheer) sauce. And so on.

Small sauces are made from béarnaise in the same way. Add the flavor and color of tomato paste to béarnaise for choron (sho-rawn) sauce (8-10a). Stir a little melted meat glaze into béarnaise to make a rich-tasting foyot (foy-oh) sauce. As with the other sauce families, seasoning is always an end process. For seasoning a hollandaise, cayenne is usually the pepper of choice, along with lemon and salt.

Another way to create different sauces is to combine sauces from different classes. For example, you can add a reduction of brown sauce and red wine to béarnaise to make medici (med-a-chee) sauce (8-10b). Or you can fold together chicken velouté, hollandaise, and stiffly whipped cream to make divine sauce (8-9b). Combine béchamel or velouté, hollandaise, and whipped cream in equal parts for a royal sauce for glazing. There is no end to the possibilities, once you know how everything works.

There are, however, limits to what you can do with the texture of a butter sauce. You can thin it with a reduction. But because of the egg you can't thicken it by cooking it down, as you can with a roux-thickened sauce. For this rea-son, in making finished sauces, keep in mind the final texture you are striving for. Reductions must be reduced accordingly. And the critical temperature must always be kept in mind, lest the egg be cooked or the emulsion broken at the last minute.

The perfect butter sauce

A good butter sauce is ultrasmooth and light in texture, similar to lightly whipped cream. It is barely pourable, yet it looks and seems fluid. It has a high gloss but never a greasy look. There is no hint of solidified butter, no bit of cooked egg, no tendency to separate or break. You taste the butter but it is not an oily taste. You know the egg is there but the sauce does not taste eggy. Its flavor will vary from delicate to robust according to the flavoring ingredients. Color will vary too for the same reasons.

Butter sauces tend to be found only in the a la carte restaurant, the banquet service, the large and fully staffed hotel kitchen. Yet even though they are not universally used, they are worth learning—for the techniques involved, for an understanding of the egg yolk and the emulsion . . . and because they are so good.

With an understanding of butter sauces even a novice can do wonders. For example, you can make a glazed fish dish by ladling a blend of hollandaise and white wine sauce over poached fish and popping it all in the salamander or overhead broiler. The high heat plus the egg in the hollandaise produce a golden-brown surface for a handsome and tasty dish. This is only one of many such wonders.

But you must master the egg-yolk-and-butter emulsion before you try working wonders. It is not easy. The temperature ranges are narrow. The checkpoints of partial cooking are difficult. Measures like "slightly thickened" are not easily grasped from a verbal explanation or even a demonstration.

Practice is the only way to master the use of such special products as egg yolks and butter. Overcook eggs, undercook them, burn

8-10 BASIC BÉARNAISE

Approximate yield: 1 pint (500 mL)

flavor, body, texture	12 oz	clarified butter	350 mL	1½ oz	liquid: 1 part lemon juice 1 part vinegar (1 part white wine)	50 mL		
	4–5	egg yolks	4–5	1 Tb	tarragon	15 mL	*flavor reduction*	
				1 Tb	minced shallots	15 mL		
				½	bay leaf, crushed	½		
				few	parsley stems, minced	few		
				few	peppercorns, crushed	few		

Basic ratio: 4–5 egg yolks / 12 oz clarified butter / 1½ oz reduction
4–5 egg yolks / 350 mL clarified butter / 50 mL reduction

Proceed as for basic hollandaise (8-8), omitting the straining in Step 4.

8-10a CHORON SAUCE

To recipe for basic béarnaise (8-10) add:

1 oz	tomato paste	25 mL
*	seasonings	*

Blend tomato paste into béarnaise. Season *to taste.

8-10b MEDICI SAUCE

To recipe for basic béarnaise (8-10) add:

Reduction of:			
2 oz	brown sauce (8-4 or 8-5)	50 mL	
2 oz	red wine	50 mL	
*	seasonings		*

1. Reduce brown sauce and red wine by two-thirds.
2. Blend into béarnaise. Season *to taste.

some butter, experience failure and success, but master these basics. The rewards will amaze you.

SPECIAL SAUCES

In addition to the five classical sauce families, other types of thickened sauces as well as some unthickened products are used in the role of a sauce to enhance a dish. This section discusses butters, both simple and compound, the sauce techniques of nouvelle cuisine, and sauces made from convenience products. Pan sauces such as gravies and others made from pan juices are discussed in Chapters 10 to 12. The cold sauces, because of their close relationship to salad dressings, are included in Chapter 14. Several one-of-a-kind sauces, such as cumberland, sweet-and-sour, and barbecue, are reluctantly omitted because space is limited. These sauces are uncomplicated and you can find recipes in other books.

Butter as a sauce

In an era when every continental chef worth his title was a master of sauce cookery, an Italian visitor to England reported that the English had 60 religions but only one sauce, and that sauce was melted butter. Today melted butter, though not a sauce, is often used in various forms to enhance a dish in the same way a true sauce is used.

Butter is a fat that comes from the milk of the cow (or the goat or the sheep or the buffalo). It is contained in the creamy part of the milk in the form of minute globules of oil suspended in emulsion with water. In butter-making the liquid is churned until the emulsion breaks; then the butter particles are gathered together and the liquid is drained off. You can see how this butter-water emulsion breaks if you overbeat whipping cream; it will separate abruptly into butter and a watery liquid.

Salt is added to butter in manufacturing. It is possible to buy unsalted butter, called **sweet butter.** This butter is very desirable for making sauces as well as for most other cooking uses.

Margarine, a butterlike fat made from hardened vegetable oils, is cheaper than butter and similar in taste. Most margarines will perform like butter in making sauces. However, to be sure of the best-tasting sauce, it is wise to use butter or, for economy, half butter, half margarine. Margarine used alone is never a substitute for butter.

Simple butters. A **simple butter** is one that contains nothing but butter; it has no added ingredients. The differences between one simple butter and another come from the way each is affected by heat. Heat will change the consistency of butter. It can change the taste and color as well.

Butter solidifies at cool temperatures, softens at room temperatures, melts when exposed to heat, and burns when exposed to extreme heat. All these reactions to temperature change are exploited by the cook as assets. They may also be limitations, and the beginning cook needs to learn how to work with them.

There are statistics on the melting, browning, and burning temperatures of butter, but they won't mean as much to you as getting the feel of butter in action with heat. How does it behave when it sits for a while in a warm room? How does it look and act in the pan as it melts, as it browns, as it burns? How quickly do the changes take place? How high have you turned the burner? Only your own experience can answer these questions, since every range is different and every set of circumstances is different, and every pan and possibly every pound of butter.

The simplest simple butter is melted butter, often called **drawn butter** (*beurre fondu* in French). Used to enhance a food, it is merely poured over the fish or vegetable or whatever, or served on the side in a small dish. Clarified butter is also used in this way and in sautéing, since it does not burn as easily as whole butter.

And, as you know, clarified butter is a major ingredient in butter sauces.

When whole melted butter is allowed to cook gently, the solid residues will brown, changing both the color and the flavor of the butter. Butter cooked to a golden brown is known as **brown butter** (*beurre noisette* in French, pronounced burr nwah-zet). It is used most often for fish and vegetables. When lemon juice and chopped parsley are added at the time of service, the combination is referred to as **à la meunière** (ah la mun-yair), meaning "in the style of the miller."

When butter is cooked until it is dark brown or just short of burned, it becomes **beurre noir** (French for black butter, pronounced burr nwahr). When beurre noir is used with a dish several ingredients may be added to it at the time of service.

Adding ingredients at the time of service takes the last two butters out of the category of simple butters, strictly speaking. However, they are more closely related to simple butters than to anything else because of the way they are made. Another such creation, traveling under the name of **amandine** (ah-mahn-deen), is made by adding sliced almonds and lemon juice to brown butter. You may run across a few others, often classed as sauces. When you recognize them for what they are you'll know you've done your homework well.

Compound butters. Compound butters are easy to understand, simple to make, handy to have on hand, and delicious. Like simple butters, they are not true sauces but they often play the role of a sauce. They differ from simple butters in two ways: they are a blend of butter and one or more additional ingredients, and no heat is used in the making.

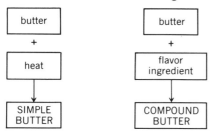

A **compound butter** is made by blending together softened butter and puréed or finely chopped ingredients. It is usually made in quantity in the mixer. It may then be spread in a long sheet pan, chilled, and cut into serving-size blocks. Or it can be rolled in paper in the shape of a long tube, chilled, and sliced in serving portions. Either way it can be frozen and brought out to be used as needed. Place a piece of the compound butter on a hot steak and it melts, transforming the steak. Twenty different butters on twenty steaks will give you twenty different-tasting dishes.

Compound butters are also used on other meats and on fish, vegetables, and eggs. They are frequently used to finish a white or brown sauce, meaning that a piece of the butter is swirled in the hot sauce at the last minute before serving (monter au beurre), much as a garniture is added to a soup. Compound butters are also often used in their softened state as spreads for canapés or for croutons such as those for French onion soup (7-1a).

Maître d'hôtel butter (8-11) is one of the most frequently served compound butters. You will probably notice its similarity to meunière, but it is most often made cold and either served cold as a spread or placed on hot food at service time. Many other butters are made in the same way using other flavorings. Anchovy, shallots, shrimp, garlic, glazes, and herbs are only a few of the possibilities.

You can use maître d'hôtel and other compound butters like mother sauces and make other butters from them, or you can make the other butters from scratch. It will depend on your menu and production needs.

A good compound butter is well blended and has the definite taste of the major ingredient added to the butter. It should not be bland; it should taste piquant, rich, and memorable.

Nouvelle sauces

The sauce families discussed so far derive from the classical or grande cuisine of nine-

8-11 MAÎTRE D'HÔTEL BUTTER

Yield: 1 pound (454 g)

flavor, body, texture	1 lb	butter, softened	454 g	2 oz	minced parsley	50 g	flavor
				1½ oz	lemon juice	45 mL	
				*	white pepper to taste	*	
				(1 oz	white wine	25 mL)	

1. Beat butter until smooth and fluffy.
2. Thoroughly blend in remaining ingredients.
3. Roll in parchment or wax paper to make a roll 1″ (2 cm) thick. Chill.
4. For service, cut into ½″ (1 cm) slices.

8-12 FRESH TOMATO SAUCE PURÉE

Yield: Approximately 2 quarts (2 liters)

flavor, body, texture	4 lb	ripe tomatoes, peeled and seeded	2 kg	12 oz	basic mirepoix	350 g	flavor builders
				1 oz	shallots, minced	25 g	
	1 qt	light stock	1 L	2	garlic cloves, puréed	2	
	1–2 Tb	tomato paste	15–25 mL	½	bay leaf	½	
				(Sachet of fresh herbs: thyme, parsley, oregano, basil, rosemary, etc.)			
				*	salt, pepper	*	
				*	oil	*	

1. Sweat mirepoix, bay leaf (and sachet) in small amount of oil until vegetables are al dente.
2. Add shallots and garlic and cook until aroma is evident.
3. Add remaining ingredients (except seasonings) and simmer just until vegetables are soft (*20–30 minutes).
4. Remove (sachet and) bay leaf. Purée ingredients.
5. If sauce is too thin, adjust texture by reducing. If too thick, thin with stock. Season to taste.

teenth-century European cooking. Heavy, smooth, and rich, they are traditionally ladled on foods to mask or cover them completely, exciting the appetite with their lavish appearance and refinement of texture. They are typically found in restaurants serving continental cuisine.

The trend today is away from the heavy roux-based sauces. The nouvelle focus is on preserving and enhancing the natural flavors and colors of fresh ingredients. Rather than covering foods with rich, heavy sauces, the emphasis is on the taste and appearance of the food itself. In sauce-making this has meant a great change in the techniques of thickening. Instead of roux, followers of the new styles use other classical techniques to thicken their sauces. Among these techniques are reducing, puréeing, and the use of natural thickeners.

For example, fresh vegetables or fruits are often simmered with stock or pan juices, puréed, and finished with cream or butter. The fresh tomato sauce in recipe 8-12 is made in this way. It differs from the classical tomato sauce in 8-6 by calling for a smaller amount of fat and by puréeing and reducing to thicken rather than using roux. Its use of fresh ingredients—fresh tomatoes, fresh herbs—is also typical of this cuisine.

Other ways of thickening use ingredients new to the American repertoire, such as crème fraîche and fromage blanc. *Crème fraîche* (krem fresh) is made by blending equal parts of sour cream and heavy cream. You let the mixture stand at room temperature until it begins to thicken (about 12 hours), then refrigerate for 24 hours until it is very thick. *Fromage blanc* (froh-mazh blahn, meaning white cheese) is made by blending a little yogurt into ricotta cheese on high speed until the mixture is smooth and velvety, then letting it stand, refrigerated, for 12 hours before using. Either of these thickeners is swirled into a sauce in the manner of monter au beurre to thicken and smooth the texture.

The presentation of sauced foods has also changed. Instead of covering a food with sauce, a contemporary chef is likely to ladle a bar of sauce across the food or pool the sauce on the plate and serve the food on top, revealing rather than concealing its natural appeal.

Sauces from convenience products

All kinds of convenience sauce products are available—paste and powder bases, concentrated sauces needing only to be thinned, and finished sauces. They have the advantage of saving both time and labor and are widely used for these reasons, especially in kitchens where low budgets prevail and the staff is not skilled in sauce-making.

Some of the convenience items, especially those for basic sauces, can be turned into very good products if properly chosen and properly used. Avoid any with a high salt content, and follow the directions on the package, since different items are reconstituted differently. As with the stock substitutes, you must determine for each product just how it fits into the overall sauce-making process, and then carry the process forward accordingly. For example, be sure you don't try to make a basic sauce using a convenience product intended to produce a finished sauce.

Once your sauce is made you must handle, hold, and store it as you would a sauce made from scratch. You can make basic sauces in volume for several days' supply, but the process is so quick and simple it is often more efficient to make a sauce as you use it.

Do not be deceived, however, by the words "quick and simple." You have to use judgment and care to achieve a sauce from a convenience product that is as good as a sauce made from scratch. The knowledge and experience you gain in making sauces from scratch will be invaluable in working with convenience products and in setting standards for convenience sauces.

HANDLING, HOLDING, AND STORING SAUCES

Starch-thickened sauces

Normally sauce cooks will make a large supply of a basic sauce at one time. They must handle and store it following the same sanitary practices used for stocks, because sauces too are ideal media for the growth of bacteria. The immediate consideration is avoiding the food danger zone of 40–140°F (4–60°C). This means that the cook must rapidly cool any sauce to be stored (Figure 6-4) and then put it in the cooler, covered. A week is the absolute maximum for storing a sauce in the cooler. Three days is safer. The efficient cook labels the container with the date, kind, and quantity of sauce.

Some stored sauces reconstitute well; others have trouble surviving cooling and reheating and sometimes develop problems of lumping and thinning. They can be strained and their consistency adjusted when they are used to make finished sauces, either by adding more thickening agent or by simmering. A sauce that becomes too thick for any reason can be thinned with the kind of stock used to make it.

Basic sauces that are to be used the same day for finished sauces can be held in stainless-steel pots in the bain-marie at a temperature above the danger zone. They may require some adjustment of texture before being used to make finished sauces.

Finished sauces too are held in the bain-marie. The professional cook will complete finished sauces about an hour before service begins. For example, the saucier may draw on the supply of basic brown sauce (made the day before or earlier that day) to make a pot of bordelaise sauce for steak bordelaise, a pot of périgourdine sauce for tournedos rossini, and a pot of bigarade sauce for duckling bigarade. A white wine sauce for sole à l'ancienne will come from a basic fish velouté. Other finished sauces for other dishes on the menu will draw on various basic-sauce supplies as needed. In an hour an experienced cook can make a dozen finished sauces.

After completing each sauce, the cook will coat the top with melted butter. Often a starch-thickened sauce exposed to the air will form a scum on top. The film of melted butter keeps this from happening.

Sauces made with cornstarch do not hold well for long periods at high heat. They tend to break down and become thin, lumpy, and weepy. Such sauces, and indeed all sauces, should be made as close to serving time as possible so that their quality will remain high throughout the serving period. If you must make a sauce to be served over a long period, you can hold a small amount in the bain-marie and store the rest, reheating it in small batches as needed.

A finished sauce should be made fresh daily in the quantity that will be used that day. Finished roux sauces left over from one day to the next lose taste and texture and may break down or lump. They can sometimes be rescued by straining, readjusting the texture, and reseasoning, but it is far better to avoid this necessity by careful planning for each day's needs. This is the only way to maintain consistency of quality from day to day.

Freshly made sauces should never be added to a supply on hand. Each should be stored separately and the old used up or thrown out. You don't want to hand on any developing problems of quality and bacterial growth.

Butter sauces

A butter sauce has a short life. It must be held at a temperature high enough to keep the butter liquid but low enough to keep the egg from cooking further. This puts it into a narrow range of perhaps 90–140°F (32–60°C)—precisely the temperature range most suitable for bacterial growth, and egg yolks are an ideal growth medium. Therefore the sauce cannot be made far ahead, not more than an hour at most.

Establishments that cannot meet these production requirements should not attempt to serve butter sauces at all. *Unless these sauces are served within a short time of creation, they are among the most hazardous foods in the kitchen.*

Butter sauces are usually held at kitchen temperatures, perhaps on the back of the range. They cannot be stored. They cannot be kept in the cooler or the freezer, because the butter solidifies, and when they are brought out and warmed the emulsion breaks.

The reductions can be made ahead in quantity, however, and kept in the cooler to be used as needed. Since they consist mainly of acids and spices, they will keep almost indefinitely.

SUMMING UP

The hundreds of sauces of classical cuisine all stem from a few basic sauces, known as mother sauces or leading sauces. The sauces deriving from them, called small or secondary sauces, are made by adding specific flavoring ingredients to the basic mother sauces.

All the basic sauces are similar in structure. Their body is a liquid. Their texture is provided by a thickening agent. Flavorings and seasonings complete the finished sauces.

The white sauces, with béchamel as the mother sauce, are made with milk and roux. The blond sauces, or veloutés, are based on veal, chicken, or fish stock combined with white or blond roux. The brown sauces are made from dark stock thickened with brown roux or cornstarch. The red, or tomato, sauces use stock or tomato juice as their liquid. The classical tomato sauce is thickened with roux, but many American versions are thickened by reducing and puréeing. The yellow sauces are thickened by emulsifying liquid butter in egg yolks. Butter is also used in the role of a sauce, both alone and in the form of compound butters piquantly flavored and placed cold on hot dishes to melt and enrich.

Today's sauces also include more than the triumphs of the past. Nouvelle followers are bringing new tastes and textures to sauces by using such classical techniques as reducing and puréeing to thicken. New and unusual flavor combinations are appearing, and sauced dishes are being presented in fresh new ways.

Many sauces today are made from convenience products; in fact, most kitchens use such products in one way or another. They can be successful when they are selected with concern for quality ingredients and a low salt content and are used with understanding of how they fit into sauce-from-scratch procedures.

In today's restaurants sauces are a very successful yet simple way of offering a menu with great variety. They are a means of presenting a single product such as veal or steak in a number of different ways, each sauce blending its special flavor with the flavor of the meat to create a distinctively different dish. There is no need to associate the perfect sauce with the expensive commercial restaurant and the extended menu. Sauce of one kind or another is invaluable in the low-budget operation. Whatever the setting, the use, or the price tag, the quality of the sauce can make or break the dish.

Now you know all about the six basic secrets of sauce cookery—the structure of sauces, the making of roux, the liaison, the seasoning, the reduction, the emulsion. But mastery of sauce cookery requires one more secret that no text or teacher can supply, and that is practice.

THE COOK'S VOCABULARY

sauce, basic sauce, finished sauce

mother sauce, leading sauce

small sauce, secondary sauce

white sauces, béchamel

blond sauces, veloutés

brown sauces, espagnole, fond lié, demiglace

red sauces, tomato sauce

yellow sauces, butter sauces, hollandaise, béarnaise

reduction, reduce

monter au beurre, bring up, finish

emulsify, emulsion

sweet butter, simple butter, drawn butter, *beurre fondu,* clarified butter

brown butter, beurre noisette, beurre noir

à la meunière, amandine

compound butter

QUESTIONS FOR DISCUSSION

1. Compare sauce-making with soup-making: consider structure, technique, versatility, holding, and storing.

2. In what types of operation would you make sauces from scratch, and in what types would you use convenience products? Are there operations that would use no sauces at all? If so, give examples.

3. Do you think it is important to learn how to make sauces from scratch even if you never have to make them? Defend your answer.

4. Discuss the various ways of controlling texture in different kinds of sauces. Is it always possible to adjust a sauce that is too thin or too thick? Explain.

WHEN it comes to vegetables, the average restaurant menu has undergone a remarkable change in the last dozen or so years. The once-prevailing side dish of overcooked green beans has given way to a great variety of well-prepared, well-presented vegetables accompanying entrées, gracing salad bars, offered as appetizers, used as colorful plate companions to tasty but drab-colored meats, and even functioning as entire meals.

Much of this change has come in response to consumer interest. People of all ages are paying increasing attention to fitness and appearance and are eating more vegetables and cutting down on meats and sweets. Vegetables have far fewer calories, more vitamins and minerals, and more fiber—all important to good looks and well-being. In addition, properly prepared, they are attractive to the eye and they taste good.

This revolution in customer tastes has been matched in today's forward-looking kitchens. Contemporary cooks have discovered the improved taste and appearance of the al dente vegetable, just as customers have. They are experimenting with interesting flavor and color combinations and with the sensory effects of cutting vegetables in different ways. They are using modern equipment—the steamer, the microwave—to solve some of the problems of vegetable cooking and holding.

It takes all this and more to put good-looking, good-tasting vegetables on the table. Good vegetable preparation is not the easiest of kitchen assignments. It takes product knowledge plus an understanding of how cooking can affect the product and an alertness to the sensory cues of doneness. It takes timing and practice.

After completing this chapter you should be able to

- Explain the effect of an acid or alkaline medium on color in vegetables.

- Discuss the nutritional importance of vegetables and explain how to retain nutrients in cooking.

9

Vegetables, Rice, Pasta

- Choose cooking methods appropriate to different vegetables and describe or demonstrate their use.
- Cite the major holding and production problems for vegetables and suggest ways of overcoming them.
- Describe or demonstrate how to cook rice and pasta.

ABOUT VEGETABLES IN GENERAL

Defining vegetables seems almost as unnecessary as defining your hands. Potatoes, carrots, onions, broccoli, and cabbage are household words. We all know what vegetables are. It is lucky we do, because it is rather hard to define them precisely.

Vegetables are edible parts of certain plants. They may be roots, tubers, bulbs, stems, leaves, flowers, fruits, seeds, or pods. As a group they are high in vitamins and minerals. They are also important sources of dietary fiber. A few of them—the dried beans and peas—contain significant amounts of high-quality protein, a factor of importance to vegetarians. The other vegetables are low in calories, a feature that appeals to dieters. But the vitamin and mineral content of all vegetables is what makes them an essential part of a balanced diet for everyone. The bright-yellow vegetables (carrots, winter squash, for example) and the deep-green leaves and flowers (broccoli, spinach, artichoke) are especially important.

Seed and pod vegetables (beans, corn, peas) contain protein, sugar, and starch. Roots and tubers (carrots, turnips, beets, potatoes), bulbs (onions, leeks), fruits (squash, tomatoes, peppers), and flowers (cauliflower, broccoli) also contain starch and sugar. Stems (celery, asparagus) are mostly cellulose and water. Leaves (lettuce, cabbage, spinach) are mostly water, but their vitamin and mineral content is high.

Vegetables have been on the menu for centuries. The lentil was a staple of the Egypt-

ian diet; onions, cabbage, and mushrooms were also eaten. The Greeks and Romans added broad beans, carrots, cucumbers, lettuce, squash, broccoli, asparagus (for the rich only), garlic, and other vegetables. It is said that the Romans ate cabbage to avoid getting drunk and to cure hangovers.

But vegetables were very unpopular in medieval Europe. They were thought to cause "wind and melancholy." Only cabbage and the onion family were grown, mostly for soup. Dried peas provided pease porridge hot, cold, and nine days old, if we can believe the nursery rhyme. Garlic was eaten to ward off the plague.

Columbus and other explorers took back to Europe the corn, potatoes, squash, tomatoes, peppers, and beans they found the Indians cultivating in the Americas. Some of the strange vegetables caught on, notably the hot peppers. Some didn't. But gradually people began to regard vegetables in general in a more favorable light. As one writer of the day put it, "Horses, Beeves, and Elephants live on plants alone and are large, fat, very strong, and rarely out of order." Vegetables became fashionable and played an important part in the developing French cuisine.

Until the development of refrigerated transportation in the twentieth century, fresh vegetables were available only in the summer near where they were grown. Today we can get almost any vegetable we want at almost any time of the year.

Vegetables come into the kitchen in three market forms—*fresh* or *raw, frozen,* and *canned.* Of the three, fresh vegetables usually produce the best finished dish in flavor, texture, appearance, and nutritive value. But they have their drawbacks. The labor cost is high. The market product varies seasonally, even daily at times, and the price fluctuates, too. Some vegetables may not be available at all at certain times of the year.

Many frozen vegetables can be almost as good as fresh ones. They are somewhat tougher than fresh vegetables owing to the acid that is commonly added in processing, and they have lost some of their nutritive values. But they have several advantages: they save preparation time and labor, they are available year-round, and they yield a standard finished product.

Canned vegetables are the most convenient, the least attractive, and the least nutritive. Like frozen vegetables, they yield a standard product, and a few of them are heavily used in the quantity kitchen, notably tomatoes, corn, carrots, and . . . green beans.

In cooking the different market forms, you have to consider the degree to which they are already cooked. Fresh vegetables are of course totally uncooked. Frozen vegetables have been partially cooked before freezing, to avoid deterioration during storage. Canned vegetables have been completely cooked; in fact, they have been unavoidably overcooked by the prolonged high temperatures of the canning process. To cook each market form you simply take it where it stands—raw, half cooked, or overcooked—and bring it to doneness.

Fresh vegetables are cooked from scratch. Frozen vegetables should be cooked from their frozen state, except for spinach and other greens and various kinds of summer squash, which are practically solid blocks of ice. These should be thawed in the cooler before cooking. Canned vegetables you merely heat to serving temperature since they are already cooked beyond doneness. Heat them in their own liquid, using only enough to cover them.

Any market form can be cooked by any cooking method, observing the guidelines for the particular vegetable. The only thing you have to be careful of in following recipes is to remember degrees of doneness in substituting one market form for another, especially if the recipe specifies a cooking time. Doneness is not a matter of time but of texture, as we shall see.

When you buy fresh vegetables and fruits from the vendor, they are called **produce.** Once in the kitchen they become different things to different cooks. In the cold preparation area, or pantry, they are raw materials for salads and other cold foods. To the soup cook and the sauce cook they are flavor-determining ingredients or flavor builders, to be orchestrated along with stocks and thickeners and spices into composite blends of foods. To the vegetable cook the vegetable is a dish in its own right. In this chapter we will talk about vegetables as seen by the vegetable cook—as dishes prepared to be served with the main part of the meal.

VEGETABLE CHARACTERISTICS AND COOKING

Color in cooking

There are several characteristics of vegetables that influence the way we cook them. One of these is color. No matter what color a raw vegetable is, we want to preserve as much of that color as possible.

Vegetables may be grouped by color into four categories:

- *Red:* beets, red cabbage, red beans
- *Green:* green beans, lima beans, broccoli, asparagus, peas, artichokes, okra, brussels sprouts, spinach, parsley, green peppers, greens (mustard, turnip, and so on)
- *Yellow:* carrots, rutabaga, winter squash, yams, sweet potatoes, corn, tomatoes
- *White:* potatoes, green cabbage, turnips, celery, summer squash, cauliflower, onions, mushrooms, cucumbers, zucchini

These colors come from substances in vegetables known as **pigments.** Certain pigments react to heat, acid, or alkali during cooking, undergoing chemical changes that cause a vegetable to change color. It is important to know which pigments are susceptible to color change and how to deal with them in cooking.

Red vegetables. The pigments in red vegetables are known as **anthocyanins.** These pigments are red in an acid medium but will change to blue or purple in an alkaline medium. They are also water-soluble and can draw the color out of the vegetable into the cooking water.

Cooking red vegetables in an acid medium intensifies their red color. Vegetables themselves contribute acid to the cooking medium. To preserve the color, red vegetables such as beets should be cooked in a covered container to keep the acid from evaporating. Beets should be cooked unpeeled, to keep the red pigment in the beet instead of letting it leach into the water. You will see these rules illustrated later in recipe 9-2.

Some water supplies are alkaline and may stay on the alkaline side during cooking in spite of the added vegetable acids. In an alkaline medium red cabbage will not only lose its redness but will turn purple, blue, and green. A small amount of vinegar, wine, or lemon juice in the water will maintain its red color. For example, in recipe 9-5 red cabbage is cooked covered (braised) with apples, wine, and vinegar providing extra acid.

Green vegetables. The pigments in green vegetables are known as **chlorophyll.** Their reaction to acid and alkalis is just the opposite of the red pigments' reactions. They tend to lose their brilliance as their acids are released into the cooking water and may turn an olive green. They keep their color best in a slightly alkaline solution. Therefore they should be cooked uncovered to allow their acids to evaporate.

You might think that since you can add lemon juice to maintain an acid solution for red vegetables, you should be able to add baking soda to create an alkaline solution for green ones. *Not so!* If color were the only quality desired, this approach would be fine. However, baking soda has other less desirable effects. It tends to destroy such nutrients as vitamins. It also makes the vegetables mushy and sometimes adds a bitter taste.

The slightest overcooking will also make green vegetables turn from bright to olive green. This is true not only in boiling but in other cooking methods too. The dark color of canned green vegetables comes from the prolonged cooking at high temperatures that is required to prevent botulism in canned goods.

Green vegetables cooked for only 5 to 7 minutes will usually retain their brilliant natural green. This is another argument for al dente or even slightly undercooked vegetables.

Yellow vegetables. The pigments in the yellow vegetable group are called **carotenes.** There are several types, ranging from the yellow of corn to the orange of carrots to the red of tomatoes. Yellow vegetables do not suffer color loss in either acid or alkaline solutions. Some of them can lose color from overcooking, however. You can see this in the tired carrot that has been used in making stock.

White vegetables. The pigments in white vegetables are known as **flavones.** They remain white in acid but turn yellow in an alkaline medium, so a bit of lemon juice or a cover on the pot is in order. Acid tends to toughen vegetables, so keep the amount small.

For white vegetables, too, time is an enemy to quality with all cooking methods. White vegetables turn gray when overcooked and develop an undesirable taste. They should be cooked as quickly as possible and only until barely tender.

Flavor

Many flavor-producing substances are lost through evaporation or by being dissolved in the cooking water and then discarded. This means that a boiled vegetable should be cooked as quickly as possible, in as little water as possible, and in a covered pot *if* color will not be affected. Above all, it should not be overcooked. The longer the cooking, the more flavor goes into the liquid or into the air.

Not only does overcooking produce flavor loss; it often creates flavor change. Some vegetables take on new, undesirable flavors when overcooked. Members of the cabbage family—cabbage, turnips, cauliflower, brussels sprouts, broccoli—will develop a strong acrid taste and unpleasant smell if overcooked, owing to chemical changes. These vegetables will taste best when cooked quickly, with the cover off the pot to allow evaporation of the strong-flavored substances. For the red and white family members this practice conflicts with covering the pot to maintain an acid solution. A little lemon juice or vinegar or another cooking method may solve this problem.

Texture

Vegetables can be grouped roughly into three textural classes: hard, soft, and starchy. As you discovered in making soup, cooking times vary according to texture. Soft vegetables cook quickly; hard and starchy vegetables take longer.

Textural change is a primary purpose of cooking vegetables, and achievement of good texture is a primary goal. Many vegetables are palatable only if their cellulose is softened by heat and if other tenderizing chemical changes take place. But we want to carry these changes only so far. Good texture for a vegetable is, as you know, **al dente**—firm to the bite, pleasantly crunchy, crisp-tender—which again means do not overcook.

In addition, we want to preserve the vegetable's own texture as much as possible. Remember that an acid cooking medium toughens the vegetable and an alkaline medium softens it.

The degree of firmness desired varies from one vegetable to another. Green beans are firmer than squash. A good boiled potato is firmer than a good baked potato. If a vegetable can be eaten raw, undercook it slightly for the best texture.

We want the vegetable to reach the diner still in that firm but tender textural state, appetizingly hot but without further cooking. This is a challenge, since the vegetable continues to cook while being held for service. For this reason it is desirable to cook vegetables as close to serving time as possible and in as small quantities as possible, so that they may be replenished frequently with a freshly cooked supply.

Some people do not like al dente vegetables and will leave them uneaten or send them back to the kitchen as "underdone." It is quite possible that they have never eaten any but overcooked vegetables. If a majority of your customers prefer such disasters, you will just have to store what you are learning here in the back of your mind and, as in Rome, do as the Romans do.

Nutrients

Vegetable nutrients can easily be lost in cooking. Many vitamins and minerals are water-soluble, some are destroyed in alkaline solutions, and some are heat-sensitive and may be destroyed by either high heat or prolonged cooking.

No one cooking method will conserve all the nutrients. In boiling you lose some that dissolve in the cooking liquid and some that are destroyed by heat. Steaming retains some nutrients better than boiling does, but some nutrients are lost: the shorter cooking time of steaming saves some nutrients, but the higher heat destroys others. Braising uses little liquid and low heat but has a long cooking time. Frying has a short cooking time but high temperatures. Baking unpeeled vegetables retains most nutrients, but the prolonged high heat destroys vitamins that lie close to the skin. So there is no one ideal method.

There are, however, ways to keep nutrient losses to a minimum. The one rule that applies to all methods is: *Do not overcook.* This cuts all types of nutrient loss. A second general rule is to cook as close to serving time as possible. During holding, nutrients continue to disappear through exposure to air, and keeping vegetables hot for service continues to cook them slightly.

Some special rules for boiling will keep nutrient loss for that method at a minimum. One rule is to use no more liquid than necessary—just enough to cover so all pieces cook evenly. Another is to keep the liquid slightly acid or neutral and avoid additives such as baking soda for green color. A third rule is to have the liquid boiling before adding the vegetable. A fourth is to keep the action of the liquid gentle. A hard boil will cause rapid evaporation and may also break the vegetable pieces, causing additional leaching of nutrients. On the other hand the lower temperatures of simmering will prolong the cooking. Most vegetables should be cooked at or just below the boiling point.

Preparation of raw vegetables can also affect the nutritive value of the cooked product. In many vegetables the vitamins are near the skin, so as little flesh as possible should be cut away in peeling. Nutrients also leach out of cut surfaces. This means that the larger the cut surface, the greater the nutrient loss in cooking. There are many times, however, when flavor, appearance, cooking time, or the requirements of a garniture will dictate the way a vegetable is cut.

When nutrition conflicts with flavor, appearance, or production needs, the choice will be made according to circumstances and the clientele being served. The hospital may choose nutrition; the continental restaurant may choose flavor and appearance. The goal should be the most of everything for everybody.

Actually, the things that make for good flavor, texture, and appearance tend to be the same things that conserve nutrients. One thing is certain: the nutrients are more likely to be eaten if the vegetable looks and tastes good.

Quality standards and cooking guidelines

Vegetable quality begins with the arrival of produce in the kitchen. Raw vegetables should be properly stored, refrigerated and covered (Chapter 3), and promptly used. Exposure to air alters flavor and texture and causes nutrient loss. The same considerations apply to holding vegetables preprepared for cooking.

Prepreparation should be scheduled as close to cooking time as possible. Raw vegetables should be thoroughly cleaned and crisply cut in uniform pieces, not only for even cooking but also for appearance on the diner's plate.

Cooked vegetables should have the same fresh, bright colors they had before they were cooked. Their flavors should be equally fresh; they should make a fresh-from-the-garden impression on the tongue and taste buds.

Most vegetables should be cooked to al dente doneness—pleasantly crunchy, never overcooked. The few that are served soft— sweet and white potatoes, winter squash, eggplant, legumes—should be soft and tender throughout but not soggy or mushy.

When served, all vegetables should be well drained and arranged attractively on the plate. Remember that they are meant to enhance the foods they are served with and often play the visual role of garnishes.

Vegetables should be chosen for both color and flavor in relation to other menu items—blending, complementing, or contrasting in pleasing fashion. Though selection may not be the cook's job, if you keep in mind their menu role you will probably do a better job of cooking: you will concentrate on maintaining and enhancing the qualities they were chosen for.

To summarize, here are the major guidelines for the cooking of all vegetables.

- Store produce properly and use promptly to avoid texture, flavor, and nutrient loss.
- Clean raw vegetables thoroughly before cooking; hold them properly to avoid color change or nutrient loss.
- Cut vegetables crisply and uniformly.
- In boiling, use as little liquid as possible.

METHODS OF COOKING VEGETABLES

Not all methods of cooking adapt well to all vegetables and not all vegetables adapt well to

9-1 BUTTERED GREEN BEANS

Yield: 25 3-oz (100 g) portions

5 lb EP	green beans, frozen or fresh	2.5 kg EP	*	butter, melted	*
			*	salt and pepper	*
			*	water, boiling salted	*

1. If using fresh beans, wash, trim off ends, and cut into uniform lengths.
2. Add to boiling salted water. Cook uncovered at a low boil until al dente. Drain.
3. Toss with a small amount of melted butter. Season *to taste.

all methods of cookery. The cook's choice of methods will be those that best suit equipment and production needs and at the same time give each vegetable perfection in the customer's eyes.

The most common methods of vegetable cookery are

- Boiling
- Steaming
- Braising
- Deep-frying
- Pan-frying
- Baking
- "Broiling"
- Sautéing

Boiling

Cooking a vegetable submerged in a liquid at or just below the boiling point is perhaps the most universal method of vegetable cookery (recipes 9-1 and 9-2). You put the vegetable into a pot of lightly salted boiling liquid (*1 tsp salt per gal or 5 mL per 4 L). Use just enough liquid to cover the vegetable (Figure 9-1). Bring it back to a boil as quickly as possible, and boil it gently to al dente doneness,

9-1a GREEN BEANS AMANDINE

To recipe 9-1 add:

| | 1 lb | slivered almonds, toasted | 500 g |

1. Follow Steps 1 and 2 in 9-1.
2. In Step 3, sauté beans with almonds in melted butter until flavors are blended. Season *to taste.

9-1b GREEN BEANS FORESTIÈRE

To recipe 9-1 add:

| | 1 lb | mushrooms, sliced, sautéed | 500 g |

1. Follow Steps 1 and 2 in 9-1.
2. In Step 3, sauté beans with mushrooms in melted butter until flavors are blended. Season *to taste.

being careful not to overcook. Cover the pot or not according to color or strong taste. You can add herbs and spices for flavor.

Drain the vegetable as soon as cooking is complete. It cannot be held in hot liquid or it will go on cooking. If you avoid overcooking

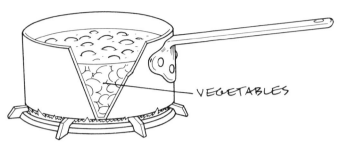

FIGURE 9-1. Boiling a vegetable. Use only enough hot liquid to cover the vegetable. This minimizes nutrient loss.

and use the right amount of liquid—no more than necessary—you will produce flavorful, good-looking vegetables.

Vegetables suitable for boiling are artichokes, asparagus, beets, broccoli, brussels sprouts, cabbage, carrots, cauliflower, corn, green beans, onions, peas, potatoes, rutabagas, summer squash, tomatoes, turnips, and zucchini.

You can serve plain boiled vegetables garnished or ungarnished; many are eye-pleasing in themselves. Or you can do other things with them to make them more glamorous. Recipes 9-1a and 9-1b give you some suggestions. You can use these recipes for many other vegetables as well. You can vary the beets in recipe 9-2 by serving them in an orange sauce made with cooking liquid and orange juice, flavored with vinegar, sugar, and orange zest, and thickened with cornstarch.

Dried legumes are also cooked in liquid in a pot. In fact, it is the only way to cook them. You have met legumes before in making potages. Cooking them is slightly different from the boiling of fresh vegetables. They should be simmered, not boiled, since the higher temperature toughens them. Use 2 to 3 quarts of stock or water to a pound of dried vegetables, and soak them in it overnight (unless the package says it isn't necessary). Lightly salt the liquid and cook the vegetables until they are done throughout but firm enough to hold

---

9-2 BOILED FRESH BEETS

Yield: 25 4-oz (125 mL) portions

7½ lb AP	fresh beets	3.5 kg AP	*	butter	*
			*	salt and pepper	*
			*	boiling water, lightly salted	*

1. Wash beets well; trim stems 2–3″ (4–6 cm) above beets.
2. Place in boiling salted water to cover. Return to a simmer, cover pot, and simmer until tender (*30–60 minutes).
3. Drain, rinse in cold water, peel, and cut into uniform slices. Heat in ⅛″ (3 mm) butter and season *to taste.

9-3 RED BEANS AND RICE

Yield: 10–12 16-oz (500 mL) servings

2 lb	dried red or kidney beans	1 kg	1 lb	light mirepoix, brunoise	500 g
(10–12	ham hocks	10–12)	2	garlic cloves, puréed	2
1 gal	water	4 L	8 oz	green pepper, brunoise	250 g
1¾ qt	cooked rice	1.75 L	2	bay leaves	2
			2 tsp	thyme	10 mL
			1½ tsp	oregano	7 mL
			1 tsp*	cayenne	*5 mL
			1 Tb*	Tabasco	*15 mL
			2 tsp	white pepper	10 mL
			½ tsp	black pepper	2 mL
			*	salt	*

1. Place all ingredients except rice in stockpot and simmer until beans (and hocks) are tender (*2–3 hours).
2. To serve, mound 6 oz (175 mL) rice in soup plate; ladle 10 oz (300 mL) beans around rice (with 1 ham hock).

their shape. For extra flavor you can cook them with smoked meat or a ham bone and flavor builders. Cooking time varies from around half an hour for dried limas to 3 hours or so for navy beans.

Because of the protein content in legumes, they are often combined with rice in vegetarian dishes. For example, beans and rice each contain certain kinds of protein that the other lacks, so when combined they supply the complete protein needed in a sound diet. An example of such a dish is given in recipe 9-3. This is a regional dish from cajun cuisine that is very popular in the southwest. Use the cayenne and Tabasco with caution! Cajun cuisine is *very* spicy.

Steaming

In today's kitchen, steaming is beginning to replace boiling as the primary method of vegetable cookery. To steam, you place the cleaned and prepared vegetables in pans, usually without water, and put them into steamer cabinets that cook them at pressures of 5 to 15 psi (pounds per square inch), or of 35 to 100 kPa in metric. The cooking is very quick; the higher the pressure, the quicker. It is so quick, in fact, that most vegetables can be steamed in small quantities as needed for service. Some vegetables can be steamed in serving pans, thus requiring less handling than most other methods. Others cook better in perforated pans where the steam can circulate all around them. The green beans in 9-1 and its variations could just as well be steamed in perforated pans.

Steamed vegetables cook so quickly that it is easy to overcook them, spoiling color, flavor, and texture and causing some nutrient loss. To avoid overcooking, follow the timing charts that apply to your own equipment. If charts are not available, test-cook a small amount. Most

9-4 STEAMED SUMMER SQUASH
Yield: 25 3-oz (100 g) portions

6 lb AP	yellow squash or zucchini	3 kg AP	*	melted butter	*
			*	salt, white pepper	*
			*	chopped parsley	*

1. Wash squash; score lengthwise with a fork or router. Trim ends. If large, cut in half lengthwise. If small, cut a thin lengthwise slice off bottom so squash will sit flat.
2. Cut into 3/8″ (8 mm) disks, keeping slices for each 3-oz (100 g) portion together as in the uncut squash. Line up portions in rows in lightly oiled hotel pan. Cover with a damp towel to help maintain form.
3. Steam until al dente. Remove towel, *season, and *butter.
4. Serve with slotted spoon. Garnish with parsley as served.

vegetables take 4 to 15 minutes at 5 psi (35 kPa) and 1 to 4 minutes at 15 psi (100 kPa).

Among vegetables that turn out well when steamed are artichokes, asparagus, broccoli, brussels sprouts, cabbage, carrots, cauliflower, green beans, lima beans, onions, peas, potatoes, rutabagas, summer squash, tomatoes, turnips, and zucchini.

Steamed and boiled vegetables can be used interchangeably in recipes calling for cooked vegetables. Recipe 9-4 is an example of a vegetable steamed in a serving pan. It is evenly preportioned for service. If you don't have steaming equipment, this vegetable can be steamed on the range by adding half an inch (1 cm) of water to the pan.

Braising
Cooking a vegetable slowly, covered, in a small amount of liquid affords some distinct advantages over boiling and steaming. The flavorful juices of the vegetable are not lost; the liquid remaining when it is done (if any) can be reduced or thickened with beurre manié and served with the vegetable. Braising is often done in the oven, with the vegetable covered with parchment paper and with stock as

the liquid. Suitable for braising are brussels sprouts, cabbage, celery, leeks, lettuce, mushrooms, onions, potatoes, summer squash, and zucchini.

Braising can also be used as a method of initial partial cooking. For example, mushrooms can be braised to 50 percent doneness in a small amount of butter, lemon juice, and water or wine and then held for up to three days to be used as needed, usually in combination with other foods. This method retains their white color.

Braised vegetables typically have added ingredients, as in recipe 9-5. Like this red cabbage dish, they often begin with flavor builders sweated or sautéed in fat.

Deep-frying
Soft vegetables, such as onions, or partially cooked hard vegetables, such as cauliflower, can be very successfully cooked by deep-frying. Most vegetables that are deep-fried are breaded or battered first; the potato is an exception. Suitable for deep-frying are cauliflower, eggplant, mushrooms, okra, onions, parsley (also unbreaded), potatoes, and summer squash.

9-5 BRAISED RED CABBAGE

Yield: 25 3-oz (100 g) portions

6 lb AP	red cabbage	3 kg AP	6–8 oz	bacon fat or oil	175–250 mL
¾ qt*	light stock or water	*750 mL	1 lb	onions, small dice	500 g
			3–4 oz	sugar	100–125 g
			1 lb	apples, peeled, cored, 1/2″ (1 cm) dice	500 g
			½ pt	red wine	250 mL
			2 oz	cider vinegar	50 mL
			*	salt and pepper	*

1. Core cabbage and shred coarsely (¼–½″ or ½–1 cm).
2. Sweat onions in fat until translucent.
3. Add remaining ingredients, adding liquid last *to 1″ (2 cm) below level of cabbage.
4. Cover with parchment paper and simmer until al dente (*20 minutes).
5. Season *to taste. Hold in braising liquid; serve with slotted spoon.

Cooking in the deep fryer is simplicity itself if you follow these rules:

- Cut uniform pieces for even cooking.
- Partial-cook hard vegetables.
- Bread carefully for a complete, even coat with no loose crumbs. Season before breading or after removing from fryer. Do not season uncoated foods; the salt will break down the fat.
- Be sure the fat is at the right temperature before immersing the food. If the temperature is too low, the food will absorb too much fat. If it is too high, the food may be overbrowned on the outside and undercooked on the inside. Vegetables cook well at temperatures of 325–350°F (160–180°C).
- Do not overload the fryer. Fill baskets only one-half to two-thirds full. Overloading will cool the fat, prolong the cooking, and produce greasy foods. Partly filled baskets allow you to shake the food occasionally to keep the pieces from sticking together.
- When the food is golden brown, lift the basket out of the fat and drain a minute or so over the kettle. Drain further on absorbent material if necessary.
- Serve immediately.

These rules apply equally well to deep-frying of all foods.

Fried eggplant (recipe 9-6) provides the contrast of soft and crunchy textures in one flavorful dish. You can substitute zucchini batonnets, small whole mushrooms, onion rings, or cauliflower flowerets. Recipe 9-6a shows the versatility of a deep-fried vegetable: you can put it together with other ingredients to create a variety of dishes. This eggplant parmesan recipe is an easy way of preparing this popular vegetable dish, used often as a vegetarian or luncheon entrée.

9-6 FRIED EGGPLANT

Yield: 25 3-oz (100 g) portions

5 lb	eggplant	2.5 kg	*	flour	*
			*	egg wash	*
			*	bread crumbs	*
			*	salt, pepper	*

1. Wash eggplant; cut crosswise into ¼″ (5 mm) round slices or french fry cuts. Hold in ice water.
2. Drain, pat dry with towels, and pass through standard breading procedure.
3. Fry in 350°F (180°C) deep fat until golden brown and tender. Drain well. Season. Serve immediately.

9-6a EGGPLANT PARMESAN

To finished eggplant from 9-6 add:

1½ qt	tomato sauce II (8-7)	1.5 L
8 oz	parmesan cheese, grated	250 g
1 lb	mozzarella cheese, grated	500 g

1. Spread a 1/4″ (5 mm) layer of tomato sauce in hotel pan or individual casseroles.
2. Place a layer of eggplant on sauce, then add another layer of sauce. Sprinkle with a layer of mozzarella and parmesan cheeses.
3. Continue layering, ending with sauce and cheeses.
4. Bake in 350°F (180°C) oven until thoroughly heated and cheese is melted (*15–25 minutes).

To refresh your memory about standard breading procedure, review the discussion of breading in Chapter 3. The quantities of breading ingredients needed will vary with circumstances. For quick breading, ingredients should be *1 to 2 inches (2–5 cm) deep in each pan. Leftover breading ingredients can be strained, the egg wash refrigerated, and everything used again for the next meal.

Pan-frying

Not many vegetables adapt well to pan-frying, but for those that do it can produce a delicious product. Thinly sliced potatoes may be pan-fried to a golden brown in butter or bacon drippings, often with onion added. Shredded potatoes are pan-fried in a browned-on-both-sides mass to make hashed browns, an indispensable breakfast dish in some regions. Onions are fried to doneness to accompany pan-fried liver. Mushrooms may be pan-fried slowly to a deep, rich brown to be served with grilled steak.

Baking

Such vegetables as squash, potatoes, eggplant, and tomatoes, which can be cooked in their skins, adapt very well to cooking by dry heat in an oven. Baking retains more vitamins and minerals than most cooking methods.

Two baked tomato dishes are given in recipes 9-7 and 9-7a. Winter squash can be baked in cut halves, buttered, and flavored with ingredients usually associated with the bakeshop—cinnamon, nutmeg, and brown sugar. Baked potatoes will be discussed in detail shortly.

Baking is also used to make vegetable casseroles. A **casserole** is a dish in which one or more cooked foods are combined with a

9-7 TOMATOES CLAMART

Yield: 24 portions (1 half tomato each)

12	whole fresh tomatoes	12	1½ lb	cooked peas, seasoned	750 g
			8 oz	bread crumbs	250 g
			*	melted butter	*

1. Core stems; cut tomatoes in half crosswise and scoop out pulp and seeds, leaving outer flesh intact.
2. Place halves cut side up on lightly oiled baking sheet.
3. Fill with peas; top with bread crumbs; drizzle with melted butter.
4. Bake at 350°F (180°C) until tomatoes are heated through and bread crumbs are golden.

sauce and heated together in the oven. Usually the dish is covered with bread crumbs and butter and sometimes cheese, and the topping is lightly browned in the salamander or under the broiler. This is known as **gratinéing,** and the dish is said to be **au gratin.**

Such a dish can be made in individual casseroles or it can be baked in hotel pans and cut into portions for serving. Recipe 9-8 is a master recipe for many different kinds of vegetable casseroles. You can substitute broccoli,

9-7a TOMATOES FORESTIÈRE

In recipe 9-7, make the following changes:

Replace peas with 12 oz (375 g) mushrooms, sliced, sautéed.

Follow instructions for 9-7, replacing peas with mushrooms in Step 3.

9-8 CAULIFLOWER AU GRATIN

Yield: 25 3-oz (100 g) portions

5 lb	cauliflower flowerets	2.5 kg	1½ qt	mornay sauce (8-1b)	1.5 L
*	water to cover, salted	*	1½ oz	bread crumbs	50 g
1 Tb	lemon juice	15 mL	*	melted butter	*
			(1½ oz	grated parmesan cheese	50 g)

1. Cook cauliflower in boiling water with lemon juice until barely tender. Drain well.
2. Place in buttered hotel pan or individual casseroles and cover with sauce.
3. Sprinkle with bread crumbs and butter (plus cheese if desired).
4. Bake in 350°F (180°C) oven until thoroughly heated (*15–20 minutes).
5. Place under salamander until top is lightly browned.

brussels sprouts, celery, leeks, or cooked diced potatoes, omitting lemon juice in all cases. Be sure vegetables are thoroughly drained so that the cooking liquid will not dilute the sauce. A casserole is one way of avoiding some of the problems of holding vegetables for service.

"Broiling"

Broiling is the term used to refer to a particular way of cooking soft sliced vegetables such as eggplant, mushrooms, onions, and tomatoes, often with a stuffing or topping. The term is a misnomer. They are cooked in the oven, with perhaps a minute or two under the broiler at the end to glaze them. If you tried to cook them under the intense heat of the broiler, the tops would burn while the bottoms would still be raw. But the menu will call these baked/glazed vegetables broiled.

Recipe 9-9 is an example of "broiled" tomatoes, a delicious and handsome addition to a plate. If you add 4 oz (125 g) parmesan cheese to the mixture in Step 3 you will be making parmesan broiled tomatoes.

Sautéing

Flipping a partially cooked vegetable in a little hot fat in a pan is a tasty way of finish-cooking it. Canned and frozen vegetables, as well as fresh vegetables partially cooked by another method, can be finished for service in this way.

Suitable for sautéing are asparagus, broccoli, carrots, cauliflower, green beans, mushrooms, onions, parsnips, potatoes, peas, brussels sprouts, turnips, and some kinds of squash.

The glazed carrot recipe, 9-10, illustrates another use of sautéing. The butter and sugar plus the high heat of sautéing add a shiny coat of glaze to the vegetable. You can use the same recipe to prepare turnips, pearl onions, or parsnips. Recipe 9-11 uses sautéing to combine two vegetables having different cooking times. This is one of the few preparations that begins and ends with sautéing. The high heat makes the tomatoes steam, which facilitates the finish-cooking.

You will find many recipes that use sautéing to add the finishing touch of a garniture to a vegetable, as in 9-1a and 9-1b.

9-9 BROILED TOMATOES PROVENÇALE

Yield: 24 portions (1 half tomato each)

12	whole fresh tomatoes	12	12 oz	bread crumbs	375 g	
			1	garlic clove, puréed	1	
			2 Tb	minced parsley	25 mL	*topping*
			1 Tb	basil or oregano	15 mL	
			½ tsp	thyme	2 mL	
			*	melted butter	*	
			*	salt, pepper	*	

1. Core stems from tomatoes. Cut in half crosswise and squeeze out seeds.
2. Place on lightly oiled baking sheet. Season with salt and pepper.
3. Mix topping with *enough melted butter to bind ingredients together.
4. Press a ¼" (5 mm) layer of topping to cover top of each tomato half.
5. Bake in 350°F (180°C) oven until heated through (*5–10 minutes).
6. Place briefly under salamander until topping is lightly golden.

9-10 GLAZED CARROTS

Yield: 25 3-oz (100 g) portions

6 lb AP	carrots	3 kg AP	1–2 oz	sugar		40–50 g
3 oz	butter	75 g	*	salt, white pepper		*
			2 oz*	chopped parsley		*60 g
			*	boiling water, lightly salted		*

1. Wash, peel, and trim carrots. Cut into uniform pieces—tourné, page 52, or ⅛" (3 mm) diagonal slices.
2. Add to boiling water; cook at a low boil until al dente. Drain.
3. Melt butter in sauteuse. Add carrots; sprinkle with sugar, salt, and pepper. Sauté until carrots are lightly golden and glazed.
4. Adjust seasoning *to taste. At service time, garnish with parsley.

9-11 SAUTÉED SUMMER SQUASH AND TOMATOES

Yield: 25 3-oz (100 g) portions

6 lb AP	yellow squash or zucchini	3 kg AP	*	salt, white pepper	*
1 lb	tomatoes, canned, drained, diced, or fresh peeled, seeded, concassé	500 g	(*	chopped parsley	*)
4 oz	butter	125 g			

1. Wash squash, trim ends, and cut into batonnets or 3/8" (8 mm) diagonal slices.
2. Melt butter in sauteuse. Sauté squash until half cooked.
3. Add tomatoes and continue sautéing until both vegetables are al dente.
4. Season *to taste. (Garnish with chopped parsley at service time.)

SEASONING, FLAVORING, AND VEGETABLE VERSATILITY

All forms of vegetables are usually served with melted butter over them, often clarified butter. They may be cooked with seasonings and spices if the cooking method allows it. In boiling and braising, seasonings and spices may be added to the cooking liquid. In steaming they may be sprinkled on top. Vegetables that are breaded for pan-frying or deep-frying may be seasoned before breading. Sautéed vegetables may be flavored by adding complementary flavors to the butter in the pan, or they may be glazed by sautéing in a butter-sugar combination, as in recipe 9-10.

If seasonings have not been added during cooking, season to taste before service. If seasonings have been added, check and adjust before serving. Don't forget fresh lemon as a seasoning, but don't add this acid to a green vegetable during cooking.

When you add flavors to vegetables compatibility is important. Table 9-1 suggests flavors that go well with specific vegetables. It is by no means a complete list, but it includes many combinations that are generally well liked.

Remember when adding flavorings that they should never drown out the vegetable's own taste but should simply provide an interesting accent. Remember too that dried herbs and spices should be cooked with the product, not sprinkled on like seasonings at the end. Freshly chopped parsley, on the other hand, should be added just before service, when it looks and tastes its best. In today's cuisine other fresh herbs are added near the end of cooking for their distinctive tastes.

Certain vegetables may be combined with others for variety and interest. Mushrooms go well with beans, peas, or squash, and the finished dish may then take on the garniture name of *forestière*. Tiny whole onions also go well with these vegetables. Lima beans and corn are served together as succotash. Carrots and peas are often partners. The vegetables

TABLE 9-1 Vegetable-and-Flavor Combinations

Vegetable	Compatible Flavors
Asparagus	lemon, brown butter, mustard
Beans, green	bacon, almonds, brown butter, onion, shallots, garlic
Beans, lima	oregano, thyme, savory
Beets	clove, onion, vinegar, dill, ginger, savory, thyme
Broccoli	lemon, brown butter, mustard, shallots, orange
Brussels sprouts	caraway seed, dill, mustard seed, savory, tarragon
Cabbage	caraway seed, dill, mustard seed, savory, tarragon
Carrots	mint, orange, clove, parsley, nutmeg, ginger root, sugar, fennel, shallots
Cauliflower	dill, nutmeg, mustard seed, parmesan
Corn	bacon, onion, red and green peppers
Cucumber	garlic, dill, tarragon
Peas	basil, dill, rosemary, sage, savory, mint
Spinach	garlic, nutmeg
Squash	onion, dill, mustard seed, savory, fennel, clove, cinnamon
Sweet potato	cinnamon, clove, brown sugar, nutmeg, orange, shallots
Tomatoes	bay leaf, garlic, basil, rosemary, thyme, tarragon

should be cooked separately and mixed at or near the end of the cooking.

Often combining vegetables involves more than one cooking method, as when boiled or steamed vegetables are finished by sautéing. Recipe 9-12 follows parboiling with sweating in butter to combine three vegetables in an interesting mix of flavors. You can vary the flavor mix by substituting mint or chervil for lettuce.

Sauces, compound butters, and garnitures are other methods of adding variety and attractiveness to vegetables, as you have seen

9-12 PEAS FRANCAISE (FRENCH GREEN PEAS)

Yield: 25 3-oz (100 g) portions

3½ lb	frozen or parboiled fresh green peas	1.75 kg	1 lb	lettuce, shredded	500 g
			4 oz	pearl onions	125 g
4 oz	butter	125 g	1 Tb	sugar	15 mL
(4 oz	chicken stock, hot	125 mL)	*	salt, white pepper	*

1. In a sautoir, sweat onions and lettuce in butter until onions are translucent.
2. Stir in peas and sugar, (moisten with chicken stock), and cook until peas are al dente.
3. Season *to taste.

in a number of recipes. Hollandaise is often served with asparagus, cauliflower, or broccoli. Spinach, peas, and green beans are enhanced by cream sauce or a hot vinaigrette sauce of vinegar, oil, and spices. Garnitures of minced hard-cooked egg, grated cheese, sliced almonds, or pimientos are often added to various vegetables. A dollop of sour cream is a standard garniture for baked potato, often topped with chopped chives or crisp crumbled bacon. Sour cream is also good with beets and spinach.

Nouvelle cuisine cooks have revived some classical practices in their treatment of vegetables. One is to use tiny vegetables or very small cuts of vegetables—baby carrots, flowerets of broccoli or cauliflower, vegetables cut julienne. A combination julienne of carrots, zucchini, and red peppers is a popular and decorative mix of flavors and colors. Vegetables are carefully chosen as much for their decorative effect on the plate as for their role in the meal.

HOLDING AND PRODUCTION PROBLEMS

Whatever the vegetable, market form, cooking method, or dish, the cook faces problems in getting vegetables onto the diner's plate at their peak of goodness. At holding temperatures the vegetables go on cooking. Within a very short time—20 minutes to half an hour—most of them change flavor, lose their bright, attractive colors, become mushy, and lose nutrients. If the cook prepares a large amount at once, all but the first few portions will be overcooked before they can be dished out.

Stagger-cooking

In many production situations the problems can be solved by **stagger-cooking,** or **batch-cooking,** fresh or frozen vegetables in small quantities as needed, using quick-cooking methods such as steaming under pressure. In this way production stays just ahead of service. Canned vegetables can also be quickly heated in small amounts as needed.

Partial-cook/quick-chill production

When thousands of portions are needed, or when several vegetables must be ready at the same time, the situation becomes more complicated. Not all vegetables cook quickly enough. Equipment and personnel may be limited or may be needed for other production. Vegetables may be needed at the same time in different service areas.

In such circumstances many large hotels use a production technique of partial-cooking and quick-chilling for vegetables having fairly long cooking times. Vegetables in large quantities are precooked to 50 to 75 percent of doneness. They are then quick-chilled with ice, either by plunging them into ice water or by plunging ice into the cooking pot. The icy bath must lower the temperature to below 40°F (4°C) within 2 minutes. This stops the cooking, preserves the color and texture, and allows the vegetables to be held in the cooler for two or three days. They can be finish-cooked quickly when and where they are needed for service, using any desired cooking method. Often they are finished by sautéing. Flavoring and seasoning can be added at this time.

In the partial-cooking step, fresh vegetables are parboiled in lightly salted water to 50 percent or more of doneness. (Exact percentages are hard to recognize and there is a range of 20 percent or so that works very well.) Frozen vegetables, since they are already partially cooked, need only to be plunged into hot water and cooked about 15 to 20 percent more—blanched—enough to separate, thaw, and bring the pieces to equal doneness. From here on, fresh and frozen vegetables are treated in the same way. Once thoroughly chilled, they are drained and held in the cooler, covered, until needed. They are ready for quick finish-cooking by any method appropriate to the vegetable, in any equipment, in any quantity needed.

This method of production spreads the use of cooks and equipment efficiently over the time available. It puts any vegetable within minutes of doneness so that the finish-cooking can be staggered as needed without dependence on one type of equipment. Or thousands of portions can be preprepared at one central location and distributed to several kitchens for finish-cooking and service.

This two-step method allows vegetables to be stored at a stage of doneness in which color and texture are intact, instead of held for service at a doneness that deteriorates rapidly to unacceptability. Wherever and however they are finish-cooked, the cook has control of that last critical percentage of the cooking process. You can send to the table vegetables that are fresh in color, al dente in texture, and full of flavor because they are freshly done in spite of the large quantities required.

This method of vegetable preparation was widely practiced in large-volume operations until the pressure steamer came along and solved many problems. Some nutritionists have frowned upon the partial-cook/quick-chill method because nutrients are tossed out along with the cooking water, but it is difficult to see how more nutrients are lost in parboiling and blanching than in boiling to doneness. In any case it is a production technique that solves some problems no other method can.

With the increasing use of microwave cooking a new version of the partial-cook/quick-chill method has developed. Instead of using ice the cook drains the three-quarters-cooked vegetables and places them in special quick-chill cabinets, where they are held until needed. They are then finish-cooked by microwave. This method is becoming popular in large hospitals where several thousand meals are served daily.

Not all vegetables are suitable for partial-cook/quick-chill treatment. The hard vegetables are the ones for which it is most useful. Soft vegetables reach doneness so quickly it would be a waste of time to precook them. They should simply be stagger-cooked as needed. Most starchy vegetables should be cooked without interruption until done, even though they do not cook quickly. The potato is an exception; it can often be treated as a hard vegetable.

THE POTATO

Americans are often said to be meat-and-potato eaters, and the reputation is well-founded. Potatoes are served three times a day in this country in all forms. Most cooks learn more ways to cook potatoes than any other vegetable.

Potatoes adapt to more styles of cooking than any other vegetable. They are baked, fried, pan-fried, boiled, braised, steamed, sautéed, mashed, and hashed. Successful cooking depends in part on choosing the right potato for the cooking method.

The many varieties of potato divide into waxy types and nonwaxy or mealy types. Mealy varieties are high in starch and low in sugar. They are best for french-fried, mashed, and baked potatoes, as well as for potato-thickened soups. Waxy potatoes, which by comparison are high in sugar and low in starch, are better for dishes requiring a firm potato that will hold its shape when cooked, such as stews, pan-fried potatoes, and potato salad.

Storage temperatures can alter the starch/sugar ratio over a period of time. Potatoes kept at 45°F (7°C) will increase in sugar in relation to starch. Potatoes kept at room temperature will undergo the opposite change. Optimum storage temperature for stability is about 60°F (16°C). Most operations use potatoes heavily and buy frequently, so starch and sugar changes are seldom a problem.

Potatoes have more nutrients than they are generally given credit for. In addition to starch and sugar they contain appreciable amounts of protein, iron, B vitamins, vitamin C, and many minerals. Many people think of potatoes as fattening, but they have far fewer calories than many of the protein foods we eat. It is the foods we add to them and the fat we fry them in that add the calories.

Potato versatility

A quick glance at a culinary dictionary shows hundreds of recipes for potatoes. Yet beneath the variety is simplicity. Most of them are cooked by everyday cooking methods but they are specially cut or shaped or breaded or dressed and given a special name.

For example, many different kinds of potatoes are really french fries cut in a special way and traveling under different names. Figure 9-2 shows several varieties. They are all cooked in the deep fryer. Their shapes may give them special textures: the thin ones cook to crispness, the larger ones are soft and mealy inside, and the soufflé potatoes, cooked with proper timing and temperatures, puff up to airy nothingness. But basically they are all simply deep-fried potatoes. French fry, by the way is a strictly American term; the French call french fries *pommes frites* (paum freet), meaning simply fried potatoes.

Beneath another group of potato dishes lies the mashed potato. Mix it with egg yolks and butter, pipe it through a pastry bag, and make such classical potato dishes as duchesse, berny, lorette, and dauphine potatoes and potato croquettes. As you can see, once the French accepted the potato they did innumerable things with it, and each time they did something they gave it a new name. As with sauces, hundreds of potato dishes derive from a few simple forms. Let us look more closely at some of them.

French fries

Whatever their cut or style, french fries are prepared by a two-step process, following the general rule for deep-frying of hard vegetables. You partially cook them first, cool them, and then finish-cook them in the deep fryer in small quantities as needed. You can do the partial cooking in water, though it is usually done in the deep fryer at a lower-than-normal frying temperature (300–325°F or 150–160°C). This allows them to cook slowly and cook through. If the fat is too hot the outside of the potato will brown before the middle gets hot enough to cook. French fries are not salted until cooking is complete, since they are not breaded and the salt would break down the fat.

You can use one side of a two-compartment deep fryer for partial-cooking and the other side for crisp-fried finish-cooking at a hotter temperature (325–350°F or 160–180°C), draining and cooling each batch briefly between steps. Or you can partial-cook

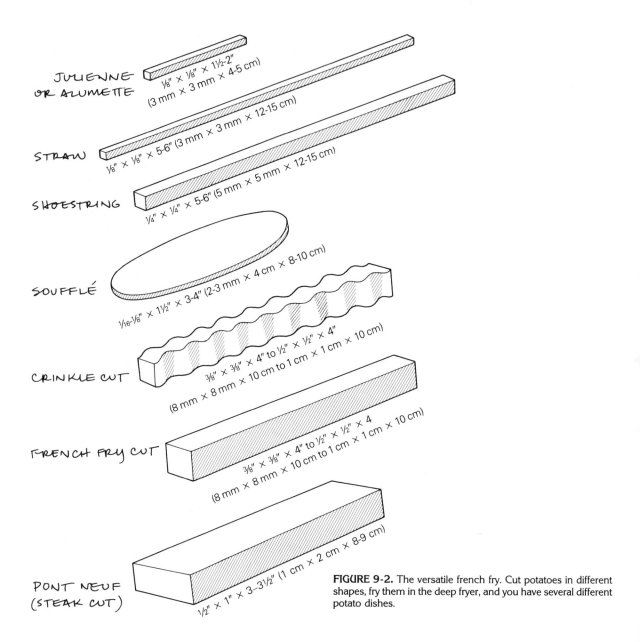

JULIENNE OR ALUMETTE
1/8" × 1/8" × 1 1/2-2" (3 mm × 3 mm × 4-5 cm)

STRAW
1/8" × 1/8" × 5-6" (3 mm × 3 mm × 12-15 cm)

SHOESTRING
1/4" × 1/4" × 5-6" (5 mm × 5 mm × 12-15 cm)

SOUFFLÉ
1/16-1/8" × 1 1/2" × 3-4" (2-3 mm × 4 cm × 8-10 cm)

CRINKLE CUT
3/8" × 3/8" × 4" to 1/2" × 1/2" × 4" (8 mm × 8 mm × 10 cm to 1 cm × 1 cm × 10 cm)

FRENCH FRY CUT
3/8" × 3/8" × 4" to 1/2" × 1/2" × 4 (8 mm × 8 mm × 10 cm to 1 cm × 1 cm × 10 cm)

PONT NEUF (STEAK CUT)
1/2" × 1" × 3-3 1/2" (1 cm × 2 cm × 8-9 cm)

FIGURE 9-2. The versatile french fry. Cut potatoes in different shapes, fry them in the deep fryer, and you have several different potato dishes.

in large quantities, hold them in the cooler or the freezer, and bring them out for finish-cooking in batches as you need them.

Many establishments buy frozen french fries. These are partially cooked, like other frozen vegetables, and are simply given the second half of the two-step treatment.

A good french fry is golden brown, cooked through, nongreasy, crisp on the outside, mealy-tender on the inside, and hot when served. It holds poorly, becoming moist and soggy on the inside while the outside becomes shriveled and dull.

Recipes 9-13 through 9-13b produce

9-13 FRENCH FRIES

Yield: 25 portions

10 lb AP	potatoes	4.5 kg AP

1. Wash and peel potatoes.
2. Cut into strips ⅜″ × ⅜″ × 4″ (8 mm × 8 mm × 10 cm) (or cut julienne for alumette potatoes).
3. Cook in deep fat at 325°F (160°C) until nearly tender. Drain.
4. Finish frying in deep fat at 350°F (180°C) until golden brown. Drain, salt, and serve immediately.

three very different potato dishes using the same product and essentially the same procedures. Recipe 9-13 is the standard procedure for french fries, from julienne on up in size.

A paper-thin cut in 9-13a, on the other hand, gives you a crisp home-style potato chip. Cut the potatoes on the slicer, then soak the slices in ice water to firm them and to remove some of the starch so they will crisp better when they cook. The cold water also keeps them white while being held. Notice that you cook these french fries only once. These chips will retain their texture better than other types of french fry.

Soufflé potatoes (9-13b) depend on precision cutting (use the slicer for these too), precision cooking, and a little bit of luck—even experts often have a few slices that fail to puff. While the potatoes are resting from their first session in fat, they will deflate somewhat, but if their coat of fat is sufficient most of them will puff up nicely in their very hot bath. Kitchen wisdom says that a starchy potato, held in the cooler for several days so the starch will turn to sugar, will give the best results.

Mashed potatoes

Potatoes used for mashing are mealy. They are boiled or steamed to doneness, then beaten in the mixer with butter and cream. The butter and cream should be added only after all lumps have disappeared.

9-13a SARATOGA CHIPS

Yield: 25 portions

10 lb AP	potatoes, washed, peeled	4.5 kg AP

1. Slice potatoes crosswise ⅛–1/16″ (2–3 mm) thick (paper-thin).
2. Cover with ice water for 30 minutes. Drain and dry thoroughly.
3. Fry in deep fat at 350°F (180°C). Drain, salt, and serve immediately.

9-13b SOUFFLÉ POTATOES

Yield: 25 portions

8 lb AP	Idaho potatoes, washed, peeled	3.6 kg AP

1. Trim potatoes into oval shape and slice lengthwise into ⅛″ (3 mm) slices.
2. In heavy saucepan, blanch in deep fat at 275°F (140°C). When potatoes float to top, turn; or shake pan to bathe both sides of each slice in fat.
3. When potatoes begin to puff, remove and drain thoroughly on absorbent paper.
4. Heat fat to *375–400°F (190–200°C) and return potatoes to fat. When potatoes are puffed up and golden brown, drain, salt, and serve immediately.

9-14 DUCHESSE POTATOES

Yield: 25 3-oz (100 g) portions

body	5 lb	peeled potatoes, concassé	2.5 kg	*	nutmeg	*	flavoring
texture	2 oz	butter	50 g	*	salt, white pepper	*	seasoning
	3	egg yolks	3	*	water, lightly salted	*	

1. Cook potatoes to doneness in lightly salted water *to cover.
2. Drain and put back on low heat to dry, stirring constantly to avoid burning, or dry in low-heat oven, stirring frequently.
3. Purée potatoes and blend in butter and egg yolks.
4. Flavor with nutmeg and season *to taste.

9-14a POTATO CROQUETTES

Yield: 25 portions (2–3 pieces each)

5 lb	duchesse potato mixture (9-14)	2.5 kg
*	flour	*
*	egg wash	*
*	bread crumbs	*

1. Using plain-tipped pastry bag, pipe long strips of duchesse mixture on sheet pans dusted with flour. Cut into 2″ (5 cm) lengths; chill.
2. Bread and deep-fry at 350°F (180°C) until golden brown. Drain.

9-14b DAUPHINE POTATOES

Yield: 10 portions (2–3 pieces each)

2 lb	duchesse mixture (9-14)	1 kg
⅔ lb	pâte à chou (15–6)	325 g

1. Fold pâte à chou into potatoes until thoroughly blended.
2. Fill plain-tipped pastry bag with mixture.
3. Hold over 350°F (180°C) deep fat; force out potatoes, cutting 2″ (5 cm) lengths with a knife and letting them drop into fryer.
4. Fry until golden; drain.

Many establishments use instant mashed potatoes to save the time and cost of preparation. To prepare, follow the instructions on the package. Adding the butter and cream and seasoning carefully will improve their flavor. Sometimes prepared instant potatoes are blended with mashed potatoes made from scratch for volume serving, as for banquets when a great quantity is needed at once.

If you use egg yolks instead of cream, you can make the mixture known as **duchesse** (due-shess), which forms the basis of the many mashed-potato dishes mentioned earlier. Recipe 9-14 spells out how it is done.

The duchesse mixture is piped through a **pastry bag** to make the shape called for in a particular dish—round, pyramid, cork-shaped, pear-shaped, crescent, whatever. Figure 9-3 illustrates some of these shapes. Figure 9-4 shows you how to use a pastry bag. Recipes

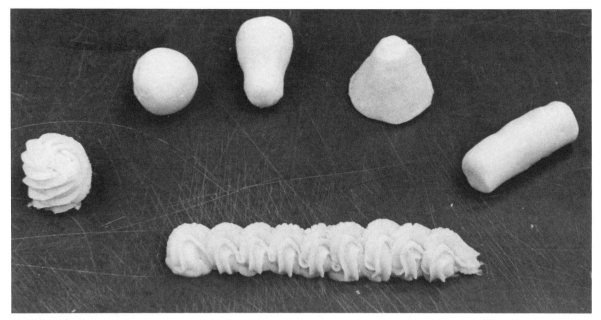

FIGURE 9-3. The versatile mashed potato.

On the left is a duchesse potato. Next are a potato berny and a potato william ready for breading. The two on the right are croquettes, also ready for breading. Down center stage is a potato border. All came from the pastry bag.

The croquettes and the berny and william potatoes were chilled and then smoothed by hand. After breading they will be deep-fried. The duchesse potato and the border will be glazed in the salamander. (Photo by David Mizer.)

9-14a and 9-14b are examples of the many potato dishes you can pipe out of your pastry bag and put on the table.

You can pipe, chill, shape, and bread duchesse potatoes for a particular dish ahead of time and then store them in the cooler or freezer for later finish-cooking. You can prepare several days' supply in this way. Duchesse potatoes will keep for several weeks in the freezer but should not be stored more than a few days in the cooler. A duchesse mixture also comes in instant form.

Good mashed potatoes, whether plain or duchesse, are smooth, free from lumps, fluffy, and mealy. Plain mashed potatoes are moist and thick enough to hold their shape but not so thick that they break apart in chunks. In color they are creamy white with no hint of gray.

Deep-fried duchesse potatoes are golden brown and crisp on the outside with a soft

yellow-white center. A duchesse mixture may be piped as a decorative border to an individual entrée or a presentation platter and glazed under the broiler. In this form it has a light-brown glossy crust atop a soft-textured interior.

Baked potatoes

The baked potato is a truly American dish. A good baked potato is fluffy, white, and mealy, almost dry. To produce such potatoes you rub the scrubbed, dry skins with oil and pierce the ends with a fork or snip them off altogether. Piercing or snipping the ends allows the potatoes to let off steam. You then bake them in a hot (400°F/200°C) oven until they are cooked through.

A certain amount of controversy has raged over whether or not to bake potatoes wrapped in aluminum foil. The anti-foil school of thought has contended that the resulting po-

FIGURE 9-4. How to use the pastry bag.

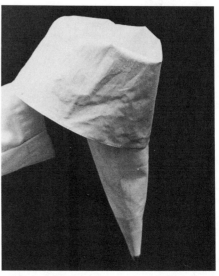

a. The **pastry bag** is a plastic or canvas funnel used to force a soft mass of food into decorative shapes through a pastry tube, or tip, fitted into its small end. An assortment of tubes with different openings make different patterns as the food is forced through.

b. Here is the bag itself, fitted with a tip and ready to be filled. About a third of the top is folded over into a collar. One hand, under the collar, holds the bag open for filling.

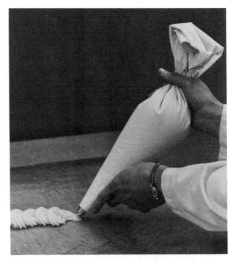

c. The other hand fills the bag, pushing the food down to make a continuous mass with no air pockets. (Fill only enough to handle easily—about one-third full for beginners.) The collar is then turned up, the food is given a final firming down from the outside, and the bag is grasped firmly at the top of the food mass.

d. Here is the bag in action. One hand squeezes the bag down from the top while the other guides the movement of the tip and steadies it. A good product comes from good coordination of pressure and movement. The two hands must work together. The whole process is called **piping.**

The third and fourth shapes in Figure 9-3 were made by pyramiding the potatoes and then shaping by hand. The second and fifth shapes were also hand-finished. The duchesse potato and the border are just as they came from the bag. (Photos by Patricia Roberts.)

9-15 STUFFED BAKED POTATOES

Yield: 10 portions

10	baking potatoes, 6–8 oz (200–250 g) each	10	2 oz	melted butter	50 mL
*	oil	*	4 oz	hot milk or light cream	125 mL
			10	egg yolks	10
			*	salt, white pepper	*
			(*	butter and paprika	*)

1. Wash potatoes well; pierce ends with skewer or fork; oil skin lightly.
2. Place on sheet pan and bake in 400°F (200°C) oven until done (*about 60 minutes).
3. Cut a lengthwise slice off each potato and scoop out pulp.
4. Purée pulp with butter, cream, and egg yolks; season *to taste.
5. Pipe back into shells with pastry bag with star tube. (Sprinkle with additional butter and paprika.)
6. Place potatoes on sheet pan and bake in 400°F (200°C) oven until thoroughly heated.

tato will be moist and soggy because it is cooked by the unreleased steam from its own moisture. Research does not bear this out if the right (nonwaxy) potato is used. In a University of Idaho experiment, baked wrapped and unwrapped potatoes had the same quality, but the wrapped potatoes took 5 to 15 minutes longer to reach doneness. After the potatoes were held for an hour, however, there was a difference: the foil-wrapped potatoes were warmer but less mealy and had begun to discolor. The soggy potato seems to be a holding rather than a cooking problem, and one that is aggravated by foil.

Holding baked potatoes *is* a problem. They take so long to cook that batch-cooking is not often practical, and any baked potato will deteriorate: it loses its fluffy mealiness and becomes moist and soggy, and its white color turns to yellow, gray, and even black. An hour of holding at 180–200°F (90–100°C) should be the limit. A lower holding temperature will not do the trick.

As for the foil, some people think that a foil-wrapped baked potato looks more attractive on the plate than the bumpy, eye-pocked skin of the vegetable itself. However, many diners prefer a nicely browned skin to a plate of aluminum foil.

Some operations solve the holding problem with the microwave. Potatoes are oven-baked to three-fourths of doneness and then refrigerated. Cooking is completed as needed in small quantities in the microwave in a matter of minutes.

Recipe 9-15 offers a delicious way of dressing up the plain baked potato. Add 2 oz (60 g) parmesan cheese to the mixture and you have potatoes jackson. Two ounces (60 g) of chives makes it potatoes georgette. Cooked bacon, mushrooms, or green pepper are other possibilities.

Recipe 9-16 is a different type of baked potato dish. Though it may look formidable, it is easy to make after you have done it once. It has the appearance and texture of fried pota-

9-16 ANNA POTATOES

Yield: 10 5-oz (150 g) portions

4 lb AP	boiling potatoes, round, uniform in size	1.8 kg AP	*	clarified butter	*
			*	salt, white pepper	*

1. Wash and peel potatoes. Cut into thin (⅛–¼″ or 3–6 mm) uniform slices. Hold in cold water.

2. Heat *⅛″ (3 mm) clarified butter in heavy 9″ skillet. Remove from heat.

3. Drain potatoes and dry with towels. Place one slice in center of skillet. Arrange slightly overlapping slices in a circle around the center slice. Reverse direction and arrange another circle next to the first circle. Continue in this way until a single layer of circles covers the bottom of the pan (see picture). Season potatoes and ladle a layer of butter over them.

4. Repeat Step 3 to form another layer; season and butter. Continue to arrange layers in this way until potatoes are mounded higher than top of pan.

5. Place pan over moderate heat until butter sizzles. Shake *lightly* to prevent sticking.

6. Cover skillet with foil and bake in a hot oven (425°F/220°C) until potatoes are tender (*about 40 minutes). Remove foil and continue to bake until golden.

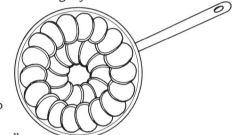

7. Drain excess butter (save for reuse) and invert potatoes onto a sheet pan. Cut round cake into wedges.

   NOTE: Individual portions may be prepared in small pans.

---

toes, but it cooks without attention in the oven, whereas fried potatoes require the cook's active attention. Furthermore, this dish holds very well.

Truly, the possibilities for presenting eye-appealing and palate-pleasing potato dishes are limited only by imagination and sometimes cost.

RICE

On the American menu **rice** is usually used as an alternative to potato when a starchy "vegetable" is desired. Technically it is classed as a cereal because it is the seed of a cereal grain. Rice was one of the earliest foods to be cultivated and is still the chief food eaten in most Asian countries. It contains protein, iron, and important vitamins in significant amounts. The kinds of protein can be paired with vegetable protein to meet nutritional requirements in a vegetarian diet. For example, rice and beans make a good vegetarian entrée, as in recipe 9-3.

Market forms

There are several market forms of rice. There are short-grain, medium-grain, and long-grain rices. The long-grain type best produces the fluffy finished product we are after. If you were cooking Chinese food you might choose the short-grain type for a somewhat stickier product suitable for eating with chopsticks. Medium-grain is somewhere in between.

Then there are enriched white rice, parboiled rice, brown rice, and instant rice. **Enriched white** is rice that has been stripped of minerals and vitamins in milling and then had them restored with a specially enriched coating. **Parboiled rice** is specially processed before milling to retain most of the vitamin-mineral content. **Brown rice** is whole-grain rice still wearing its bran coating with its vitamins and minerals. **Instant rice** is completely precooked. Parboiled long-grain rice is the kind most commonly used in industry.

Cooking rice

The vegetable cook is responsible for rice preparation. The goal of rice cookery is a tender but al dente product in which each grain stands out separately and the whole is fluffy and moist but not sticky.

Rice is always cooked in liquid. This can be done in different ways producing different textures. The **pilaf** method yields a fluffy al dente rice. Various methods of boiling and steaming produce rices ranging from al dente to soft and moist.

In the pilaf method rice and salted liquid in a 1-to-1½ or 1-to-2 ratio (by volume) are cooked covered in the oven. Recipe 9-17 illustrates the method. Liquids used with the method range from water to the best of stocks. The rice absorbs all the liquid, and the grains stand out separately, firm but tender. This method works best with parboiled long-grain rice.

Many combinations of meat or vegetables can be added to pilaf, such as cooked peas, sautéed mushrooms, dried ham or bacon, sliced green onions, pimientos, spinach, raisins, or chopped nuts. One such dish is risi bisi (recipe 9-18). In this instance flavor builders are cooked with the rice, and fresh vegetables, cooked separately, are tossed with the rice at the end of the cooking. The dish is seasoned to taste when done.

A two-step boiling-and-steaming method is occasionally used to cook rice. First the rice is boiled in salted water, using 1 part rice to 2 parts water. When the rice is al dente a third part of water is added. The rice is brought to a boil again; then it is covered and allowed to cook over low heat until all water is absorbed. This produces a very soft, moist rice of the type used in oriental cuisine.

The same result can be achieved in a single step using a cabinet-type steamer and a 1-to-2 ratio of rice and water. The rice grains

---

9-17 RICE PILAF

Yield: 25 4-oz (125 mL) portions

2 lb	rice	1 kg	6 oz	onions, small dice	175 g
2 qt	boiling chicken stock	2 L	*	salt	*
4 oz	butter	125 g			

1. Melt butter in heavy saucepan and sweat onions until translucent. Add rice, stirring until grains are coated with butter.
2. Add boiling stock, salt *to taste, and return to a boil.
3. Cover and bake in 350°F (180°C) oven until liquid is absorbed and rice is tender (*15–20 minutes).

9-18 RISI BISI

Yield: 25 4-oz (125 mL) portions

2 lb	rice	1 kg	6 oz	butter	175 g
2 qt	boiling chicken stock	2 L	4 oz	onions, small dice	125 g
½ pt	cooked green peas, hot	250 mL	1	garlic clove, minced	1
3 oz	pimientos, small dice, hot	75 g	4 oz	ham, small dice	125 g
2 oz	sliced mushrooms, sautéed, hot	50 g	½	bay leaf	½
			*	salt, white pepper	*

1. Sweat onion in butter until translucent. Add rice and stir until grains are coated with butter.
2. Add garlic, ham, and bay leaf. Cook until aroma is evident (*3–5 minutes). Add stock; return to boil; cover.
3. Bake in 350°F (180°C) oven until rice is dry and fluffy (*20–30 minutes).
4. Remove bay leaf. Toss hot vegetables with rice. Season *to taste.

absorb moisture from the steam as well as the water, yielding the same soft, moist rice texture.

Boiling rice is a common method of cooking rice in large quantity. The rice is boiled in a large volume of salted water until tender. The excess water is drained off and the rice is rinsed with cold water until the rinse water runs clear and colorless. This keeps the rice from becoming sticky, but it also washes away the nutrients in the cooking water. It is probably the least desirable method of rice cookery.

Brown rice is cooked in the same ways as white rice, except that it requires more liquid and a longer time—about twice as long. Instant rice is cooked according to the directions on the package.

Wild rice

Wild rice is not a true rice but the seed of a grass that grows wild in the marshes of the Great Lakes region. It is harvested exclusively by Indians of the region, who travel the marshes in canoes and shake off the ripe grains. It has a high price tag and high nutritive value and a strong flavor that goes well with game. Wild rice is often cooked by boiling until it pops open; then it is rinsed, drained, sautéed, and seasoned. Or it may be prepared by washing, soaking, and steaming. It is often served combined with white rice, because it is so expensive. The two kinds of rice are cooked separately and combined after cooking.

PASTA

When we hear the word pasta we relate it quickly to Italian cuisine. Granted, the Italians do have a great deal of pasta in their diet. But a good look at the American menu shows that we too eat a great deal of pasta.

About pasta

In this country **pasta** refers to the large group of products made from a paste of flour and water. We know pasta best in the form of

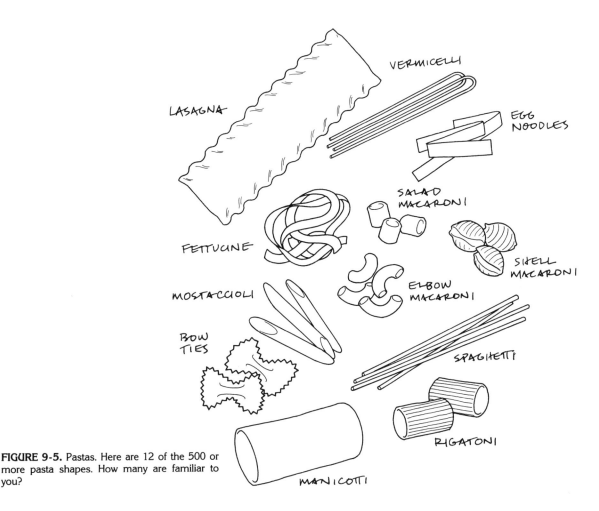

FIGURE 9-5. Pastas. Here are 12 of the 500 or more pasta shapes. How many are familiar to you?

spaghetti, macaroni, and noodles. Pasta is made from hard flours, mainly farina and semolina, which keep the product in shape. The macaronis and spaghettis are flour and water alone. The noodles have egg added. Taking them all together, there are more than five hundred kinds. The differences are mostly in the sizes and shapes of the product, not in their composition. Even the difference between spaghetti and macaroni is one of shape: spaghetti is a string and macaroni is a tube. Figure 9-5 shows some commonly used pasta shapes.

Pasta, like rice, is an alternative to the potato as a menu starch. Combined with other foods it is a popular and versatile low-budget entrée (macaroni and cheese, spaghetti with meat sauce, and many others). Like rice, pasta has several desirable nutrients. Most pasta has been enriched with B vitamins and iron. The flour from which it is made contributes protein. Pasta, like rice, is an important protein resource for vegetarians.

Pastas are usually dried when they arrive in the kitchen. There are exceptions. Ravioli is a soft dough, stuffed with a filling. It may be made in the kitchen or purchased ready-made and frozen. Spaetzle and gnocchi are also soft pasta doughs. Fresh pasta has recently become a popular market form. It is available as

9-19 FETTUCINE ALFREDO

Yield: 12 5-oz (150 mL) portions

3 lb	fettucine, cooked al dente, warm	1.4 kg	1 pt	heavy cream	500 mL	
			3 oz	butter	100 g	*alfredo sauce*
			12 oz	grated parmesan cheese	375 g	
			*	salt, black pepper	*	
			pinch	nutmeg	pinch	

1. Over medium heat, simmer half the cream with the butter until slightly thickened (*5 minutes).
2. Pour butter/cream over warm fettucine; add remaining cream and cheese.
3. Place over low heat and toss to coat fettucine thoroughly with sauce.
4. Add nutmeg and season *to taste. Serve with additional parmesan.

dough or in shapes and comes colored and flavored by eggs, spinach, tomato, or even pumpkin.

Cooking pasta

Pasta, like rice, is prepared by the vegetable cook. The steps are not at all complicated. Here are a few simple rules you should learn for successful cooking:

- Cook in a large amount of water. Use a 4-to-1 ratio (by volume) of water to pasta.
- Use salt and a little oil in the water (1/4 cup of oil to the gallon or 50 mL to 4 L).
- Submerge pasta in water that is already boiling, keeping the pieces separated as much as possible.
- Cook at a boil and stir gently to keep the pieces from sticking to the pan and to each other.
- Always cook al dente, or a little short of al dente if it is to be held. (The term al dente originated with the cooking of pasta.)
- Drain and rinse thoroughly with cold water until the rinse water runs clear.
- If held, coat lightly with oil or butter to prevent sticking.

Learning to identify the point just under al dente is the most important part of cooking pasta. You can do this by pushing it against the side of the pot with a knife or spatula and feeling the delicate balance between resistance and give. Army cooks used to say that if you throw the pasta at the ceiling and it sticks, it's done, but feeling or tasting it is a more reliable test. When you are cooking a big kettleful of spaghetti, it is critically important to open the drain valve at the right time. You can ruin the spaghetti by being a few seconds too late.

To reheat pasta for service you place the amount needed in a china cap or strainer and submerge in hot water.

Pasta is usually served with a sauce that determines the character of the dish. It may be a simple tomato sauce to which various garnitures are added to make different dishes. Or it may be created especially for a given dish, as in recipe 9-19. Add diced cooked bacon and beaten eggs to alfredo sauce and you have carbonara. These dishes may be served as an entrée, or made in smaller portions and served as a first course preceding the entrée.

Contrast the making of the alfredo sauce with the sauce-making of Chapter 8. Here it is made by mixing its ingredients one by one with the food the sauce accompanies. Obviously no other thickening is necessary.

Recipe 9-20 illustrates another popular way of serving pasta. It is stuffed with a hearty filling and covered with a plain sauce. Many shapes of pasta are suitable for filling, and all kinds of fillings may be used. Here is another challenge to the cook's ingenuity.

9-20 MANICOTTI

Yield: 24 portions (2 shells each)

	48	manicotti shells	48	1½ qt	tomato sauce II (8-7)	1.5 L	sauce
filling	4 lb	ricotta cheese	1.8 kg	*	parmesan cheese	*	
	4	eggs	4				
	2 lb	spinach, cooked, well drained, chopped	900 g				
	8 oz	parmesan cheese	250 g				
	*	nutmeg	*				
	*	salt	*				

1. Cook manicotti shells in boiling salted water until al dente. Drain.
2. Mix filling ingredients together. Season *to taste.
3. Using a pastry bag with a plain tip, fill each shell with *3 oz (75 mL) filling and place on lightly oiled hotel pan.
4. Ladle ¾ oz (25 mL) sauce over each shell and sprinkle with parmesan cheese.
5. Bake in 350°F (180°C) oven until filling and sauce are thoroughly heated and cheese is golden (*15 minutes).

SUMMING UP

The menu role of cooked vegetables is usually to accompany the entrée. Their function is to enhance the entrée by providing complementary flavors, textures, visual variety, and additional nutrients, especially vitamins and minerals.

Cooking vegetables is a real challenge to the cook because so many undesirable changes can take place if they are not cooked properly. Colors can change from bright green to olive drab, from white to yellow or gray, and from red to pink, purple, green, and even blue. Fresh flavors can fade or change to something entirely different and unpleasant. Textures can become soft and mushy. Nutrients can be lost. The one single all-embracing rule is: *Do not overcook!*

Because of these hazards of cooking, holding for service is a problem, since at safe temperatures vegetables go on cooking. To minimize these problems, you can cook vegetables in small batches as needed or partially cook them ahead and finish-cook them just before service.

Vegetable cookery utilizes nearly all cooking methods. The method should be suited to the vegetable. Often the choice of method will solve the holding problem.

Vegetables are versatile. Besides the variety you can achieve with different cooking methods, you can combine vegetables, add flavoring ingredients, or add sauces, always keeping in mind the compatability of flavors, textures, and appearance. Properly cooked, vegetables are among the most attractive of foods on the plate, often taking the place of a garnish.

Rice and pasta, like vegetables, often supplement the entrée on the menu. They can, however, assume the entrée role when combined with other foods. This is especially true of pastas, which are only the beginning of many main dishes. Rice and pasta are not difficult to cook; the essentials are to follow the rules and to make accurate judgments about doneness.

The things you can do with five hundred kinds of pasta boggle the mind. The same is true of rice. The same is true of vegetables.

Learn textures, tastes, and cooking methods. Learn what spices enhance what vegetables. Experiment. Use your imagination. You will be in good company. Some of today's best cooks are focusing their efforts on vegetables and the good things that can be done with them.

THE COOK'S VOCABULARY

produce

pigments, anthocyanins, chlorophyll, carotenes, flavones

al dente texture

casserole

gratiné, au gratin

stagger-cook, batch-cook, partial-cook/quick-chill

duchesse potatoes

pastry bag, piping

rice: enriched white, parboiled, brown, instant

pilaf

wild rice

pasta

QUESTIONS FOR DISCUSSION

1. Discuss the importance of color in cooking a vegetable. How would you maintain color when cooking cauliflower? Red cabbage? Spinach? Carrots?

2. Explain the problems in holding cooked vegetables for service, and suggest ways to solve them.

3. How does the potato differ from other vegetables? Explain how differences in cutting potatoes for deep-frying can produce such varied results.

4. Discuss the menu roles of rice and pasta. What nutritional role does rice play when paired with legumes?

5. To what extent are different market forms of vegetables (fresh, frozen, canned) already cooked? How do you deal with the differences when you cook them?

MANY people, when seafood is mentioned, think of rich and exotic dishes dripping with butter, loaded with calories, and available only regionally in expensive restaurants. Others think only of fast-food deep-fried shrimp or fish sticks with catsup on a bun. Yet in between is the whole world of fish cookery. There is something for every type of meal—from the low-budget school lunch to the specialty of the house, from the hospital tray to the charity-ball buffet.

The cook who can prepare fish and sauces well has an inexhaustible source of entrées. They are quick and some are relatively inexpensive, yet they taste delicious, look elegant, and can command a good menu price. Both fish and shellfish also make good appetizers, soups, salads, sandwiches, casseroles, garnishes, and garnitures. Once you know the basic methods of cooking and the strengths and limitations of the product, all these uses are open to you.

This chapter begins our study of the flesh foods—fish, poultry, and meat—the mainstays of the menu. Along with the fundamentals of cooking flesh you will have the fun of learning how to use your stocks and sauces with basic entrées. And then you will *really* be cooking!

After completing this chapter you should be able to

- Understand the special characteristics of fish and explain how these influence fish cookery.

- Describe the different market forms of fish, and specify how to handle, store, and prepare each type for cooking.

- Select fish types and forms appropriate for broiling, baking, deep-frying, poaching, and pan-frying, and describe or demonstrate each process.

- Identify different kinds of shellfish, and specify how to handle, store, and prepare each type for cooking.

- Understand and follow the basic guidelines for fish and shellfish cookery.

10

Fish Cookery

ABOUT FISH IN GENERAL

Fish as a food includes both **fin fish**—the smooth, slippery kind that swim about in fresh or salt water by moving their tails—and **shellfish,** which are fish that have shells. Another term you will meet is **seafood,** which refers to saltwater fish of both kinds. Let us look first at what they all have in common.

There is one thing very special about fish, and that is its delicate and fragile quality. Fish of all kinds have little or no connective tissue, and even the raw flesh is fragile. They have a high moisture content that evaporates readily, carrying much flavor away with it. The flavor of fish is delicate; its texture is ultra-tender if properly cooked; its shelf life is short. Some shellfish are not edible if they die before they are cooked.

You might expect fish to have a strong and indestructible fishy taste, but properly cooked fish tastes like a tender and delicately flavored meat dish. Fresh uncooked fish has a sweet and pleasant odor and does not smell fishy at all. The tastes and odors we call fishy come primarily from fish-oil products and from fish that are somewhat less than fresh.

Getting fresh fish and keeping it edible has always posed a problem. Wealthy Romans raised their own fish in specially built reservoirs or had relays of slaves bring fish fresh from the sea in buckets of water. Medieval monasteries had their own ponds to supply live fish. A Portuguese abbey boasted a trough running from a trout stream right into the kitchen, where a trapdoor could be opened to let in the day's supply. Problems of supply caused one famous tragedy: a fine chef named Vatel, supervising a banquet for Louis XIV, fell upon his sword and killed himself when the fish for the first course failed to arrive in time.

The railroad and the development of canning and refrigeration put most fish within the reach of most places by 1900. A man named Clarence Birdseye completed the process. Fishing through the ice in Labrador, he caught a fish that froze stiff in the cold air before he could get it off his hook. He discovered that such quick-frozen fish, when thawed and cooked weeks later, tasted as though they were freshly caught. In 1930 Birdseye launched the frozen-foods industry. Today you can get almost any fish you want to cook—if not fresh, then frozen or canned.

These delicate creatures are excellent sources of protein. Most of them are low in fat and calories, which makes them very desirable menu items for diet-minded customers. (Of course the ingredients you use with them in preparing menu dishes can pile on the calories quickly.) Many are also good sources of the B vitamin niacin and certain trace elements such as fluoride, iodine (seafood only), and selenium.

HANDLING AND STORING FISH

The handling and storage of fish are of great importance because of the delicate nature of the flesh and the short shelf life of fish products. The fragility of the flesh, the high moisture content, and the readiness with which the moisture evaporates—these characteristics underlie the handling and storing of fish.

Fish do not have to undergo the same federal inspection for product purity and plant sanitation that is required by law for meat, poultry, and eggs. Fresh fish at present are not subject to federal inspection. For many kinds of processed (canned and frozen) fish products voluntary inspection is provided by the National Marine Fisheries Service. Processors who use the service may mark their products "Packed under federal inspection." Voluntary quality grading is also available. Figure 10-1 shows federal inspection and grading marks.

Plants not so inspected are spot-checked periodically by the federal Food and Drug Administration. The less rigid inspection system for fish products means that the cook must take special responsibility for checking fish coming into the kitchen. The buyer for a food-service establishment should specify inspected products when buying items for which inspection is available.

Fish come into the kitchen fresh, frozen, smoked, cured, and canned. Special considerations apply to each form.

Canned fish

Canned fish should always be checked upon receipt to make sure there are no swollen or damaged containers. Swollen cans indicate spoilage. Damaged cans may have air leaks that allow the fish to spoil—and it will spoil quickly. Undamaged goods are kept in dry storage.

Once a can has been opened, its contents will keep two to three days in the cooler. Store the fish in a glass or plastic container, covered tightly so that it will not dry out and will not lend its special aroma to other foods.

Frozen fish

Frozen fish products should be examined immediately to make sure they are solidly frozen when delivered. Then they should go right into the freezer, well wrapped to prevent freezer burn. The flesh of fish does not freeze at 32°F (0°C), the freezing point of water. Store it at 0°F (−18°C) or below. Once thawed, fish should never be refrozen.

The safest and best method of thawing is to let the fish thaw at ordinary cooler temperatures. This may take some time, depending on the size of the frozen item, the temperature of the cooler, and other variables. A common practice is to move the fish from the freezer to the cooler the day before use.

Putting the frozen fish in hot water or soaking it in tepid water is the wrong way to thaw it. These methods encourage bacterial growth by raising the temperature of the fish. They also allow the flavor to drip away and sometimes cause partial cooking.

Another method of thawing is to put the product, in its original wrappings, under cold running water. This is better than soaking but not as safe and satisfactory as thawing in the cooler.

Whenever possible, do not thaw small pieces such as steaks and fillets. As fish thaws

FIGURE 10-1. Federal inspection and grading of fish.

a. Each fish product processed under constant federal inspection is entitled to carry this seal. It certifies that the product is clean, safe, wholesome, properly labeled, and meets commercial standards of acceptability. *b.* This federal grade symbol indicates that the product meets not only all federal inspection standards but top quality standards for uniformity, appearance, and flavor as well.   (Seal and symbol courtesy U.S. Department of Commerce, National Marine Fisheries Service.)

it loses moisture and a great deal of flavor, so cook small pieces such as fillets up to 8 ounces (250 g) right from the frozen state. Once fish are thawed you should treat them like fresh fish, which is what they are.

Many frozen fish products are available that fall into the category of convenience foods, meaning that they have been partly or completely prepared for cooking or service. They range from prebreaded fish fillets or shrimp to finished menu items such as sole florentine or lobster newburg that need only to be heated. Often such items are manufactured to the buyer's specifications. They are widely used in such large institutions as hospitals and restaurant chains where their higher costs are balanced against savings in time and labor, reductions of loss and waste, and consistency of product.

The cook's concern with convenience products is to handle and prepare them properly. Keep them frozen until use. Read the label to see exactly what the product is and how much preparation has been done: for example, is it raw or cooked? Then follow carefully all the standard guidelines for whatever cooking method is to be followed.

Fresh fin fish

Fresh fin fish should come into the kitchen really fresh—as soon as possible after catch and definitely within 24 hours. Since they are not federally inspected it is up to you to know quality and freshness.

Here are some measures of freshness:

- Tight scales
- Bright-pink to red gills
- Clear, almost transparent flesh, firm but elastic to the touch
- Firm adherence of flesh to bone
- Bulging, bright, shiny eyes with an expression of alarm
- Pleasant, sweet smell

As a fish ages, the gill area grays. Scales become loose. Eyes flatten and look dull and expressionless. The flesh is cloudy or milky and pulls easily from the bone. The fish develops a fishy smell.

It is also important for you to check the delivery to see that you get what you ordered. If you order red snapper, for example, and receive flounder instead, you may not be able to make the dish your menu calls for.

Fresh fish should always be stored on shaved or crushed ice in the cooler. Place the fish in drip pans (pans with holes that fit into another pan) so that they do not stand in water as the ice melts. Change the ice daily, discarding the water. Proper storage keeps fish fresh longer and odor to a minimum.

How long fish will stay fresh cannot be stated in absolute terms. If it is not used within two or three days, fresh fish can be cooked and stored in the cooler for a few more days, or frozen and kept for a few weeks.

Market forms of fresh fish. Fresh fin fish are available processed in several different ways. Figure 10-2 illustrates the different market forms.

Whole, or **round,** fish are not processed. They are simply caught, iced, and delivered.

Drawn fish are eviscerated (that is, relieved of their viscera or entrails—gutted), then iced and delivered.

Pan-dressed fish are eviscerated and scaled or skinned. They may also be headless, tailless, finless, boned, or any combination of these less-than-whole states.

A **steak** is a crosscut of the body of a large pan-dressed fish, such as salmon and halibut.

A **fillet** or **filet** (both pronounced fil-lay) is a side of a fish that has been removed from the bones.

Sticks are crosscuts of fillets.

A **butterflied** fish consists of fillets from both sides removed together and still attached to one another.

Processing a whole fish. Although fish is usually bought in the market form in which it is to be used, it is still handy to know how to process a fish from the whole state. If you are going to do this, there are three things you must always keep in mind:

- Cut on a clean surface.
- Use clean knives.
- Clean everything thoroughly after cutting and before other food products are processed at the same station.

The reason for such care is that fish is easily contaminated, spoils quickly, and readily leaves behind these sanitary shortcomings along with its taste and its smell.

Fish have two kinds of bone structure, flat and round, as Figure 10-3 shows. The type of fish you have makes a difference in how you go about processing it, especially in filleting. **Flatfish** such as sole and flounder (*a* in the picture) have four fillets, two on top and two on the bottom. **Round fish** (*b*) have two fillets, one on each side. Figures 10-4 and 10-5 show how to fillet the two types of fish. A knife with a flexible blade is best.

How you intend to serve the fish will determine how much processing you must do. Trout, for example, is usually cooked with the head, tail, and skin left on and needs only to be eviscerated. Large fish are often pan-dressed

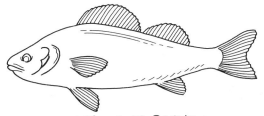

a. WHOLE OR ROUND

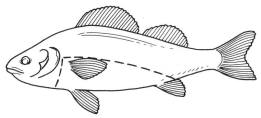

b. DRAWN

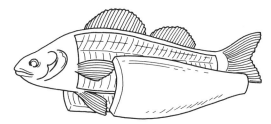

e. FILLETS

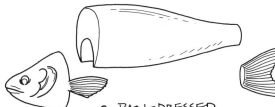

c. PAN-DRESSED

f. STICKS

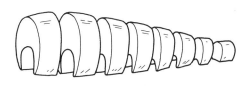

d. STEAKS

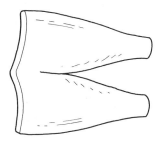

g. BUTTERFLY FILLETS

FIGURE 10-2. Market forms of fresh fin fish.

FIGURE 10-3. Bone structure of fish.

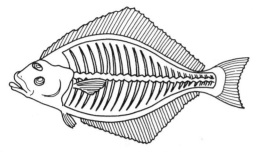 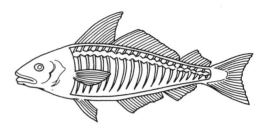

a. This bone structure is characteristic of flatfish, such as sole, flounder, and turbot.

b. This bone structure is characteristic of round fish, such as trout and salmon.

FIGURE 10-4. How to fillet a flatfish.

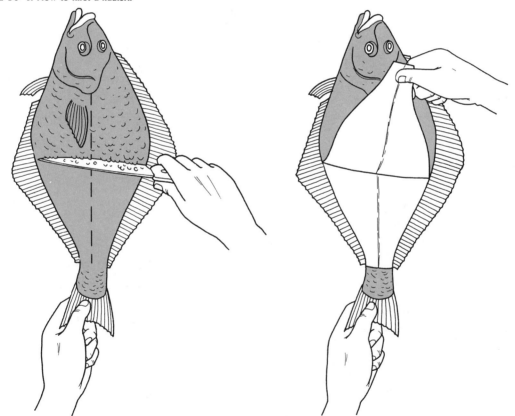

a. If skin is to be left on, scale it by rubbing a knife blade against the scales from tail to head until they flake off.

b. To take the skin off, first cut through it near the tail. Hang onto the tail and pull the skin toward the head.

(skinned, definned, eviscerated) and cooked whole. You can cut off the fins with scissors. To eviscerate, slit open the belly, pull out the sac of viscera, and clean the cavity. To cut off the head, use a cleaver or the big end of your knife blade.

The head, skin, and skeleton of the fish contain a great deal of flavor and are used in making fish stocks. Entrails are discarded.

Smoked and cured fish

A number of popular fish products are smoked or salt-cured or both, or they are dried, pickled, or otherwise treated to enhance their taste and prolong their usability. Smoked salmon, smoked oysters, and lightly smoked and cured haddock—known as finnan haddie—are common. Caviar (salted fish roe) and pickled herring belong with this group of fish foods. Many such products are used as appetizers because of their piquant flavor.

These products come in three forms: canned, frozen, and unfrozen. The canned products keep until opened, the frozen ones until thawed. Unfrozen smoked and cured fish products stay wholesome longer than fresh fish do, but longer should not be confused with indefinitely. A week is safe. They must be kept refrigerated like fresh fish.

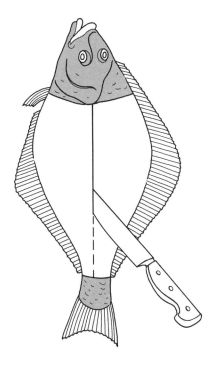

c. To remove the fillets, first cut along the backbone from head to tail. This is the bone running between head and tail along the middle of the fish. A line along the flesh parallels it exactly, so cut along this line.

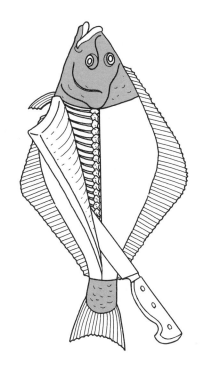

d. Holding the knife flat on the rib bones, cut outward to the edge of the fish. Repeat for the other three fillets.

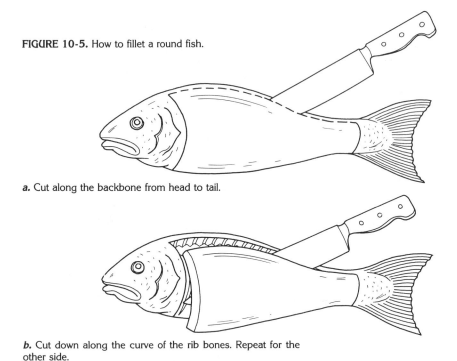

FIGURE 10-5. How to fillet a round fish.

a. Cut along the backbone from head to tail.

b. Cut down along the curve of the rib bones. Repeat for the other side.

We will discuss handling and storing shell-fish later in the chapter.

COOKING FIN FISH

With the cooking of the flesh foods—fish, poultry, and meat—we approach the flavor, body, and texture of foods from a different angle. In soups and sauces these characteristics are built into dishes by the cook. In flesh foods the basic flavor, body, and texture are built into the product by mother nature. The cook's job is to maintain and bring out the best that is there.

In fish this means preserving the delicate flavor, the fragile texture, the succulence, the tenderness by careful cooking with a suitable method. Because fish has so little connective tissue, careless cooking will make it fall apart. Because it has a high and volatile moisture content, much of its flavor can evaporate or drip away. Fish cooks quickly and dries out quickly: as its muscle proteins coagulate they

become hard and chewy. *Overcooking is the most common sin of fish cookery.* Fish is done if it is opaque and gently firm; if it is flaky it is past the point of perfection.

Small pieces of fish need special care, not only because of their fragility and quick cooking but because a single piece may not be the same size throughout. Thus the thin tail of a fillet may dry out during cooking before the thickest part reaches doneness. To avoid this in poaching or baking you can tuck the tail under to equalize the thickness (Figure 10-6a).

Another problem with fillets is their tendency to curl toward the dark, or skin, side of the fillet. One way of dealing with curling is to take advantage of it. This has led to several different ways of presenting the fish to the diner. In Figure 10-6b the raw fillet (fresh or thawed) is folded in thirds with its dark side in. The curling that takes place during poaching holds the fillet in shape. In 10-6c the fillet is rolled, dark side in, into a cylinder shape called a **paupiette** (pope-yet), usually fastened with string or a pick during cooking. You can put another kind of seafood inside, such as an oyster or a piece of lobster or fish meat. Each variation creates a new dish.

In the cooking of flesh foods, seasoning has the same role as it does in soups and sauces: it brings out the food's natural flavors. The big difference in seasoning flesh foods is that seasonings are usually added at the beginning of cooking instead of at the end. This gives them a chance to penetrate the flesh.

For fish one thing is common to all cooking methods—lemon. In fish cookery lemon should become second nature, like putting on your shoes in the morning. Season with it, flavor with it, serve it with the fish. A traditional accompaniment, its sharp taste enhances the delicate, sweet fish flavor.

Almost any cooking method can be used for fish as a class, but few fish can be cooked by almost any method. The choice depends on the nature of the fish, and especially on whether it is fat or lean.

To understand fish cookery let's look first at the fat and lean in fish, and which kinds of fish are which. Then we will see how fat and lean relate to choosing a cooking method, and we will examine the following common methods of fish cookery:

- Broiling and grilling
- Baking
- Deep-frying
- Poaching
- Pan-frying
- Steaming

Fat and lean in fish cookery

A fish is either lean or fat, but you can't tell which by looking at it. Fish do not have the kind of fat covering over the entire body that land animals do. For the most part fat is distributed throughout the fish in the form of oil. On a few fish, such as salmon, you will find a fat layer running along each side. The percent-

FIGURE 10-6. Ways of shaping fish fillets.

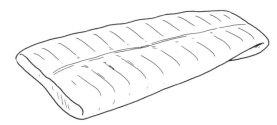

a. Tail folded under for even cooking.

b. Folded in thirds.

c. Rolled (paupiette).

age of fat in a fish may vary from 0.1 to 20 percent.

Table 10-1 lists some common fish and shellfish. You can see from the table that most fin fish and all shellfish are lean. The important thing to understand about fat or its absence in a fish is how it will affect cooking.

Fat fish cook best by such dry-heat methods as broiling, grilling, and baking. Their fat content enables them to tolerate drier heat and longer cooking times or higher temperatures than lean fish can. The dry heat in turn helps to get rid of excess oiliness.

Lean fish cook better by moist-heat methods, such as poaching and steaming, or by

TABLE 10-1 Fat and Lean Fish

Fin Fish	Fat	Lean
Bass (sea)		x
Catfish		x
Cod, scrod		x
Flounder		x
Haddock		x
Halibut		x
Herring	x	
Mackerel	x	
Ocean perch		x
Pompano	x	
Red snapper		x
Salmon	x	
Sole		x
Swordfish	x	
Trout (rainbow)	x	
Trout (brook)		x
Turbot		x
Whitefish	x	

Shellfish		
Clams		x
Crab		x
Lobster		x
Mussels		x
Oysters		x
Scallops		x
Shrimp		x

such quick-cooking methods as pan-frying and deep-frying. These methods enable them to retain their moisture and tenderness. If lean fish are cooked by dry heat—baked or broiled—they must have special treatment to keep them from becoming dry and tough.

Broiling and grilling

Fish are usually broiled in an overhead broiler. This means that they are cooked quickly by direct heat at a high temperature. The fish should be 5 inches (12 cm) or less from the heat source. The high temperature, normally taboo in fish cookery, is offset by the quick cooking. A broiled fish cooks in a very few minutes.

Fat fish pose no problem in broiling. The high oil content in the flesh, plus the short cooking time, keeps them from drying.

Lean fish are not barred from broiling, but they require special care. A lean fish should be coated with butter, margarine, or oil. Watch it closely: it cooks so fast it will dry out before you realize it. Here are the important steps.

- Use steaks or fillets.
- Season before broiling with salt, pepper, and lemon.
- Coat lean fish with melted butter, margarine, or oil before cooking. Often a compound butter is used. For fat fish the butter coating is optional.
- Place on a greased pan, skin side down for fillets. The skin may be left on a fillet to help hold it together. The skin side of a skinned fillet has darker flesh than the bone side.
- Broil on one side only unless fish is very thick.
- Cook only until done. Fish is done when the flesh turns color and becomes opaque, and when it springs back to the touch.

Recipe 10-1 gives you a formula for broiled lean fish fillets. The cod or snapper fillets it calls for are fairly thick. You can substitute thinner fillets such as sole or flounder, but you must watch them carefully because they cook so fast. Recipe 10-1a takes the formula one step further to produce a very tasty dish. You can substitute any other compound butter to produce a variety of broiled and grilled fish dishes. A light topping of bread crumbs and paprika may also be used to coat the top (or presentation) side.

10-1 BROILED FISH FILLETS

Yield: 10 6-oz (175 g) portions

10	6-oz (175 g) fish fillets (red snapper or cod)	10	*	clarified butter or oil	*
			*	salt, pepper	*
			*	lemon juice	*
			(*	paprika	*)

1. Brush both sides of fillets with melted butter or oil. Season *to taste.
2. Place on baking pan; broil at medium-hot temperature till gently firm. If very thick, turn once.

10-2 GRILLED FISH STEAKS

Yield: 10 6-oz (175 g) portions

10	6-oz (175 g) fish steaks (salmon, swordfish, mackerel, halibut, etc.)	10	*	clarified butter or oil	*
			*	salt, pepper	*
			*	lemon juice	*
			(*	paprika	*)

1. Brush both sides of steaks with melted butter or oil. Season *to taste.
2. Place directly on medium-hot grill and broil, turning once. Fish is done when gently firm.

10-1a BROILED FISH MAÎTRE D'HÔTEL

To broiled fish fillets from 10-1, add:

10	½-oz (15 g) slices maître d'hôtel butter (8-11)	10

Place 1 slice of butter on each portion immediately after removing from heat.

10-2a GRILLED FISH STEAKS GRATINÉ

To grilled fish steaks from 10-2, add:

1–1¼ pt	royal sauce:	500–600 mL
	1 part velouté	
	1 part hollandaise	
	1 part whipped cream	

Stripe or cover steak with sauce. Place under salamander till lightly glazed.

Lean fish that are overcooked or held after cooking may curl or dry out. Flavor and appearance diminish with time, so timing of cooking in relation to service is of the utmost importance.

Sometimes steaks from such fat fish as salmon or swordfish are cooked on an open grill with heat from below, as in recipe 10-2. For this method oil or butter must be used to keep the fish from sticking to the grill. The steaks are turned to cook both sides. This type of broiling takes longer than cooking with heat from above. It requires skill to bring the steak to doneness while still keeping it moist and whole. Usually the steak is marked with grid marks as well, a technique explained in Chapter 12.

These fish steaks may be served at once as they come from the grill, or they may be turned into many different dishes by adding sauces or garnitures. Recipe 10-2a is an example. Almost any type of sauce, especially the butter sauces, will complement grilled or broiled fish.

Baking

Baking a fish in the oven, another dry-heat cooking method, is a good deal slower than broiling. Although the cooking temperature is much lower, the longer cooking time in the hot, dry air of the oven can cause lean fish to

10-3 BAKED SEA BASS

Yield: 10 6-oz (175 g) portions

10	6-oz (175 g) portions fresh sea bass	10	*	clarified butter or oil	*
			*	salt, pepper, lemon juice	*
			(*	paprika	*)

1. Place sea bass portions on oiled or buttered baking sheet.
2. Brush with melted butter or oil; season. (Dust with paprika.)
3. Bake in 350°F (180°C) oven until done (*10–15 minutes).

10-3a BAKED SEA BASS PORTUGAISE

To baked sea bass from 10-3 add:

1½ pt	portugaise sauce (8-6c)	750 mL

Ladle sauce over sea bass after baking.

become too dry unless you take special care. So baking is usually more appropriate for fat fish than for lean fish.

Large whole fish or large pieces of large fish are often baked. Salmon and tuna are good examples. To bake a large fish:

- Use fat fish, either whole or in large pieces.
- Season before baking, using salt, pepper, and lemon. If the fish has not been skinned, season the inside of the fish.
- Bake in a moderate oven (350°F or 180°C) until done. The signs of doneness are the same as for broiling.

Portion-size fish pieces are sometimes baked using oil or butter to keep them from drying out. Even lean fish can be baked in this way if they have enough thickness to stand up to the baking process. Recipe 10-3 is a good example. It is important to keep an eye on the fish as it approaches doneness, so that it does not cross that line between tenderness and toughness. Baking small portions of fish is actually very quick, even though it is slower than broiling and grilling. The recipe can also be used for such other fish as cod, snapper, flounder, perch, haddock, and swordfish.

Sauce is often added after baking, as in recipe 10-3a. It is one way of adding visual interest to a flat and colorless piece of fish, and it complements the delicacy of the fish's flavor. The paprika in 10-3 serves the same purpose. Be cautious in using paprika: too much will give a bitter flavor. Other appropriate sauces are creole (8-6b), hollandaise (8-9), and white wine (8-3).

Another oven-cooked fish dish is one in which fillet portions are breaded as for frying, placed on heavily buttered sheet pans, brushed with butter on top, then cooked in a hot oven (380–400°F or 190–200°C) until the crust is crisp. The fish stay moist under the protection of the breading, provided they are not cooked too long. This is a very good way of cooking fish for large-volume production. The result is like fried fish but it can be produced quickly in far greater quantities than it can by either pan-frying or deep-frying.

Deep-frying

Lean fish adapt well to the deep-fry method. The chief reason is that when fish are deep-fried they are either battered or breaded, which helps to retain their moisture and flavor. For the same reason fat fish are not suitable for deep-frying; their fat would be retained and they would taste oily and fishy.

To deep-fry:

- Use small lean fish or portions: shrimp, scallops, clams, oysters, fish sticks, fillets, portion-size pieces of large lean fish.
- Season with salt, pepper, lemon.

10-4 SEAFOOD PLATTER

Yield: 10 portions, 7–8 oz (200–250 g)

body of dish	10	shrimp, medium size, peeled and deveined	10	*	flour	*		breading ingredients
	20	oysters	20	*	egg wash	*		
	10	2–3 oz (50–75 g) fillets (sole, cod, or catfish)	10	*	bread crumbs, cornmeal, or cracker meal	*		
	20–30	clams	20–30	1½ oz	tartar sauce	50 mL		sauce and garnish per portion
				1½ oz	cocktail sauce	50 mL		
				1	half lemon or wedge	1		
				1	parsley sprig	1		

1. Bread all fish items thoroughly.
2. Deep-fry at 350°F (180°C) until golden brown, as close to service time as possible.
3. Arrange on each platter 1 shrimp, 2 oysters, 1 fillet, 2–3 clams. Add sauces in individual cups. Garnish with lemon and parsley.

- Bread or batter.
- Deep-fry at 350°F (180°C) until golden brown.
- Serve at once.

Fish should be fried separately from other foods.

Recipe 10-4 is a well-known deep-fried fish dish—a seafood platter. Any combination of fish and shellfish may be used. The platter should include at least four kinds of fish. The variety offered in a single dish is part of its appeal.

Deep-frying is one of the most popular methods of fish cookery in America today. It is fast and efficient, it is easily mastered by most cooks, and it yields a tasty product.

Poaching

Poaching a fish means cooking it in a flavored liquid at temperatures of 160–180°F (71–82°C). A moist-heat method, it is most commonly used to cook lean fish, but fat fish do well with it too. Poaching cooks a fish gently at low temperatures, yet because it is surrounded by hot liquid it cooks quickly, thus retaining maximum flavor and moisture.

Poaching is often confused with boiling. In fish cookery boiling will cause great flavor losses. The fish flavor will be dissipated in the liquid or evaporated altogether. In addition, the delicate texture of the fish can be damaged. Fish falls apart easily, so the action of boiling water is a natural enemy.

Fish of any size may be poached, either fresh or frozen. Large fish should be thawed before poaching.

Many cooks and connoisseurs consider poaching the best way of cooking fish. Certainly it offers many avenues that other cooking methods don't. For example, poached fish can be served either hot or cold. Another option is the use of the cooking liquid as a vehi-

10-5 COURT BOUILLON

Approximate yield: 2 quarts (2 liters)

1½ qt	water	1.5 L	8 oz	mirepoix, ⅛″ (3 mm) slices	250 g
1 pt	vinegar (or equal parts vinegar and white wine)	500 mL	5–6	parsley stems	5–6
			5–6	peppercorns, crushed	5–6
			½	bay leaf	½
			pinch	thyme	pinch
			2	lemons, thinly sliced	2
			½ tsp	salt	2 mL

Combine all ingredients and simmer *15–20 minutes.

NOTE: For salmon or tuna, red wine may be used in place of white.

cle for adding flavor to the fish. Sometimes a sauce can be made from the cooking liquid, as you will see shortly.

Fish is often poached in a liquid known as **court bouillon** (recipe 10-5). This is a liquid with several flavorful acid ingredients and a number of other flavor builders. It is typically used to poach large whole fish such as salmon or turbot or smaller pieces such as steaks. It may be used to cook fish to be served either hot or cold, but it is not generally used in making sauce.

Usually you should cook the court bouillon before you add the fish. With a little thought you can see the logic of precooking the bouillon. If you intend to extract any flavor from its flavor builders, you must simmer it long enough to allow the flavors to blend. Yet small fish may cook to doneness even before the boiling point is reached. They should be poached in hot precooked bouillon, as in recipe 10-6.

If a fish is large and takes an hour or so to cook, you can cook the court bouillon and the fish together. It will take this long for the court bouillon to develop its full flavor and convey it to the fish.

A large fish is often covered with a poach-

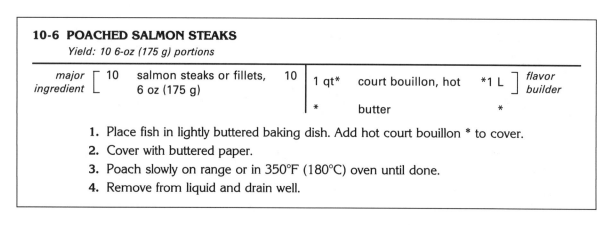

10-6 POACHED SALMON STEAKS

Yield: 10 6-oz (175 g) portions

major ingredient				flavor builder	
10	salmon steaks or fillets, 6 oz (175 g)	10	1 qt*	court bouillon, hot *1 L	
			*	butter *	

1. Place fish in lightly buttered baking dish. Add hot court bouillon * to cover.
2. Cover with buttered paper.
3. Poach slowly on range or in 350°F (180°C) oven until done.
4. Remove from liquid and drain well.

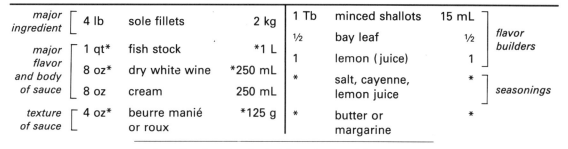

10-7 SOLE IN A WHITE WINE SAUCE

Approximate yield: 10 8-oz (250 g) portions

major ingredient	4 lb	sole fillets	2 kg	1 Tb	minced shallots	15 mL		*flavor builders*
				½	bay leaf	½		
major flavor and body of sauce	1 qt*	fish stock	*1 L	1	lemon (juice)	1		
	8 oz*	dry white wine	*250 mL	*	salt, cayenne, lemon juice	*		*seasonings*
	8 oz	cream	250 mL					
texture of sauce	4 oz*	beurre manié or roux	*125 g	*	butter or margarine	*		

Basic ratio: 4 parts stock / 1 part wine / 1 part cream

1. Coat the bottom of a pan with butter or margarine; sprinkle with shallots.
2. Season fillets *lightly and place in pan with remaining flavor builders. Add wine and stock *to cover.
3. Bring liquid to a boil; then reduce to a low simmer and poach until done.
4. Remove fillets from liquid and add cream to pan.
5. Reduce the combined liquid to *about half its volume.
6. Add beurre manié or roux a little at a time *to produce the desired sauce thickness. Simmer until no flour taste remains.
7. Strain and season *to taste.
8. Coat fillets with hot sauce and serve at once.

ing paper to retard evaporation and help keep the fish intact. Sometimes a whole fish is wrapped in cheesecloth or placed on a rack to keep its shape and to simplify handling.

Cooking a large fish may take anywhere from 20 minutes to an hour and a half, depending on its size. You can tell when a whole large fish is done by squeezing it gently at its thickest part. It should feel firm but not hard. Or you can use a meat thermometer, placing the bulb in the thickest part. Fish is edible at an internal temperature of 140°F (60°C) and begins to break down and lose flavor and juices at 150°F (70°C).

When the fish is done, remove it immediately from the bouillon if it is to be served hot.

If it is to be served cold, stop the cooking at once by adding ice to the court bouillon. Then cool the fish quickly *in the liquid* to keep its moisture and flavor from evaporating.

Small fish portions such as small fillets, cuts of larger fillets, or steaks are frequently poached in a flavorful fish stock with spices and often white wine added. This liquid may then become the body of a sauce to be served with the fish. The classical term for this liquid is **fumet** (fue-may). Recipe 10-7 describes these procedures: they combine flesh cookery and sauce cookery in a single dish. Let us examine the recipe in some detail.

First of all, the amounts marked * are *guideline* amounts. The amount of poaching liquid (stock plus wine) that you will need is whatever will *cover the fish. It will not necessarily be the exact amount given here but may vary with the size and shape of your pan. If you use either more or less, you should increase or decrease the remaining ingredients accordingly to keep the same proportions.

Likewise you may not need exactly 4 ounces of beurre manié or roux. Use what is necessary *to produce the desired sauce thickness.

Now for the steps of the cooking. Step 1 is a method right out of the French kitchen. The shallots add flavor to both fish and sauce. The butter keeps them from burning or sticking to the bottom as the liquid is heated. Of course it keeps the fish from sticking too.

The fish is seasoned only lightly in Step 2 because the seasonings dissolve in the liquid. Since the liquid will be reduced in making the sauce, you want only enough seasoning to bring out the fish flavor without spoiling the sauce.

The other ingredients in Step 2 will function in several ways. The liquid will cook the fish. The wine and stock and flavor builders will also give it extra flavor. At the same time they will build the flavor and body of the sauce to be served with the fish.

Step 3 describes the basic poaching process. You bring the liquid to the point of general agitation, then reduce the heat immediately. The temperature you want will cause bubbles on the pan bottom and slight action in the liquid, but the surface will be calm. The fillets will poach to doneness very, very quickly. They are done when they become firm and opaque and lose their sheen.

While you are cooking the fish you are also beginning the sauce. Its flavors are being blended and the liquid is becoming somewhat reduced. You will not need to make a separate flavor reduction because all the ingredients are already there.

With Step 4 you end the cooking of the fish and concentrate on the sauce. You add cream for body and also because cream is

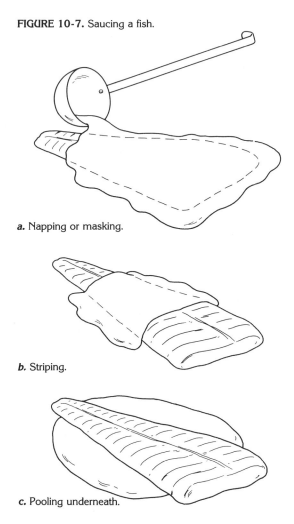

FIGURE 10-7. Saucing a fish.

a. Napping or masking.

b. Striping.

c. Pooling underneath.

always an integral part of a white wine sauce.

In Step 5 you reduce the fumet and cream further for greater flavor concentration. *Half its volume is a guideline figure. To be more precise, you want to end up with 1 to 2 ounces of sauce per serving of fish, so you reduce the liquid to roughly that volume.

In Step 6, you make the sauce as you would a basic velouté, using beurre manié or roux as thickening. Be sure to cook out the raw-flour taste.

Straining and seasoning (Step 7) are the final steps of preparation. Strain the sauce for smoothness. Season it to achieve the flavor most suitable to the fish. A slight taste of lemon does a great deal for fish, so use lemon as much for flavoring as for seasoning.

Step 8 combines both fish and sauce into the final dish. To coat the fish evenly with the sauce is to **nap** or **mask** it. Napping is a special technique: using a single swift stroke, you move the ladleful of sauce above the food from one end to the other, emptying it evenly with a smooth rotation of the wrist. For a traditional poached fish dish the sauce will cover the entire serving. Today the sauce may be served under the fish or as a broad stripe across it (Figure 10-7).

This dish is a sample of what you can do with a poached fish and a sauce made in the same process. Not only does this method capture every bit of flavor from the fish, but it retains the nutrients dissolved in the poaching liquid.

You can go further with this simple beginning. For example, you can create a sole pierre le grand by blending hollandaise with the velouté made in Step 6, folding in whipped cream, napping the fish with the sauce, covering half with chopped ham and half with chopped truffles, and running it all under the salamander for a golden-brown glaze. Any number of different dishes can be made by varying flavor builders, combinations of sauces, and garnitures. Recipes 10-7a and 10-7b give you two popular examples.

Pan-frying

Pan-frying is a common method of cooking fish and a good one. The oil or butter added for frying aids in keeping the fish moist. Lean fish do well with this style of cooking. It is especially good for small whole fish and fillets. Frozen fish should be thawed for pan-frying.

Fish to be pan-fried are first seasoned, then dredged or breaded, and then fried on both sides to a golden brown. The fire under the pan is moderate, and the fish cook quickly. The coating helps them keep their shape and moisture and gives them color.

10-7a PAUPIETTES OF SOLE BONNE FEMME

To recipe 10-7 add:

1 lb	mushrooms, sliced	500 g

1. Add mushrooms to pan with shallots.
2. Form fillets into paupiettes as in Figure 10-6c.
3. Proceed as in basic recipe.

10-7b SOLE FLORENTINE

To recipe 10-7 add:

20 oz	cooked spinach, well drained, buttered, hot	600 g
4–6 oz*	mornay sauce, thick	*125–175 mL

1–5. Follow basic recipe 10-7.
6. Strain reduced liquid; add mornay sauce *to produce desired consistency. Season *to taste.
7. Place fillets on a bed of hot spinach, 2 oz (60 g) per portion. Coat with sauce.
8. Glaze under broiler or salamander until lightly golden.

Pan-fried fish may be served without further elaboration, or they may be embellished in a number of ways. Often they appear on the menu under the name à la meunière. This means they have been dredged in flour and pan-fried in brown butter, with fresh lemon and chopped parsley added at the end. You'll recognize this style from Chapter 8.

A closer look at a meunière trout (recipe 10-8) will not only explain this particular dish but give you a good grasp of the whole pan-frying process. Look closely at each step.

To season the trout (Step 1) you sprinkle salt, pepper, and lemon juice on the inside of the fish. A pan-dressed trout still has its head, skin, and tail, but its fins, bones, and entrails

10-8 TROUT MEUNIÈRE

Yield: 4 portions

4	trout, 8-oz (250 g), pan-dressed	4	1	lemon (juice)	1
			2 Tb	parsley, minced	25 mL
			*	salt, pepper, lemon	*
			*	butter	*
			*	flour	*

1. Sprinkle trout inside with salt, pepper, and lemon.
2. Dredge trout in flour.
3. Pan-fry in butter *¼" (5 mm) deep over low heat, turning once. Use care not to overbrown butter.
4. Remove trout to serving plates. Add lemon juice and parsley to hot pan; deglaze pan and cook mixture a few seconds.
5. Pour butter mixture over trout and serve at once.

10-8a TROUT BELLE MEUNIÈRE

To recipe 10-8 add:

4 oz	sautéed mushrooms	125 g

Add mushrooms to pan in Step 4 of recipe.

10-8b TROUT AMANDINE

To recipe 10-8 add:

4 oz	sliced or slivered almonds, toasted	125 g

Add almonds to pan in Step 4 of recipe.

have been removed. The seasoning would not penetrate the skin to season the flesh.

Dredging the trout (Step 2) is no different from dredging other products. The only caution is to dredge just before cooking so that the flour does not have time to become soggy.

In Step 3 you use butter as the frying fat, with a low heat to keep the butter from burning. For this dish you want the butter to develop a golden-brown color during cooking (*beurre noisette*). Many pan-fried dishes are prepared with half butter and half oil, which can be cooked over moderate heat without burning.

Pan-frying is defined as cooking to doneness in a small to moderate amount of fat in a pan over moderate heat. Doneness for the pan-fried fish happens quickly, as one student discovered who went off to make a phone call while the fish was cooking.

As the fish approaches doneness the translucent flesh turns an opaque white. You can see this on the trout by examining the inside. When the flesh is all opaque and the texture is gently firm the fish is done. If the texture becomes hard the fish is overdone.

If you have a big fish and the butter is beginning to get too brown before the fish reaches doneness, you can put the whole pan in the oven for a few minutes. This will finish the cooking without further browning the butter. Then return the pan to the range and go on with Step 4.

The lemon juice in Step 4 is used to deglaze the pan and salvage all the flavorful buttery juices. The lemon and parsley contribute extra flavor. The parsley is added after the fish is cooked because it might burn if added sooner.

In Step 5 the butter is put back over the trout to add both flavor and moisture. If you don't like the vacant eye staring at you from the plate, you can cover it with a slice of lemon as a garnish.

Many other items can be sautéed and added to pan-fried fish, as is done in recipes 10-8a and 10-8b. As usual, the name of the dish changes with each addition—à la belle meunière with the mushrooms, amandine with the almonds. Many other classical garnitures may be used. You can substitute other fish in the recipes—sole, flounder, perch, snapper, and other white fish.

At the other end of the scale of elegance and range of price, cooked fish may be mixed with duchesse potatoes and pan-fried as fish cakes for a delicious luncheon dish (recipe 10-9). This is a popular dish in some types of operation and a good way to use canned fish or high-quality leftovers. Crab cakes and codfish cakes make good regional house specialties, but any cooked fish may be used.

Steaming

Fish are seldom cooked in a cabinet steamer: they tend to overcook in its high heat, and their flavor leaches out. There are, however, delicious ways of steaming them in their own juices. One of these is to cook them in a covered pan with just enough hot butter, oil, or liquid to trigger the release of their own flavorful moisture in the form of steam.

Another way is to enclose each individual portion of fish tightly in parchment paper and bake it in a hot oven. This cooking method is called **en papillote** (on pop-ee-yote). Again it is the fish's own moisture that steams the flesh to doneness. This method can produce some of the tastiest fish dishes imaginable, as every bit of the fish's own special flavor is captured

---

10-9 FISH CAKES

Yield: 25 5-oz (150 g) portions (2 cakes 2½ oz or 75 g)

4 lb	fish, cooked and flaked	2 kg	(4 oz	green pepper brunoise, sautéed	125 g)
4 lb	duchesse potatoes (9-14)	2 kg	(4 oz	onion brunoise, sautéed	125 g)
			(*	nutmeg	*)
			*	salt, white pepper	*
			*	standard breading ingredients	*
			*	oil	*

1. Mix well fish, potatoes (sautéed pepper, onion, and nutmeg). Season *to taste.
2. Shape into 2½-oz (75 g) patties and chill until firm. Bread.
3. Pan-fry in *⅛" (3 mm) oil over moderate heat until well browned and heated through. Drain well.

10-10 POMPANO EN PAPILLOTE BELLA VISTA

Yield: 10 portions, 6–7 oz (175–200 g)

10	pompano fillets, 6–7 oz (175–200 g)	10	1 oz	minced shallots	25 g
*	melted clarified butter	*	*	chopped parsley	*
			10	bell pepper slices, ¼″ (5 mm)	10
			10	onion slices, ¼″ (5 mm)	10
			10	tomato slices, ¼″ (5 mm)	10
			10	lemon slices, thin	10
			*	salt, white pepper	*

1. Cut parchment paper in a heart shape large enough for a fillet to fit on one side with ½″ (1 cm) to spare all around. Oil the paper.

2. Place a fillet on one side of heart (see diagram). Brush with melted butter, season, and sprinkle with shallots and parsley.

3. Overlap 1 slice each of pepper, onion, and tomato across fillet lengthwise. Center lemon slice on top.

4. Fold empty side of heart over fillet and begin making small overlapping folds around edge to enclose fish tightly (refer to diagram).
   Fold point under to hold in place.

5. Place half hearts (papillotes) on lightly oiled sheet pan.

6. Bake in hot oven (400–425°F/200–225°C) until paper is puffed and brown (no more than *5–8 minutes).

7. To serve, slide portion onto plate and cut open in front of customer.

and blended with the butter, lemon, and other added flavor builders. The paper envelope is opened at the table when served, and the delicious aroma is released to add to the diner's anticipation and pleasure.

An example of this cooking method is given in recipe 10-10. Pompano en papillote is a famous dish and can be made in many other versions by using such flavor builders as herbs, anchovies, shrimp, or crabmeat. It can also be made with other fish such as mackerel or with less expensive fish such as sole or flounder.

One of the problems in preparing this dish is that you cannot see the fish itself to tell when it is done. This is the reason for the time guide-line in Step 6. You would use the lower limit for thin fillets such as sole or flounder and the higher limit for thicker pieces.

You can substitute foil if you do not have parchment paper, folding it carefully in the same way so that no steam escapes. But you will lose the doneness clue of having the paper puffed and brown.

Shellfish are also steamed in their own juices by cooking them in their shells. We'll look at that process when we discuss shellfish cookery.

Quality standards and guidelines

Cooked fish should be moist, sweet, and tender. They are done when they are opaque and gently firm. Fish that is flaky is still edible but has gone beyond perfection. Dry, chewy fish is unacceptable.

Fish should be served as soon as possible, or it will lose the qualities that make it perfect. Presentation is important: a pale, flat fish on a plate needs something to give it height and color—a garnish or garniture, a sauce, a contrasting accompaniment. Butter sauces go especially well with fish. Gratinéing is another way to add color. Lemon is a must, both in cooking and in presentation.

But no matter how elaborate the dish or what you do to dress it up, preserving the fish's own flavor, body, and texture underlies the quality of the product you serve.

HANDLING AND STORING SHELLFISH

Types of shellfish

Thus far we have talked mostly about fin fish. Shellfish are different creatures. Figure 10-8 shows the most commonly served shellfish.

Some shellfish live inside a pair of shells, as clams, oysters, mussels, and scallops do, or underneath a single shell, as the abalone (ab-a-lo'-nee) does. These are **mollusks.** The whole clam or oyster or mussel is edible, but what we eat as a scallop is only the muscle that opens and closes its shells. The shells themselves are often used as dishes for vari-

FIGURE 10-8. Commonly used shellfish.

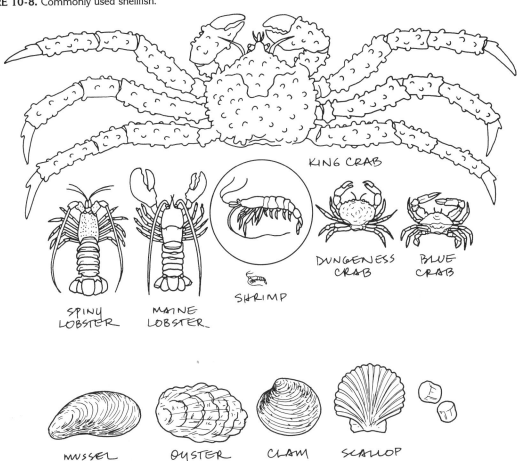

KING CRAB

SPINY LOBSTER

MAINE LOBSTER

SHRIMP

DUNGENESS CRAB

BLUE CRAB

MUSSEL

OYSTER

CLAM

SCALLOP

Handling and storing shellfish / 255

ous sauced fish delicacies, which are then called **en coquille** (on ko-keel). Abalone steaks are also only one muscle, sliced and pounded thin.

Other kinds of shellfish wear jointed suits of armor. These are **crustaceans** (krus-tay-shuns). The ones we eat are crabs, lobsters, shrimp, and crayfish. Shellfish of both types have a prominent place in fish cookery, and they have characteristics all their own.

Shellfish enter the kitchen in three forms—fresh, frozen, and canned. Canned shellfish are treated like any other canned fish. Some frozen shellfish come in cans; they are treated as frozen products, not as canned goods.

Frozen shellfish

Frozen shellfish come both raw and cooked. Crustaceans come both with and without their shells. All kinds should be stored at 0°F (−18°C) or below.

Frozen cooked shellfish such as shrimp and crab are often used after thawing without further cooking or heating. Thaw them in the cooler and serve them immediately to prevent loss of moisture and flavor. If allowed to stand, these products dry out rapidly.

Frozen raw shellfish can often be cooked without thawing. They will taste better because there will be no drip loss of flavorful juices.

Fresh shellfish

Fresh shellfish have special requirements. Most of them must be alive at delivery to ensure quality. If they aren't alive you can't tell how long they have been dead, and they deteriorate almost instantly. Some kinds must be alive until cooked or eaten. The flesh of a dead lobster falls apart when cooked.

So check at once upon delivery. Here are the signs of life.

- Shells tightly closed on oysters, mussels, and clams. If a shell is open, joggle it. If the fish is alive it will close the shell. If the shell stays open the fish is not fit to eat.

- Visible life in lobsters and crabs.
- Pleasant, sweet smell for all kinds.

Store live shellfish in a cool wet area and maintain life by keeping them wet. Leave them in the seaweed or wet sacks in which they arrive. Do not put clams, oysters, and mussels in fresh water. Oysters will keep two or three weeks if properly stored. Some of our ancestors used to keep an oyster barrel in the root cellar as part of their supplies for the winter.

Some establishments that serve lobster regularly have found it profitable to install salt-water holding tanks to keep the lobsters alive until use. Often the customers pick out their own lobsters from the tank, then meet them a short time later on the table, transformed.

Oysters, clams, and mussels in the shell should be scrubbed well before use—the shells, that is. The clam spent its life half buried in the sand and may have brought a good deal of it along. The clam will rid itself of this sand if you put it in several changes of salt water for 15 or 20 minutes at a time: it has a set of siphons that pull water in and out. Or you can sprinkle cornmeal in a pail of clams submerged in brine and let them sit in the cooler for 3 to 12 hours. The same treatment is necessary for mussels. Rinse the shells with fresh water before use.

Clams and oysters are removed from their shells, or **shucked,** by prying the shells open with an oyster knife. It isn't easy, because the live little fellow inside clams up and hangs on. Figure 10-9 illustrates the technique of shucking oysters. Mussels are not shucked, but the "beards" hanging out of the shell are removed.

Clams and oysters are often served raw on the half shell as appetizers. In the nineteenth century oysters with champagne were status symbols for the rich. At the same time they were being peddled to the poor on the streets of London and large American cities—"all you can eat for 6 cents."

Oysters and clams may also be bought already shucked, either fresh or frozen, in con-

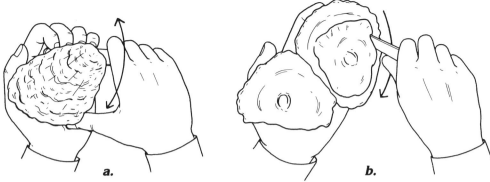

FIGURE 10-9. How to shuck oysters. **a.** Insert an oyster knife between the shells at the hinge and twist to pry open. Cut the muscle away from the upper shell, keeping the knife close to the shell to avoid piercing the juicy body. **b.** Open the shell and cut the muscle away from the bottom shell.

FIGURE 10-10. How to peel and devein shrimp.

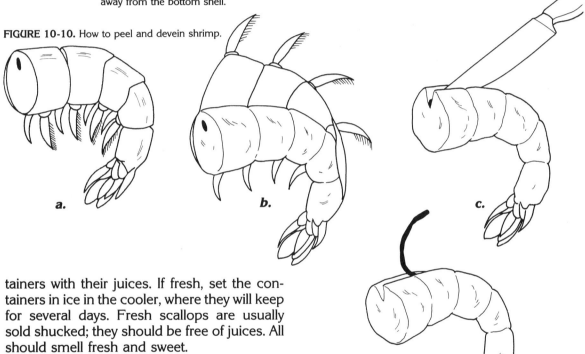

tainers with their juices. If fresh, set the containers in ice in the cooler, where they will keep for several days. Fresh scallops are usually sold shucked; they should be free of juices. All should smell fresh and sweet.

Shrimp do not arrive live. The fishermen cut their heads off right on the shrimp boat, or else this is done in the packing plant. They may be bought raw in their shells—called **green**; or **P&D**—peeled and deveined; or **PDQ**—peeled, deveined, and quick-frozen; or **IQF**—individually quick-frozen. They are purchased by **count per pound**—the higher the count per pound, the smaller the shrimp.

Cook green shrimp in the shell for greatest flavor. Figure 10-10 shows how to peel and devein them.

a. Headless shrimp with shell on. **b.** Pull off the shell beginning at the leg side. It will come right off. **c.** To devein, cut along the curved surface to the black vein, which is the intestine. **d.** Pull the vein away or run a knife tip under it.

10-11 BOILED SHRIMP

Yield: 3 servings of 6 each

1 lb	shrimp (15–20 count)	454 g	½	lemon, sliced	½	
1 qt	liquid:	1 L	½	bay leaf	½	
	4 parts water		2 oz	carrot, sliced	60 g	
	1 part wine		4 oz	onion, sliced	125 g	flavor builders
			5–6	parsley stems	5–6	
			5–6	peppercorns	5–6	
			pinch	thyme	pinch	
			(*	other spices	*)	
			½ tsp	salt	2 mL	

Basic ratio: 1 qt liquid / 1 lb shrimp
1 L liquid / 454 g shrimp

1. Add flavor builders to liquid.
2. Bring to a boil; reduce heat and simmer a few minutes.
3. Add shrimp. Bring back to boiling point but do not boil.
4. As soon as shrimp are firm remove from hot liquid. Do not overcook! Plunge into ice water if shrimp are to be served cold. Serve immediately if they are to be served hot.

COOKING SHELLFISH

Steamed clams, boiled shrimp, boiled live lobster—these terms express two things common to all shellfish cookery: moist heat and low temperatures.

Shellfish are all very lean. Dry heat, high heat, and long cooking times will make them tough and rubbery. Ideally they should be either steamed or simmered in the temperature range of 190–210°F (90–99°C). All shellfish cook very quickly.

"Boiling"

Although boiled shrimp is the accepted term for shrimp cooked in hot liquid, the cooking method is really simmering. Recipe 10-11 is a formula for boiling shrimp. You will probably notice immediately how similar it is to poaching fish in a court bouillon. The method is essentially the same with a different liquid and different flavor builders and a somewhat higher temperature. You cook the liquid and flavor builders for a few minutes before adding the shrimp, in order to blend and develop flavors. Then you cook the shrimp at a simmer only until they are done.

Use this method for either green or peeled shrimp. Cook green shrimp in the shell; the shells have a great deal of flavor.

Boiled live lobster is cooked in the same way. You plunge the lobster headfirst into enough boiling salted water to cover (it dies immediately). Bring the liquid back to the boiling point, then reduce it to a simmer. The greenish-brownish shell turns bright red as it cooks. A 1-pound (454-g) lobster (called a chicken lobster), the normal size for one serving, will take only 6 to 8 minutes of simmering.

When the lobster is done, remove it immediately from the cooking liquid, cut it in half (lay it back side down and use a heavy knife), and crack the claws. Serve at once with lemon and a dish of melted butter. The guest dips bits of lobster in the butter.

The "boiling" method can also be used for live crab and crayfish. Simmering time is adjusted to the size of the fish. Crab shells are cracked for service.

Steaming

Steaming is a good, quick, moist-heat method for certain forms of shellfish. It is an excellent way to prepare lobster tails. The tails come frozen and must be thawed shortly before cooking. Recipe 10-12 shows how they are prepared by steaming. Let us look at each step in detail.

Step 1: Figure 10-11 shows how to **saddleback** the lobster tail.

Step 2: The seasoning is done at this point so that it will penetrate the flesh during cook-

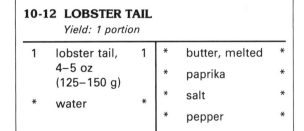

10-12 LOBSTER TAIL
  Yield: 1 portion

1	lobster tail, 4–5 oz (125–150 g)	1	*	butter, melted	*
*	water	*	*	paprika	*
			*	salt	*
			*	pepper	*
			*	lemon	*

1. Saddleback the lobster tail.
2. Sprinkle with seasonings, coat with melted butter, and sprinkle with paprika.
3. Place in a pan with a small amount of water (*½–¾″/1–1½ cm deep). Cover and steam until done.
4. Serve immediately.

ing. Butter is added for both visual and taste appeal; paprika is largely for looks.

Step 3: The function of the water is to create steam in the covered pan, not to boil the fish. Since the flesh has been placed on top of the shell, it is not immersed in the water. "Done" is when the flesh is firm and opaque. It takes only a few minutes.

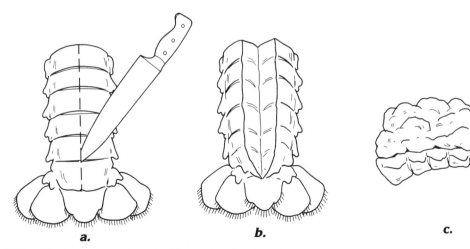

FIGURE 10-11. How to saddleback a lobster tail. *a.* Cut through the top shell of the tail (dotted line). *b.* Spread the shell open. *c.* Pull the flesh out and arrange on top of the shell.

10-13 BROILED SHRIMP, SCAMPI STYLE

Yield: 10 portions (5 pieces each)

50	shrimp, P&D (16–20 count), tails left on	50	8 oz	clarified butter	250 mL
			½ oz	puréed garlic	15 mL
			1 oz	lemon juice	25 mL
			(1 oz	white wine	25 mL)
			*	chopped parsley	*
			*	salt, white pepper	*

1. In small casseroles, place 5 shrimp per portion with tails up.
2. Sauté garlic in butter until aroma is evident. Add lemon juice (and wine). Season *to taste.
3. Pour butter sauce over shrimp and cook under broiler at medium heat until shrimp are done (pink and firm). Sprinkle with chopped parsley.

Step 4: Serve at once for flavor and eye appeal. Lemon and melted butter (drawn butter, *beurre fondu*) are indispensable accompaniments to plain hot lobster meat no matter how it is cooked.

Clams are cooked by steaming in their shells, either in a cabinet steamer or in a covered stockpot on the range with a small amount of water on the bottom. The shells open when they are done. Serve them in the shell along with a cup of the rich broth that results from their cooking. Do not season them. Mussels are also steamed in this way, often using a flavored cooking liquid similar to a court bouillon.

Other methods of cooking shellfish

Broiling and baking, although dry-heat methods, may be used with care and plenty of butter for whole lobster, lobster tails, and oysters and clams on the half shell. The main thing is to cook them quickly with added moisture. Oysters baked in their shells were part of the first Thanksgiving dinner; in this cooking method the oysters provide their own moisture. It is really steaming rather than baking.

The popular "broiled live lobster" of the menu card is really cooked by a two-step method. The lobster is first "boiled" live, then split open, coated with melted butter, sprinkled with paprika, and glazed under the salamander.

Another broiled seafood dish is broiled shrimp scampi style (recipe 10-13). In this procedure the shrimp are literally immersed in garlic butter as they cook. The tails stiffen and stand up, providing a handsome and striking presentation for this rich dish.

Scallops may also be broiled in casseroles using the techniques of the shrimp scampi recipe. They are covered with a layer of bread crumbs before the garlic butter is poured over them, which gratinées as they are broiled. The crumbs also protect them from high heat and moisture loss.

Scallops may also be sautéed (recipe 10-14)—still another method for cooking seafood. The secret here is very quick cooking in butter and oil. Herbs and wine provide a rich and special taste.

Another famous seafood recipe—coquilles st. jacques—blends a number of cooking methods and techniques. Recipe 10-15

10-14 SAUTÉED HERBED SCALLOPS

Yield: 10 6-oz (200 g) portions

3¾ lb	scallops	1.8 kg	4 oz	butter	125 g
			1 oz	olive oil	25 mL
			4 oz	white wine or sherry	125 mL
			4 oz	chives	125 g
			4 oz	chopped parsley	125 g
			*	salt, white pepper	*
			*	flour or dry bread crumbs	*

1. Dredge scallops in flour or bread crumbs.
2. Heat oil and butter in a sauteuse and sauté scallops over high heat until lightly golden on all sides (*1 minute). Remove scallops from pan and keep warm.
3. Deglaze pan with wine. Add chives and parsley and pour over scallops. Season *to taste. Serve at once.

10-15 COQUILLES ST. JACQUES

Yield: 10 5-oz (150 g) portions

major ingredient	3 lb	scallops	1.5 kg	½ lb	mushrooms	250 g	flavor builders
sauce	1¼ qt	fish velouté, hot	1.25 L	1 oz	minced shallots	25 g	
				4 oz	lemon juice	125 mL	
liaison	¾ pt	heavy cream	375 mL	8 oz	white wine	250 mL	
	3	egg yolks	3	*	salt, white pepper	*	
				(*	parmesan cheese	*)	
				4–6 oz*	melted butter	*125–175 mL	

1. Sauté mushrooms and shallots in butter (*⅛"/3 mm deep in pan) until light golden.
2. Add scallops and extra butter if needed. Cook until scallops *begin* to firm and change color.
3. Add lemon juice and wine, deglaze pan, and simmer until liquids are reduced by one-third.
4. In another pan, temper liaison into hot velouté. Add to scallop mixture. Season *to taste.
5. Place portions in individual shells (coquilles) or small casseroles. (Sprinkle with cheese.) Gratiné under broiler or salamander.

10-16 SEAFOOD NEWBURG

Yield: 10 7-oz (250 mL) portions

2 lb	cooked lobster, crab, shrimp, and scallops, mixed	900 g	2–4 oz*	clarified butter	*50–125 mL
			½ oz	paprika	15 g
2 qt	cream sauce (8-1a)	2 L	4 oz	sherry	125 mL
			1 oz	lemon juice	25 mL
			*	salt, white pepper	*

1. Sauté cooked seafood in *⅛″ (3 mm) butter until hot.
2. Add paprika, sherry, and lemon juice; mix well.
3. Add cream sauce. Bring to a simmer. Season *to taste.

shows you how the dish is built. It begins by adding the scallops to sautéed flavor builders for very brief cooking. The pan is then deglazed with wine and lemon juice and the liquids are reduced, during which the scallops finish cooking by simmering. They are then combined with a liaison-enriched sauce, portioned into scallop shells, and gratinéed. They may be further embellished with cheese. Obviously the scallops must be watched at each step in order not to overcook them.

Cooked seafood may be turned into still another famous dish by combining with a sherried cream sauce. Recipe 10-16 offers a simple way to do it. This memorable combination of flavors may be served in small casseroles or patty shells, on toast, or in a rice ring.

A richer version adds a liaison of cream and egg yolks to the simple cream sauce.

There is scarcely any limit to what you can do in building mouth-watering, calorie-laden, profit-producing shellfish dishes. But underneath everything you do in cooking these delectable creatures are five simple things to remember.

- Shellfish are very lean.
- Moist-heat methods are best.
- Quick cooking is best.
- Lemon should be part of cooking and service.
- Shellfish should be served immediately.

SUMMING UP

Fish is one of the trio of flesh foods (fish, poultry, meat) that form the backbone of the American menu and provide much of the protein in the typical American diet. Cooking these foods is rather different from making a soup or a sauce: instead of building flavor, body, and texture, these characteristics are a natural part of the product, and the cook's job is to preserve and enhance them.

The flavor, body, and texture of all kinds of fish and seafood are delicate and fragile. In flavor, fish is delicate and sweet. It has a high water content that readily evaporates, carrying much flavor with it. In body, fish has little connective tissue, which makes it fall apart easily unless gently handled and gently cooked. It cooks quickly: its muscle tissue coagulates readily and it is done when opaque and gently firm. In texture, fish is tenderness itself if cooked quickly at low temperatures. If overcooked, its texture becomes tough, dry, and chewy.

The choice of cooking methods for a particular kind of fish depends on what will best preserve and enhance its flavor, body, and texture. This depends partly on the fat content of the fish. Fat fish may be cooked with either moist-heat or dry-heat methods. Lean fish do best with moist-heat methods but may be broiled, baked, or fried if protected by butter or oil or a coating of some kind.

All kinds of fish respond especially well to the use of lemon. They are also compatible with many flavor builders, especially wine, butter, mushrooms, herbs, and sauces. As a menu item fish is versatile: the same fish may be prepared in many different ways, and a given recipe can be varied by substituting different fish.

If you understand fish cookery you are well on the way to understanding the handling and cooking of all flesh. The effect of heat on flesh, the importance of moist and dry heat, and the special concepts of doneness all apply to cooking poultry and meats as well as fish. Each type of flesh cookery has special twists of its own, however, and we'll pursue these in the next chapters.

THE COOK'S VOCABULARY

fish, seafood, fin fish, shellfish

market forms: whole, round, drawn,
    pan-dressed, steaks, fillets, sticks,
      butterflied, convenience

flatfish, round fish

fat fish, lean fish

court bouillon, fumet

paupiette, en papillote, en coquille

nap, mask

mollusks, crustaceans

shuck (clams, oysters)

shrimp: green, P&D, PDQ, IQF

count per pound

saddleback (lobster tail)

QUESTIONS FOR DISCUSSION

1. How does the cooking of flesh foods differ from the making of soups and sauces? Explain why product knowledge is so important in cooking flesh foods.

2. What are the major considerations in cooking fish? In choosing a cooking method, what difference does it make whether a fish is fat or lean?

3. Suggest ways of preparing and presenting fish to compensate for their flat, colorless appearance.

4. How do shellfish differ from fin fish? What are the best cooking methods for shellfish?

A bird in the hand is worth two in the bush. So goes the ancient proverb. You might say that poultry consists of birds in hand, since poultry is raised to be eaten. The two in the bush that the hunter hopes to bag are game.

Early human beings recognized the advantages of the bird in hand when they gave up nomadic life and settled down to raise their own food. Thousands of years ago they tamed the jungle fowl of India, ancestor of today's chicken. Indians in ancient Mexico tamed the wild turkey.

By the time of the great Middle East civilizations not only did the well-to-do have birds in hand but these birds were being specially fattened to satisfy gourmet tastes. "Fatted fowl" was part of the daily fare at King Solomon's court. Peacocks were raised in the Egyptian empire and geese were force-fed to produce *foie gras* (fwah grah), the fat goose liver that has remained a symbol of elegant cuisine. The Roman pigeon had its wings clipped or its leg broken to keep it quiet while it was fed chewed bread to fatten it.

Birds raised for today's market lead similarly restricted lives devoted to getting fat quickly. Confined in small cages and fed special high-vitamin health diets, tender-fleshed chickens and ducklings are ready for market in a matter of weeks, turkeys in four to seven months. So efficient has the poultry industry become that these specially nurtured birds with flesh fit for a king's table are among the most economical of protein foods on the market. And they are universally popular. Americans eat billions of pounds of poultry in a year.

High popularity, high protein, and low price make poultry a good item on any menu, whether for the low-budget school or hospital or the profit-oriented restaurant. In addition it is versatile. It adapts to almost any cooking method. Hundreds of different dishes can be made with it, from fast-food fried chicken to elaborate creations from classical cuisine and intriguing menu items from all parts of the world.

There is much about working with poultry

11

Poultry Cookery

that is similar to dealing with fish, and much that is different. By comparing the two you may understand each one better. That in turn should help you when we discuss meats in the next chapter.

After completing this chapter you should be able to

- Identify the kinds and classes of poultry and suggest appropriate cooking methods for each.
- Discuss the handling and storage of fresh and frozen poultry and explain how to avoid the health hazards associated with poultry.
- Compare fish and poultry in terms of menu uses, nutritional roles, and special cooking requirements.
- Describe or demonstrate how to roast, poach, pan-fry, deep-fry, broil, bake, and braise various poultry dishes.
- Discuss the preparation of dressings and the hazards of cooking a stuffed bird.

ABOUT POULTRY IN GENERAL

The term **poultry** refers to edible birds domestically raised for human consumption. Often the word is used loosely to include wild birds such as pheasant and wild duck. Such birds are hunted for sport and are more correctly classified as **game.** A few farm-raised game birds such as pheasant, squab, and quail are now on the market.

Poultry, like fish, is an excellent source of energy (calories), provided by a high protein content and a moderate fat content. The protein, along with the flavor, body, and texture of the flesh, casts poultry in the menu role of an entrée. Most of the fat is concentrated in the skin of the bird or just under it. Because of this, poultry can be made into low-calorie dishes by cooking the skinless flesh without adding calorie-laden breading, sauces, and so on. White meat (breast, wings) has less fat than dark

meat (leg quarters). Duck and goose have more fat than other kinds of poultry. Poultry is also a source of some B vitamins and of such minerals as phosphorus, iron, zinc, and selenium.

Inspection and grading

All poultry shipped from one state to another must be inspected both before and after kill by an agent of the U.S. Department of Agriculture. The poultry must be processed under sanitary conditions and must meet federal standards of wholesomeness. Approved poultry products must carry the USDA mark of inspection (Figure 11-1).

State governments have similar regulations that vary from one state to another. Some cities also have regulations. A poultry product must meet whatever standard is highest—federal, state, or local—in the place where it is produced and the place where it is sold.

Poultry is also graded for quality by the USDA. There are three grades—A, B, and C—with A at the top of the scale. The factors that determine grade are conformation (shape of the carcass), fleshing (amount of flesh on the carcass), fat coverage, absence of pinfeathers, and freedom from damage such as skin tears, cuts, blemishes, broken bones, and freezer burn. Poultry graded by the USDA must carry the grade shield illustrated in Figure 11-1— with the appropriate grade, of course.

Federal poultry grading is not required by law. Some packinghouses have established

FIGURE 11-1. Federal inspection mark and grade shield for poultry. (Courtesy USDA.)

their own grades, which may or may not correspond to federal grades. Most poultry used in the food-service industry is federally graded.

Grade is not an evaluation of wholesomeness. In fact, each bird must pass inspection for wholesomeness *before* it can be graded. Look for both stamps when you check a delivery.

Market forms

Many varieties of poultry are available, and each has characteristics that relate to handling, storage, and cooking. In order to grasp the distinctive characteristics of each, you need to understand several terms that look confusingly alike but actually have specialized market meanings:

- Kind
- Class
- Style
- Type

Kind refers to the species of bird—the names most familiar to us. Chicken, turkey, duck, pigeon, goose, and guinea hen are the kinds available on today's market.

A **class** of poultry is a subgroup of a kind. Each class has clearly defined standards or characteristics that have to do mainly with age, sex, weight, and tenderness. It is important for the cook to be familiar with the different classes because each may have particular cooking requirements or special uses.

In each kind of poultry the classes progress from tender-fleshed, soft-skinned young birds, a delight to cook and eat, to tough old birds that have little or no use in the kitchen. The young turkey, duck, goose, and squab are usually roasted; the old birds are usually avoided—and should be.

Chicken has the greatest variety of classes.

- *Cornish game hen:* a specially bred young female chicken usually five to seven weeks old weighing not more than 2 pounds (ready-to-cook weight). Most cornish game hens used in industry are less than 1 pound (454 g). They are very tender and can be cooked by any method.

- *Broiler* or *fryer:* a young chicken of either sex usually nine to twelve weeks old. The skin is soft and smooth, the meat is tender, and the breastbone cartilage is flexible. In spite of its name, this chicken is not limited to broiling and frying but can be prepared by any cooking method. It is the most often used class of chicken.

- *Roaster:* a young chicken of either sex usually three to five months old. A roaster also has soft, smooth skin and tender flesh, but its breastbone cartilage is less flexible than the fryer's. You would not use this bird for broiling or frying but you can cook it by any other method.

- *Capon:* a desexed male chicken. The capon, at eight months or less, is older than the game hen, fryer, and roaster, but it too is tender-fleshed with soft, smooth skin. It has a rather large body and is good for roasting, but its very tender flesh can be fried, broiled, braised, or poached as well.

- *Stag, hen* (sometimes called *fowl*), and *cock:* older chickens with coarser flesh, tougher skin, and hardened breastbone cartilage. They adapt best to poaching and braising, if used at all.

Turkeys are classed as *fryer-roaster, young hen* and *young tom, yearling hen* and *yearling tom, old hen* and *old tom.* Ducks are classified as *broiler* or *fryer duckling, roaster duckling,* and *mature* (or *old*) *duck.* Geese and guineas are classed as *young* and *mature* (*old*). Pigeon classes are *squab,* an extra-tender bird about four weeks old weighing usually less than a pound, and *pigeon,* mature, coarse-skinned, and tough. It is seldom used.

Style of poultry refers to the degree of cleaning or processing. Style applies to all kinds and classes. The styles available are live, dressed, ready to cook, and convenience.

Live poultry is not commonly bought by the industrial consumer. Not many cackling birds are delivered to receiving areas of today's food facilities.

Dressed poultry is not common either. A dressed bird is one that has been killed, bled, and plucked, with craw removed. Since it is not eviscerated it cannot be shipped across state lines and is no longer in general use. It is usually available only from a local supplier and probably has not been inspected.

Ready-to-cook poultry is the most common style on the market today. Ready-to-cook poultry is completely processed: bled, headless, footless, plucked, and eviscerated, with the giblets wrapped in oiled paper and put back inside the bird if purchased whole.

Ready-to-cook poultry can be purchased either whole or cut up into individual pieces. Figure 11-2 shows three ways in which a whole bird is commonly **broken down**—that is, cut up into portions. You can also buy packages containing only certain parts—breasts, thighs, wings, and so on. Portion-control items such as boneless breasts in specific weights are also available. Ready-to-cook poultry rolls are available consisting of white meat or combined white and dark. The dishes you intend to make will determine which is the most economical form to buy.

Many convenience products—processed past the ready-to-cook stage—are also available, some fresh, some frozen. These include cooked and diced meat, raw or cooked

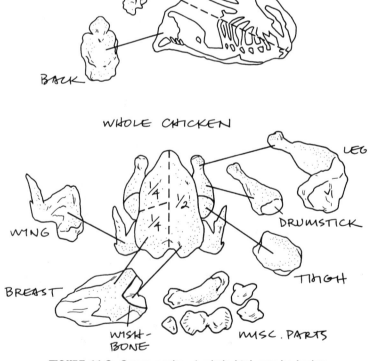

FIGURE 11-2. Cut-up poultry. A whole bird may be broken down into halves, quarters, or parts.

breaded or battered products, cooked breasts and rolls, and finished menu dishes that need only heating, such as braised items in sauce with or without rice, noodles, dumplings, or other starch. The same general rules for convenience bases (Chapter 6) and fish products (Chapter 10) apply to poultry convenience products. Check the list of ingredients so you know what you are dealing with. Store and handle properly. Observe all the general rules for whatever cooking method is needed to finish the product for presentation to the customer.

Type of poultry refers to whether it is *fresh* or *frozen*. The state of the bird is important to the cook because of its handling and storage requirements.

HANDLING AND STORING POULTRY

Fresh poultry should be checked over upon delivery, even though it is inspected and graded. Like fresh fish, it has a very limited shelf life, though the reasons are somewhat different. With fish we are concerned primarily with flavor change. With poultry the main concern is with health hazards: poultry is a frequent carrier of salmonella and offers a good growth medium unless properly handled.

Fresh poultry should be delivered packed in shaved ice, and it should be kept on ice until used. Ideally, fresh poultry should be used within 24 hours of receiving.

With frozen poultry the hazards lie not in storing but in thawing and in handling during preparation. Many cooks fail to carry out these processes properly.

Do *not* thaw poultry by soaking it in water. This practice can quickly create a health hazard. As the surface of the bird thaws, its temperature rises to the bacterial growth range, where it remains while the inner flesh thaws. The surrounding water in turn becomes a medium for bacterial growth and cross-contamination. Meanwhile the bird becomes water-

logged, a very undesirable development from the cooking point of view.

Thawing the bird by letting it sit at room temperature, another common practice, creates the same likelihood of bacterial growth on the surfaces before the inner parts are thawed. So does leaving it under running water, though this is less risky than the other two methods. In any case, the larger the bird the greater the hazard.

The best way is to thaw the frozen bird in the cooler, allowing **slack time**—that is, time for slow thawing. This may take as long as three to five days for large birds such as turkeys and geese.

All frozen poultry should be thawed before cooking. Once a bird is thawed it should be treated as a fresh bird. A thawed bird should not be refrozen unless it has been cooked.

Cooked poultry may be safely kept up to three days in the refrigerator. It can be frozen and kept several weeks longer.

But the greatest health hazards in handling poultry occur during prepreparation. Any salmonella bacteria a bird carries will multiply at kitchen temperatures while it is being prepared for cooking. Furthermore, these bacteria are easily transferred to fingers, knives, cutting boards, towels, and anything else a raw bird touches. These items in turn may pass the salmonella along to contaminate other foods.

To prevent such bacterial growth and spread from developing into a full-blown episode of food-borne disease, the cook must take constant precautions. The raw flesh should be rinsed and patted dry before preparing. Hands must be washed and work surfaces and utensils must be sanitized as soon as preparation is complete, and the poultry must be either cooked immediately or returned to refrigeration. Large quantities should be prepared in small batches at a time and returned to refrigeration as completed. Once cooked, poultry should be served at once or held in the upper safe zone at 180°F (82°C) or above.

Improperly handled, poultry is one of the most hazardous foods in the kitchen. The poultry cook must think about this all the time and consciously follow all sanitary practices.

UNDERSTANDING DONENESS IN POULTRY

The cooking of poultry is challenging because there are so many ways it can be prepared. But whatever the kind, class, and cooking method, one concern must always remain uppermost in the cook's mind: doneness.

Poultry must always be cooked done. "Done" is the point at which the meat is cooked through but not dried out. A common pitfall of poultry cooking is inability of the cook to distinguish between done and ruined. If a once-succulent breast of chicken tastes like a mouthful of sawdust, it is overcooked. Poultry takes longer to reach doneness than fish because it has more connective tissue. But small pieces of young birds cook surprisingly fast.

There are several indicators of doneness:

- Firmness of flesh. Underdone flesh will feel soft to the touch; done flesh will remain firm (but not hard) when pressed. On a whole bird the leg and thigh are the best places for touch testing.
- Visual change of flesh color.
- Joints becoming loose. You can feel this by twisting the leg slightly.
- Flesh beginning to separate from the bone.
- In roasted poultry, clear, translucent juices inside the bird. Before doneness is reached the juices will be opaque and brown.
- Internal temperature of 180–185°F (82–85°C). In roasting, use a meat thermometer in the thickest part of the breast or the inner part of the thigh. The bulb should not touch bone.

All these indicators can be used, depending on the cooking method. The degree of accuracy depends on the skill and experience of the

cook. The thermometer is the safest and most accurate method.

For volume production it may be difficult to use a thermometer for each of 40 or so birds, so random placing of a few is a good method. Birds should be grouped according to size, with a thermometer in one bird of each size.

One common method of testing doneness is definitely not recommended for a roasted bird, and that is to stick it with a meat fork. If you do this, the bird's good juices will run out of the holes you have punched. Poultry loses enough moisture in cooking without having the cook provide another avenue of loss.

METHODS OF COOKING POULTRY

Cooking methods suitable for poultry include all the methods there are. All kinds and most classes of poultry can be cooked by almost any method. Some common methods are

- Roasting
- Poaching
- Pan-frying
- Deep-frying
- Broiling and grilling
- Braising

Roasting

Roasting is a way of cooking poultry that is near and dear to the American heart. Roast turkey on the Thanksgiving table is a must.

Poultry is usually oven-roasted. It may also be smoked, barbecued, or spit-roasted. Whole young birds do very well in this dry-heat process because of their tender flesh and the protection of a layer of fat between it and the skin. The skin and fat form a coating that conserves the juices, thus keeping the flesh moist as it cooks.

The procedures for roasting poultry are the same for all kinds of birds, except for one thing: cooking time. The larger the bird, the longer the time.

Recipe 11-1 is a typical formula for roasting poultry. Let us review the basic steps.

Step 1 is primarily for appearance. Oil added to the skin will give the roasted bird a golden-brown color. In addition it will prevent the skin from cracking and blistering and will help to keep the flesh moist. Notice that the recipe makes no mention of basting the bird with water or stock. Basting is totally unnecessary. Worse, it introduces moisture into dry-heat cooking—not needed, not wanted.

In Step 2 the seasoning is put inside the bird, not on the skin. Seasonings will not penetrate the skin, so there is no need to season the skin unless it is to be served.

Trussing the bird (Step 3) ensures even roasting. The object is to make the bird a solid piece by tying the legs and wings neatly to the body. Extended wings or legs will cook done before the breast is cooked, which means they will be overcooked when the breast is done. Trussing will prevent this and maintain uniform quality. Figure 11-3 shows a quick and easy method of trussing a bird.

Many turkeys come from the market with a wire clip holding the legs in place. These birds do not need trussing; just turn the wing tips under.

Roasting the bird back side down (Step 4) steadies it on the rack and gives the breast its crisp golden coat.

A bird should rest for a short time after cooking before it is carved (Step 5). This allows the juices to settle into the flesh, keeping it moist, instead of running out. Twenty to 30 minutes is enough for a large bird to rest. If poultry is to be stored after roasting, place it breast side down. This will keep the juices from draining away from the breast.

The temperature for roasting given in this recipe is common, but other temperatures can be used. A temperature of 250°F (120°C) will preserve more moisture, but it will require a good deal longer cooking time—enough longer, in fact, to put it out of reach of many kitchen schedules. Higher temperatures up to 400°F (200°C) are used—and should be—for roasting small poultry such as squab, quail,

---

11-1 ROAST CHICKEN

Yield: 6–8 portions

1	roaster	1	*	seasonings	*
			*	vegetable oil	*

1. Oil chicken skin with vegetable oil.
2. Rub inside of bird with seasonings.
3. Truss the bird.
4. Roast back side down on rack in roasting pan at 300–350°F (150–180°C) until done.
5. Let chicken rest 15 minutes before carving.

11-1a ROAST CHICKEN WITH BRANDY SAUCE

Yield: 6–8 portions chicken
1 pint (500 mL) sauce

To recipe 11-1 add:

1 lb	mirepoix, ½" (1 cm) concassé	500 g
Sauce:		
1 oz	brandy	25 ml
¾ pt	chicken stock	375 mL
2 oz*	beurre manié or roux	*50 g
1 oz	heavy cream	25 mL
*	salt, white pepper	*

1. Complete Steps 1–3 of 11-1 and begin Step 4.
2. Forty-five minutes before you expect the chicken to be done, add mirepoix to pan.
3. Remove chicken when done. Pour off fat and deglaze pan with brandy. Add stock.
4. Thicken with beurre manié or roux *to desired consistency. Simmer to blend flavors and remove starchy taste.
5. Add cream and simmer until hot. Strain. Adjust seasoning and texture as necessary. Serve each portion of chicken with 2 oz (50 mL) sauce.

FIGURE 11-3. How to truss a bird.

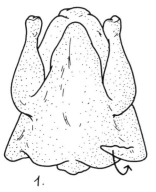

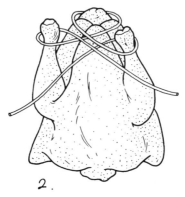

1.

2.

3.

Step 1. Place the bird on its back with the neck toward you and tuck the wing tips under the Vs of the wings, pointing them toward the tail.

Step 2. Take a piece of butcher string about three times the

length of the bird and loop it around the tail and under and over the ends of the legs.

Step 3. Pull the legs together tightly, tuck the strings under the breastbone cartilage, and run the two strings toward you beside the thighs.

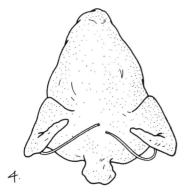

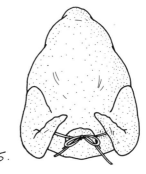

4.

5.

Step 4. Hook them through the Vs of the wings and turn the bird over.

Step 5. Tie the strings firmly just below the neck opening and tuck the neck skin under the string to close the neck cavity.

and game birds. This is another way of minimizing moisture loss because these small birds cook very quickly at the higher temperatures.

The 300–350°F (150–180°C) temperature range is the most logical for quantity cooking from the point of view of oven use. Often all meats and poultry for a given meal are cooked at the same time in one or two ovens. A temperature that adapts to all kinds eliminates constant oven adjustment and production problems.

Approximate times for the roasting of poultry are handy to use as guidelines for production scheduling. You cannot use them as guarantees of doneness, however. The only absolute measure of doneness is the internal temperature of 180–185°F (82–85°C).

Table 11-1 shows approximate cooking times per pound (500 g) for poultry at an oven temperature of 325°F (160°C). Look closely for a moment at the first three sizes of bird listed in the table. Notice how widely the total cooking time for doneness may vary for birds

**TABLE 11-1 *Guideline Timetable for Roasting Poultry
(Oven Temperature 325°F or 160°C)**

Weight				Cooking Time per lb (500 g)	Total Cooking Time
1–2	lb	0.5–1	kg	30–40 min	½ to 1⅓ hr
2–3	lb	1–1.5	kg	30–40 min	1 to 2 hr
3–4	lb	1.5–2	kg	30–40 min	1½ to 2⅔ hr
4–10	lb	2–4.5	kg	30–40 min	
10–14	lb	4.5–6	kg	approx. 20 min	
14–20	lb	6–9	kg	approx. 18 min	
20–30	lb	9–14	kg	approx. 15 min	

*For use only in production planning. Do not use for determining doneness.

that are more or less the same size. It illustrates clearly the reason you cannot cook by time charts but must look for concrete evidence of doneness.

After you roast your chicken you can combine the techniques of roasting and sauce-making in an easy and tasty dish (recipe 11-1a). The mirepoix is added in Step 2 to enrich the pan juices; it does not flavor the chicken meat. In Step 3 the pan is deglazed with brandy to capture all this rich flavor. Deglazing incorporates the **fond**—the pan drippings and the bits of food clinging to the pan bottom. The remaining steps of gravy-making follow the usual sauce-making techniques.

You can apply both the roasting method and the sauce techniques to make a great variety of dishes. The well-known duckling à l'orange, for example, is made on the same pattern, using a brown sauce flavored with orange juice and caramelized sugar and enriched with the deglazed fond. Because the duck is so fat, it is roasted at the high temperature of 425–450°F (220–230°C) for the first 15 minutes and then at 375° (190°C) until done. This helps to render the fat from beneath the skin and produce a crisp covering that intensifies the special duck flavor.

In addition to oven roasting, smoking and barbecuing are special methods of roasting poultry. The roasting process is the same as for ordinary oven roasting, except that the temperature is lower, the cooking time is therefore longer, and smoke is infused to give the flesh distinctive flavor. Often spices are added to the bird to create specific flavors.

Spit-roasting is another special method, used mainly for show. It requires special equipment but no special knowledge or technique. Small birds are trussed, oiled, and placed on spits that revolve before a hot fire. Basting with a spicy sauce is common.

In all these special roasting methods the chief consideration is doneness. The tests for doneness are the same as those for conventional roasting.

Dressings and stuffings

Roast poultry served with a dressing is a traditional American dish. A bird roasted whole seems to invite stuffing with a flavorful dressing. There is no question that this makes a tasty dish, but cooking stuffing in a bird is surrounded with question marks. Let us look first at the nature of dressings and then at the question marks that apply to cooking them inside birds.

A poultry dressing is usually made with a starch for body and texture, such as bread or rice (cornbread in the South), plus a flavor

11-2 BREAD DRESSING

Yield: 20 3-oz (100 g) portions

2 lb	bread, cubed	1 kg	1 lb	onions, small dice	500 g
1 pt	stock	500 mL	½ lb	celery, small dice	250 g
4	eggs, lightly beaten	4	*	sage	*
			*	chopped parsley	*
			*	seasonings	*
			*	fat (bacon fat, chicken fat, or butter)	*

1. Cook onions, celery, and herbs in fat until vegetables are done.
2. Cool this flavor base and add to the cubed bread.
3. Add hot stock, toss to combine, and cool.
4. Mix in eggs.
5. Season *to taste. Bake in hotel pans at 350°F (180°C).

base of pan-fried onions and often celery with various spices and herbs such as thyme and sage. Some sort of fat and often stock are included to add moisture. Some cooks add eggs for binding. Many other things can be added—fruits, nuts, seafoods such as oysters or shrimp, tasty meats such as sausage or ham. Such additions can create many interesting flavors to complement the flavor of the bird itself.

A tasty product like this is called a **stuffing** if it is stuffed into a cavity in a bird, fish, meat, or vegetable. It is called a **dressing** whether it is stuffed into another food or is cooked and served separately. Recipe 11-2 gives you a basic formula.

Now let us consider whether to roast such a dressing inside the bird following American family tradition or to bake it separately. From a production standpoint, it makes sense to stuff a bird only if it is to be presented whole and will hold enough dressing to accompany all the meat from the bird. This is generally true only of small birds intended to serve one or two persons.

The far more serious questions have to do with what happens in cooking a stuffed bird. Consider these important factors.

- Stuffing a bird will prolong its cooking time—by as much as an hour for a big bird.
- The temperature of the stuffing inside the bird will rise very slowly and it will remain in the ideal range for bacterial growth for most of the cooking period.
- The ingredients in the stuffing will undergo little or no cooking.

The primary problems come from improper handling and use of ingredients that pose health threats—specifically eggs and egg-based products that are used incorrectly and meats that are insufficiently cooked. The length of time it takes to bring a cold, thick mass of stuffing surrounded by a cold, thick mass of poultry flesh out of the bacterial growth range poses a real risk of food-borne disease. To give you a feeling of how easily the

11-3 ROAST ROCK CORNISH GAME HENS, STUFFED

Yield: 4 portions

4	rock cornish game hens, 12–16 oz (350–450 g) each	4	*Stuffing:*			
			1 pt	cold cooked rice, pilaf style	500 mL	
8 oz	mirepoix, ½″ (1 cm) concassé	250 g	2 oz	chopped parsley	50 g	
1 pt	stock (chicken or light)	500 mL	4 oz	pine nuts, toasted	125 g	
			*	salt, pepper	*	

1. Season insides of game hens. Combine stuffing ingredients and stuff cavities loosely.
2. Truss birds. Place mirepoix in pan. Set birds on rack above.
3. Roast in 350°F (180°C) oven until done (golden brown and tender).
4. Remove birds. Pour off fat and deglaze pan with stock. Strain.
5. Remove trussing strings and serve birds with pan juices.

worst can happen, let us assume you are going to use recipe 11-2 as a stuffing. The problems come up one after another like this.

- In Step 1 the vegetables are often undercooked. They will not cook any further inside the bird. Onions that are not properly cooked will give a bad flavor to the stuffing. They are not a health hazard, but what cook wants poor flavor?

- In Step 2 the vegetables are often added to the bread while still hot. They shouldn't be; they should be cooled to room temperature. This will help prevent spoilage if the product is to be stored. *Keep it cool.*

- In Step 3 the stock is added hot so that the bread will absorb it quickly and evenly. The problem comes if the dressing is not allowed to cool before the eggs are added in Step 4. The eggs will bring their salmonella bacteria into a warm, cozy medium ideal for multiplying. Cool the dressing after adding the stock and you will have no problems in Step 4.

- If Steps 2 and 4 are done incorrectly, you are going to put warm or hot stuffing into a cold bird. Then, if the bird is stored for later roasting, the egg stuffing cools far too slowly while inside the bird. Or, if the bird is roasted right away, the stuffing starts out in the critical temperature range and stays there far too long.

The following rules will eliminate these problems:

- Combine the problem ingredients with starches at cool temperatures.
- Don't use eggs if you can do without them.
- If sausage or other meats are used, cook them fully before adding.
- Make stuffing only as needed and cook immediately.

Dressing that is cooked separately cooks far more quickly and avoids the prolonged period of hazardous temperatures. Bake it in shallow pans so that all of it will make a quick trip through the danger zone.

If you do stuff a bird, put the stuffing loosely in the body and neck cavities. It expands during cooking, and if you pack it in, it will be heavy and soggy.

The stuffed birds in recipe 11-3 are another way of preparing roast stuffed birds.

11-4 POACHED BREAST OF CHICKEN

Yield: 10 portions

flavor and body of dish	10	chicken breasts, 6 oz (175 g), boneless and skinless	10	½ pinch pinch 1	bay leaf thyme rosemary clove	½ pinch pinch 1	flavor builders
flavor and body of sauce	1 qt* (8 oz* 8 oz	chicken stock white wine cream	*1 L *250 mL) 250 mL	* *	salt, pepper butter or margarine	* *	seasoning
texture of sauce	4 oz*	beurre manié or roux	*125 g				

Basic sauce ratio: 4 parts stock / 1 part wine / 1 part cream

1. Sprinkle seasonings on the inside (the bone side) of each breast and tuck the edges under to make a compact piece.
2. Place the breasts close together in a *buttered pan, add flavor builders, and *cover with cold stock (and wine). Use *enough to make 1–2 oz (25–50 mL) of sauce per serving. (If you must change the amount of liquid, adjust the other sauce ingredients to keep the same proportions.)
3. Bring to a simmer and poach until breasts are done. Remove from liquid.
4. Add cream to liquid and reduce by about one-third.
5. Thicken with beurre manié or roux *to desired consistency. Cook until no starch taste remains.
6. Strain sauce. Adjust seasoning *to taste.
7. Serve the breasts napped with the sauce.

11-4a POACHED CHICKEN PRINCESSE

To recipe 11-4 add:

30   cooked asparagus spears   30

Place poached breasts on asparagus spears before napping with sauce in Step 7.

11-4b POACHED CHICKEN FLORENTINE

In recipe 11-4 make the following changes:

Add 20 oz (625 g) spinach, cooked and buttered, hot.

Add 4–6 oz* (125–175 mL*) mornay sauce (8-1b), thick.

Omit beurre manié/roux.

1. Substitute mornay sauce for beurre manié/roux in Step 5 of 11–4.
2. Place breasts on bed of hot spinach.
3. Coat with sauce and glaze under salamander.

11-5 "BOILED" CHICKEN

Yield: approximately 1 lb (450 g) meat

1	broiler or fryer chicken, whole	1	1 lb	mirepoix, ½" (1 cm) concassé	500 g	flavor builders
			*	stock herbs and spices (6-1)	*	
			*	water	*	

1. Place chicken in stockpot with flavor builders. Add water *to cover.
2. Simmer until done (*45–60 minutes), skimming as necessary.
3. Chill quickly. When chicken is cool enough to handle, remove skin, bones, and tendons. Cut meat into pieces of desired size and shape.

They do not run the risks of food-borne disease because they are small and cook quickly and because the stuffing is already cooked and contains no problem ingredients. Again, the mirepoix is added to enrich the pan juices and does not flavor the meat of the birds.

Poaching

The poaching of poultry is very similar to the poaching of fish. The only real difference is in the kinds of flavor builders selected to enhance the taste. If you compare recipe 11-4 with 10-7, you will see that the basic method is the same. The flesh is cooked done, the stock is reduced and thickened, and you have your dish.

Many cooks have a tendency to overcook the product. Poultry poaches very quickly, not as quickly as fish but faster than you might think. The chicken in this recipe cooks done in 30 minutes or less, even when you are cooking a large quantity. It is done when the flesh changes color and feels firm but not hard. When poached flesh is overcooked it is dry, even though it has been cooked in liquid and even when it is covered with a sauce.

White wine is optional in poultry poaching. (If you omit it you may need to increase the chicken stock to meet the guidelines.) The flavor builders given here are good ones but certainly not the only ones you can use. Different dishes may call for different flavor builders, different sauces, or additional ingredients.

Recipes 11-4a and 11-4b are adaptations of the basic recipe. Asparagus turns the dish into chicken princesse. The addition of spinach makes it florentine (compare the chicken dish with sole florentine (10-7b). If you add mushrooms to the sauce after straining you will make it into chicken forestière—a familiar name by now.

Poaching is also the method of choice for cooking whole birds for salad or cooked-chicken dishes. The birds are placed in water or stock with a mirepoix and stock herbs and spices and are poached until done—no longer (recipe 11-5).

The usual tests for doneness are hard to practice on a big bird in a poaching kettle. One way is to remove the bird from the liquid and apply the touch test. If the breast feels firm the bird is done. Another way is to test with a meat thermometer.

When you need to use the meat right away, remove the chicken from the broth and place it in the refrigerator, covered, until cold enough to handle. Strain the broth, cool it

11-6 CHICKEN TETRAZZINI

Yield: 10 portions

body and flavor	1½ lb	boiled chicken meat cut in strips ¼ × 2" (½ × 4 cm)	675 g	1 pt	chicken stock	500 mL	sauce
				2 oz*	roux or beurre manié	*60 g	
	1 lb	mushrooms, sliced	450 g	4 oz	cream	125 mL	liaison
	2 oz*	butter	*60 g	1	egg yolk	1	
	1 lb	spaghetti or vermicelli, cooked	450 g	1 oz	sherry	25 mL	
				*	salt, cayenne	*	
				8 oz	parmesan cheese	250 g	

1. Sauté mushrooms in butter until golden.
2. Add chicken stock and thicken with roux or beurre manié *to make sauce. Simmer until no starch taste remains.
3. Temper in liaison. Add sherry and season *to taste.
4. Add chicken and heat but do not boil.
5. Divide spaghetti into individual casseroles. Put chicken mixture in center and sprinkle everything with parmesan cheese.
6. Gratiné under salamander or heat in oven until golden brown.

quickly, and refrigerate. If the cooked meat is not needed immediately, cool the pot quickly in cold running water with the bird in the broth, then refrigerate—bird, broth, pot, and all. This keeps the bird from drying out. The poaching liquid can be used to produce a sauce or to fortify a stock or a soup, since it has a great deal of flavor.

Notice that in this recipe the chicken is unseasoned. You leave the seasonings out of this preparation because you want the chicken to be uncommitted in flavor, just as you want a basic sauce to be uncommitted. You add your seasonings when you use the chicken in a dish, and you season according to the needs of that dish.

One such dish is given in recipe 11-6. It is one of many casserole-type dishes you can

make with chicken or turkey meat. Cooked chicken, in fact, has many menu uses, especially for luncheon or buffet service—chicken salad, chicken à la king, chicken pot pie. You cut your cooked meat as required by the dish you will make, and season and flavor it accordingly.

In making the chicken tetrazzini, if you had a pot of chicken velouté on hand you would add it to the mushrooms in the pan in Step 2 in place of the stock and thickener. In a real-life kitchen situation a pot of velouté would probably be a part of your mise en place.

Pan-frying

The pan-frying of poultry is similar to the pan-frying of fish, except that it takes longer to

11-7 PAN-FRIED CHICKEN

Yield: 4 portions

1	chicken, cut up	1	*	salt and pepper	*
			*	milk or egg wash	*
			*	flour for dredging	*
			*	butter/oil (equal parts)	*

1. Sprinkle the chicken pieces with salt and pepper.
2. Dip in milk or egg wash.
3. Dredge in flour.
4. Pan-fry in half butter/half oil (*to ¼"/5 mm deep in pan) over low to moderate heat until done.

achieve doneness. Low to moderate temperatures are necessary to keep the surface of larger pieces such as the breast and thigh from overbrowning before the center reaches doneness. Wings and drumsticks cook through more quickly. Recipe 11-7 gives you a step-by-step procedure for pan-frying poultry.

Sprinkling the seasonings on the chicken (Step 1) assures an even distribution of the seasoning on the bird. Many cooks season the flour and thus season and dredge the chicken at the same time. Although this may save time, it does not assure even seasoning. Salt is heavier than flour and will settle to the bottom of the dredging pan.

Dipping the pieces in milk (Step 2) before dredging them in flour (Step 3) will assure that the flour sticks to the chicken to give it a golden-brown crust.

The use of half butter and half oil in Step 4 eliminates rapid browning or burning of the butter before the chicken reaches doneness. Cook both sides to a golden brown, turning as necessary. Use tongs for turning. Test for doneness by feel.

On completing a pan of fried chicken you can apply your basic sauce techniques to make a delicious gravy from the cooking fat and the fond. Recipe 11-7a shows you how.

11-7a PAN GRAVY FOR PAN-FRIED CHICKEN

Yield: ½ pint (250 mL)

2 Tb	pan fat plus fond from recipe 11-7	25 mL
2 Tb	flour	25 mL
½ pt	milk, light cream, or stock	250 mL
(4 oz	onion, small dice	125 g)
(1 tsp	thyme or other herbs	5 mL)
*	salt and pepper	*

1. Remove chicken pieces from pan and drain off all but 2 Tb (25 mL) fat.
2. (Sweat onions with herbs in fat until onions are translucent.) Stir in flour to make a blond roux, scraping pan to incorporate all the fond.
3. Add liquid, stirring until smoothly blended.
4. Simmer *15 minutes to remove starchy taste. Adjust texture if necessary. Season *to taste.

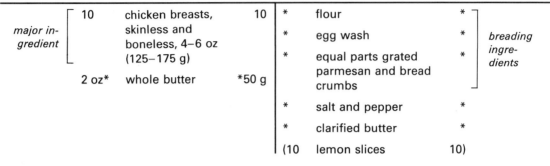

11-8 CHICKEN SUPRÊMES MILANESE STYLE

Yield: 10 portions

major ingredient	10	chicken breasts, skinless and boneless, 4–6 oz (125–175 g)	10	*	flour	*
	2 oz*	whole butter	*50 g	*	egg wash	*
				*	equal parts grated parmesan and bread crumbs	*
				*	salt and pepper	*
				*	clarified butter	*
				(10	lemon slices	10)

breading ingredients

1. Season chicken breasts. Bread, using cheese–crumb mixture in last breading step. Chill.
2. Heat clarified butter in heavy pan (*⅛"/3 mm deep) and cook breasts over moderate heat until chicken is done and coating is lightly brown.
3. Remove chicken from pan. Swirl in *enough whole butter to serve 1 oz (25 mL) beurre noisette per portion. (Garnish with lemon slices.)

You will find the gravy-making process familiar. This technique is used to make all **pan gravies.**

For quantity production pieces of poultry can be browned in the pan and then placed in an oven to cook through. It is a way of producing "fried" chicken in volume, often referred to as **ovenizing** or **oven-frying,** though it is actually baking. It is also a way of avoiding the pan-frying problem of overbrowning the surface of large pieces while cooking the center to doneness. Temperatures of 300–350°F (150–180°C) are appropriate for this type of cooking.

Many different entrées made with chicken breasts are cooked by pan-frying. In recipe 11-8 the boneless breast of a half chicken, known on the menu as a **suprême** (soo-prem), is breaded with a special coating and served with a garniture of brown butter and lemon. You can vary this basic formula with other coatings and garnitures to make other dishes.

In other pan-fried chicken entrées the breasts (suprêmes) are stuffed before breading—with ham and cheese, for example, for chicken cordon bleu, or with other flavorful stuffings.

Deep-frying

Deep-frying is a very common method of cooking poultry. It is not at all difficult and the product is very popular.

Two forms of poultry are deep-fried. One is whole pieces—chicken breasts or thighs, for example—that are either battered or breaded. The other is croquettes, which are made of cut-up cooked meats bound with a heavy béchamel sauce, shaped, and breaded.

Good frying temperatures usually range from 325 to 350°F (160–180°C). At these temperatures small pieces pose no problem. Larger pieces may not reach doneness internally before the surface becomes too brown. To achieve doneness you can finish-cook

11-9 TURKEY CROQUETTES

Yield: 25 portions (two 2-oz/60-g croquettes each)

major flavor and body	4 lb	cooked turkey meat, small dice	1.8 kg	8 oz	celery, brunoise	250 g		flavor builders
				8 oz	onions, brunoise	250 g		
body and texture	12 oz	clarified butter	350 g	2 oz	parsley, chopped	60 g		
	12 oz	flour	350 g	*	seasonings	*		
	1 qt	milk	1 L	*	standard breading ingredients	*		
				(2 qt	suprême sauce, 8-2b	2 L)		
				(*	chopped parsley	*)		

1. Sweat celery and onions in clarified butter until translucent.

2. Stir in flour and cook to make a blond roux.

3. Add milk, stirring until smoothly blended with roux. Simmer to blend flavors and cook out starch taste (*10–15 minutes).

4. Add turkey and parsley; season *to taste. Cover and chill until firm (*1–3 hours).

5. Using a No. 20 scoop, portion mixture into 50 2-oz (60 g) croquettes. Shape for uniform size and appearance; bread.

6. Deep-fry at 350°F (180°C) until golden brown. Drain. (Serve with suprême sauce and garnish with more chopped parsley.)

such pieces in the oven, as you may do with pan-fried chicken, especially when a large quantity is required. But if you want to limit your frying to a single step, the solution is to use only pieces small enough to cook to doneness in the fryer.

A typical recipe for croquettes is given in 11-9. You will recognize the flavor-building and body-building techniques from several earlier chapters, as well as the heavy béchamel from Chapter 8. The cooking may remind you of the potato croquettes in 9-14a, though the preparation techniques are different. You may substitute other poultry meat for turkey, and you may use high-quality leftover meats.

Some specialty poultry dishes are deep-fried. One such dish is chicken kiev (recipe 11-10). The thinned-out breast meat cooks quickly. The meat and the breading seal in the butter even though it melts. This dish can also be pan-fried in clarified butter or oil to brown it quickly, then finished in the oven.

Like all other deep-fried foods, deep-fried poultry dishes should be served promptly. If they are held, their crust becomes soggy and loses all its charm.

Broiling and grilling

Poultry can be broiled or grilled with great success. It is much easier to broil poultry than fish. The fat tissue in poultry allows it to be broiled fairly slowly without drying out, whereas fish must be broiled fast at high heat. Indeed, poultry *must* be broiled at a lower temperature and a slower rate than fish to prevent drying while ensuring doneness in the center.

11-10 CHICKEN KIEV
Yield: 4 portions

4	chicken breasts, 4 oz (125 g), boneless, skinless	4	2 oz	butter (room temperature)	60 g	
			2	garlic cloves, puréed	2	*stuffing*
			2 tsp	minced chives	10 mL	
			*	salt, pepper	*	
			*	standard breading ingredients	*	
			(8 oz	allemande sauce, 8-2a	250 mL)	

1. Combine garlic and butter. Form into 4 equal "fingers" about 2 × ½" (5 × 1 cm). Roll in chives. Chill.

2. Place chicken breasts skin side down between sheets of waxed paper. Flatten with mallet to ¼" (5 mm) thickness.

3. Place a finger of butter in the center of each chicken breast. Roll breast to enclose butter, folding in ends to seal in butter completely.

4. Pass through standard breading procedure. Chill.

5. Deep-fry until coating is golden brown and breast is done (*8–12 minutes). Drain well. (Serve with allemande sauce.)

Recipe 11-11 gives you the basic method for broiling chicken. The mechanics are simple, but you can run into hidden problems.

PROBLEM: The outside may cook done before the inside does.

SOLUTION: Use a lower temperature. You can lower it either by turning down the heat or by moving the cooking surface farther from the heat.

PROBLEM: The meat may stick to the grate of the broiler.

SOLUTION: Be sure to brush with butter or oil, maintain a moderate to low temperature, allow the meat to cook to the halfway point before attempting to move it or turn it, and keep the grate clean at all times.

A few more observations:

• Seasoning is done before cooking.

• Coating the surface with butter will do three things: prevent surface drying, add flavor, and keep the chicken from sticking. Oil may be used instead for cost reasons, but it will not add flavor.

• Using tongs for turning is a must. Or, more accurately, not using a fork is a must. Piercing the flesh with a fork will release the sealed-in juices.

• If you are grilling the chicken, you may move the skin side once to produce criss-cross marks. (This technique is spelled out in Chapter 12.)

Once you get the feeling of the cooking temperature, you will find broiling a simple way to cook poultry, and the results are excellent.

Broiled chicken may be dressed up for variety and excitement. Chicken diable (dee-ah-bla, meaning devil) is one such variation (11-11a). You can also experiment with your own combinations of herbs, compound butters, or other flavorers to add zest to plain broiled or grilled chicken.

Braising

In braised poultry dishes the cut-up bird is cooked slowly in a small amount of liquid in a covered pot, usually with other ingredients that form part of the dish. Such dishes are descended from the peasant's pot-on-the-fire of ancient times, and the method was often used to cook a tough old bird that only slow, moist-heat cooking could tenderize. Contemporary cooks choose tender birds and use the method for other reasons. For one thing, braising produces a soft, moist texture. Even more important, it provides a method of flavoring the flesh by cooking it with flavorful ingredients such as wines, stocks, and flavor builders, which usually become part of a sauce served with the bird.

The typical braised poultry dish is really a two-step process in which the cut-up poultry pieces are first sautéed or seared before braising. Often flavor builders are cooked in the sauté pan and the pan is then deglazed with a liquid that becomes the body of a sauce. Everything is then cooked together with a cover on the pan, in a slow oven or over low heat on the range.

Reading through the steps in recipe 11-12 you will see that this is exactly what happens when you make the famous French dish coq au vin. Not only are you cooking a chicken slowly with flavor builders to enrich its taste; the same ingredients are building the flavor and body of a sauce at the same time. This pattern of building a dish is a familiar one in braising. You will meet it again.

Although there are many steps in this preparation, they are all familiar. You know

about precooking such flavor builders as garlic, onions, and mushrooms to maximize their flavor contribution to the dish. You know about incorporating the pan scrapings (fond) into a liquid; you did this in making pan gravy. You also did this in making stocks in Chapter 6 when you deglazed the pan. You know about adjusting the sauce texture and seasoning: the sauce should be the consistency of es-

---

11-11 BROILED HALF CHICKEN
Yield: 1 portion

½	chicken	½	*	salt, pepper	*
*	butter or oil	*	(*	lemon	*)

1. Sprinkle seasonings on chicken. Brush with melted butter or oil.
2. Put skin side down on a moderately hot broiler or grill.
3. Cook until half done—that is, until done on the side exposed to the heat source.
4. Turn, using tongs. Finish cooking and serve.

11-11a CHICKEN DIABLE

To recipe 11-11 add:

	1 Tb	mustard	15 mL
	1 oz	bread crumbs	25 g
	(*	cayenne	*)

1. Follow Steps 1–3 in 11-11.
2. After turning in Step 4, lightly coat skin side with mustard, then dredge in bread crumbs. (Sprinkle with cayenne.)
3. Finish cooking. If grilling, glaze in salamander.

11-12 COQ AU VIN ROUGE

Yield: 4 portions (2 pieces chicken, 2 oz/50 mL sauce)

major in-	1	fryer, cut into 8 pieces	1	1–2	garlic cloves, puréed	1–2	
gredient							
	4 oz	salt pork, rind re- moved, small dice	125 g	(1 oz	tomato, concassé or paste	25 g)	
				Sachet of:			flavor builders
flavor and body	12	pearl onions	12	1	parsley sprig	1	
				½–1	bay leaf	½–1	
	8 oz	mushroom caps, small or quartered	250 g	½ tsp	thyme (or ½ sprig fresh)	2 mL	
				*	salt and pepper	*	
flavor, body	1½ pt	dry red wine	750 mL	*	flour	*	
	½–1 pt	brown stock	250–500 mL	*	clarified butter	*	
texture	*	beurre manié	*				

1. In a sautoir, render fat from salt pork over moderately high heat. Remove pork from pan.
2. Season chicken parts and dredge in flour. Sear on both sides until well browned. Remove from pan.
3. Reduce heat and cook garlic in fat until aroma is evident.
4. Add pearl onions to pan and cook until lightly caramelized on all sides.
5. Add mushrooms and cook until light golden, adding butter *as necessary.
6. Stir in stock, wine, (and tomato), scraping with a wooden spoon to incorporate fond.
7. When liquid reaches a simmer, return chicken to pan, add sachet, cover, and simmer on range or in 350°F (180°C) oven until done (*30–45 minutes).
8. Remove sachet. Degrease and adjust seasoning and texture of sauce with beurre manié *as necessary.

pagnole. The only technique that may be new is searing. This is hotter and quicker than pan-frying. It is a partial-cooking process for browning the chicken, producing both color and flavor in the final dish. The braising step is, as you know, low-heat cooking in a covered pot. With chicken it produces a melt-in-the-mouth product in which all flavors are blended.

You can also make coq au vin with white wine instead of red. It then becomes coq au vin blanc (white) instead of rouge (red).

SUMMING UP

Poultry is one of the easiest foods to cook well, and one of the most widely used. It is a desirable menu item for just about any type of food-service establishment. It is inexpensive; it is popular both for its taste and for its nutritional values; and it is versatile. It is at home in the fast-food operation in the form of fried chicken, and it is equally at home in the elegant restaurant, appropriately selected, cooked, sauced, and garnished.

Poultry adapts to all cooking methods. It may be roasted, poached, fried, broiled, grilled, braised, or prepared by combining methods, such as frying/baking, poaching/baking, or sautéing/braising. The chief challenge to the cook is achieving the moist and tender quality that goes with the right degree of doneness—fully cooked but not overcooked.

Poultry is easier to cook than fish because it is less fragile. Yet many of the same techniques are used in preparing special dishes from these two flesh foods, such as making a sauce from the poaching liquid or the pan drippings, breading, glazing, and napping with sauce. Once you master these techniques and understand how to adapt them to the special qualities of the product you are cooking, you have a wealth of delicious dishes at your fingertips.

The chief caution to bear in mind in working with poultry is the health hazards it poses if not handled properly. Every cook must take constant, scrupulous care to avoid cross-contamination and danger-zone temperatures in preparing, holding, and serving poultry dishes.

If you want to venture beyond the usual American fare, you will find poultry a popular food in almost any country. Using your basic skills, try the popular Indian chicken tandoori, marinated in yogurt and braised or roasted; the Spanish arroz con pollo, rice with chicken; doro wat, an Ethiopian chicken stew; chicken marengo from France—chicken braised in brown sauce with tomatoes and mushrooms. But don't forget how good the simple dishes taste—plain broiled chicken, plain roast turkey, duck, or squab—when they are cooked to perfection.

THE COOK'S VOCABULARY

poultry, game

kind, class, style, type

chicken: cornish game hen, broiler, fryer, roaster, capon

slack time

broken down (cut up)

truss

dressing, stuffing

ovenize, oven-fry

suprême

fond

pan gravy

QUESTIONS FOR DISCUSSION

1. In what ways are the cooking of poultry and the cooking of fish similar? In what ways are they different?

2. Suppose you want to prepare duckling à l'orange, chicken with dressing, and baked potatoes for the same meal. Can you do them all in the same oven? If not, what additional equipment will you need?

3. Give examples of several ways in which sauces are made for poultry dishes. Explain how they differ.

4. Of the poultry dishes discussed in this chapter, which, in your opinion, needs the most attention to avoid health hazards? What are the potentially hazardous points in preparation of this dish and how will you deal with them?

MEAT cookery began in ancient China, so one story goes, when a young boy accidentally burned down his father's house and with it a litter of suckling pigs. Discovering the irresistible flavor of the burnt flesh, he and his father, and their neighbors too, burned down their houses whenever they had a litter of pigs.

Spit-roasting of meat goes back to prehistoric times and carried right through to the days of Escoffier and beyond. In medieval times the great banquet dishes were the whole ox, the wild boar, the boar's head (served with garlands and ushered in with trumpets), the suckling pig spit-roasted over the open fire.

In the 1600s and 1700s fresh meat became more available and a new cuisine emerged featuring a great variety of meat dishes. As classical cuisine developed, meat dishes multiplied through the use of different sauces and garnitures. So many ways to fix meat were invented that when the food supply of Paris was cut off during the Franco-Prussian War in 1870–1871, resourceful restaurateurs had no trouble devising delicious ways to serve the animals from the zoo—elephant trunk with sauce chasseur, roast bear chops with poivrade sauce, haunch of wolf with venison sauce, stuffed donkey's head.

Today's American cook is the beneficiary of several revolutions in meat production—in feeding, transporting, preserving, aging, grading, and marketing. The United States is a world leader in the production of quality beef, pork, and veal, and one of the world's top consumers of meat.

Meat is by far the most expensive item the cook prepares. In almost every kitchen the dollars spent on meat far exceed those spent on any other item. It becomes very important, then, to cook it well so that this high-cost menu item can pay its own way.

Meat cookery should come easy if you have a thorough grasp of fish and poultry preparation. Many important concepts and techniques are common to all three. The differences in cooking stem from characteristics of meat itself.

12

Meat Cookery

After completing this chapter you should be able to

- Choose appropriate cooking methods for different cuts of meat.
- Describe the different degrees of doneness in red meats and determine when the desired degree of doneness has been reached.
- Describe or demonstrate how to braise, "boil," broil, grill, pan-fry, sauté, and roast appropriate cuts of meat.
- Describe or demonstrate how to make sauces, gravies, and jus using cooking liquids, pan juices, and fonds.
- Handle and store raw and cooked meats properly.

ABOUT MEAT IN GENERAL

Meat is the flesh of domestic animals—beef and veal from cattle, pork and ham from hogs, lamb and mutton from sheep. Venison, hare, squirrel, and coon are also spoken of as meats, but from a cook's point of view they are game and do not belong in our discussion.

Meats are divided into two groups, **red** and **white,** based on the color of their flesh. The red meats are beef, lamb, and mutton. The white meats are veal, pork, and ham. Don't be fooled by the color of ham. It began its career as a white meat and achieved its distinctive pink color while being cured. Corned beef acquired its dark-redness the same way. It is classed as a red meat because of the meat's origin and not because of the color produced by curing.

A third group of meats, known as **variety meats,** consists of such things as liver, kidneys, heart, tongue, and sweetbreads, which are organs of the animal. Meat mixtures such as sausage meat and cold cuts are also classed as variety meats.

Meats are the major source of protein in the American diet. They are also typically high in fat. The fat content will depend on the kind

of meat, the amount of fat trimmed away, and to some extent the method of cooking. Some meats are also good sources of the B vitamins and some minerals, notably iron, copper, and phosphorus.

Meats are generally high in calories and in saturated fatty acids, which some health-conscious patrons try to avoid. This accounts for the growing interest in fish and poultry. However, meat is still the leading entrée choice.

The various kinds of meat are very individual in flavor, but their cooking is similar. Lamb is roasted the same way as beef. Veal stew, beef stew, and lamb stew all use the same techniques of cooking. For this reason we do not need to talk about cooking each different kind of meat in turn. It makes more sense to talk about meats as a group, to look at the things about meat that affect the cooking, and to learn how to deal with them.

If you are going to get a good meat dish on the table you need to know quite a bit about the raw product. What makes it tender? What makes it tough? How do you tell which is which, and how do you deal with it?

We'll talk about raw meats under the following broad topics. Each of them has a bearing on cooking methods and final product quality.

- Structure of meats
- Aging
- Inspection and grading
- Cuts of meat and how to use them
- Handling and storage

Structure of meats

Meat is the muscle of the animal. The muscle is composed of fibers—tubelike strings held together by connective tissue. The texture of the fibers and the amount and kind of connective tissue determine the tenderness of the meat.

Young animals, females, and males castrated when young have finer muscle fibers and are therefore more tender. Uncastrated males and mature animals have coarser fibers and therefore less tender meat. The texture of the muscle fiber also varies from one part of the animal to another.

Connective tissue is a factor the cook does not have to cope with when cooking fish and poultry. In meat it makes a big difference in what you choose to cook and how you choose to cook it. Connective tissue is tough. The more a muscle has been exercised and the older the animal, the more connective tissue there will be.

There are two kinds of connective tissue—**collagen** (kol'-a-jun), which is white, and **elastin** (ee-lass'-tun), which is yellow. Collagen can be tenderized by proper cooking. If cooked a long time at a low temperature by moist heat, it gradually breaks down and turns to gelatin and water. Meat cuts that are high in collagen, such as brisket, plate, and chuck, are therefore cooked by moist-heat methods. Cuts that are low in collagen and have fine-textured fibers, such as steaks and loin cuts, can be cooked by dry-heat methods.

Elastin remains tough no matter how it is cooked. The only way to deal with elastin is mechanically—by cutting it away or by grinding, for example.

Fat in meat also differs from fat in poultry and fish. There is a fat layer all around the meat carcass (called **finish**) as well as fat distributed throughout the meat, called **marbling.** Fat in meat is associated with tenderness. It melts at low temperatures and encircles the muscle fibers, thus preserving their juices. Hot fat and hot juices cook the fibers to a moist tenderness.

Aging

Shortly after an animal is slaughtered a stiffening of the muscles occurs called **rigor mortis.** In red meats it takes three or four days for substances within the flesh called enzymes to soften the rigid muscle tissue. In white meats there is little rigor and it disappears more quickly. The practice of holding meats long enough for enzymatic action to be effec-

tive is called **aging.** During aging the meat is held at cool temperatures to prevent bacterial growth.

Meats that are not allowed time to soften are called **green meats.** Cooked green meat is tough. Since it usually takes several days for meats to reach the market, green meat is not a common problem.

White meats such as pork and veal are not aged beyond the time it takes for rigor to disappear. Red meats, on the other hand, can be aged for several weeks, allowing enzymatic action to increase tenderness and flavor. The difference is that red meats are protected from bacterial action by a layer of fat. Veal does not have much fat covering. Pork does, but pork fat quickly becomes rancid. Actually both pork and veal are tender to begin with and do not need aging.

There are a number of ways of aging meats. In frontier days the hunter used to hang his kill on the back porch in 30 to 40°F weather and let it ripen. Today meat carcasses may be similarly hung in coolers for three to six weeks with carefully controlled temperature, air flow, humidity, and bacteria-killing ultraviolet light. This method is known as **dry aging.** Another method uses higher temperatures and high humidity, which speed enzymatic action and reduce aging time to one to two weeks.

But most often meat is **Cryovac-aged.** In this process the carcass is broken down into smaller cuts that are vacuum-packed in moisture-vapor-proof plastic bags and aged under refrigeration. The removal of oxygen reduces mold and bacterial growth and fat rancidity, while allowing enzymatic action to continue.

Aging does not affect quality grading, but it can affect quality eating. It contributes to the tenderness and flavor that no grade stamp can guarantee.

Inspection and grading

All meats must be inspected for wholesomeness. They are inspected by the federal government if they are shipped interstate. If

FIGURE 12-1. Federal inspection mark. The number refers to the establishment where the meat was inspected. (Courtesy USDA.)

they are sold within the state where they are produced, they are inspected either by the state or by the federal government, whichever has the higher standard. Animals are inspected before slaughter and again after kill. An inspection mark (Figure 12-1) certifies that the meat is wholesome and has been processed under sanitary conditions.

Meats that pass inspection are usually graded, although grading is not required by law. Most meat sold to food-service operations is graded by the U.S. Department of Agriculture (USDA) and bears their grade shield (Figure 12-2). USDA grade standards are based on quality of exterior fat (finish), quality and distribution of interior fat (marbling), and quality of flesh.

The grades are important to the cook because they influence the choice of cooking method. Higher grades are juicier and tenderer than lower grades. But a good cook can create a palatable dish from any grade of meat by choosing an appropriate way to cook it.

There are several grades of meats, but from the kitchen standpoint there are only a few of any importance. For beef, lamb, and veal there are three primary grades.

Prime grade is the highest in quality as well as in price. Prime meat has a good-quality fat cover (thick, white, brittle), fine-textured flesh, and abundant marbling. Most prime cuts are both tender and juicy.

Choice-grade meat is high in quality. It has good brittle fat and good marbling, and most cuts are tender and juicy. Choice is the most commonly used grade. It is usually in abundant supply, so the price is within reason.

Good-grade meats may have lower-quality fat or less fat cover and less marbling than the two higher grades. The meat fibers are not always smooth and tender. Lack of fat and coarser flesh texture will not yield as tender and juicy a product as will choice and prime. The price is correspondingly lower.

Cuts of meat and how to use them

In addition to grade, the cook must consider the cut of meat to be cooked. The charts in Figures 12-3 through 12-6 show how the beef, veal, lamb, and pork carcasses are divided into **primal cuts**—large divisions—and how the primal cuts may be further divided into cuts of meat for cooking. Generally speaking, the tender cuts come from the part of the animal getting the least exercise. You can prove this to yourself by studying the charts. An exercised muscle has built up tough connective tissue while muscles that have been idle have remained fine-grained with a minimum of connective tissue.

Meat cuts fall neatly into three groups—tender, moderately tender, and less tender. *Tender* cuts include rib steaks and roasts and loin-cut steaks such as T-bone, sirloin, and tenderloin. Generally speaking, meat that touches the backbone is tender, suitable for steaks and quick cooking. You can cook the tender cuts by dry-heat methods in any grade.

Moderately tender cuts include rump, sirloin tip, chuck, and top-round roasts, plus steaks cut from the round and chuck. You can cook any of these cuts from prime- and choice-grade meats by dry-heat methods, but the same cuts from a lower grade need moist-heat cooking.

Less tender cuts include shoulder, arm, flank, and brisket. These cuts need moist-heat cooking in all grades.

Smoked and cured meats

Another market form of meat is the group of products that are **smoked** or **cured.** Smok-

FIGURE 12-2. Federal grade shields. Federally graded beef, veal, and lamb are stamped with the appropriate quality grade shield. A meat grader rolls a choice veal carcass with the USDA shield. (Photo and shields courtesy USDA.)

ing and curing serve the dual purpose of preserving meats from spoilage and adding flavor. Meats may be either cured or smoked or both.

Hams, shoulders, bacon, spareribs, loins, and sausages are among the pork products that arrive in the kitchen smoked or cured. Many are ready-to-eat items to be served either cold or hot.

Bacon arrives in kitchens in one of two ways: whole slab or sliced. The cook has to slice the whole slab bacon. Sliced bacon comes by the count—that is, so many slices to the pound. Common sizes are 18 to 22 slices to the pound. The larger the number the thinner the slice.

Ham is available in several market forms—cooked and uncooked, bone-in and boned, rolled and tied or canned. Most hams arrive in today's kitchen already cooked. Cooked hams come both bone-in and boned. Canned hams are boned and cooked and

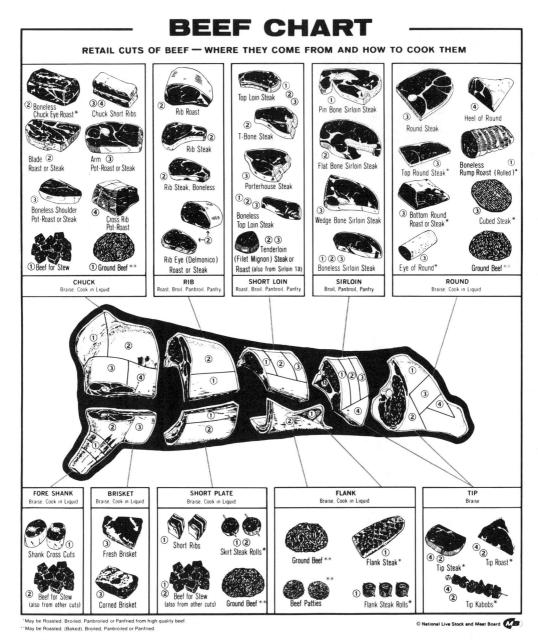

BEEF CHART

RETAIL CUTS OF BEEF — WHERE THEY COME FROM AND HOW TO COOK THEM

CHUCK
Braise, Cook in Liquid

- ② Boneless Chuck Eye Roast*
- ③④ Chuck Short Ribs
- ② Blade Roast or Steak
- ③ Arm Pot-Roast or Steak
- ③ Boneless Shoulder Pot-Roast or Steak
- ④ Cross Rib Pot-Roast
- ① Beef for Stew
- ① Ground Beef**

RIB
Roast, Broil, Panbroil, Panfry

- Rib Roast
- Rib Steak
- Rib Steak, Boneless
- Rib Eye (Delmonico) Roast or Steak

SHORT LOIN
Roast, Broil, Panbroil, Panfry

- ① ② Top Loin Steak
- ② T-Bone Steak
- ② Porterhouse Steak
- ① ② ③ Boneless Top Loin Steak
- ② ③ Tenderloin (Filet Mignon) Steak or Roast (also from Sirloin 1a)

SIRLOIN
Broil, Panbroil, Panfry

- ① Pin Bone Sirloin Steak
- ① Flat Bone Sirloin Steak
- ② Wedge Bone Sirloin Steak
- ① ② ③ Boneless Sirloin Steak

ROUND
Braise, Cook in Liquid

- ③ Round Steak
- ④ Heel of Round
- ③ Top Round Steak*
- ① Boneless Rump Roast (Rolled)*
- ③ Bottom Round Roast or Steak*
- ③ Cubed Steak*
- Eye of Round*
- Ground Beef**

FORE SHANK
Braise, Cook in Liquid

- ① Shank Cross Cuts
- ② Beef for Stew (also from other cuts)

BRISKET
Braise, Cook in Liquid

- ③ Fresh Brisket
- Corned Brisket

SHORT PLATE
Braise, Cook in Liquid

- ① Short Ribs
- ① ② Skirt Steak Rolls*
- ① Beef for Stew (also from other cuts)
- Ground Beef**

FLANK
Braise, Cook in Liquid

- Ground Beef**
- Flank Steak*
- Beef Patties
- ① Flank Steak Rolls*

TIP
Braise

- ④ ② Tip Steak
- ④ ② Tip Roast*
- ④ ② Tip Kabobs*

*May be Roasted, Broiled, Panbroiled or Panfried from high quality beef.
**May be Roasted, (Baked), Broiled, Panbroiled or Panfried.

© National Live Stock and Meat Board

FIGURE 12-3. This is a side of beef—one-half of the animal carcass. The large divisions (chuck, rib, round, and so on) are known as **primal cuts.** They are broken down into smaller cuts according to how they will be used. The ones shown in this chart may be seen in the supermarket. For commercial and institutional use the primal cuts are usually broken down differently. (Photo courtesy National Live Stock and Meat Board.)

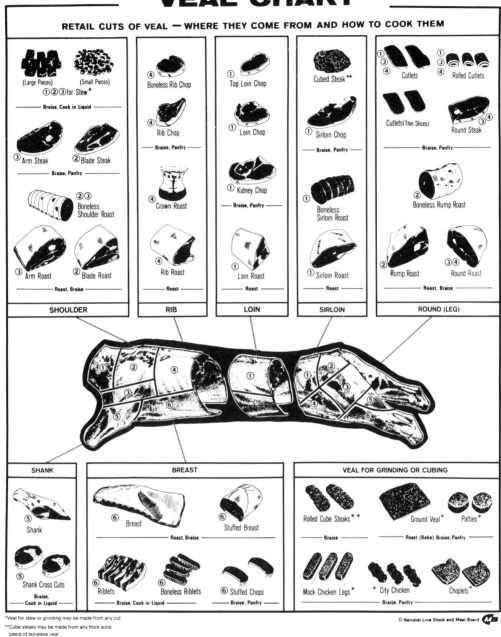

FIGURE 12-4. This is a whole veal carcass. All of it is tender and can be cooked by any method. Food-service operations use veal from all parts of the animal, though not usually in the retail cuts shown here. (Photo courtesy National Live Stock and Meat Board.)

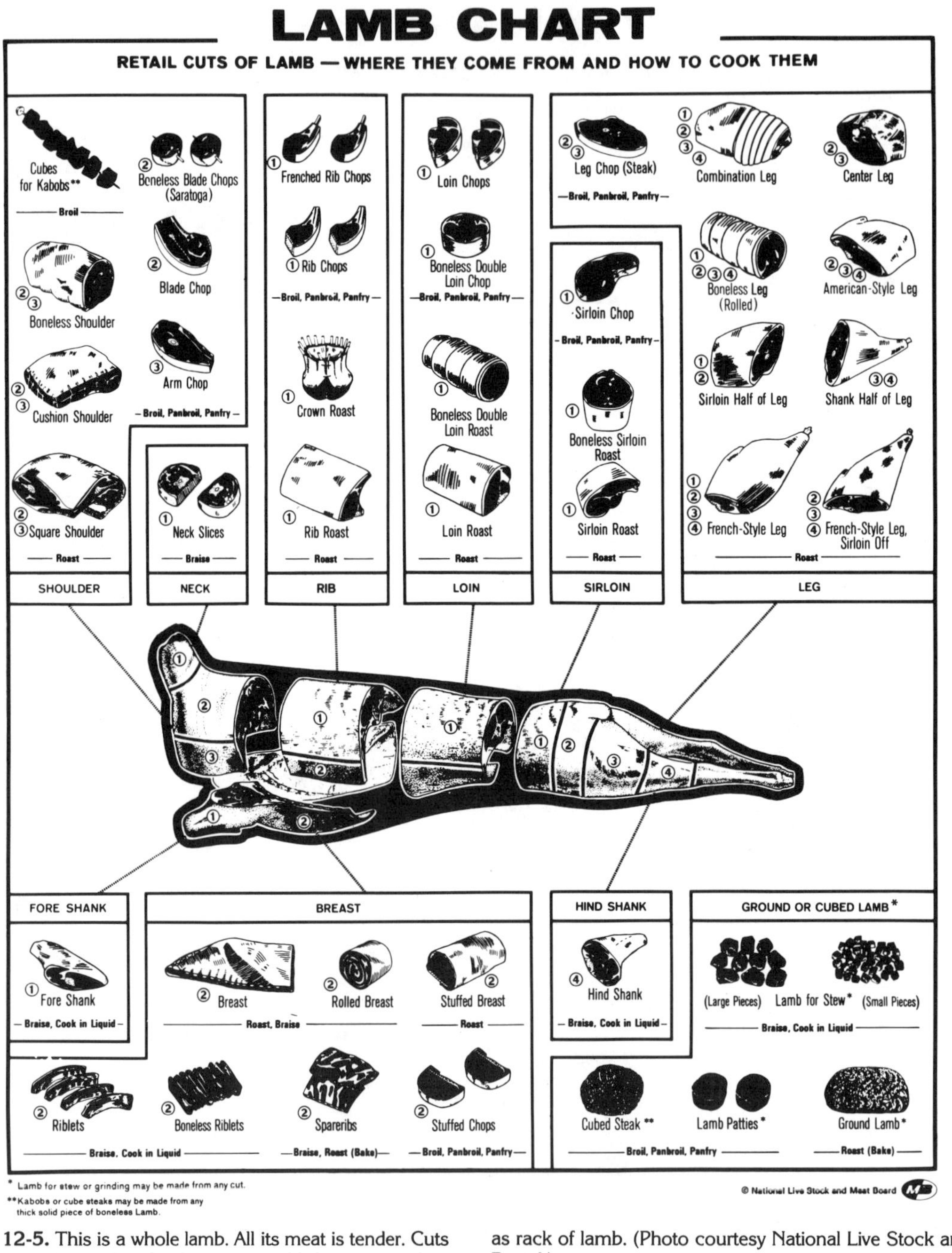

LAMB CHART

RETAIL CUTS OF LAMB — WHERE THEY COME FROM AND HOW TO COOK THEM

SHOULDER

Cubes for Kabobs**

② Boneless Blade Chops (Saratoga)

— Broil —

②③ Boneless Shoulder

② Blade Chop

② Arm Chop

②③ Cushion Shoulder

— Broil, Panbroil, Panfry —

②③ Square Shoulder

— Roast —

NECK

Neck Slices

— Braise —

RIB

① Frenched Rib Chops

① Rib Chops

— Broil, Panbroil, Panfry —

① Crown Roast

① Rib Roast

— Roast —

LOIN

① Loin Chops

Boneless Double Loin Chop

— Broil, Panbroil, Panfry —

Boneless Double Loin Roast

① Loin Roast

— Roast —

SIRLOIN

① Sirloin Chop

— Broil, Panbroil, Panfry —

① Boneless Sirloin Roast

① Sirloin Roast

— Roast —

LEG

②③④ Leg Chop (Steak)

— Broil, Panbroil, Panfry —

①②③④ Combination Leg

②③ Center Leg

②③④ Boneless Leg (Rolled)

②③④ American-Style Leg

①② Sirloin Half of Leg

③④ Shank Half of Leg

①②③④ French-Style Leg

②③④ French-Style Leg, Sirloin Off

— Roast —

FORE SHANK

① Fore Shank

— Braise, Cook in Liquid —

② Riblets

— Braise, Cook in Liquid —

BREAST

② Breast

② Rolled Breast

② Stuffed Breast

— Roast, Braise — — Roast —

② Boneless Riblets

② Spareribs

② Stuffed Chops

— Braise, Cook in Liquid — — Braise, Roast (Bake) — — Broil, Panbroil, Panfry —

HIND SHANK

④ Hind Shank

— Braise, Cook in Liquid —

GROUND OR CUBED LAMB*

(Large Pieces) Lamb for Stew* (Small Pieces)

— Braise, Cook in Liquid —

Cubed Steak **

Lamb Patties *

Ground Lamb *

— Broil, Panbroil, Panfry — — Roast (Bake) —

* Lamb for stew or grinding may be made from any cut.

**Kabobs or cube steaks may be made from any thick solid piece of boneless Lamb.

© National Live Stock and Meat Board

FIGURE 12-5. This is a whole lamb. All its meat is tender. Cuts most commonly used in food-service establishments are loin chops for broiling, the leg for roasting, and the rib roast served as rack of lamb. (Photo courtesy National Live Stock and Meat Board.)

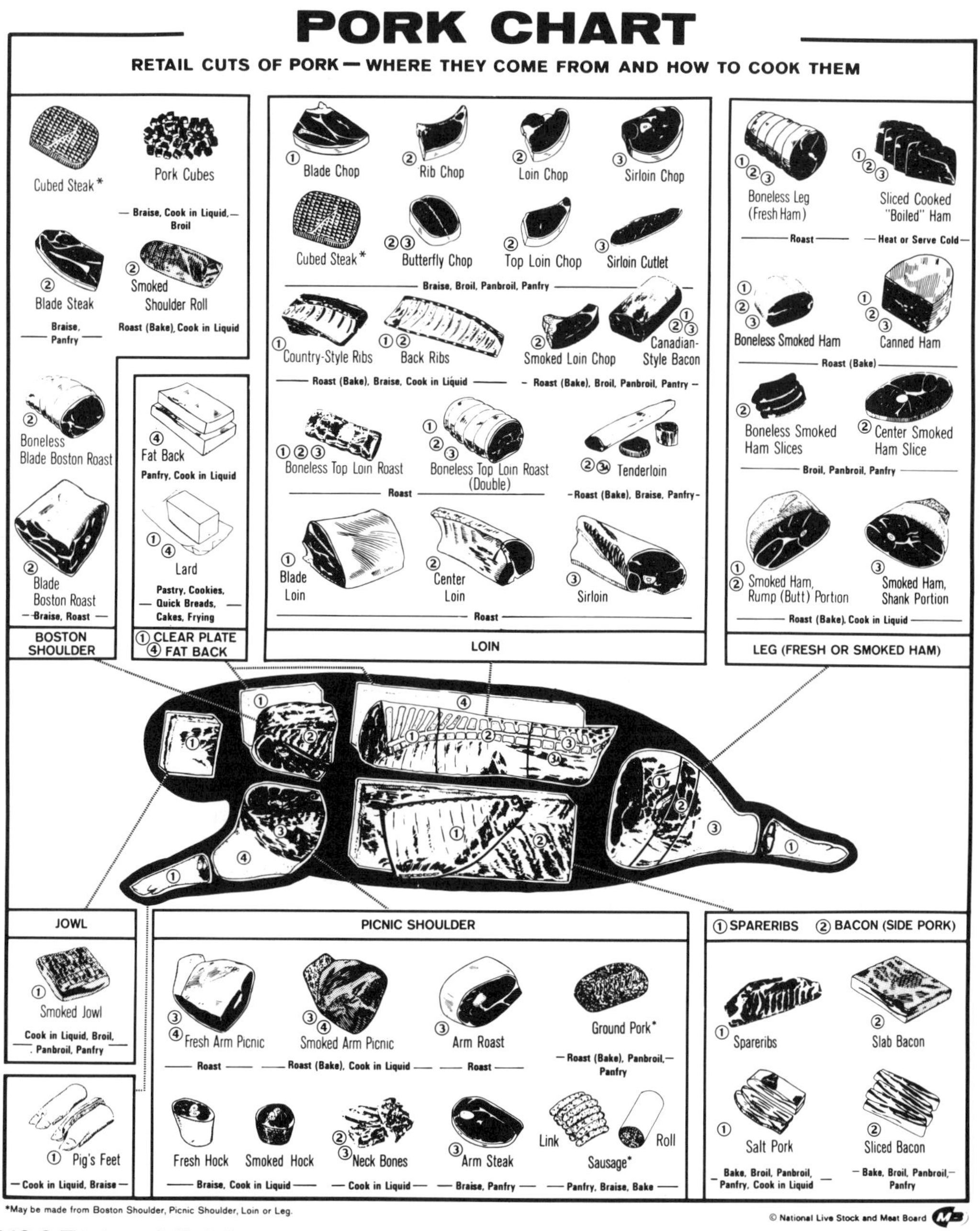

PORK CHART

RETAIL CUTS OF PORK — WHERE THEY COME FROM AND HOW TO COOK THEM

BOSTON SHOULDER

Cubed Steak *

Pork Cubes

— Braise, Cook in Liquid, Broil —

Blade Steak ②

Smoked Shoulder Roll ②

Braise, Panfry

Roast (Bake), Cook in Liquid

Boneless Blade Boston Roast ②

Blade Boston Roast ②

— Braise, Roast —

BOSTON SHOULDER

CLEAR PLATE / FAT BACK

Fat Back ④

Panfry, Cook in Liquid

Lard ④

Pastry, Cookies, Quick Breads, Cakes, Frying

① **CLEAR PLATE**
④ **FAT BACK**

LOIN

Blade Chop ①

Rib Chop ②

Loin Chop ②

Sirloin Chop ③

Cubed Steak *

Butterfly Chop ②③

Top Loin Chop ②

Sirloin Cutlet ③

— Braise, Broil, Panbroil, Panfry —

Country-Style Ribs ①

Back Ribs ①②

Smoked Loin Chop ②

Canadian-Style Bacon ②③

— Roast (Bake), Braise, Cook in Liquid —   — Roast (Bake), Broil, Panbroil, Panfry —

Boneless Top Loin Roast ①②③

Boneless Top Loin Roast (Double) ②③

Tenderloin ②③④

— Roast —   — Roast (Bake), Braise, Panfry —

Blade Loin ①

Center Loin ②

Sirloin ③

— Roast —

LOIN

LEG (FRESH OR SMOKED HAM)

Boneless Leg (Fresh Ham) ①②③

Sliced Cooked "Boiled" Ham ①②③

— Roast —   — Heat or Serve Cold —

Boneless Smoked Ham ①②③

Canned Ham ①②③

— Roast (Bake) —

Boneless Smoked Ham Slices ①

Center Smoked Ham Slice ②

— Broil, Panbroil, Panfry —

Smoked Ham, Rump (Butt) Portion ①②

Smoked Ham, Shank Portion ③

— Roast (Bake), Cook in Liquid —

LEG (FRESH OR SMOKED HAM)

JOWL

Smoked Jowl ①

Cook in Liquid, Broil, Panbroil, Panfry

Pig's Feet ①

— Cook in Liquid, Braise —

JOWL

PICNIC SHOULDER

Fresh Arm Picnic ④

Smoked Arm Picnic ④

Arm Roast ③

Ground Pork* ③

— Roast —   — Roast (Bake), Cook in Liquid —   — Roast —   — Roast (Bake), Panbroil, Panfry —

Fresh Hock ③

Smoked Hock ③

Neck Bones ③

Arm Steak ③

Link / Sausage* / Roll

— Braise, Cook in Liquid —   — Braise, Panfry —   — Panfry, Braise, Bake —

PICNIC SHOULDER

SPARERIBS / BACON (SIDE PORK)

① **SPARERIBS**   ② **BACON (SIDE PORK)**

Spareribs ①

Slab Bacon ②

Salt Pork ①

Sliced Bacon ②

Bake, Broil, Panbroil, Panfry, Cook in Liquid   — Bake, Broil, Panbroil, Panfry —

*May be made from Boston Shoulder, Picnic Shoulder, Loin or Leg.

© National Live Stock and Meat Board

FIGURE 12-6. This is one-half of a hog carcass. The flesh of the animal is very tender. Even the feet are edible. The heavy layer of fat surrounding the lean flesh gives us bacon, salt pork, fatback, and lard. (Photo courtesy National Live Stock and Meat Board.)

commonly come in two shapes. The pullman ham is rectangular and slices uniformly for easy preparation. The other common canned ham is pear-shaped.

The distinctive flavor in a ham comes either from the curing method or from smoking. Most hams used today are cured but not smoked. Smoked hams cost more and are usually used only for specialty dishes. Cured uncooked hams, sometimes referred to as country hams, include the famous Smithfield ham from Virginia. These hams are dry-cured in salt, rubbed with a seasoned coating, smoked, and aged for up to two years. They must be soaked for 12 to 24 hours and scrubbed before cooking. Then they are roasted like any other raw meat.

Partially cooked hams usually carry the phrase "Cook before eating." Fully cooked hams are labeled "Ready-to-eat" or "Heat and serve." Many imported hams of high quality (and cost) are used for their specialized flavors—produced by different smoking and curing methods and ingredients. Danish hams, Westphalian hams from Germany, and prosciutto from Italy are some examples.

Smoked or cured sausages that originated in many different countries are now produced domestically as well as being imported. Among the choices are frankfurters, salami and summer sausages, braunschweiger (liver), bologna, pepperoni, and Thuringer. Some are smoked or cured but not fully cooked. Make sure you know which of these need to be cooked to safe internal temperatures.

Corned beef—usually cured from the brisket—smoked tongue, and dried, cured, and smoked sliced beef are also used in the kitchen. They should be refrigerated, but they have a slightly longer shelf life than fresh beef.

HANDLING AND STORING UNCOOKED MEATS

Meat used to be bought by the whole carcass, and each establishment butchered its own meat. Even today a few large operations maintain their own butchers, but the practice is dying out in this country. Today many establishments buy their meats in **portion-control cuts** ready for use, and the cook is not faced with the problem of what to do with pig's trotters or the tail of the ox.

It goes without saying that raw meats should be refrigerated. Meats that arrive in the kitchen Cryovac-wrapped should remain wrapped until use. Unwrapped meats should be stored loosely to allow good circulation of air. Air circulation will dry the meats to some extent. Although this may cause some shrinkage, it will retard bacterial growth, since bacteria thrive in moisture. Cut surfaces should be covered with plastic wrap.

If you must keep meats for any length of time, wrap them well and freeze them to 0°F (−18°C). But even in a freezer meats do not have an indefinite shelf life.

Different meats have different shelf life, both in the freezer and in the cooler. Table 12-1 gives some recommended guidelines.

Meat should always be thawed before cooking. To thaw meat, use the same precautions and procedures you use for fish and poultry. Meats are subject to the same hazards of bacterial growth and cross-contamination. Thaw at refrigerator temperature, allowing slack time (up to three days for large pieces). Do not thaw at room temperature and do not thaw in water. Once meats are thawed, treat them as fresh meats.

TABLE 12-1 **Shelf Life of Meats**

Meat	Unfrozen	Frozen*
Pork	2–5 days	1–6 months
Veal	2–5 days	1–6 months
Lamb	2–5 days	1–6 months
Beef	2–5 days	1–6 months
Ham	1 week	1–2 months

*Purchased frozen. Meat you freeze yourself should be used within a few weeks.

All smoked and cured meats should be refrigerated. The preservative processes do not substitute for refrigeration and cooking, but they do prolong shelf life. Canned ham must be refrigerated like any other ham.

UNDERSTANDING DONENESS IN MEATS

In poultry and fish cookery only one degree of doneness is acceptable—total cooking throughout the flesh. In meats this is not always the case.

In meats you will work with several degrees of doneness. This phrase refers not to degrees of temperature but to the changes in the physical state of the meat itself as it progresses from rawness to total doneness. It is true that degrees of temperature can be an index to degrees of doneness. But think of doneness first in terms of the meat itself.

Degrees of doneness

Degrees of doneness may be described as follows.

- *Rare:* cool and red in the center
- *Medium rare:* slightly warm in the center, with deep-pink or pale-red center color
- *Medium:* warm and pink in the center
- *Medium well:* slightly hot and slightly pink in the center
- *Well done:* fully cooked, hot in the center with no pink, but still moist

As a meat progresses from rare to well done the outside becomes brown and the meat shrinks somewhat and gradually becomes drier. A sixth degree of doneness—overdone or ruined—causes the meat to shrivel, dry out, and toughen.

Degrees of doneness apply to the cooking of red meats—that is, to beef and lamb. This is not to say that red meats *must* be cooked something less than well done, but that they *can* be. White meats such as pork and veal, as well as variety meats, are generally cooked well done for tenderness and taste.

For pork, there is also a health reason for well-done cooking. At one time undercooked pork carried the parasite causing trichinosis. Though none has been found in federally inspected pork for many years, it is still safer to cook pork to temperatures that will kill the parasite. Besides, people are used to eating pork well done and do not enjoy it rare, even though rare pork is tender.

Why varying degrees of doneness for red meats? Cooked less than well done, they are juicier and possess a flavor many diners enjoy. Furthermore, a good cut of red meat cooked less than well done is definitely more tender. If cooked all the way to doneness it dries out and begins to toughen. Many restaurants will not guarantee the tenderness of steaks cooked beyond medium well. Notice that the relationship between tenderness and doneness in red meat is the reverse of this relationship in poultry and fish and in pork and veal. With these the flesh is not tender until it is fully cooked. However, overdoneness is tough in all types of flesh.

Identifying doneness

But enough about what and why. The next question is: How do you cook to the right degree of doneness and no more? There are three good methods for identifying the degree of doneness:

- Internal temperature
- Time/weight
- Feel

Let's examine these one at a time and then apply them to specific situations.

The internal-temperature method. Table 12-2 shows the internal temperatures at which various meats reach various degrees of doneness. The only method for checking internal temperature is to insert a meat thermometer into the flesh with the point in the center of the meat. Many meat thermometers have done-

TABLE 12-2 Internal Temperatures for Degrees of Doneness

Meat	Rare °F	Rare °C	Medium °F	Medium °C	Well °F	Well °C
Beef	125–140	52–60	140–160	60–71	170–180	77–82
Lamb	160	71	170	77	180	82
Pork	–	–	–	–	185	85
Veal	–	–	–	–	180	82
Smoked pork	–	–	–	–	170–180	77–82
Ham, uncooked	–	–	–	–	185	85
Ham, fully cooked	–	–	–	–	140	60

ness readings for different kinds of meats marked on the face or dial, like the one in Figure 12-7. Some doneness readings differ from one thermometer to another. Some dials are simply marked in degrees Fahrenheit or Celsius or both. In such cases you must use a chart like Table 12-2 or, better still, memorize the information.

Achieving the right degree of doneness has one complicating factor known as **carry-over cooking.** Simply stated, the inside of the meat goes on cooking after you remove it from the heat source. This happens through conduction of heat through the meat from outside to inside. Thus the internal temperature will rise anywhere from 5°F (3°C) in small cuts to 25°F (15°C) in very large roasts after removal from heat. The average rise is 10–15°F (6–9°C). This means that in order to have a final temperature of 125°F (52°C) for a rare roast, you would remove the meat at 110–115°F (45–48°C) and its internal temperature would increase to 125°F (52°C) after resting 30 minutes.

Internal temperature is certainly the most accurate indicator of doneness, but you need to know the other two methods as well. Each one has its uses.

The time/weight method. According to the time/weight method, you achieve the de-

gree of doneness you want by computing the time necessary to do the job and then cooking the meat for that length of time. To do this you must know the time it takes for a pound of meat to cook at a given temperature to the degree of doneness you want. Table 12-3 illustrates how this works.

As you can see, you have to have many kinds of information in order to use this

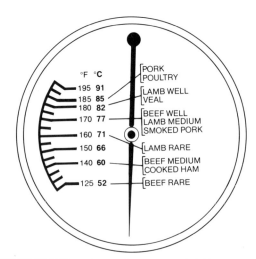

FIGURE 12-7. Typical meat-thermometer dial. Many meat thermometers tell you everything you need to know about internal temperatures. Others give you only temperature readings, so you must know degrees of doneness in degrees Fahrenheit or Celsius.

TABLE 12-3 *Guideline Timetable for Roasting Meats

Meat	Cut	Approximate Weight		Temperature		Minutes per pound (approximate)
		lb	kg	°F	°C	
Beef	Prime rib, rare	15–20	7–9	325–350	160–180	10–11
	medium	15–20	7–9	325–350	160–180	11–12
	well	15–20	7–9	325–350	160–180	12–14
	Prime rib, rare	15–20	7–9	250	120	12–13
	medium	15–20	7–9	250	120	13–15
	well	15–20	7–9	250	120	15–17
	Steamship round medium	40–50	18–23	250	120	12–13
	well	40–50	18–23	250	120	13–15
	Sirloin (top)	3–5	1.5–2.25	325–350	160–180	8–10
	Tenderloin	3–5	1.5–2.25	400	200	7–9
Pork	Loin	4–5	2–2.25	325–350	160–180	30–35
	Shoulder	3–5	1.5–2.25	325–350	160–180	35–40
	Fresh ham	10–15	4.5–7	325–350	160–180	28–32
	Fresh ham, boneless	8–10	3.5–4.5	325–350	160–180	38–40
	Cured ham	10–15	4.5–7	325–350	160–180	3–5
Lamb	Leg	5–10	2.25–4.5	325–350	160–180	28–32
	Rack	2–4	1–2	325–350	160–180	15–20
Veal	Rib (rack)	4–6	2–2.75	325–350	160–180	30–35
	Loin	5–7	2.25–3	325–350	160–180	25–30

*Guidelines for planning only! These are average times for one to four roasts in the oven. Times may not fit larger quantities or large ovens.

method: kind and cut of meat, total weight of cut, oven temperature, degree of doneness desired. In addition, the number of roasts in the oven, the size and type of oven, the position of the roast in the oven, and other products being cooked in the same oven can all affect the actual cooking time of roasted meats. Carry-over cooking comes into play with this method also.

The feel method. The use of feel as a check for doneness is just that. You feel for a particular texture that tells you what degree of doneness has been reached.

Meat as it cooks becomes firmer in texture. The more it cooks, or the closer it gets to well done, the firmer it gets. Well-done meat is firm to the touch; it resists pressure. Medium meat feels medium firm; there is some resistance to pressure but also some give. Rare meat feels soft; there is little resistance.

With practice a cook can quickly learn to judge with reasonable accuracy the doneness of a steak, remembering that some carry-over cooking will take place. A broiler cook with oversensitive fingers may dip them into a pot of ice water to keep them from being well done after four hundred steaks.

Which method when? Just which method of checking for doneness is the best? All three methods are good, but what's best depends on the circumstances.

Internal temperature is certainly the most accurate test, but it may not always be the best method. Imagine a broiler cook trying to measure the internal temperature of four hundred steaks to be cooked to different degrees of doneness in a one-hour period. He or she would feel like a mosquito in a nudist colony, not knowing where to start.

To make the matter simple let's list the situations in which each method would be best and see just how to use it.

Internal temperature is best . . .

- When large pieces of meats are being roasted.
- When different meats and other products are being roasted at the same time in the same oven—for example, prime rib, leg of lamb, and turkey. Each kind must have its own thermometer.
- When large numbers of different-size pieces of the same item are being roasted—say 20 prime ribs of varying size. In this case you would stagger the thermometers according to the sizes of roasts as you do in poultry roasting. Place one in a small roast, one in a medium size, and one in one of the larger pieces. Then consider each thermometer as representing all roasts of a similar size. In this way you can achieve consistency in doneness for all the meats.
- Whenever you *can* use it.

Time/weight is best . . .

- When all meats being roasted will be done

at the same time, and your ovens have been time-tested and calibrated so that you know they will perform according to the table you are using.
- When a thermometer is not available.

Feel is best . . .

- When small pieces of meat are being cooked—steaks or chops, for example.
- When different items are being cooked with the same equipment starting at different times—for instance, rare, medium, and well-done steaks, two or three chateaubriands, and some hamburgers, all being cooked to order.
- When there is doubt about the accuracy of the first two methods. In this case feel is a good final check. However, it is not an accurate substitute for either of the other methods. For example, as large roasts are roasting, they may feel firm to the touch. Allowed to stand, they will once again feel soft and you may find you are serving meat that is much less done than you intended.

It takes practice to learn how to choose the most appropriate method for each meat-cooking situation, and then how to put each method to work with accurate results. But these are the keys to successful meat cookery. Good meat, the right cooking method, and the right degree of doneness are the three secrets of tenderness and flavor.

Anyone can put meat into an oven, but it takes a good cook to take it out at the right degree of doneness.

METHODS OF COOKING MEATS

Choosing the right method of cooking depends on the cut of meat you are going to use and the dish you are going to make.

The better cuts and higher grades of meat are cooked by dry-heat methods such as broiling and roasting and by pan-frying. These meats are tender to begin with, and the cook's chief concern is to achieve the desired degree of doneness while preserving tenderness and flavor.

The less tender, less expensive cuts are cooked by moist-heat methods such as braising and simmering. The cook's goal here is to create tenderness, and the way to achieve it is to use moisture, low temperatures, and prolonged cooking. This combination of conditions breaks down tough connective tissues (collagen) while avoiding the toughening of muscle fiber that takes place at higher temperatures.

The choice between dry-heat and moist-heat methods is of the greatest importance. Roasting or broiling less tender cuts of meat would never make them tender, no matter how long you cooked them. Cooking a tender cut by braising or simmering would be wasting the very quality of instant tenderness that makes it so desirable.

Let's look at moist-heat cooking first.

Braising

Braising is a means of creating delicious dishes from less tender cuts of meat by cooking them covered in a small amount of liquid. The meats may be either bite-size pieces, which become a stew, or larger pieces such as pot roasts, which are cooked whole. The latter are served sliced, often with a sauce made from the cooking liquid. All kinds of meats may be braised.

As in braising poultry, the meat is usually seared over high heat to brown it before the liquid is added and the pot is covered and the long, slow braising process begins. The braising can be done in a slow oven or over low heat on the range or in a covered tilting fry pan.

Testing doneness in a braised meat is rather different from the methods described earlier. Braised meat is done when it is tender, and the best way to test tenderness is by feel with a fork. When the prongs go into the meat

easily and come out easily the meat is done. Because of the slow moist cooking you do not have to worry about releasing juices by probing with the fork. They have already blended with the liquid in the pot—and vice versa.

Even a braised dish can be cooked too long, so that tenderizing ceases and toughening begins. It is important to know when to begin testing for doneness. Table 12-4 gives approximate cooking times for some braised meats.

Pot roasts are among the most common of braised dishes. The label is not a cooking term but a dish name. A pot roast is not roasted; it is cooked in a pot. It is a large cut of meat cooked whole and sliced for service, but there its similarity to roasted meat ends. It is selected from less tender cuts of meat such as brisket or round, and slow moist-heat cooking makes its flavor very different from that of roasted meats. Recipe 12-1 makes a typical pot roast of beef.

When you examine the T format you can see that you are preparing two things at the same time, a meat and a sauce. The stock, thickening ingredients, and mirepoix are all sauce ingredients, and the proportions given represent the proportions for a good sauce.

In order to get the best interaction of meat and moisture during cooking you need *enough liquid to submerge half to three-fourths of the roast. The quantity required to do this will vary with the shape of the roast and the size of the pan.

Estimate the amount of sauce you need before you begin to cook, using pan capacity and roast size to make your judgment. You do not need to be exact. But if it is apparent that 2 quarts will be either far too much or far too little, decrease or increase the sauce part of the recipe. Remember also that you need a minimum amount of 1½ to 2 ounces of sauce per serving. If this minimum threatens to submerge the whole roast, choose a larger pan.

Going back to the cooking instructions, you see that cooking begins with the high-heat

TABLE 12-4 *Guideline Timetable for Braising Meats

Meat	Cut	Average Weight U.S.	Metric	Minutes per pound (approximate)
Beef	Large cuts	5–10 lb	2.25–4.5 kg	50–55
	Pot roast	3–5 lb	1.5–2.25 kg	50–55
	Corned beef	5–7 lb	2.25–3 kg	40–45
	Steak, round or flank	½–1 lb	250–500 g	40–60
	Cubes for stew	1–2 oz ea	25–50 g ea	50–60
	Ribs	4–8 oz	125–250 g	90–120
Pork	Smoked ham	10–15 lb	4.5–7 kg	16–20
	Picnic ham	5–10 lb	2.25–4.5 kg	40–50
	Pork ribs	2–4 lb	1–2 kg	30–40
	Pork chops	6–8 oz	175–250 g	50–60
Lamb	Breast	1–3 lb	500 g–1.5 kg	90–120
	Leg	6–8 lb	3–3.5 kg	40–50

*Guidelines only! Use this table for planning and as a guide for when to test for doneness. Times are averages for weight ranges given. Large quantities of small cuts will not increase cooking time proportionately.

process of searing (Step 1). This is done mostly for color, both for the meat and for the sauce. It does not affect the meat texture or its juiciness. Notice that you do not season the meat before searing. This is because salt will draw out the meat juices and interfere with browning.

In Steps 2 to 4 you make the sauce, converting the quantities of the ingredients if you need more sauce or less. You cook the mirepoix slightly as usual, to mellow and blend the flavors, and you make the roux and sauce in the usual way.

In Step 5 you cook the meat. The time will vary with the size and cut. It is done when it is fork-tender.

Step 6 is old stuff to you by now. It is the final step in sauce-making.

In Step 7, slice the meat across the grain and serve your sauce over the slices but not masking them.

We have given you the traditional way to make a pot roast—that is, cooking it in the sauce. Some cooks prefer to cook it in the unthickened stock and make the gravy at the end. It is less messy when it comes to removing the meat from the pot and slicing it for service.

If you want to prepare it this way, use less butter in Step 2 of the directions and skip Step 3. Add the stock in Step 4 and cook as in Step 5. Then remove the roast from the pot, skim the excess fat, and add beurre manié or cold roux to the hot liquid to make the gravy.

Individual portions of meat may also be braised—for example, the chops in recipe 12-2. The structure of this dish is very much like that of the pot roast: meat is browned, then cooked slowly in a sauce that conveys delicious flavors to the meat and is served over the finished dish. Notice that the method of cooking the chops parallels the pot roast rec-

12-1 BEEF POT ROAST

Yield: 10–12 8-oz (250 g) portions
1½–2 oz (50–60 mL) of sauce each

major in-gredient	1	rump roast, 5–8 lb (2.25–3.5 kg)	1	1 lb	basic mirepoix	500 g		
				2 oz	tomato concassé	50 g		
body of sauce	2 qt*	dark stock	*2 L	1	garlic clove	1		*flavor builders*
texture of sauce	5 oz	butter	150 g	pinch	thyme	pinch		
	4 oz	flour	120 g	5–6	peppercorns	5–6		
				*	salt, pepper	*		
				*	oil	*		

Basic sauce ratio: 1 lb roux / 1 gal stock
500 g roux / 4 L stock

1. Coat pan with oil and sear roast on all sides until brown. Remove from pan and discard oil.
2. Add butter and mirepoix and sauté mirepoix until lightly caramelized.
3. Add flour and make a brown roux.
4. Add stock to make sauce. Use *enough liquid to submerge half to three-fourths of the roast.
5. *Season roast and return to pan. Cover pan and braise in a low-heat oven (300–325°F/150–160°C) for *3 to 4 hours until done.
6. Strain sauce, adjust consistency, and season *to taste.
7. Slice beef across the grain. Serve sauce over meat.

ipe, and the only real difference in the recipes is in the ingredients. If you place a julienne of sour gherkins on the chops before adding the sauce, you will make it *charcutière*.

Many braised dishes are descended from the peasant's pot-on-the-fire and are made by the same methods as the first two recipes. Each region has its own variation. For example, in a carbonnade of beef flamande (a Flemish or Belgian dish), cubes of beef are braised in a sauce made of beer, brown stock, espagnole, and the fond from searing the meat and sautéing the onions. Tomato purée and bouquet garni herbs complete the medley of flavors, and meat and sauce are served to-gether. In beef bourguignon, from the Burgundy region of France, julienne of salt pork provides the fat, red wine deglazes the pan, and the cubes of beef are simmered in the wine, fond, and demiglace. Mushrooms and pearl onions, cooked separately, complete the finished dish.

Notice how closely the method follows the making of the other braised dishes. Compare it also with the coq au vin (11-12), a braised poultry dish. You will find striking similarities.

In recipe 12-3 we have a braised dish that departs from the pattern we have observed so far: it is not browned before braising. It is simply simmered with flavor builders in a light

12-2 BRAISED PORK CHOPS, SAUCE ROBERT

Yield: 10 portions

10	pork chops, 4–6 oz (125–175 g)	10	2 oz	shallots, minced	50 g
			1 Tb	dry mustard	15 mL
8 oz	dry white wine	250 mL	*	salt, pepper, lemon juice	*
8 oz	cider vinegar	250 mL	*	chopped parsley	*
1½ pt	espagnole	750 mL	*	oil	*

1. In heavy sautoir, sear chops in oil until well browned. Remove chops and hold.
2. Drain off all but ⅛″ (3 mm) of fat. Sweat shallots in remaining fat until translucent.
3. Deglaze pan with wine and vinegar, incorporating fond. Reduce liquid by half over high heat.
4. Stir in espagnole and mustard. Season chops lightly and return to pan. Cover and cook at low heat until chops are tender.
5. Remove chops. Adjust sauce texture and seasoning if necessary.
6. Strain sauce over chops. Garnish with chopped parsley.

stock until tender, then thickened with a white roux and enriched with a liaison. The liaison and the distinctive color elevate this classical dish to the level of elegance.

This dish may also be simmered uncovered if the level of the stock remains enough to keep the meat surrounded with liquid. If frequent skimming is necessary, as it may be with veal, it is simpler not to replace the cover each time.

Many other meal-in-a-pot dishes may be made by braising or simmering cut-up meats, adding other ingredients, and serving them in the cooking liquid, thickened or unthickened. They may go by various names—stew, ragoût, fricassee (usually white), navarin (a brown lamb dish), and so on depending on their origin and their specific ingredients. You can make a family-style stew as you would a soup, first braising cubes of meat and then adding vegetables—carrots, celery, turnips, potatoes, and so on—in the order in which they will

cook to doneness. Serve it in soup plates or bowls.

All these braised dishes are a way of turning less tender meats into delicious dishes through long, slow cooking with moist heat. You can even turn a braised dish into a pot pie by topping each serving with a pie crust.

"Boiling"

Lower grades and tougher cuts of meat are usually cooked by simmering. Low temperatures and longer cooking time in a moist medium tenderize their coarser fibers and their collagen. Beef brisket and the less tender variety meats, such as tongue, fall into this category. They are referred to as "boiled" meats, even though the careful cook never allows the liquid to reach a boil. Cooking below the boiling point prevents shrinkage and toughening and minimizes flavor loss. The simmering of meat is similar to the poaching

12-3 BLANQUETTE DE VEAU (VEAL IN WHITE SAUCE)

Yield: 10 5-oz (150 mL) portions

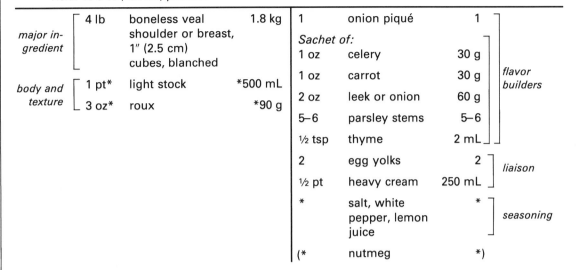

major in-gredient	4 lb	boneless veal shoulder or breast, 1″ (2.5 cm) cubes, blanched	1.8 kg	1	onion piqué	1	
					Sachet of:		
body and texture	1 pt*	light stock	*500 mL	1 oz	celery	30 g	flavor builders
	3 oz*	roux	*90 g	1 oz	carrot	30 g	
				2 oz	leek or onion	60 g	
				5–6	parsley stems	5–6	
				½ tsp	thyme	2 mL	
				2	egg yolks	2	liaison
				½ pt	heavy cream	250 mL	
				*	salt, white pepper, lemon juice	*	seasoning
				(*	nutmeg	*)	

1. Cover veal with stock, add flavor builders, and simmer, covered, until tender (*1½ hours). Skim frequently.

2. Remove meat to another pan and keep warm.

3. Blend cold roux into the hot liquid *to produce desired texture. Simmer to blend flavors and remove starch taste. Remove flavor builders and discard.

4. Temper in liaison. (Add nutmeg and) season *to taste.

5. Strain sauce over meat. Reheat for service, being careful not to boil.

NOTE: Instead of a sachet you can use a bouquet garni of 1 celery rib and ½ small carrot tied together with the parsley, thyme, and bay leaf as in Chapter 6.

of fish or poultry, but meats need the slightly higher temperatures of simmering.

A typical example of a "boiled" meat is given in recipe 12-4. You can see its similarity to the braising of a pot roast, but the meat is entirely covered with liquid, and no sauce is made from it. You can use the same recipe for such variety meats as tongue.

The small pot (Step 1) is efficient. Use water *to cover, with half an inch to an inch (1–2 cm) above the meat to be sure it remains submerged during the cooking.

In Step 2, adjust the amounts of the flavor builders in proportion to the amount of water you use. (You may notice that there is no salt in this recipe, since corned beef is well equipped with its own salt. For a fresh brisket you would add an ounce or so of salt, or about 25 g.)

Cooking time (Step 3) may be a matter of hours. Test tenderness by fork or by feel. The meat will first become firm and rubbery; then it will feel less firm to the touch as it becomes tender to the bite.

12-4 "BOILED" BRISKET

Yield: 16 4-oz (125 g) servings

major ingredient	5 lb	corned beef brisket	2.25 kg	2 oz	carrot, concassé	50 g	
				2 oz	celery, concassé	50 g	
cooking medium	1 gal*	cold water	*4 L	4 oz	onion, concassé	125 g	
				4 oz	leek, concassé	125 g	*flavor builders*
				6	parsley stems	6	
				½	bay leaf	½	
				2–3	cloves	2–3	
				5–6	peppercorns	5–6	

1. Place meat in a small pot and add *enough water to cover meat, plus ½–1″ (1–2 cm) more.
2. Bring to a boil and skim. Add flavor builders.
3. Reduce heat, cover, and simmer until tender.
4. Serve hot, sliced, or cool rapidly in cooking liquid for use as cold cuts. Store in liquid.

In Step 4, cool the meat in the cooking liquid for flavor and for moisture. Cool it rapidly for wholesomeness by surrounding the pot with cold running water. Refrigerate it at once if it is not to be used immediately.

Tender variety meats such as sweetbreads and brains are also simmered, but only briefly and for different reasons. They are blanched for a few minutes to firm them up so they can be skinned or otherwise handled. They are then usually finish-cooked by some other method, such as broiling or pan-frying.

Broiling and grilling

We turn now to dry-heat methods of cooking, suitable only for tender cuts of meat. Of these methods, broiling and grilling head the list in customer popularity. Almost every menu includes broiled or grilled meats, and many specialty restaurants such as steakhouses serve nothing else. The broiler station is one of the most common areas of specialization in the kitchen.

In broiling and grilling, degree of doneness is 95 percent of the game. You have tenderness to begin with, so the task is to produce the degree of doneness the diner orders and to recognize it when it is reached.

You already know how the various degrees of doneness are defined. (Let us hope the diner agrees with the definitions. Some diners have their own firm convictions about medium rare and medium well, which can cause frustration all around when cook and diner disagree.)

You know, too, how to determine doneness. Since you are usually broiling or grilling small pieces—steaks, chops, liver—you use the feel method.

How do you cook to the right degree of doneness? You season the meat and put it in the overhead broiler or directly on the grill. You cook it, touch-testing it frequently, until it feels like the degree of doneness you want. Then you turn it over, using tongs, and cook the other side the same way. Recipe 12-5 sums things up.

There are some fine points to the cooking:

- Always preheat the broiler or grill.
- Use lower temperatures for medium well and well done. Use higher temperatures for meats at the other end of the scale. You can control the temperature either by turning the heat up or down or by moving the meat toward or away from the heat source.
- Pay attention to the thickness of the cut. Thin cuts cook rapidly and thick cuts take longer.
- A grill marks the meat as it cooks. To make crisscross grid marks, place the meat on the grill diagonally. When you are halfway through cooking the first side, rotate it 60 to 90 degrees. When you turn the meat over, the marked side becomes the presentation side of the finished product (Figure 12-8).

Successful broiling and grilling take practice and learning from your mistakes. You have to become fairly expert before you can distinguish medium well and medium rare by feel. Mastery of rare, medium, and well done is more than enough for the beginning broiler cook.

A piece of meat that has been perfectly broiled will stand alone, but it can be enlivened

12-5 BROILED LAMB CHOPS					
Yield: 10 portions					
10	lamb chops, 4–8 oz (125–250 g) each	10	*	salt and pepper	*

1. Season chops and place on preheated grill or broiler.
2. If grilling, mark presentation side with crisscross grid marks. Turn with tongs to cook second side.
3. Cook to desired degree of doneness.

by imaginative accompaniments. Try choosing contrasting or complementary flavors for broiled steaks, lamb chops, pork chops, or liver from the following list.

- Compound butters of various flavors
- Chutneys—sweet–sour preserves from east Indian cuisine
- Sautéed or puréed fruits such as apples or peaches
- Puréed vegetable or fruit sauces finished with butter
- Marinated vegetables or relishes
- Mint sauce (for lamb)

FIGURE 12-8. How to make grid marks.

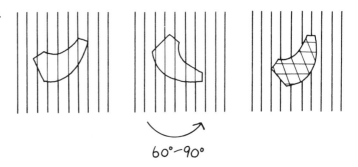

60°–90°

12-6 LONDON BROIL (MARINATED FLANK STEAK)

Yield: 10–14 portions

major ingredient	5	flank steaks, 1½–2 lb (675 g–1 kg) each	5	1 pt	oil	500 mL	
				½ pt	lemon juice or vinegar	250 mL	
				1 or more of:			
				1 tsp	puréed garlic	5 mL	
				2 oz	soy sauce	50 mL	*marinade*
				2 Tb	honey	25 mL	
				2 oz	sherry	50 mL	
				1 Tb	fresh ginger	15 mL	
				1 tsp	thyme, rosemary, or other herb	5 mL	
				*	salt and pepper	*	

1. Combine marinade ingredients.
2. Lightly season flank steaks, place in shallow pans, and pour marinade over them. Turn and coat thoroughly. Marinate in refrigerator, covered, 1–8 hours.
3. Remove from marinade and place on preheated grill or broiler. Cook quickly to desired doneness, turning once.
4. Cut across the grain in very thin diagonal slices.

A recent trend that has moved into the restaurant from the backyard barbecue is the use of hickory, mesquite, or other types of wood to impart their distinctive flavors to foods being grilled.

A few less tender cuts of beef may be broiled or grilled if marinated first to tenderize them. The tasty favorite known as london broil is made by marinating flank steak in a zesty marinade for several hours and then broiling quickly over high heat. The outside should be well browned and the inside rare. Medium rare is recommended for maximum tenderness and juiciness. Recipe 12-6 gives you a formula. Thick cuts of round or chuck steak can also be used successfully in this broiling method.

Pan-frying and sautéing

You know how to sauté flavor builders and how to pan-fry fish and poultry, so you are familiar with these cooking methods. Applying them to meats is not a problem once you separate the two methods.

Sautéing, a quick flip in a bit of hot fat, is usually a partial-cooking process, but it can be a finish-cooking process too for meats so thin they cook almost instantly, as you will see shortly. Pan-frying involves larger cuts of meat, more fat in the pan, a more moderate temperature, and a somewhat longer cooking time.

Meats that are pan-fried are tender cuts such as steaks, chops, cutlets, sliced liver. The cooking process is virtually the same as the pan-frying of fish and poultry. Meats are often

12-7 BREADED VEAL CUTLET

Yield: 10 portions

10	veal cutlets, 6–8 oz (175–250 g)	10	*	salt and pepper	*
6–8 oz*	clarified butter or oil	*175–250 mL	*	standard breading ingredients	*

1. Flatten cutlets to ¼″ (5 mm) thickness. Season *lightly; bread.
2. Heat oil or butter. Pan-fry cutlets until coating is golden brown and meat is tender.

pan-fried without breading or dredging, but they are sometimes breaded or otherwise coated for variety and flavor.

Recipe 12-7 is a dish with a coating—a familiar coating and an easy dish. The coating allows you to season the meat before cooking, because it is not the meat that must brown but the coating. You can turn this simple dish into the elegant and famous Wiener Schnitzel by topping each serving with an anchovy rolled around a caper on top of a peeled lemon slice, and arranging chopped hard-cooked egg yolks, chopped hard-cooked egg whites, and parsley to accompany it.

The pepper steak in recipe 12-8 also has a coating. You could not broil this steak without

12-8 STEAK AU POIVRE MARCHAND DU VIN

Yield: 1 portion

1	boneless sirloin steak, 8 oz (250 g)	1	1 Tb	black pepper, coarse grind	15 mL
			1 Tb	minced shallots	15 mL
			1 oz	dry red wine	25 mL
			2 oz	demiglace or espagnole	50 mL
			*	salt, lemon juice	*
			*	oil or clarified butter	*

1. Press pepper into both sides of steak to coat evenly.
2. Heat fat in pan. Sear both sides of steak.
3. Reduce heat and pan-fry to three-fourths of desired doneness. Remove and drain excess fat from pan.
4. Sweat shallots in remaining fat until translucent.
5. Deglaze pan with red wine, incorporating fond. Reduce liquid by half over high heat.
6. Blend in demiglace. Return steak to pan. Simmer to blend flavors (*5–10 minutes).
7. Remove steak to serving plate. Season sauce *to taste, and strain over steak.

12-9 CALF LIVER WITH ONION AND BACON

Yield: 10 portions

10	slices calf liver, 5 oz (150 g), ¼" (5 mm) thick	10	2–4 oz*	brown stock	*50–125 mL
			*	salt and pepper	*
1½ lb	onions, thinly sliced	750 g	*	clarified butter	*
10–20	bacon slices, cooked	10–20	*	flour	*
			*	oil	*

1. Sweat onions in ⅛" (3 mm) butter until lightly golden. Add *enough stock to moisten and simmer briefly to blend flavors. Keep warm.
2. Season liver slices *lightly and dredge in flour.
3. In another pan, heat oil and pan-fry liver on both sides to desired doneness. Maintain moderate heat to avoid a hard crust.
4. Serve each portion with 1–1½ oz (25–40 g) onions and 1 or 2 slices cooked bacon.

losing at least some of its peppery coat. Nor could you add a sauce made in the pan from its fond to intensify the flavor. This is a dish that is usually cooked to order. The techniques are familiar to you by now; the skills come with practice.

Recipe 12-9 illustrates how the simple, familiar techniques of pan-frying are adapted to another kind of meat, and how you can add complementary ingredients for a hearty and satisfying dish.

Turning from pan-frying to sautéing, let us look at the veal dish in recipe 12-10. The veal slices are cooked quickly to maintain their delicacy and tenderness, using the sautéing technique you already know. You also know about deglazing, reducing, swirling in butter, and making a special butter to serve as a sauce over the meat. Compare it with dishes à la meunière. Dozens of other veal dishes are made following the same pattern. For example, you can omit the lemon juice, deglaze the pan with marsala wine, reduce by half, and finish with butter for veal alla marsala.

Meats are seldom deep-fried. The one exception is cooked meats used in croquettes. This is not really a way of cooking meat but a way of making a dish out of a meat that is already cooked.

Roasting

Roasting is a common method of meat cookery and a good one. Tender meats roast well to produce good dishes.

The rules for doneness that apply to different types of meats are very important in roasting. Red meats *can* be cooked from rare to well done, but white meats *must* be cooked well done.

Roasting meat is very simple, so simple that the procedure is all contained in the first two steps of recipe 12-11. Everything else has to do with making the jus to be served with the meat.

Notice that you do not season the roast. In a prime rib it would be a waste of seasonings. Since it has a thick layer of fat on the top and sides and a layer of bones on the bottom, the

12-10 VEAL FRANÇAISE (FRITTURA PICCATA)

Yield: 10 portions (2 pieces each)

20	veal scallopine, 2 oz (50 g) each	20	2 oz	butter	60 g
6–8 oz*	light stock	*175–250 mL	3 Tb	lemon juice	45 mL
*	flour	*	*	salt and pepper	*
*	oil or clarified butter	*	10	thin lemon slices	10
			*	chopped parsley	*

1. Flatten scallopine to ¼″ (5 mm) thickness, taking care not to tear. Season *lightly. Dredge in flour.
2. Sauté in hot fat until lightly golden on both sides (*3–5 minutes). Remove to warm platter.
3. Drain excess fat from pan. Deglaze with light stock and reduce liquid by one-third.
4. Swirl in butter and cook until nut-brown (beurre noisette). Stir in lemon juice.
5. Serve sauce over veal. Garnish with chopped parsley and lemon slices.

salt would not penetrate to the meat except on the ends.

In other roasts seasoning may be appropriate. If a surface is edible or servable it should be seasoned. In most instances an edible, servable surface will allow seasoning to penetrate the flesh to some extent and bring out the flavor of the meat. However, if a sauce is to be made from the pan juices, salting the meat may make the drippings too salty to be used. Salt also interferes with browning by drawing the juices to the surface.

In the roast beef au jus, all logic tells us not to season. Let us go on to make the jus. The **jus** (zhue) means the natural juices from the meat, enhanced with appropriate flavor builders and served over the meat—**au jus** (oh zhue).

In Step 3 you begin to make the jus by adding mirepoix to the pan. Notice that the mirepoix is added only after the roast is cooked. Some cooks like to roast the meat in a bed of mirepoix from the beginning. However, this adds no flavor to the roast, overcooks the mirepoix, and spoils the pan juices with the flavors of overcooked onion, celery, and leek.

When you first add the mirepoix to the roasting pan they cook briefly in the fat from the roast, since there is virtually no other liquid in the pan. In effect you are sautéing them as you do your flavor builders when you are making a soup or sauce.

Pouring off the fat in Step 4 is easy because it is the only liquid in the pan. The juices are neatly preserved in the crust on the bottom of the pan, and you recover them by deglazing in Step 5.

In deglazing you add *enough liquid to make the quantity of jus you want, allowing for 40 to 50 percent evaporation. Then you simmer it until the mirepoix has contributed its best flavors to the jus—up to *30 minutes (Step 6). If necessary you can add a little meat base to increase quantity and flavor. Strained, degreased, and seasoned (Step 7), the jus is ready for the table at the same time as the roast.

The roast, meanwhile, has been standing—a necessary step. When first removed

12-11 ROAST PRIME RIB AU JUS

Yield: 18 6-oz (175 g) portions
1–2 oz (25–50 mL) jus per portion

1	prime rib, 14 lb (6.3 kg), oven ready	1	1 lb	mirepoix, ½″ (1 cm) concassé	500 g	
			*	salt and pepper	*	
2 qt*	stock or water	*2 L				

Basic jus ratio: 1 lb mirepoix / 2 qt stock
500 g mirepoix / 2 L stock

1. Place meat thermometer in center of roast, place roast in roasting pan, and roast in a preheated moderate oven (350°F/180°C).
2. When meat reaches the desired internal temperature, remove it from the pan and let it stand.
3. Add mirepoix to pan and cook it in the fat until lightly caramelized.
4. Pour off fat, keeping mirepoix in pan.
5. Return pan to heat. When hot, add cold stock or water and deglaze pan.
6. Simmer liquid and mirepoix in pan until vegetables are fully cooked (*20–30 minutes).
7. Strain and degrease jus and season *to taste.
8. Slice roast and serve with jus.

from the oven, it goes on cooking and its temperature continues to rise (carry-over cooking). You must give it about 30 minutes to stop cooking so that the juices will settle before you carve it. If you cut it too soon the juices shoot out under pressure and are lost to the meat forever.

The French term *au jus* refers to the manner of serving the meat—roast beef served with juice—and not to the juices themselves. You will hear people refer to these as "the au jus," pronouncing it "oh zhoos," "oh joos," and even "ah juice." The faulty usage and pronunciations jar the ears and sensibilities of people who know French, but the distortions are so common they have become part of the jargon of the trade in some places.

Another source of confusion is the meaning of the word prime in roast prime rib. It does not refer to the grade of meat, as many people assume. It applies rather to the cut of meat, a seven-rib cut from the forequarter.

Whatever you think it is and however you pronounce it, roast prime rib au jus is a dish of both substance and elegance that is simple to prepare—a good one to master.

Lamb, ham, pork, and veal, as well as other cuts of beef, are roasted the same way as prime rib. The pork loin roast in recipe 12-12 applies the basics of roasting to a meat that must be cooked well done. This recipe includes a special sauce of jus and a garniture of prunes. For a nouvelle version, purée the cooked prunes with the jus and finish with butter.

Roast meat can be turned into a meal-in-a-pot dish by roasting it on top of vegetables that are braising in stock beneath it. Leg of

12-12 ROAST PORK LOIN WITH PRUNE SAUCE

Yield: 10–15 6-oz (175 g) portions

1	boneless pork loin, 4–6 lb (2–3 kg)	1	1 lb	mirepoix, ½″ concassé	500 g
1 qt	stock, light or dark	1 L	(*	rosemary, sage	*)
			*	salt and pepper	*
			20–45	prunes, pitted	20–45

1. Season pork with salt and pepper (and rub in herbs as desired).
2. Roast on rack in 350°F (180°C) oven for 1 hour. Turn roast and add mirepoix to pan.
3. Roast meat until well done (185°F/85°C). Remove from pan and keep warm.
4. Drain off excess fat. Deglaze pan with stock and simmer to blend flavors. Strain into another pan and degrease.
5. Add prunes and simmer until prunes are tender.
6. Serve each portion of meat with 2 or 3 prunes and 2 oz (50 mL) sauce.

lamb boulangère is such a dish. After roasting by itself for an hour or so, the meat is placed on top of a pan of sliced potatoes, onions, and stock and roasted to doneness. Gravy is made in the usual way and served over the sliced lamb and potatoes. This down-home dish is incredibly good.

If you are going to roast a ham for a "baked ham" entrée, you need to know whether it is fully cooked, partially cooked, cured uncooked, or fresh uncooked. Fresh uncooked hams are easily identified: they are the color of pork and are treated like any other fresh pork roast. Cured uncooked hams must reach an internal temperature of no less than 170°F (77°C) and no more than 185°F (85°C). Partially cooked hams are brine-cured and have reached only 148°F (65°C) in processing, so they must be cooked to 185°F (85°C). Fully cooked hams to be served as baked ham should be heated to 140° (60°C) to improve their flavor. If you have any doubts about the degree of processing of the ham you are preparing, treat it as uncooked pork.

Any ham that is cured includes salt in the process, so no more is needed for seasoning.

HANDLING AND STORING COOKED MEATS

Meats reach their upper limits in quality as soon as cooking is completed. Ideally service immediately follows readiness. Realistically it may not. Two such situations are common in quantity production. One is left-over meats. The other is extremely large volume that cannot be handled all at once—a thousand steaks for a banquet, for example.

Any cooked meats that are to be served at a later time must be first quickly chilled to room temperature, then either covered or wrapped, and then stored in a cooler or freezer.

If you do not cool these products before covering or wrapping you are inviting great losses from bacterial growth and spoilage. A warm, moist, enclosed place is the ideal breeding ground for bacteria that feed on meat. It is entirely possible that in a careless or slovenly operation the difference between profit and loss lies right here.

SUMMING UP

Since meat is the centerpiece of the menu in most food services as well as the most expensive item, it is critical for you to know how to cook it well. It is important to the budget, the balance sheet, and the customers. They are not likely to return if the meat is overcooked, undercooked, too salty, tasteless, tough, dry, or unattractive.

The two secrets of good meat cookery are knowing how to cook the different cuts of meats and being able to cook them to the right degree of doneness. The right degree of doneness for the white meats (pork and veal) and for less tender cuts of red meat (beef and lamb) is well done—cooked through. Tender cuts of red meats may be cooked from rare to well done according to customer preference. Generally the less well done a steak, chop, or roast from a tender cut of red meat, the more tender, juicy, and flavorful it is.

Many meat dishes include sauces that incorporate the fond from roasted, pan-fried, or sautéed meats or are made from liquids in which the meat was braised. In many braised dishes meat and sauce are cooked together, enriched by the same flavor builders and enriching each other. The structure of most meat dishes and the techniques used to make them are familiar to you from earlier chapters. Each dish simply puts together in an individual way things you already know.

Meat cookery is a special skill but it is not complicated. If you know your product, choose the right cooking method, and cook to the right degree of doneness, you can hardly miss. At today's prices you had better not.

As with fish and poultry, there are many ways of creating different entrées with butters, sauces, marinades, dressings, garnitures, and special flavor combinations from cuisines of other countries. The techniques you have learned in this and earlier chapters put all kinds of meat dishes within your reach.

THE COOK'S VOCABULARY

meat: red meat, white meat, variety meats

elastin, collagen, marbling, finish

aging, rigor mortis, green meat, dry aging,
   Cryovac aging

primal cuts, portion-control cuts

meat grades: prime, choice, good

smoked meats, cured meats

degrees of doneness: rare, medium rare,
   medium, medium well, well done

carry-over cooking

jus, au jus

QUESTIONS FOR DISCUSSION

1. Discuss the importance of meat on the menu and the role of meat cost in the profitability of an establishment.

2. What meat cuts are naturally tender and why? How would you cook them? What cuts are less tender and why? What are the best methods of cooking them?

3. How can you tell when meat is done? What method would you use for steaks? For roasts? For braised dishes?

4. Suggest several ways of building in extra flavor when cooking meats.

5. What nutrients does meat contribute to the diet? Why do some people avoid eating it?

BREAKFAST is often defined as the first meal of the day. You probably think of it in terms of 6 to 9 A.M. But in today's world breakfast may be served at noon, at 9 in the evening, or at 3 A.M. to top off an evening out. It is much more than the day's first meal; it is a group of foods cooked and served in a particular way.

Usually it is eggs with bacon, sausage, or ham, and maybe with hash browns, french fries, or grits, and toast or muffins or cornbread, with fruit or juice to begin with and coffee before, during, and after. The alternative to eggs seems to be pancakes with sausage, or with bacon, or with ham. Or cereal, hot or cold. Or a light continental breakfast of rolls and coffee, or danish and coffee, or doughnuts and coffee. Or just coffee.

In recent years another popular meal period has evolved. **Brunch,** a combination of breakfast and lunch, is served from late morning until midafternoon, usually on weekends. Here you will find dishes that take off from breakfast eggs and pancakes and bacon and ham and fruit to make light and appetizing luncheon entrées, along with such familiar light luncheon fare as cold seafoods, cheese boards, salads, canapés, and quiche. Sometimes such a meal is displayed on an eye-catching buffet with ice sculptures and fruit displays—a visual feast.

What will you cook for breakfast and brunch? Many operations use convenience items. They buy ready-made danish, doughnuts, and rolls. They make cereals, muffins, cornbread, and grits from mixes, flakes, or powders needing only to be baked or boiled as the package directs. They use frozen hash-browned potatoes and canned or frozen fruit juices.

So what is left for the cook to do? You will put to work your skills and knowledge to prepare

13

Breakfast and Brunch

- Eggs
- Breakfast meats
- Pancakes, waffles, french toast, crêpes
- Beverages
- Brunch dishes

317

You will learn more about some familiar foods, practice some old techniques, learn some new ones, and get some experience on the griddle. After completing this chapter you should be able to

- Describe the similarities between breakfast and brunch and the differences between them.
- Describe or demonstrate the principal ways of cooking eggs to order.
- Describe or demonstrate how to use the griddle to cook eggs, breakfast meats, pancakes, and french toast.
- Describe or demonstrate how to prepare breakfast ham, bacon, and sausage.
- List the principal breakfast beverages and describe how to use them.
- Name and describe a dozen kinds of cheese.

ABOUT EGGS

An egg is made up of the albumen, or white; the yolk, or yellow; and a porous shell. It is at its best right after it is laid. A cross section of an egg is shown in Figure 13-1. In a fresh egg, the two ropes of chalazae (ka-lay'-zee) hold the yolk firmly in the middle of the egg. There is more thick white than thin white, and the air cell is small.

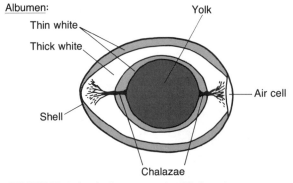

FIGURE 13-1. Inside the egg—a simplified version.

Eggs lose their firmness by the escape of carbon dioxide through the porous shell. As this happens, the air cell enlarges, the chalazae relax, the yolk moves off center, the thick white lessens, and the thin white increases. You can see off-center yolks and large air-cell indentations in hard-boiled eggs that have lost quality. Notice the thick white and thin white as you fry and poach eggs, and you'll see why freshness is important.

Quality and size

Eggs are graded AA, A, or B under a federal–state program administered by the U.S. Department of Agriculture. You can check for high quality and freshness by noting the egg's appearance when broken. Its yolk should remain whole and stand high, and the white should stand high and close to the yolk.

Proper handling can preserve freshness. Stored in coolers at 36°F (2°C), eggs have a shelf life of several months with little loss of quality. At room temperature they deteriorate rapidly. When you hold eggs at the grill for cooking you are exposing them to rapid quality loss. Store them away from strong-smelling foods. They absorb odors through the shell.

The color of the shell has no relation to quality. Shell color is determined by the breed of hen.

Eggs are classified by size as well as by quality. The two classifications have nothing to do with each other. Size classification is actually by weight per dozen, not by the egg, and the eggs in a dozen may not all be the same size. Table 13-1 shows the classification of eggs by size.

Market forms

In addition to fresh eggs, there are several other market forms. Dried eggs and frozen eggs are available whole or separated into whites and yolks. The biggest demand for processed eggs is in the baking industry, but whole dried and frozen eggs are being used more and more in large operations such as airline catering and hospitals. Such products

TABLE 13-1 Eggs Classified by Size

Size	Minimum Weight per Dozen	
Jumbo	30 oz	849 g
Extra large	27 oz	768 g
Large	24 oz	672 g
Medium	21 oz	588 g
Small	18 oz	504 g
Peewee	15 oz	425 g

are useful for eggs cooked in quantity and in mass, such as scrambled eggs and omelets. Use only pasteurized dried eggs.

All frozen eggs must be stored at 0°F (−18°C), thawed in the cooler, and stirred well before use. Dried eggs must be stored in the cooler and reconstituted according to package directions.

All eggs except the frozen pasteurized form are likely to bring salmonella bacteria with them into the kitchen. This is another reason for keeping them refrigerated and handling them with respect at all times.

Uses of eggs

The egg is versatile. You have already met it as an emulsifier in making butter sauces. You have seen it in the liaison as a binding agent and creator of smooth texture for soups and sauces. You know that it is used to clarify liquids such as consommés. You have used it to hold breading together and make it adhere to the product, and to bind duchesse potatoes.

It has still other uses. Egg thickens custards and puddings. Egg white leavens batters and soufflés and is the essence of meringue. Egg can be brushed on foods to be baked, or added to sauces to be glazed, to produce a shiny golden-brown crust.

Nutritionally eggs are good sources of protein, vitamin A, iron, and some B vitamins. The yolk is high in fat and in cholesterol, a fatty substance some people avoid for health reasons. Economically eggs are an inexpensive meat substitute and make excellent luncheon entrées as well as being the backbone of the breakfast menu. Let us now focus on this last role and see how to cook the egg as an egg.

COOKING EGGS

Eggs cooked for breakfast are high-grade whole fresh eggs prepared in a number of ways:

- Eggs to order (fried)
- Poached eggs
- Boiled eggs
- Shirred eggs
- Omelets

The most important rule for cooking eggs of any kind is to use low to moderate temperatures and short cooking times. Overcooking and high heat cause toughness and loss of flavor.

Eggs to order

Eggs fried to order are the heart of the typical American breakfast. The phrase "to order" refers mainly to different degrees of firmness of the yolk and white, depending on the guest's specifications. There are also some differences in style in some of the variations. Here are the more common ones.

- *Sunny side up* or *eyes open:* fried, *not* flipped over, the white cooked firm and yolk cooked medium.
- *Basted:* pan-fried, *not* flipped over, the top cooked by exposing to heat from above in the salamander or by adding a small amount of water to the pan, covering, and steaming. Eggs may also be basted by spooning hot fat from the pan over the yolk while the egg is frying.
- *Over easy:* fried and flipped over, the white barely firm and the yolk just warm.

FIGURE 13-2. Flipping eggs in a pan.

a. Cook the eggs on one side until the white is set.

b. Lift the pan and tilt it away from you so that the eggs begin to climb the far rim of the pan.

c. Flip your wrist upward, pulling the pan toward you, and the eggs will turn over. (Photos by Patricia Roberts.)

- *Over medium:* fried and flipped over, the white firm and the yolk partially cooked.
- *Over well:* fried and flipped over, both yolk and white cooked firm.
- *Scrambled:* whites and yolks beaten together to an even yellow color, then fried and broken up while cooking. Scrambled eggs may be ordered soft, medium, or hard, which simply means cooked to varying degrees of doneness.

Cooking eggs to order requires both practice and patience. The cook must learn to achieve a good-looking finished product as well as one that tastes good. An egg to order should be glossy, moist, and tender no matter what its degree of doneness.

Here are some techniques essential to success.

Cook two eggs at a time. Break them into a bowl first. If anything is wrong, such as a broken yolk or a blood spot, you can save them for another use.

Use a well-primed fry pan 6 to 8 inches across at the bottom, just the right size to accommodate the eggs in a nice round shape. Heat the pan over low heat and add ⅛ inch (3 mm) or so of fat—butter, margarine, or a mixture of butter and oil. When the fat is hot (but not hot enough to sizzle), add the two eggs simultaneously. Cook the first side to the desired degree of doneness.

Flipping eggs is an art that scares and frustrates many novice cooks. The object is to get the eggs turned over without redecorating the floor, range top, or ceiling, and without damaging the eggs. Yolks must remain whole and white unfolded.

To flip eggs successfully, follow the steps below. They are illustrated in Figure 13-2.

1. Cook the eggs on one side, as described, until the white is set.

2. Lift the pan, tilting it away from you so that the eggs start to slide toward the far side of the pan.

3. Flip your wrist quickly upward while pulling

the pan toward you, and the eggs will turn over. Do not toss them in the air; they should scarcely leave the pan.

Once the eggs are flipped, cook the second side to the desired degree of doneness. Then flip the eggs back again to serve the best-looking side to the guest.

You might practice with a slice of bread rather than eggs until you have the feel for flipping. If you have trouble, you are in good company. Napoleon, cooking eggs for Josephine, sent them right onto the floor.

You can also cook eggs to order on a griddle. Figure 13-3 shows you how, from beginning to end. Use a low heat and flip the eggs with a spatula. Sometimes they are cooked in an egg ring to keep them in a perfect round shape.

To scramble eggs, mix yolks and whites well and add to the pan as for fried eggs. Place a plastic spoon or spatula in the middle of the pan and shake the pan back and forth over the burner, stirring occasionally, so that the eggs are broken up and cook evenly.

Here are some common pitfalls and ways to avoid them.

- *Eggs brown and crisp:* Too much heat. Use a low heat. Eggs cook at 140–158°F (60–70°C).

- *Egg white blistered:* Too much heat or too much fat. Cut down accordingly.

- *Eggs odd shapes:* Eggs not fresh enough. Use only high-grade fresh eggs; they are well shaped and stand tall.

- *Eggs sticking:* Too much heat, too little fat, or a porous cooking surface.

A porous cooking surface is a constant nightmare for the egg cook. A primed surface, whether griddle or pan, is absolutely necessary. A **primed,** or **seasoned, surface** is one that has been polished at a high heat with salt and fat or oil to overcome its porousness.

To prime a pan follow these steps.

- Heat the pan on a hot fire.

- Remove the pan from the fire and add to it a few drops of oil and a handful of salt.

- With a soft cloth, rub salt and oil vigorously and with pressure into the surface of the hot pan, as though you were scouring it with cleanser.

- Discard the salt-and-oil mixture and wipe the pan very clean with a soft, dry cloth.

- Repeat until you can cook an egg in the pan without its sticking anywhere.

Water destroys a primed surface; even steam basting can do it. A common cry in the breakfast kitchen is, "Who washed my egg pans??!" Cooking a hamburger or anything else in an egg pan causes the same frustration. Egg pans should be used *only* for eggs.

Wash your own egg pans when you are through for the day; dry them properly and reprime them. To dry an egg pan put it on the heat. When it is dry and hot, reprime it before storing and it will work just fine. For extra security rub it again with oil before you start cooking your next egg.

Fried eggs are best cooked by the individual serving, but scrambled eggs may be cooked in quantity. You can shell the eggs and mix them ahead of time, using a wire whip. Cook them in a shallow pan in a thin layer, stirring constantly, and remove them before they are quite done, because they will go on cooking somewhat. If they must be held, place them in earthenware containers.

Scrambled eggs held on a steam table can turn an unappetizing green. To avoid this, blend in a small amount of cream or béchamel sauce after they are cooked. This will not only prevent the green but will keep them moist.

Poached eggs

A poached egg is a shelled egg cooked in hot liquid. To poach an egg, you drop it gently into hot liquid and let it stand until it reaches the desired doneness.

FIGURE 13-3. Cooking eggs on a griddle.

a. First crack the eggs into a bowl.

b. Holding the bowl close to the griddle surface, tip the eggs all together onto the griddle.

c. When the white is set, place a spatula under one edge of the eggs.

d. Flip them over with a smooth, quick lifting and turning motion so that they scarcely leave the griddle.
(Photos by Patricia Roberts.)

It is a simple process. But there are several factors of critical importance in achieving a good-looking poached egg—one that has a compact, glossy, obviously tender white surrounding an unbroken, somewhat thickened yolk.

The first is the quality of the egg. Only a fresh, high-quality egg will emerge from its hot bath in a state of togetherness. In an older or lower-grade egg part of the white will be thin and wispy and wrinkled, with ragged edges, so unattractive it is best to cut it away before you serve the egg.

The second factor is the poaching liquid. This liquid is water with a small amount of distilled vinegar or salt added to encourage shapeliness. Half an ounce (15 mL) of vinegar or a teaspoon (5 mL) of salt to a quart (1 L) of water will help firm up the white and keep it from spreading.

The third consideration is the temperature. It needs to be hot enough to begin cooking the egg as soon as the egg hits the liquid, but not hot enough to produce agitation. Action in the liquid will tend to tear the egg or spoil its shape. What you want is small bubbles rising from the bottom but no agitation. You can use the same criteria you used for poaching fish or poultry.

The fourth point of concern is the amount of liquid. It should be 3 or 4 inches (7–10 cm) deep in the pan to be sure the egg is completely covered while cooking. It should also be deep enough to cook the egg slightly before it reaches the bottom of the pan, so that it does not stick to the bottom. There should be enough liquid altogether to ensure that adding the egg does not drop the temperature below the 150–160°F (66–71°C) necessary for cooking. The amount you need will vary with the number of eggs being poached in one pan.

A fifth factor is the way you put the egg into the pan. Slip it in gently toward the side of the pan. It may be easier to do this from a bowl or saucer than directly from the shell. You'll see the yolk sink quickly to the bottom, with the white flapping upward.

Poached eggs too can be cooked to varying degrees of doneness. The minimum is enough firmness to be removed from the liquid without breaking. Take them out with a skimmer or perforated spoon, draining them well.

Eggs for quantity service may be poached in advance and held in ice water. For poaching large numbers of eggs you need a large shallow pan or kettle with a continuous heat source—that is, the heat must be distributed evenly to all parts of the pan. A tilting fry pan is ideal for this purpose. You slide the eggs carefully into the liquid one after another, remove them individually when barely done, and slip them into ice water, which stops the cooking. At serving time you can reheat them for 30 to 60 seconds in simmering liquid.

Poached eggs can be served plain on buttered toast or english muffins, or you can combine them with other ingredients as in recipes 13-1a and 13-1b. The holland rusk in 13-1a resembles a round thick piece of melba toast and comes ready to serve. You can use english muffins in either recipe. A variation on 13-1b is to make containers of duchesse or baked potatoes or of grilled tomato halves. Or you can substitute other vegetables and sauces to create your own house specialty. The many poached egg dishes you can make as variations of these recipes give you a wealth of entrées for brunch menus.

"Boiled" eggs

Boiled eggs are also cooked in a hot liquid. They differ from poached eggs in that they are cooked in their shells in hotter water. But though they are called boiled, the water should not boil; it should simmer. The rapid action of boiling water will crack the shells as they bump each other.

Eggs to be simmered should be at room temperature. This will help prevent the shells from cracking when they hit the hot water.

13-1a EGGS BENEDICT

Yield: 1 portion

1	egg, poached, drained	1
1	canadian bacon slice, 2 oz (60 g), grilled	1
1	holland rusk or toasted english muffin half, buttered	1
1½ oz	hollandaise sauce	45 mL

1. Place rusk or muffin on serving plate and lay hot bacon on top. Center a well-drained poached egg on meat.
2. Nap with sauce and serve immediately.

13-1b EGGS FLORENTINE

Yield: 1 portion

1	egg, poached, drained	1
2 oz	cooked chopped spinach, seasoned	60 g
1½ oz	mornay sauce	45 mL
(*	parmesan cheese	*)

1. Make a nest of hot drained spinach on serving plate. Place poached egg in center of spinach.
2. Nap with sauce. (Sprinkle with cheese and gratiné lightly.)

Boiled eggs, like other kinds, are cooked to varying degrees of doneness, usually spelled out in minutes. The times given here refer to eggs at room temperature placed in water that is already at a simmer.

- 3 to 5 minutes in simmering water produces a soft egg.
- 7 to 8 minutes produces a medium egg.
- 10 to 15 minutes produces a hard-cooked egg.

The time spans given are broad. For smaller eggs use the lower limits and for larger eggs use the upper limits.

The problems with boiled eggs are not with the soft egg but with the hard one. Don't overcook it. An overcooked egg will darken around the yolk and have a tough white.

If you are making hard-cooked eggs for something other than breakfast and plan to use them cold, cooling them quickly in ice water will help avoid the dark color around the yolk. Peeling them right away under cold running water is easier than peeling them later. Another way to keep a hard-cooked egg free of that dark area is to start it in cold water, simmer it for 5 minutes after it comes to a boil, remove the pan from the heat and let the egg sit in the same hot water for another 5 minutes, then cool it in ice water. This works beautifully for a few eggs. Larger numbers require extended cooking times of up to 7 minutes.

Hard-cooked eggs in quantity are sometimes done in the cabinet steamer. Use single layers in shallow pans. Otherwise they do not cook evenly and you do not get a uniform product.

Shirred eggs

Shirred eggs are eggs cooked and served in the same dish, usually a shallow flat-bottomed earthenware dish. You coat the dish with melted butter and break the eggs into it. For speed, you set it directly on the range until the whites begin to firm. Then you transfer it to a moderate oven (350°F/180°C) for finish-cooking or run it under the salamander to cook the top. Be careful not to overcook. Shirred eggs should have the same qualities as eggs sunny side up.

You can make many different brunch dishes with shirred eggs by first placing the raw eggs on hash, bacon, diced tomatoes, or cheese and preparing them the same way. Or you can cook them first and then surround them with mushroom or tomato sauce, grilled meat, hot cream, or asparagus tips.

Omelets

Of all egg dishes the omelet is the most difficult to master. Mastery takes patience, practice, and timing. To understand the omelet, study recipe 13-2 step by step. An omelet pan, by the way, is a primed fry pan slightly larger than a two-egg pan. Figure 13-4 illustrates the last half of the story, from Step 4 to completion.

A perfect omelet is fluffy, moist, and tender, soft in the center, yellow in color with no brown at all or just a hint of it, oval in shape, and all in one continuous piece. You can fill it with meat, cheese, jelly, mushrooms, shrimp, or other good things whose flavors complement the eggs. You add the filling before you make the first fold. Or you can make an herb omelet by mixing herbs into the eggs before cooking begins. Some cooks add two or three drops of water per egg before beating them. It makes a somewhat lighter, fluffier omelet.

Recipes 13-2a through 13-2d give you four more techniques for adding flavorful foods to omelets. In the cheese omelet you cook the added ingredient as part of making the omelet. In the western omelet you add a precooked mixture of ingredients during cooking. In the currant jelly omelet you fill the completed omelet, and in the Spanish omelet you ladle a sauce over it after cooking is done. All make delicious dishes for breakfast, brunch, or lunch.

You can vary the form of the omelet if you wish. Leave it flat and cook it like eggs to order or cook the top under the salamander. Or add ingredients to make an Italian-style frittata or a Chinese egg foo yung and serve it flat. Or fold the omelet in half to make it "American style." However, the form we have pictured here, with the two folds, usually called a french omelet, is the one most people expect an omelet to be.

Like eggs to order, omelets must be made individually. You can, however, preprepare the eggs in quantity, shelling and mixing them as you do for scrambled eggs, then measuring them into individual pans as the omelets are ordered. Where large quantities are required, omelets may be made ahead, chilled, and reheated at service time. This is how some airline caterers prepare omelets. Flight attendants reheat them on the planes.

The omelet is both versatile and challenging. It is well worth the time and practice it takes for mastery.

BREAKFAST MEATS

Any meat can be served for breakfast, but there are some kinds we identify with the breakfast menu. Ham-and-eggs, bacon-and-eggs, pancakes-and-sausage—all are breakfast go-togethers. These products of the pig fall into two groups: ham and bacon, which are smoked or cured, and sausage, which is usually raw fresh pork.

Breakfast ham is typically sliced cooked ham grilled or broiled to order. You need only enough cooking to get it thoroughly hot and to brown the fat around the edges. Use a moderate heat and cook both sides. Two to 4 ounces is a typical breakfast portion.

The typical portion of bacon is 2 to 4 slices. The best way to cook bacon is in a moderate oven. You can lay the slices out on sheet pans or on racks placed on sheet pans, or you can buy it already laid out on parchment paper that can go right into the oven on a sheet pan. Any of these ways will give you a consistent product, evenly cooked without turning. It looks 400 percent better than pan-fried bacon because it does not curl.

The most difficult part of the cooking is pouring off the grease, which must be done when cooking is complete. Handling a large amount of hot grease in a shallow pan is extremely dangerous and calls for all your caution and skill. Using a rack avoids this problem because you just pick the rack up off the pan, leaving the grease to be dealt with when it is cooler.

Drain the cooked bacon on paper towels or racks. Bacon holds well and can be prepared ahead in considerable quantity.

FIGURE 13-4. Cooking and folding an omelet.

a. When the edges curl and cook firm . . .

b. . . . place a spoon or spatula in the center of the pan and vigorously slide the pan back and forth so that the raw eggs spill over the cooked edges.

c. When the bottom is firm but the top is still moist, remove from the heat and fold one edge to the center of the pan or a little beyond.

d. Slide the other edge onto a plate and . . .

e. . . . roll the folded part over on top of it—all in one motion.

f. "A perfect omelet is fluffy, moist, and tender. . . ." (Photos by Patricia Roberts.)

13-2 THREE-EGG OMELET

3	eggs	3	(*	seasonings *)
*	butter	*		

1. Break eggs into a bowl (add seasonings *to taste), and beat vigorously with a fork or whip, aerating the eggs slightly.
2. Heat an omelet pan until hot. Add butter to the hot pan (*about ⅛"/3 mm) and allow time for the butter to get hot.
3. Add the eggs to the center of the omelet pan.
4. When the edges curl and cook firm, place a plastic spoon or spatula in the center of the pan and vigorously slide the pan back and forth so that the raw eggs on top spill over the cooked edges and cook.
5. When firm on the bottom but still moist on top, remove from heat and fold one edge of the omelet to the center of the pan or a little beyond, using the spatula or spoon.
6. Slide the other edge of the omelet onto a plate and roll the folded part over on top of it to make a second fold—all in one motion.

13-2a CHEESE OMELET

To recipe 13-2 add:

2 oz	cheddar or swiss cheese, grated	60 g

Step 4a. Sprinkle cheese in a 2" (5 cm) stripe (perpendicular to handle) across center of pan.

Step 4b. Place under salamander until cheese is barely melted. Continue with remaining steps.

13-2b WESTERN OMELET

To recipe 13-2 add:

2 oz	*western mixture:* equal parts small dice ham, onions, and green pepper, sautéed	60 g

Step 4a. Add a stripe of hot mixture across center of pan and proceed.

13-2c CURRANT JELLY OMELET

To recipe 13-2 add:

1 oz	red currant jelly	30 g

Step 6a. Cut a slot in center of finished omelet and spoon jelly into it.

13-2d SPANISH OMELET

To recipe 13-2 add:

2 oz	spanish sauce (8-6a)	60 mL

Step 6a. Nap finished omelet with spanish sauce.

A second way of cooking bacon is to fry it in a pan or on a griddle. This method is used only for small amounts cooked to order. Preheat the pan, use moderate heat, and turn the slices so as to cook both sides. Bacon may also be broiled to order on the broiler rack of the salamander. It cooks well in the microwave oven too.

Whatever cooking method you use, cook the bacon to crispness, or a little short of crispness if it is to be held. It should never be allowed to reach the point at which it suddenly turns brown and brittle and changes flavor. It may take a little experience to know how to stop just before the turning point.

One other smoked-pork item used for breakfast and brunch is smoked pork loin that has been boned and rolled. This cut of meat is called *canadian bacon*. It comes precooked and is handled, stored, sliced, and heated the same way as ham. Look back at recipe 13-1a for one way to use it.

Sausage used as a breakfast meat comes in two forms: links and patties. Sausage patties can be compared to hamburger patties with one major difference: sausage is fresh pork and must always be cooked well done. This is true for the links too.

Sausage is cooked like bacon. You pan-fry it or cook it on the griddle for small amounts, and cook it in the oven for larger quantities. Take great pains to cook it done yet not overdone. It is done when it becomes firm and the color is totally changed from gray to brown. Overcooked sausage becomes very dry, crisp, and hard. Crispness may be desirable in bacon but not in sausage.

Other meats too can be served for breakfast, and often are—steak, pork chops, chipped beef in white sauce, corned beef hash, chicken livers. Fish are also offered on some menus: mackerel and smoked salt fish such as kippered herring and finnan haddie. Meats and fish are prepared for breakfast and brunch exactly as they would be for other meals, except that the portions are smaller—usually 2 to 4 ounces (50–100 grams).

PANCAKES, WAFFLES, FRENCH TOAST, CRÊPES

Waffles and pancakes, sometimes called griddle cakes or flapjacks, are typically American breakfast fare. Both are made from batters, but they differ in the way they are cooked.

13-3 PANCAKES

Yield: 1 quart (1 liter) = 16 3" (7 cm) pancakes

dry							liquid
	8 oz	flour	250 g	2	eggs	2	
	1 oz	sugar	30 g	1 pt	milk	500 mL	
	½ tsp	salt	2 mL	2 oz	oil or melted butter	60 mL	
	1 Tb	baking powder	15 mL				

1. Sift dry ingredients together.
2. Mix liquid ingredients, stirring until blended.
3. Add liquid to dry ingredients and mix until barely combined.
4. Using a 2-oz (60 mL) ladle, pour onto griddle set at low to moderate heat, turning when holes begin to appear on top.
5. Cook until bottom is browned. Serve immediately.

13-4 FRENCH TOAST

Yield: 25 portions

50	day-old bread slices	50	(1 Tb	nutmeg or cinnamon	15 mL)
20	eggs	20	(1 Tb	vanilla	15 mL)
1½ qt	milk, half-and-half, or cream	1½ L	(2–4 oz	sugar	60–120 g)
			½ oz	salt	15 g

1. Mix eggs, milk or cream, (flavorers), and salt until thoroughly combined.
2. Soak bread slices in egg mixture until moistened throughout.
3. Cook on griddle over moderate heat, turning once, until lightly golden on both sides.

Pancakes are made from a batter consisting of eggs, flour, water or milk, seasoning, and a leavening agent to make them puff or rise as they cook. The most common leavening agent is baking powder. You can make the batter from recipe 13-3 or use a prepared mix. In either case do not overmix it: too much mixing will make it tough. Stop as soon as it is well blended.

To cook pancakes use a 2-oz (60 mL) ladle to pour small quantities of batter on a slightly oiled griddle set at low to moderate heat. When they are brown on the bottom and begin to form holes on top, flip them over and brown them on the other side. Serve them immediately—piping hot in a stack with butter and syrup or jellies and preserves.

Good pancakes are light and slightly spongy in texture. Add pecans or fruit for a special flavor treat.

Waffles are made from a similar but slightly heavier batter with fat or oil added. They are cooked with a waffle iron, a piece of small equipment that has only one use: making waffles. It cooks the batter on the top and bottom simultaneously and makes the waffles look like large plaid pancakes.

You can make waffles from a mix, or use one of the recipes from the baking chapter (15-1, 1a, 1b). Cook them in a preheated waffle iron.

A good waffle is light to medium brown, with a crisp, light texture. It should have the exact shape of the waffle iron, with no ragged edges. Serve it like a pancake with butter and syrup or preserves or even fresh strawberries.

To clean the waffle iron, simply brush out any crumbs. The iron has a preprimed surface that will be spoiled by water. An occasional light oiling may be necessary.

French toast is a complete breakfast in itself. You may wonder how French french toast is, but there is no doubt how American it is. In France it is called *pain perdu* (pan pair-due), meaning lost bread, because you can use up day-old, slightly stale bread and turn a loss into a profit. Day-old bread absorbs more egg mixture than fresh bread and produces the best french toast.

French toast (recipe 13-4) is made by soaking bread in seasoned beaten eggs often flavored with vanilla or nutmeg or cinnamon, and then griddling or pan-frying it to a golden brown. Include cream for an extra-rich flavor. French toast is served dusted with powdered sugar with syrup on the side.

We turn now from french toast to a type of pancake from France—**crêpes**. These are

13-5 BASIC CRÊPES

Yield: 25 6" (15 cm) crêpes

	8 oz	flour	250 g	6 oz	eggs	185 g		
dry	1 tsp	salt	5 mL	1 lb	milk	500 g		liquid
	(1 oz	sugar	30 g)	2½ oz	clarified butter, melted	80 mL		
				(*	water	*)		

1. Sift dry ingredients into a bowl.
2. Stir eggs into dry ingredients.
3. Add enough milk to make a paste and stir until smooth.
4. Gradually blend in remaining milk and butter.
5. Strain through a china cap. If necessary *adjust texture with water. Batter should be consistency of heavy cream.
6. Cover and refrigerate at least 2 hours or overnight.

To fry:
7. Coat a seasoned 6–7" skillet very lightly with butter or oil.
8. Heat over moderately high heat until very hot. Remove from heat.
9. Using a small ladle, pour about 1½ oz (45–60 mL) batter into pan. Immediately swirl pan so that batter coats bottom with a thin, even layer. Pour off excess.
10. Return to heat and cook until bottom is light brown.
11. Turn crêpe and brown second side. Slide onto flat surface.
12. Continue in this way, stacking crêpes with parchment or waxed paper between. Oil pan lightly as needed.
13. Wrap in plastic wrap and refrigerate or freeze until needed.

quite different from American pancakes: they are very thin, and since they contain no leavening they are flat. They do not make a dish by themselves but are usually rolled around fillings and napped with sauce. Savory fillings produce dishes for brunch, lunch, or appetizers. A few of the possibilities are creamed chicken, seafood newburg, or creamed spinach, often topped with a sauce such as mornay and gratinéed lightly.

By adding sugar to the batter you can make sweet crêpes for desserts. Fill them with fruit, ice cream, preserves, or pudding, then roll them and top with a dessert sauce or confectioner's sugar.

Before you let your imagination run wild,

let us examine the crêpe-making procedure. It is nowhere near as simple as our American pancake. Recipe 13-5 spells it all out.

In Step 1, sift the dry ingredients to distribute them thoroughly, just as you did for American-style pancakes. (The sugar is included for dessert crêpes, though some cooks use up to a tablespoon (15 mL) in the basic mix to aid in browning.)

At this point the method begins to differ. With a wire whip, either by hand or in the mixer, stir in the eggs (Step 2) and add 2 to 4 oz (60–120 g) of the milk (Step 3). Make sure this mixture is very smooth and lump-free before adding the rest of the liquids (Step 4). Strain through a fine-mesh china cap (Step 5). You need a smooth texture to make the very thin pancake desired.

But all this mixing causes a substance in the flour called gluten to develop. If you used the batter immediately, this gluten would give you a thin but tough crêpe. This is why you refrigerate the batter (Step 6). By letting it rest, you give the gluten time to relax. Then you are ready to try your hand at cooking the crêpes.

Frying crêpes, like making omelets, takes practice to produce a perfect one. Even experienced French chefs say that the first of any batch is "for the cat" because it is seldom right. After some practice many cooks can produce crêpes assembly-line style with five or more pans on the fire simultaneously. The first pancake is ready to flip as the batter is poured into the last pan.

The first step is to choose a well-seasoned pan and oil it lightly (Step 7). The crêpe may tear if it sticks, but it will be greasy if you use too much fat. Heat the pan (Step 8). As you ladle the batter in, tilt the pan and swirl the batter gently as it reaches the hot pan (Figure 13-5a) so that a thin, round, even coat will "set" on the bottom of the pan (Step 9). Pour off the excess. All this is accomplished almost in one motion taking only a few seconds.

Return the pan to the heat for a minute or so until the crêpe is a light golden brown (Step 10). Use your fingertips to pull one edge gently

---

13-5a CRÊPES SEAFOOD NEWBURG
Yield: 1 portion

2	crêpes	2
3 oz	seafood newburg (10–16)	90 mL
2 oz	mornay sauce (8-1b)	60 mL

1. Place 1½ oz (45 mL) hot newburg mixture on each crêpe. Roll up.
2. On serving plate, place rolled crêpes side by side with seam on bottom.
3. Nap with sauce. Gratiné under salamander until light golden.

Production method: Fill and refrigerate until needed. Heat in oven. Nap with sauce and gratiné.

---

up from the side of the pan (Figure 13-5b) to flip the pancake over (Step 11). Cook until it has browned lightly, then use the pan to slide it onto the stack (Figure 13-5c). The first side browns more evenly than the second one. It is used as the *presentation side*—the outside of the rolled crêpe—so that it looks more attractive to the diner.

Crêpes can be made ahead of time because they store well in the refrigerator or freezer when tightly wrapped and protected from air (Steps 12 and 13). When you have become a confident crêpe maker, you can use some fillings and sauces from previous chapters to create dishes for brunch, lunch, and appetizers—for example, crêpes seafood newburg in recipe 13-5a. And keep crêpes in mind for delicious sweet combinations when you reach the dessert chapter.

You will find other batter-based products for breakfast and brunch discussed in Chapter 15—muffins, cornbread, sweet rolls, coffee cake, biscuits, brioche. In most kitchens such products are bought or made from mixes. Certain other prebaked products are standards on most breakfast menus—buttered toast, english muffins, doughnuts, danish pas-

FIGURE 13-5. Frying crêpes. (Photos by Patricia Roberts.)

a. Ladle the batter into the pan while tilting and swirling to make a thin, even coating.

b. When the first side is a *light* golden brown, peel it away from the pan to turn it over.

c. When the second side is light golden, slide it onto the stack.

tries. You simply toast and butter the bread or the muffin, heat the doughnut or danish, and serve it forth.

BEVERAGES

To many people a cup of coffee is the essence of breakfast. Others may feel the same way about tea, but coffee is the great American beverage.

Coffee

The one thing most likely to leave a lasting impression of the place where it is served is coffee. There's a good chance it will be both the first and the last thing a customer tastes, especially at breakfast. To ensure a good after-image, good coffee is a must.

Coffee is made with two ingredients, ground coffee and hot water. It is brewed by passing the water over the coffee in a machine that does most of the work. Simple? It isn't simple at all. Yet many food-service operations let the least-qualified people make the coffee. They consistently serve bad coffee as a result.

A good cup of coffee is a clear, rich-brown, steaming-hot brew with an inviting fragrance. To make good coffee you must give careful attention to absolutely everything that has to do with making it—equipment, time, temperature, water, as well as the ground coffee and the method of making the brew. Let's look at the basic rules.

Use clean equipment. Coffee leaves a barely visible oily residue that will spoil the next potful if it is not cleaned away. One spot can do it. All coffeemakers must be cleaned after each brewing, and cleaned thoroughly once a day. Large urns must be taken apart and cleaned with a special compound after each brewing.

Use fresh coffee. Only fresh coffee will give you fresh taste. Ground coffee loses flavor quickly. A few weeks to a few months is the most shelf life you can expect. Store coffee in a cool, dry place.

Use the right grind. The right grind is what-

ever is recommended by the manufacturer of your equipment. Regular, or medium, grind is best for most types. Too coarse a grind will give you weak, flavorless coffee. Too fine a grind will give you bitter flavor plus the chance of fine grounds in the bottom of the cup.

Use the right proportions. A good proportion of coffee to water is 1 pound to 2–2½ gallons (450 g to 8–10 liters). Establish exact amounts for your coffeemaker and your clientele by taste and experience.

The proportion of brewed coffee to the size of the coffeemaker is also important. It is best to use the equipment at its full capacity, or at three-quarters capacity at the very least.

Use fresh water. Draw fresh water for each batch of coffee. Boiled water that stands becomes stale. Use water from the cold tap. Hot tap water may contain residues from the hot-water tank.

Use the right water temperature. Water temperature for brewing should be between 195 and 203°F (91–95°C). Water that is not hot enough will not extract the flavors you want. Water that is too hot can extract some flavors you don't want.

Use a pour-over or drip method of brewing. Hot water should pass over the ground coffee *one time and one time only.* Two types of modern pour-over equipment are shown in Figure 13-6. For small amounts of coffee the 10-cup pour-over machine is popular. Many models have as many as six burners for keeping fresh-brewed coffee hot. For larger volume, an urn such as the one pictured brews by spraying hot water over the ground coffee. Urns vary in size from 2 to 100 gallons, but the basics of brewing are the same.

Do not overbrew. Brewing time must be long enough to extract the flavorful soluble solids but not long enough to extract the less soluble and unpleasant-tasting solids. Total brewing time should not exceed 8 minutes. Most coffee is brewed in 4 to 6 minutes. Less than 4 minutes will underextract; more than 8 will certainly overextract.

Remove the grounds as soon as brewing

is complete. This prevents further unintentional brewing. Hot brewed coffee will send steam up through the grounds, which condenses and drains back again, leaching undesirable flavors from the grounds.

Do not hold coffee more than an hour—certainly never more than 1½ hours. Coffee that stands loses both flavor and aroma and actually undergoes chemical changes that alter its taste. Holding temperature should be 185–195°F (85–91°C).

Cost is often the reason given for not throwing out stale coffee and making a fresh pot. Consider which cost is greater, a few cups of coffee or a customer. Improved planning and timing will solve the waste problem better than pretending stale coffee is good to the last drop.

Most operations experience a modest demand for decaffeinated coffee. Many use instant decaffeinated made to order by the cup, or, when demand is greater, they brew it from ground decaffeinated beans using the same precautions as for regular coffee. The alternative is to serve a packet of decaf with a pot of hot water and let the diner mix it at the table.

Tea

Another standard hot beverage at breakfast, brunch, and in the afternoon is tea. In fact, a new serving period—afternoon tea—is making its appearance.

Tea is made from the crushed dried leaves of oriental shrubs and comes in many different flavors and blends. It is commonly bought in

FIGURE 13-6. Typical coffeemakers.

a. A 10-cup pour-over model. You place premeasured coffee in the basket and flip a switch. The machine draws the right amount of water, heats it to the right temperature, and makes the coffee. A warming plate on the top keeps one pot hot while the second pot is making.

b. A double spray-over urn. You place premeasured coffee in the basket at the top of the urn, position the spray over it, and flip a switch. Water is heated to the proper temperature in the middle section. (Photos courtesy Bunn-O-Matic Corporation.)

portion-size bags and in larger bags for quantity production.

Like coffee, tea is a brew made by exposing the product to hot water over a period of time. However, the tea leaves stand immersed in hot water rather than having the water seep through them and drain off as in coffeemaking. The process is called **steeping.**

A good cup of tea is a clear, fragrant liquid with a taste often described as brisk—somewhat sweet, somewhat tart, but never bitter. Flavor, aroma, and color vary with the kind and blend of tea, and strength varies with the taste of the diner.

To make good tea, you pour boiling water over the tea bag in a preheated pot, let it steep for 3 to 5 minutes, and remove the bag.

As in making coffee, there are some important rules:

- *Use the right proportions.* A teaspoon (5 mL) of tea, or one portion-size tea bag, makes one cup of strong tea or two cups of mild tea. An ounce of tea makes a gallon (6–8 grams make a liter).

- *Use boiling-hot water, freshly boiled,* for maximum flavor extraction.

- *Do not overbrew.* Tea steeped more than 5 minutes becomes dark and bitter. Remove the tea bag from the pot at the end of the brewing period.

- *Use only pottery, china, glass, or stainless steel* for brewing. Metals react with a substance in tea called tannin to produce a metallic taste.

Actually, most operations do not make tea this way. They serve the diner a cup or pot of hot water with a tea bag beside it. They do this for two reasons—because people like their tea in different strengths and because Americans are not great tea drinkers and demand is light. Perhaps dumping a whole shipload of tea into Boston Harbor two hundred years ago influenced our drinking habits.

This type of service does not make very good tea because the water is tepid by the time it is served. An individual pot is better than a cup because it keeps the water hotter and allows the diner to pour it over the tea rather than dunk the bag in the tepid water. Preheating the pot helps too.

There aren't any good solutions to the problem of what to do with the soggy bag when the tea is made.

Iced tea is made the same way as hot tea, doubling the proportion of tea to water (2 oz to a gallon or 15 g to a liter) and using the maximum steeping time. It is made in quantity and held at room temperature. It holds well, up to 4 hours. Pour it over ice just before service. Instant iced tea is often used today to cut preparation time.

Juices

Cold fruit and vegetable juices are a very American way to begin breakfast or brunch. Tangy orange, grapefruit, and pineapple juices as well as ice-cold tomato and V-8 juices are excellent stimulators of the appetite. Chill canned juices thoroughly; reconstitute frozen juices according to package directions and chill. Serve in chilled glasses.

For a festive holiday brunch, orange juice or tomato juice is sometimes combined with an alcoholic beverage to make a house specialty. The screwdriver (orange juice with vodka), the bloody mary (tomato juice with vodka, suitably spiced), and the mimosa (orange juice and champagne) are often offered to spark the holiday appetite. Sometimes a complimentary glass of champagne is a festive come-on for a buffet spread.

Milk and its relatives

Milk is always on hand as a beverage at every meal, especially in establishments with a family clientele. Usually it is *whole milk,* which has a fat content of 3 to 8 percent. Some operations such as hospitals also offer *skim milk* (1/2 percent fat or less) and *low-fat milk* (1/2 to 3 percent fat). Other milk products served to the customer include *light cream* (16 to 22 percent fat) and *half-and-half* (10 to 12 percent fat), both served with coffee or cereal. Many operations substitute nondairy creamer to go with coffee.

Among other milk products are three items made by combining friendly bacteria with a milk product. *Buttermilk* is skim milk that is cultured with bacteria to produce a tangy beverage. *Yogurt* is made by fermenting whole or low-fat milk. It is sometimes sweetened and flavored and served by itself or as part of another dish. *Sour cream* is 18 percent fat cream, fermented. It has a thick, spoonable consistency and a delicious flavor. It is used in dips and dressings.

Milk products must always be refrigerated. They are among the foods most likely to encourage bacterial growth. They deteriorate rapidly.

Then there is cheese, an important milk product and an ideal candidate for the brunch menu.

CHEESE

Cheese is a high-protein dairy product made from milk of domestic animals: cows, sheep, and goats. It is made by curdling milk—that is, separating it into curds and whey—by adding rennet or bacteria or both. The liquid whey is drained off, and the solid mass of curd, or coagulated milk protein, is used to make cheese.

Legend has it that the first cheese was made accidentally from goat's milk that an Arab merchant was carrying in a saddlebag. The jolting of his camel in the hot sun separated the milk into curds and whey. The fact that the saddlebag was made of animal innards may have had something to do with it. Most of the rennet used in cheese-making today comes from the lining of a calf's stomach.

Kinds of cheese

There are literally hundreds of different kinds of cheese. They range in taste from mild to sharp and in texture from soft to hard—

usually referred to as *soft, semisoft, firm,* and *hard.* They are also divided into two groups— **ripened** (fermented with bacteria or molds) and **unripened** (fresh, untreated). Cheeses ripened over a period of time are said to be **aged.** The longer they age, the sharper their flavor— and the higher their cost. Let's take a look at just the few you are most likely to serve or to use in the kitchen.

Cheddar, often called American cheese, is the best-seller of cheeses. A firm ripened type, it comes in many varieties, ranging in flavor from very mild to the very sharp "rat cheese" sold by the old-time butcher. Cheddar is used in sandwiches and appetizers and as a dessert cheese. It is also the most-used cooking cheese, the one the cook uses when the recipe says just "cheese."

Swiss is another popular type of firm ripened cheese. It is immediately recognizable by its holes, which come from gases that develop during fermentation. The swisses have a variety of mild flavors. Two kinds of imported swiss are frequently used in the kitchen: *emmenthal* (em'-un-tahl) and *gruyère* (groo-yair). They are the cheeses of choice for the cheese–fruit plate and the buffet, as well as for the soufflé, the fondue pot, and the sauce pot. Domestic swiss is usually used in sandwiches.

A group known collectively as *blue cheese* are ripened semisoft cheeses with blue-green veins of mold in them. They have a sharp, peppery flavor and crumbly texture that make them look and taste very similar. Among them are some well-known imports—*roquefort* from the town of Roquefort, France, *gorgonzola* from Italy, and *stilton* from England—that could be featured as stars on your buffet, fruit–cheese plate, or dessert menu. The less famous domestic blues are popular in salad dressings, canapé toppings, salads, and sauces, as well as in their own right.

Another well-known flavorer of salad dressings and sauces is *parmesan* (par'-ma-zan), a hard, ripe cheese with a sharp and piquant flavor. This is the cheese you shake onto spaghetti. It comes pregrated in a soft powdery form, but it is even more delicious if you grate it fresh from the hard piece. Originally an Italian cheese, it is now produced domestically, like nearly all other cheese types. *Romano* (roh-mahn'-o) is very similar to parmesan with a slightly sharper, saltier flavor.

Compatriot to parmesan is *mozzarella* (motz'-a-rel'-a), the pizza cheese. An unripened cheese of semisoft-to-firm texture, it has a mild but distinctive flavor. No pizza tastes right without it.

Of the other unripened (fresh) cheeses, the most familiar are *cottage cheese* and *cream cheese,* both native American products, both versatile mainstays of the cold kitchen. Cottage cheese is primarily a salad cheese; cream cheese is used in sandwiches, canapés, hors d'oeuvre, and dips and is an essential ingredient in cheesecake. They are the only cheeses you could call inexpensive.

At the luxury end of the scale are three soft—almost sauce-soft—dessert cheeses: *brie* (bree), *camembert* (kam'-um-bare), and *limburger* (pronounced as spelled). You'll find them in restaurants catering to connoisseurs of food. They taste much better than their aroma and rather unattractive appearance would lead you to believe. But an odor of ammonia tells you when they are past their prime.

Two red-jacketed cheeses from the Netherlands, on the other hand, make bright and attractive buffet items. They are *gouda* (goo'-da) and *edam* (ee'-dum). They have the firm texture and good cheese color of a pale cheddar, and they offer mild but subtly different flavors that are welcome in a dessert cheese or on a cheese board.

There you have a baker's dozen of what are called the **natural cheeses.** Then there is process cheese.

Process cheese is made by adding an emulsifier and water to grated natural cheese and heating and mixing it all until it becomes homogeneous. One cheese connoisseur has called it "solidified floor wax." But it does have some endearing qualities: it does not spoil easily, it stays moist, it melts well, and it is cheaper than natural cheese. It should never be used as a dessert cheese, but it is found at

sandwich bars and atop the meat in a cheeseburger.

Holding, storage, and service

Cheeses are both held and stored under refrigeration. They can also stand in bulk at room temperature for several hours, which makes them good buffet items (Figure 13-7). Their most significant limitation is that they dry and harden when exposed to air. This means that as soon as you cut into a cheese you must either use it or wrap it tightly with plastic wrap to exclude the air.

Hard and firm cheeses, properly wrapped, keep from a week to several months in the refrigerator. Even with the best of care, once a whole cheese has been cut it tends to dry out, grow sharper in flavor, and develop inedible molds around the edges. Semisoft and soft cheeses keep one to two weeks refrigerated. Fresh cheeses should be kept no more than a week.

Cheeses should be served at room temperature. Slices and bite-size pieces of cheese must be cut just before service. Once dried out, they are useless except in sauces and cooked products. This is fine if you serve a lot of cheese sauce. But cheese is too expensive to waste.

Cooking with cheese

As you may have already discovered, cheese cookery poses no problems so long as you keep the temperature low or the cooking time short, or both. The high-protein content of cheese means that it becomes tough and stringy with high temperatures and prolonged cooking. Its fat content may also separate out.

Cheese used in a starch-thickened sauce must not be added until after the thickening process is completed.

Cheese for gratinéing should be added near the end of the cooking period if it is an oven-cooked product. A glaze administered in the salamander is always a quick trip, whatever the product.

To top off the subject of foods for break-

FIGURE 13-7. Cheese-and-fruit tray. This display uses blocks of cheese and fruit pieces like sculptural forms to set the stage for portioned slices. Since slices dry out quickly, only a few are presented. (Photo courtesy Wall's Catering, Dallas, Texas.)

fast and brunch, you can combine cheese and egg cookery in a cheese quiche (recipe 13-6). A **quiche** (keesh) is a savory pie with a custard base.

Use a frozen prepared pie shell or jump ahead to Chapter 16 and make your own shells with mealy pie dough (16-15). Of course you already know that you must make a paste of the starch (Step 1) to avoid lumps when you mix the starch with the liquids in Steps 2 and 3. The seasonings and the optional herbs and spices are added to the basic custard. You can add paprika for improved color, but don't add too much or it will be bitter.

Different kinds of quiche can be made by varying the major flavor. Recipes 13-6a and 6b give you two ideas. You can use cheese alone as the major flavor, or combine it with other major flavors, or leave it out entirely. Seafood, meat, poultry, and vegetables such as mushrooms, broccoli, or cauliflower can also be used to good advantage.

Bake the pies on the bottom shelf or directly on the floor of a stack oven. This allows the dough to bake fairly quickly and thus avoids a soggy bottom crust. The filling is set when the center no longer jiggles but is firm without being rubbery.

13-6 QUICHE AU FROMAGE (CHEESE PIE)

Yield: five 8" (20 cm) pies or one half sheet pan

	5	8" (20 cm) pie shells, unbaked	5	1 lb 4 oz	gruyère or swiss cheese, grated	600 g	major flavor	
flavor, body, texture	*Custard:*			*	nutmeg	*		
	8	eggs	8	(1 tsp	paprika	5 mL)	flavorers	
	1 qt	milk or half-and-half	1 L	(4 oz	chopped parsley or other herb	125 g)		
	2 oz	cornstarch or flour	60 g	*	salt, white pepper	*		

1. Make a paste of cornstarch or flour with a little of the milk.
2. Add to eggs and stir to blend.
3. Stir in remaining milk, flavorers, and seasonings.
4. Spread a 4-oz (120 g) layer of cheese into each pie shell.
5. Fill each shell with custard.
6. Bake in 350°F (180°C) oven until filling is set (*25–30 minutes).

13-6a QUICHE LORRAINE

To recipe 13-6 add:

1 lb	diced bacon, cooked, drained	500 g

(Cheese may be omitted.)

In Step 4, divide bacon evenly among pie shells (placing on top of cheese if used).

13-6b QUICHE FLORENTINE

To recipe 13-6 add:

2 lb	onions, small dice, sautéed	1 kg
1½ lb	cooked chopped spinach, drained	750 g

(Cheese may be omitted.)

In Step 4, divide onions and spinach among pie shells (placing on top of cheese).

SUMMING UP

Breakfast, first meal of the day, is made up of groups of foods traditionally cooked and served together. Brunch builds on the breakfast menu and moves it to span the middle of the day. Breakfast is likely to be a wake-up, hurry-up affair. Brunch, usually a weekend offering, is a leisurely meal with the accent on pleasure and the chance to explore new dishes.

For both meals, eggs and egg-based dishes are the heart of the menu. Egg cookery is the single most important skill for the breakfast cook to master. Once you are comfortable with the egg, you can combine it with your other cooking knowledge and skills to produce any number of egg dishes—many kinds of omelets, many poached-egg and shirred-egg dishes, scrambled eggs, savory quiches.

Another group of breakfast dishes centers around waffles, pancakes, and french toast, with breakfast meats to accompany them. For such dishes the cook must know how to make a batter that will produce a light and tender product, how to cook on the griddle, and how to prepare the different kinds of breakfast meats. The thin French pancakes known as crêpes offer the cook a real challenge, along with the chance to fill them with delicious mixtures for brunch dishes.

The beverage side of breakfast is making good coffee and good tea and serving the hot beverages hot and the cold ones cold—juices and iced tea and milk. Beverages are routine and unchallenging and are therefore often neglected, but they can make all the difference in the world to the customer—especially the coffee.

Many other foods can be served for breakfast—potatoes, tomatoes, cheese, cornbread, muffins, oysters, champagne. Regional preferences often determine the selection of offerings. In some parts of the South, for example, grits are standard breakfast fare; elsewhere a plate of eggs would be unthinkable without french fries or hash browns.

Many breakfast foods can be featured in other settings. Omelets and shirred eggs are excellent luncheon dishes. Bacon, ham, and sausage are great to use in sandwiches, canapés, salads, and entrées. Hard-cooked eggs go anywhere anytime. Waffles and pancakes, suitably sweetened and flavored, double as desserts. Coffee and tea are universal 24-hour pick-me-ups.

Once you can cook them well, use basic breakfast foods as starters for your own creations, and let your imagination run.

THE COOK'S VOCABULARY

breakfast, brunch

eggs to order, sunny side up, eyes open, basted, over easy, over medium, over well, scrambled

poached, "boiled," shirred, omelet

bacon, canadian bacon, sausage

pancakes, waffles, french toast, crêpes, quiche

primed or seasoned surface

steep

cheese: natural, processed, unripened, ripened, aged

QUESTIONS FOR DISCUSSION

1. Describe how a French crêpe differs from an American pancake. Why does the crêpe make a more suitable luncheon dish than the pancake?

2. In your opinion which menu items discussed in this chapter make the most suitable brunch dishes? Explain your views.

3. Which food items do you think are most suitable for buffet service? Give reasons for your choices. Which items would not be appropriate and why?

4. Name several ways in which the tasks of the breakfast cook are different from those of the soup or sauce cook.

WITH this chapter we enter another realm of the kitchen—the area where cold foods are prepared. It is known variously as the cold kitchen, the pantry, or the garde manger department. What you call it will depend on the kind and size of the operation and on local jargon.

This is not to say that no cooking goes on here. It does. In fact, the cold-foods expert must be a master of all the techniques of the kitchen.

Cold foods are important to any food-service menu. Today's American diner responds to foods that are crisp, fresh, and natural—foods that have lost nothing in cooking and processing but retain their original color, shape, and flavor. But there is more to cold foods than uncooked fruits and vegetables. To a far greater degree than hot foods, cold foods offer opportunities for interesting harmonies and contrasts of textures and tastes as well as of color and shape and pattern. And some popular cold foods are as sophisticated as others are fresh and simple.

The products of the pantry fill many menu roles. Some are used to open a meal—fresh, colorful fruits and vegetables that awaken the appetite, or tangy tidbits that hint of pleasures to come. Some are served with drinks, not only to heighten the enjoyment but also to cushion the effect of the liquor. Some may accompany an entrée or follow it as an accent or a change of pace. Some may be entrées in themselves. Whole meals may be provided from the cold kitchen, from inexpensive salad bars to elaborate party buffets.

We will begin our exploration of cold food preparation with that most universal of all cold foods, the salad. Then we'll have a look at salad dressings and their close relatives cold sauces, and we'll consider how to put salads and dressings together. We'll conclude with a look at another important responsibility of the pantry department—cold appetizers, canapés, and hors d'oeuvre. After completing this chapter you should be able to

• Identify greens commonly used in salads.

14

Pantry Production

343

- Describe or demonstrate how to prepare the major salad types.
- Explain and illustrate the principles of salad presentation.
- Describe or demonstrate how to make the major types of salad dressings and cold sauces.
- Describe the characteristics of appetizers, canapés, and hors d'oeuvre, and explain how to prepare them in quantity.

SALADS AND SALAD-MAKING

The first salads were simply greens dipped in salt. In fact, the word salad comes from a Latin word meaning "salted." Roman dinners often had a separate salad course of raw greens with a dressing.

Salads vanished from the European diet for a thousand years or more but reappeared in the seventeenth century. At one time it was not unusual to include flowers such as nasturtiums, marigolds, rose petals, and violets in salads. But though it become common in Europe, salad was seldom the focus of interest for either the cook or the diner.

It was not until the salad crossed the ocean to America that it came into its own. One true claim to fame of the American cook is ingenuity in the preparation of salads. We have gone far beyond the simple salted greens of the past to vegetables of every species, shape, and flavor, and to meats, fish, fruits, cheeses, eggs. We have moved the salad all over the menu, from appetizer to accompaniment to entrée to dessert to meal-in-itself. And we have taken it from obscurity to stardom. Many a salad is a work of art.

How do we define this versatile food? A **salad** is a dish that is almost always served cold, usually accompanied by a cold dressing made of oil, vinegar, special flavorings, and often eggs. It usually takes off from a leafy green base and is likely to be piquant in flavor. There are four parts to the structure of the typical salad:

- The **base,** or **underliner:** usually a leafy green such as a lettuce cup or a fine layer of shredded lettuce.
- The **body:** the major ingredient or mixture of ingredients.
- The **dressing:** sometimes part of the salad, more often not, but always planned to be compatible with it.
- The **garnish:** a colorful accent providing eye appeal (often omitted if the salad itself is colorful).

Salads are held in high regard by the health-conscious American customer, and rightly so. Leafy greens and other salad vegetables and fruits are good sources of many essential vitamins and minerals. They also contain cellulose (fiber), an important aid in digestive function. Salads containing meat or cheese contribute protein to the diet, and dressings can provide desirable unsaturated fat.

But salads are not always the low-calorie foods many people think they are. Most dressings are high in calories, and so are many ingredients—meats, cheeses, eggs, nuts, pastas, shellfish, many fruits, and even some vegetables, such as avocados, beans, and corn. To design salads as weight-watching specials, you would have to plan knowledgeably and count calories per portion.

Let us explore the essentials of good salad-making by examining some different kinds of salads. We'll group them according to their ingredients and the way they go together.

- Leafy green
- Vegetable
- Combination
- Cooked
- Fruit
- Congealed

Leafy green salads

The **leafy green salads** are made of raw leafy green vegetables, usually of the lettuce or endive families. The most common of these salad greens are listed below, grouped according to type. They are pictured in Figure 14-1.

Crisphead lettuces
- **Iceberg:** a crisp, green-white lettuce, very mild in flavor
- **Romaine** or **cos:** a crisp, coarse lettuce with long, flat, bright-green leaves, full of flavor

Butterhead lettuces
- **Bibb** or **limestone:** a small, loose-leaved head lettuce having soft, smooth, buttery leaves, yellow-white to dark green in color
- **Boston:** similar to bibb but less sweet, and having a slightly larger head with more yellow tones

Leaf lettuces
- **Green leaf:** tender, curly-edged, crisp, but softer than the crisphead lettuces; many varieties of many shades of green
- **Red leaf:** curly green leaves with fragile red tips

Endive
- **Chicory (curly endive):** a bunched head having crisp, narrow, curled, feathery dark-green leaves and a slightly bitter taste
- **Escarole:** flat-headed, similar in appearance to chicory but with larger, coarser, firmer, and darker-green leaves; distinctively bitter in taste
- **Belgian endive:** a pointed cluster of crisp, fleshy, waxy white leaves looking like a short spear; actually the specially cultivated shoot of the curly endive

Variety greens
- **Spinach:** flat or crinkled dark-green leaves, crisp and flavorful
- **Watercress:** small dark-green leaves on a crisp stem, strong and zesty in flavor; used occasionally in salads, more often as a garnish

These greens can be served separately or in combinations offering texture and color variety. Usually they are served in bite-size pieces (except, sometimes, belgian endive and some of the soft lettuces) with a dressing that is added at the moment of service.

The primary areas of concern to the salad maker are in the handling and serving of a green salad. It goes without saying that the greens should be fresh, high-quality produce. They should be thoroughly washed as described in Chapter 3.

All green salads should be served well chilled. Green salads should be crisp, unless they are made entirely of soft lettuces such as boston, bibb, and leaf. These soft lettuces should be fresh and unwilted. Naturally crisp salad greens such as iceberg and romaine should be very crisp when served. If the greens lack crispness, both they and the salad lack quality.

To maintain crispness in cut greens, cut them as close to serving as possible. You can also put them in ice water to crisp them, draining them well before dishing them out. Iceberg lettuce has been held in ice water for as long as two days in preparation for a banquet serving thousands. But normally holding time should be a matter of hours at most.

For true quality in a salad, greens must be cleanly and evenly cut with a sharp stainless-steel cutting edge. The size of the cut pieces is very important. Nothing is more frustrating to the diner than to be served a salad of crisp greens with pieces too large to be maneuvered gracefully from plate to mouth.

Controversy has raged for years over whether to cut or to tear lettuce for salads. But try tearing lettuce for a thousand salads—it would take you all day. You can cut it in one-tenth the time.

Consider another factor: crisp vegetables depend for their crispness on their high water content. When this diminishes they wilt. Greens that are torn lose their water faster than greens that are cut. It is almost impossible to tear them without bruising the leaves.

A common problem in holding salad

FIGURE 14-1. Leafy greens for salad.

a. Iceberg lettuce. (Photo courtesy Burpee Seeds.)

b. Romaine lettuce. (Photo by Patricia Roberts.)

c. Bibb lettuce. (Photo courtesy Burpee Seeds.)

d. Boston lettuce. (Photo courtesy Burpee Seeds.)

e. Green leaf lettuce. (Photo by Patricia Roberts.)

f. Red leaf lettuce (Photo by Patricia Roberts.)

g. Chicory. (Photo by Patricia Roberts.)

h. Belgian endive. (Photo by Patricia Roberts.)

i. Spinach. (Photo courtesy Burpee Seeds.)

j. Watercress. (Photo courtesy USDA.)

greens is the appearance of rust color on the edges. To prevent discoloration you can rinse them in a light ascorbic acid solution. But proceed with caution: too strong a solution can produce a bad taste.

Precut, prewashed lettuce is available in plastic bags in many areas. It keeps two to three days, and the labor it saves is worth its price for many operations. Once you open a bag, however, the lettuce loses quality quickly.

Leafy green salads are served in various ways. They may be tossed together in a large container until they are evenly mixed, then served on individual plates or perhaps in a large serve-yourself bowl. Or they may be arranged carefully on individual plates for artistic effect. Sometimes greens and dressing are tossed together at tableside. But no dressing is ever added to a tossed salad until the very last minute; it will wilt the lettuce in no time.

Let us look at a basic green salad—mainstay of the typical American menu. The combination of greens in recipe 14-1 provides variety in color and flavor. The paleness of the

14-1 BASIC GREEN SALAD

Approximate yield: 25 3-oz (90 g) portions

body				garnishes		
	2 heads	iceberg, cored	2 heads	25	tomato wedges	25
	2 heads	romaine	2 heads	25	black olives	25
	1 bunch	watercress	1 bunch			

1. Wash and drain all greens, discarding unusable portions.
2. Cut into bite-size pieces.
3. Toss gently to distribute all greens evenly.
4. Cover with damp towels and plastic wrap and refrigerate.
5. Shortly before service, portion onto chilled plates and refrigerate.
6. Add garnishes and dressing at time of service.

iceberg contrasts with the strong green colors of the romaine and watercress, and the iceberg's bland taste is a foil for their assertive flavors. There is textural contrast, too, in the fragile leaves of the watercress among the crisp lettuce pieces. (You will discard the tough watercress stems, using the thinner branches and leaves.)

Notice the care taken to keep greens fresh and crisp. If holding time is short, you may skip Step 4 and portion the greens directly after tossing, holding the plated portions in the refrigerator. You will add the garnishes as the salad is served so that their moisture will not wilt the lettuces.

There are countless variations for this recipe. For the watercress you might substitute a pound of spinach or half a head of curly endive; either of these will give color and flavor contrasts to the lettuces. You might use different garnishes—cucumber or radish slices, a bell pepper ring, a cherry tomato. Try developing your own basic green salad recipe; the possibilities are practically endless.

Vegetable salads

A **vegetable salad** has one or more non-leafy vegetables as its main ingredients. It does not contain leafy vegetables at all. It may have leafy greens as a base, or underliner, but not as part of the body.

Many vegetable salads are made of raw vegetables cut into various shapes. When two or more vegetables are combined they should be chosen for their complementary flavors and colors. The following raw vegetables are commonly used in vegetable salads:

cabbage	mushrooms
carrots	onions
celery	radishes
cucumbers	tomatoes
green peppers	zucchini

Cut raw vegetables, like leafy greens, do not hold well. Cut them as close as possible to serving time and place them in ice water so that they do not dry out or shrivel. Wilting and rusting are not the major problems they are with the leafy vegetables, but certain kinds do not hold their color well. White vegetables, such as celery and especially mushrooms, can turn dark or rust. You can prevent this by the same means used for leafy greens—cutting with stainless steel, using (with caution) an ascorbic acid solution, and storing correctly.

Many cooked vegetables are also used as main ingredients in vegetable salads. Such vegetables are cooked because they are not suitable for salad in their raw state. They too may be used singly or in combination. Again the choice is based on compatible flavors and colors. Among the most popular are:

artichoke hearts	carrots
asparagus	corn
beans (all kinds)	hearts of palm
beets	peas

Both raw and cooked vegetables for salads are often marinated to give them special flavor. If this is done, the problem of discoloration in raw vegetables is solved by the marinade, which protects the cut surfaces from the air.

Vegetable salads, both raw and cooked, are generally arranged on a leafy-green liner, with or without a dressing added at the time of service. One very common vegetable salad—coleslaw, made from shredded cabbage—has a dressing mixed in as an integral part of the salad. If vegetables have been marinated, the marinade replaces a dressing.

Recipe 14-2 is a marinated vegetable salad. You will remember the principles of marinating from Chapter 3 and the partial-

---

14-2 VEGETABLES Á LA GRECQUE

Approximate yield: 25 2½-oz (75 g) portions

body	2 lb	mushrooms, small whole or large quartered	900 g	1 qt	water or chicken stock	1 L		
	1 lb	carrots, ⅛" (2 mm) slices	450 g	1 pt	olive oil	500 mL		
	1 lb	green beans, 2" (5 cm) pieces	450 g	6 oz	lemon juice	175 mL		
base	25	lettuce cups	25	1	celery rib, 6" (15 cm)	1		
				2 tsp	salt	10 mL	marinade (flavor builders)	
				Sachet of:				
				1 tsp	minced garlic or shallots	5 mL		
				1 tsp	crushed peppercorns	5 mL		
				2 tsp	coriander seeds	10 mL		
				1	bay leaf	1		
				1 tsp	thyme	5 mL		
				*	chopped fresh parsley	*	garnish	

1. Wash and dry mushrooms and trim ends.
2. Parboil carrots and green beans separately until 50–75% done. Remove from heat and add ice to chill. Drain.
3. Place all marinade ingredients, including sachet bag, in stainless-steel pan and bring to boil. Simmer 15 minutes.
4. Add mushrooms, carrots, and green beans to marinade and simmer 5 minutes. Remove from heat.
5. When cool, remove sachet and celery. Marinate vegetables overnight in refrigerator.

cook/quick-chill method of cooking vegetables from Chapter 9. Assembling the chilled ingredients on lettuce cups is the final move that turns it all into a salad. In serving marinated salads, remove the vegetables carefully from the marinade with a slotted spoon to keep the plate free of excess liquid. To assemble, place a 2½-oz (75 g) portion on a lettuce cup on a chilled plate and sprinkle with chopped parsley.

Combination salads

A **combination salad** is just what the name implies—a combining of two or more kinds of ingredients. It may combine leafy greens and vegetables as well as foods from this list:

relishes	fruit
pickles	meats
olives	poultry
eggs	fish
cheese	bread

This is by no means an exhaustive list. Added to leafy greens and vegetables, these foods multiply the number of potential salad combinations, since each item can combine with many others.

Certain salad combinations have become so popular they are considered standards. For instance:

- *Lettuce, tomato, and cucumber*
- *Tossed garden salad:* a combination of garden vegetables in season
- *Chef's salad:* leafy greens, ham, turkey, and cheese, with often a vegetable or egg garnish

Depending on its nature, a combination salad may be combined in a careful arrangement on its serving plate or it may be mixed together in random fashion by tossing. The chef's salad in recipe 14-3 is an example of an arranged salad. It contains the standard combination of ingredients plus a variety of garnishes chosen for compatibility of flavor as well as eye appeal. A chef's salad is an entrée salad, traditionally served in a bowl with the greens on the bottom. The other major ingredients and garnishes are carefully arranged to form a pleasing pattern. A dressing of the customer's choice is added at the time of service or served separately.

Salads are usually tossed only to mix leafy greens or to mix other foods with leafy greens. But many foods that combine well with greens in flavor and texture do not toss well. Heavy or bulky items sink to the bottom. Juicy foods wilt the greens. Tomato, for instance, has too much juice for tossing in a garden salad. It is best to add the tomato as a garnish after the other ingredients are tossed together. And cucumber used with soft lettuce will deflate the lettuce very quickly.

Occasionally a salad is tossed at tableside not only to mingle its ingredients but also to blend a dressing with the salad. The caesar salad described later is often served this way.

The possibilities for combination salads are limited only by the imagination. Let taste and color again be your guides when combining different kinds of foods. Don't put fish with meat or pimientos with blueberries.

Cooked salads

Cooked salads are those that use a single cooked food as the major ingredient. Macaroni salad, tuna salad, and potato salad are everyday examples. It is true that combination salads may have cooked ingredients in their makeup, but such foods are only part of the salad and do not provide its characteristic body and flavor.

Some of the foods commonly cooked to become salads are

potatoes	ham
rice	poultry (chicken, turkey)
pastas	fish (tuna, salmon)
eggs	shellfish (shrimp, lobster, crab)

Cooked vegetable salads may be classified as either cooked or vegetable, since they have characteristics of both.

14-3 CHEF'S SALAD

Yield: 1 portion

body							
	5 oz	basic green salad (14-1)	150 g	2	tomato wedges	2	
	¾ oz	chicken or turkey white meat, julienne	25 g	2	hard-cooked egg quarters	2	*garnishes*
	¾ oz	ham, julienne	25 g	4	cucumber slices	4	
	¾ oz	swiss cheese, julienne	25 g	1	olive, black or green	1	
	¾ oz	cheddar, julienne	25 g				

1. Place basic green salad mixture in chilled bowl.
2. Arrange julienne of meats and cheeses on greens as shown.
3. Place garnishes on salad as shown.

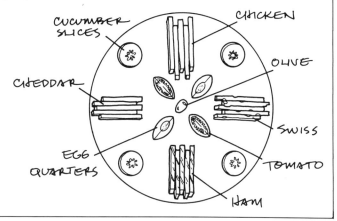

Cooked salads usually have another feature that sets them apart: they include a dressing as an integral part of their makeup. This dressing provides another characteristic of the cooked salad—its cohesiveness. This quality of sticking together allows it to be portioned with a scoop. It can also be spread as a sandwich filling if the major ingredient is suitable. Egg, ham, chicken, and tuna salad sandwiches are familiar examples.

You can create many variations of the basic cooked salads by using different dressings and different flavor additions. A common addition is something to give crunch, providing texture contrast to the soft cooked food. It might be raw celery, for example. Or it could be crisp pickle or minced onion if the flavor is right for the salad.

14-4 CHICKEN SALAD

Yield: 20 3-oz (90 g) portions

major flavor, body	2¼ lb	cooked chicken, medium dice	1 kg	½ tsp	worcestershire sauce	2 mL	*flavoring*	
texture	¾ lb	celery, small dice	375 g	1 tsp	salt	5 mL	*seasoning*	
				⅛ tsp	white pepper	0.5 mL		
				1 pt	mayonnaise	500 mL	*dressing*	

1. Mix chicken, celery, flavoring, seasonings, and dressing.
2. Cover and refrigerate 4–6 hours to blend flavors.

Recipe 14-4 shows the structure of a typical cooked salad. Its major ingredient, chicken, is enhanced by the addition of celery for texture contrast and worcestershire sauce for extra flavor.

The main ingredient in a cooked salad can be marinated to give it special flavor. This is often done with shellfish. A similar trick for flavoring potato salad is to add an oil-and-vinegar dressing to the cooked potatoes while they are hot, so that they soak up the dressing.

Cooked salads are among the hearty salads that can be served as entrées. They are also a pleasing and acceptable way of using suitable leftover cooked foods of high quality.

Recipe 14-5 shows you a popular way to dress up a cooked salad entrée. Though the tomato traditionally gets top billing on the menu, it is the cooked salad that provides the character of the dish. The tomato functions as a combination of base, body, and garnish that enlarges the salad to entrée size, both colorfully and economically. It could provide a convenient frame or format for almost any cooked salad. Consider the variations shown in 14-5a and 14-5b.

14-5 STUFFED TOMATO SALAD

Yield: 20 portions (3 oz/90 g stuffing)

body	3½ lb	chicken salad (14-4)	1.8 kg	20	black olives	20		
base	20	tomatoes, cored	20	20	cucumber slices	20	*garnish*	
	20	lettuce leaves	20	20	parsley sprigs	20		

1. Prepare chicken salad as directed in recipe 14-4.
2. Cut tomatoes into quarters, leaving sections attached at bottom; spread apart.
3. To serve, place tomatoes on lettuce leaves and, using a No. 10 portion scoop, center 3 oz (90 g) chicken salad in each tomato. Arrange garnish.

Other cup-shaped foods may play the same role—avocado halves stuffed with shrimp or crab salad, pineapple halves filled with fruit salad. The main consideration is the appropriateness of the container to the salad it contains.

Fruit salads

Fruit on the table is certainly not new. Beginning with Eve and the apple, fruit was a popular food in ancient civilizations. Today's table offers fruit in great variety from all parts of the world. But it has usually been served as a cocktail, a dessert, or a breakfast food. Fruit as a salad course is fairly recent. Demand has burgeoned as the popularity of fresh natural foods has increased and fresh fruits have become available year round. Today fruit salads have become standard menu items—as appetizers, as accompaniments to the main course, as entrées in their own right, and as desserts.

A **fruit salad** is any salad in which fruit predominates. It is generally composed of cut or sectioned fruits served separately or combined. Berries of many varieties are sometimes added to create good flavor and color. Some of the fresh fruits commonly used in salads are

apples	honeydew melon
apricots	kiwi (kee-wee)
avocados	mango
bananas	oranges
blueberries	peaches
cantaloupe	pears
grapefruit	pineapple
grapes (red,	strawberries
green, dark)	watermelon

Handling fruits for salads requires some special product knowledge and techniques. Certain fresh fruits—apples, pears, peaches, bananas, avocados—discolor when exposed to air. Like the lettuces, they must be cut with stainless-steel cutting edges. If you combine

---

14-5a TUNA SALAD STUFFING

Replace body of recipe 14-5 with:

2¼ lb	tuna	1 kg
¾ lb	celery, diced	375 g
2 oz	onions, diced	50 g
2 oz	lemon juice	50 mL
1 tsp	tarragon	5 mL
1 pt	mayonnaise	500 mL
*	salt	*

Mix ingredients as in 14-4. Serve as in 14-5.

14-5b BEEF SALAD STUFFING

Replace body of recipe 14-5 with:

2½ lb	cooked beef, julienne	1 kg
¾ lb	onions, chopped	375 g
1 pt	vinegar–oil dressing	500 mL
*	salt, black pepper	*

Marinate for 24 hours. Serve as in recipe 14-5.

---

such fruits with citrus fruits, the high acid content of the latter prevents the rapid discoloration of the fruits that are vulnerable to air. Or you can rinse vulnerable fruits in lemon juice and water or an ascorbic acid solution, though this does compromise their flavor.

Fruits that are not peeled should be washed as close to use time as possible. Berries in particular, especially strawberries and raspberries, do not hold well. Wash them just before use, drain them well, and add them just before service.

Many canned fruits are good salad material—mandarin oranges, peaches, pears, apricots, grapefruit, pineapple, sweet cherries.

14-6 FRESH FRUIT PLATTER

Yield: 1 portion

body	2 oz	cantaloupe wedges	50 g	½	strawberry	½	garnish
	2 oz	pineapple sticks	50 g	1	parsley or mint sprig	1	
	2 oz	watermelon cubes	50 g	2 oz	yogurt dressing (14-11)	50 g	dressing
	2 oz	orange slices	50 g				
	2 oz	apple or pear slices	50 g				
	2 oz	grapefruit segments	50 g				
	2 oz	grapes	50 g				
base	2	lettuce leaves	2				

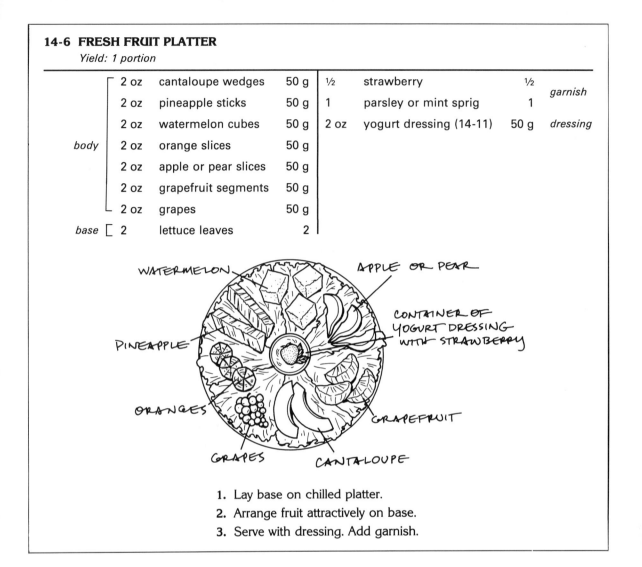

1. Lay base on chilled platter.
2. Arrange fruit attractively on base.
3. Serve with dressing. Add garnish.

Drain them carefully or they will make for a watery plate. Dried fruits—dates and prunes—are also used.

Almost any fruits may be combined. Flavor, color, variety, and availability will determine your choices. The fresh fruit platter in recipe 14-6 is a colorful arrangement designed as a luncheon entrée. Fruit may vary with seasonal prices. A yogurt dressing (14-11) complements the fruit.

Other foods may be added to a fruit salad to spark flavor or texture. For example, the famous waldorf salad combines apples with celery and walnuts. The diced apples, celery, and chopped nuts are mixed with a mayonnaise or chantilly dressing to hold the salad together.

Fruit salads are usually served on lettuce, but not always. They are usually accompanied by a dressing (sometimes a sweet one), but by no means always.

Congealed salads

A **congealed salad** is any salad that has gelatin in its makeup to hold it together. Gelatin comes in three primary forms: clear or un-flavored, fruit-flavored, and aspic.

Clear or **unflavored gelatin** comes in two principal forms, powder and leaves. The leaves look like heavy plastic film. Good-quality powdered gelatin has a softness and sheen referred to as *bloom*.

Fruit-flavored gelatin comes in powdered form in assorted flavors under many familiar brand names. It contains sugar as well as color and flavor.

Aspic is a powdered meat-flavored gelatin. It is usually beef-flavored, but it also comes in fish and poultry flavors.

There are two methods of handling gelatin, one for clear gelatin and the other for fruit-flavored gelatin and aspic. For clear gelatin the first step is to mix it with cold water. Then you stir the mixture into boiling-hot water, dissolve it completely, and cool. Dispersing the gelatin in cold water first will keep it from lumping. Then dissolving it in boiling-hot water, as many product labels advise, will give you the best end results. Technically, gelatin will dissolve at 100°F (38°C), but it may take forever and you may not have that much time.

For aspic and fruit-flavored gelatin only one step is necessary: dissolve the powder in very hot water, then cool.

The end product for all gelatins is a jellied substance that forms when the mixture is cold. It is important to get the right proportion of liquid to gelatin. Too much liquid will make the gel wobbly; too little will make it rubbery. You can substitute fruit juice or another suitable liquid for part or all of the water.

The tomato aspic in recipe 14-7 is an example of a salad made with clear gelatin. As you can see, tomato juice provides most of the liquid, as well as the flavor and body of the salad.

Many different fruits, vegetables, and other foods can be added to gelatin as it begins to jell. Drain them well, so that the proportion of

---

14-7 TOMATO ASPIC

Approximate yield: 3 quarts (3 liters)

body	2 qt	tomato juice	2 L	4 oz	onion concassé	125 g		
	2 oz	unflavored gelatin	60 g	2 oz	celery concassé	50 g		
texture	1 pt	cold water	500 mL	1	bay leaf	1	flavor builders	
				4	cloves	4		
				1 tsp	dry mustard	5 mL		
				7 oz	sugar	200 g		
				½ pt	lemon juice	250 mL	flavoring	
				*	salt	*		

1. Sprinkle gelatin on cold water and let stand 10 minutes.
2. Simmer tomato juice with flavor builders for 5 minutes.
3. Strain mixture and add to gelatin, stirring until gelatin is dissolved.
4. Stir in lemon juice; season *to taste.
5. Pour into two half-size (10 × 12"/25 × 30 cm) hotel pans or decorative molds and refrigerate until firm.

liquid to gelatin does not change and spoil the consistency. You can add almost any fruit or vegetable. The few exceptions are raw pineapple, figs, and papaya. These fruits contain certain enzymes that keep the gelatin from congealing. The same fruits cooked or canned cause no trouble.

If you add things before the gelatin has begun to set, some kinds of foods will float to the top. For a good mix, wait until setting begins before adding anything.

After you have added everything and the product is beginning to jell, pour it into individual molds or, for volume production, into large pans. Cut the panful of salad into serving portions after it is firmly jelled—6 to 8 hours at least. It is best to make congealed salads a day ahead.

To unmold individual salads, dip each mold into hot water for a second or two, then flip over onto the salad plate. If you have trouble getting the hang of this, you can invert the plate over the upright mold and then turn everything over together. Refrigerate unmolded salads to restore any firmness they may have lost.

Congealed salads, except dessert salads, are usually served on lettuce. Sometimes congealed salads are served without a dressing. If a dressing is used it is generally a mayonnaise or another dressing with considerable body.

Congealed salads must be kept refrigerated until the moment of service or they may lose their firmness. Covered and kept in the cooler in their pans or molds, they will hold well for several days.

Salad on the menu

In discussing various salads we have noted that many of them can play several menu roles. To adapt them to different roles you would make several kinds of adjustments. You would use smaller portions for an appetizer or accompaniment, larger portions for an entrée. You might extend an entrée salad by adding extra ingredients (such as tomato to chicken salad in recipe 14-4) or by using hearty garnishes such as hard-cooked egg quarters or a small bunch of grapes. You might use a different dressing for each different menu role—a tangy one for an appetizer salad, a hearty dressing for an entrée, perhaps no dressing at all for a leafy green served between courses to cleanse the palate.

Another menu use of salads is to make them part of a buffet or salad bar. In this case you will not worry about the underliner and the plate garnish; you will prepare only the body of the salad, though you may use greens and garnish for the serving piece. (You may have noticed that our recipes have usually omitted the base, dressing, and garnish where these do not really affect the nature of the salad. These salad elements will vary from one operation to another and will be included on the standardized recipe card.)

A luncheon plate is another popular menu use of salad: combine several salads or use them with other cold foods. A typical cold luncheon plate might contain a small sandwich and three salads, such as mixed-fruit salad, potato salad, and vegetable salad. Another might have a salad of avocado stuffed with shrimp accompanied by fruit and relishes.

Still another luncheon plate might be made up entirely of fresh fruits, such as the fruit platter in recipe 14-6. A fruit salad platter often includes a scoop of cottage cheese or a small serving of yogurt to provide the protein usually associated with an entrée. Or it may have a scoop of sherbet as a flavor-texture complement.

When you plan a cold luncheon plate, the most important considerations are a good balance of flavors and attractive visual presentation. The same two things hold for all salad-making. You already know a good deal about flavor; let's focus on the very important subject of presentation.

SALAD PRESENTATION

Eye appeal is the purpose of every presentation, whether the food is hot or cold. It is espe-

FIGURE 14-2. Actual height in a salad arrangement. The romaine leaves on the right, arranged for maximum height, make a far more interesting salad than the flat arrangement on the left. Both quantities are the same. (Photo by Patricia Roberts.)

cially important for cold foods because they lack the come-on of an appetizing aroma. On the other hand, the fresh colors and textures of many cold foods offer more visual potential than most hot dishes.

There are three essentials to consider in presentation: *height, color,* and *unity.*

Height

Height gives a salad interest and importance. A raised surface or high point calls attention to itself. A flat and level surface is monotonous and self-effacing.

Height in a salad can be in one of two forms: actual or implied. Actual height in a leafy salad, for example, may be achieved by loosely arranging the greens on the plate so that they are higher in the center than toward the edges of the plate. Figure 14-2 shows the difference this makes.

Another way of achieving height is by adding a garnish that has some height. For instance, a plate of sliced cucumbers may be given actual height by adding a bouquet of parsley.

Where actual height is difficult to attain, implied height, or an illusion of height, can often be achieved by causing the eye to focus on a particular point. This can be done in sev-eral ways. One is by arranging ingredients in a pattern that guides the eye to that point, as in Figure 14-3. Another is to use an eye-catching ingredient or garnish to establish a focal point. If the point is near the center the salad will appear tall.

Color

Color is very, very important in cold foods. Take a plain, ungarnished coleslaw and see how dull it looks. Add a wedge of tomato, serve it on bright romaine lettuce, and see how color transforms it.

Many people feel the more color in a salad the better, but this philosophy doesn't work out well in practice. Too many colors tend to confuse the eye and dissipate the attention. Three colors are really all that are needed. They can even be various shades of the same color, such as the three greens of a cucumber salad served on lettuce and garnished with parsley.

A limit of three colors is not a hard-and-fast rule. There will be salads whose flavor combinations override the color rule, as in a mixed-fruit salad that might have a whole rainbow of color. But as long as a salad has at least three colors, there is no need to add ingredients or garnishes just to add more color.

FIGURE 14-3. Implied height. A pinwheel arrangement gives the effect of height on the plate by focusing the eye on a central point.

FIGURE 14-4. Odd shapes can form a circular pattern.

FIGURE 14-5. Circles in circles on a circle.

There are no precise formulas for choosing and arranging colors in a salad. Colors are like flavors: some go well together and some don't. Bell pepper and tomato colors complement each other; carrot and tomato together create color confusion. The way to learn to handle color in a salad is to experiment with it and follow good examples of other people's work.

Unity

Creating unity in a food presentation can be compared to putting round pegs in round holes. Unity refers to the relationship of the whole salad to the serving piece on which it is presented. The layout of the salad must fit the shape of the salad plate.

Salads are usually presented on round plates. This means that the lines, forms, and shapes of the salad ingredients must be arranged in a pattern that fits harmoniously into a circle. The pattern may repeat the curve of the plate's edge, or echo its roundness on a smaller scale, or complement it with balance and symmetry.

The pattern begins with the rim of the plate. Never place anything on the rim; it is the frame of your design. If you use a lettuce liner you can arrange it in a circle within the rim to repeat the shape.

The examples on these pages illustrate how various patterns can be used to complement the circular shape of the plate. Figure 14-4 is a salad of sliced tomato served with egg wedges. Not all these items are round, but they are placed in a circular pattern. This not only unifies the salad but also adds implied height by focusing the eye on the center of the plate.

Figure 14-5 is an arrangement of cucumber slices. They themselves are little circles, and when placed in a circular arrangement they echo and re-echo the roundness of the plate, creating a unified presentation. Parsley sparks the pattern with contrast.

The cold luncheon plate follows the same rules of presentation. Figure 14-6 shows a harmonious arrangement of the salad–sandwich luncheon plate described earlier.

Often a round lettuce liner can help to unify a salad composed of stiff linear shapes or a diversity of shapes. Or, if the ingredients are grouped symmetrically and there is a focal point in the center of the plate, the effect is one of unity in spite of the awkward shapes. The salad in Figure 14-7 a shows asparagus spears and tomato slices in a unified arrangement with a bouquet of parsley in the middle for height and focus.

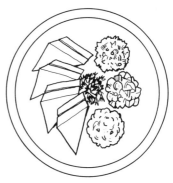

FIGURE 14-6. Symmetrical arrangement for a salad–sandwich plate.

Garnishing

Many a salad is brought to life by an appropriate garnish used as an accent, a color contrast, a focal point. On the other hand, there is no need to garnish a salad that is already colorful and well designed. Often an ingredient of the salad itself can take over the function of a garnish by its position, shape, and color, and there is then no point to adding a further garnish.

The most effective garnish is something bright, eye-catching, contrasting in color, pleasing in shape. The foods you can use are unlimited. Here are some of the most popular:

parsley	lemon slice or wedge
watercress	
mint	hard-boiled egg slices, halves, quarters
olives, green or black	
radishes	berries
pickles	cherries
cherry tomatoes	grapes
tomato wedges	fruit wedge
pepper rings	nuts, chopped or whole
mushrooms	
pimiento	paprika

But don't limit your imagination to these. Look at the raw materials available to you in terms of bits of shape and color and be creative. Do limit your choice to things compatible in taste and spirit with the salad itself.

Use your garnishes in odd numbers—one, three, five. Stick to one garnish or a group of such go-togethers as a black olive, a green olive, and a cherry tomato. Place the garnish or group of garnishes in one spot only. To make this point clear, look at the bad example in a and the good example in b in Figure 14-7. The one on the bottom scatters the attention; the one on the top concentrates the attention and thus helps to unify the presentation. The garnish must always be planned as part of the total presentation.

Keep in mind that a garnish should play the role of an accent and should not steal the show. Garnishes cut into fancy shapes may draw attention to themselves and diminish the salad, as an overdressed woman is outdone by her jewels and furs. In addition, the labor cost of creating such garnishes cannot be justified for the individual salad plate.

Guidelines for making good salads

The job of making salads can be a challenging, enjoyable, and creative endeavor. Here is a summary of the essentials for producing eye-catching, appetizing, and tasty products:

- Use fresh, high-quality ingredients.

- Choose ingredients for compatibility of flavors, textures, and colors.

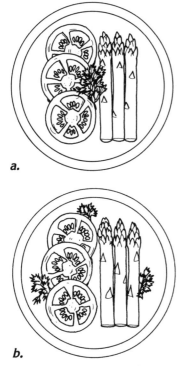

FIGURE 14-7. Placing the garnish. *a.* Grouping the parsley sprigs in the center pulls the salad together. *b.* Placing them symmetrically around the edge dissipates the attention and creates a helter-skelter effect even though the arrangement fills out the round form of the plate.

- Plan your presentation carefully in terms of *height, color,* and *unity.* Keep it simple. Do not overcolor. Do not overgarnish. Do not cover the edge of the plate.
- Serve salads well chilled on chilled plates.

SALAD DRESSINGS

Most salads include a dressing. Sometimes it is an integral part of the salad, as in coleslaw or tuna salad or marinated vegetables. More often the dressing is a separate companion to the body of the salad. We can define a **salad dressing** as a liquid or semiliquid served with or on a salad to give it specific flavor.

Most salad dressings fall into two categories, those having a vinegar-and-oil base and those based on an egg-and-oil emulsion. Most unthickened dressings have a base of vinegar and oil, while most thickened dressings are emulsion-based. Let us examine each type in turn.

Oil-and-vinegar dressings

The simplest group of salad dressings consists of those having a vinegar-and-oil base—the unthickened dressings. These date back to ancient history. Olive oil with lemon was used in the ancient Persian empire. Greeks and Romans ate salads dressed with olive oil and vinegar. They dipped their bread in the same mixture.

The primary ingredients of this group of dressings are oil, vinegar, and water. Each ingredient has its variations. There are, for example, many oils. Some common ones are

- Corn oil
- Vegetable or salad oil (a blend)
- Olive oil
- Peanut oil
- Walnut oil

The first two are the oils most widely used in American dressings. Olive oil is used more extensively in Europe and is an important ingredient in many dishes of European origin. Olive, peanut, and walnut oils have distinctive flavors that limit their uses to products in which the specific flavor is desired.

The vinegars commonly used are fewer in number. You should learn to recognize these by color as well as by taste:

- Wine vinegar
- Cider vinegar
- White vinegar

Both wine and cider vinegar are made by fermentation and carry the flavor and color of the fermented food—wine flavor and color in wine vinegar; apple flavor and the brown color of apple juice in cider vinegar. White vinegar is distilled from a fermented product (usually molasses), so that it has no color and no flavor other than its acid tartness. Because of its neutral flavor it is a better all-round vinegar than the other two, especially for basic dressings. In this text the term vinegar means distilled white vinegar unless another vinegar is specified. Many fruit and herb vinegars, such as tarragon and raspberry, can provide special flavors.

Water as a salad-dressing ingredient is variable not in taste but in amount, which will depend on the strength of the vinegar.

The difficult part of making a vinegar-and-oil dressing is achieving the proper balance of the primary ingredients. If the oil predominates, it gives the dressing an oily taste. If there is too much vinegar, it drowns out everything else. Recipe 14-8 gives you a good basic ratio. This simple dressing is called a **vinaigrette.**

The standard ratio here is the oil/vinegar. The water ratio will vary *according to the strength of the vinegar. The ratio given should be used only as a guideline.

The amount of water to be used is determined in the making of the dressing. You add it little by little to the other ingredients, always tasting as you go. The proper way of tasting is to blend all ingredients well, put a small amount on your tongue, and take in air as you

taste. If the vinegar taste is too strong it will take your breath away. If the vinegar is too weak the dressing will have a flat or oily taste.

To make a vinegar-and-oil dressing, blend everything together vigorously at room temperature until an emulsion forms. The emulsion will be very temporary and must be reformed at the moment the dressing is served. There is an old saying that you need a miser to pour in the vinegar, a spendthrift to add the oil, a counselor for the salt, and a madman to shake it all up.

Basic vinegar-and-oil dressing can be used to create many different dressings by adding ingredients to alter the flavor. Here are a few common additives:

chopped onion	sugar
chopped egg	Tabasco
chopped pickles	roquefort cheese
chopped capers	parmesan cheese
chopped parsley	lemon
chopped herbs	lime
chopped chives	bacon, crumbled
crushed	honey
peppercorns	worcestershire
crushed garlic	sauce
paprika	dill
mustard	anchovy paste

The most common vinegar-and-oil dressings are given in recipes 14-8a and 14-8b. These are not standard recipes and there are many variations. Another common one is roquefort made with basic vinegar-and-oil plus crumbled roquefort cheese and seasoned to taste.

Oil-and-vinegar dressings are not as perishable as the emulsified dressings because they contain no eggs and have a high acid content. However, they deteriorate in flavor rapidly. For this reason it is advisable for optimum flavor to make no more than a day's supply at a time, although many operations do. If kept overnight, such dressings should be refrigerated. They must be brought to room

---

14-8 VINEGAR-AND-OIL DRESSING (VINAIGRETTE)

3 parts	oil	(*	flavorings to taste	*)
1 part	vinegar			
0.5 part*	water	(*	seasonings to taste	*)

Basic ratio: 3 parts oil / 1 part vinegar

1. Blend ingredients together vigorously until a temporary emulsion forms.
2. Repeat just before use.

14-8a VINAIGRETTE II
Yield: 1+ quart (1+ liter)

1½ pt	oil	750 mL
½ pt	vinegar	250 mL
2	eggs, hard-cooked, chopped	2
1 oz	onion, chopped fine	25 g
2 Tb	minced parsley	25 mL
2 tsp	minced chives	10 mL
*	seasonings	*
*	water	*

14-8b ITALIAN DRESSING
Yield: 1 quart (1 liter)

1½ pt	olive oil	750 mL
½ pt	wine vinegar	250 mL
1½ tsp	puréed garlic	7 mL
1 Tb	oregano	15 mL
*	coarse black pepper	*
*	seasonings	*

temperature before service so that the temporary emulsion with its blend of flavors can be re-created.

Emulsified dressings

Mayonnaise. The prototype of all the emulsified dressings is **mayonnaise** (may-a-nayz), which is a flavored, seasoned emulsion of egg yolks and oil. If you can make mayonnaise you can make all the others.

Mayonnaise is a base, or mother sauce, for many salad dressings as well as some important cold sauces. It is also a dressing in its own right.

The origins of mayonnaise go back to a sauce the Romans made by adding egg yolks to an oil-and-garlic sauce that they had borrowed from the Egyptians. Somewhere along the way the garlic was dropped but the emulsion was kept, thus creating mayonnaise.

It later became a custom in many European towns to have an annual mayonnaise parade. Every chef in town would enter the parade with his bowl of mayonnaise, each one a little bit different, a little bit special. Today's garde manger too is likely to have a specially flavored version.

Recipe 14-9 provides a formula for a basic mayonnaise. Before studying it you may want to review the principles of emulsion in Chapter 8.

Let us review the recipe a step at a time. You begin with the egg yolks, using five large or six small ones per quart of oil. You whip them with the flavorings you've added until the mixture is smooth and well blended.

Add the oil very slowly (Step 2), especially in the beginning, to keep the emulsion from breaking. Add it in a slow, steady stream, whipping all the time, as you did when adding butter in butter sauces (Figure 8-6). If you are making the dressing by hand, place a folded wet towel under the bowl to steady it.

Adding the remaining vinegar and lemon juice midway (Step 3) will tend to stabilize the emulsion. You can add them earlier if your dressing becomes too thick to whip.

The finishing step is to season to taste (subdued taste for a basic dressing) when your emulsion is complete.

If these procedures and precautions look familiar it is because they should. The making of mayonnaise is very similar to the making of a butter sauce. But there are some major differences. The eggs are not cooked, the flavor base is not a reduction, and the proportions are different. Egg yolks will hold far more oil than warm butter—about twice as much.

One more precaution: the ingredients for the mayonnaise should be at room temperature before you start. The reason for this is that

14-9 MAYONNAISE

Yield: 1+ quart (1+ liter)

body and texture	5–6	egg yolks	5–6	1 oz	lemon juice	25 mL		
	1 qt	salad oil	1 L	1 oz	vinegar	25 mL	*flavorings*	
				1 tsp	dry mustard	5 mL		
				*	salt, cayenne	*		
				(*	white pepper or hot pepper sauce	*)	*seasoning*	

Basic ratio: 5–6 egg yolks / 1 qt (1 L) oil

1. Add half the vinegar and lemon juice and all the mustard to the egg yolks and whip until blended and light in color.
2. Very slowly add oil, whipping rapidly to make an emulsion.
3. When you have added half to three-fourths of the oil, whip in the balance of the vinegar and lemon juice; then slowly whip in remaining oil.
4. Season *to taste.

14-9a THOUSAND ISLAND DRESSING

Yield: 1+ quart (1+ liter)

1½ pt	mayonnaise	750 mL
¼ pt	chili sauce	125 mL
¼ pt	catsup	125 mL
6	eggs, hard-cooked, brunoise	6
2 oz	onion, brunoise	50 g
2 oz	dill pickles, brunoise	50 g
*	seasonings	*

Blend mayonnaise, chili sauce, and catsup. Fold in remaining ingredients. Season *to taste.

14-9b BLUE CHEESE DRESSING

Yield: 1+ quart (1+ liter)

½ pt	mayonnaise	250 mL
½ pt	blue cheese	250 mL
1 pt	sour cream	500 mL
1–2	lemons (juice)	1–2
1 Tb	crushed black pepper	15 mL
2 tsp	puréed onion	10 mL
1	garlic clove, puréed	1
*	seasonings	*

Blend mayonnaise, cheese, sour cream, and flavorings. Season *to taste.

cold oil does not readily separate into the tiny fat droplets that are necessary for a stable emulsion. The other ingredients should be the same temperature as the oil in order for emulsion to take place.

You can thin mayonnaise if it is too thick by beating in a few drops of water. If it is too thin you can thicken it by starting over with new egg yolks and whipping the thin dressing into them. As with butter sauces, this can also be a way of dealing with a broken emulsion.

Mayonnaise is a basic dressing and should be treated as such. Be very careful not to over-flavor it with specific ingredients. Keep it un-committed—bland—so it can go in any direction. For the same reasons use a mild-tasting vegetable oil rather than olive oil. The latter has a distinctive flavor that is not usually appropriate in a basic dressing.

Seasoning a basic mayonnaise is simpler than seasoning a hot sauce because there is no cooking. The sauce will not be reduced, so there will be no change in the proportion of seasoning to volume of sauce. Therefore seasoning can be done either before or after the basic mayonnaise is used to make finished dressings. The one potential problem might come in adding a flavoring having a high salt content, such as anchovies, to an already salted mayonnaise.

Finished dressings are made from basic mayonnaise in the same way that finished sauces are made from mother sauces—by seasoning or by adding specific flavors and ingredients to a basic dressing. When we look at finished dressings as a group, however, we find that there are few standard recipes. Each person or establishment may take great pride in a particular recipe for a dressing. Such a dressing is often referred to as a *house dressing,* and its individuality may well contribute to the success of the house.

Although specific recipes are often well-guarded secrets, there are some general characteristics for certain popular dressings. One or two ingredients may vary but the general concept is the same. Recipes 14-9a and 14-9b give you two examples made from basic mayonnaise. In addition, you can make

- *Russian:* mayonnaise, pickle relish, chopped egg, chopped pimiento, seasonings
- *Creamy roquefort* (roke-furt): mayonnaise, sour cream, roquefort cheese crumbled, seasonings
- *Chantilly:* mayonnaise, whipped cream, lemon juice, nutmeg
- *Green goddess:* mayonnaise, sour cream, anchovy, garlic, tarragon, parsley, chives, seasonings
- *Dill:* mayonnaise, chopped fresh dill

Emulsified french dressing. Another base used for thickened dressings is a basic **emulsified french dressing.** A typical recipe is given in 14-10. To make it, you apply techniques similar to those used in making mayonnaise to ingredients that are similar to those in oil-and-vinegar dressings. The result is that the oil and acids and flavorers are held in suspension in the correct proportions, emulsified by the eggs. This makes a dressing that doesn't have to be blended every time it is served, as an oil-and-vinegar dressing must be, with the chance of too much oil or vinegar being served on a salad. Yet the dressing is thin enough to coat leafy greens.

Paprika, garlic, shallots, herbs, and flavored vinegars and oils offer many ways to vary this basic recipe. The dressing that Americans term French (and the French call American) is a tomato-flavored, sweetened version of this basic dressing. Try using the flavorings from 14-8a and 14-8b in the emulsified french recipe and compare the texture and flavor differences in the two types of dressing.

Here are some of the flavorful finished dressings made from basic emulsified french:

- *Anchovy:* french dressing, anchovy paste, seasonings.

14-10 BASIC EMULSIFIED FRENCH DRESSING

Yield: 1 quart (1 liter)

body, texture	2	egg yolks	2	(½ tsp	dry mustard	2 mL)	flavor
		OR		*	salt	*	
	1	whole egg	1	*	pepper (white or cayenne)	*	seasoning
	1½ pt	oil	375 mL				
flavor	4 oz	vinegar	125 mL	*	water	*	
	2 oz	lemon juice	60 mL				

1. Add half the vinegar and lemon juice to eggs and whip until blended and light-colored.
2. Add oil slowly to make an emulsion.
3. When half the oil has been added, blend in remaining vinegar and lemon juice.
4. Whip in remaining oil. Adjust texture by whipping in water or additional lemon juice or vinegar a few drops at a time until thin enough to pour.
5. For a finished dressing, season *to taste.

- *Russian:* french dressing, red caviar, seasonings.
- *Herb:* french dressing, parsley, chervil, oregano, chives, thyme, seasonings. Herbs should be fresh if possible.

Literally hundreds of other finished dressings can be created by adding one or more of the following items to either basic emulsified french or basic mayonnaise—and this list is by no means exhaustive:

blue cheese	caviar
roquefort cheese	sweet relish
parmesan cheese	dill relish
other cheeses, shredded	sweet pickles
	dill pickles
sour cream	brandy
whipped cream	vinegars of
hard-cooked eggs	different flavors

worcestershire sauce	mustard
Tabasco sauce	fruit juices
catsup	fruit rind
chili sauce	grapes
anchovies	avocado
capers	diced vegetables
ham	curry powder
garlic	chili powder
fine herbs	currant jelly

Handling and storing emulsified dressings

Mayonnaise and emulsified french dressing have limited shelf life. They must be refrigerated because of their raw-egg content. Although they cannot be frozen successfully, they may be kept in the cooler for up to a week, which is longer than most raw-egg products can be stored. The vinegar and lemon juice they contain retard bacterial growth. However, they really should be used within three or four days because they lose flavor.

Emulsified dressings actually improve in the first 24 hours as their flavors blend. Then they begin to suffer flavor loss or change. This is particularly true of finished dressings containing onions, garlic, fresh herbs, parsley, and anchovies, all of which turn bitter after a short time. Emulsified dressings should be stored tightly covered in glass or plastic containers, away from foods having odors.

Prepared dressings

In the modern kitchen there are other options in the making of salad dressings. Basic dressings can be purchased in prepared form. Prepared mayonnaise is common in institutional outlets. Prepared salad dressing, which is similar to mayonnaise but has more filler and less oil and egg, is also a widely used base. Basic vinegar-and-oil dressing is also available.

Prepared dressings are frequently used as bases to which specific ingredients are added to make special finished dressings. It is common, for example, to stock mayonnaise in quantity and make it into thousand island, blue cheese, and other dressings as needed.

Various finishing ingredients are also available as dried dressing mixes, and they are becoming very popular. You simply add X number of packages to Y amount of basic dressing according to package instructions, and the job is complete. Some of these may be added to buttermilk or cottage cheese as a base to produce tasty low-calorie dressings. All kinds of prepared finished dressings are also becoming more and more common.

A special type of salad dressing on the market is a cooked dressing made by thickening a body of milk or fruit juices with a starch thickener and sometimes eggs, with appropriate flavorings and seasonings added. This type of dressing is seldom used in commercial establishments, but it does offer an alternative for special diets, since it is usually made with little or no oil. It is also used to give a particular consistency or flavor to a particular salad dish, such as a coleslaw or a fruit salad, and it can substitute for mayonnaise in a product that is to be frozen, since mayonnaise does not freeze well.

This type of salad dressing may also be made from scratch. Though it is often referred to as *boiled dressing,* it is not boiled but is made in a double boiler over hot water. Made-from-scratch cooked dressings must be kept refrigerated at all times. They have a short shelf life of no more than two or three days.

All prepared dressings, especially those with an egg base, should be kept in the cooler once the jar is opened or the product is reconstituted. Their shelf life at this point becomes the same as that of a product made from scratch. They should be freshly opened or reconstituted as needed.

The motivations for using prepared products are certainly valid. Labor is a prime cost in all food industry, and there is a lot of labor in the making of salad dressings. As a result, unless a particular establishment uses enough of the product to warrant the labor, it is likely to choose packaged products.

In terms of quality the dressings made from scratch are often better than commercially prepared dressings, though the commercial product tends to be more consistent. Dressings made from scratch allow for the expression of individual skill and the creation of that certain flavor people will come back to savor again.

The imaginative cook can also use other commercial products as bases for dressings. Sour cream and yogurt as well as cottage cheese and buttermilk may be used alone as bases or mixed with other dressings. In fact, you can try almost anything that has a promising texture and a suitable flavor.

Recipe 14-11 is an example of a dressing using sour cream and yogurt as a base. Honey is added to tame the tart yogurt flavor to go with a fruit salad such as the fruit platter in recipe 14-6.

PUTTING DRESSING AND SALAD TOGETHER

Some people think a salad is not a salad until it has a dressing on it. Others prefer their salad with no dressing at all. Still others will eat only one kind of dressing, no matter what the salad. Because of this variety of tastes it is customary in American restaurants to offer the guest a salad with a choice of dressings. And since most salads require the dressing to be added at the last minute, it is often the customer who adds it.

In planning a dressing or a choice of dressings for a salad, keep in mind the purpose of any dressing: it is meant to dress a salad. The dressing should not mask or overwhelm the body of the salad but should blend, contrast, complement, or otherwise enhance it. For example, salads made from mild, tender lettuces such as boston and bibb should not be subjected to dressings whose strong taste or heavy texture disguises or drowns the very qualities for which the lettuces are chosen.

There are few rules to curb your imagination in putting dressings and salads together, but some things do go together better than others.

- Vegetables, both raw and cooked, go well with dressings having an acid taste such as vinegar or lemon.
- Meats, fish, shellfish, and poultry typically have dressings with subtler flavorings— herbs, curry, condiments such as mustard or horseradish, tomato (for fish or shellfish), brandy.
- Fruits go well with such sweet–tart dressings as poppy-seed or honey-lime.
- Emulsified dressings are usually used when the salad is intended to stay together, as most cooked salads are. They are also typical choices for gelatin salads.

14-11 YOGURT DRESSING
Yield: 1¾ quarts (1.75 liters)

1 pt	plain yogurt	500 mL	*	nutmeg	*
1 qt	sour cream	1 L	1–2	lemons (juice)	1–2
½ pt	honey	250 mL			

Blend all ingredients thoroughly. Flavor with nutmeg and lemon juice *to taste.

- Oil-and-vinegar dressings or very thin emulsified dressings are usually used when a salad is tossed at tableside.

But in most instances the cook does not choose a specific dressing for a salad. Instead the diner is offered a choice of three or four. For example:

- An oil-and-vinegar dressing, probably a basic dressing or an italian
- An emulsified dressing, such as french, thousand island, or russian
- The most popular dressing in town
- A house dressing—the cook's specialty

The cook may choose the dressing for a banquet where a single fixed menu is served. In this case both dressing and salad should be selected in relation to the entrée—a light salad and dressing with a heavy meal, a more substantial salad and dressing with a light meal. A steak entrée would call for an oil-and-vinegar dressing on the salad. A fish or poultry entrée could handle a salad with an emulsified dressing. The most important consideration of all, however, is the taste of the people you are serving. If it is the custom in your area to serve steak with baked potato and a tossed green salad with an emulsified blue-cheese dressing, forget the oil-and-vinegar dressing and serve the menu your customers will expect.

There are very few salads for which there is one specific dressing and no other. Of the few whose body and dressing are inseparable, the most familiar is the caesar salad. It was invented, so the story goes, by a restaurateur named Caesar in Tijuana, Mexico, who was faced with unexpected numbers of guests and ran out of everything but eggs, romaine, and some stale bread. His solution was to toast cubes of the bread with oil and garlic, coddle the eggs (he simmered them 1 minute), and toss it all together with a flourish, along with some zesty flavorings—crushed peppercorns, lemon juice, parmesan cheese—and serve it as the specialty of the house. The tableside ceremony of putting it all together with a flourish is traditionally as much a part of this salad as the romaine and the dressing.

COLD SAUCES

Cold sauces are thickened, seasoned liquids that are used like hot sauces to enhance dishes of meats, poultry, fish, and vegetables. The reason you find them in this chapter is that most of them are like emulsified dressings in every way but use. In fact, most of them are made from basic mayonnaise as the mother sauce. Like salad dressings, cold sauces are a product of the garde manger or pantry department.

The cold sauces that derive from mayonnaise are just like the emulsified salad dressings from the standpoint of production, handling, and storage. The difference is in their use and in the requirements imposed by use.

The key factors to consider when preparing a cold sauce are

- The base consistency
- The kind of meat or other product it is to enhance
- A logical balance of flavors

The consistency must meet the description of an ideal sauce, one that seems to be in motion. Because the sauce is cold it will not run as freely as a hot sauce, but it should be pourable.

The kind of dish with which the sauce is to be served will determine the kinds of products used to flavor it. For example, lemon and dill will complement fish. Fruit flavors will complement game. The options are wide open, but logic must be used in making choices.

Here are a few well-known cold sauces that have mayonnaise as the mother sauce. The mini-recipes show you their structure and proportions.

- *Tartar* (14-12a). Generally served with fried fish.
- *Rémoulade* (ray-ma-lahd) (14-12b). Served with shellfish; often offered as a "choice of" cocktail sauce along with red sauce.
- *Sauce verte* (vairt) (14-12c). Served with fish, cold meats and poultry, cold vegetables.

Another widely used cold sauce is the cocktail sauce for cold shrimp and crab, often called red sauce. It is not based on mayonnaise but uses a blend of tomato products such as catsup, chili sauce, tomato paste or

---

14-12a TARTAR SAUCE

To 1 qt (1 L) mayonnaise (14-9) add:

1 oz	onion, chopped	30 g
1 oz	dill pickles, chopped	30 g
1 oz	capers, chopped	30 g
1 tsp	dry mustard	5 mL
*	salt, white pepper, lemon	*

Blend all ingredients.

14-12b RÉMOULADE SAUCE

To 1 qt (1 L) mayonnaise (14-9) add:

4 oz	creole style mustard	120 g
2 oz	green onions, finely chopped	60 g
1 oz	capers, finely chopped	30 g
1 oz	celery, finely chopped	30 g
½ oz	garlic, puréed	15 g
1 oz	lemon juice	30 mL
*	salt, white pepper	*

Blend all ingredients.

14-12c SAUCE VERTE

To 1 qt (1 L) mayonnaise (14-9) add:

5 oz	parsley	150 g
10	spinach leaves	10
1 tsp	lemon juice	5 mL
*	salt, white pepper	*

Purée greens in food chopper or blender and squeeze juice through cheesecloth into mayonnaise along with lemon juice. Season *to taste.

purée, flavored with horseradish and fresh lemon juice and seasoned. Like many of the hot tomato sauces it does not derive from a mother sauce. It is made from scratch or bought in prepared form.

Cold sauces are handled and stored following the same rules that apply to salad dressings. Anything having a mayonnaise base must be kept under refrigeration. Cocktail sauce, with its many acid ingredients, is much less susceptible to spoilage and health hazards. But it too should be refrigerated, not only for health reasons but because it is served with chilled foods.

APPETIZERS

Appetizers are another type of food created in the pantry or garde manger department. They are bite-size pieces or small portions of foods served to stimulate the appetite. Usually they are very sharp or spicy in taste to wake up the taste buds and make the diner hungry—or thirsty, as the case may be. The ancient Greeks called them "provocatives to drinking" and served them at their version of the cocktail party—a bring-your-own-goatskin-of-wine affair. Included were such items as roasted grasshopper, marinated octopus, and spiced meats wrapped in grape leaves.

Appetizers may be served as the opening part of a meal, or they may be the entire menu, as at a cocktail buffet. It would be impossible to list the many different kinds: they range all the way from a simple glass of tomato juice to medallions of goose-liver pâté in aspic. But certain kinds can be grouped together. Let's look at the following types:

- Cocktails
- Canapés
- Hors d'oeuvre
- Dips

Cocktails

Most people are familiar with the cocktail via the ever-popular shrimp and crab cocktails. The **cocktail** is usually served at table as the opener to a meal. The typical cocktail consists of several bite-size pieces of meat, fish, shellfish, or fruit served with a highly flavored sauce. In the fruit cocktail the "sauce" would probably be fruit juice flavored with a liqueur, or perhaps a bite-size topping of tangy sherbet. Oysters and clams on the half shell belong to this group of appetizers. The familiar crab cocktail is presented in recipe 14-13.

Canapés

A **canapé** (can-a-pay) is a bite-size or two-bite-size finger food consisting of three parts: a

14-13 CRAB COCKTAIL

Yield: 1 portion

body	1 ½ oz	crabmeat	45 g	1 oz	red or rémoulade sauce	25 mL		*sauce*
base	1	lettuce leaf	1	1	lemon wedge	1		*garnish*
	1 oz	iceberg lettuce, shredded	25 g	1	parsley sprig	1		

1. Pick over crabmeat to remove shells.
2. Line plate or cocktail glass with lettuce leaf. Top with mound of shredded lettuce.
3. Arrange crabmeat attractively on shredded lettuce. Top with sauce; garnish with lemon and parsley.

base, a spread or topping, and a garnish or garniture. Designed for eye as well as taste appeal, canapés are made in assorted shapes, arranged attractively on trays, and served from the cocktail buffet or passed to the guests.

Canapé bases can be made from a number of foods:

- Breads—pullman, rye, boston brown, french, pumpernickel
- Croutons
- Pastry bases
- Melba toast
- Crackers of many varieties

Melba toast and crackers make the simplest bases. They come in assorted standard sizes, shapes, and textures and are all ready for topping and garnish. Breads are more trouble; they must be sliced and cut into shapes—squares, rectangles, circles, triangles, diamonds, and so on. Pastry bases are usually purchased ready-made. They come in various shapes ready to hold spicy or cheesy fillings or meat pastes. Croutons are usually made from scratch and commonly take the most preparation time of all the bases.

The **crouton** (kroo-tahn) is a buttered bread shape baked in the oven until crisp and brown. Like other types of canapé base, croutons are made in a great variety of shapes. (Small cubes of bread fried with herbs and spices and used as garnitures for soups and salads are also called croutons.)

The best way to make croutons for canapé bases is to start by cutting pullman bread lengthwise, as Figure 14-8 shows. You can freeze the bread lightly and use a slicing machine for even thickness. Then you cut your circles, squares, or other shapes from these large slices. Figure 14-9 shows some pleasing shapes.

Once you have cut the crouton shapes, use recipe 14-14 to finish them. Croutons made this way can be stored dry for several days and remain crisp.

But once you have made a crouton into a canapé you can run into a major problem—keeping it crisp when it is in contact with a moist spread or topping. One way to avoid this problem is to brush the croutons with egg white before they are baked. The baked egg white provides a coating that prevents the croutons from absorbing moisture.

Now let's consider the second part of the canapé—the topping or spread. It should be something that clings nicely to the base and holds the garnish, so that the canapé does not fall apart in the guest's fingers. Choose it together with the garnish with two things in mind—eye appeal and taste. "Eye-appealing" and "appetizing" go together; we eat with our eyes as well as our taste buds.

Canapés should be sharp in flavor. Often sharp contrasting flavors are used together on the same piece. In creating contrast you may use sweet/sour, salty/bland, strong/mild, but avoid flavors that do not blend well. Don't, for example, mix fruit with fish or caviar with pickles.

Here are some examples of topping–garnish combinations:

Topping	Garnish
lemon butter	red and black caviar
caviar butter	egg slice
lemon butter	chopped onion, caviar
anchovy butter	sliced egg, caper
pimiento butter	smoked oyster
mustard butter	ham slice rolled around asparagus
butter	salami, pickle slice
parsley butter	sardine, capers
lobster butter	shrimp, parsley
cream cheese	smoked salmon, chopped onion, chopped parsley

The examples given do not express fixed relationships. You can use any base of any shape with any topping and any garnish. The sole requirement is harmony of taste and appearance.

Most of the toppings in the examples are butters. In addition to these you can use any kind of meat spread and garnish it appropriately. (The term meat here includes fish, shellfish, and poultry.) Recipe 14-15 is an example of such a spread.

You can vary this formula with any other tasty meat. The other ingredients are also variable. For example, butter, cream cheese, or sour cream could substitute for the mayonnaise. The flavorings are also variable, con-

14-14 CROUTONS

bread shapes	*	melted butter	*

1. Coat a sheet pan with butter.
2. Lay croutons on buttered pan and brush with melted butter.
3. Bake at 450°F (230°C) until crisp and brown (*5–8 minutes).

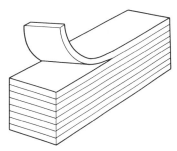

FIGURE 14-8. Slicing a pullman loaf for canapés—lengthwise.

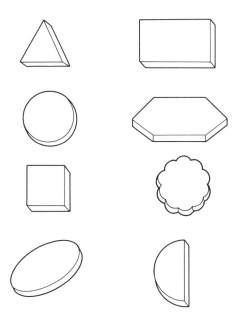

FIGURE 14-9. Popular shapes for canapé bases.

14-15 SHRIMP SPREAD

Approximate yield: 1 quart (1 liter)

1 lb	cooked shrimp	500 g	2 oz	minced onion	50 g
¼ qt	mayon-naise	250 mL	½ oz	chopped capers	15 g
			*	salt, white pepper, lemon juice	*

1. Purée shrimp.
2. Blend mayonnaise, onion, and capers with shrimp.
3. Season *to taste.

trolled only by what belongs with what, such as olives with meat, capers with fish, onions with caviar, and so on.

Make each small creation neat, trim, fresh, bright, precisely garnished, and exactly like its brothers of the same kind. They are then ready for arrangement on a tray.

Canapés can be made with inexpensive ingredients and efficient use of labor and equipment. At the other end of the scale are the expensive shellfish, caviar, smoked salmon, and puréed meat creations, garnished with precision and flair by the skilled garde manger. Enormous amounts of time and labor can be spent in creating mouth-watering, eye-appealing canapés, and the price per bite can be high indeed.

To the cook or garde manger they are a versatile and challenging species. Let your taste and imagination run wild. Then work with precision and care to make a fresh, attractive, professional-looking product even from such everyday ingredients as cream cheese, eggs, and olives.

Hors d'oeuvre

An **hors d'oeuvre** (pronounced or durve) is similar to a canapé and is used for the same purposes. The two are often confused. The primary difference is that hors d'oeuvre are not served on a bread or crust base. Another difference is that they are not finger foods but are eaten with picks or a cocktail fork. A third distinction is that the major ingredient of the hors d'oeuvre is usually served whole rather than puréed or chopped and made into a spread.

Some familiar examples of hors d'oeuvre are

- *Cheese:* bite-size cubes. Cut them shortly before serving because they dry out quickly when exposed to air.
- *Whole shrimp:* marinated or served with an accompanying sauce such as rémoulade or red sauce.
- *Deviled eggs:* hard-cooked eggs—the whites stuffed with a spread made from the yolks (14-16), or with a spicy meat or fish spread.
- *Cheese balls:* bite-size balls made of cheese blends such as crumbled roquefort, cream, and grated cheddar. Chill them; roll them in finely chopped nuts or parsley just before service.
- *Ham rolls:* thin slices of cold ham rolled around pickles or asparagus spears or filled with a spread or mousse.
- *Antipasto* (ann-tee-pass'-toe or ann-tee-pahs'-toe; Italian for "before the food"): a small plate or tray of flavorful bite-size cold foods: smoked oysters, olives, marinated vegetables, spicy cold meats, fish, shellfish, cheese, and such. The origin of this elegant hors d'oeuvre was an Italian chef's ingenuity in using far-from-elegant leftovers.
- *Liver pâté* (pah-tay): specially seasoned chicken-liver or goose-liver paste glazed or baked in a crust, sliced, and served cold.

Hors d'oeuvre may be hot as well as cold. Among the hot hors d'oeuvre are cream puffs filled with spicy meat mixtures, bite-size meatballs served in a spirited sauce, oysters rockefeller, miniature beef kebabs, and many more. Hot hors d'oeuvre are prepared in the hot kitchen.

Preparing and holding appetizers

One person at a party may be expected to eat a total of five or six different hors d'oeuvre and canapés. As you can see, serving a party of 500 could mean making and arranging 3000 or more. The cold-food expert must work with patience and staying power as well as skill and care.

Production must be planned carefully because most canapés and hors d'oeuvre do not hold well. Crisp canapé bases will absorb moisture from their toppings or from the moist air of the cooler. Soft bread canapé bases will dry out quickly if exposed to air. Toppings and garnishes will soon lose their fresh look, and even their contrasts of flavor can blur in time. Cheese cubes will harden and develop ugly, brittle edges. The peaks and ridges of deviled-egg fillings will become crusty.

The solution is to prepare the various parts of these mini-foods separately ahead of time and assemble them as close to serving time as possible. Dry canapé bases, stored dry, keep well for several days. Bread bases may be cut ahead, but must be kept moist or frozen. Some bread-based canapés can be made ahead and frozen, if their toppings are foods that freeze well. Butters and spreads hold well in the cooler (cover them); some even improve in flavor. But bring them to room temperature before attempting to apply them. Garnishes may be cut ahead, meats sliced, sauces prepared.

Many canapé and hors d'oeuvre ingredients are good bacteria growers—fish, poultry, meats, eggs, egg products—and must not stay long at kitchen temperatures. Keep both raw ingredients and assembled products out of danger-zone temperatures while you are working. Chill finished platters before service: once served they may have to stay at room

14-16 DEVILED EGGS					
Yield: 25 portions (2 halves each)					
25	eggs, hard-cooked	25	1 tsp	dry mustard	5 mL
2 oz	milk, hot	50 mL	2 oz	vinegar	50 mL
6 oz	mayon-naise	175 mL	*	salt	*

1. Peel eggs and cut in half lengthwise. Reserve whites.
2. In mixing bowl, mash yolks. Blend in milk, then mayonnaise, mustard, and vinegar. Season *to taste.
3. Using pastry bag with plain or star tube, pipe about 1½ Tb (20 mL) of yolk mixture into each half egg white.

temperature for an hour or more before being eaten.

Summing up, here are some general rules for holding:

- Keep holding times for finished products as short as possible.
- Keep moist ingredients moist and dry ingredients dry, and assemble the two kinds as close to use time as possible.
- Keep cold foods cold and hot foods hot, not only for taste and eye appeal but for safety's sake.
- Plan production carefully, with all these other rules in mind.

Dips

Dips are informal appetizers made with softened cheese, sour cream, mashed avocado, bean purée, or foods of similar consistency flavored to complement crisp, bite-size foods that are dipped into the product. Recipe

14-17 ROQUEFORT OR BLUE CHEESE DIP

Yield: 1 pint (500 mL)

8 oz	cream cheese	250 g	2 tsp	lemon juice	10 mL
6 oz	roquefort or blue cheese, crumbled	175 g	2 Tb	onion, finely chopped	25 mL
4 oz	light cream	125 mL			

Beat cream cheese until soft and fluffy. Blend in remaining ingredients.

14-17 is an example. The dippers can be chips, crackers, or **crudités**—crisp raw vegetables such as carrot sticks, celery, cauliflower.

Dips are inexpensive, easy to make in volume, and simple to serve—a bowl of dip, a dish of dippers. They hold well and make good buffet items.

Appetizers of all kinds provide an avenue for using leftovers and odds and ends, *if these are fresh and attractive.* This adds profitability to the virtues of these delightful foods. Wide variety and attractive presentation contribute to the success of any party and any operation.

SUMMING UP

The pantry area of the kitchen produces some of the most interesting and attractive foods on the menu. Here the cook works not only with flavor and texture but with color and shape and visual harmony as well. The products of this kitchen area fill many menu roles—openers, entrées, accompaniments, whole meals, party fare. The principal categories are salads, salad dressings, cold sauces, and appetizers, including cocktails, canapés, and hors d'oeuvre.

Salads fall naturally into six categories—leafy green, vegetable, combination (more than one ingredient type), cooked, fruit, and congealed (made with gelatin). Within each category the possibilities of tasty and attractive ingredient combinations are almost limitless.

Most salads are served with a dressing, usually added at serving time. Dressings are of two types—oil-and-vinegar and emulsified.

Oil-and-vinegar dressings require only the right proportions and vigorous blending. Making an emulsified dressing, such as mayonnaise, is more complicated, rather like making a butter sauce. A wide variety of flavorful ingredients can produce hundreds of different dressings, including house specialties.

Most cold sauces are made by adding distinctive ingredients to a basic mayonnaise. A few are made with tomato products as the base. Cold sauces typically accompany fish, seafood, cold meats and poultry, or cold vegetables.

Appetizers include cocktails (usually served at table), and canapés and hors d'oeuvre, party foods typically served on a buffet or passed on trays. Party foods require especially careful planning, handling, holding, and storing, to maintain maximum appeal and to avoid the risks of food-borne disease.

In all cold foods, presentation shares top honors with flavor in creating customer-pleasing products. A well-presented salad or buffet tray will have color, height, and unity to please the eye and stimulate the appetite.

To the uninitiated, the amounts of time, labor, and tender loving care that go into foods that never get near the fire can be eye-opening. Cold-food production is a facet of food preparation that can challenge both the innovative culinary artist and the lover of tradition. This area of specialization is in continuing demand at all skill levels. The payoff for such efforts is obvious as salads and other cold foods increase in popularity almost before our eyes.

THE COOK'S VOCABULARY

pantry

salad: base, underliner, body, dressing, garnish

salad greens: iceberg, romaine, bibb, boston, green leaf, red leaf, chicory, escarole, belgian endive, spinach, watercress

salad types: leafy green, vegetable, combination, cooked, fruit, congealed

gelatin: unflavored, fruit-flavored, aspic

salad dressing: oil-and-vinegar, vinaigrette, mayonnaise, emulsified french

cold sauce

appetizer, cocktail, hors d'oeuvre, canapé, crouton, dip, crudités

presentation: height, color, unity

QUESTIONS FOR DISCUSSION

1. In your opinion, what makes a salad bar appeal to customers? Consider actual items that might be offered as well as presentation and freedom of choice.

2. Do the principles of height, color, and unity apply to foods other than salads? If so, which ones and why? If not, why not?

3. If you were asked to use fruits in a cocktail, a salad entrée, and an accompaniment to a poultry entrée, what fruits would you choose for each, how would you present each one, and how would the portions compare?

4. What cold sauces, if any, would you serve with a hot dish?

5. What is it about cold-food preparation that challenges creativity?

IN this chapter and the next we look at still another specialized area of cooking—the production of breads, rolls, pies, cakes, and other dessert items. Baked goods and desserts are often neglected menu items that require only a little knowledge and creative flair to become people-pleasing stars. Even small operations can produce freshly baked bread or rolls and specialty desserts to increase profits and keep customers coming back.

Bread has a long history as a staple food, beginning with grain-and-water pastes baked on a hot flat stone—the ancestor of griddle cakes. Some form of pancake is found in every culture of the world.

Early Egyptians were probably the first to produce leavened bread by using wild yeasts and saving a bit of the fermented dough from one batch to start the next—the original sourdough "starter." The Egyptians also invented the oven. Rich Egyptians enjoyed some 30 different kinds of breads and cakes and even measured their wealth in loaves of bread.

Desserts and sweets originated with combinations of nuts and nut pastes, honey, milk, spices, fruits, and meal. Cheesecake was popular in both Greece and Rome. Baked custards were made in Greece and Rome but were considered suitable only for women and children. The art of puff pastry comes to us from Persia by way of ancient Greece.

Until the nineteenth century, methods of baking changed very little. The baker's oven, a dome-shaped brick structure, was still heated with hot coals, and the bread or pastry was set on the oven floor or hearth after the coals were scraped out. There was no way to control the temperature. During the nineteenth century a stove with a coal-burning fireplace below the oven was invented. Gas and electric ovens soon followed. During the same period chemical leaveners and commercial yeasts were developed, easing the baker's task.

Today's large commercial bakeries have specialized equipment for almost everything you can think of. But you can make most breads and pastries and sweets with the ovens

15

The Bakeshop

and mixing equipment you find in the typical quantity kitchen, even without a separate bakeshop area. What you need is to know your ingredients well, to understand how they act and react in the heat of the oven, and to learn a few special techniques.

After completing this chapter you should be able to

- Understand and explain what happens in a dough or batter as it is baked.
- Describe the principal baking ingredients and explain the roles they play in baking.
- Scale ingredients accurately.
- Describe the differences in the major types of batters and doughs, and explain or demonstrate mixing methods used for each type.
- Explain what is meant by makeup and how this process can turn out different products from the same batter or dough.

THE BAKING PROCESS

You are already familiar with baking as a cooking method—a dry-heat method in which heat is applied to a product by surrounding it with the hot air of an oven. You have learned how to bake vegetables, meats, poultry, fish, and casserole combinations of precooked foods to bring them to the desired degree of doneness.

But in baking the products that we refer to as baked goods, the transfer of heat brings about far more complicated changes than the simple cooking to doneness that happens in baking a potato or a ham. Baked goods start out as doughs and batters, which are primarily flour-and-water mixtures with other ingredients added. When the heat of the oven travels through these mixtures, it brings about complex physical and chemical changes. The nature of the end product depends on many interactions between ingredients and on the way they are put together, and even small differences in ratios and proportions or in methods of mixing will produce very different results.

Doughs and batters are varied from the basic flour-water mix by using another liquid in place of water or by adding other ingredients—eggs, salt, sweetening, fats, leavening, flavoring—any or all of these. Yet all doughs and batters undergo the same basic changes as heat is conducted to and through the product and its temperature rises. In order to control these changes and produce consistently well-made baked goods, it is important to understand what takes place during **the baking process.**

As heat is applied and the temperature of the product rises, gases, such as carbon dioxide, steam, and bubbles of air, form and expand. These gases create the **leavening,** or increase in volume, that occurs during baking. They also increase digestibility and palatability by making the product tender and light.

As these gases expand, they are held within the dough or batter by certain protein substances in the flour known as **gluten.** Gluten has an elastic structure that stretches with the expanding gases yet is strong enough to contain them, forming a network of cells within the dough or batter. If all the gases escaped, the product would be heavy and tough.

As the temperature rises, starches in the flour absorb moisture, and at 150°F (65°C) they begin to firm, or gelatinize. When the product reaches 165°F (74°C), the proteins in the flour, and in eggs if they are present, begin to coagulate, and the elastic gluten stops expanding and becomes rigid. Gelatinization and coagulation contribute to the structure and chewiness of the finished product.

In this development of leavening and structure, correct baking temperatures are crucial. If the oven temperature is too high, coagulation will occur too quickly, the gases won't be able to expand enough, and the baked product will have insufficient volume. If the temperature is too low, coagulation may not occur soon enough and the product may collapse.

Along with these developments in leavening and structure, fats in the batter or dough melt and coat cell walls, which aids in tenderizing. Some fats, as they melt, release air bubbles that help to leaven batters, puff pastry, pie dough, and sponge cakes. Since different fats have different melting points, it is important to choose the correct fat for each use.

As the baking proceeds, some of the surface moisture evaporates and a crust forms on the outside of the product. The crust browns as certain ingredients react to the increase in the temperature of the product, caramelizing or undergoing other chemical changes that produce **browning.** Sugar is often responsible for this turn of events, but milk solids, gluten, and egg proteins also contribute to browning.

When all these processes have been completed, the dough or batter has become a loaf of bread, a cake, a batch of muffins, or whatever, and the product is *done.*

It is not surprising that bakers and pastry chefs call their recipes **formulas,** referring to the chemical reactions that must take place. There is no leeway in baking: the specific ingredients, the amounts, and their proportions must be followed exactly or the proper reactions will not happen and the product will not turn out as it should. Baking is a precise form of art.

INGREDIENTS AND THEIR FUNCTIONS

Let us look more closely at the most-used baking ingredients and the roles they play in the character of the finished product.

Flours

Flour of one kind or another is *the* basic ingredient in baked goods. It performs many functions. As we have seen, it provides the structure and backbone of the finished product: it acts as a body builder as well as a binding agent. It also provides texture, flavor, absorbency, and keeping qualities. Nutritionally flour contributes starch and protein, as well as small amounts of minerals, vitamins, sugar,

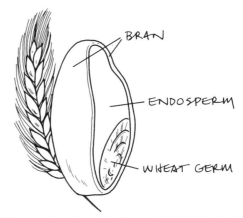

FIGURE 15-1. Wheat kernel. White flours are made from the starchy endosperm. Whole wheat flours are made from the entire kernel.

and fat. Some flours are enriched with additional vitamins and iron.

Flour is a cereal product made by milling (grinding) the kernel of the grain (Figure 15-1). The flours most used in the bakeshop are made from wheat, because wheat contains the highest proportion of the proteins *gliadin* and *glutenin,* which combine to form gluten in the batter or dough.

White flours are made from the starchy interior of the wheat kernel, which contains the gluten-forming proteins. There are two types of wheat, hard and soft, which make the flours used in every bakeshop—bread flour, cake flour, and pastry flour. Each provides the different qualities needed for different types of doughs and batters.

Bread flour is a strong flour made from hard wheat. It is capable of forming the long, strong gluten strands needed for such crusty, chewy products as French bread and hard rolls.

Cake flour, on the other hand, is known as a weak flour because it is made from soft wheat, which has a good deal less protein. This flour is useful in making soft, tender products such as high-quality cakes and doughnuts.

Pastry flour, another weak flour, has a slightly higher protein content. It is used in pie doughs, quick breads, muffins, biscuits, pastries, and some cookies—products that need a somewhat firmer structure than cakes.

A fourth familiar type of flour, **all-purpose flour,** or Hotel and Restaurant flour, is a combination of 40 percent strong and 60 percent weak flours. Because it is all-purpose, it does not serve any one purpose as well as a specific flour type but can be used in formulas calling for pastry flour.

Whole wheat flours are milled from the entire kernel. This makes them more nutritionally complete than white flours, but they make a heavier, denser product because their gluten is less elastic. For this reason they are usually combined with a white flour in making muffins, breads, rolls, and even pie doughs.

Flours made from rye, soybeans, oats, and barley are sometimes chosen for specialty items or to provide menu variety. All these flours have protein, but it is not the gluten-forming kind. They are usually combined with a strong flour to provide gluten.

Meal, especially cornmeal, may also be used in combination with wheat flour. **Meal** is a cereal product that is not as finely ground as flour. Cornmeal makes pleasantly coarse-textured products with a special flavor, such as cornbread, corn sticks, and muffins.

Liquids

Moisture is necessary to gluten development. Moisture means water specifically, not just any liquid. Oils, for example, are liquids, but they contain no moisture.

Most dough and batter formulas specify water or a milk product, which is mostly water. Other ingredients—eggs, butter, honey, molasses—may also contribute water. You will remember from Chapter 4 that water is the major ingredient in most foods.

Many milk products are used to add flavor, food value, and keeping qualities. They also improve texture. Here are the milk products most commonly used in baking.

Whole milk contributes both water and fat to the batter or dough. *Skim milk* has had most of the butterfat removed. If you want to exchange these two milks in formulas, you must adjust the amount of fat in the formula accordingly.

Buttermilk, since it is slightly acid, is often used when the leavening agent in a formula is baking soda, which requires an acid to work with. Buttermilk also adds a special flavor and contributes to the tenderness of the finished product.

Dry milk powder, usually made from nonfat (skim) milk, has had all but a fraction of its water removed. It can be added with the dry ingredients in a formula that uses water as the liquid, or it can be reconstituted and added as liquid skim milk.

Cream is seldom an ingredient in batters and doughs but is used in the bakeshop in such dessert items as custards, puddings, fillings, and toppings. Its fat content is important. Half and half is 10 to 12 percent fat. It can replace heavy cream in some recipes for lower cost and fewer calories but will not whip up. Heavy cream and whipping cream have a range of 30 to 40 percent butterfat.

Eggs, being 75 percent water, contribute liquid in formulas. Other liquids are occasionally used in baking, such as beer in a coating batter or orange juice, molasses, or burnt sugar syrup for a special flavor.

Leaveners

Leavening is the process by which doughs or batters increase in volume through the addition of bubbles of gas. A **leavener** or **leavening agent** initiates the increase in volume by producing the bubbles. As you know, leavening is not complete until the bubbles have been trapped by the structure and the product can hold its shape. Without leavening, baked goods would be heavy, dense, and unpalatable.

Leavening can be achieved in four ways: with yeast, with chemical leaveners, mechanically—that is, by the mixing method—and by turning moisture into steam. The amounts of leaveners are small in comparison with the major ingredients, but the ratios are just as important as any other. Be very careful in measuring these critical ingredients!

Yeast. Yeast is a living plant that multiplies under favorable conditions, produces the gas carbon dioxide, and thereby creates light and appetizing rolls, breads, and sweet rolls from heavy doughs. Yeast also has other virtues. It increases digestibility, adds flavor, and contributes small amounts of protein, minerals, and vitamins.

The process by which yeast works is called **fermentation.** Three factors are necessary to this process: the right food, the right amount of moisture, and the right temperature. The right food is provided by sugars in wheat flour and by sugar itself. Moisture comes from liquids in the formula. The right dough temperature is 70–90°F (20–32°C). During fermentation the yeast breaks down the sugars into carbon dioxide, alcohol, and water. Rising dough indicates the progress of this leavening action, which takes 1 to 3 hours.

Fermentation continues until the dough is baked. At 140°F (60°C) the yeasts are killed, but by this time the bubbles they have made are trapped safely in a strong gluten framework. The alcohol evaporates during the baking.

There are two forms of yeast, compressed and active dry. *Compressed yeast* comes in a springy yet firm grayish cake. To add it to the dough you dissolve it in warm liquid from the formula—twice its weight or more. A temperature of 90–100°F (32–38°C) makes a good start. *Active dry yeast* is compressed yeast with the water removed. It is granulated and is either mixed with warm liquid from the formula or added to the dough with the dry ingredients. Since there are many different types of dry yeasts, you must follow the manufacturer's instructions carefully. Compressed yeast should be stored in the refrigerator. Active dry yeast should be stored in a cool, dry place.

Chemical leaveners. The principal chemical leaveners are baking soda and baking powder. **Baking soda,** like yeast, releases carbon dioxide to create its leavening action. To do this it needs moisture and an acid ingredient to work with. Any of several things could provide the acid—cocoa or chocolate, honey, molasses, buttermilk, or fruit.

Unlike yeast, baking soda produces carbon dioxide without depending on heat. This means that batters made with soda must be baked very soon after mixing or the gases will escape. Baking soda is often used in cookies, muffins, and quick breads.

Baking powder is a combination of 1 part baking soda and 2 parts acid, usually cream of tartar. It is more stable than soda and it requires heat for maximum gas production. A baking powder batter can be held for a time without loss of its leavening power. Baking powder is used in biscuits and cakes whose formulas do not have the acid needed by soda.

Mechanical leavening. Air bubbles may be incorporated mechanically into batters by two different mixing methods—creaming and foaming. In the heat of the oven these air bubbles expand and act as leaveners.

The **creaming method** consists of whipping air into a fat–sugar combination until the mixture is light and fluffy. Pound cakes and some cookies rely on this method. The **foaming method** incorporates air by beating it into eggs. Whole eggs provide the foam that leavens sponge cakes, and foams from egg whites raise angel food cakes, soufflés, and meringues.

Steam. Steam may be used as a leavener by vaporizing the moisture in the batter or dough during baking. Water converted to steam can expand up to 1600 times its original volume. This takes a high initial baking temperature: the water must reach 212°F (100°C) to vaporize. Products leavened by steam include pie doughs, cream puffs, popovers, and puff pastry.

Eggs

Eggs are versatile additions to batters and doughs, playing many roles in support of the major ingredients. Egg proteins assist gluten in providing structure. Eggs contribute moisture, since they are three-fourths water. The fat in the yolks can play the role of a shortening in some formulas. And, as noted, eggs become important leavening agents when whipped to incorporate air. Whole eggs when whipped can increase to four times their original volume, whites can reach eight times theirs, and yolks can achieve two and a half times their original volume.

In addition to these major functions, eggs add color, flavor, and texture to baked goods. They can turn a plain white batter golden or produce a shiny golden-brown crust on a pie or puff pastry. Eggs in a batter or dough enrich the flavor of the finished product.

Eggs have the remarkable quality of producing different textures. Whipped egg whites folded into batters make lighter, fluffier products. The yolks are natural emulsifiers: when whipped together with other ingredients, they help to hold batters together.

Besides whole fresh eggs the bakeshop uses frozen eggs, both whole and separated. They save time and labor, provide consistent quality, and avoid waste since whites or yolks can be bought separately when whole eggs are not needed. But whole fresh eggs are essential when fresh flavor is important to the product.

In baking you measure eggs by weight rather than by numbers of eggs because not all individual eggs or parts of eggs are the same size. Egg quantities in formulas are given by shelled weight. Chapter 13 contains more information on eggs.

Fats

Bakers use several types of fat, some vegetable and some animal. Their most important function is to shorten gluten strands. This enables a batter or dough to rise higher before the gluten becomes rigid, thus adding bulk as well as softening texture and tenderizing the product. Fat also enhances the keeping quali-

ties of baked goods by retaining moisture.

Fats assist in leavening when they are used as creaming agents. Butter used in pie and puff pastry doughs also leavens by releasing steam, but fats that contain no water do not have this capability. Butter also adds flavor, and even fats with no flavor of their own subtly enhance the flavor of the finished product.

As you can see, the various kinds of fats do not perform alike in baking and are not interchangeable. Let us look at them individually.

Butter is a natural fat with a melt-in-the-mouth quality and flavor that is very desirable in certain desserts and pastries. It is about 80 percent fat, 5 percent milk solids, and 15 percent water, which gives it its leavening ability. Its low melting point has its drawbacks: it makes doughs based on butter more difficult to handle. Butter is also expensive. Often it is mixed with shortening or margarine to lower the cost while retaining some of butter's best qualities.

Margarine is a butter substitute made from hydrogenated animal or vegetable fats. Like butter, it contains some water (about 14 percent). It can sometimes replace butter or be mixed with it, but it lacks the distinctive butter flavor.

Shortenings are fats made especially for baking by hydrogenating animal or vegetable fats. They are practically 100 percent fat and contain no water. They have higher melting points than butter or margarine. There are several kinds, falling into two groups:

Regular shortening has a tough, waxy texture, a bland flavor or no flavor, and a high melting point. Shortenings of this class can form small particles that will produce the flaky texture of pie doughs and biscuits. They are also good at absorbing and retaining air when creamed, making them good leavening agents. This type of shortening is the one most widely used in baking.

Emulsified shortening, also called **high-ratio shortening,** is softer than regular shortening. It emulsifies easily with other ingredients and can incorporate more air than other shortenings when used in creaming. It is used in formulas having more sugar than flour and in cakes and icings high in sugar and liquid because it can hold everything together without breaking or curdling.

Oils are liquids at room temperature. They are almost 100 percent fat and contain no water. They are seldom used in doughs and batters but are useful in oiling pans, in deep-frying, and sometimes as a wash.

Sugars

Sugars are included in baked goods primarily for flavor and tenderness. They also add color either through caramelization or by contributing their own color, as brown sugar and molasses do. Sugar will absorb and retain moisture, which influences texture and keeping qualities. Sugars also provide food for yeasts. Sometimes sugar assists in leavening by acting as a mixing agent with butter or as a foaming and stabilizing agent with eggs to incorporate air into batters.

Sugars have different textures and different levels of sweetness, and some have very individual flavors. Here is a rundown on the most-used sweetening agents.

Granulated sugars are white sugars made from sugar cane or sugar beets. There are various degrees of refinement. *Fine granulated,* or *table sugar,* is most commonly used. *Confectioners' sugars* are white sugars ground to fine powder. The degree of fineness is identified by the number of Xs on the package. Number 10X is the finest and is used in icings, toppings, and fillings.

Brown sugar comes from the same sources as white sugar but is less highly refined and contains caramel and molasses. It is chosen for its flavor, color, and moisture-retaining ability. *Molasses* is a liquid by-product of sugar refining. Its color and flavor are important in gingerbread, cookies, and rye breads. It also has high moisture-retaining ability. It is an acid and is often paired with baking soda.

Honey is a natural liquid sugar made by bees. It is used in special cakes and cookies for its flavor. It is also acidic.

Corn syrup, used in candies and icings, is made from cornstarch. Because of its chemical makeup it inhibits crystallization and produces a smoother texture than other sugars.

Salt

Salt acts as a seasoning, bringing out the flavor of baked goods just as it does in other areas of cooking. In the bakeshop it also has other important functions, especially in yeast products. Salt inhibits the action of yeast, controlling its rate of growth. It also strengthens gluten, which helps it to trap carbon dioxide more effectively, thus improving texture. It is important to weigh the salt in a formula accurately to ensure the right fermentation rate and the desired texture of the final product.

Flavorings

Most flavorings do not affect the chemistry of baking. Their role is simply to provide interesting flavors and to contribute variety to the baker's output.

Ground *spices,* especially cinnamon, allspice, ginger, cloves, and nutmeg, are used in a number of products. Use the best quality possible and weigh spices whenever you can rather than measuring them by the spoonful.

Two kinds of liquid flavorings, extracts and emulsions, are used in baked goods and desserts. *Extracts* are oils dissolved in alcohol. Familiar examples are vanilla, lemon, and almond. *Emulsions* are oils emulsified with water. Lemon, orange, and mint emulsions are those most commonly used.

Many other ingredients not limited to the bakeshop are used for flavor and textural variety. They include fresh and dried fruits, nuts, coconut, chocolate, cocoa, cheeses, herbs, vegetables, and even meats. Most do not affect the baking chemistry, but they do contribute bulk and increase yield to some extent.

FIGURE 15-2. How to use the balance beam scale.

a. A balance beam scale with scoop and counterweights. The scale is balanced and ready for weighing (Step 1). If you use a different container, place it on the left-hand platform and move the beam weight along the bar until the scale balances.

b. Set the scale for the amount you need (Step 2). For 1 lb 4 oz flour you will put a 1-lb weight on the right-hand platform and add 4 oz on the beam. Use the same procedure for metric scales.

SPECIAL BAKING CONCEPTS AND PROCEDURES

Scaling

Now that we have reviewed ingredient roles, you can appreciate even better the concept of recipes as chemical formulas and the necessity for maintaining accurate ratios and proportions. The most accurate method of controlling amounts and proportions is to weigh all ingredients. This is called **scaling.** Accurate weighing is even more important in baking than in other types of cooking. Dry ingredients must always be weighed. Certain liquid ingredients—water, milk, and eggs—can be measured either by weight or by volume. For these ingredients and these only, "a pint's a pound the world around" is a handy rule to remember.

Scaling is done on a special **baker's balance beam scale** such as the one shown in Figure 15-2. It contains two platforms, a balance beam with a sliding weight for measuring ounces or grams, and several counterweights for measuring pounds or kilograms. A scoop for scaling dry ingredients, shown on the left-

hand platform, comes with the scale, along with a counterweight for the right-hand side to balance it exactly.

The principle of using this scale is to set up the right-hand side to the weight desired by using counterweights and the weight beam, and then to add the ingredient on the left-hand side until the scale balances. The illustrations show a step-by-step procedure for scaling.

The term scaling applies to the entire process of measuring ingredients. This includes measurement of the completed batter or dough when it is **panned**—that is, put into pans for baking. Measuring the dough or batter for each muffin or roll or loaf of bread is essential to a uniform product—each muffin like every other muffin in size and appearance, each one baking at the same rate. Scaling each one also guarantees that you will produce the number intended.

In scaling the finished dough or batter you do not always use a scale. You may use a measure such as a scoop or ladle that is equal to the weight of the batter desired per muffin, or a biscuit cutter that produces the size biscuit you want. In making bread or rolls you will use

c. Add the ingredient until the scale balances (Step 3).

d. To weigh additional ingredients increase the amount needed with counterweights and beam. Then add the new ingredient carefully to the container until the scale balances. If you reach 16 oz on the beam, put a 1-lb weight on the right-hand platform and reset the beam to zero so you can use it again. (Photos by Patricia Roberts.)

a **dough cutter** (Figure 15-3) as well as a scale to divide the dough into equal parts of the required weight.

Baker's percentages

A system known as **baker's percentages** is another concept that is unique to baking. It is a way of expressing ratios or proportions of ingredients in a given formula. In each case 100% represents, *not* the total of all ingredients in the formula, but the amount of flour alone. Other ingredients are then expressed as percentages of this amount. For example, if a formula calls for 10 lb flour and 4 lb shortening, the flour is 100% and the shortening is 40%. If a formula specifies 130% sugar for 10 lb flour, you will need 13 lb sugar.

You may find all this confusing at first. Just remember that it expresses ratios, not total percentages. An experienced baker or pastry chef uses baker's percentages when creating new formulas or making major adjustments to old ones.

In this book we will not be using baker's percentages. But it is a concept you will meet if you pursue a baking career.

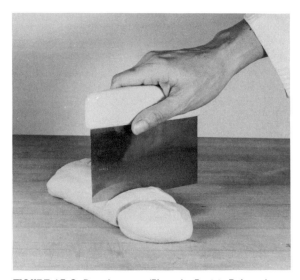

FIGURE 15-3. Dough cutter. (Photo by Patricia Roberts.)

15-1 WAFFLES I

Approximate yield: 1 quart (1 liter) batter

8 oz	flour	250 g	12 oz	milk	375 g
½ oz	baking powder	15 g	3	eggs	3
½ tsp	salt	2 g	4 oz	melted butter or oil	125 g
1 oz	sugar	30 g			

1. Sift dry ingredients together.
2. Combine eggs with milk and butter/oil and fold into dry ingredients until lightly blended.
3. Oil waffle iron lightly and pour on enough batter to cover two-thirds of the surface. (Batter will spread to fill.)
4. Close iron and cook until steaming stops and waffles are light brown and crisp.

15-1a WAFFLES II

In procedures for 15-1, make these changes:

Omit sugar in Step 1.

In Step 2, separate eggs. Combine yolks with other liquids and fold into dry ingredients.

Step 2a. Whip egg whites to a soft peak. Add sugar and whip again just until combined. Fold gently into moistened mixture.

Continue with Steps 3 and 4 of 15-1.

15-1b WAFFLES III

To ingredients in 15-1, add:

1 tsp	cinnamon	5 g
4 oz	nuts, chopped	125 g
6 oz	fruit, small pieces, drained	175 g

Follow instructions in 15-1 or 15-1a, adding cinnamon in Step 1 and folding in nuts and fruit at end of Step 2.

POUR BATTERS

Batters and doughs are typically grouped according to the texture of the mixture, which derives mainly from the proportion of flour to liquid. **Pour batters** have the lowest ratio of flour to liquid. They can be poured easily in a steady stream.

You have already produced pour batters if you made the pancakes and crêpes in Chapter 13 (13-3 and 13-5). Another pour batter is given in the formula for waffles (15-1). Comparing it with the pancake formula, you will see that it is very similar except that it contains more fat and less liquid.

In pour batters the dry ingredients are sifted together to mix them well, as in Step 1 of the waffle formula. They are then mixed with the liquids just until they are moistened, as in Step 2. Overmixing would develop the gluten, which would make these products tough and chewy. This two-step mixing method is often called the **muffin method** because this is how muffins are made, as we shall see shortly.

You may remember that crêpes are an exception to this method: they must be mixed until they are smooth in order to produce a thin product. Because this develops the gluten, a crêpe batter must rest before baking so that the gluten can relax and yield a tender crêpe as well as a thin one.

To make waffles (Step 4), preheat the iron and pour enough batter on the middle of the bottom to cover about two-thirds of the surface. Close the top and cook. Up-to-date waffle irons signal when done and turn off automatically. If yours doesn't, wait until things stop steaming; then lift the top. It should come up easily. If it resists you, cook another 30 seconds and try again. Lift the waffle out carefully, working from one edge. It should emerge all in one piece.

Both pancakes and waffles can be made lighter and fluffier when whipped egg whites are folded into them, as in formula 15-1a. This is the foaming method of leavening discussed earlier. Make sure that no yolk is present in the whites and that utensils and mixing bowl are grease-free. Even the tiniest bit of yolk or fat keeps the egg whites from attaining volume.

To determine a soft peak (Step 2a), lift a small amount of beaten white above the surface. If it stands up but the top or peak falls over, you have reached this consistency.

Making waffles with whipped egg whites takes extra preparation time, and the batter does not hold quite as well, a consideration when you are cooking to order. There are other ways of dressing them up, such as adding extra flavor and texture ingredients. Formula 15-1b is one suggestion.

Crisp and tender waffles, a delicious addition to the breakfast menu, can also function as a dessert with ice cream and fruit sauce. Some establishments use waffles to replace toast under creamed chipped beef or chicken.

Popovers (15-2) are made from a pour batter mixed by a completely different method (Steps 1–3). They are leavened entirely by steam. Because of this, bread flour must be used for its stronger gluten content, and the dough must be well mixed until very smooth (Step 3) so that the gluten is well developed and will form a strong structure to trap the rapidly expanding gases. The popovers are baked at a high temperature to promote quick formation of the steam and coagulation of the proteins in the flour and eggs. The result is a light and airy puff, a dramatic illustration of the leavening power of steam.

Popovers may be used as an accompaniment to a meal or as an interesting container for meat or vegetable salads. For a delicious

---

15-2 POPOVERS

Yield: 2 lb 6 oz (1185 g) batter = about 36 4" (10 cm) popovers

8 oz	eggs	250 g	1 oz	melted butter or shortening	30 g
1 lb	milk	500 g	12 oz	bread flour	375 g
½ oz	salt	15 g			
½ oz	sugar	15 g			

1. In mixer, using low speed and paddle attachment, blend well the eggs, milk, salt, and sugar.
2. Pour in melted fat and combine on low speed.
3. Add flour and mix on second speed until very smooth.
4. Oil alternate muffin cups in tin to allow for expansion. Fill oiled cups three-fourths full, about 1 oz (30 g) each—a No. 32 scoop.
5. Bake at 425°F (220°C) until firm with a dry, medium-brown crust (*30–40 minutes).

15-3 PLAIN MUFFINS

Yield: 3 lb 5 oz (1649 g) batter = 24–30 muffins

1 lb 4 oz	pastry flour	600 g	4 oz	eggs	120 g
1 oz	baking powder	30 g	1 lb	milk	475 g
6 oz	sugar	180 g	6 oz	melted butter or shortening	180 g
¼ oz	salt	7 g			

1. Sift dry ingredients into a large bowl.
2. In another bowl beat eggs. Stir in remaining liquids.
3. Fold liquids into dry ingredients until barely blended.
4. Scale 1½–2 oz (50–60 g) batter into each greased or paper-lined muffin cup.
5. Bake at 400°F (220°C) until firm but springy (*20 minutes).

15-3a WHOLE WHEAT MUFFINS

In formula 15-3 make these changes:

Reduce pastry flour to 14 oz (420 g).

Add 6 oz (180 g) whole wheat flour.

Reduce baking powder to 3/4 oz (22 g).

Add 1 tsp (5 mL) baking soda.

Add 2 oz (60 g) molasses or honey.

In Step 1, mix dry ingredients by stirring thoroughly. Do not sift.

In Step 2, add honey or molasses with milk and fat. Proceed as in 15-3.

15-3b BLUEBERRY NUT MUFFINS

To formula 15-3 add:

8 oz	blueberries, well drained	240 g
6 oz	walnuts or pecans, chopped	180 g

Follow instructions for 15-3. Fold in berries and nuts in Step 3.

luncheon entrée try filling them with such things as chicken à la king or seafood newburg. When popover batter is made with beef drippings and served with a roast, it is called yorkshire pudding.

DROP BATTERS

A great variety of products are made from the somewhat rough-textured, often lumpy semi-liquids known as **drop batters.** The differences in product may come from diversity of ingredients or simply from the mixing, panning, or baking method. Ranging from muffins and tea breads to gingerbread, scones, dumplings, and coating batters, they have in common a similar batter texture and most of them use the muffin method of mixing.

Many of these products belong to a group known as *quick breads* because they are quickly and easily put together and they are breadlike in texture and in menu use. The chief reason they are quick and easy is that they are leavened with a chemical leavener. This is simply added to the dry ingredients, and there is no need for the time and activity required by other leavening methods.

In the muffin formulas (15-3 and 15-3a and b) you see the muffin mixing method in

FIGURE 15-4. Muffin mixing method.

a. Sift the dry ingredients.

b. Fold liquids into dry ingredients to barely combine. Batter should be lumpy.

action again. Figure 15-4 illustrates the essential steps. First the dry ingredients are sifted together to ensure even distribution in the batter. The liquids are blended together and then folded in, mixing only enough to barely combine the ingredients. Don't worry if a few small lumps remain; they will disappear during baking. To produce a tender product you want to avoid overmixing: once the gluten has access to moisture it will begin to develop if manipulated, thus diminishing tenderness.

In mixing the whole wheat muffins, you do not sift the dry ingredients because this would sift out the wheat germ, which is an integral part of the flavor and texture. Baking soda is used to take advantage of the acidity of the molasses or honey and to bring out its special flavor.

Because of the type of leavener used, all three of these batters must be baked very soon after mixing, especially the whole wheat muffins, so that no volume is lost.

Formulas for muffins can be baked as loaf breads or sheet cakes and vice versa. They can be varied by replacing part of the liquid with fruit juice or buttermilk and by adding nuts, bran, fruit, and spices, or even cheese,

c. To make up, portion into prepared pans. (Photos by Patricia Roberts.)

15-4 COATING BATTER

Approximate yield: 1 quart (1 liter)

12 oz	flour	360 g	8 oz	eggs, beaten	240 g
¾ oz	baking powder	22 g	12 oz	milk	360 g
¾ tsp	salt	3 g	*	flour for dredging	*
¾ oz	sugar	22 g			

1. Sift together dry ingredients.
2. Mix beaten eggs and milk. Fold into dry ingredients.
3. Refrigerate, covered, 4–8 hours.
4. Dredge product in flour and dip in batter to cover completely.
5. Fry in deep fat at 350°F (180°C) until golden. Drain well and serve at once.

15-4a FRUIT FRITTERS

Yield: about 24 fritters

To formula 15-4 add:

¾ oz	sugar (1½ oz/44 g total)	22 g
1 lb	diced fruit (apples, berries, pineapple, etc.) well drained	480 g

Dredge fruit in flour and fold into batter at end of Step 2.

In Step 5, using a No. 24 scoop, drop batter directly into deep fat.

15-4b VEGETABLE FRITTERS

Yield: about 24 fritters

To formula 15-4 add:

1 lb	diced cooked vegetables (corn, carrots, zucchini, eggplant, etc.)	480 g

Dredge vegetables in flour and fold into batter at end of Step 2.

In Step 5, using a No. 24 scoop, drop directly into deep fat.

herbs, and vegetables, to produce breads to be served at lunch, tea, and dinner as well as breakfast. The added ingredients will not change the basic chemistry of the formula but may increase the yield slightly. Formula 15-3b is one of dozens of possible variations.

The last drop batter we will examine (formula 15-4) has many uses in the hot-food kitchen. You can use it as a coating for all sorts of deep-fried foods, such as onion rings, frog's legs, mushrooms, or rounds or batonnets of zucchini or eggplant, or you can add things to the batter to make fritters. Fruit fritters (15-4a) can be dusted with powdered sugar and served at breakfast with syrup or preserves, or at lunch or dinner to accompany entrées. Vegetable fritters (15-4b) or batter-fried vegetables are popular snacks or side dishes.

This batter is made with the by-now-familiar muffin method. Refrigerating it for several hours relaxes the gluten, increasing tenderness. Like pancake or waffle batter, it can be made lighter by separating the eggs and folding in stiffly beaten whites separately. You can make a beer batter from this formula by omitting the baking powder and replacing the milk with beer. The carbonation in the beer acts as the leavener and the beer adds its distinctive flavor. Both these variations increase the crisp texture so desirable in fried foods. Some cooks add a small amount of paprika to coating batters to aid in coloring.

Avoid frying these products at too high a temperature or making the fritters too large because the outside will darken too quickly before the interior is cooked. Like other fried foods, these products are at their peak when served immediately but can be held successfully for a short time in a warm place, uncovered.

PASTES

Pastes have a texture that is stiffer than batters and softer than doughs. They are usually piped from a pastry bag and are firm enough to maintain their shape. The best-known paste, **éclair paste,** is a flour–liquid mixture like the other doughs and batters. Cookie pastes, which require different ingredients and a different mixing method, are discussed later.

Éclair paste is also called **chou paste,** from the French *pâte à chou* (pot a shoo)

meaning cabbage paste, so called because the mounds of paste look like little cabbages. Familiar chou paste products include cream puffs and éclairs—tender puffed-up crusts with hollow centers like popovers—and crullers or french doughnuts.

Chou paste makes a great variety of menu items. Small cream puffs, called profiteroles, are served with soup. Bite-size cream puff shells can be flavored by stirring grated cheese, herbs, minced meat, seafood, or poultry or combinations of these into the mixture before cooking, or the shells can be filled after baking with savory mixtures for delightful hors d'oeuvre. And of course there are éclairs and cream puffs for dessert, filled with delicate cream fillings. You have also met chou paste in an entirely different role—providing structure and texture in duchesse potatoes (9-14).

Formula 15-5 details the ingredients and procedures for chou paste. You will notice that this formula is not unlike the other baking mixtures you have dealt with, except for the large amount of butter and eggs. Like pop-

---

15-5 PÂTE À CHOU (CHOU PASTE, ÉCLAIR PASTE)

Approximate yield: 3½ lb (1800 g) paste

1 lb	milk and/or water	500 g	12 oz	bread flour	375 g
8 oz	butter or shortening	250 g	1 lb 4 oz	eggs	625 g
1 tsp	salt	5 mL			
1½ oz	sugar (see note)	45 g			

1. In trunnion kettle or heavy pan, bring liquid, fat, salt, and sugar to a full boil.
2. Remove from heat and add flour all at once, stirring rapidly with a wooden spoon.
3. Over moderate heat, continue to cook and stir until mixture is smooth, pulls away from pan, and forms a ball-like mass.
4. Remove from heat. Continue stirring, by hand or in mixer with paddle, until mixture cools to 140°F (60°C).
5. Beat in eggs a little at a time, incorporating them completely each time until batter is smooth and glossy. When all eggs are absorbed, mixture should be thick and able to stand alone.
6. Pipe or pan out into desired shape and size.
7. Bake at 400°F (200°C) until crisp, brown, and dry.

   NOTE: For duchesse potatoes and savory preparations omit sugar.

overs, it uses bread flour because, like popovers, chou paste is leavened by steam and needs the extra gluten to contain the tremendous expansion. The butter and eggs are for tenderness, flavor, and texture. The eggs also emulsify the butter–flour–liquid mixture and hold it together. Milk is used for flavor too, especially for dessert items, but water also makes an excellent product. Sugar is used for a sweet product and omitted for a nonsweet or savory item.

The procedures, on the other hand, are something new. Let us go through them step by step.

Make sure the liquid is at a rolling boil in Step 1. The fat must be completely melted and mixed with the liquid before the flour is added, so that the ingredients are evenly distributed. In Step 2, removing the mixture from the heat, adding the flour all at once, and stirring like crazy is the easiest way to produce the smooth, lump-free mixture.

In Step 3, rapid stirring continues over moderate heat (to avoid scorching) to begin gluten development and to allow the flour to absorb moisture and gelatinize. (Does this remind you of making roux?) When the mixture forms a ball, you know the process is complete. At this point (Step 4), remove the mixture from the heat and let it cool slightly so that the eggs won't cook when you add them. You can transfer the mixture to a mixer with the paddle or continue stirring by hand.

Perhaps you can guess why you add the eggs little by little in Step 5—to avoid lumping. They must be evenly distributed to form a uniform emulsion. When all the eggs have been beaten in, you should have a thick, smooth, glossy paste, able to stand alone, ready to be piped out. With a little practice, pâte à chou takes only a few minutes to prepare and should be piped out (Step 6) and baked as soon as possible.

To form cream puffs, use a plain tip to pipe out quarter- to half-dollar-size rounds, depending on the final size desired. A mound about 1½" (4 cm) in diameter is usual; a well-made paste will increase three to five times

when baked. Space on pans to allow for expansion. Use paper-lined sheet pans: oiled pans will cause the paste to flatten out. For éclairs, pipe out 1 × 4" (2½ × 10 cm) oblong shapes, using the same procedure.

In baking (Step 7), the oven temperature is high in order to create the steam that expands and puffs the paste. The continued heat coagulates the gluten and the egg protein to firm and set the structure. Some chefs bake at 425°F (220°C) for 10 minutes and reduce the temperature to 375°F (190°C) for the remaining time. Baking time varies according to product size. Cream puffs and other chou paste products must be thoroughly baked— well browned and crisp—and cooled slowly or they will collapse.

Cream puffs and éclairs may be filled with whipped cream, pastry cream (16-11), ice cream, or a fruit filling. They are then dusted with confectioners' sugar or topped with a dessert sauce or chocolate fondant (more on these good things later). Hold them in the refrigerator or, for an ice cream filling, in the freezer.

Unfilled pâte à chou products that have been thoroughly cooled may be placed in plastic bags and stored in the refrigerator for up to a week, or frozen and stored longer. They keep very well and can be freshened by heating in a moderate oven for a few minutes.

SOFT DOUGHS

Soft doughs include biscuits and yeast breads and rolls. A **soft dough** has a higher flour-to-liquid ratio than a drop batter—enough to make a firm but elastic dough that is soft to the touch. These doughs can be rolled, cut, or formed into various shapes and sizes to make a variety of products. They are also varied by the use of different ingredients and mixing methods.

Biscuits

Biscuits (formula 15-6) are usually considered quick breads because they are fast

15-6 BISCUITS

Yield: 4 lb 5 oz (2150 g) dough = about 48 2" (5 cm) biscuits

1 lb	bread flour	500 g	10 oz	butter and/or shortening	310 g
1 lb	cake flour	500 g	1½ lb	milk or buttermilk	750 g
2 oz	baking powder	60 g	*	milk or egg wash	*
½ oz	salt	15 g			
½ oz	sugar	15 g			

1. Sift together dry ingredients.
2. Cut fat into dry ingredients.
3. Fold in liquid until barely combined.
4. Turn out onto lightly floured surface and knead lightly, making four quarter turns of the dough.
5. Roll out to ½" (1 cm) thickness.
6. Cut into desired shape and place on paper-lined or lightly oiled baking sheets.
7. Brush tops with milk or egg wash.
8. Bake at 425°F (220°C) until doubled in height and golden brown (*15–20 minutes).

and simple to make, whereas yeast breads take 2 to 3 hours and require more preparation. The mixing method used for biscuits is called the **pastry method** because it is also used for pie doughs, as you will see in the next chapter. It requires that the fat be rubbed or cut into the dry ingredients before liquids are added. You can **cut in** the fat with a fork, pastry cutter, or mixer, or by rubbing the fat and flour together between the palms of your hands.

Let us look at the formula in detail. The mixture of flours is used for two different but complementary purposes. Bread flour contributes the stronger gluten structure needed during leavening. Cake flour moderates this effect, allowing the biscuit to be tender and flaky. The other ingredients perform their usual functions: baking powder for leavening, salt and sugar for flavor, fat for tenderness, milk to provide liquid for the gluten and for starch gelatinization, as well as to add flavor. Butter will add flavor too.

Now let us examine the mixing method

15-6a SWEET BISCUITS

In formula 15-6 make these changes:

Increase sugar to 4 oz (125 g).

Add 6 oz (175 g) raisins.

In Step 2, stir raisins into dry ingredients after cutting in fat.

15-6b SAVORY BISCUITS

To formula 15-6 add (any or all):

1–2 oz	parsley or other herb	30–60 g
10 oz	cheese, grated	300 g
10 oz	ham, brunoise	300 g

In Step 2, stir added ingredients into dry ingredients after cutting in fat.

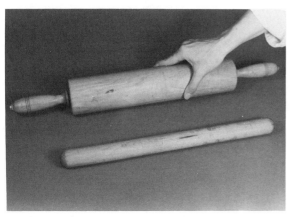

FIGURE 15-5. Rolling pins. Top, ball bearing pin. Bottom, broomstick pin. (Photo by Patricia Roberts.)

step by step. In Step 1, you sift the dry ingredients to distribute them evenly, as in the muffin method. It is equally important to distribute the fat throughout (Step 2) until the mixture resembles a coarse meal or, for a flakier biscuit, until the fat is pea-sized.

When adding the liquid ingredients (Step 3), mix as little as possible because this is when the gluten begins developing and you want to control this development. At this point the dough will resemble a drop batter and can be treated like one. You can drop 2-oz biscuits onto paper-lined pans, skipping Steps 4–7, and bake them in this form. They will be very tender but irregular in appearance.

Beginning in Step 4, traditional biscuits differ from most quick breads. A *moderate* amount of gluten development is desirable to support the structure during leavening. You accomplish this by kneading. **Kneading** manipulates the dough to stretch the gluten strands and develop their elastic qualities. For biscuits the kneading is gentle. Place the dough in one lump on a lightly floured surface and use the heels of your hands to push the bulk of the dough away from you. Fold it in half back on top of itself and turn the dough in a quarter circle. Repeat three times until the circle is completed.

This is the entire kneading procedure for biscuits. We will see in the next section that yeast products require more gluten development, and the kneading takes place in the mixer.

After kneading, the dough is ready to be rolled out to a uniform thickness (Step 5). This is done with a small broomstick pin (Figure 15-5) and is known as **pinning out.**

Cut the biscuits into the desired shape (Step 6) using a lightly floured cutter. If you use a round cutter, cut the biscuits as close together as possible. The scraps between the biscuits have to be reworked and won't be as tender. You can avoid this problem by cutting the biscuits in squares or triangles with a floured knife or dough cutter. Whatever their shape, space the biscuits ½″ (1 cm) apart on a lightly oiled or paper-lined sheet pan. For softer, less crusty biscuits, place them almost touching each other.

A milk or egg wash (Step 7) helps to produce an attractive, shiny brown crust. Milk wash makes a softer top crust, and egg wash produces a crisper, browner crust. Baking temperature is high (Step 8) to make the biscuits rise quickly and to create a firm structure.

Biscuits are traditionally served at breakfast in certain areas of the country. You might want to try some variations to produce a sweet shortcake for fruit (15-6a) or bite-size savory biscuits to serve as an hors d'oeuvre (15-6b). Any of these biscuits can be a welcome addition to the bread basket at any time of day.

Yeast doughs

Most soft doughs are yeast doughs. The products they make range from French and Italian loaves to sweet rolls and danish pastry. As in other types of baked products, the differences come from ingredients and makeup.

Differences in ingredients produce two types of yeast doughs—lean and rich. **Lean doughs** are low in fat and sugar. They include crusty breads and rolls and pizza dough as well as whole wheat and rye bread and rolls. **Rich dough** formulas contain more fat and sugar and often include eggs. Brioche, challah breads, sweet rolls, and coffee cakes are examples.

All doughs, lean or rich, go through the same series of production steps—12 of them. It is a long process, but the baker is actively involved only a small part of the time. It is an in-and-out process in which the baker is very busy for short periods. In between, the baker puts the dough to work by itself. It goes like this:

Baker	Dough alone
1. Scaling ingredients	
2. Mixing	
	3. Fermenting (1–2½ hours)
4. Punching	
5. Scaling the dough	
6. Rounding	
	7. Bench proofing (10–20 minutes)
8. Makeup and panning	
	9. Proofing (1–2 hours)
	10. Baking (20–90 minutes)
	11. Cooling (30–45 minutes)
	12. Storage

The baker is responsible for beginning and ending the "dough alone" steps properly but is not actively involved.

Let us look at these steps briefly to gain an overview of the process. Then we will examine some formulas to gain a better understanding of what goes on and why.

Scaling ingredients (Step 1) is already familiar to you. In yeast doughs as elsewhere, careful weighing is essential, especially for salt, which affects both fermentation and gluten development.

Mixing (Step 2) is the most complex and possibly the single most important step. It must accomplish two things of key importance to the finished product. First, it must distribute all ingredients evenly throughout the batter, for correct leavening action and a uniform product. Second, it must develop the gluten properly.

Two major mixing methods are used. The **straight dough method** has one step: you place all the ingredients in the mixer bowl and combine them, using the dough arm. Some rich doughs require a **modified straight dough method** in which the ingredients are combined in installments to ensure that such ingredients as fat and sugar are completely integrated into the dough.

The second major method—the **sponge dough method**—has two steps. In the first step the liquid, part of the flour, and the yeast are mixed to a smooth, thick batter, or sponge, which is fermented until doubled in volume. The sponge is then mixed with the remaining flour and other ingredients to form the dough.

Fermenting (Step 3) follows mixing in the straight dough method. Fermentation begins during mixing and continues until the yeast is killed when the dough temperature reaches 140°F (60°C) in the oven. Between these two events it needs time to work its chemical magic. So you place the dough in a proof box—a special cabinet with controlled temperature and high humidity. If you do not have a proof box, you place the dough in an oiled container, oil the dough surface, and cover the container to prevent a crust from forming. You let it ferment until it has doubled in volume and does not spring back but remains indented when you press it lightly with your fingertips (Figure 15-6). The best temperature for fermenting is to keep the dough at about 80°F (27°C).

In the sponge method, the sponge alone is fermented. After the remaining ingredients are added, another brief fermentation period usually follows.

Punching (Step 4) is the next step in the straight dough method. This is done by pulling up the sides of the dough mass and pushing them down into the center until the dough has deflated. This equalizes the temperature, allows the gluten to relax, and redistributes the yeast so the dough will rise again.

You do not punch the sponge after it ferments. Mixing in the remaining ingredients accomplishes the same things.

Scaling the dough (Step 5) comes next—weighing it into portions of the desired size. The dough is divided on the **bench**, the baker's wood-surfaced worktable. You dust the surface lightly with flour, cut the dough with a dough cutter or sharp knife to avoid stretching it, and weigh it on the balance scale. After you weigh out the first portion correctly, you can use it as a counterweight and weigh the remaining portions against it.

Rounding (Step 6) is a preliminary makeup technique. Your aim is to form each portion into a round ball with a smooth skin that will contain the gases effectively. You use the cupped palm of your hand to roll the dough around on the bench while pressing it against the bench surface with the outside edge of your hand.

Bench proofing (Step 7) means fermenting at the bench. The balls of dough are covered and allowed to rest at the bench for 10 to 20 minutes as fermentation continues. This relaxes the gluten and makes makeup easier.

Makeup and panning (Step 8) bring you

FIGURE 15-6. Testing the rising.

closer to the final product. Makeup means forming the dough into its final shape. The goal of this step is familiar: uniformity of size and appearance to produce attractive, evenly baked portions. An immense variety of shapes and sizes is possible. After makeup, bread and rolls are placed in pans or molds or properly spaced on sheet pans. Those baked on sheet pans are called *hearth breads,* from the days when they were placed directly on the oven floor or hearth for baking.

Proofing (Step 9) is another fermentation period. Bakers use the term **proofing** to distinguish this leavening period from the first fermentation. The best conditions for proofing are a humidity of 85 percent and a temperature of 90–100°F (32–38°C) to keep the dough at 80°F (27°C). If a proof box is not available, duplicate these conditions as closely as possible and cover the dough to retain moisture and prevent a skin from forming. Proofing is "done" when the dough has doubled and remains indented when pressed. Handle with care: it is very fragile and is easily deflated.

Baking (Step 10) comes next. Before going into the oven, loaves and some rolls are **cut** or **docked** by slashing the top with a sharp knife. This allows even expansion in the oven. Most products are brushed with a wash to provide shine, crispness, browning, or all three. Pans are then placed carefully in the oven. Lean doughs and small rolls bake quickly at high temperatures, but rich doughs and large loaves bake at lower temperatures for a longer time.

Yeast products rise rapidly in the oven at first as gases expand. Fermentation ends as the temperature rises, and the product firms as the starches gelatinize and the proteins coagulate. The crust forms and browns. Doneness is signaled when the crust is golden brown and the loaves sound hollow when tapped lightly.

You may think of baking as the final step,

but two more steps are the baker's responsibility in order to preserve that fresh-baked quality.

Cooling (Step 11) allows excess moisture to escape. Products baked in molds should be removed and placed on screens or racks so that air can circulate around them. Bread and rolls baked on sheet pans can be left on the pans to cool. Keep drafts away from hot breads or the crusts may split.

Storage (Step 12) is the final step for all baked goods. Its goal is to inhibit **staling**—deterioration of texture and aroma caused by loss of moisture and changes in the structure of the starches.

Staling begins very soon after baking, but bread, rolls, biscuits, and quick breads to be served within 8 hours can be stored at room temperature. If they must be kept longer, wrap them in plastic wrap or place in plastic bags after they are thoroughly cool. If they are not cool, moisture will collect and make the product soggy—particularly undesirable in hard-crusted goods. *Always store them in the freezer.* Refrigeration actually increases staling, so don't follow this common practice. Freshen frozen baked goods in the oven at a low temperature for a short time, or simply let them thaw.

Making yeast products

Now let us examine some formulas for different types of breads and rolls. You will see that they all have the basic steps in common; the only differences are in mixing method and makeup techniques.

Hard roll dough. Hard roll dough (formula 15-7) is a lean dough that makes chewy, hard-crusted rolls or French or Italian type bread. True French bread has only flour, yeast, water, and salt. The small amounts of fat and sugar in this formula contribute to keeping qualities. Bread flour is used for its strong gluten content.

This formula is an example of the straight dough method. After dissolving the yeast in part of the water (Step 1), you place all the ingredients in the bowl of the mixer. Don't let the yeast come into direct contact with the salt; this would inhibit fermentation.

During mixing (Step 2) the ingredients are distributed evenly in the first few minutes, and the dough forms a mass around the dough hook. The slapping of dough against the sides of the bowl kneads and stretches the gluten strands, making them stronger and more elastic. If the dough has not lost its sticky look and feel when two-thirds of the mixing time is up, you should add a little more flour.

Twelve minutes for mixing is only a guideline. Watch for clues: lean doughs when properly mixed look and feel smooth and resilient. The dough clears the bowl in a smooth mass. Both undermixing and overmixing can produce poor volume and texture in the final product.

During fermentation (Step 3) the yeast multiplies and produces carbon dioxide, causing the dough to rise. Punching in Step 4 deflates it. Punching, along with scaling, rounding, and bench proofing, prepares the dough for makeup. If you take special care during rounding to form smooth balls, makeup will be much easier and will produce more attractive finished products. (You could even choose to bake these balls as buns or round loaves without further handling.)

For Step 5, makeup technique for club rolls is illustrated in formula 15-7a. The technique of rolling and sealing (Steps 5a, b, and c) is the same for French and Italian style (hearth) loaves and pan bread (bread baked in loaf pans). This technique produces a uniform roll or loaf with a smooth, even surface—one that will keep its shape.

Use the same steps for hearth and pan breads. These breads are scaled at anywhere from 12 to 16 oz (360–500 g) or more depending on the size loaf desired. For pan breads the width of your rectangle in Step 5a is

15-7 HARD ROLL DOUGH

Yield: 4 lb 7½ oz (2145 g) dough

2 lb 10 oz	bread flour	1260 g	1 lb 8 oz	water	720 g
1 oz	salt	30 g	1½ oz	compressed yeast	45 g
1 oz	sugar	30 g	*	lean egg wash or water	*
1 oz	shortening	30 g	*	cornmeal, for pans	*
1 oz	egg whites	30 g			

1. Dissolve yeast in 3 oz (100 mL) of the water, warmed to 90°F (32°C).
2. Using straight dough method, mix all ingredients at medium speed for *12 minutes.
3. Ferment at 80°F (27°C) until doubled (*1 hour).
4. Punch down, scale, round, and bench proof 10–20 minutes.
5. Make up as desired and pan.
6. Proof at 90°F (32°C) until doubled. Test with fingertips.
7. Slash top, brush with wash, and bake at 400°F (200°C) with steam for 10 minutes. Continue without steam until crust is firm and golden brown.

the length of the loaf pan. The made-up loaf should touch the ends of the pan.

Rolls and loaves from this dough are traditionally baked with a thin layer of cornmeal on sheet pans. This practice stems from the days when cornmeal was sprinkled on the hearth to keep the bread from sticking. The cornmeal on the pan still performs this function as well as adding texture and flavor. If you use loaf pans or molds, oil them lightly instead. Placing

15-7a CLUB ROLLS

Yield: about 4 dozen rolls

Using hard roll dough (formula 15-7):

In Step 4, scale at 1½ oz (45 g) per roll.

In Step 5, make up and pan as follows:

a. Roll each round into a rectangle twice as long as wide and the thickness of a finger.
b. Tightly roll up the strip of dough, sealing it to itself with your fingertips as you roll.
c. Stretch end of strip to width of roll and seal.
d. Sprinkle cornmeal on sheet pans. Place rolls 2″ (5 cm) apart with seam on bottom.

Total baking time: *15–20 minutes.

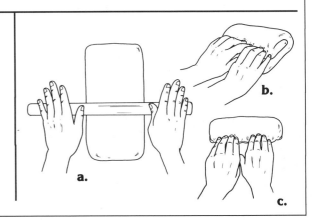

15-8 SOFT ROLL DOUGH

Yield: 4 lb 13 oz (2310 g) dough

2 lb 8 oz	bread flour	1200 g	2 oz	dry milk solids	60 g
1 oz	salt	30 g	1 lb 8 oz	water	720 g
4 oz	sugar	120 g	2 oz	compressed yeast	60 g
4 oz	shortening/butter/ margarine	120 g	*	water, milk, or lean egg wash	*

1. Dissolve yeast. Using straight dough method, mix all ingredients at medium speed for *about 12 minutes.
2. Ferment at 80°F (27°C) until doubled (*1 hour). Test with fingertips.
3. Punch down, scale, and round. Bench proof 10–20 minutes.
4. Make up as desired. Place on paper-lined sheet pans or in greased molds.
5. Proof at 90°F (32°C) until doubled. Test with fingertips.
6. Brush with wash. Bake at 400°F (200°C) until golden.

the rolls or loaves seam side down makes the dough rise evenly and keeps the crust from cracking during baking. Spacing on the pan must allow for expansion.

Now, going back again to the dough formula in 15-7, you proof the made-up dough (Step 6). If you don't have a proof box, put the pans in a warm place and cover the dough with plastic wrap or lightly dampened towels. If a crust forms before baking, the dough cannot expand properly.

In Step 7, cut a lengthwise slash on top for club rolls, or two or three diagonal parallel cuts in loaves. Without any cut, a crack appears on the side of a loaf as it rises and forms its crust. Rolls are cut mainly for appearance. Brushing with wash helps create a thin, crispy crust during baking. Use your pastry brush with a light touch to avoid collapsing the dough. Place your pans gently in the oven. If the dough is banged or knocked around, the fragile structure will collapse, ruining all your hard work.

Lean doughs are the only kind that use steam in baking. Some stack ovens have a generator that can inject steam into the oven. This helps these doughs develop a thin, crispy crust. If steam is not available you can still produce an excellent product, but it will have a slightly thicker crust. Total baking times will be *15 to 20 minutes for rolls and *40 to 75 minutes at 375°F (190°C) for loaves and pan breads, depending on size.

Soft roll dough. Soft roll dough (15-8) creates a softer, less chewy texture than hard roll doughs because of the higher sugar and fat content. The milk solids also give it a slightly different flavor and texture. Use the straight dough method, observing the same guidelines as in mixing the hard roll dough. You can either dissolve the milk powder in the water or simply add it directly to the mixing bowl.

As with other yeast doughs, you have your choice of many sizes and shapes of finished products. Among these are single-knot rolls (15-8a) and butterflake rolls (15-8b). Other possibilities are buns, figure 8s, and braided rolls. Most rolls from soft dough are spaced

15-8a SINGLE-KNOT ROLLS

Yield: about 6 dozen rolls

Using soft roll dough (15-8):

In Step 3 scale at 1 oz (30 g).

In Step 4 make up and pan as follows:

a. With your palms, roll each piece of dough into a rope 5″ (12 cm) long and ½″ (1 cm) thick.

b. Form one half into a doughnut shape.

c. Roll other half over and then under the doughnut and push end up through center to form a button.

d. Place on paper-lined sheet pans 2″ (5 cm) apart.

Baking time: *15–20 minutes.

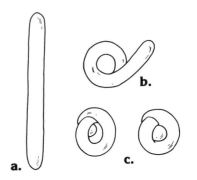

15-8b BUTTERFLAKE ROLLS

Yield: about 6 dozen rolls

Using soft roll dough (15-8):

In Step 3 scale three 24-oz (720 g) pieces of dough.

In Step 4 make up and pan as follows:

a. Roll out dough into a very thin rectangle 12 × 18″ (30 × 45 cm). Brush with melted butter and cut into lengthwise strips 1 × 18″ (2½ × 45 cm).

b. Make stacks of 6 strips each. Cut each stack into 1½″ (3½ cm) pieces.

c. Place pieces on end in greased muffin tins.

Baking time: *15–20 minutes.

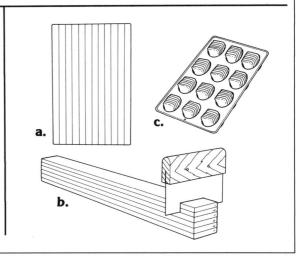

about 2¼″ (5 cm) apart. Rolls baked closer together or in molds have less crust.

Brush rolls with a wash for a shiny glazed look when baked. A lean egg wash is made with water and has more whites than yolks. Baking time for rolls is usually *15 to 20 minutes.

You can also make white pan bread—the familiar American style loaf—with this formula. Makeup and panning are the same as for hard roll dough. Baking time for loaves is *45 to 75 minutes at 375° (190°C).

You can make whole wheat bread and rolls from this formula by adding 1½ lb (720 g) whole wheat flour and reducing the bread flour to 1 lb (480 g). These items too can be made up in all these different ways.

Sweet roll dough. Doughs used for sweet rolls and coffee cakes need the modified straight dough method in order to incorporate the fat, sugar, and eggs evenly. Formula 15-9 is a typical sweet roll dough illustrating this method. You add the ingredients step by step for thorough mixing, and you mix the first three groups of ingredients with the paddle, which does a better mixing job than the dough arm.

You switch to the dough arm when you add the flour in Step 2d because the paddle would cut the gluten strands. You can see why when you compare it with the dough arm in Figure 3-19. A short mix with the dough arm develops the gluten to the proper degree for this dough.

Notice that the fermentation period is longer than that for the other two doughs. It is harder for the yeast to expand this sweet, rich dough.

Rich doughs generally use the familiar egg wash of 2 parts egg to 1 part water. For an extra-rich wash, use milk in place of water, or add extra yolks, or do both. Egg wash provides extra browning of the crust as well as a very shiny look.

For special flavors you can add spices such as nutmeg and cinnamon along with the fat and sugar in Step 2a. Or you can use special fillings such as cinnamon sugar when you make up the dough. To make cinnamon sugar, mix ½ oz (15 g) cinnamon with 1 lb (480 g) of sugar.

Formula 15-9a makes this dough into cinnamon rolls. Roll up the dough tightly and evenly, but seal only the seam. This makes an attractive swirl when the dough is cut. You can add raisins, chopped dates, or nuts with the cinnamon sugar.

You can produce a variety of pastries for breakfast and coffee break by adding fillings of caramel, nuts, cheese, dried fruit, or preserves. You can make up the dough like cinnamon rolls, or flatten 1½-oz (45 g) rounds of dough and put the filling in an indentation in the center. You can make it into a coffee cake.

Brioche. The rich, delicate roll known as brioche (bree-ohsh) is often served at breakfast in Europe, but it can be served with lunch or dinner or used as a container like popovers. As you can see by scanning the formula (15-10), it is made by the sponge dough method. This allows the best fermentation for a formula rich in eggs and butter.

Remember that in this method the sponge is fermented before all the ingredients have been added to the dough. Butter, which inhibits yeast growth, is not included in the sponge. Mixing time for the sponge is short to avoid gluten development (enough gluten will develop during fermentation). Even with all these conditions favorable to yeast growth, the fermentation time is long.

When the rest of the ingredients are added, the mixing time is short. The paddle mixes better than the dough arm, and since strong gluten development is not wanted in a tender roll, cutting the gluten strands is not a concern. Mixing ends when the butter is absorbed. The dough will be very soft and sticky.

Because of this soft, sticky consistency many bakers cover the dough at this point and put it in the refrigerator, where it will ferment very slowly. The cold dough will be easier to handle during the remaining steps. If not refrigerated, doughs made by the sponge

15-9 SWEET ROLL DOUGH

Yield: 5 lb 1½ oz (2540 g) dough

1 lb	milk	500 g	6 oz	eggs	185 g
3 oz	compressed yeast	90 g	1 lb 12 oz	bread flour	875 g
8 oz	butter/margarine/shortening	250 g	12 oz	pastry flour	375 g
8 oz	sugar	250 g	*	egg wash	*
½ oz	salt	15 g			

1. Heat milk to 100°F (38°C) and dissolve yeast in it.
2. Mix using modified straight dough method:
   a. In mixer, using paddle, combine fat, sugar, and salt at low speed.
   b. When smooth add eggs; mix thoroughly.
   c. Mix in liquid and yeast.
   d. Add flour and mix with dough arm 4–5 minutes at medium speed.
3. Ferment at 80°F (27°C) until doubled (*1½ hours). Test with fingertips.
4. Punch down, scale, and round. Bench proof 10–20 minutes.
5. Make up as desired and pan.
6. Proof at 90°F (32°C) until doubled. Test with fingertips.
7. Brush with egg wash and bake at 375°F (190°C) until golden brown.

15-9a CINNAMON ROLLS

Yield: 48–50 rolls

Using sweet roll dough (15-9):

In Step 4, scale four 1¼-lb (635 g) pieces.

In Step 5, make up as follows:

a. Roll out each round into a rectangle 12 × 8 × ½" (30 × 20 × 1 cm). Brush with melted butter and sprinkle with cinnamon sugar.
b. Roll lengthwise tightly; seal seam.
c. Slice into 1¼" (2½ cm) pieces.
d. Place in oiled muffin tins or on sheet pans 1" (2½ cm) apart.

Baking time: *20–25 minutes.

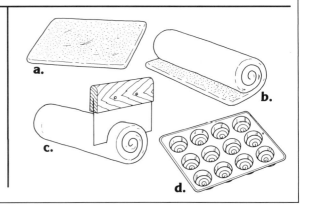

15-10 BRIOCHE

Yield: 3 lb 2½ oz to 3 lb 6½ oz (1685–1810 g) dough

Sponge:					
			10 oz	eggs	310 g
8 oz	milk	250 g	1 lb	bread flour	500 g
1 oz	compressed yeast	30 g	1 oz	sugar	30 g
8 oz	bread flour	250 g	½ oz	salt	15 g
			10–14 oz	butter, softened	300–425 g
			*	egg wash	*

1. Heat milk to 100°F (38°C). Stir in yeast and flour to form the sponge.
2. Cover and let ferment until doubled (*1½–2 hours).
3. In mixer with paddle at medium speed, gradually add eggs to sponge. Beat in dry ingredients. Add butter little by little until absorbed.
4. Ferment covered in refrigerator overnight or at 90°F (32°C) for 20 minutes.
5. Punch down, scale, and round. Bench proof 10–20 minutes.
6. Make up and pan as desired.
7. Proof at 90°F (32°C) until doubled. Test with fingertips.
8. Brush with egg wash. Bake at 400°F (200°C) until golden and firm.

15-10a TRADITIONAL BRIOCHE

Yield: 3 dozen rolls

Using brioche dough from 15-10:

In Step 5 scale at 1½ oz (50 g).

In Step 6 make up and pan as follows:

a. Using the edge of your hand, roll one-fourth of the rounded dough away from the rest without separating. Continue rolling until both pieces are smooth and round.

b. Place large-end-first into oiled fluted tin and lightly press the small ball into the larger ball.

Baking time: *20–25 minutes.

a.

b.

method will follow mixing with the usual fermentation step, but the dough will double in half the usual time.

The traditional brioche shown in 15-10a is made up in a fluted tin, with a small round piece on top of a large ball as shown in the drawing. Pressing down the small ball keeps it from separating too much during proofing and baking. Egg wash helps provide the shiny golden-brown color of the finished roll. Brioche can also be baked in loaf pans, as muffins, or in many other shapes.

Rolled-in yeast doughs. Croissants and danish pastry are made with rich yeast doughs into which butter is rolled in the makeup process. After a short mixing and chilling period the dough is rolled out, the butter is applied, and dough and butter are folded into layers and refrigerated for 3 to 4 hours. The rolling, chilling, and folding are repeated twice, trapping 300 layers of butter between thin layers of dough and creating a tender, flaky roll.

These delectable rolls are seldom made in the ordinary kitchen; they require a great deal of time and a certain amount of skill. It is more practical to buy the frozen dough or the fresh-baked product.

Problems in yeast products

By scaling accurately and following procedures carefully you can avoid most problems in your finished breads and rolls. But sometimes things don't come out well and you wonder what went wrong. Here are some common problems and their causes. You can use them to analyze your less-than-perfect products and improve them the next time around.

PROBLEM: Incorrect volume.
CAUSES: Too much or too little salt, yeast, or dough scaled. Improper mixing or fermentation. Weak flour.

PROBLEM: Poor shape, split or blistered crust.
CAUSES: Careless molding and shaping. Underproofed or overproofed. Too much liquid. Weak flour.

PROBLEM: Texture too dense.
CAUSES: Not enough yeast. Underproofed.

PROBLEM: Crumbly texture, gray color.
CAUSES: Incorrect mixing. Too much dusting flour. Overproofed. Fermentation temperature too high. Fermentation time too long. Baking temperature too low.

PROBLEM: Crust too dark.
CAUSES: Baking time too long. Baking temperature too high. Too much milk or sugar.

PROBLEM: Crust too pale.
CAUSES: Baking time too short. Baking temperature too low. Overfermented. Too little sugar or milk.

PROBLEM: Poor flavor.
CAUSES: Poor quality ingredients. Too little salt. Improper fermentation. Poor sanitation. Improper storage.

STIFF DOUGHS

Stiff doughs, when made up, have the firmest texture and the highest flour-to-liquid ratios of all the baking mixtures. The major types are pie doughs, short dough, and puff pastry. They are all composed mainly of flour, fat, and liquid. The wide variety of products you can make from them comes mainly from mixing and makeup techniques as well as final assembly with other preparations.

Pie doughs and short doughs are used mostly for desserts, and are treated in detail in the next chapter. Puff pastry dough, on the other hand, is used almost as much in the hot-food kitchen as for desserts. For **puff pastry** fat—usually butter—is rolled into the dough as for croissant and danish pastry, but puff pastry depends solely on steam from the butter for its leavening. When properly made and baked it can rise up to eight times its thickness!

The dough consists of flour, liquid, salt, and a small amount of butter, mixed until combined. After a period of relaxing, a large amount of additional butter is rolled into the dough in the manner of rolled-in yeast doughs. The amount can range from 50% to 100% of the weight of the flour. Since it is the steam from the water in the butter that provides the leavening during baking, 100% butter yields the largest increase in volume.

The dough is rolled and folded from four to six times, depending on whether it is folded in quarters (called 4-folds) or in thirds (3-folds). Since this makes 1280 layers, it is easy to see why the French give the name *mille-feuilles*—a thousand leaves—to desserts made with this pastry.

Napoleons, tart shells, cheese straws, turnovers, and cream horns are a very few of the desserts made with this amazing dough. In the hot-food kitchen you can make patty shells and *vol-au-vents* (vo-lo-von) as containers for sauced foods, or bake chicken breasts, fish fillets, or beef tenderloin wrapped in puff pastry for elegant *en croûte* (on kroot, meaning "in crust") entrées. Figure 15-7 illustrates a few of these possibilities.

Puff pastry dough demands not only time but skill. The rolling-out must be uniform and the corners must be kept square and the edges even or the layers will not build up evenly and the dough won't rise uniformly in baking. You must avoid pulling and stretching. The temperature must be just right so the butter is neither too firm nor too soft. All in all, this is a dough for the experienced pastry chef.

Most kitchens without pastry chefs take advantage of the frozen puff pastry dough products available. These include 15-lb blocks of dough that can be rolled, shaped, or cut. Even easier are prerolled 10 × 15″ (25 × 37 cm) sheets and 5″ (12½ cm) squares.

Here are some guidelines for working with puff pastry:

- Avoid pulling or stretching the dough when rolling or shaping it; it will cause shrinking and toughening.

- For proper rising during baking, keep the dough cool while you are working with it. Don't let egg wash or your fingers touch the edges, or the layers may stick together. Make straight, even cuts with a sharp knife.

- Refrigerate items before baking. Bake at 400°F (200°C) until thoroughly done. Products should be very crisp and brown or they will be too chewy.

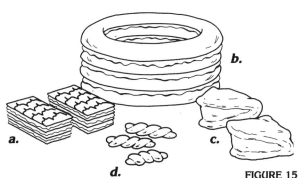

FIGURE 15-7. Puff pastry dough products. *a.* Napoleons. *b.* Patty shells (*vol-au-vents*). *c.* Turnovers, sweet and savory. *d.* Cheese straws.

SUMMING UP

Baking is very different from making a soup or a sauce or cooking a steak to doneness, even though many of the same physical and chemical reactions take place in the cooking. In baking it is essential to use exact ingredients and amounts to achieve a successful product. You can add salt to a soup at the end of cooking. But if you forget to put salt in the bread dough, the baked bread is a failure.

There is a definite pattern to the baking process. As heat is applied, the rising temperature within the dough or batter causes bubbles of gas provided by leaveners to form and expand. The elastic gluten in the flour expands to contain the bubbles and form a network of cells around them. As the internal temperature continues to rise, starches absorb moisture and gelatinize, proteins coagulate, the gluten becomes rigid, the inner structure of the finished product firms, and the outer crust browns. When all these processes are completed, the product is done.

Batters and doughs are primarily flour-liquid mixtures with one or more added ingredients—leavening, eggs, fat, sugar, salt, flavorings. Each ingredient contributes certain qualities, and in each product the proportions of ingredients are critical to the final product. If you understand your ingredients and what they are supposed to do, you will know how to use them properly and can avoid faults in the finished product.

The basic flour—liquid mixtures vary in texture from the thin pour batters that make pancakes and popovers to the stiff doughs that make pie crust, tarts, and puff pastry. Different mixing methods are called for, appropriate to the batter type. The goal is to distribute the ingredients evenly and at the same time achieve just the right gluten development—a neat trick.

When the dough or batter is properly mixed, it is prepared for baking by makeup into rolls, loaves, muffins, or whatever the product is to be. This is done by scaling the mixture into equal pieces, forming these pieces into the proper shapes, and panning them for baking. Some, especially yeast doughs and stiff doughs, can be turned into many different products simply by making them up differently.

After baking, the product must be cooled and stored properly to keep staling to a minimum. Products like waffles, pancakes, and fritters are cooked to order and served at once (have you ever tasted a cold pancake?). Products to be stored any length of time must be frozen.

Some of the products we have explored in this chapter are complete in themselves. Others, such as chou paste products and puff pastry, are only the starting point for delectable desserts and pastries. We will have more to say about these in the next chapter.

THE COOK'S VOCABULARY

the baking process: leavening, gelatinization, coagulation, browning

gluten

bread flour, cake flour, pastry flour, all-purpose flour

whole wheat flour, meal

yeast, fermentation

chemical leavener: baking soda, baking powder

mechanical leavening: creaming, foaming

regular shortening, emulsified shortening, high-ratio shortening

scaling, baker's balance beam scale

formula, baker's percentages

pour batters, drop batters, pastes, soft doughs, stiff doughs

muffin method, pastry method, creaming method

straight dough method, modified straight dough method, sponge dough method

chou paste, éclair paste

knead, cut in, pipe out, pin out, make up, pan, cut, dock

lean dough, rich dough, sweet dough, rolled-in dough, puff pastry

ferment, proof, bench proof, punch, round

staling

QUESTIONS FOR DISCUSSION

1. What do you think is the greatest difference between baking and other kinds of cooking? Explain your answer.

2. Describe the changes that heat brings about during baking, and explain why bakers call their recipes formulas.

3. Explain the role of gluten in baking. Mention several ways to develop gluten and several ways to relax it or avoid its development.

4. How do leaveners increase volume?

5. What are the biggest differences between yeast doughs and other doughs and batters? How do these differences affect the product?

FOR centuries people have been putting together delicious combinations of fruits, sugars, eggs, milk, butter, and grain products to satisfy their sweet tooth. An array of such dishes appears today on the typical menu card for a delightful finish to a dinner, lunch, or brunch. These dishes are mostly products of the bakeshop, whether they are bought from a bakery or come out of a special corner of the kitchen.

This chapter completes the story of basic bakeshop production, building on the knowledge of ingredients, mixing methods, and techniques you gained in Chapter 15. You will find it useful to dip back into that chapter now and then to reinforce your understanding of the baking process and of baking ingredients, mixing methods, and such techniques as whipping eggs, scaling, makeup, and panning.

Even though you may never become a baker, you can use your knowledge, understanding, and baking skills in the hot-food kitchen. They will enable you to make great quiche, pancakes, popovers, patty shells, biscuits, fritters, savory soufflés, en croûte entrées, and many other products featured on other parts of the menu. And when you see in this chapter how hundreds of products are made by putting together a few basic components in different ways, you can apply this idea not only to creating your own dessert specialties but also to making all kinds of menu dishes.

After completing this chapter you should be able to

- Describe three cookie mixing methods and seven cookie makeup styles and apply them in making cookies.

- Describe three mixing methods for cakes, explain when and why they are used, and apply them in making cakes.

- Explain how to make icings, fillings, toppings, and glazes and how to use them in finishing cakes and cookies.

- Explain the roles of eggs in making custards, meringues, and soufflés, and deal

16

Desserts

409

with eggs correctly in making these products.

- Describe or demonstrate how to make pie doughs, fillings, and finished pies.

COOKIES

Fresh cookies can provide a special accompaniment to ice cream or sherbet, variety on a dessert buffet, or even treats "to go." Cookies are made in more sizes, shapes, flavors, and textures than any other type of baked item. Several factors account for this great variety. One is differences in ingredients and proportions. Another is three different mixing methods. Still another is seven different makeup styles. When you add to all this the many different flavorers you can use and the many ways you can decorate cookies, you have infinite variety at your fingertips.

About cookies in general

Cookies draw on the same groups of ingredients as the baked goods in Chapter 15, but as desserts they are higher in fat and sugar, and they avoid high-gluten flours in favor of melt-in-the-mouth tenderness. They have their own special mixing methods—three of them—since certain combinations of ingredients must be put together in a certain way or they won't form a smooth, uniform dough. So we have

- **The creaming method,** used for doughs that are high in fat. In this method you cream fat, sugar, and flavorings together with the paddle, add eggs and liquid, and mix in flour and leavener last.

- **The one-stage method**—the simplest and quickest—used for doughs that are low in moisture, high in fat and sugar, and can stand some gluten development. In this method you mix everything together at once.

- **The foam method** (sometimes termed *sponge* method), used for doughs that are high in eggs and low or lacking in fat. In this method you whip the whole eggs, yolks, or whites with sugar and carefully fold in the remaining ingredients by hand.

The texture of cookie doughs varies from soft but firm to very stiff according to the proportions of flour, sugar, fat, and liquid. The creaming and one-stage methods are used for firm and stiff doughs. Doughs made by the foam method resemble the pastes in Chapter 15 and can be piped out like pâte à chou. The texture of the doughs does not necessarily correspond to the texture of the finished cookie, which may be *crisp, soft,* or *chewy* depending on such factors as the characteristics of the ingredients, the amounts of sugar, fat, and liquid, the makeup style, the size of the cookie, and the baking time.

We will examine each of the three mixing methods in detail by following a formula through all the procedures. We will also examine the seven makeup styles: drop, bar, bagged, rolled, icebox, molded, sheet. Meantime let us look at some guidelines that apply to all kinds of cookies made in all kinds of ways.

- In all three methods, ingredients must be at room temperature before mixing. Otherwise they will not mix properly, and if they are not properly mixed they will not turn into the excellent product you want to serve your guests.

- All ingredients must be scaled accurately and all instructions must be followed carefully. Cookies are no different from any other baked product: they are chemical formulas and must be followed exactly.

- Scale all cookies in a batch to a uniform size. This makes an attractive appearance and ensures even baking.

- Before baking you may decorate cookies with nuts, candied fruit, sugar, coconut, or chocolate sprinkles. After baking you can ice them with frosting or melted chocolate or dust them with powdered sugar.

- Many cookie doughs made by the one-stage or creaming method can be refrigerated or frozen before baking. This allows you to bake them as needed. Foam-method cookies must be baked immediately.
- Choose clean pans that are not warped. Line them with parchment paper (for most cookies). It eliminates the need to grease or flour and saves time, money, and labor.
- Doughs that are very rich in fat may burn on the bottom. To prevent this, **double-pan** them: place a second pan of the same size under the pan with the cookies.
- Baking times are short with relatively high temperatures. Most cookies have reached doneness when the edges and bottoms take on a light golden color. Watch them very carefully because they can overbake in as little as one minute.
- Cookies continue to bake after you take them out of the oven because of heat stored in the pan. Allow for this in judging doneness.
- Cool cookies slowly away from drafts or they may crack. Soft cookies should cool and firm up before you remove them from the pan. Others can be removed while still warm. Like bread, cookies should be completely cool before being stored so that moisture won't accumulate and make them soggy.
- All cookies should be wrapped with plastic film when cool. Exposure to air increases staling.
- When carefully wrapped, cookies can be held or stored at room temperature for two days to a week, depending on the type of cookie. All cookies can be frozen after baking to maintain freshness. Simply let them thaw, or reheat them very briefly at a low temperature.

The creaming method

Now let's take a step-by-step look at cookies mixed by the creaming method. Formula 16-1 gives us the ever-popular chocolate chip cookie as an example. You start with all ingredients at room temperature and you scale them accurately, of course.

In Step 1a the fat and sugar are beaten with the paddle at medium speed to form an emulsion that will hold the liquids when they are added. At the same time the paddle beats in bubbles of air, which are held in the emulsion and will provide leavening during baking to lighten texture. You use the paddle rather than the whip because this mixture is too stiff for the whip and may break it. Do not use high speed for creaming, thinking you will save time. Not as many air cells will form.

Notice the instruction to **scrape down** at the end of Step 1a. For this you stop the motor, and you use a plastic dough scraper (Figure 16-1a) or rubber spatula to scrape the bottom and sides of the bowl and the paddle completely. If you skip this step, some ingredients will cling to the bowl and paddle and will not be incorporated completely into the dough. You will use this important technique in many kinds of dessert formulas. *Always turn the motor off before scraping down* to avoid accidents.

In most cookies made by the creaming method, the butter and sugar are mixed until the volume has increased considerably and the texture is light and fluffy. The exceptions are dense, chewy cookies, such as oatmeal cookies, that need to keep their shape during baking; they are mixed only until a paste is formed. The paste will not spread as much

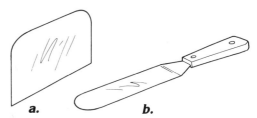

FIGURE 16-1. Dessert equipment. **a.** Dough scraper, a flexible piece of plastic 4 × 6″ (8 × 12 cm) used for scrape-down and folding. **b.** A cake spatula, used to smooth cake batters and to apply icings and fillings.

16-1 CHOCOLATE CHIP COOKIES

Yield: 6 lb 13 oz (3.4 kg) batter = 9 dozen 1-oz (30 g) cookies

1 lb	butter, margarine, or regular shortening	500 g	8 oz	eggs	250 g
			4 oz	water	125 g
12 oz	brown sugar	375 g	2 tsp	vanilla	10 mL
12 oz	granulated sugar	375 g	1 lb 8 oz	pastry flour	750 g
½ oz	salt	15 g	2 tsp	baking soda	10 mL
			1 lb 8 oz	chocolate chips	750 g
			8 oz	nuts, chopped	250 g

1. *Creaming method:*
   a. Place fat, sugars, and salt in mixer bowl and blend with paddle on medium speed until light and fluffy (*8–10 minutes). Scrape down bowl.
   b. On medium speed, blend in eggs, water, and vanilla little by little. Scrape down bowl.
   c. Sift together pastry flour and soda. Add to bowl and blend on low speed just until combined.
   d. On low speed, stir in chocolate chips and nuts.
2. *Drop makeup method:*
   Portion with a No. 30 scoop onto paper-lined pans, spacing evenly.
3. Bake at 375°F (190°C) until edges are lightly colored (*8–12 minutes).

during baking. Salt, flavoring, and spices are often added at this stage to distribute them evenly.

In Step 1b, you add the eggs and other liquids little by little to give them time to be absorbed completely. Continue mixing until light and fluffy—as much as 5 minutes—to increase the eggs' ability to emulsify and hold the other ingredients without curdling. Don't forget to scrape down.

Sifting the flour and soda in Step 1c distributes the soda evenly. Add the sifted mixture all at once, mixing on low speed to avoid flour dust flying everywhere! To avoid toughness in the finished cookies, mix only until combined so that gluten will not build up. Add the choco-

late chips and nuts last, and again mix only until they are distributed evenly.

The **drop method** of makeup (Step 2) is one of the fastest and easiest. Use a portion scoop for uniformity. A No. 30 scoop makes 1 oz (30 g) of dough that will spread into a fairly large chocolate chip cookie. Space evenly about 2″ (5 cm) apart for a cookie this size. For smaller cookies use a higher-numbered scoop.

The drop method can be used for almost every kind of cookie. Likewise cookies made by the creaming method can be made up by any other method.

Bake these chocolate chip cookies only until the edges have colored and firmed slightly (Step 3). Remember that they will continue to bake somewhat after you take them out of the oven. Cool them on the pan.

The one-stage method

The next formula (16-2) illustrates the one-stage mixing method. You may recognize this method as a counterpart of the straight-dough yeast method (Chapter 15). Before you begin the mixing there are two preliminary steps: preparing the raisins and sifting the dry ingredients. Then you just mix everything together thoroughly on low speed (Step 3), scraping down midway in the process. Fin-ished dough will be blended but not ultra-smooth. Don't overmix or the gluten will develop too much.

You may notice that there is no milk or water in this formula. Liquid is provided by the eggs and butter. This is a very stiff dough.

The **bar method** of makeup is used in Step 4. You could also make up these cookies with the drop, sheet, icebox, rolled, or molded method, but this dough is too stiff to bag.

The bar method requires chilled dough for easy handling. Form it into rolls on a dusted bench. Space the rolls across the sheet pan, and flatten them with your fingers or a pin.

16-2 RAISIN SPICE BARS

Yield: 5 lb 8¾ oz (2770 g) batter = 6 dozen bars 1 × 3" (2.5 × 8 cm)

8 oz	butter, margarine, or regular shortening	250 g	1 lb 8 oz	pastry flour	750 g	⎤
1 lb	granulated sugar	500 g	¼ oz	baking soda	7 g	
8 oz	brown sugar	250 g	¼ oz	salt	7 g	
8 oz	eggs	250 g	¼ oz	cinnamon	7 g	⎦
1 lb 8 oz	raisins	750 g	*	egg wash	*	
			*	confectioners' sugar	*	

1. If raisins are hard, soak in hot water until soft. Drain and dry thoroughly.
2. Sift together flour, soda, salt, and cinnamon.
3. *One-stage mixing method:*
   a. Place all ingredients in mixer bowl and mix with paddle on low speed.
   b. When partially combined, scrape down bowl.
   c. Continue mixing until blended.
4. *Bar makeup method:*
   a. Scale dough into four equal units. Chill thoroughly.
   b. Form chilled dough into rolls as long as the width of a sheet pan. Space rolls evenly on paper-lined pan.
   c. Flatten each roll until about 3" (8 cm) wide.
5. Brush tops with egg wash.
6. Bake at 360°F (180°C) until firm and lightly golden (*12–15 minutes).
7. When cool, cut into 1" (2.5 cm) bars. Ice or dust with confectioners' sugar.

16-3 LADYFINGERS

Yield: 2 lb 4 oz (1080 g) batter = 8 dozen ladyfingers

8 oz	egg yolks	240 g	10 oz	egg whites	300 g
8 oz	granulated sugar	240 g	2 oz	granulated sugar	60 g
8 oz	pastry flour, sifted	240 g	*	powdered sugar	*

1. *Foam mixing method:*
   a. In mixer bowl, using whip, whip egg yolks with 8 oz (240 g) sugar on high speed until very thick and light (*10–12 minutes).
   b. Remove bowl from machine. With scraper or spatula, fold in sifted flour.
   c. In another mixer bowl whip egg whites on high speed to a soft peak. Add 2 oz (60 g) sugar and whip to stiff peak.
   d. By hand, carefully fold whites into yolk mixture.
2. *Bagged makeup method:*
   a. Place mixture in pastry bag fitted with a large plain tube.
   b. Pipe out 3 × ¾″ (8 × 2 cm) strips onto parchment-lined sheet pans.
   c. Dust lightly with powdered sugar.
3. Bake at 375°F (190°C) until edges are very light brown (*10 minutes).

Brush the tops with egg wash for a shiny look, but don't let the wash drip down the sides or the bars will stick to the paper. Bake these strips until firm but still springy and lightly colored on the edges. Let them cool completely in the pan, then cut crosswise into uniform bars, using a sharp or serrated knife. Dust with powdered sugar or use an icing to frost them.

The foam (sponge) method

Formula 16-3, ladyfingers, demonstrates the foam, or sponge, method. Notice that the formula contains no butter, no milk or water, and no leavening other than the air you will beat into the batter. It is all eggs, sugar, and flour. The foam method whips and folds them step by step into a soft, delicate batter. The method is not limited to fat-free batters, however; brownies, which are heavy in butter and chocolate, are often made by the foam method. The key to foams is the role of the eggs, which emulsify the other ingredients and add leavening at the same time.

You begin by whipping yolks and sugar at high speed, maximizing the emulsifying power of the yolks and incorporating the most air possible. The mixture will be very thick and pale yellow and should double or triple its original volume.

Before adding the flour in Step 1b, you sift it to eliminate lumps and to lighten it. Carefully fold it in by hand (Figure 16-2), maintaining as much volume as possible. This is the folding technique described in Chapter 3.

To fold in flour use a plastic scraper or rubber spatula. Sift the flour onto the top of the batter. Start folding by moving the scraper down the side and across the bottom of the bowl. Then bring it up the opposite side, bringing batter with it, and turn it to spread the batter over the flour on top. Continue this motion, moving around the bowl, until the flour is blended with the foam. Avoid cutting through the batter. The goal is to avoid deflating it as much as possible.

Whipping the egg whites (Step 1c) also deserves special attention. Soft peak and stiff peak can be considered "degrees of doneness" for egg whites. You will remember from making waffles in Chapter 15 that egg whites beaten to a soft peak will stand up but the top will curl over. In many formulas for cakes and cookies, after the soft peak stage is reached, part or all of the sugar from the formula is added and the mixture is then whipped to a stiff peak, meaning that the top or peak will stand up without curling over. It is very important to stop beating as soon as a stiff peak will form. If you are not careful you can very quickly overbeat the whites. They should look moist and shiny. If they look dry and form large lumps or curds, they are overbeaten and much of their leavening ability is lost.

After you have whipped the egg whites with the sugar to a stiff but moist peak, fold them in until no streaks remain. Use the same folding technique, and once again keep as much volume as possible.

In Step 2 you make up the ladyfingers using the **bagged method.** This method can be used for almost any kind of dough that is soft enough to bag out, but it is used most often for doughs made by the foam method.

Follow the steps in the formula. You may want to glue the corners of the parchment to the pan with a dab of the mixture. This keeps the paper from pulling up when you pull up with the bag at the end of each strip of dough. Dust lightly with confectioners' sugar, and bake at once.

Foam cookies must be baked immediately because the air incorporated in beating, which will turn to steam in the oven, is often the only leavening agent. A high temperature is needed to create the steam. Cooking time is

FIGURE 16-2. Folding. To fold ingredients into a mixture, use a spatula to go down the side, across the bottom, and up the opposite side as you rotate the bowl.

short: these cookies will be done when they are a very pale golden brown. Cool completely before removing them from pans for storing.

Makeup methods

The mixing method for any given formula depends on ingredients and ratios. The makeup method, on the other hand, usually depends on how the cookie should look. Most cookie doughs can be made up by nearly all the seven methods, with a different look for each. The method chosen will often depend on what the cookies will be used for and the demands of production as much as on the traditional look of the particular cookie.

Here is a quick summary of the seven makeup styles, including those you have already examined closely.

- **Drop.** Use a portion scoop to place uniform amounts of dough onto sheet pans.

- **Bar.** Form equal pieces of chilled dough into cylinders. Space three or four logs crosswise on a sheet pan. Flatten with fingers or roll to make strips. Cut strips into 1" (2.5 cm) pieces after baking.

- **Bagged** (sometimes called *spritz* or *pressed*). Use a pastry bag to press out onto sheet pans uniform amounts of dough in the size and shape desired. To use this method, the dough must be soft enough to pipe. Foam cookies are most often bagged.

- **Rolled.** Chill a stiff dough. On a lightly dusted bench with a lightly dusted pin, roll dough to a uniform thickness of ⅛ to ¼" (3–6 mm). Press cookie cutters dipped in flour into the dough as close together as you can. Slide a straight cake spatula (Figure 16-1*b*) under the cutout cookies to lift them and place on paper-lined pans.

    Rolled cookies are often decorated before baking with nuts, sugar, and so on. After baking they can be iced and decorated, or you can put two together with frosting or melted chocolate for a delicious sweet sandwich.

- **Icebox** or **refrigerator.** Scale a stiff dough into equal units and form them into cylinders of uniform dimensions—usually 1 to 2" (2–5 cm). Wrap in parchment or waxed paper and chill at least 4 to 6 hours. Slice into uniform slices and place on paper-lined sheet pans.

    These cookies can also be decorated. Or you can color part of a batch and form it into logs. Pin out remaining dough ¼" (5 mm) thick and the same length as the logs. Brush lightly with egg wash to act as glue, and wrap around the logs (Figure 16-3*a*). Wrap, chill, slice, and bake.

    To make pinwheels, pin out equal-size sheets of colored and white dough. Egg-wash the colored sheet, place the white sheet on top, and roll up to form a log (Figure 16-3*b*). Wrap, chill, slice, and bake.

- **Molded.** Shape uniform portions of dough by hand or place in special molds to bake.

    Madeleines, for example, which are made from a sponge dough, are baked in special molds. The familiar peanut butter cookie, made from a stiff dough, is also molded. To mold it, place balls of ½ to 1 oz (15–30 g) on paper-lined pans 1 to 2" (2–5 cm) apart. Dip a fork in sugar to prevent sticking and press down on each ball to flatten and make the traditional criss-cross marks. Other molded cookies may use a weight or the bottom of a glass to flatten.

- **Sheet.** Spread or roll dough evenly into sheet pans lined with parchment or greased and floured, making sure the dough fills the corners completely. After baking, cool and cut into squares or rectangles.

The word cookie means "little cake." We will see in the next section that the two have more similarities than differences.

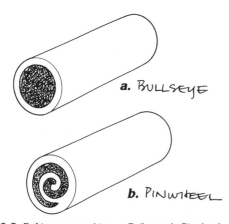

FIGURE 16-3. Refrigerator cookies. *a.* Bullseye. *b.* Pinwheel.

CAKES

Cakes are another baked product made in incredible variety using a few basic methods and the same kinds of ingredients used for all baked goods.

About cakes in general

Cakes, like cookies, are high in sugar and usually in fat and low in gluten, since tenderness is the goal. Most are made with cake flour, which has the least gluten of the white flours.

The biggest difference between cake and cookie batters is in the amount of liquid used. Most cake batters are thin and pour readily. They typically have high ratios of liquid to flour, sugar, and fat. Incorporating all this liquid without making the mixture curdle requires special care in mixing.

Like cookies, cakes are mixed by three basic methods. They correspond fairly closely to the three cookie-mixing methods, but you will see some definite differences. The **creaming method** is essentially the same as the creaming method for cookies. The **two-stage method** is similar to the one-stage cookie method, but it incorporates the liquid in two distinct stages—hence its name. The **foam method** corresponds to the foam method for cookies.

We will look at the three methods in detail, using a formula as an example for each. But first, here are some guidelines for making cakes by any method.

- Have all ingredients at room temperature and scale them accurately.
- Follow instructions carefully. Do not try to take shortcuts or combine steps. Cake emulsions must be built little by little.
- Scale batter uniformly into pans lined with parchment or greased and floured (except for foam cakes, which require ungreased pans). Smooth batter in pan.
- Rap pans sharply on the bench (again, except for foam cakes) to release large air bubbles that may be trapped in the batter. They will make tunnels in the finished cake.

- Bake *promptly*.
- Don't let pans touch each other in the oven; the heat cannot circulate and the cakes will not bake evenly.
- The correct temperature is very important: too high and the crust will form too early, too low and the dough will not expand properly.
- There are three tests of doneness. The sides begin to pull away from the edges of the pan. The center is firm and springy. A wooden toothpick inserted in the center comes out clean.
- When the cake is done, remove it from the oven and let it cool in the pan away from drafts. Cakes are tender and fragile and will break or crack if removed from the pan when more than barely warm. After the initial cooling, turn cakes out of pans bottoms up onto racks or cardboard cake circles to cool completely. This allows air to circulate around them, preventing a soggy bottom.
- When completely cool, wrap cakes in plastic wrap and hold in a cool place or in the freezer.

The creaming method

Pound cake (formula 16-4) is an example of the many butter cakes made by the creaming method. It is one of the oldest and simplest cakes. This method of mixing was the only one available for high-fat cakes until the development of emulsified shortening. It produces a coarser, slightly less tender cake than the other two methods.

Compare the instructions for pound cake with those for chocolate chip cookies. You will find them similar except for Step 3, where you add just a little of the flour. This prevents the mixture from curdling when the rest of the eggs are added.

To scale the cakes, set the scale for 1 lb (500 g) and place a prepared pan on the left platform and a pan on the right to act as a counterbalance. Pour batter into the left-hand

16-4 POUND CAKE

Yield: 9 lb 5¾ oz (4675 g) batter = 12 8" (20 cm) round layers

1 lb	butter or butter/shortening	500 g	1 lb	eggs	500 g
1 lb	sugar	500 g	1 lb	cake flour	500 g
2 tsp	vanilla	10 mL			

1. In mixer bowl cream fat, sugar, and vanilla with paddle on medium speed until light and fluffy (*8–10 minutes). Scrape down.
2. Add one-fourth of the eggs and blend until incorporated.
3. Blend in a little (2 oz/60 g) of the flour.
4. Continue adding eggs a little at a time, blending each addition until incorporated. Scrape down.
5. Beat until light and fluffy (*5 minutes).
6. Mix in remaining flour on low speed until barely blended.
7. Scale cakes at 16 oz (500 g) of batter for pans 2¼ × 3½ × 8" (6 × 9 × 20 cm).
8. Bake at 350°F (180°C) until done (*1 hour).

pan until the scale balances. Then place the filled pan on the right side, return the scale to zero, and balance the remaining pans against the first one. Smooth the batter, rap the pans sharply against the bench, and bake.

This cake can be flavored with nutmeg or finely grated orange or lemon zest. Raisins, nuts, and candied fruit are other possibilities. To make into a chocolate cake, replace 4 oz (125 g) of the flour with the same amount of cocoa.

You can also make a marble cake from this formula. Add 2 oz (60 g) cocoa to half the batter and mix until smooth. Scale the white batter into pans at half weight. Pour chocolate batter in puddles into white batter. Swirl a cake spatula through the batters to distribute chocolate through white for a marbling effect.

The two-stage method

The two-stage method of mixing cakes was developed when emulsified shortenings became available. You will remember from

Chapter 15 that this type of fat can carry a higher percentage of sugar to flour and larger amounts of liquid without curdling. This mixing method corresponds to the one-stage cookie method, except that the liquids are added in two stages. The method and the shortening type produce a smooth, liquid batter that bakes into a moist and tender cake with a texture like velvet.

The general pattern of the two-stage method is to mix the dry ingredients, the fat, and part of the liquid for 7 to 8 minutes with several scrape-downs. This is Stage 1. Sometimes the mixing is broken into several steps, with the liquid added as a separate step. In Stage 2 additional liquid is mixed with the eggs and added in three parts.

Everybody's favorite, chocolate cake (16-5), is an example of the two-stage method. It breaks Stage 1 into three steps, with the chocolate added as a separate step to incorporate it thoroughly before the liquid is added. Low speed is used throughout the mixing.

A series of thorough scrape-downs is one

of the most important features of this method, to keep the ingredients within reach of the paddle. They are especially important in Stage 2 when the batter becomes more liquid with each egg–milk addition. Ingredients left on the sides of the bowl do not emulsify properly and may form lumps that will cause faults in the cake. Continue mixing after the last addition *until a smooth liquid batter forms.

Two-stage cakes are usually scaled with a volume measure because the batter is so thin. You balance the scale with an empty volume measure on the left. Place the desired weight on the scale and pour batter into the measure until it balances. Note the volume level that equals the weight desired, then pour the batter into a pan, using a rubber spatula to empty the measure completely. Scale the rest of the batter by using the volume measure at the level noted. For this very liquid batter this method is much quicker and easier than weighing out.

Both creamed and two-stage batters can easily be turned into cupcakes and sheet cakes. Scale cupcakes at 1½ oz (45 g) into paper-lined or greased and floured pans. Bake them at 385°F (195°C) until done (*15–20 minutes). Scale sheet cakes at 6 to 8 lb (3–3.6 kg) into paper-lined sheet pans. Bake at 360°F (180°C) until springy in the center (*35 minutes).

16-5 CHOCOLATE CAKE

Yield: 9 lb 5¾ oz (4675 g) batter = 12 8" (20 cm) round layers

2 lb	cake flour	1000 g	1 lb 4 oz	eggs, lightly beaten	625 g
¾ oz	salt	20 g	12 oz	skim milk	375 g
¾ oz	baking powder	25 g			
¼ oz	baking soda	7 g			
2 lb 8 oz	sugar	1250 g			
1 lb	emulsified shortening	500 g			
8 oz	bitter chocolate, melted	250 g			
1 lb 4 oz	skim milk	625 g			

1. *Stage 1*
   a. Sift flour with salt, baking powder, and soda. Place with sugar and fat in mixer bowl and mix with paddle on low speed for 2 minutes. Scrape down.
   b. Add melted chocolate and blend on low speed for 2 minutes. Scrape down.
   c. Add the first amount of skim milk and blend on low speed for *3–5 minutes, stopping mixer to scrape down several times during this mixing period.
2. *Stage 2*
   a. Combine eggs with remaining skim milk. Add this mixture in three parts with machine running on low. Scrape down after each addition is blended in. Total mixing time for this step should be *5 minutes.
3. Scale at 12 oz (375 g) into 8" (20 cm) round pans.
4. Bake immediately at 375°F (190°C) until done (*25 minutes).

The foam method

Cakes made by the foam method are leavened primarily by air whipped into an egg foam. They contain little or no fat compared to other types of cakes. *Sponge, angel food,* and *chiffon cakes* are the kinds made by this method. Formula 16-6 shows the techniques this method requires.

Butter sponge cake, called *genoise* (zhun-wahz) by the French, uses whole eggs for the foam. The eggs must be at room temperature or warmed slightly to aid in increasing the volume. To warm them (Step 1) place the mixer bowl in water just below a simmer either in a pan on the stove or in a bain-marie. Keep stirring and do not overheat or you will make sweetened scrambled eggs. The egg mixture should reach 110°F (43°C)—slightly warmer than body temperature. You can sense a change when it is ready: it will feel looser and less viscous.

This step can be omitted, but mixing times will be longer and volume and texture will suffer. With warmed eggs, an increase in volume of three times or more is possible in Step 2. (You can also use this technique in making ladyfingers.)

Steps 3 and 4 use the folding technique described for mixing ladyfingers. In formulas having other dry ingredients, such as cocoa, cornstarch, or chemical leaveners, these would be sifted with the flour in Step 3.

In order to handle the batter as little as possible during scaling (Step 5), use a volume measure as in the two-stage scaling method. Weights for round layers are 10 to 16 oz (280–450 g), sheet cakes scale at 2½ lb (1.2 kg), and cupcakes at 10 oz (280 g) per dozen. Only the bottoms of the pans are greased or lined with paper because this batter needs to cling to the sides slightly during baking in order to rise properly.

Bake immediately. Foam batters require a higher temperature than most cakes to create the steam needed for leavening and setting. Cakes are done when the center is springy and

---

16-6 BUTTER SPONGE CAKE (GENOISE)
Yield: 5 lb 8½ oz (2765 g) batter

2 lb	eggs	1000 g	1 lb 8 oz	cake flour	750 g
1 lb 8 oz	sugar	750 g	8 oz	butter, melted	250 g
½ oz	vanilla or other flavoring	15 g			

1. Place eggs, sugar, and flavoring in mixer bowl. Place bowl in bain-marie. Heat to 110°F (43°C), stirring constantly.
2. Using whip attachment, whip on highest speed of mixer until increased in volume, thick, and light in color (*15–30 minutes).
3. Sift flour onto top of foam and carefully fold in with rubber spatula until no streaks remain.
4. By hand fold in melted butter just until combined.
5. Scale batter into pans prepared on the bottom only. Spread smooth.
6. Bake at 375°F (190°C) until done (*20–25 minutes).

a toothpick in the center comes out clean. This type of cake does not pull away from the sides as much as the other two types. Run a cake spatula around the sides to loosen if necessary. Cool slightly, then turn out onto racks to complete cooling.

You can make a chocolate sponge cake from formula 16-6 by substituting 4 oz (125 g) of cocoa for 4 oz of the flour. Sift the cocoa together with the remaining flour in Step 3.

You can also make a rolled cake from a sponge cake—a product of great versatility. In order to roll it you must omit the butter from the formula to keep the cake from cracking. You scale 2½ to 3 lb (1–1½ kg) of dough into a paper-lined sheet pan and bake as usual. Immediately after baking follow the steps in Figure 16-4.

Angel food cakes are made from egg white foams that require some variations in technique. You whip warmed egg whites on high speed, adding salt, cream of tartar, and flavoring when they are foamy. Continuing to whip, you add half the sugar gradually, and whip until a stiff peak is reached. Mix the remaining sugar with the flour for even distribution, and fold in, using the same technique as for a sponge cake. Bake in ungreased tube pans, scaling 1½ to 2 lb (700–900 g) for a 10″ (24 cm) tube pan. Bake at a lower temperature, 350°F (180°C), to avoid early crust formation. Cool cakes completely upside down on racks to maintain their volume. Loosen with spatula to remove from the pan.

For chiffon cakes, sweetened whipped egg whites are folded into a batter of flour, liquid, eggs, and oil. They are baked and cooled the same way as angel food cakes.

Convenience mixes

Many convenience mixes are available for all types of cakes. They save a great deal of time and labor. Follow their instructions carefully and apply your knowledge of mixing methods, baking, and cooling to produce a consistently reliable result.

The cake is baked. Now let's look at some icings and see how to assemble everything for a popular finishing touch to any meal.

ICINGS AND TOPPINGS

Icings, also called **frostings,** are used to top or coat a cake and are sometimes spread between layers as a **filling.** They are made primarily of sugar, with fat, eggs, and flavorings often added. Icings serve three functions:

- They make cakes more attractive and decorative.
- They add flavor and richness.
- They improve keeping qualities by forming a protective coating around the cake.

The six basic types are fondant, flat, buttercream, royal or decorator's, boiled or foam, and fudge.

Fondant is a smooth, shiny white icing made of very fine crystallized sugar. It is difficult to make, and most bakeshops buy it as a moist paste or a dry powder to which water is added. Store both types covered at room temperature.

Fondant is sometimes thinned with **simple syrup.** This syrup is made with equal parts sugar and water heated and stirred until the sugar has dissolved and combined with the water. It is a basic preparation of many uses that should be a part of every baker's mise en place. Cover and store it at room temperature.

Here are the procedures for using fondant.

- Heat and stir the desired amount over hot water. Do not heat over 100°F (38°C) or fondant will lose its shine.
- If necessary, thin with water or simple syrup until icing is easily pourable.
- Stir in flavoring and coloring as desired.
- Pour fondant over a cake set on a rack over a sheet pan. Smooth with a cake spatula dipped in hot water (Figure 16-6). You can scrape up the excess and strain for another use.

FIGURE 16-4. A rolled cake.

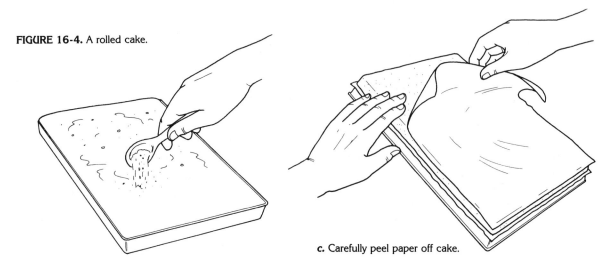

a. Sprinkle top lightly with granulated sugar.

c. Carefully peel paper off cake.

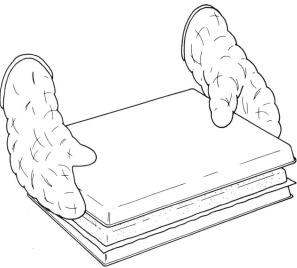

b. Place clean parchment paper on top of cake and place an inverted sheet pan over it. Turn cake out of pan onto inverted sheet pan.

d. Roll up cake in the clean parchment paper and cool.

e. To assemble, unroll and spread an even layer of jelly, preserves, buttercream, or ice cream.

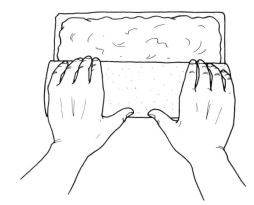

f. Reroll. Ice and decorate as desired.

To make chocolate fondant, stir in 3 oz of melted bitter chocolate per pound of fondant (90 g per 500 g) and thin to the right consistency. Many other colors and flavors can be used. For all icings, use a light hand with color and the best-quality flavors possible. Pastel colors and delicate flavors are preferred.

Flat icing (formula 16-7) is almost a simple fondant and can be substituted for it in an emergency. Simply combine all ingredients until smooth, juggling the amounts of sugar and water to achieve a fairly stiff consistency. It will become more liquid when it is warmed for use. Stir in egg whites for a lighter, more stable icing. You can replace part of the water with milk, cream, or fruit juice, and color or flavor it as desired.

This icing is often used on coffee cakes and sweet rolls. It can also provide a simple coating for pound cakes, angel food cakes, cupcakes, and cookies.

Buttercreams are the most familiar frostings. Formula 16-8 gives a basic recipe. Butter provides the most desirable flavor, but you can mix it with margarine for economy or with emulsified shortening for a more stable emulsion, especially in hot weather. Salt and lemon juice function as they do in other kitchen areas—as seasonings. Egg whites help lighten the mixture. French buttercreams use whole eggs for an extra-rich flavor and texture.

If you have fondant on hand, use formula 16-8a for the easiest basic buttercream. Formula 16-8b calls for cream cheese for a specialty flavor popular on carrot cakes and others.

Buttercream is made in many flavors: in place of vanilla use lemon, orange, almond, peppermint, and so on. For chocolate buttercream add sweet chocolate (16-8c). For coffee, make with instant coffee as in 16-8d. Combine the two and you have mocha!

Any basic buttercream can be made up in quantity and used to make many different flavors, as you would make a large supply of a basic sauce for many small sauces. Cover and store in the refrigerator, where it will keep several days. Bring to room temperature, add the desired flavor, and apply to the waiting cake.

16-7 FLAT ICING

Yield: 5 to 6 lb 4 oz (2640–3140 g) icing

4–5 lb*	confectioners' sugar	*2–2.5 kg	1 Tb	vanilla or other flavoring	15 mL
12 oz*	hot water	*375 g	(4 oz	egg whites	125 g)
4 oz	corn syrup	125 g			

1. With paddle, on low speed, mix all ingredients until smooth. (Include egg whites if used.)
2. To use, heat over low heat or in bain-marie and apply as for fondant.

16-8 BUTTERCREAM I

Yield: 8 lb (4050 g) icing

5 lb	confectioners' sugar	2.5 kg	8 oz	egg whites	250 g
2½ lb	butter/margarine/ emulsified shortening	1.25 kg	½ oz	lemon juice	15 mL
¼ oz	salt	7 g	2 Tb*	vanilla or other flavoring *to taste	*30 mL

1. In mixer, using paddle, cream fat, sugar, and salt on medium speed until combined thoroughly, texture is light, and volume is increased.
2. Stir in remaining ingredients on medium speed.
3. Beat on high speed until very fluffy.

16-8a BUTTERCREAM II

equal parts	fat
	fondant

1. Cream fat until light and fluffy.
2. Add fondant by handfuls and beat until fluffy.

16-8c CHOCOLATE BUTTERCREAM

1 lb	buttercream icing	500 g
4 oz	sweet chocolate	125 g

Melt chocolate and cool. Blend into buttercream.

16-8b CREAM CHEESE ICING

In 16-8 make these changes:

Replace fat with cream cheese.

Omit egg whites.

Proceed as in 16-8.

16-8d COFFEE BUTTERCREAM

1 lb	buttercream icing	500 g
1½ Tb	instant coffee	25 mL
2 tsp	hot water	10 mL

Mix instant coffee into hot water. Blend into buttercream.

Royal icing is made by beating together confectioners' sugar, egg whites, and cream of tartar until stiff. It becomes hard and brittle when dry and is used only on cakes that will be served immediately. It is also called **decorator's icing** and is often used for flowers and other decorative work.

Boiled icing is a foamy, airy icing used on angel food and chiffon cakes. To make it you mix hot simple syrup into whipped egg whites, then flavor and color as desired. It must be used the day it is made because it breaks down overnight.

Fudge icing also uses a hot simple syrup. It is mixed slowly into fat, sugar, and cocoa. A dense, rich, candylike icing results, which must be warmed slightly to spread. Store it in the refrigerator, covering it to prevent a crust from forming.

Some other coatings and toppings are often used to enrich and enhance cakes and other pastries. Among these are **glazes**—transparent coatings that take the place of icings and display the product instead of covering it up. They are brushed on rich cakes and fruit tarts for a simple yet elegant topping and a dazzling shine.

Apricot glaze is among the most popular. It is usually bought ready-made, and you simply melt it over low heat or in a water bath, thin with water or simple syrup, and apply with a pastry brush. You can make this glaze by melting and thinning apricot preserves and straining or puréeing them. Red currant jelly and some other jellies are also used in this manner.

Sweet sauces made with butterscotch, fruit, chocolate, caramelized sugar, and custards are another category of coatings and toppings. They can be napped across or pooled under slices of pound cake and cheesecake, for example. They are often purchased ready-to-use, but you will have a chance to make at least one kind of sweet sauce later in this chapter.

Simple syrup also has its own roles in finishing desserts for service. European style cakes often use simple syrup flavored with liqueur or wine to saturate cake layers before assembling. This has the added advantage of maintaining a moist, fresh taste and appearance longer on the pastry cart or display case. Flavored simple syrups are also used to poach fruits. These may be served as simple fruit compôtes or combined with cake or a frozen product for a more elaborate dessert.

ASSEMBLING AND DECORATING CAKES

Putting cake and icing together to make a handsome product has secrets of its own. Here are the major procedures and techniques for combining icings with sheet, layer, or cupcakes.

Choose icings and fillings that complement the cake in color, flavor, and texture. Sponge cakes are iced and filled with fruit, buttercream, fondant, pastry cream, or whipped cream. Angel food and chiffon cakes need only flat, fondant, or fluffy boiled icings. Heavier cakes made by the creaming or two-stage methods can carry a denser buttercream or fudge icing or any of the other icing types.

Cool cakes completely before finishing. Icings will not maintain their texture if applied when the cake is even slightly warm. Cakes can be wrapped when completely cool, frozen for a short time, and assembled and finished as needed with good results.

Remove crumbs from cakes by brushing or tapping gently. Loose crumbs give a messy look when they become mixed with the icing.

Trim ragged or crusty edges evenly from layer and sheet cakes, if necessary. This helps make a uniform, attractive appearance in the finished cake.

Split round cakes into layers if you are going to use a filling. Figure 16-5 shows you how to do this.

Place the bottom layer cut side down on a cardboard cake circle on a turntable or serving plate. Spread a thin, even layer of filling to within ⅛ to ¼" (¼–½ cm) of the edge. Place the top layer cut side down on the filling.

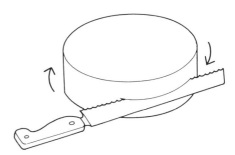

FIGURE 16-5. Splitting a cake into layers. Rotating the cake, use a serrated blade to cut in 1 inch (2 cm) all around edge. Without removing the knife, continue to rotate and cut until cake is cut through in even layers.

To apply fondants and flat icings, pour onto the center of the cake. Use a cake spatula dipped in hot water to spread to the edges and down and around the sides (Figure 16-6a). For the other icing types, place some of the icing in the center and spread to the edges. Dip out more with the spatula as needed to cover the entire cake with an even coat.

To avoid getting crumbs mixed with the icing, always push it ahead of the spatula (Figure 16-6b). Do not let the spatula touch the surface of the cake.

Cupcakes can be iced by either of the methods described, or you can use the faster, more efficient technique shown in Figure 16-6c. For volume service, use sheet cakes iced on the top only.

For all kinds of cakes, you can either swirl the icing into peaks, or smooth it and practice your pastry bag techniques of pressure, motion, and release to perfect the simple decorations and borders illustrated in Figure 16-7.

For inscriptions and finer designs, make a paper cone as shown in Figure 16-8. Fill it two-thirds full and fold the corners and top to close. Using the right hand to exert pressure and the left hand to guide (as you do with the pastry bag), write Happy Birthday or make designs. The paper cone can also be used with pastry tips.

FIGURE 16-6. Assembling cakes and icings.

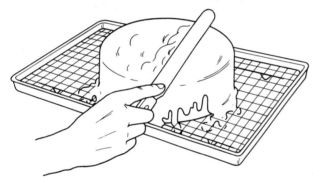

a. Pour icing in center of cake and spread to edge and around sides.

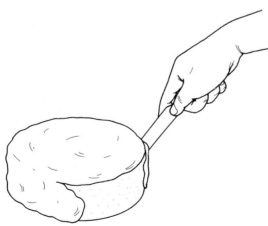

b. Push icing ahead of spatula to keep it free of crumbs.

c. Dip tops of cupcakes into softened icing, twist a quarter turn, and remove with a quick, smooth motion.

FIGURE 16-7. Simple decorations and borders.

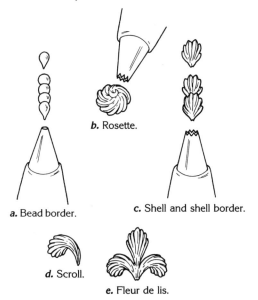

b. Rosette.

a. Bead border.

c. Shell and shell border.

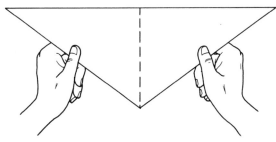

d. Scroll.

e. Fleur de lis.

Whatever decorations you choose, *keep them simple* in kind, amount, and color, just as you do for salads, buffets, and garnishing. This not only saves time and labor but results in a more attractive and professional-looking cake.

Divide cakes into uniform portions, marking them into halves, then quarters, with the dull edge of a long knife. Mark each quarter into the number of portions desired.

Cut the cake as close to service time as possible to prevent drying. Dip the knife into hot water after each cut.

FIGURE 16-8. Paper cones.

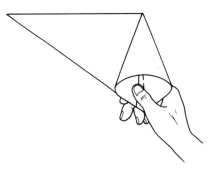

a. Cut a triangle from parchment paper.

b. Roll into a cone beginning at a point slightly left of center.

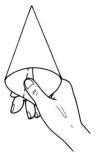

c. Finish rolling the cone, pulling it to close tip completely. Fold in flap at open end to prevent unrolling.

d. Fill two-thirds full and fold over corners and top to close. Snip off point for desired-size hole. Use gentle pressure to apply inscriptions and line designs.

16-9 BASIC BAKED CUSTARD

Approximate yield: 3½ quarts (3½ liters) = 28 4-oz (125 g) portions

2 lb	eggs	1 kg	2 qt	milk, scalded	2 L
1 lb	sugar	500 g			
1 tsp	salt	5 mL			
1 oz	vanilla	30 mL			

1. In mixer bowl, with whip, mix eggs, sugar, salt, and vanilla on low speed until blended.
2. Continue mixing while gradually pouring in hot milk until combined.
3. Skim foam from surface. (Strain through fine-mesh china cap.)
4. Pour into prepared pans or molds placed in hot water. Remove any bubbles. Bake at 325°F (160°C) until done (*45 minutes).

16-9a CRÈME CARAMEL

To formula 16-9 add:

*	caramelized sugar syrup	*

1. Heat syrup and pour to ⅛–¼″ (¼–½ cm) depth in pan or molds.
2. Prepare custard through Step 3.
3. Pour unbaked custard on top of caramel syrup. Bake as in Step 4.

16-9b BREAD PUDDING

To formula 16-9 add:

2 lb	sliced bread	900 g
12 oz	melted butter	350 g
*	cinnamon	*
*	nutmeg	*

1. Brush melted butter on both sides of bread. Lay out overlapping slices in hotel or baking pan.
2. Prepare custard through Step 3.
3. Strain custard over bread. Dust with spices. Bake as in Step 4.

CUSTARDS, MERINGUES, AND SOUFFLÉS

In this section we encounter once again the versatility of the egg and its key role in dishes for every part of the menu. Three types of dessert preparations are built almost entirely on its ability to incorporate air, to emulsify, to coagulate, to thicken, and to develop a product with a delightfully smooth and tender consistency.

Reviewing the nature and behavior of the egg and the techniques of egg cookery will help you tackle these formulas. Follow sanitation rules carefully in handling eggs to avoid the hazards of bacteria they are likely to carry.

Custards

Sweet custards are mixtures of eggs, milk, sugar, and flavorings. They take advantage of the egg's emulsifying ability to make a variety of toppings, fillings, puddings, and sauces. Two preparation techniques produce two types of custards. *Baked custards* (formula 16-9) are baked in an oven until they are set. *Stirred custards* (formulas 16-10 and 16-11) are stirred over gentle heat until the eggs coagulate.

You have met a savory baked custard in the quiche filling in Chapter 13. Formula 16-9 is a sweet baked custard. You can readily see both similarities and differences between the two. These custards are easy to make; they need only thorough blending of ingredients.

The mixer does the blending. Scalded milk (heated to just below a simmer) helps the custard to set more quickly in the oven. Add it slowly, remembering that an egg mixture must absorb a hot liquid slowly or it will curdle.

Skimming the air bubbles and foam formed during mixing is always a necessary step. Some bakers feel that straining gives a silkier texture to the finished product.

Custards are baked in individual metal or porcelain cups, hotel pans, or other baking pans and molds. They can be served in the mold but are more often unmolded. If custards are to be unmolded, butter the molds lightly. After pouring the custard into the pan or molds, remove any bubbles that formed when pouring. The bubbles will scorch and spoil the texture. Place the pan or molds in a larger pan, put in the oven, and add hot water to reach halfway up the sides of the custard pan or molds. Baking in hot water moderates the heat and keeps the egg protein from toughening. The water should stay just below a simmer during baking.

The test for doneness is a knife inserted an inch or two (2–5 cm) from the edge. If it comes out clean, the custard is done. The center won't be as firm as the edges but will finish cooking after you take it out of the oven.

Remove the custard pans from the hot water, cover, and store in the refrigerator. Serve cold, unmolding at service time if desired. To unmold, gently loosen the edges with a cake spatula, place the serving plate over the mold, and reverse with a sharp, jerking motion to release the custard in one piece.

Crème caramel (16-9a) turns a plain baked custard into a dish with great style. To make the **caramelized sugar syrup,** you heat 3 to 4 parts sugar to 1 part water in a heavy saucepan, stirring until sugar is dissolved, then cook at a low boil. As the temperature increases, the water evaporates and the sugar

begins to brown. The syrup reaches the amber-colored caramel stage at the high temperature of 320–340°F (160–170°C), so handle it very carefully. It must be poured into the pans while hot because when cool it is unpourable, hard, and brittle. Don't cook it past the amber color or it will be bitter. Crème caramel is always served unmolded so that the caramel syrup forms the topping.

This caramel syrup is usually made up in quantity and forms a standard part of a bakeshop mise en place. You can make it into a dessert sauce of many uses. Heat until liquefied, and carefully thin the hot mixture with regular simple syrup, water, or cream until it reaches the desired consistency.

A heartier version of baked custard is bread pudding (16-9b)—a delicious and profitable way to use up day-old bread. It is usually portioned and served with a dessert sauce. You can add raisins or nuts for extra flavor.

Now let us look at a stirred custard. The **custard sauce** in formula 16-10 is a basic preparation served with cakes, puddings, ice creams, and pastries. Making a custard sauce takes advantage of the emulsifying and thickening ability of eggs and uses techniques similar to those used in butter sauces.

Whipping the egg yolks and sugar in Step 1 starts emulsification. When the mixture has lightened and thickened enough to show traces of the whip, add the milk slowly to avoid scrambled eggs. This is the same technique you used in Chapter 6 in adding a liaison to a hot liquid.

In Step 3, heat makes the eggs coagulate, thickening and binding the mixture. The heat must be gentle and you must stir constantly to prevent scorching and overheating. If the sauce gets too hot, it will curdle. When the sauce will lightly coat a spoon, it has reached the right consistency. If the sauce does begin to curdle, you have a chance to bring it back by taking it off heat and whipping it little by little into a tablespoon (15 mL) of cold milk, either by hand or in a blender.

Cool quickly, stirring so that a crust

16-10 VANILLA CUSTARD SAUCE (CRÈME ANGLAISE)

Yield: 2½ pints (1.25 liters)

| 6 oz | egg yolks | 185 g | 1 qt | milk or half-and-half, scalded | 1 L |
| 8 oz | sugar | 250 g | 1 Tb | vanilla | 15 mL |

1. Whip yolks and sugar by hand or in mixer until *pale* yellow and thickened.
2. Temper in hot milk.
3. Place in trunnion kettle or place bowl in hot water on stove. Using low heat (185°F/85°C), stir constantly until thickened.
4. Remove from heat. Stir in vanilla.
5. Cool by placing bowl in cold water, stirring occasionally.

16-10a CHOCOLATE CUSTARD SAUCE

To formula 16-10 add:

| 6 oz | sweet chocolate | 180 g |

Melt chocolate and stir into warm sauce in Step 4.

doesn't form, and refrigerate, covered, as soon as possible, remembering the health risks of keeping egg products at room temperature. Store this sauce a few days at most, and never mix new with old for sanitation safety.

Custard sauces can be flavored in the same ways as buttercreams. Formula 16-10a is one example.

Pastry cream is another stirred custard used as is or flavored to produce cake and pie fillings, puddings, fillings for éclairs, or, when thinned with milk, a light custard sauce. As you see in formula 16-11, it is made by the same basic technique as custard sauce but contains starch and flour and must be heated to a higher temperature to reach its firmer consistency.

A trunnion kettle is easiest to use, but a heavy saucepan produces good results with careful heating and constant stirring. In Step 1, some sugar heated with the milk helps prevent scorching. While the milk is heating, mix the eggs in another bowl and blend in the dry ingredients (Steps 2 and 3). In Step 4, stir in the hot milk slowly to raise the temperature gradually, and then put everything back into the kettle or pan. Slowly cook and stir the mixture until it *reaches a full boil*—but no longer. The custard will be firm and thick and the starchy taste will be gone. (Don't go on cooking it as you would a soup or sauce. The cornstarch and the slow cooking make the difference.)

After blending in the butter and flavorings, pour into shallow pans. The melted butter or sugar in Step 7, along with the paper, prevent a filmy crust from forming. Refrigerate for a quick exit from the danger zone.

Formulas 16-11a and b show two popular ways to vary the basic pastry cream. You can substitute other flavorings for the vanilla, such as almond, orange, or lemon.

Before we leave custards, let's look at a popular dessert that is normally thought of as a cake—*cheesecake* (formula 16-12). Despite its name, it is a form of baked custard since its structure is provided by coagulation of the eggs during baking. The cheese provides the major body, and the cornstarch and flour act as thickeners and binders. All this gives the cheesecake a very different texture from other baked custards.

The mixing method is more like making a

16-11 BASIC PASTRY CREAM (CRÈME PÂTISSIÈRE)

Approximate yield: 2½ quarts (2½ liters)

2 qt	milk	2 L	4 oz	butter, softened	125 g
4 oz	sugar	125 g	½ oz	lemon juice	15 mL
1 lb	eggs	500 g	½ oz	vanilla	15 mL
5 oz	cornstarch	150 g	*	melted butter	*
5 oz	cake flour	150 g	*	sugar	*
12 oz	sugar	375 g			

1. In a trunnion kettle or heavy saucepan, heat milk and 4 oz (125 g) sugar to a low boil.
2. In a mixing bowl, stir eggs with a whip until blended fairly smooth.
3. Sift cornstarch, cake flour, and sugar together over eggs. With whip, blend until very smooth and thoroughly combined.
4. Temper in hot milk.
5. Return to pan or kettle and heat slowly, stirring constantly, until mixture thickens and reaches a full boil. Remove from heat.
6. Stir in butter, lemon juice, and vanilla until combined.
7. Pour into shallow pan. Brush lightly with melted butter or sprinkle with granulated sugar to prevent crust. Cover with paper and refrigerate immediately.

cake than a custard: it is similar to the creaming method. As in cakes, scrape-downs are important in producing a smooth, homogeneous, lump-free mixture.

Cheesecakes are often baked in springform pans, which make it easy to remove the baked cheesecake. If you use this type of pan, place the panned cakes on a rack in the oven with a pan of hot water underneath. If you use solid pans, put them right in the pan of water. The steam from the water will keep the custards from cracking during baking.

Bake until the center is set and the sides have pulled away slightly from the pan. Cool the cakes completely in the pans. When cool, invert onto cardboard cake circles, wrap, and refrigerate until needed—up to several days.

Use a long-blade knife dipped in hot water to cut each piece cleanly and neatly. Serve with a choice of fruit sauces for an added treat.

16-11a CHOCOLATE PASTRY CREAM

To formula 16-11 add:

8 oz	semisweet chocolate, melted	250 g

Stir chocolate into hot pastry cream in Step 6.

16-11b CHANTILLY PASTRY CREAM

To formula 16-11 add:

½–1 pt	heavy cream	250–500 mL

Whip cream and fold into chilled pastry cream.

16-12 CHEESECAKE NEW YORK STYLE

Yield: four 10" (25 cm) round cakes

4½ lb	cream cheese	2250 g	12 oz	eggs	375 g
5 lb	sour cream	2.5 kg	8 oz	lemon juice	250 mL
8 oz	cornstarch	250 g	8 oz	heavy cream	250 mL
5 oz	bread flour	150 g			
2½ lb	sugar	1250 g			
¼ oz	salt	7 g			

1. In mixer, using paddle, beat cream cheese on medium speed until soft, light, and fluffy.
2. Stir in sour cream until combined. Scrape down.
3. Sift dry ingredients together. Stir in on low speed until combined. Scrape down.
4. Add eggs little by little, waiting until each addition is absorbed. Scrape down.
5. Stir in juice, then cream until combined.
6. To scale, fill four 10" (25 cm) pans to the top. Set them in or over a pan of hot water.
7. Bake at 375°F (190°C) until set (*1 hour). Cool completely in pans.

Some other familiar desserts use custards as a base. *Bavarian creams* are flavored light custard sauces with gelatin and whipped cream. *Chiffons* are a stirred custard base with gelatin and beaten egg whites. Many types of dishes are called *mousses,* but the sweet ones are often stirred custards with whipped cream or stiff egg whites or both.

Meringues

Meringues are egg whites whipped with sugar, which produces still another multiuse preparation. They come in two types—soft and hard—and are made by three procedures.

Soft meringues are made with equal parts of sugar and egg whites. Pie toppings are their most common use. They are also folded into cakes, soufflés, and icings.

Hard meringues contain up to twice as much sugar as egg whites. They are usually formed into shells, nests, cookies, or layers (Figure 16-9) and are baked in a low-heat oven (200°F/100°C) for 1 to 2 hours until dry and crisp without browning. They are combined with ice cream, fruit sauces, and other preparations for finished desserts.

The three procedures—common, Swiss, and Italian—are spelled out in formula 16-13. As you can see, meringues are quickly and easily made. Make sure that all equipment is clean and grease-free and that no traces of yolk are present in the whites. As you know, fat prevents egg whites from stiffening.

All three procedures can be used for either hard or soft meringues. They are spelled out separately in our formula.

Common meringue is whipped to soft peak with the sugar added gradually for full absorption. Whipping continues until the mixture is stiff but still looks moist and shiny. (This is true for all meringues. Watch carefully because a dry, lumpy texture can happen quickly.) This is a fairly stable meringue, especially when a higher percentage of sugar to egg whites is used.

FIGURE 16-9. Meringues.

a. Meringue shells.

b. Meringue cookies.

c. Meringue layers.

d. Meringue nests.

16-13 MERINGUE

Yield: 2 to 3½ lb (1000–1750 g)

1 lb	egg whites	500 g	*For Italian meringue only:*
1–2 lb*	sugar (see note)	*500–1000 g	8 oz water 250 g

Procedure for **COMMON MERINGUE**

1. In mixer, with whip, whip egg whites on high speed to soft peak.
2. Gradually add sugar while continuing to whip on high speed.
3. Whip to stiff peak. Use immediately.

Procedure for **SWISS MERINGUE**

1. Place sugar and whites in mixer bowl, place bowl in hot-water bath, and whip by hand until mixture is warmed to 120°F (50°C).
2. Place bowl on machine and whip on high speed to stiff peak.

Procedure for **ITALIAN MERINGUE**

1. In a mixing bowl, place sugar and water in hot-water bath. Heat until sugar dissolves.
2. In mixer, whip egg whites on high speed to soft peak.
3. Continue whipping, gradually adding hot sugar syrup.
4. Whip mixture to stiff peak.

NOTE: Use 1 lb (500 g) for soft meringues. Use up to 2 lb (1000 g) sugar for hard meringues.

16-14 VANILLA SOUFFLÉ

Yield: 10 4½-oz (125 g) portions

3 oz	flour	100 g	8–10 oz	egg whites	250–300 g
3 oz	butter, softened	100 g	6 oz	sugar	200 g
8 oz	milk, scalded	265 g	2 tsp	vanilla	10 mL
6 oz	egg yolks	200 g	(*	salt	*)
			*	butter	*
			*	sugar	*

1. Make a paste of flour and butter (beurre manié).
2. In heavy saucepan, add beurre manié to hot milk, whipping until smooth. Simmer, stirring, until no starch taste remains.
3. Cool to warm. Stir in egg yolks until blended.
4. Whip egg whites to stiff peaks with sugar, vanilla (and salt). Fold into base mixture.
5. Place in buttered and sugared baking dishes, smoothing tops carefully.
6. Bake at 375°F (190°C) until puffed and golden (*15–20 minutes for individual portions).

16-14a CHOCOLATE SOUFFLÉ

To formula 16-14 add:

5 oz	bitter chocolate, melted	150 g

Add chocolate at end of Step 3.

16-14b CHEESE SOUFFLÉ

In formula 16-14, make these changes:

Omit sugar.

Add 8–10 oz (250–300 g) grated cheese.

Add seasonings.

Stir in cheese at end of Step 2, off heat, and season as for a béchamel.

In Step 5, replace sugar with finely grated cheese.

Swiss meringue is heated before whipping. This gives it greater volume and stability.

Italian meringue uses a hot syrup that cooks the egg whites, producing the most stable form. Flavor this meringue with vanilla or other extracts and you have made the boiled icing discussed earlier in the chapter.

Soufflés

Soufflés have a formidable reputation among beginners. But examine formula 16-14. In it you can see that a **soufflé** has a base of white sauce, flavored. A meringue is folded in and the mixture is baked. What could be easier since you are combining familiar products and basic techniques?

The basic procedures are indeed familiar and uncomplicated, and if you carry out the techniques correctly, your soufflé will not fall. Here are some points to watch.

- Don't overbeat the egg whites and sugar.
- Fold them in carefully to maintain volume.

- Bake at the correct temperature to create the steam for leavening.
- Handle carefully when putting a soufflé into the oven and removing it. Don't bang the oven door.
- Don't open the oven door until the guideline time is nearly up.

Soufflés can hold without collapsing in a turned-off warm oven for a short time, but careful coordination of timing with service personnel gets the soufflé to the guest with all its impressive height.

Formulas 16-14a and 16-14b are easy variations. In savory soufflés such as 16-14b you merely omit all the sugar and use cheese in place of sugar to coat the pans. You can also use a thick béchamel sauce as a base and stir in cooked, drained chopped vegetables or other flavor ingredients.

PIES AND TARTS

Pie doughs

Pies, tarts, tartlettes, and quiche (as in Chapter 13) are only a few of the good things to eat that come from pie or pastry dough. Two types of this stiff dough—**flaky** and **mealy**—are needed to make good pies. Both are mixed by the pastry method used in making biscuits. The difference between them comes in mixing the fat and flour and in the amount of liquid used. In flaky dough you leave the fat in larger pieces. This forms layers of fat and flour that produce flakiness when rolled and baked. Flaky dough is used for top crusts and unfilled or prebaked shells. In mealy dough you mix the fat into the flour more completely. This dough is more tender and less likely to absorb moisture and is therefore used for bottom crusts. Formula 16-15 includes both types.

16-15 PIE DOUGH

Yield: 4 lb 7–11 oz (2205–2315 g) dough = 9 bottom crusts or 12 top crusts for a 9" pie

2 lb 8 oz	pastry flour	1250 g	10–12 oz*	water or milk, 40°F (4°C) or below	*300–360 g
1 lb 4 oz	shortening/butter	625 g	1 oz	salt	30 g
			(1–2 oz	sugar	25–50 g)

1. Place flour and fat in a large bowl.
2a. For flaky crust, rub fat and flour until ¼" (5 mm) particles of fat are evenly distributed.
2b. For mealy crust, rub fat and flour until mixture has a coarse, crumbly texture.
3. Dissolve salt (and sugar) in three-fourths of liquid and add to flour mixture. Use the lower amount of liquid for mealy dough.
4. Toss mixture, adding more liquid as necessary, until it will form a mass of dough.
5. Cover and refrigerate 4 hours or more.
6. Dust bench, rolling pin, and dough lightly with flour.
7. For a 9" (23 cm) pie, scale 8 oz (250 g) for bottom crusts, 6 oz (200 g) for top crusts.
8. Roll each crust into a circle ⅛" (3 mm) thick, working from the center outward. Turn, lift, and dust dough if necessary to prevent sticking.
9. Place in pan. Trim or flute as desired. (Refrigerate again.)

As we examine the formula, look first at the ingredients. Pastry flour is used for its moderate gluten content. You have a choice of fats. Regular shortening is most often the choice for cost and consistency. Emulsified shortening should not be used. Butter combined with shortening gives a pleasing flavor and an easily handled dough. If you use all butter, you have a very tender, rich dough that is more difficult to handle. It will require less liquid because of the moisture in the butter.

You also have a choice of liquids. Water is used most often. Milk adds flavor and strength but browns more quickly than water. Whatever the liquid, it must be cold—40°F (4°C) or less—to help keep the dough cool. The dough should stay at or below 60°F (15°C) to keep the fat soft but not too soft and to prevent gluten from developing too quickly. Salt, and sugar if used, is dissolved in the liquid for even distribution. (Sugar may be added for flavor; it also increases browning.) Notice that the formula has no leavener: this is a dough that is leavened by steam.

Now for the action. Beginning with Step 1, you can mix a large amount (at least three times this formula) as quickly and easily by hand as in the machine with the dough hook. It is also easier to judge the readiness of the dough. Place a dampened towel under the bowl to keep it steady. (When using an extra-large bowl for a big batch, you can even use a clean trash can as a stand.) Rub the flour and fat together with the palms of your hands (Step 2), until you achieve the consistency you want (a or b) and the fat and flour are evenly distributed.

Proceed with Steps 3 and 4. Make a hole in the middle of the mixture and pour in most of the liquid. Use your fingertips to go down the sides of the bowl to the bottom and then up. As the water is absorbed, begin to try to shape the dough into a solid mass. Add the rest of the water as necessary to form a ball. If you use too little liquid, the baked crust will crack and fall apart. If you use too much, the crust is tough. Mealy dough requires less liquid than

flaky. Do not overwork the dough. If you over-mix it after adding the liquid, you end up with a tough piece of shoe leather instead of a tender container for the filling.

Some gluten development is unavoidable, so the dough is allowed to relax in the refrigerator (Step 5). Cover it well with plastic film so that a crust doesn't form.

Steps 6 through 9 carry the dough through makeup and panning. Use as little flour as possible to dust the bench, dough, and pin. Scale the dough. Shape the crust into a flattened ball, and roll out. Steady, even pressure from the center outward in all directions makes it easiest to roll a perfect circle of uniform thickness (Figure 16-10a). Lift the dough once or twice to make sure it isn't sticking, and dust if necessary. Avoid pulling or stretching the dough here or gluten will develop. Roll it as close as possible to the size you need. Allow an extra 2″ (5 cm) for a bottom crust.

In Step 9, roll up the circle of dough around the rolling pin and unroll it into the pan (Figure 16-10b). Use gentle pressure to eliminate air pockets and shape the dough into the pan. Again, avoid stretching or pulling or the crust will shrink during baking.

A single-crust pie can now be fluted or crimped and trimmed. To make a *fluted* edge, place a thumb or finger inside the edge of the crust. Use the forefinger and thumb of the other hand to pinch up the dough (Figure 16-10c). Continue this process around the crust, spacing evenly. You can make a simpler edge by *crimping*—pressing the tines of a fork around the rim (Figure 16-10d).

To pinch off excess dough, press your palms against the rim while rotating the pie plate. Another technique is to use a knife to cut against the rim while rotating the pie above the bench with the other hand. Either way, make a neat and even edge with no jagged pieces.

Tarts, cream pies, and chiffon pies, among others, require a *prebaked shell* for filling. With a fork, dock the bottom of the unbaked crust

FIGURE 16-10. Makeup for pie crusts.

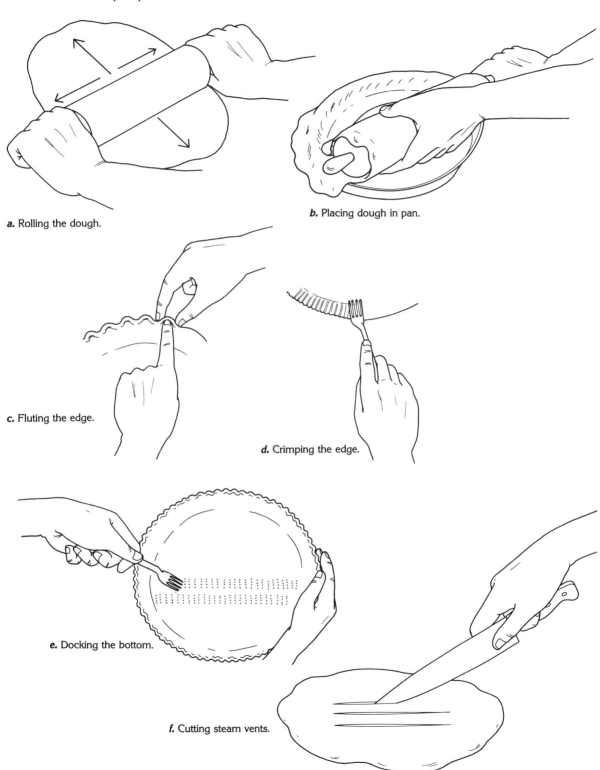

a. Rolling the dough.

b. Placing dough in pan.

c. Fluting the edge.

d. Crimping the edge.

e. Docking the bottom.

f. Cutting steam vents.

by piercing rows of evenly spaced holes (Figure 16-10e). This will prevent air pockets and blisters in the finished crust. Place another pie pan of the same size inside the dough. Put pans and dough upside down on a sheet pan and bake until done. This procedure keeps the crust from shrinking.

A double-crust pie begins by placing the rolled-out mealy dough in the pan and shaping it. Fill the pie carefully. Don't let any filling get on the edges or the steam from the pie as it bakes will break through the sealed edge and leave more filling on the outside than the inside. Brush the rim with egg wash; it will act as glue to seal the top to the bottom and keep the bubbling liquid from escaping during baking. Roll out flaky pie dough, dock the crust or cut decorative steam vents (Figure 16-10f), and place on the pie. Use the techniques for finishing and trimming single crusts, making sure the edges are well sealed.

Colorful fruit pies (cherry, blueberry) may have a *lattice crust* of crisscross strips of pie dough to show off their beauty. Either type of crust can be brushed with milk or egg wash and sugar to aid in browning and produce a shiny crust.

Short dough

Short dough is another type of stiff pastry dough, used mainly for tartlettes and tarts. These are European style pastries finished with a custard type filling, fruit, or both. This dough is actually considered a rich cookie dough and can be used for sugar cookies and other types of rolled or molded cookies. You can use your cookie expertise with this dough by adding flavoring ingredients and decorating the finished cookies for an array of delicious little pastries.

Short dough, also known as sweet dough, is a very tender, sometimes fragile dough. In addition to the flour and butter of pie dough, it contains sugar and eggs. It is mixed by the creaming method and chilled. If it warms as you work with it, the dough becomes very sticky and hard to handle. For tarts, the dough is rolled out thicker than pie dough—about 1/4" (5 mm) thick. If it is not thick enough, the tart shells you make with it may crack and fall apart after baking. The fragility of this dough requires very gentle handling.

Pie fillings

The dough is relaxing in the cooler, but you can't relax until you know how to fill the pies. But don't panic. You will discover in this section that assembling a baked or unbaked pie is simply a matter of putting together several different preparations you have already learned how to make.

Unbaked pies are baked, cooled shells that are filled with a finished filling. Often the filling is topped with meringue, sweetened whipped cream, or other ingredients such as fruit, coconut, or nuts.

A variety of *cream pies,* for example, are easily made by using a filling with a pastry cream base. Here are a few.

- *Chocolate cream pie.* Fill baked pie shells with chocolate pastry cream (16-11a). Chill.
- *Banana cream pie.* In baked pie shells, layer one sliced banana per pie with vanilla pastry cream (16-11).
- *Coconut cream pie.* Stir 8 oz (250 g) toasted coconut into vanilla pastry cream (16-11). Fill baked pie shells.

Lemon pie filling (16-16) is a stirred, thickened custard just like pastry cream. Water replaces milk, and of course lemon provides the major flavor. You can make an orange or lime pie filling by substituting orange or lime zest and juice. To intensify the flavor of a citrus filling, increase the amount of zest. It is the zest, not the juice, that imparts the characteristic flavor.

For a lemon meringue pie—or for any meringue pie—use a common or Swiss soft meringue (16-13). Spread a generous coating in a decorative manner over the cooled filled pie. Make sure the meringue is spread all the

16-16 LEMON PIE FILLING

Approximate yield: 1 quart (1 liter)

1 qt	water	1 L	4	egg yolks	4
8 oz	sugar	250 g	2	eggs	2
			3 oz	cornstarch	90 g
			2 Tb	grated lemon zest	30 mL
			4 oz	lemon juice	125 mL

1. Bring sugar and water to a low boil.
2. Mix remaining ingredients together and temper in hot syrup.
3. Return to heat and cook, stirring constantly, until thickened.
4. Cool slightly before pouring into baked pie shells.

way to the edges of the shell with no gaps, to keep it from slipping. Place in a hot oven (400°F/200°C) for a few minutes until light golden.

Chiffon pies are made by adding gelatin to a stirred, thickened custard base and folding in whipped cream, meringue, or both before the gelatin sets. This combination produces a filling that is both firm and fluffy.

Baked pies start with unbaked single mealy-dough shells. These are filled with an uncooked mixture and then baked. They include pourable fillings that set during baking when the eggs coagulate—in other words, custards. Here are three examples of custard pie.

- *Custard pie.* Fill unbaked pie shells with the mixture for baked custard (16-9). Dust with nutmeg. Bake for 10 minutes at 400°F (200°C). Reduce to 325°F (160°C). Bake until filling is set at edges.
- *Pecan pie.* Mix sugar, butter, and salt. Mix in eggs, corn syrup, and vanilla, and pour this translucent custard over pecan

pieces spread in shell. Bake as for custard pie, dropping the temperature to 350°F (180°C) after 10 minutes.
- *Pumpkin pie.* Mix canned puréed pumpkin with brown sugar, spices, and a little bit of flour. Mix in eggs, milk, and corn syrup for a custardlike batter. Bake as for custard pie, dropping the temperature to 350°F (180°C) after 10 minutes.

You will notice that at first a high temperature is used to bake these pies. This is to set and seal the mealy dough and avoid a soggy, unappetizing crust. Use the baked custard test for doneness to prevent overbaking and curdling.

Fruit pies use an unbaked shell of mealy dough that is filled with fruit and usually topped with a flaky top crust or lattice. Formula 16-17 gives a basic method for making a fruit filling. The method can be used with fresh, canned, or frozen fruit. In effect, you are making a dessert sauce to which you add fruit. Since the fruit is not cooked before baking, it

16-17 FRUIT PIES

Yield: four 9" (23 cm) pies

1 No. 10 can	fruit, water pack	1 No. 10 can	1 lb 8 oz*	sugar	*750 g
3 oz*	cornstarch	*90 g	1 tsp	salt	5 mL
1 qt	drained juice and water	1 L	*	lemon juice	*
			*	flavorings	*

1. Drain fruit liquid into volume measure. Add water to juice to equal 1 qt (1 L).
2. In a heavy saucepan bring 1½ pt (¾ L) liquid to boil.
3. Mix remaining liquid with cornstarch and stir into hot liquid.
4. Simmer until thickened to consistency desired.
5. Stir in sugar, salt, and flavorings *to taste. Bring back to a simmer, then remove from heat.
6. Gently combine with drained fruit. Cool slightly.
7. Fill and top pies. Bake at 400°F (200°C) for 10 minutes. Reduce heat to 350°F (180°C) and bake until crust is golden.

NOTE: Five pounds (2.5 kg) fresh or frozen fruit may be substituted for canned fruit. Appropriate fruits are apples, cherries, peaches, berries, etc.

retains a firm texture instead of becoming mushy.

The variable amounts of sugar and starch depend on the natural sweetness and thickening ability of the fruit chosen (for example, apples and peaches are high in pectin, a natural jelling ingredient, so they require less starch). If you use fresh fruit, you can sprinkle it with some of the sugar to draw out juices. Drain and combine with water in Step 1.

Choose flavorings—cinnamon, nutmeg, cloves, extracts, lemon zest—compatible with each fruit. Salt and lemon juice bring out the natural flavor.

COMBINING DESSERTS AND BAKED PRODUCTS

All the techniques, ingredients, methods, and finished products may be a jumble in your mind by now. But when you analyze the roles of ingredients and the methods of mixing and assembling, you can see there are only a few. Even a small bakeshop area can produce a few basic items in a multitude of ways to add sparkle and variety to a dessert menu.

Here are a few suggestions to get you started—but don't limit yourself to these!

- *Black forest cake.* Soak split chocolate cake layers with kirsch-flavored simple syrup. Fill with dark sweet cherry filling. Ice with sweetened whipped cream. Decorate with shaved chocolate and additional cherries.

- *Pear belle hélène.* Place a poached pear on a slice of pound cake. Top with chocolate sauce.

- *Napoleons.* Sandwich pastry cream between three layers of thin baked puff pastry. Ice with fondant.

- *Boston cream pie.* Fill split layers of white or yellow cake with pastry cream. Frost with fudge icing.
- *Vacherin.* Sandwich layers of ice cream between baked meringue layers. Ice and decorate with whipped cream.
- *Charlottes.* Line a mold with ladyfingers. Pour in bavarian cream. Chill and unmold for service.
- *Éclairs or cream puffs.* Fill baked pâte à chou shapes with pastry cream. Ice with chocolate fondant.
- *Crêpes.* Fill with mousse, ice cream, or fruit and top with appropriate sauce.

SUMMING UP

Desserts—sweet selections on the menu to finish the meal—complete the story of bake-shop production. This side of baking is referred to as the pastry shop, though the kinds of products described in this chapter can be made in any kitchen. In addition to such baked goods as cookies, cakes, and pies, dessert production includes icings, custards, pastry creams, pie fillings, and meringues—everything you need to make dozens of different desserts.

Cookies are easily made. They are mixed by the creaming method, the one-stage method, or the foam method, depending on ingredient combinations. There are seven methods of makeup—drop, bar, bagged, rolled, refrigerator, molded, and sheet.

Cake batters are high in sugar, fat, and liquid and need special care in mixing. Three cake-mixing methods—creaming, two-stage, and foam—are appropriate to different ingredient combinations. For icing on the cake there are six choices—fondant, flat, butter-cream, royal, boiled, and fudge. Coatings and toppings such as glazes and sweet sauces are also used. Assembling cake and icing is a skill in itself and must be done with care and precision.

Custards can be complete desserts in themselves, or they can be used as pie fillings, toppings, and sauces, or even baked as cheesecake.

Meringues—hard and soft—are egg whites mixed with sugar. They combine with many other pastry shop products to create finished desserts.

Soufflés are made by folding meringue into a thick béchamel and baking—good for luncheon items as well as desserts.

Pie and short doughs are stiff doughs used to make shells for tarts, cream pies, custard pies, chiffon pies, fruit fillings, and countless other variations. You can use them for quiche at lunch as well as for dessert.

All the products of the bakeshop and pastry shop require the utmost care and concentration at every step to prepare them correctly. Baking is, as we have said, a precise form of art. But most of the products we have examined here are within reach of the professional cook in the typical kitchen. The career of pastry chef has a much broader repertoire and requires considerable additional training and experience, but the rewards and satisfactions are great.

THE COOK'S VOCABULARY

mixing methods: creaming, one-stage, two-stage, foam

cookie makeup methods: drop, bar, bagged, rolled, icebox, molded, sheet double-pan, scrape down, fold, skim

icing, frosting: fondant, flat, buttercream, royal, boiled or foam, fudge

filling, simple syrup, glaze, caramelized sugar syrup

baked custard, stirred custard, custard sauce, pastry cream

cheesecake, bavarian cream, chiffon, mousse

meringue: soft, hard, common, Swiss, Italian

soufflé

flaky pie dough, mealy pie dough, short dough

pie shell, prebaked shell, fluted or crimped crust, lattice crust

unbaked pies: cream, chiffon

baked pies: custard, fruit

QUESTIONS FOR DISCUSSION

1. What are the differences and similarities in mixing and makeup for cookies and cakes?

2. What other makeup methods could be used for ladyfingers? Raisin spice bars? Chocolate chip cookies?

3. Why are two methods necessary in producing pie doughs? Name pies that use each method.

4. What are the tests of doneness for cookies? Cakes? Custards? Soufflés? Describe the differences in the textures of these products.

5. What other flavors of cream pie filling could you make? How does a fruit pie differ from a custard pie?

NOW that you know a good deal about foods and how to prepare them, it is time to put all this knowledge into the context of the real kitchen in the real working world. The key to success in the working world is the ability to produce good food both efficiently and profitably.

When you cook in the laboratory you cook to learn. Your goals are to understand foods and cooking and to develop skills. The time you take to prepare something in the lab is the time it takes you to learn how to do it. The quantity you prepare is an amount suitable for learning. The quality is the best you can achieve with what you have to work with. Usually you prepare one thing at a time.

In a working kitchen your goals will be quite different. You will prepare food to be served. You will prepare definite quantities, to be ready at definite times, to meet definite quality standards set by the operation for which you work. You will usually prepare not one dish but several. You will be involved in production.

Production is that part of a food-service operation responsible for transforming foods from the market into finished dishes for service. Production is the heart of the food-service industry. You can see that the cook, as a member of a production staff, plays an important role in the success of the operation.

As a cook you will be responsible only for your own station and your own set of tasks. But you will not be a good production cook unless you understand the goals of the operation as a whole and relate your own work to them. So let's first look at these overall goals and their effect on the cook's job. Then we will see how cooks manage their own stations and their daily responsibilities.

After completing this chapter you should be able to

- Understand management goals and explain how the work of the cook relates to meeting these goals.
- Explain the meaning and importance of

17

Out of the Lab and into Production

cost control, quality control, and quantity control, and cite ways in which the cook must carry out such controls.

- Describe common ways of communicating production responsibilities and assignments.
- Describe how to use and interpret common kitchen forms and records and explain the importance of each.
- Plan your own production and set up your production station efficiently.

GOALS AND CONTROLS

The goal of a commercial restaurant is to make a profit for its investors. Its profit is the difference between its costs and its sales. The goal of a nonprofit operation such as a school or hospital is to provide a certain group of people with food of a certain quality within a certain budget. In both types of operation the responsibility for meeting goals lies with management.

In order to meet its goals management develops techniques for controlling those variables within the operation that may keep them from reaching their goals. To management, controls are insurance policies, ways of guaranteeing success.

Production involves several variables that are subject to such controls. The three most important variables are

- Cost
- Quality
- Quantity

Every production job, from the scrubbing of potatoes to the making of a pie, can affect cost, or quantity, or quality, or all three, and no production manager can effectively control any of these unless the staff understands the necessity for controls and carries them out. Let's look at each in turn.

Cost and its control

Cost control is a complex subject whose intricacies are not appropriate to this book. It is

a management responsibility and it deals with all costs of an operation, not just those of production. However, the costs involved in production can be critical to success or failure. It is important for you to understand some general concepts of cost control and to realize what part the production worker plays in controlling costs.

In production there are two prime costs: food cost and labor cost. What the cook does affects both costs directly.

Food cost is defined as the cost of the edible products purchased for production—the dollars-and-cents value of products used by the cook. For each operation there is a certain minimum spread between total food costs and income that represents a break point between success and failure. To maintain this spread, the goal is to keep food costs down while maintaining or increasing income.

Management determines the food-cost standard (minimum spread) and keeps close track of actual costs and dollar sales. When they find the spread between costs and income dropping below the standard, they take corrective action. They may, for example, change certain dishes on the menu, substituting a lower-cost item for an expensive one. They may raise menu prices. They may fire the cook. It all depends on what is out of line.

Why would they fire the cook? The reason would be that what the cook has done in the kitchen has raised food costs without increasing sales. Since it is the cook who works most closely with food, it is the cook who controls its efficient care and use. When food is wasted, more must be bought, and the food-cost figure rises.

Thus, while management sets the food-cost standard, it is the production crew who actually carry out controls for costs that are due to waste. Firing the cook may be an extreme form of action, but a cook who is careless about controlling waste may not be worth the salary.

Waste means you are throwing away food that was purchased for use. It is caused by improper storage and handling of foods, spoilage, carelessness in preparing raw materials, careless sanitary practices, overproduction, oversupplying, and poor cooking. Waste is also caused by pilferage. In day-to-day terms, here are things the cook can do to hold costs down by keeping waste to a minimum.

- Store both cooked and uncooked foods properly to prevent spoilage. Store them at proper temperatures, properly wrapped or covered. Improper storage shortens shelf life. Careless wrapping for the freezer causes freezer burn. Don't keep foods beyond their normal shelf life; not only will you waste them but they may contaminate others.
- Rotate supplies to make sure the most recently received is not the first used. *First in, first out* is a rule of thumb in any operation. It ensures that a food with a short shelf life gets used before it spoils.
- Report to your supervisor any change in the quality of raw supplies being received. A lower-quality product may yield a smaller amount, thus increasing costs.
- Clean and cut each food carefully to get the most out of it. Don't take half the potato along with the peel; don't create uneven shapes or slices that must be discarded.
- Use your product knowledge to recognize further uses for trimmings. Use parsley stems and celery trimmings for flavor building; stems of mushrooms, asparagus, broccoli for soups; lemon and orange peels and green onion tops for garnishes; poultry, meat, and fish bones and fish heads for stocks. Check with your supervisor before discarding such trimmings.
- Cook and handle all foods properly to avoid producing foods that must be discarded. Don't prepare more than is needed. Don't burn the beans.
- Make good use—and only good use—of leftovers. Use good-quality leftovers as quickly as possible.

- It goes without saying that you do not take food from the kitchen for your own use.

Your pride as a true professional cook should allow you to accept nothing less than an effective control of all food within your sphere of responsibility.

Labor cost refers to the wages and salaries that are paid to the people who produce the food—you and your coworkers. Again there is a certain minimum spread between labor cost and dollar sales that must be maintained for financial success. Labor cost can also be related to specific dishes by figuring how long it takes a cook to make a given dish and how much this cook is paid for this time. The labor cost involved may make the dish cost more than it can be sold for. This is one reason why many classical dishes have disappeared from the average restaurant menu. It is why many convenience foods are used even when they are more expensive than the unprocessed products they replace.

The overall control of labor cost is a management function. But all cooks have the power to affect labor cost by the way they produce. If you produce efficiently you help to control labor cost. If you are inefficient you may increase it. You may have heard it said of a good worker, "She does the work of two people." It is a comment on all three of them.

Here are some ways in which your efficiency can help control labor cost.

- Follow your work schedule faithfully. When you are on time and on the job you are producing.
- Understand your job so that you spend your time in production and not in confusion.
- Set up your work station with both supplies and equipment necessary to do your job. This enables you to work efficiently.
- Meet your production deadlines. Your own inefficiency is bad enough, but it can be compounded by affecting other workers

and other segments of production. For example, if the salad dressing you are supposed to make is not going to be ready on time, someone else must be assigned to help you in order to meet the deadline and serve the salad. That person's work is then off schedule and other assignments may have to be rearranged to meet other deadlines. Usually someone ends up working overtime, and up goes the labor cost.

• Be constantly aware of how you stand with respect to your assignments. If it is your responsibility to produce 300 salads by 11:00 A.M. and you are behind at 10:15, report your position to your supervisor or adjust your own method or work speed to meet your schedule.

A food-service operation has other production-related costs besides those of food and labor. The cook who takes the extra steps necessary to conserve energy, avoid breakage, and maintain equipment is helping management to control these costs.

Quality and its control

Quality in production refers to the taste, texture, appearance, nutritional value, and level of excellence of the food served. **Quality control** means assuring day-in-day-out consistency of quality in each product offered for service.

Many people in the industry consider product consistency the single most important factor in the continued success or failure of a commercial operation. A restaurant is known by its food. People come back to enjoy tastes and textures they remember with pleasure from their last visit, and they tell their friends. Good food and sales go hand in hand.

Quality and consistency are just as important in a nonprofit operation as they are in a commercial restaurant, though the feedback supplied by the profit motive is absent. The quality of food in a hospital contributes directly to patient recovery. Good food in a school affects student health: the typical school lunch is carefully designed for nutritional value, which is wasted if the students don't eat it. The food served day after day to captive clienteles, such as employees in a company dining room or military personnel on base, is tremendously important to morale, and management in such places is deeply concerned with morale. If the food is consistent but consistently bad, they've got a problem.

The standards of quality are set by management, but their achievement is in the hands of the cook. The task is complicated by the very nature of quality. It is hard to keep personal opinion out of quality judgments.

To make the difficult task of quality control a little easier, here are some important guidelines.

• Be sure you understand the quality standards set by management for each product. There are various ways these standards may be communicated to you—by recipes, by photographs of completed dishes, best of all by demonstration and taste.

• Accept these quality standards as they are defined by management. In any well-run operation they reflect the preferences of the clientele. Follow these standards to the letter. Some dishes may not be to your taste. They may even be contrary to some of the teachings of this text. But that doesn't mean you can change them, unless you have been given specific authority to do so. You can suggest changes, however, and make them if your supervisor approves.

• Follow good production techniques from prepreparation to final product to ensure consistently high quality. Often the quality of the finished dish can be lowered by carelessness in the early stages of preparation. Poor breading technique, for example, can make an otherwise perfect chicken kiev look ragged and splotchy.

• Sample finished products even when they are made from standardized recipes, so that you can test the quality and make any necessary adjustments before the food is served. If, for example, your cream soup has a scorched taste you don't want to learn about it from an unhappy customer. A poor-quality product presents a real dilemma: should you throw it out and waste all those materials and labor, or serve it and risk losing sales and customers? You had better throw it out.

Countless other things contribute to quality and its control—proper setup for production, proper use of tools, good-quality raw materials, proper cleaning, good timing, almost everything you do. You have to think about quality all the time.

Quantity and its control

The term **quantity** in the context of production refers to the amount of a product to be produced for service in a given production period. **Quantity control** means producing the exact amount—no more, no less. Again management sets the standard and the cook has actual responsibility for control.

Quantities are usually expressed in numbers of portions of a standard size. Each number represents a careful forecast based on known needs (such as banquet orders in a hotel or student population in a school) or on careful projections based on records of past sales. The care with which the figure is set reflects management's concern with quantity control. If it is too low there won't be enough of the product for everyone who wants it. If it is too high there will be too much, and overproduction can affect both quality and cost.

The same things happen if the figures are correct but the cook does not meet them. There may be a guest who drove 50 miles for a cup of the soup you have just run out of. Or you may end up with 2 quarts of hollandaise that won't keep until tomorrow.

There are several things you can do as a cook to keep your own production on target.

- Be sure there is good communication between you and your supervisor on the number of portions to prepare.
- Be sure you understand the portion sizes needed. If 100 4-ounce portions are called for and you prepare enough to serve 100 5-ounce portions, you will have enough for 25 portions left over. If 100 5-ounce portions are specified and you prepare only enough for 100 4-ounce portions, you will be short 20 portions.
- Prepare foods in logical quantities and numbers. For example, make soup in quarts and gallons. Make round numbers of portions, such as 250 or 500, not 248 or 492. Round numbers are easy to calculate and measure and there is far less chance of making a mistake.
- Know raw products and their yields. This will save you unpleasant surprises. Yield as served, or **edible portion (EP),** compared with the raw product **as purchased (AP)** is sometimes as little as 40 or 50 percent. The difference represents bone, fat, shell, peelings, trimmings, or shrinkage during cooking, depending on the product. Table 17-1 gives you yields of commonly served foods.
- As always, use good cooking techniques and controls to avoid unservable products or short yields such as shrinkage of meats.
- Stagger-cook whenever necessary to avoid having products lose servable quality before they are used. If they should become unusable, you will either run short or be forced to prepare extra amounts.

All these practices are essential for good quantity control. Now let's look more closely at why quantity control is so important.

Quantity control is directly related to profit. Overproduction affects cost. Underproduction affects sales. And profit, as you know, is the difference between the two.

Underproduction reduces sales. Not only are the current sales of the missing portions

TABLE 17-1 Approximate Yields of Raw Products in Common Use*

Raw Product as Purchased (AP)	Yield as Served (EP)	Raw Product as Purchased (AP)	Yield as Served (EP)	Raw Product as Purchased (AP)	Yield as Served (EP)
BEEF		LAMB		Lettuce, boston	70–75%
Strip loin (boneless)	70–75%	Leg (roast)	40–50%	Lettuce, iceberg	70–75%
Pot roast (flank and brisket)	55–65%	Rack	40–50%	Lettuce, romaine	60–65%
Chopped beef, 80% lean	70–75%	Lean stew meat	75–85%	Mushrooms	60–70%
Corned beef brisket	60–65%	POULTRY		Okra	90–100%
Beef liver	80–90%	Chicken fryers	90–100%	Onion	75–80%
Tenderloin steak	85–95%	Chicken roasters	70–80%	Peas, green, shelled	75–80%
Strip steak	75–80%	Turkey	40–50%	Potato, baked	95–100%
Stew meat	65–75%	FISH		Potato, deep-fried	50–70%
Beef round	45–55%	Round fish	50%	Tomato	90–95%
Prime rib	50–60%	Portioned fish	90–100%	Turnips	70–75%
PORK		VEGETABLES, FRESH		FRUIT, FRESH	
Pork chops	75–85%	Asparagus	45–55%	Apples	70–75%
Pork loin (roast)	45–55%	Beans, green	85–88%	Avocado	70–75%
Fresh ham (roast)	45–55%	Beets, no tops	70–75%	Banana	65–70%
Sausage	50–55%	Broccoli	60–65%	Cantaloupe	50–55%
Pork ribs	55–65%	Brussels sprouts	70–75%	Cranberries	90–100%
Ham	60–80%	Cabbage	75–85%	Grapefruit	45–50%
VEAL		Carrots	70–75%	Honeydew melon	55–60%
Calf liver	70–80%	Cauliflower	45–50%	Lemon	45–50%
Rack (rib)	70–80%	Celery	70–75%	Mango	60–70%
Veal chop	75–85%	Cucumber	80–90%	Orange	50–60%
Leg roast	50–60%	Eggplant	70–80%	Strawberries	85–90%
Loin roast	50–60%	Endive, curly	75–80%	Watermelon	75–80%

*Yields vary according to processing procedures, cooking methods, and product grades.

lost, but future sales may be lost as well. Disappointed customers often do not come back.

Overproduction increases cost. It takes increased labor as well as an increase of raw materials to overproduce. One of the best ways of controlling cost is to produce only what is needed when it is needed. What is overproduced is wasted or left over.

Leftovers relate quantity control directly to quality control. When you have a fixed menu it is difficult to use all leftovers effectively without loss in quality. Warmed-over leftovers do not maintain product consistency.

Many people make a great mistake in attempting to control production costs by focusing their efforts on how to utilize leftovers instead of concentrating on how to prevent them. Granted, we must deal with leftovers if we have them, but it is far more practical to avoid them in the first place.

A second aspect of quantity control is portion control. It comes into play when the cook has made the assigned quantity and the food is being served to the diner. **Portioning** is the breaking down, or dividing up, of large quantities into specific serving quantities, or **portions. Portion control** refers to the measurement of portions to guarantee that the quantity planned is the quantity actually served.

Poor portion control is without a doubt one of the primary factors causing food-service establishments to operate in the red. The most accurate of cost projections is only as valid as the strictness with which portion control is enforced in the kitchen.

The only way to control portions is to use tools and equipment designed to do the job. It is true that portioning a small quantity of food is often possible without measuring. You can guesstimate the division of a dish into two, three, or four portions with reasonable accuracy. Large amounts are a different story. Try dividing a big kettle of beef burgundy into 300 *equal* portions without measuring. Finishing the job with 295 portions is an unforgivable sin.

What may look like a small loss today—a few pennies here and there—multiplied by day after day after day, can grow into hundreds, even thousands, of dollars. To keep this kind of loss at a minimum, you must follow the specified serving portion to the letter and use portion-control equipment properly. You must be familiar with the various scoops, ladles, and serving spoons. You must know how to divide a pan of food into the right number and size of portions based on its capacity. You must be able to cut a pie or a cake into the right number of *equal* pieces.

Tables 17-2 through 17-5 give you much of the information you will need for practicing portion control. Study them with the actual equipment at hand, so that you become familiar with real sizes of real portions.

As we have seen earlier, many items can be purchased in specific portions or weights. It is part of the cook's job to verify from time to time that these portions are accurate.

Production schedules and deadlines

A fourth control essential to the success of any operation is the production schedule. It is a means of controlling time or, more precisely, the way time is spent. A **production schedule** is a plan for a specific production period stating who is responsible for what products and when each product must be ready.

As with quantity, quality, and cost controls, management (in this case the person in charge of the kitchen) sets the goals and the production workers share the responsibility for achievement. There is one big difference. Quantity, quality, and cost are variables, and the goals of controls are targets to aim for. But time is not a variable, and the goals of control, the production deadlines, are not targets but requirements.

Time of service is an unalterable, inescapable daily reality, the beginning and end point of all production schedules. There is no give. The food *must* be ready to serve at the appointed time.

The scheduling of production is an intricate balancing of personnel, product flow, equipment usage, and available time. Every person in production must meet his or her own deadline or the whole structure is affected. In a large operation, because the schedule is complex, one worker's failure to produce on time can upset the flow of products and the work of many other people. In a small operation one person's performance may be even more important, since each person has a larger share of the work and there are fewer people to help out if someone falls behind. *Meeting production deadlines is the single most important concern in any kitchen.*

The production schedule sets the deadlines for production, but within its framework you have the responsibility for organizing and scheduling your own work. You will remember from Chapter 3 that organizing your work is

TABLE 17-2 Common Pan Capacities

Pan	U.S.		Metric	
	Depth (inches)	Approximate Capacity (quarts)	Depth (centimeters)	Approximate Capacity (liters)
Steam table inserts:				
Full size (12 × 20″)	2½	7½	6¼	7½
(30 × 50 cm)	4	14½	10	14½
	6	22	15	22
⅔ size	2½	6¾	6¼	6¾
	4	10	10	10
	6	14½	15	14½
½ size	2½	4¼	6¼	4¼
	4	6½	10	6½
	6	11	15	11
⅓ size	2½	3	6¼	3
	4	4⅓	10	4⅓
	6	6⅔	15	6⅔
¼ size	2½	2½	6¼	2½
	4	3⅓	10	3⅓
	6	4¾	15	4¾
⅙ size	2½	1⅓	6¼	1⅓
	4	2	10	2
	6	2¾	15	2¾

TABLE 17-3 Common Ladle Sizes

1 oz = ⅛ C	30 mL
2 oz = ¼ C	50 mL
4 oz = ½ C	125 mL
6 oz = ¾ C	200 mL
8 oz = 1 C	250 mL

the key to good production. It is up to you to plan carefully, so that you can work efficiently and meet your deadlines comfortably.

HOW PRODUCTION RESPONSIBILITIES ARE COMMUNICATED

Controlling costs and quality and quantity and time are general responsibilities that apply to everything in production. Like sanitation, these things should become habits, applied automatically to any task. But what about the specific daily responsibilities of each individual worker? Each job is different. Each day is different. How do you know what to do when?

There are several ways in which your own responsibilities may be communicated to you. They begin with your job description, written or unwritten. They may include printed forms or written schedules of various types from which you extract the information that applies to you. They may be verbal instructions. They may be daily routines you simply learn.

Job descriptions

Each job in industry has specific duties and requirements. These duties and requirements vary widely with the type and size of the establishment. Many employers have written job descriptions, especially in large operations such as restaurant and fast-food chains, large hotels, hospitals, and big-city school systems. Because of the diversity of operations and jobs, it would be hard to cite a typical example, but we can look at the kinds of information you might find in a job description.

- Time schedule and hours of work.
- Skill levels required on the job.
- Title of your immediate supervisor.
- Span of supervision (that is, your area of responsibility and the people you supervise).
- Types of products you are responsible for in production.
- Flow of supplies: where and how raw materials are obtained, and where finished products are to be placed.

A job description can be brief, or it can be very detailed. In any case your first responsibility is to understand completely everything the job entails.

Helpful as job descriptions are, many operations do not put them in writing. When a job description is not available you can create your own by asking specific questions that will

TABLE 17-4 Portion Scoops and Capacities

Number*	Level Measure	Ounces	Milliliters
6	⅔ C	6	165
8	½ C	4	125
10	⅜ C	3–4	100
12	⅓ C	2½–3	80
16	¼ C	2	60
20	3 Tb	1¾–2	50
24	2⅔ Tb	1½–1¾	40
30	2 Tb	1–1½	35

*Scoop number indicates approximate number of portions in level quart or liter.

TABLE 17-5 Common Can Sizes

Can Size	Average Net Weight*		Average Volume	
	U.S.	Metric	Pints	Liters
No. 10	6 lb (96 oz) to 7 lb 5 oz (117 oz)	2.72 kg to 3.31 kg	6 to 7	2.84 to 3.24
No. 5	56 fl oz		3½	1.66
No. 3 Cyl	51 oz (3 lb 3 oz) or 46 fl oz (1 qt 14 fl oz)	144 kg	2⅞	1.36
No. 2½	26 oz (1 lb 10 oz) to 30 oz (1 lb 14 oz)	737 g to 850 g	1¾	0.83
No. 303	16 oz (1 lb) to 17 oz (1 lb 1 oz)	453 g to 481 g	1	0.47

*Net weight on labels varies according to density of contents.

define your duties. Some important questions are

- What are my hours of work?
- What is my work area?
- What products am I responsible for?
- Who is my supervisor?
- Who are my coworkers and how do my responsibilities relate to theirs?
- How does my job fit into the overall picture?
- Where do I get supplies and equipment?
- Where are my storage areas?

Work schedules

Even though your job description outlines your hours of work, there is often another schedule issued periodically by management that details the work hours for each person on the entire production staff. Figure 17-1 is a typical example of a work schedule showing working hours as well as days off. In many operations this schedule is changed frequently.

Management spends a great deal of planning time to ensure that the maximum work force is available when the production commitment is at its peak. It is important for you to study the schedule whenever a new one is issued and look for changes that could affect you or your job. The very nature of the food business often calls for irregular schedules as well as last-minute changes.

Production assignments

The next kind of information you need is what is expected of you in a given shift or production period. There are several methods of communicating such information.

In a simple operation a verbal instruction for the day may be all that is needed. In a restaurant with a fixed menu, for example, the kinds of foods produced are usually the same from day to day and only the amounts to prepare will change. Management keeps sales-history records that provide accurate predictions of quantities needed for a given day. In some cases these predictions become a fixed weekly schedule. On Tuesdays, for instance, 200 portions of a certain dish may be needed, but on Fridays and Saturdays 350 portions

Weekly Schedule Salad Dept.							
Name	Mon.	Tue.	Wed.	Thurs.	Fri.	Sat.	Sun.
D. Conley	On duty	On duty	On duty	On duty	On duty	On duty	Off
J. Smith	8:00-4:30	8:00-4:30	OFF	OFF	8:00-4:30	8:00-4:30	8:00-4:30
B. Risner	8:00-4:30	8:00-4:30	8:00-4:30	8:00-4:30	OFF	OFF	8:00-4:30
J. Horne	OFF	OFF	8:00-4:30	8:00-4:30	8:00-4:30	8:00-4:30	8:00-4:30
D. Muncy	3:30-11:00	3:30-11:00	3:30-11:00	3:30-11:00	OFF	OFF	8:00-4:30
E. French	OFF	OFF	3:30-11:00	3:30-11:00	3:30-11:00	3:30-11:00	3:30-11:00
D. Odum	3:30-11:00	3:30-11:00	OFF	OFF	3:30-11:00	3:30-11:00	3:30-11:00

Date   2/5 - 2/11   Dept. Head   M. Parker

FIGURE 17-1. A weekly work schedule.

Production Sheet

Department ___Salad___   Date __4/15__

Product	Number Portions	Portion Size	Type Function	Time Needed
tossed salad	200	6 oz	banquet	7:00 PM
shrimp cocktail	200	4 oz	banquet	7:00 PM
thousand island	200	1½ oz	banquet	7:00 PM
cocktail sauce	200	1 oz	banquet	7:00 PM
Plus daily setup for a la carte --- 250 lunch --- 325 dinner				

Special Instructions

Dressings and sauces to be added by waiters before service.

FIGURE 17-2.
A production
worksheet.

may be standard. In many kitchens the cook's production instructions are simply a word-of-mouth communication of how many portions to make for the day.

Other operations may use a daily **production worksheet,** a work schedule for each person or each department. Such worksheets may vary in format but they always include all the information necessary for production—the food, the quantity (usually given in number and size of portions), and the time. They will also contain any additional information that varies from day to day, such as place needed and style of service in an operation having several dining rooms. Figure 17-2 shows an example of a production worksheet.

How production responsibilities are communicated / 455

Event Order

Person Making Reservation: __D. Jones__ Date: __3/11__

Address: __3311 Park Ave__

Date of Event: __4/15__ Time of Event: __7:30__

Type of Service: __banquet__ Guarantee: __200__

Billing Address: __3311 Park Ave__ Price/Person: _____

Room or Place of Event: __Regency__ Person in Charge: __D. Miller__

Menu

Shrimp cocktail

—

Tossed salad
Thousand island dressing

—

Roast sirloin of beef
Berny potato
Buttered asparagus

—

Orange sherbet

Rolls   Coffee   Iced tea

Open bar after dinner
for meeting

Room Setup

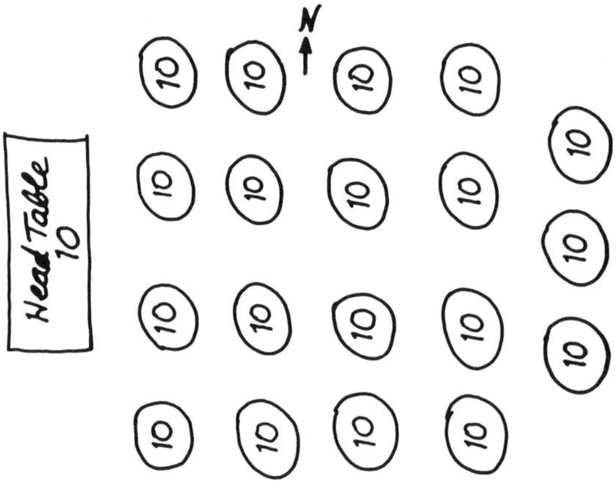

Head Table 10

N

(tables of 10 arranged in the room)

Special Instructions and Equipment

1) Have podium and sound equipment at head table.
2) Room decoration supplied by Jones Florist
3) Have two portable bars available for service during meeting after dinner. Should be available at __8:15__.
4) Price $25.00/person + 16% grat. + tax
   Drinks $3.00 ea.

FIGURE 17-3. A function sheet. Items to be prepared by the salad department have been circled for attention.

Another common method of communicating production needs is the **function sheet,** sometimes called an **event order.** It is an order form for one-time special events, such as banquets and receptions, at which a specific group of guests is served a specific menu at a specific time and place. A completed function sheet contains all the data the facility needs to put on the party, including the information necessary for kitchen production.

Figure 17-3 is a typical function sheet. Notice the many kinds of information it includes. Not all of it is pertinent to the individual cook. Sometimes you must look carefully for the facts that are important to you:

- Number of people
- Date of service
- Time of service
- Place of service
- Style of service
- Menu
- Special instructions

This method of communication is often used in hotels, clubs, and restaurants where special events are booked frequently. A copy of the original is given to each cook or department (and sometimes to both), so that nothing is garbled as it passes through channels, which can happen with verbal instructions or hand-copied information. The items the department or individual is responsible for may be underscored or circled.

The individual function sheet will not give you your schedule for a given production period. You may have to combine it with other instructions.

Specifications for individual dishes

The next type of information the production cook needs is the specifications for individual dishes or foods. Here again we have several forms of communication. The first of these is the standardized recipe. Figure 17-4 is one example.

Many standardized recipes contain additional information for the cook, such as preparation time, equipment to be used, people or stations involved in preparation, even photographs of the finished product. The cook should use all such data to maintain the controls necessary for good production.

You will notice that the example contains cost information that is not used by the cook. It is used by management in reviewing and projecting costs for control purposes. This type of standardized recipe card is a centralized record of much valuable data used by others. Use the card carefully and return it to the file as quickly as possible.

Many commercial operations do not use standardized recipes but employ skilled cooks who can prepare a standardized version of any common dish having universal standards, such as the dishes that form the body of this text. In this case communication becomes a matter of conveying the requirements for special house dishes or the special tastes, textures, or plate arrangements for standard dishes as made by that particular house. Experienced cooks can often learn all they need to know by tasting the product of the cook who is leaving. In other cases the house secrets may be conveyed by the departing cook or the executive chef. In any event, the skilled cook can produce a consistent, standardized product even though no written recipe is available.

Some small operations with fixed menus may not use standardized recipes but rely on verbal instruction and demonstration to teach new employees the dishes they serve. The cook simply learns the method of preparation and the basic ratios and proportions and converts these to daily needs.

Obtaining supplies

Getting the supplies needed to carry out the production assignment is usually, in one way or another, the responsibility of the cook.

Getting these supplies from market is a management function that is seldom carried out by the cook except in a very small operation. However, getting supplies to your work

Recipe for:	Thousand Island Dressing			
Yield: 5½ gallons			**Portion Size:** 1½ oz	
Ingredient	Amount	Unit Cost	Total Cost	Instructions for Preparation
Mayonnaise	4 gal	$5.21	$20.84	1. Chop onion, eggs, and pickle or use dill relish.
Chili sauce	2 qt	1.19	2.38	
Catsup	2 qt	1.09	2.19	2. Blend all ingredients thoroughly.
Hard-cooked eggs, chopped	30	0.08	2.40	3. Season to taste.
Onion, chopped	2 lb	0.11	0.22	
Dill pickle, chopped	2 lb	0.99	1.98	
Salt				
Pepper				
Lemon				
		TOTAL	30.01	
Special Notes:				

FIGURE 17-4. A standardized recipe. The recipe gives ingredients and quantities for the yield most commonly prepared in the operation. Some operations give figures for several yields if they are needed. Details such as pan sizes, mixer speeds, oven temperatures, and plate layouts may be given when they are appropriate to the dish. Cost data are used by other departments.

area is likely to be your responsibility. This may simply mean taking these supplies from a storage area such as the cooler or freezer or storeroom. Or it may require the use of a requisition.

A **requisition** is an in-house form the cook or supervisor uses to tell a storeroom or purchasing department what items are needed for the day's production. It is not only a communication tool; it is also a record of what supplies were used on a given day, who used them, and how much they cost. Figure 17-5 shows a typical requisition.

To use this requisition form you begin by recording the department and the date. You fill out the first three columns, listing all your needs for the entire day, and have your supervisor sign it. You then present it to the person in charge of issuing supplies. When you receive the supplies you complete the last column, either initialing each item or noting any variation in amount or kind of supply received. The cook is not responsible for completing the two cost columns or the grand total; these are completed by the issuing department. When you have received every-

458 / **Out of the lab and into production**

	Requisition for Supplies					
Department *Salad*				Date *4/15*		
No.	Item Description	Unit	Quantity	Unit Cost	Total Cost	Received
1	*shrimp 21-25c*	#	45			
2	*lemons 152c*	case	1			
3	*iceberg lettuce*	case	3			
4	*romaine lettuce*	case	1			
5	*cherry tomatoes*	flat	2			
6	*black olives 152c*	#10can	2			
7	*parsley*	case	1			
8	*cocktail sauce*	#10can	3			
9	*mayonnaise*	gal.	2			
10	*relish*	gal.	1			
11	*chili sauce*	#10can	1			
12						
13						
14						
15						
16						
17						
18						
19						
20						
21						
22						
			Grand total			
Approval *D. Paul* Supervisor			Received			

FIGURE 17-5. A requisition form as it might be filled out by a cook making the cold foods for the menu in Figure 17-3. Notice that the cook seems to have a few supplies on hand.

thing you ordered, you sign the requisition and return it to the department issuing supplies. When you sign the requisition you are assuming responsibility for these supplies from this point on.

In making out a requisition you must figure out what ingredients you need, in what quantities, for each dish you are scheduled to produce. You must also include supplies that require preprepration that day for use on another day. (You may be making congealed salads today for lunch tomorrow.) Requisition foods in terms of package sizes—a case of eggs, not half a dozen; a No. 10 can of tomatoes, not a quart or a liter.

Requisition only the products you need in the quantities you need that day. Check your own storage areas for unused supplies before requisitioning more.

In large operations the requisition form is absolutely essential. Data from completed requisitions become the basis of cost reports allowing management to keep close tabs on daily or weekly costs of supplies issued. They also aid in forecasting supply needs and in controlling quantity.

A word about kitchen paperwork

Still other forms may be used in particular operations to communicate information or to make requests. It may strike you that there can be a great deal of paperwork just to get food on the table. This is true. But where forms are used they usually simplify rather than complicate. For one thing, there is no doubt about information in writing. It is there to refer to if you forget something or if a misunderstanding arises. For another, information on a filled-out form is likely to be more specific and complete than verbal instructions. The printed form acts as a checklist for the person filling it out.

A third advantage of communications on paper is that they can be used as records. The standardized recipe is a record of a given dish as produced by a given operation. A requisition is a record of quantities, costs, and rates of use. Many forms also become records of

who was responsible for what on any given day.

This is not to say that every production kitchen should put everything in writing and keep it all. In many operations this would be absurd. There are even disadvantages to some of the paperwork for establishments that use it. It is expensive to handle and store. It can overstandardize procedures, stifling response to changing needs. It can create confusion if mistakes are committed to paper, if records are misfiled, if recipe cards are not kept up to date to accord with changes made in ingredients, portion sizes, or procedures.

These, of course, are not the cook's headaches. But you can make someone else's head ache if you don't respect the purpose of the written communication or the printed form, use it with precision, and fulfill the responsibilities it assigns to you.

PRODUCTION FOR DIFFERENT SERVICE STYLES

The way you carry out your production assignments will be influenced greatly by the style of service in the operation where you work. The service style will determine whether you prepare foods as individual servings or in bulk amounts from which servings will be portioned—perhaps in counter pans for the steam table or in bowls or platters for buffet service. This in turn will influence your choice of equipment and utensils, your timing, and whether you complete a preparation or leave the finish work for another time or another person.

For table service, some menu items—such as soups, roasts, braised dishes, baked potatoes—are completely cooked, timed to be ready shortly before serving time begins. Most vegetables are batch-cooked, with the first batch ready in the steam table at serving time. Hot foods are held in holding cabinets set at 180°F (82°C) or on the steam table in the service area of the kitchen. Some foods may be held in the refrigerator and reheated portion by portion as ordered, by microwave or some other method.

Other foods are cooked to order (a la carte)—hamburgers, broiled and fried entrées, grilled steaks, and so on. All foods are dished out by the cook or cook's helper in a specified arrangement on the plate, and the server picks up the plates and serves them.

On the other hand, in several styles of service all the foods will be served at once. In hospitals, for example, all the food is prepared in large volume. At serving time the hot food is reheated and the trays are made up individually to the doctor's specifications and the patient's order. They are delivered by moving belts or mobile cabinets to the hospital floor.

In banquet service too the food must all be ready at once. It is typically cooked in large quantities, then plated in the kitchen assembly-line fashion and delivered to the banquet in large mobile cabinets.

In cafeteria service the food is also prepared in large quantities—often cooked in the steam table pans from which it will be served. Salads are typically presented in large bowls that will be set on ice rather than arranged in individual portions.

Buffet service is the presentation of foods in volume from which the customer makes a selection. The cafeteria is really a type of buffet. Other familiar types are the luncheon or brunch buffet, the salad bar—usually a mini-buffet combined with table service for the main part of the meal—and the cocktail buffet. Beyond all these is the show buffet—usually the centerpiece of an opening, a fundraiser, or a diplomatic affair. It is typically a full meal made up of delicious, unusual, and often expensive foods artistically presented to create an air of elegance and opulence. The big thing is the show. Great pains are taken to fashion elaborately decorated pieces of culinary art.

For buffet service of all types, the food must be completely prepared and set up before the guests arrive. The whole production process is geared to this reality. Since visual presentation replaces the menu card, buffet production will include the final arrangement of each bowl or platter of food on the buffet table or serving line.

The necessity of holding foods on a buffet or cafeteria line is important in preparing them. The cafeteria steam table, which keeps foods appetizingly hot, also continues to cook them slightly. This is where bright-colored al dente vegetables are difficult to manage. Tender loving care and attention will put them on line slightly underdone, never, never overdone.

When the serving period or the serving lines are long, so that platters and chafing dishes are replaced several times, the finish-cooking of items that do not hold well may be staggered so that a new batch is ready just as the old one is running out. Nothing sparks the appetite like steaming-hot rolls fresh from the oven or a sizzling-hot pan of onion rings, with aromas to match the sight and sound effects. Foods with a particularly short holding span may be served in smaller dishes and replenished more often. Bring on the new pan just before the line would be held up without it.

Stagger-cooking takes good coordination between kitchen and service. Timing, communication, and good cooking are the keys to success.

In production for buffet service the cook must pay special attention to sanitation because foods sit for some time on the buffet table before being eaten. Even before it reaches the buffet, a single platter may have been time-consuming to assemble, so if you are not careful the foods you are working with may sit at kitchen temperatures until they lose their cool. Finished platters of cold meats and bowls of salad must be kept refrigerated until placed on the buffet. Foods in the chafing dishes on the buffet tables must be kept at safe temperatures, and so must hot foods waiting in the kitchen as replacements.

One problem of buffet production is how to achieve an effect of plenty for the last guest without having to deal with mounds of leftover food. Actually you can't avoid leftovers. But careful planning can keep them from being a problem. "Leftovers," said Carême, "must be used with caution, ability, and above all silence."

One way is to offer at least some foods that will store well for another 24 hours and have further potential for use. Roast beef and ham can be used the next day for cold platters, sandwiches, or hors d'oeuvre. Large blocks of cheese, wrapped carefully and refrigerated, can be reused the next day simply by cutting off the thin layer that may have dried overnight. A large molded salad can be used whole one day for decoration and the look of abundance, and be cut up the next day into serving portions. Chicken and fish can often be turned into casserole dishes or croquettes.

A second way to deal with leftovers is to throw them out. This is the proper treatment for any food that has passed its limit in quality—cooked vegetables, pork chops, dried-out foods, wilted foods, and anything that has already been reworked. Don't make soup from tired leftover vegetables, or add them to a casserole, or cover them with mayonnaise.

A third way of dealing with leftovers is to minimize them by careful production planning. Although production planning is not the cook's job, within your own sphere of responsibility there is much you can do. You can complete your preprepreparation according to the production schedule but hold off finish-cooking or setting up a cold platter until you determine whether it is actually needed. A blizzard or a hurricane might reduce your customers to a handful.

Still another style of service is tableside service. This is found occasionally in continental restaurants at the luxury end of the scale and is usually limited to the final preparation of such showy dishes as caesar salad, crêpes suzette, flaming coffees, or the finish-cooking of special sauced dishes such as steak diane. In this service the mise en place is set up on a movable table called a **gueridon** (gair-ee-don). When the dish in question is ordered, the gueridon is moved beside the guest's table and

the captain of a service team completes the preparation while the customer (and everyone nearby) watches admiringly. This is the territory of trained service personnel, but the mise en place will be prepared in the kitchen.

PLANNING YOUR OWN PRODUCTION

Depending on your job, your particular production responsibility may be large or small: it may be anything from washing vegetables or making sandwiches to cooking foods to order or preparing platters for an elegant buffet. Whatever your assignment, your goal is to work cleanly and efficiently to meet all your production deadlines.

Working cleanly includes order as well as sanitation. You cannot work efficiently if your station is a clutter of dirty utensils and waste.

Working efficiently means completing each task with a minimum of time and motion. Efficiency depends on good production planning and good setup.

Steps in planning

There are several steps essential to a good production plan:

1. Get all your information together. You need to know what is required in the way of *products, amounts, preparation methods, equipment, style of service,* and *times needed.* You will recognize the list from Chapter 3. Make it a mental checklist for planning.

2. Determine what supplies you need and how much you need of each, and make out your requisition for the day.

3. Divide your tasks into subtasks and arrange these roughly in the order in which you will carry them out.

4. Working backward from your deadline for each product, make out a time schedule for your subtasks. Rearrange the order of subtasks if necessary.

Planning a station setup

A **station** is any area set up with supplies and equipment in order to complete a production job. It may be a fixed station such as a broiler station or a grill. It may be a temporary station such as two tables put together at which several people are preparing salads in assembly-line fashion. It may be an area of variable size that includes the slicer and the counter beside it. It may simply be the place you put your cutting board and the parsley you are going to mince and the dish to put it in as you mince it.

Any place in the kitchen that is set up to complete a particular task is a work station as long as it is so set up. The term station is also used, as you know, to describe specific areas of a particular kitchen layout—the salad station, the sauce station, the vegetable station, and so on.

Where and how you set up a work station depends on the specific task. You may set up several times in the course of one production assignment. If you are doing canapés, for example, you may set up once to make croutons, several times to make different spreads, again to make garnishes, and a last time to assemble the canapés on trays. Clearly there is no one right way to set up that would satisfy all tasks.

There are, however, certain common elements in any setup that you must handle well in order to achieve efficiency. The two main considerations are

- The flow of supplies from raw materials to finished product
- The motions you will make in production

In planning the flow of supplies, you need to establish a layout that includes an area for supplies, an area in which to work, a holding area, and a means of keeping these areas free of waste and dirty dishes. In a la carte cooking you may also need a dish-out area. In a fixed production station such as a grill these areas are already laid out. In other situations you must lay out your own. In either case you need

to arrange your supplies and movable equipment in these areas in such a way that the supplies can flow into production and out again as finished products with a minimum of motion, like an assembly line in a factory.

In thinking through the motions you will make, consider both your hands and your body. You want to make as few movements as possible, reach as short a distance as possible, use both hands cooperatively (your right hand must know what your left hand is doing). Your body motions should be smooth, comfortable turns, with no bending or reaching in uncomfortable or tiring postures and no running back and forth. All your motions should expedite the flow of supplies.

To set up for slicing salami, for example, you will plan your supply area on the right side of the slicer, so that you can pick up your salami and place it on the slicer with a minimum of motion. To plan the salami arrangement you need to decide where and how you will remove the casing, whether you will slice the whole salami or cut it in half first, and whether you will need both hands to place the salami on the slicer. Your work area will include the slicer itself plus a stack of trays for receiving the slices. Beyond this you need a holding area for filled trays. To plan this holding area you must know whether your slices go into someone else's production or into the cooler, and you must decide how to get them there with a minimum of time and motion. Your total setup will vary with the counter space available, the amounts needed, and the flow of the product after it leaves you. Figure 17-6 shows one solution.

Setting up for mincing parsley is much simpler, since it requires no large equipment, but the principles are the same. Your arrangement of supply area, work area, and finished-product area should have a smooth flow from left to right or right to left, so that your motions are limited to getting the parsley with one hand, mincing it, and scooping up the product and putting it in the container you have set up to receive it.

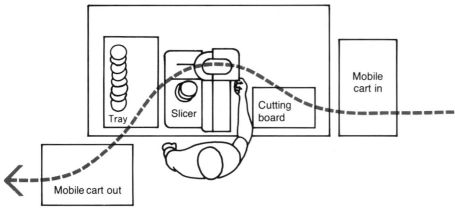

FIGURE 17-6. Flow of supplies in a production station. In this setup for slicing salami the flow of supplies goes from the mobile cart on the right containing whole salamis, to the cutting board, where the salami is cut in half and the casing is removed, to the slicer, to the holding tray, then to another mobile cart and out to another phase of production.

If you are making sandwiches in quantity you have a whole series of supplies and motions to deal with and a large number of finished products to be plated, wrapped, or held. Again your supplies and equipment must be arranged for a smooth flow. But before you can do this you need to think through your motions very carefully. What are the basic motions of making a sandwich? Will you make fewer motions if you make one sandwich at a time or several? If several, how many? Can you break down the motions into logical steps? How far can you reach to scoop up the filling or put a finished sandwich on a tray? How can you plan your motions so that you can use both hands to best advantage? How will you slice, plate, or wrap the sandwiches? How will you set up your supply and holding so that the bread stays moist and the tuna salad cold?

Sandwich production has been studied by efficiency experts and there are standard solutions for such problems. One of these is illustrated in Figure 17-7.

Setups for simple tasks are simple to plan, and if you keep in mind the two essentials—supply flow and motions of production—they will become almost automatic. In more com-plicated assignments that are new to you, the planning of your setup is well worth a detailed analysis of the task. The time you take to make a good plan will be saved in efficient production. In working out complicated or unusual setups you can call on the experience of your supervisor for suggestions.

Setting up for a la carte cookery
In a la carte cookery setting up is the key to production success or failure. A good setup depends on essentially the same elements and procedures as any other setup.

1. Efficient station layout for supplies, cooking, holding, and dish-out
2. Knowledge of production requirements
3. Analysis of the task and the motions necessary to complete the task in actual production
4. Efficient setup of supplies and equipment to facilitate these motions

Let's take a specific fixed station as an example and see how it can be set up to handle a hypothetical production requirement. Figure 17-8 is the broiler station of a steak-

FIGURE 17-7. How to make 24 sandwiches at a time: maximum production with minimum motion.

a. Cut packages in half. Place cut side down on tray, leaving bread in wrappers until needed.

c. Place a scoop of sandwich filling in upper right corner of each of the eight center slices (left-handers place in upper left corner). Spread with S motion.

b. Taking four slices of bread in each hand, lay out two rows across of four slices each, a row at a time, dropping off the center slices first. Then pick up four more slices in each hand and complete two more rows for a square of 4 × 4 slices.

d. Using both hands, close sandwiches with bread slices from outside rows.

Repeat Step *b,* placing the center slices on top of the completed sandwiches; then repeat Steps *c* and *d.* Then do Steps *b, c,* and *d* again, so that you end with four stacks of three sandwiches each.

e. Cut each stack of sandwiches diagonally with a single downward stroke of the french knife. Steady the stack with your thumb and forefinger straddling the knife.

(Photo © by Patricia Roberts. Remaining photos and sandwich method courtesy American Institute of Baking.)

house where several kinds of steaks—New York strips, filets, and top sirloins—are cooked a la carte to the specification of each guest. The work load is 350 to 400 steaks over a 3-hour period.

Step 1 is to *examine the station layout.* It is a fixed reality. Fortunately the layout of this facility is an efficient arrangement that allows the supplies to flow smoothly from supply area (refrigerator) to work area (broiler) to holding area to dish-out. The cook's body motions can be limited to smooth turns to left or right. You will not need to cross your own path as you use different areas. You are in luck. In many facilities stations were originally laid out for a different production goal. When the goal changes, the station has outlived its own efficiency, but the cook has to work with what is there.

Step 2 is to *determine production requirements.* Using your mental checklist, you establish the following:

- *Product:* 3 kinds of steaks (top, filet, strip) × 5 degrees of doneness = 15 possibilities for any one order
- *Amounts:* 350–400 total
- *Preparation method:* grill
- *Equipment:* grill, refrigerator, tongs, plates for dish-out, area for holding until pickup
- *Style of service:* a la carte (random ordering)
- *Times needed:* random

Step 3 is to *analyze the task and the motions of production.*

The task is to cook the right kind of steak at the right time to the right degree of doneness and deliver it to the right order—four hundred times. As you can see, there are several real problems:

- Random timing of orders
- Random selection of products
- Varying degrees of doneness
- High volume

You cannot precook. You cannot time the cooking. It is out of the question to keep track of each individual order. The task is complicated.

Now look at the motions of production. Reduced to their minimum, these are, for each order:

1. Remove steaks from supply area and put them on the grill.
2. Cook them.
3. Remove them from the fire and hold for pickup.
4. Serve them.

The motions of production are simple.

Step 4 is to *set up supplies and equipment for efficiency.* Efficiency = minimal error = the right kind of steak at the right time to the right degree of doneness for the right customer.

The secret is to set up so that all the cook has to do is concentrate on cooking steaks. No keeping track of which is which and for whom and when. There is a way to do this. If you divide the supply area into kinds of steaks, and the broiler and holding area into degrees of doneness, and place the steaks accordingly in each area, you don't have to keep track of anything. There will always be a steak of the right kind and doneness ready for pickup. It may not be the very steak you put on the fire when the order came in, but that does not matter.

Figure 17-9 shows the setup of each area. Here is the way you will use it.

In the refrigerator you separate the three kinds of uncooked steaks. No need to look around for a particular kind; you know exactly where it is. You put the highest-demand item in the easiest area to reach. This setup means that when a table order comes in you can simply reach in the refrigerator and get out the right kinds of steaks—two strips, one top, four filets, or whatever the order is—and put them on the fire.

You divide the broiler into five areas, one

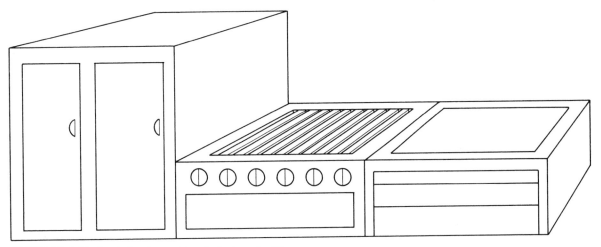

FIGURE 17-8. Broiler station for cooking steaks to order. The flow of supplies moves from refrigerator (left) to grill to holding area (right).

FIGURE 17-9. Setup for production.

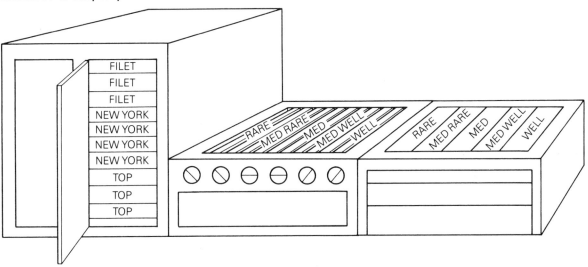

In the refrigerator, steaks are arranged on trays according to type, with the most-ordered steak in the easiest-to-reach position.

On the broiler, degrees of doneness go in order from rare to well done. Note that the two left-hand controls are set at high for the rare steaks, the two middle controls are on moderate settings, and the right-hand controls are set on low for slow cooking of medium-well and well-done steaks. The system can work with any number of controls from two on up.

On the holding area, degrees-of-doneness areas are laid out in the same order. First-off-the-fire steaks are placed in the front of their appropriate row, with others lined up behind. Steaks are plated in first-in, first-out order when the server picks up.

for each degree of doneness. You set the temperature controls for one end of the broiler on high heat for the rare steaks, the controls for the other end of the broiler on low heat for the well-done steaks, and the middle controls on moderate heat for medium steaks. You lay out your areas accordingly, with the medium rare between the high and moderate heats and the medium well between moderate and low. Now all you have to think about is putting each steak ordered on the right area of the grill as soon as it is ordered.

You cook all the steaks on the rare area to rareness, all the steaks on the medium area to medium, and so on. You do not need to keep track of the orders; whatever was ordered will be ready when the server comes to pick it up. You do not need to keep track of the kinds of steak; you can identify them by sight at pickup time. You just cook each steak on the broiler to the right degree of doneness for its broiler area, determining doneness by the feel method.

You also divide the holding area into degrees of doneness, arranged in the same order as the areas of the broiler. As each steak reaches the right degree of doneness for its area on the grill, you place it in the corresponding doneness section of the holding area. Within each section you place the steaks in the order in which they are finished, so that the first steak done is the first served—rotating the stock, so to speak. Again you pay no attention to the kind of steak you are handling. You don't need to.

At pickup time, either the order ticket or the server tells you the kinds of steaks being picked up. You simply set out the right number of plates, take the right kinds of steaks from the front of the right degree-of-doneness holding areas, and put them on the plates.

Any a la carte station has similar problems of random ordering, random timing, holding, and dish-out. Every station must be set up with the same attention to flow of supplies and economy of movement. In addition, many stations require considerable prepreparation. This is part of setting up the station, so that only finish-cooking and assembly remain to be done in production. Whatever the station, the way you set it up—your mise en place—will determine whether you have smooth sailing or kitchen chaos.

SUMMING UP

When you go to work in a production kitchen, your focus widens and you concentrate not only on producing good food but on producing it both efficiently and profitably. You become aware of what management expects from you, and you learn how your work fits into the achievement of management goals.

Three management goals set standards for your work: cost control, quality control, and quantity control. To help management control costs, you are expected to keep waste to a minimum, to make the best and fullest use of each product, and to work quickly and efficiently. To help control quality, you are expected to produce food that *consistently* meets the standards set by the operation. To help control quantity, you are expected to produce foods in the amounts specified—no more, no less—and to portion them accurately. To make the operation run smoothly and economically, you are expected to perform the tasks assigned to you efficiently and to meet your production deadlines.

The responsibilities assigned to you may be communicated through your job description and by work schedules, production sheets, function sheets, word of mouth, recipes, and special forms for special purposes. You in turn may communicate with others by means of special forms such as requisitions for getting supplies. It is important that you understand and use these forms of communication correctly so that you receive the messages sent to you and send your own messages clearly and accurately.

The way you plan and set up your own work is the most significant part of producing efficiently and profitably. Gather your information and your supplies, analyze your assignments, make yourself a schedule, and set up your station in the way that will provide the best product flow with the least motion.

When you realize all that goes into the planning of a single station setup, you can see that a thorough knowledge of cookery is basic to production planning of any kind on any level. Only the person who understands cooking knows everything involved in a given cooking task. The person who has mastered the basics of cooking, and who has learned and practiced efficient planning of individual production assignments, is the person who will make the most efficient production manager.

THE COOK'S VOCABULARY

production

cost control, food cost, labor cost

quality, quality control

quantity, quantity control

as purchased (AP)

edible portion (EP)

portioning, portion, portion control

production schedule

production worksheet

function sheet, event order

standardized recipe

requisition

production station

gueridon

QUESTIONS FOR DISCUSSION

1. In what ways does the cook's performance affect cost? Food quality? Supplies used? Quantities served? Describe any examples you have observed.

2. Pick a production task not discussed in the text, and outline the steps you would take to plan and organize it. Describe how you would set up a production station for this task.

3. In your kitchen experience, how good have communications been between production supervisors and cooks? How can communications go wrong, and how can they be improved?

4. Discuss the advantages and drawbacks of kitchen paperwork.

NOW that you know how to prepare so many different menu items, you are ready to look at the menu as a whole. You have no doubt, as a diner, done some looking at menus. Some of them are displayed in plastic letters above a take-out counter; others are presented on oversize fold-out cards that send your elbows into your table companions as you open one out to order your meal. You know why a menu is important to the diner, but do you know how its contents are chosen and how the menu functions in the running of an operation?

Historically the menu was written by the chef and was often a showcase for his own creations. This worked well in the private kitchens of aristocrats where money was no object and a meal was looked upon as a work of art. After the French aristocrats were beheaded or impoverished by the revolution, some of their chefs opened restaurants in Paris and continued to write menus built around their own culinary masterpieces. But even these menus were drastically modified by the necessity of making ends meet, and many of the restaurants did not long survive.

The tradition lingers of the master chef who writes the menus, creates new dishes, and runs his kitchen with his boot, and there are a few restaurants today that are built around the fame and skills of a particular chef. But they are not at all typical.

In this chapter you will discover that the menu is far more than a showcase for the creations of a master chef. It is, in fact, the hub of the wheel of every food-service enterprise, and its planning is an intricate process with input from all sides. After completing this chapter you will be able to

- Explain why the menu is called the core of the food-service operation.
- Define static, cycle, a la carte, and table d'hôte menus and cite typical uses of each.
- Explain the importance of the clientele in planning the menu.

18

Planning and Presenting the Meal

- Discuss the various aspects of menu balance.
- Explain the role of the budget in menu planning.
- Cost a menu.
- Design plate and platter presentations and plan buffet setups.

THE CENTRAL ROLE OF THE MENU

A **menu** is a list of the dishes offered for service at a meal. To different parts of the food-service establishment the menu means different things. To the production worker it is a brief description of work to be done. To the guest it is a written presentation of available foods from which to choose. To the operation it can be the difference between success and failure.

Each food-service facility has its own special menu or group of foods, chosen to fill its own needs and objectives. The hospital, the fast-food franchise, the resort hotel, the luxury dining room, and the little Italian restaurant on the corner have widely differing menus because their purposes are different. The menu expresses the character of an operation; it builds its reputation, good or bad.

The menu is the point of departure for all aspects of the business, the core around which everything revolves. It controls the purchasing and production; it provides the framework for the budget; it generates the income. In a new operation it determines the equipment and its layout, and may even determine whether a bank will finance the project.

Because of its central importance, today's successful menu is a carefully researched document prepared by management. There is as much input from the business side of the operation as from the food specialist, sometimes more.

Today a menu reflecting only the skills of the chef is a chancy document. The chef's input may be important, but it is only one consideration among many. A commercial operation will consult specialists in cost control, marketing, customer appeal. A hospital operation must have input from nutritionists and the medical staff as well as the business department. The apparently simple choice of what to cook for dinner is a vastly complex and intricately balanced decision.

Even a simple menu planned by the most skillful of menu writers is a venture into the future, like opening a new play on Broadway. Until it has been offered to the people it is designed to please, no one knows exactly how well it will all work. The proof of this pudding is literally in the eating.

Most new menus have some rough spots in the beginning. Customer response may be better than anticipated for some items and not as good for others. Food cost and availability of supplies can change overnight. One small menu change may require several others. The skilled person who originally wrote the menu watches it closely during its early days in action, analyzing the problems and continuing to make adjustments. Over a period of time the rough spots are smoothed out and a final document represents the essence of the establishment.

Though each menu is unique, the way each establishment goes about its menu writing is not so very different from one operation to another. There are certain questions all must ask and answer. If they don't, they don't last long.

Here are the most important questions to be raised and answered in the development of a successful menu:

- The kind of menu
- The kind of meal the menu is to cover
- The clientele: its needs, tastes, and willingness to pay
- Menu structure
- Menu balance
- Portion size

- Availability of products, equipment, and production skills
- Profitability
- Presentation

These and other considerations, such as style of service and number of people to be fed, are all interdependent. Each must be considered in relation to the others in order to achieve a workable menu. As we focus on each one in turn you will begin to see how difficult it is to isolate any one from the others.

KINDS OF MENUS

The term menu refers both to the list of items offered for service and the card on which the list is printed for the guest. Not every operation gives a printed menu to the guest, but every one has a written menu that it follows. It is the writing of this menu we will discuss. The guest menu card is a marketing tool beyond the scope of this book.

Static and cycle menus

Although there are as many kinds and styles of menus as there are operations, they fall into two basic groups: static (or fixed) and cycle (or cyclical).

A **static menu** is one that offers the same dishes day after day. Such menus are used by restaurants, hotels, and other facilities that have specialties to offer and a varied clientele. The static menu is likely to offer its dishes **a la carte**—that is, separately priced and often cooked to order.

A **cycle menu** is really a series of menus that are different from one day to the next for a certain period of time; then they reappear in the same order for an equal period. The cycle may rotate weekly, biweekly, or over any other interval. Thus a three-week cycle menu would have 21 different menus; on the twenty-second day it would start over again. There might

even be a different cycle for each season of the year—a cycle of cycles. Cycle menus are typically used in hospitals, schools, and employee food-service facilities that feed the same people day after day. They allow such facilities the luxury of variety within a controlled system.

The menu for each meal is worked out with the same consideration for content, customer appeal, production capability, balance, and cost as is given a static menu. Then each menu must be related to those preceding and following it. But once successfully planned, the sequence of menus functions just as effectively as a static menu does in controlling production and pleasing customers.

Some operations have a combination of static and cycle menus. Many cafeterias, for example, have a few standard foods day after day but rotate other foods on a weekly basis. In this way regular customers will enjoy more variety than a static menu would offer.

Choice, no choice, or modified choice

Some operations do not offer the diner any choice of foods. This is known as a **nonselective menu.** It is used in many school cafeterias, military feeding facilities, and hospitals. Airlines may offer only a choice of entrées, with the remainder of the menu nonselective. This does not necessarily make the menu writing any less complicated; it simply presents the basic concerns in a slightly different setting.

The **a la carte menu** is at the opposite end of the scale. On an a la carte menu each item is offered separately, priced separately, and selected separately by the diner. This type of menu is used in some commercial restaurants.

Many restaurants used a modified a la carte menu that groups certain parts of the meal together as one offering at one price. The two most common groupings are the meat–starch–vegetable entrée with salad and the two- or three-course dinner, priced according to the entrée. Within each grouping the customer selects from several offerings.

A complete multicourse dinner at a fixed price is sometimes referred to as a **table d'hôte** (tobbled oat) **menu** or meal. The phrase literally means "table of the host" and refers to a nonselective, fixed-price meal served at a specific time to all guests in a club or a resort hotel. However, the term is also applied loosely to restaurant menus on which prices are given for whole dinners, even though more than one such dinner is offered. In this sense it simply means the opposite of a la carte.

KINDS OF MEALS

Each meal of the day has special menu requirements. These tend to be dictated by habit, culture, and way of life. The traditional American meal pattern for away-from-home dining is a quick breakfast, a light noon meal, and a heavy meal in the evening.

The breakfast menu, for example, is a wake-up, get-to-work offering. Breakfast foods are usually eye-openers—coffee to widen the eyelids, fruit to spark the appetite, eggs and toast to fill the empty stomach. A hurry-up meal is called for—foods quickly prepared, quickly eaten. The American breakfast is traditional: fruit, cereal, eggs, breakfast meats, breads, coffee. Few menus depart far from these standard offerings. Brunch, in contrast, is a leisurely weekend substitute for the traditional breakfast meal, offering a much more varied selection of foods.

A lunch is usually a light, fast meal. The mainstay of the luncheon business is the working force. Typical lunch breaks range from 30 minutes to an hour, meaning that quick foods must be offered—ready to eat or quickly prepared, and easy to eat quickly. The content of the luncheon menu is far less traditional than the dishes offered for breakfast. In fact, variety is highly desirable, since often the same customers eat lunch at the same place day after day. These people,

who at breakfast were intent only on getting to work, are now wide awake and ready for a change. Imagination is a necessary ingredient in the writing of good luncheon menus. However, a complicated menu with vast numbers of dishes is seldom as successful as the careful selection of a few items that go well together and have customer appeal. Soup–sandwich, soup–salad, and salad-combination plates, omelets and other egg dishes, and diet specials are among today's luncheon leaders, along with luncheon standards such as the hamburger plate.

Dinner in the evening is the main meal of the day. The traditional American dinner has an entrée of meat, fish, or poultry, usually served with vegetables. It may be preceded or followed by other courses.

Unlike breakfast and lunch, the dinner hour is a time for relaxation and enjoyment. The need to hurry is gone. There is time to savor good food, time to travel far for something special to eat. The meal becomes an event, not just a necessity for survival.

Because of the special character of this meal many commercial operations devote most of their menu-making efforts to the dinner menu. It must attract and hold customers, since time and location are not the automatic advantages they were at breakfast and lunch. It must meet or beat the competition. The pressure for successful menu writing is increased by the fact that dinner foods are more expensive, there are more dishes in the meal, and fewer meals are sold per serving period because the meal takes longer to eat. The restaurant menu is typically printed on a handsome menu card; this makes change expensive, so the menu had better be workable to begin with.

CONSIDERING THE CLIENTELE

The people to be served are the most important consideration in menu design. They are, after all, the reason for each operation's existence.

Differing needs and tastes

In some types of operation you know quite well whom you are serving. A hospital serves patients, staff, and sometimes visitors. A club serves a membership with fairly predictable tastes. A school cafeteria serves students with limited time and money and hearty appetites. A highway restaurant serves travelers in a hurry. A big-city hotel serves conventions, expense-account executives, potential big spenders. A neighborhood cafeteria serves families who may dine there several times a week.

In each operation the particular clientele dictates certain things about the menu. In the hospital the primary consideration is the health of the patients. The menu must provide for three meals a day of a nutritionally balanced diet, with special versions for special needs—low-fat, low-sodium, liquid, and so on. The menus for staff and visitors will probably be spin-offs from the general patient menu. Although the patient may not have a choice of foods, the menu is still intricate in design because of the variety of special needs. In addition, the menu offerings change from one day to the next, so that the patients won't get tired of the food.

A menu for a school cafeteria would typically be a low-budget, nutritionally balanced meal consisting of foods most students like—nourishing foods easily served and quickly eaten. Specific offerings would depend on whether you were serving persons less than three feet tall, or college athletes in training, or junior high students in their hungry years.

A travelers' restaurant might have a fast-food menu limited to one or two types of entrée with optional take-out service. A club's menu will depend on the kind of club it is and the income level of its members. A cafeteria with a family trade will offer family-type meals at modest prices, with some offerings changing from day to day. A big-city hotel will have menus for three meals a day plus a la carte room service, and will typically have both a coffee shop and a dining room of some elegance to cater to the needs and desires of several potential clienteles. You can readily picture differences in such menus. (Can you also think how the various hotel menus might be coordinated for production efficiency?)

Less predictable than hospital, school, club, and traveling clienteles are the customers of specialty dinner restaurants. Many such operations depend on the once-or-twice-a-month customers, the out-of-towners, the special-occasion party. They are a dining-for-pleasure clientele, and the menu is designed to attract them and bring them back again.

How to attract customers is a riddle to which all food people would like to have a magic key. The answer is elusive and changeable. Restaurateurs must keep their antennae out, watch sales to see which dishes are popular and which aren't, keep up with changes in customer taste, keep track of the competition. It is this aspect of menu planning that calls for the marketing specialist.

Many of today's dinner customers like a food-and-atmosphere combination in which menu, decor, service, and perhaps entertainment carry out a theme—an olde English tavern, a European-style café, a Swedish smorgasbord, an exotic national theme such as Mexican, Polynesian, Japanese, and so on. The menu is designed accordingly.

The most successful restaurant dinner menus contain a variety of selections, including dishes of proven popularity. A choice between old favorites and unusual dishes—foods the diners would not cook themselves—makes it a pleasure for customers to plan their own menus for the evening.

Most customers, in fact, tend to be comfortable and happy with foods they understand and are used to. The new cook must remember this. New cooks have a tendency to try to make their mark in history by giving birth to a new dish—something different and unusual. This can get out of hand. Never forget that you are in a service industry. Your responsibility is to give the customers what they want. Set aside your personal tastes and dreams of glory and learn to know the customer who is paying for your food.

Customer tastes may be motivated by needs, habits, ethnic traditions, regional preferences. Working people may need fast foods because of limited time, or heavy foods because of physical labor and hearty appetites. Temperature and seasons of the year affect customer preferences. Cold weather requires more hot dishes on the menu, hot weather more cold dishes.

Different foods are in demand in different areas of the country. In the Southwest people lean toward spicy foods such as chili; in the Northeast they prefer blander flavors. Seafood is popular on both coasts; roast meat and potatoes and apple pie are chosen by Middle America. City tastes are different from small-town tastes, though the fast-food franchises are making us all more and more alike.

The cook as well as the menu writer must understand the styles and tastes of various dishes in different areas. Chili does not mean the same thing to a Texan and a Midwesterner. Milk shakes get thicker the farther west you go. You must take great care not to disappoint the customer's expectations.

The money for the meal

Perhaps the most important thing about the customer is the amount of money he or she is willing to spend. This immediately puts brackets around the kind of food the menu will feature. The family cafeteria does not have lobster and beef tenderloin on its menu, nor dishes requiring the salaries of highly skilled cooks. The federal school-lunch program requires a certain amount of protein in a lunch that typically sells for around 50 cents, thus reducing its menu choices to a very small number of entrée foods with inexpensive vegetables. At the other end of the scale, the well-heeled customer will demand every dollar's worth and expects a menu worthy of its high price tag in product quality, cooking skills, and presentation. Such customers will not come back unless they have experienced something on the menu worth remembering.

MENU STRUCTURE

Whatever the meal or the menu type, there is a common method of constructing a menu. The offerings are grouped into the courses in which the meal is to be served, and the courses are listed in order of service. The customer selects one item per course.

A menu may offer only one course or as many as 12. An eggs–toast–coffee breakfast is a one-course meal; a dinner menu in the classical French style may have as many as 12 separate courses. Most menus offer two, three, or four courses. The number of courses depends to a large extent on the type of operation and the clientele.

Breakfast

Here are some examples of breakfast menus:

Structure	Courses	Type of Selections
1-course	Main dish	Typical breakfast dishes: Eggs to order, served with toast; Eggs with meat, toast; Pancakes; Pancakes with meat
2-course	Appetizer	Fresh and cooked fruits; Fruit and vegetable juices
	Main dish	Egg, meat, pancake combinations
3-course	Appetizer	Fruits and juices
	Main dish	Egg, meat, pancake combinations
	Sweet	Breakfast pastries; Croissants with preserves

Many other variations are possible, depending on the operation.

Lunch

The types of menu structure illustrated here are typical of the luncheon menu:

Structure	Courses	Type of Selections
1-course	Main dish (luncheon entrée)	Light entrées: Omelet Sandwich Quiche Salad entrée Hamburger with french fries Spaghetti with meatballs Meat–vegetable plate (small/ medium portion)
2-course	Soup	Soup du jour and others
	Main dish	Light entrées
2-course	Salad	Tossed salad with choice of dressings
	Main dish	Light entrées
2-course	Main dish	Light entrées
	Dessert	Pie, cake, ice cream, pudding
3-course	Soup	Soups
	Salad	Tossed salad, dressings
	Main dish	Light entrées
3-course	Soup	Soups
	Main dish	Light entrées
	Dessert	Pie, cake, ice cream, pudding

Today's luncheon menu often combines on a single plate foods that are usually served as separate courses. You might find such combinations as soup–sandwich, main-dish–salad, salad–sandwich, or several salads. This saves the customer's time and provides the operation with cost savings and quick turnover.

Dinner

The dinner menu runs the gamut from the hamburger plate to the multicourse meal. Here are some examples of dinner menus:

Structure	Courses	Type of Selections
1-course	Main dish (dinner entrée)	Heavy entrée: Meat–starch–vegetable combinations (dinner portions)
2-course	Soup Main dish	Soups Meat–starch–vegetable combinations
2-course	Salad	Green salads, dressings
	Main dish	Meat–starch–vegetable combinations
2-course	Appetizer	Cocktails or hors d'oeuvre such as: Shrimp cocktail Suprême of fresh fruit Cherrystone clams Antipasto
	Main dish	Meat–starch–vegetable combinations
3-course	Soup Salad	Soups Green salads, dressings
	Main dish	Meat–starch–vegetable combinations

3-course	Appetizer	Cocktails, hors d'oeuvre
	Salad	Green salads, dressings
	Main dish	Meat–starch–vegetable combinations
3-course	Appetizer	Cocktails, hors d'oeuvre
	Soup	Soups
	Main dish	Meat–starch–vegetable combinations
3-course	Soup or salad or appetizer	Soups, salads, cocktails, hors d'oeuvre
	Main dish	Meat–starch–vegetable combinations
	Dessert	Pies, pastries, ice creams, mousses, sherbets, soufflés, cheeses
4-course	Soup	Soups
	Salad	Green salads, dressings
	Main dish	Meat–starch–vegetable combinations
	Dessert	Sweets and cheeses
6-course	Appetizer	Cocktails, hors d'oeuvre
	Soup	Soups
	Fish	Small fish dishes such as: Seafood cocktail Shrimp rothschild Fish pâté Poached fish
	Salad	Green salads, dressings
	Main dish	Meat–starch–vegetable combinations
	Dessert	Sweets and cheeses

The mainstays of the American dinner menu are the three- and four-course combinations. A few specialty restaurants offer as many as six courses.

Classical menus

An elaborate classical menu consists of many possible courses and is usually presented at the dinner hour. It is written for special occasions and usually does not allow the diner a choice of foods. The meal is the entire experience of the evening, lasting up to four hours. Writing a classical menu requires broad food knowledge and skill.

Here is a list of typical courses for a classical menu given in French and English:

1. *Hors-d'oeuvre froid* (cold hors d'oeuvre)
2. *Potage* (soup)
3. *Hors-d'oeuvre chaud* (hot hors d'oeuvre)
4. *Poisson* (fish)
5. *Pièce de résistance* (main course)
6. *Entrée chaude* (hot entrée)
7. *Entrée froide* (cold entrée)
8. *Sorbet* (sherbet)
9. *Rôti, salade* (roast, salad)
10. *Légume* (vegetable)
11. *Entremets de douceur* (sweet)
12. *Fromage* (cheese)
13. *Dessert* (small pastries and candies with coffee)

You are familiar with the first three courses, though perhaps not in this context. The fourth item is a serving of fish, either hot or cold.

Items 5, 6, 7, and 9 may puzzle you, since they all sound like what we know as the main dish. Historically the main dish was Item 5, the *pièce de résistance* (pyess da ray-zee-stahns), a large piece of poultry, meat, or game elaborately presented—a roast suckling pig, a saddle of venison. *Entrées* (on-tray) were portioned pieces of meat or game that had been boiled, braised, grilled, or pan-fried. The *rôti* (ro-tee) was another portion of meat, roasted, served with a salad. The *légume* (lay-guym) course (Item 10) is a vegetable. It would probably be served with the *rôti* even though it would appear on the menu as a separate course.

Items 8, 11, and 13 may also seem to overlap. The *sorbet* (sore-bay) of Item 8 is not a dessert but a light course separating two heavier ones. The sweet and dessert are considered two separate categories. Sweets are hot and cold pastries, puddings, and frozen dishes; desserts are small pastries and candies with coffee.

Menus in the classical style do not necessarily have all these courses, and the courses are not necessarily in the order given. Here is a classical-style menu that might be served today:

Hors-d'oeuvre froid	Oysters au Naturel (on half shell)
Potage	Consommé Célestine
Hors-d'oeuvre chaud	Croquette de Volaille (Chicken Croquette)
Poisson	Shrimp Rothschild
Entrée chaude	Tournedos Rossini
Entrée froide	Pâté of Duck en Croûte, Sauce Cumberland
Sorbet	Sorbet Champagne
Rôti	Saddle of Veal Oscar
Salade	Belgian Endive Vinaigrette
Légume	Tomato Clamart; Potato Château
Entremets	Charlotte Russe
Fromage	Cheese with Fresh Fruit
Dessert	Petit Fours, le Café (Small Pastries with Coffee)

Bread and beverages

All menus, whether classical or contemporary, one course or 15, usually include bread and beverages in addition to the separate courses, and some include wines. Such items are chosen on the basis of customer tastes and expectations and their suitability to the main part of the menu.

BALANCING THE MENU

Once the menu planner has established the kind of menu, the kind of meal, the clientele, and the menu structure, the next thing is to think in terms of specific dishes. The balancing of a menu is in essence the selection of its dishes in relation to one another. This requires a knowledge of what foods go well together.

There are several aspects of menu balance. There is the balancing of heavy foods with light foods, of spicy with bland, of light with dark, of soft with crispy or chewy. There is the blending and contrasting of colors. There are some foods that go well together for no observable reason, and some that do not, also for no apparent reason. There is nutritional balance. There is the goal of total satisfaction: a guest prefers to feel pleasantly satisfied, neither stuffed nor starved.

The successful balancing of a meal depends to a great extent on the amount of selection allowed the guest. In a nonselective menu it is possible to balance everything that requires balancing. Thus a hospital having a nonselective menu can provide a nutritionally balanced diet for its patients because it feeds them three meals a day. Hospitals that offer a limited selection of foods can offer alternative choices that fill the same nutritional needs. The nonselective menu can also balance tastes, textures, colors, and heavy and light foods. This is a matter for intensive study in preparing an elaborate banquet menu.

At the opposite extreme is the menu on which everything is a la carte—individually priced and individually ordered. Here the menu planner has no control over what the customer will put together to make a meal. The most the menu writer can do is to offer selections that make it possible—even probable—that the customer will put together a meal with balance.

In between is the menu that precombines certain parts of the meal for the diner. Its entrées, for example, are meat–starch–vegetable combinations that can be carefully planned for a good balance of tastes, textures, colors, and so on. The guest may then select from the appetizers, soups, and desserts offered. Usually the salad is planned in relation to the entrées, with the dressing the only selection to be made.

Let's look more closely at some of the elements of balance.

Taste

You want a certain amount of contrast in tastes so that one food enhances another. Here are some specific rules.

- Balance spicy foods with something bland. Notice that the hot curries and the heavily spiced foods of some Far Eastern cuisines are usually served with plain rice.
- Balance bland foods with something flavorful or spicy. A meal of roast veal, plain rice, and boiled zucchini would put the taste buds to sleep.
- Do not repeat items in the same meal. If tomato soup is served, don't serve tomato sauces or a tomato vegetable dish.
- Avoid serving foods of similar tastes together. Cauliflower, broccoli, cabbage, and turnips, for example, all belong to the same group of tastes.
- Avoid more than one fried item on the same plate. This is a matter of both taste and texture. Fried foods tend to have a similarity of taste when eaten together. The exception to this rule of menu planning is the popular fried-fish platter of the seafood restaurant.

Texture

With texture, too, balance means contrast. Every food combination should have something you can get your teeth into, but not everything should be chewy.

- Balance soft foods with something crisp or chewy and vice versa.
- Don't serve cream soups with sauce-base entrées.
- Don't serve sauces on breaded items. The sauce will spoil the texture of the breading. If sauce must be served, put it under the breaded item.
- Serve one starch and only one. Starches are similar in texture; they are also universally heavy.

These rules do not apply, of course, to situations in which the customers choose their own food combinations. A cafeteria line will offer several starches, and you might find a cream soup and a sauce-base entrée on the same a la carte menu along with other selections.

Color

Color in itself and the balancing of colors served together should be planned right into the menu.

- Put bright-colored foods on the menu. Don't depend on the cook's garnish for sprucing up a plate.
- Choose foods with color contrast for service together.
- Don't serve all dark or all light foods. The veal–rice–zucchini meal mentioned earlier would put the eyes as well as the taste buds to sleep. Pot roast and gravy served with beets wouldn't be too great to look at either.

The balance of light and heavy

Foods served together on a plate should have a balance between light and heavy items. There should also be an alternation of light and heavy from one course to the next—light soup, heavy entrée (clear soup with prime rib, for example); heavy soup, light entrée (cream soup with broiled fillet of sole). If you turn back to the classical menu discussed earlier, you will see how carefully this balance has been carried out.

The balancing of light and heavy foods is more than a convention dictated by tradition. The light food complements the heavy one when they are eaten together—like peanut butter and jelly. Balance also contributes to the pleasant feeling of satiety—not stuffed, not starved—that the diner should have at the end of the meal. It is doubtful that anyone could complete a 12-course dinner if the courses were not well balanced.

On an a la carte menu it is impossible to balance courses for the guest. But the menu can and should be written so that guests can achieve such a balance in their selections. A banquet menu, and any other nonselective menu, should observe this balance of courses.

Foods that go well together

Now look at some foods that are natural partners. Table 18-1 lists foods generally accepted as going well together for various reasons of balance or for the simple reason that people like them together. The table is meant for study and reference, however, and not as a rule of thumb. There are many unusual combinations of foods that have great appetite appeal as well as the excitement of novelty.

It is in the balancing and pairing of foods in menu writing that knowledge of foods and cooking is most important. Though the menu may not be left to the cook to write, it must certainly have input from the kitchen.

Nutritional balance

Establishments that feed the same clientele three meals a day must plan nutritionally balanced menus. Operations serving people only one meal out of three cannot guarantee that their customers will order nutritionally balanced meals, but they can and should provide a selection of healthful foods that make it possible.

What is nutritional balance? You may remember from Chapter 4 that, in a well-balanced diet, protein should provide 10 to 15 percent of the calories (energy), carbohydrates 55 to 58 percent, and fats and oils not more than 30 percent. The foods chosen should supply not only energy but adequate amounts of all the vitamins and minerals and enough fiber to keep the digestive system in good working order. In addition, certain foods should be avoided as much as possible: refined sugar, saturated fats (butter, cream, animal fats, egg yolk, shortenings, some margarines, coconut and palm oils), and too much salt. These foods increase the long-range risks of heart disease, cancer, and stroke.

How can these requirements be translated into menus? Experts in nutrition recommend that daily choices follow the pattern shown in Table 18-2. Balancing menus, then, becomes a matter of providing enough of the recommended items and avoiding foods too heavy in sugar, saturated fat, salt, and calories. Overall, the daily menu should provide roughly 2300 to 3100 calories for an adult male and 1600 to 2400 for an adult female.

The guidelines sketched in this table represent a day-in, day-out diet for good health. Unfortunately, this diet plan does not represent the current eating habits of today's typical Americans, who generally eat twice as much protein as they need, get 40 percent of their calories from fat, eat too much sugar and too little complex carbohydrate from the bread–cereal group, and consume far more salt than is good for them.

Too much protein is hard on the liver and kidneys. Refined sugar offers nothing but calories and is likely to be eaten in place of foods that provide needed nutrients. Too much sugar and fat of any kind are converted into body fat, and too much body fat is another hazard to good health. Too much salt can cause high blood pressure, heart attack, and stroke.

But today more and more people are becoming interested in following a balanced diet. When they go to restaurants they look for low-fat entrées, well-cooked vegetables, and meals

TABLE 18-1 Popular Main-Dish Menu Combinations*

Main Dish	Goes Well With . . .	Flavor Accents
Beef, grilled and broiled	Green vegetables Tomato Sautéed potato Green salads Fruit salads	For all beef dishes: Herbs such as thyme, rosemary, bay, basil Red wine Brandies
Beef, roasted	Braised vegetables Green vegetables Soft-centered potatoes Green salads Combination salads	
Beef, braised	Braised vegetables Pasta Rice Braised potatoes	
Pork, roasted	Green and yellow vegetables Braised potatoes	For all pork dishes: Sweet-sour Apple Pineapple Spiced fruit Port and madeira wines
Pork, broiled and grilled	Fruit (pineapple, apples, crabapple) Green and yellow vegetables	
Fish and shellfish	Lemon Rice Boiled potato Green vegetables Green salads	Herbs White wine Lemon
Poultry, roasted	Rice pilaf Dressing All vegetables Vegetable salads Combination salads	For all poultry: Allspice Curry Chutney White wine Port and madeira wines
Poultry, fried	Mashed potatoes Cooked salads Slaw Green vegetables	
Game	Deep-fried potatoes Fruit Nuts Green vegetables Tart sauces	Fruit Sweet wines Brandy

Lamb, grilled and broiled	Green vegetables	For all lamb dishes:
	Tomato	Garlic
	Sautéed potato	Mint
	Green salads	Herbs
	Fruit salads	White and red wines
Lamb, roasted	Braised vegetables	
	Green vegetables	
	Soft-centered potatoes	
	Green salads	
	Combination salads	

*This table was compiled from popular menu combinations served by Advanced Foods classes in El Centro College's faculty food facility.

that add up to good health. These people will not patronize restaurants that offer nothing but thick steaks, deep-fried foods, rich sauces, and desserts loaded with sugar and whipped cream.

In the past most restaurant menus have paid little attention to nutrition, but more and more of them are responding to nutrition-conscious customers. It is not difficult to adjust almost any menu to fill their needs. Add baked or broiled fish, chicken suprêmes. Offer smaller portions of leaner steaks (tenderloin instead of ribeye), baked potatoes instead of french fries, low-calorie salads and dressings. Serve fruits and angel cake for dessert in addition to your chocolate mousse house special.

TABLE 18-2 Essentials of a Balanced Diet

Food Group	Servings per Day	Main Contributions
Fish, poultry, lean meat	Two servings (3 oz/85 g each for meats)	Protein and fat (energy)
Eggs, cheese, nuts		Iron and other minerals
Legume–cereal combinations such as beans and rice		B vitamins
Fruits and vegetables	Four or more servings, including at least one good source of vitamin C daily and one good source of vitamin A three times a week	Vitamins
		Minerals
		Fiber
Complex carbohydrates:	Four or more servings	Starches, unrefined sugars, and some protein (energy)
Breads (especially whole-grain)		
Cereals (especially whole-grain)		B vitamins, iron
Rice (especially parboiled long-grain)		Fiber
Pasta (especially enriched)		
Dairy products: milk, cheeses (especially cottage and low-fat), yogurt	Two or more servings	Calcium, B vitamins, minerals
		Protein, fat (except skim milk products)
		Vitamin D if enriched

No one expects the cook to give up the egg yolk, whose talent for emulsification is so valuable, or the foods whose flavor, texture, and aroma depend so much on fat; it isn't necessary. Many customers deliberately choose a restaurant for its thick steaks or its classical cuisine or its hollandaise or its pastries. They may choose rich foods from habit or preference or for an occasional splurge. The commercial operation must serve its customers what they want, not necessarily what they need, or it won't be in business for long. It is the customer who makes the choices from your menu, but the healthful choices should be available.

Where nutritional balance must be observed, as in hospitals and nursing homes, the menu writing must include nutritional expertise. Certain other types of operation also feed the same people three meals a day every day—school and college catering services, prisons, the armed forces, cruise lines and resort hotels. While such operations do not need the same degree of nutritional knowledge as medical facilities, they must be able to plan nutritionally balanced menus. In fact, food-service personnel in all types of operations who have anything to do with menu planning need some knowledge of the nutritional values of foods.

PORTION SIZES

Not only the nature of the dishes on the menu but also the sizes of the portions must be established as part of the menu writing. Fixed and appropriate portion sizes are important for many reasons. From the guests' point of view, a good balance of the amounts of different foods is important to enjoyment of the meal. They may not be aware of portioning—portion sizes are seldom mentioned on the menu card, except for steaks. But a diner may be unhappy if there is too much gravy and not enough meat in an order of pot roast, or if the fruit salad–sandwich luncheon plate is mostly peanut butter sandwich with a dab of salad.

There is also the subtler measure of how the customer feels at the end of the meal. Suitable portion sizes can help to avoid the extremes of stuffed and starved.

Some restaurants are experimenting with menus offering a choice of portion sizes for the entrée, with a corresponding difference in price. Some also offer smaller-size portions for children. Many operations serve larger portions than they need to, and food is left uneaten on the plate. Food thrown away is profit thrown away. Smaller portions would have filled the need as well. Some restaurants will give customers doggy bags for taking home the food they can't finish. This shouldn't be necessary if the menu is well planned, though there may be customers who consider it a plus.

Portion sizes are important to plate layout. One more asparagus spear on the plate, or a smaller ear of corn, or a little more shrimp on a little less rice may make all the difference.

To purchasing and production, specific portion sizes are absolutely essential. They determine amounts of foods to be purchased and produced. The kitchen would be chaos without them.

Established portion sizes also make it possible to figure costs accurately and set suitable prices of individual dishes and the menu as a whole, as you will see shortly. Changing portion size is also one way of adjusting a cost/price ratio that is off balance, though it is not always the best way.

Finally, established portion sizes provide the basis for portion control. We discussed in the previous chapter how important this is in the management of both quantity and cost.

There are no absolute rules for portion sizes for every food and every menu. But there are some guidelines for quantities that represent general acceptability. Table 18-3 gives you suggested portion sizes for various foods. Notice that many portion sizes vary according to the meal, the course, or the time of day. A luncheon filet of beef, for example, would be 4, 5, or 6 ounces, whereas a dinner portion

TABLE 18-3 Common Serving Portions*

Breakfast

Eggs	2–4 oz (1–2 eggs)	50–125 g
Meat	2–4 oz	50–125 g
Fruit	½ C	125 mL
Cereal	¾ C	175 mL
Juice	½–¾ C	125–175 mL
Bread	1–2 slices (1–2 oz)	(30–60 g)

Lunch

Soup	4–6 oz	125–175 mL
Salad	4–8 oz	125–250 g
Salad dressing	1–2 oz	25–50 mL
Main dish	4–6 oz	125–175 g
Starch	2–3 oz	50–100 g
Vegetable	2–3 oz	50–100 g
Sauce	1–2 oz	25–50 mL
Bread	1–2 oz	30–60 g
Dessert	2–4 oz	50–125 g

Dinner

Soup	6–8 oz	175–250 mL
Salad	4–8 oz	125–250 g
Salad dressing	1–2 oz	25–50 mL
Main dish	6–8 oz	175–250 g
Sauce	1–2 oz	25–50 mL
Starch	2–3 oz	50–75 g
Vegetable	2–3 oz	50–75 g
Bread	1–2 oz	30–60 g
Dessert	2–4 oz	50–125 g

Hors d'oeuvre and Canapés**

Lunch, with meal	2–4 per person
Lunchtime, without meal	4–6 per person
Dinner, with meal	4–6 per person
Before-dinner reception	6–8 per person
After-dinner reception	4–6 per person

*Quantities given reflect general practice. Specific needs will vary.
**Average size is 1 oz (30 g). Total number reflects combined hot and cold items.

would be from 6 to 8 ounces. Sometimes restaurants will offer extra-large portions as a special feature, such as a 12- or 16-ounce steak on a steakhouse menu.

PRODUCTION CAPABILITY

In choosing specific dishes the menu writer must consider another set of questions. Can each dish be produced successfully, and can they all be produced successfully together? Three things must be available: the products, the equipment, and the production skills.

The menu planner must establish that the products to be used are readily available in the area. Though a restaurateur may have a burning desire to open a great seafood restaurant in a small Midwestern town, it could be difficult to get good seafood at realistic prices.

Many foods are perishable and seasonal. When such items are being considered it is essential to make sure they are continuously available. Fresh fruit and vegetables make good menu items, but it may be difficult to serve fresh strawberry shortcake in January.

Unless you can produce a product exactly as it is stated on the menu, don't state it. Seasonal foods should be added to a printed menu in the form of a flyer or insert that can be removed when the product is not available.

The proposed menu must be reviewed, item by item and as a whole, in the light of the equipment and labor it takes to prepare it. In a new operation there is the option of designing the kitchen to accommodate the menu. In an existing kitchen the menu must be producible with the existing equipment. Often an establishment will attempt a menu item that is too difficult to produce profitably with limited equipment. If you are given the responsibility of selecting items for a menu, be sure you can make them readily with the equipment you have.

The professional skill level of an operation is just as important to menu writing as its equipment capability. Complicated dishes that require special skills fit only in operations that

have the personnel with these skills. An added consideration in any operation is the spread of the work load among employees to take maximum advantage of the work hours available.

MEETING BUDGET GUIDELINES

The final test of a menu is whether it can be produced within the budget guidelines set by management. In a nonprofit operation the cost of all the food on the menu must be within the limit of so much per person, or per meal, or whatever standard management has set. In a commercial operation the menu must maintain the minimum spread between food cost and sales—at menu prices the customer is willing to pay. No sales, no restaurant. Sales but not enough profit, no restaurant. The unskilled menu writer can write himself or herself right out of a job.

Before a menu can be launched, then, both the individual dishes and the menu as a whole are carefully costed to make sure they can be served within the guidelines. **Costing** a menu means figuring the raw-food cost of each product as served.

Bringing costs and prices into line

When you are planning a menu there are two ways of working with menu costs. You can find out what you will be able to spend first and then pick menu items you can produce for that price, or you can decide on specific items you think will fall within the guidelines and then check them out.

Suppose you have been given a food-cost allowance of 30 percent of menu price and a sales-price limit of $5.95. To find out how much you can spend you multiply the *price* by the *percentage:*

$5.95, rounded to $6.00   menu price
           ×   0.30   percentage
              $1.80   food-cost
                         allowance

This means that the cost of raw food must not exceed $1.80 to stay within budget.

Or you can figure it the other way around. Take the *raw-food cost* of the dish as served and divide it by the *cost percentage,* and you come up with the necessary menu price:

$$\frac{\text{Cost}}{\text{Percentage}} \quad \frac{\$1.80}{0.30} = \$6.00 \quad \text{menu price}$$

Costing a menu

Because raw-food prices fluctuate constantly, menus are costed and recosted frequently. Consider the following menu:

Tossed salad
Thousand Island dressing
_____

Onion soup
_____

Prime rib au jus
Baked potato
_____

Pineapple sherbet

To cost this menu you begin by computing separately the portion (EP) cost of each item. You do this by costing the recipe for each dish, using the procedure illustrated in Figure 5-6. You figure the EP cost of each raw ingredient in a given dish, add these costs together, and divide the total by the yield to determine the individual portion cost for that dish. When you have the cost for each dish, you add these costs together to determine the total cost of this meal for one person. For example,

Tossed salad	$0.159
Dressing	0.111
Onion soup	0.327
Prime rib	1.926
Jus	0.048
Baked potato	0.166
Sherbet	0.283
	$3.020

To establish a tentative menu price for this dinner, you would divide the total cost of the dinner by the cost percentage as you did for the single dish:

$$\frac{\text{Cost of meal}}{\text{Cost percentage}} \quad \frac{\$3.02}{0.30} = \$10.06 \text{ menu price}$$

This might be translated into a typical menu figure of $10.25. Such a price would include a small allowance for cost changes.

The actual pricing of a menu includes many factors besides cost/price ratios, and the cost/price ratio used here is an arbitrary example of a budget goal. The whole subject of pricing is complicated and well beyond the scope of this text. What is important for you at this point is to grasp the mechanics of costing and pricing and to understand their importance as tools in menu development.

Checking menu costs

Costing a menu or a dish is also used as a tool of cost control to determine whether costs and prices are maintaining the minimum spread necessary to successful operation. Suppose, for example, that the menu we have been costing is one you have been serving at a price of $9.50, and you are recosting the menu to see if your cost/price budget ratio of 30 percent is holding. To find the current percentage you divide the *cost* by the *price:*

$$\frac{\text{Current menu cost}}{\text{Current sales price}} = \frac{\$3.02}{\$9.50} = \frac{0.318 \text{ or}}{31.8 \text{ percent}}$$

Your costs, you find, have risen above the 30 percent of sales that was your target.

When such changes occur, management may decide to raise the menu price, or to make changes in menu ingredients to reduce food costs, or to let the cost/price ratio rise. Sometimes popular high-priced items are allowed to rise above an overall cost/price percentage goal because their dollar return is high. A best-selling steak whose cost/price ratio is 45 percent still brings in more dollars than an inexpensive chicken dish with smaller sales at a 30 percent cost/price ratio. The right decision depends on the circumstances. The important thing to realize is that costing a menu and looking at cost in relation to dollar sales will give the facts needed to make the decision.

You can see that the costing of menus is an essential ingredient in the success of an operation. You can also see that the process does not end once the menu is written. In commercial menus the pricing is as important as the costing. Successful menus stay within budget guidelines, and successful pricing includes allowances for cost changes.

You can see too, by this time, why menu writing is not left entirely to the chef, no matter how skilled that chef may be in the kitchen.

PLATE PRESENTATION

The best-planned menu may falter and fail at the moment the food is presented to the diner unless the presentation is well done. A haphazard arrangement of food on a plate can turn off the appetite. An aesthetically pleasing plate can sharpen it. The menu writer should make plate layout a part of menu planning, while menu changes to improve a presentation are still possible. The look of the plate—the diner's first impression of the food on it—is a matter well worth the most careful thought and study.

But not all menu planners design plate layouts, and not every menu is planned with plate presentation in mind. Some a la carte menus, in fact, do not offer groups of foods together, and a plate's contents may not be known until the order is turned in to the kitchen. The look of the plate becomes the cook's responsibility.

Though the cook has less flexibility than the menu planner, many a cook has devised many an attractive plate presentation using only foods the menu dictates plus an occasional garnish. With a good knowledge of foods, some rules, and some practice, the cook is well equipped to do a good job.

It is also up to production personnel to see

that planned plate layouts are carried out with precision at dish-out time. Some of the remarks in the following discussion apply as much to carrying out a plate design as they do to planning it.

You have learned a good deal about presentation in making salads. Many of the same rules apply to main-dish presentation. In addition there are a few special ones. Let's talk about the following:

- Don't cover the plate edges.
- Keep garnishes simple and use only when necessary.
- Consider color and unity.
- Position all foods on the plate for the diner's convenience.
- Preserve the identity of individual foods.
- Plan portion sizes in relation to one another.
- Use hot plates for hot food and cold plates for cold.

The border of the plate should never have food on it. Not only should the layout be planned within the borders, but the drips of sauce or juices that might be spilled during dish-out should be carefully removed. Clean plate edges are mandatory.

Garnishes used properly can be profitable. Unnecessary garnishes are costly. To add a garnish simply because you feel you need to garnish everything is a useless and wasteful practice. Many plates do not need garnishes. If they are full and the foods themselves possess all the color necessary, a garnish simply adds confusion. Where a garnish is needed, it should be planned into the layout and its cost should be included in the menu price.

Providing color for a plate of hot foods presents more of a challenge than working with color in cold foods. Many cooked foods have brown and gold tones. Brilliance of natural color is often lost through cooking.

The careful menu writer plans the vegetable accompaniments for main dishes specifically to give color. Two yellow vegetables, for example, do not provide color contrast. When a yellow or red vegetable is served, a green vegetable will give the necessary color contrast.

When the menu writer has not considered color, it becomes the responsibility of the cook to add imaginative garnishes to give the color needed.

Unity is provided by the arrangement of food on the plate. As with cold foods, you want a pattern harmonious with the shape of the plate. The trick is to use food shapes and relationships to create this harmony. Keep the center of the plate in mind and work around it. At the same time you should balance the colors in the arrangement. Sometimes an awkward combination of shapes can be avoided by cutting the vegetable differently. Sometimes it is better to change the vegetable or to add a second vegetable or a garnish. This is a good reason for planning plate layouts before the menu is frozen on a printed card. Sometimes an oval plate substituted for a round one will solve the problem.

Look carefully at the plate layout patterns in Figure 18-1 to see how food combinations can be laid out to maintain unity and color balance. Notice how color and color contrast have been supplied either by the menu or by the addition of garnishes. The ingredients tend to rotate around the center of the plate, creating unity.

There are rules of service that may complicate the plate layout. The main dish or meat is presented directly in front of the guest, as the illustrations show.

When meat having a fat or bone side is presented, that side should be turned away from the guest. If there is no fat or bone there is no problem.

These rules force you to work with the meat in a more or less fixed position. It becomes your focal point, which is what you want it to be anyway.

Notice that the individual items in the drawings maintain their separate identities be-

FIGURE 18-1. Plate presentation.

a. New York steak, baked potato, asparagus, broiled tomato.

b. New York steak, baked potato, broiled tomato, parsley. Notice that color contrast is supplied by adding a garnish.

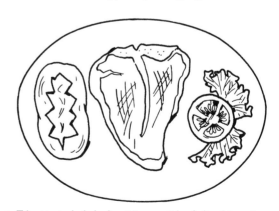

c. T-bone steak, baked potato, garnish of sliced tomato and curly endive.

Plate presentation / 489

d. Chicken stew in tureen, noodles, parsley.

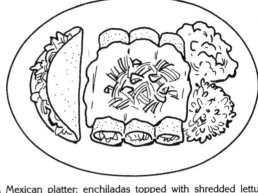

g. Mexican platter: enchiladas topped with shredded lettuce, cheese, diced tomato with taco, rice, beans.

e. Potato salad, sandwich.

h. Sliced calf liver with onions, noodles, sautéed pineapple rings, parsley.

f. Chicken kiev, rice, belgian carrots, asparagus.

i. Lobster tail, cup of butter, parsley, half lemon.

490 / **Planning and presenting the meal**

cause they are neatly arranged. You can further maintain identity by straining excess liquids from vegetables and using no more than the proper amount of a sauce that is part of a dish.

When determining portion sizes the menu writer should think of them in relation to one another on the plate, and the production crew should carry out the specifications to the letter. Otherwise it is possible for the wrong item to become the main object on the plate. Too large a baked potato could make a steak look like a garnish.

Last but not least, always present hot foods on hot plates and cold foods on cold plates. You can blow the whole thing—the days of planning, the hours and hours of production—by allowing a hot meal to be served cold.

BUFFET PRESENTATION

A good buffet sells itself by its visual presentation—the appeal to the senses that whets the appetite. It must be designed as a whole for continuous visual impact. Within the overall design individual dishes should be designed according to their position on the buffet.

Here are the main considerations that underlie the visual art of buffet presentation:

- Height, color, and unity
- Simplicity
- Lasting appeal
- An effect of plenty

Height, color, and unity

The concepts that govern the design of individual salads apply equally to the design of the whole buffet. Height gives the buffet stature and focus; color sparks interest; unity provides harmony and order.

Height is achieved in many ways. Built-up shelves or empty soft-drink boxes, suitably covered, are often used to add actual height. Tall floral arrangements, candelabra, and even ice carvings are used to lift the line of sight.

Color is essential to a good buffet, but it should be kept simple. Because of the great variety of foods on a buffet, the salad rule of no more than three colors is impractical; nevertheless food colors should not reach the stage of riot and confusion. There should be a sense of plan and order. This means careful menu design with color in mind and careful layout so that colors next to one another harmonize rather than clash, complement rather than cancel one another out.

Unity on the buffet as a whole means unity in the style of service and in the dishes and utensils. If elegance is the keynote, food will be served on silver, mirrors, and crystal, with silver serving utensils. A buffet for a German Oktoberfest party might use homespun tablecloths and wooden serving dishes and utensils. Platters and bowls should be similar in shape—all curves or all rectangles, not a hodgepodge of shapes and sizes. As with color, the goal is order and harmony. The appointments should complement the food, not detract from it.

Simplicity

Simplicity in everything is the rule of thumb in setting up the buffet. Each individual dish must be developed in relation to the whole buffet. Garnishes must be kept simple on such items as salad bowls, relish trays, meat trays, and hot foods. If every dish is overgarnished, the combining of overgarnished dishes multiplies confusion and clutters the buffet.

You can see this in the salad bowls in Figure 18-2. The one on the left is garnished with tomato wedges around the edge, nothing more. This presentation is simple. The bowl on the right is elaborately garnished with cherry tomatoes, black olives, parsley, and whatever else the cook could find.

Although the second bowl may be attractive by itself, when displayed on a buffet it is bad for two reasons.

- It is so outstanding it does not complement the buffet as a whole.

FIGURE 18-2. Simplicity. The garnish for the salad bowl on the left will still be there when the bowl is three-quarters empty. The one on the right will be a jumble after the first serving or two.

• As soon as the first person is served it loses all its beauty.

Simplicity can have interesting effects on the guests' attitudes. It is much easier to make choices from foods that are simply presented and easily identifiable than from presentations where design and color have taken over and the food is secondary. Timid guests may skip their favorite foods rather than spoil your platter designs, and then they'll feel frustrated with themselves and you.

Lasting appeal

It may seem impossible to expect lasting appeal in something that is being constantly diminished by hungry guests. Yet each person viewing the buffet and eating from it has as much right to have the total visual experience as the first person to pass. Remember too the guests at a buffet who wait in line gazing at the food while others are making their selections. You want their appetites to be heightened as they survey the display and plan their own selections. Poor layout and platters that lose their looks with the first few servings can easily take the appetite away.

A well-designed buffet will have elements and patterns that hold throughout service—its focal point, its height, its color, its unity, its overall harmonious arrangement of dishes and trays of food. Simplicity is important here. A simple layout will hold its pattern. It is easy to replenish. Platter arrangements of good, simple design will retain rhythm and color and focus when portions are gone. Even an empty tray will still function as part of the overall design.

An effect of plenty

A good buffet is always full. This will do more than anything else to achieve lasting appeal. Nothing is more discouraging to the appetite than a series of almost empty serving dishes. Good planners in cafeterias, restaurants, and all kinds of buffet establishments make backup platters, bowls, and chafing dishes and hold them in readiness to replace a dish that runs out.

Some tricks of the trade can create the effect of plenty without risking large amounts of leftovers. A plate inverted in the bottom of a salad bowl will make a modest supply look inexhaustible. Platters placed fairly close together give a look of abundance, whereas too much bare tablecloth between dishes makes the total offering look skimpy. Whole foods such as a ham, a whole fish, or a large salad mold may share a platter with serving portions of the same food; these pieces help to fill the plate visually even when the serving portions are almost exhausted. Displays of whole fruits and blocks of cheese from which the guests cut their own portions give a continuing appearance of plenty.

Presentation of individual dishes

Each individual platter, bowl, or tray should take its starting point from its position in the overall buffet layout. The part the dish plays in the overall design can affect the size of the dish itself, the placement of its focal point, the type and size and color of its garnish, and the arrangement of portions on the dish. When you arrange a serving dish for buffet presentation, you must always think of how it will be viewed by the guest and how it will look in relation to its neighbors and to the buffet as a whole.

Salads form a major part of most buffets. They are usually presented in large bowls. These in turn are set on a bed of ice, as in the typical cafeteria, or with each salad bowl set in a larger bowl containing ice, as on a typical buffet. Congealed salads are often made in large molds of decorative shapes and presented on well-chilled platters laid on ice. Ring molds are popular, with a bowl of dressing or a contrasting garnish in the center.

Each salad bowl should have its simple garnish to complement the food or accent it. The most successful is a row of a suitable garnish arranged around the edge of the bowl (Figure 18-2). Helpings of the salad will be taken mostly from the middle of the bowl, especially if it is mounded to begin with, so chances are good that the ring of garnish will remain relatively unspoiled. For a coleslaw, for example, you might stand a row of overlapping pineapple slices along the rim. You might ring a bowl of potato salad with halves of hard-cooked eggs, a bowl of mixed-fruit salad with a single row of whole strawberries.

Salad dressings should be placed near the salads they are to dress. If this detail is left to someone who does not understand foods, you may have guests eating apricot glaze on a green salad and vinaigrette on a bavarian cream.

Cold meats and vegetables, canapés and hors d'oeuvre, and many baked desserts are typically arranged in serving portions on flat serving dishes such as platters, trays, and mirrors. Some basic rules of presentation apply to all.

The basic design of a platter is a matter of using lines or rows of foods to create a simple, rather formal pattern. The rim of the platter is the frame of your design. Keep the food patterns within the rim. Not only does this look better, but it makes for easier service and fewer spills.

Once again in platter design you meet the basics of height, unity, and simplicity. On a platter, height may be something that is physically higher than the rest of the platter or it may be implied height. The function of height is to give focus. You can supply height in several ways. You can use an unportioned piece of a food as a background to arranged portions of the same food, such as a piece of a whole ham on a platter of sliced ham. Or you can use a bowl of cold sauce, or a simple garnish such as parsley, or a cluster of small garnishes of a strong contrasting color—black olives, for example. Whatever it is, it should provide the focal point of your design.

You may have encountered the following problem before:

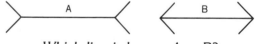

Which line is longer, A or B?

The answer is that they are the same length. Line A looks longer because the angles at each end carry the eye outward. The angles on B hold the eye to a smaller dimension.

Thus the eye can be made to flow in the direction desired. By using patterns consisting of curves or lines that carry the **eye flow** in the direction you want it to go, you can make platters both interesting and effective.

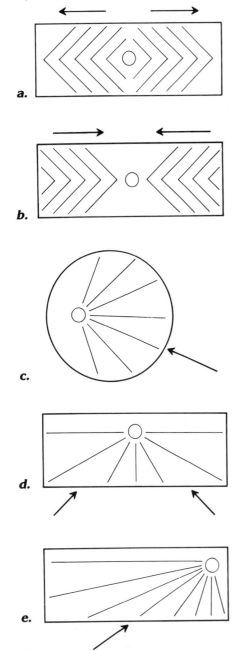

FIGURE 18-3. Eye flow. The eye follows the lines. Eye flow gives a flat design the illusion of height when the eye follows lines to a single point as in *b, c, d,* and *e*. Eye flow does nothing for *a,* because the eye does not focus on the center point but is led away.

a.

b.

c.

d.

e.

Examine the patterns in Figure 18-3. Notice how, in all the figures but *a*, the tendency is for the eye to flow toward the circle. In *a* the eye flows away. The effect is to sharpen the design in *b, c, d,* and *e* and to dissipate or flatten it in *a*.

In designing a platter, then, establish a focal point and lay out lines that cause the eye to flow to and from that point to create balance and height. Even if your focal point is physically as flat as the rest of the platter, eye flow will create the illusion of height.

Unity means the same thing in platter arrangement as it does in salads. The lines of your design—that is, your rows of food—should relate to the shape of the platter (Figure 18-4). On a round plate they may be curves of a circle, or radiating spokes of a pinwheel, or S curves, or straight lines whose length and arrangement are fitted into the roundness. On a rectangular platter straight or angled lines are harmonious with the shape. So are repeating curves that fit the shape neatly and fill it visually. The portions of food should be uniform in shape and size for a crisp, clean, linear look in your design.

Simplicity of design is important. The pattern should be straightforward and repetitive. This not only gives a pleasing rhythmic look but maintains the basic design while the food is disappearing from the platter.

The position of the platter on the table, plus the direction of traffic flow, will determine where you place your platter's focal point. Plan your presentation from the point of view of the guests as they first see it. Then you can plan your eye flow accordingly. In Figure 18-5, for example, the traffic is approaching from the left and the platter is angled toward the guest. The focal point is placed at the back of the platter, and the rows of food are arranged to face toward the guest and draw the eye toward the focal point.

Another factor to consider is the shape of the food items. You want to angle their best features toward the guest. For example, you would usually arrange wedge-shaped pieces

FIGURE 18-4. Unity. Simple line patterns that accentuate platter shape give unity to each design.

so that the high back of the wedge is away from the guest and the triangular shape slopes forward. Likewise you would layer rows of sliced foods, such as cold meats, so that the layers face the guests.

Sometimes a platter is positioned so that it is seen from all sides. You would then place your focal point in the center and work outward instead of from the corners or back line of the platter and buffet table.

No matter how you plan your design, the platter must be easy to serve. If getting a portion off the platter disrupts either the whole arrangement or the guest's composure, you have defeated the entire purpose of your display.

The professionally designed platter in Figure 18-5 was a prizewinner in a culinary competition. Notice how the skilled specialist follows the simple basic principles of any buffet or platter presentation. Of course the person who can do show work has added the mastery of advanced techniques and long experience, plus hours and sometimes days of labor for a single piece. But the techniques, experience, and labor are of little value without the basic principles. And these you can apply right now with simple foods using techniques you have already mastered.

Presentation of hot foods

Most hot foods on the buffet are served from chafing dishes. Whenever possible, hot foods are arranged in portions. This not only looks attractive and makes service easy; it also provides some degree of portion control for these more expensive items. Often hot foods are served by staff, even when the rest of the buffet is serve-yourself. This also helps in controlling portion size.

The fact is that hot foods are difficult to present visually. For appetite appeal they depend more on their aroma and their reputation than they do on their natural beauty. They are not easily garnished for buffet service: parsley wilts, and most of the other colorful garnishes used on cold foods do not go well with hot foods or, like parsley, lose their freshness with continued heat. Occasionally chopped parsley is successful, or slices of parsleyed lemon with fish, or glazed fruits with ham or pork, or pimiento with vegetables or rice, or a bright cheese topping or buttery brown crumbs on a casserole. But in general garnishes on chafing dishes begin to look tired very quickly.

However, most hot foods do not need a great deal of attention to visual presentation. If they look as they should—fresh, hot, the fried chicken crisp, the asparagus plump and green, the rice light and fluffy, the baked potatoes mealy-white—they sell themselves.

FIGURE 18-5. Hors d'oeuvre parisienne—a simple, straightforward design. Rows of beef medallions are interspersed with rows of complementary food portions—stuffed artichoke bottoms, tomato cases filled with asparagus, stuffed eggs. The fat sculpture provides focus and height. Its classic look blends with the simplicity of the tray design, yet softens the tray's repetitive regularity. Presentation on a mirror heightens the effect of simple elegance. (Photo by James C. Goering.)

SUMMING UP

The menu is the hub of the food-service enterprise. It controls the purchasing and production, provides the framework for the budget, and generates the income. It expresses the character of the establishment and builds its reputation and its clientele. Though the chef's input is essential, its objectives, its character, and its budget are developed by management.

Many factors go into the planning of a successful menu. The kind of menu is important—whether static or cycle, selective or nonselective. The kind of meal is important—breakfast, lunch, dinner, brunch. The clientele is especially important—their habits and tastes, what they are looking for, what they will spend. The menu structure is important—the number and kinds of courses to be offered. Balance is important in the menu as a whole and in the individual dishes—balance of tastes, textures, colors, light and heavy foods, go-together foods, portion sizes. Production capability is important—the equipment, skills, and products necessary to produce the meal.

The cost of the food on the menu is perhaps the most important factor of all. Can it be sold at menu prices that will meet budget guidelines and produce a profit? The final moment of truth is in presenting the meal to the diner. Will the visual presentation excite the appetite and please the guest?

The more you learn about menus, the better off you will be, whether you are headed for a management position or advanced culinary studies. You can learn a great deal by studying the menus of successful operations. If you can analyze what makes them work well, they will teach you more than you can learn from books.

Menu planning brings our study of food preparation full circle. In visiting kitchens in Chapter 1 you saw how equipment and layout and stations and staff differ according to the menu of each operation. As you progressed through this text learning how to cook different foods and make different dishes, you also learned how to prepare the major types of menu items—appetizers, soups, salads, main dishes, vegetables, breakfast items, beverages, desserts. Now you have a good understanding of how they all go together to make customer-pleasing meals. You may well be on your way to a very successful career!

THE COOK'S VOCABULARY

menu

static menu, cycle menu

a la carte menu, table d'hôte menu, nonselective menu

menu balance

costing, cost percentage

presentation, height, color, unity, eye flow

QUESTIONS FOR DISCUSSION

1. What is meant by the statement that the menu is the hub of the food-service enterprise? Give details.

2. Why doesn't the chef have charge of menu planning in the typical food-service enterprise?

3. What is the contribution of the chef to menu planning? What are the goals and limiting factors for the chef's input?

4. Why is presentation important? What are the essentials in a successful plate or buffet layout?

Glossary

Acid A term applying to certain chemical characteristics of foods. The opposite of acid is alkaline, and the degree of acidity or alkalinity is expressed by the chemical symbol pH and measured on a scale of pH 0 to pH 14, with 0 being most acid and 14 most alkaline. A pH of 7 is neutral, below 7 is acid, and above 7 is alkaline. Lemon and vinegar are highly acid foods; baking soda is the most familiar example of an alkaline food substance. Acid foods taste sharp, tart, or sour. Acidity and alkalinity can affect cooking outcomes, changing colors, textures, and nutritive values. Acid foods can cause protein to coagulate, as in the curdling of milk.

Aging Holding of meats over a period of time long enough for enzymatic action to tenderize them.

A la carte (ah la kart) (1) Cooking: Cooked to the order. (2) Menu: A menu on which each item is offered separately, priced separately, and selected separately by the diner.

À la meunière (ah la mun-yair, meaning "in the style of the miller") Dredged, pan-fried, served with brown butter, lemon juice, and chopped parsley.

Al dente (ahl den'-tay) Firm to the bite, crisp-tender; an Italian term referring originally to pasta, now applied broadly, especially to vegetables.

Alkaline A term referring to certain chemical characteristics of foods; the opposite of acid. See **Acid.**

Allemande (alla-mahnd) German style.

Amandine (ah-mahn-deen), also **almondine** Made or garnished with almonds.

Anglaise (ahn-glez) English style, usually boiled.

Anthocyanins: Pigments in red vegetables; red in an acid medium, changing to blue or purple in an alkaline medium.

Antipasto (ann-tee-pahs'-toe, Italian for "before the pasta") A small plate or tray of flavorful bite-size cold foods such as smoked oysters, olives, marinated vegetables, spicy cold meats, fish, shellfish, cheese.

AP As purchased, referring to a product as it comes from the purveyor before it undergoes any processing.

Appetizer A bite-size piece or small portion of food served to stimulate the appetite.

Arrowroot A starch from the root of a tropical plant; used as a thickening agent.

Aspic (ass-pik) (1) Powdered meat-flavored gelatin. (2) Plain or colored jellied aspic, often used in decorating cold foods. (3) A cold dish consisting of ingredients bound in jellied aspic.

Au gratin (oh grat'-un) Having a glazed or crusty top surface, especially a sauced food topped with bread crumbs or cheese and baked in a hot oven or glazed under the broiler.

Au jus (oh zhue)   Served with its natural juices, which are usually mixed with stock and enriched by simmering with a mirepoix.

Bacteria   Microscopic organisms, some of which can produce food-borne disease; others cause fermentation, both desirable and undesirable.

Bacterial growth range   Temperatures between 40 and 140°F (4–60°C), known as the **danger zone.**

Bain-marie (ban′-ma-ree′)   Vat of hot water kept at 180°F (82°C), or thereabouts, for holding hot liquids such as soups or sauces in readiness for service.

Bake   To cook by heated air in an enclosed area called an oven.

Baker's percentages   A system for expressing ratios of ingredients in baking formulas: the weight of the flour is always 100%, and the weight of each other ingredient is expressed as a percentage of the weight of the flour.

Baking powder   A chemical leavener composed of baking soda and an acid; it releases carbon dioxide gas in the presence of moisture and heat.

Baking soda (sodium bicarbonate)   An alkaline chemical leavener; it releases carbon dioxide in the presence of moisture and acid.

Banquet chef   Person responsible for coordinating food production for all special events.

Barbecue   To slow-roast a product at low heat in or over a pit infused with smoke to add flavor.

Bard   To cover meat with a layer of fat for cooking.

Barquette (bar-ket′)   A small boat-shaped pastry shell used for hors d'oeuvre.

Base, meat or **soup**   A convenience product made by cooking a stock down to a thick gelatin concentrate and adding salt and other preservatives.

Base, sauce   A convenience product containing both flavoring and thickening for making a sauce.

Basic sauce   An unseasoned sauce used for making one or more finished sauces.

Baste   To pour drippings or liquid over a food before or during cooking.

Batch-cook   To cook in small amounts as needed for service; to stagger-cook.

Batonnet   A precision cut ¼″ × ¼″ × 3″ (6 mm × 6 mm × 8 cm).

Batter   A semiliquid mixture of flour, liquid, and eggs, used to make cakes, cookies, and quick breads or as a coating for foods to be fried. **To batter** is to coat with batter for frying. A **drop batter** is a semiliquid batter, often rough-textured or lumpy. A **pour batter** is one having a low ratio of flour to liquid that can be poured easily in a steady stream.

Bavarian cream   A dessert made of custard mixed with gelatin, whipped cream, and flavor ingredients.

Béarnaise (bare-naze or bay-er-nez)   A butter sauce made with an emulsion of egg yolks, clarified butter, and a reduction containing tarragon and other finely minced herbs, unstrained.

Beat   To move a paddle, whip, or spoon back and forth to blend foods together or to achieve a smooth texture.

Béchamel (bay-sha-mel or besh-a-mel)   A white sauce made by thickening milk with white roux. Basic béchamel is one of the five mother sauces.

Beurre manié (burr man-yay—literally, worked or kneaded butter)   A thickening agent of butter and flour in a 1-to-1 ratio by weight, made by kneading ingredients together to form a paste.

Beurre noir (burr nwahr—literally, black butter)   Butter cooked until it is dark brown, or just short of burned.

Beurre noisette (burr nwah-zet)   Brown butter or nut butter; butter cooked gently to a golden brown.

Bind   To cause a mixture of two or more ingredients to cohere as a homogeneous product, usually by adding a binding agent such as starch or gelatin.

Bisque (bisk)   A thickened shellfish soup.

Blanch   To plunge into boiling liquid and cook 10 to 20 percent of doneness.

Blanquette (blahn-ket)   A braised dish made with white meat and a white sauce.

Blend   To mix two or more ingredients so completely that they lose their separate identities.

Blond sauce   A sauce made by thickening a light stock with blond roux; a velouté. A basic velouté is one of the five mother sauces.

Body   That quality of a dish providing its substance and volume; physical substance plus strength or richness of flavor.

Boil   To cook a product submerged in a boiling liquid. The body of a boiling liquid is in turmoil; its surface is agitated and rolling. Its temperature is a constant 212°F (100°C) at sea level.

Boiled dressing   A cooked salad dressing with little or no oil, made by thickening milk or fruit juices with starch or eggs or both.

Boiling point   The point at which a liquid bubbles and turns to vapor. The boiling point of pure distilled water is 212°F (100°C) at standard atmospheric pressure (the pressure exerted by the atmosphere at sea level). The higher the altitude, the lower the atmospheric pressure and therefore the lower the boiling point.

Bone   To remove flesh from the bone or bones from flesh.

Botulism (botch-a-lizm)   A food-borne disease caused by a family of bacteria that produce deadly toxins in nonacid foods in the absence of air; usually associated with improperly processed canned goods.

Bouchée (bou-shay)   A round puff-pastry shell.

Bouillon (bull-yon)   Seasoned stock.

Bouillon cubes, bouillon powders   Convenience products made from dehydrated finished bouillons.

Bouquet garni (boo-kay gar-nee—literally, garnished bouquet)   (1) Classically, sprigs of parsley, bay leaf, and thyme, tied together in a bundle with string, often with a celery rib; used as a flavor builder in stocks, soups, and sauces. (2) Any aromatic vegetable–herb–spice combination so used.

Bouquetière (boo-ket-yair)   A selection of three or more vegetables to accompany an entrée.

Braise (brayz)   To cook food at low heat with a small to moderate amount of liquid in a covered container.

Breading   A coating for a product to be fried, usually consisting of a coat of crumbs on top of a coat of egg wash on top of a coat of flour, a three-step process known as **standard breading procedure.**

Break down   (1) To divide—for example, to cut a meat carcass into smaller cuts. (2) To disassemble—for example, to take apart a display platter after the buffet line has closed and store or dispose of the remaining food.

Brigade de cuisine (bree-gahd de kwee-zeen)   Crew or team of chefs, station heads, cooks, and helpers in a classically organized kitchen.

Brine   Heavily salted solution for pickling or corning foods.

Brochette (bro-shet)   A small skewer. Foods **en brochette** are usually bite-size pieces of meat and vegetables cooked and served "on the spear."

Broil   To cook by direct heat from above, a radiant-heat process.

Broiler   A tender young bird of either sex. Chicken broilers are also called **fryers.**

Broth   The liquid in which a food, usually flesh or vegetable, has been cooked.

Brown sauce   A sauce made by thickening a dark stock with brown roux or cornstarch.

Brunoise (broon-wahz)   (1) A cube-shaped cut ⅛" (3 mm) in size; fine dice.

Butter   A fat derived from the creamy part of milk. **Brown butter** is whole melted butter cooked gently until golden brown; *beurre noisette*. **Clarified butter** is liquid butterfat separated from the water and solids in ordinary butter. A **compound butter** is a blend of softened butter and one or more puréed or finely chopped ingredients.

Simple butter is heated butter with no added ingredients, used in the role of a sauce. **Sweet butter** is unsalted butter.

Butterfly fillets or **butterflied fish**   Fillets from both sides of a fish connected by a strip of flesh.

Butter sauce   A sauce made by emulsifying egg yolks and butter.

Calorie (kal-a-ree)   A unit that measures the energy value of a food. If you consume more calories than you expend in energy, your body stores the excess in fat.

Canapé (can-a-pay)   A bite-size or two-bite-size finger food consisting of a base, a spread or topping, and a garnish.

Capon (kay-pon)   A desexed male chicken, noted for its tender flesh.

Caramelize   To heat sugar until it liquefies. For a caramel flavor you must heat it further until it turns brown.

Carbohydrates   Starches, sugars, and cellulose or fiber, found mainly in plant foods, in milk, and in manufactured starch products. Starches and sugars supply energy to the body; fiber aids in digestion. The behavior of all three carbohydrate types in the presence of heat is very important in cooking.

Carotenes   Pigments in yellow vegetables.

Carry-over cooking   The increase in internal temperature of a food (usually a roast) after removal from the heat source.

Casserole   A food or mixture of foods bound by a sauce, baked or heated in the oven.

Cauldron   Large pot formerly used for cooking over an open fire.

Caviar   Salted fish roe (eggs).

Cellulose   The fiber found in fruits, grains, and vegetables, which provides their texture. A form of carbohydrate.

Celsius (sel'-see-us) **scale** (abbreviated **C**)   The system of temperature measurement used in most countries, also called the **centigrade scale.** It sets the freezing point of pure distilled water at 0° and the boiling point at 100° at standard atmospheric pressure. One Celsius degree equals 1.8 Fahrenheit degrees.

Centigrade scale   See **Celsius scale.**

Chaudfroid (show-frwah) **sauce** (literally, hot–cold sauce)   White or brown sauce combined with aspic, used to coat culinary showpieces before decorating them.

Cheese   A dairy product made from coagulated milk protein (curd); used as a flavorer, a meat substitute, a topping, an appetizer, a cold buffet food, a sandwich filling, a salad ingredient, a dessert.

Chef (1) A person in charge of a production station. (2) A person of recognized superiority in a specialized area of cooking—a pastry chef, for example.

Chef de cuisine Head chef, working chef.

Chemiser (shem-ee-zay) To coat the inside surface of a mold or dish with aspic or gelatin (for a cold food) or sugar or flour (for a hot food).

Chiffon (1) A light, fluffy custard or pie filling containing egg white and gelatin. (2) A light cake made by folding a meringue into a flour–egg yolk–oil batter.

Chiffonade (shif-a-nod) Shredded lettuce, meat, or vegetable.

China cap A cone-shaped strainer, also called a **chinois** (sheen-wah).

Chlorophyll Pigment that makes vegetables green, which changes to olive green in an acid medium.

Choice grade The second-highest USDA quality grade for meat, indicating good brittle fat, good marbling, and good-textured flesh; the most commonly used grade of meat.

Chop (1) To cut into pieces of no specified shape. (2) A tender portion-size crosscut of meat from the rib, loin, or shoulder, usually including the bone.

Chou (shoo) **paste** A paste of flour, butter, egg, and water or milk, used for cream puffs and certain potato dishes.

Chowder A hearty soup made of fish or vegetables or both, with a large proportion of solid ingredients served in the liquid.

Clarify To clear a liquid of all solid particles. To clarify butter is to heat it and remove the clear oil from the milky residue at the bottom of the pan. To clarify stock is to remove particles by simmering it with a ground-meat-and-egg-white mixture.

Classical cuisine (kwee-zeen) Style of cooking developed in France in the eighteenth and nineteenth centuries, characterized by elegance, refinement of flavor, delicacy of texture, richness of ingredients, an abundance of sauces, rigid rules for the makeup of each dish, the endless multiplication of such dishes by minute variations in ingredients, and the need for advanced cooking skills for their preparation.

Clearmeat (cleer-meet) A mixture of lean ground meat, mirepoix, water, and egg white, used to make consommé.

Clear soup An unthickened soup, usually translucent.

Clostridium perfringens (klos-trid′-ee-um per-frin′-junz) Disease-causing bacteria that can survive cooking temperatures and multiply in cooked meats and sauces left at room temperatures.

Coagulation (co-ag′-u-lay′-shun) A process in which proteins, when exposed to heat, become firm and gather together into a thickened mass, as egg proteins do when heated or gelatin does when it jells.

Cocktail An appetizer typically consisting of several bite-size pieces of meat, fish, shellfish, or fruit with a highly flavored sauce, usually served at table as the opener to a meal.

Cold sauce A cold, usually thickened, seasoned liquid used to enhance a meat, poultry, fish, or vegetable dish or a sweet.

Collagen (kol-a-jun) White connective tissue in meats, capable of tenderization by moist-heat cooking.

Complement To add a second food or flavor that goes so well with the first that both are enhanced.

Concasser (kon-kass-ay) To cut rough-shaped but even-size pieces. **Concassé** means having been so cut.

Condiment A highly flavored bottled "sauce" that is added to a dish as flavoring, usually after cooking is complete.

Condition See **Prime.**

Conduction The transfer of heat from something hot to something touching it that is cooler. A pot conducts heat from the fire to the product inside it.

Consommé (kon-sum-may) Double-strength clarified stock.

Convection In cooking, the spread of heat by a flow of hot air or steam or liquid.

Convenience food A food product that is purchased partly or wholly processed.

Converting a recipe Increasing or decreasing the amounts of ingredients in the correct proportions to produce a larger or smaller quantity of the same product.

Cook To bring about change in a food product by applying heat over a period of time, usually to make the food more palatable.

Cook's helper Worker of limited skill or experience who works under the direction of a station head. Also **apprentice, aide.**

Coquille (co-kee) A sea shell such as a scallop or oyster shell, often used to serve seafood. **En coquille** Served in a shell.

Cost To cost a recipe is to figure the raw-food cost of one portion of the product as served. To cost a menu is to cost each dish and the menu as a whole.

Cost control Policies and practices for ensuring that the necessary relationship is maintained between costs and income.

Count The number of items in a given unit of a given product, such as shrimp in a pound or apples in a crate;

a way of indicating size. Individual items in a recipe are sometimes given by count—that is, by number—rather than by weight or volume.

Court bouillon   An acid and highly flavored poaching liquid used to cook fish.

Cream   To work to a smooth paste or a fluffy texture in order to incorporate air as a leavener in doughs and batters. Fat and sugar are creamed for cakes, cookies, and icings.

Cream soup   A soup thickened with a thickening agent.

Crécy (kray-see)   Served with carrots.

Crêpe   A thin pancake used for both desserts and entrées.

Croissant (krwa-sahn)   A light, flaky, crescent-shaped roll made from a rolled-in soft dough.

Croquette (kro-ket)   A mixture of minced or puréed cooked food, bound, shaped, breaded, and fried.

Cross-contamination   The spread of bacteria from one food to another via a dirty knife, towel, counter, sink, dish, cutting board, or hands.

Crouton (kroo-tahn)   (1) A small cube of bread fried with herbs and spices, used as a garniture for soups and salads. (2) A buttered bread shape baked in the oven until brown and crisp, used as a canapé base.

Crudités (krue-dee-tays)   Attractively cut raw vegetables often used as an accompaniment to a dip.

Crustaceans   Shellfish whose shells are like jointed suits of armor, such as shrimp, lobsters, crabs.

Cryovac aging   The aging, under refrigeration at controlled temperatures, of meats that are broken down into wholesale cuts and vacuum-packed in moisture–vapor-proof plastic.

Cube   A cube-shaped cut ⅛ to ½″ (3 mm–1 cm). **To cube** is to cut into cubes; to dice.

Cuisine (kwee-zeen)   Style of cooking—of a restaurant, a region, or a whole culture.

Curd   The protein in milk when coagulated.

Curdle   To form curds through coagulation of proteins.

Cure   To preserve by salting, pickling, or drying.

Custard   An egg-and-milk mixture that is either stirred over heat or baked until the eggs coagulate.

Cutlet   A lean slice of meat, often pounded or tenderized.

Cycle menu   A rotating series of menus that are different from one day to the next; the series extends over a certain number of days and then repeats.

Danish   A large flat sweet roll made from a rolled-in soft dough, typically served at breakfast.

Deep-fry   To cook food submerged in hot fat.

Deglaze   To dissolve the glaze of drippings (fond) in the bottom of a pan by adding cold liquid to the hot pan and stirring.

Degrease   (1) To remove the fat from the top of a liquid such as a sauce or stock. (2) To remove excess fat from the bottom of a pan after cooking a fat food, such as a steak, if another product, such as a sauce, is to follow in the same pan.

Demiglace (dem-ee-glass or dem-ee-glaze)   A sauce made from equal parts espagnole and brown stock, reduced by half; often used as a base for other sauces.

Dessert (des-sair in French, da-zert′ in English)   (1) On a classical menu, a final course consisting of a small pastry or candies. (2) On a typical American menu, a final course consisting of a sweet dish, fruit, or cheese.

Dice   To cut into small uniform cubes. **Brunoise** is ⅛″ (3 mm). **Small dice** is ¼″ (6 mm). **Medium dice** is ½″ (1 cm). **Large dice** is ¾″ (2 cm).

Dietitian   Person degreed in a four-year program in food and nutrition or institutional management who has met the requirements of the American Dietetic Association and state licensing requirements.

Dock   To cut a bread dough with a knife or perforate a pie dough with a fork to allow steam to escape.

Dough   A flour–liquid mixture, thicker than a batter, used to make biscuits, breads, rolls, pies, and pastries.

Drawn   Eviscerated, relieved of entrails.

Dredge   To pass a product through a fine, dry or powdery substance such as flour, cornmeal, or ground almonds to coat it lightly.

Dress   To prepare for cooking or service.

Dressed poultry   Killed, bled, and plucked with craw removed, but not eviscerated.

Dressing   (1) For salads, a flavorful liquid or semiliquid used to enhance a salad. (2) For poultry, an accompaniment or stuffing consisting of a bread product or rice mixed with flavorful foods such as onions, herbs, sausage, usually moistened with fat or stock, sometimes bound with egg.

Drippings   Juices and fat from a cooked product.

Dry aging   The aging of meat by hanging the carcass for three to six weeks in a refrigerator with carefully controlled temperature, air flow, and humidity.

Dry-heat method   Any cooking method in which heat is transferred to food without use of water or steam. Baking, roasting, barbecuing, broiling, grilling, and frying are all dry-heat methods.

Du barry   Served with or containing cauliflower.

Dust   To sprinkle a fine substance such as sugar or flour gently on a surface.

Duxelles (dook-sells) Stuffing made by sautéing in butter mushrooms, shallots, and chopped parsley, flavored with cayenne and wine.

Edible portion (EP) The weight or quantity of food remaining after trimming and processing.

Egg wash A mixture of eggs and liquid used in breading a product for frying; also used in baking for coating doughs to produce good color and gloss.

Elastin (ee-lass'-tun) Tough yellow connective tissue in meat, which cannot be tenderized by cooking.

Émincer (ay-man-say) To mince; to slice very thin or cut into thin uniform strips. **Émincé** Minced or sliced very thin.

Emulsified dressing Any salad dressing based on an emulsion of egg and oil.

Emulsified french dressing A thin emulsified salad dressing made by whipping oil and vinegar slowly into whipped egg yolks or whole eggs and thinning to a pourable consistency.

Emulsify To form an emulsion.

Emulsion A mixture of two liquids in which one, evenly dispersed in the other, is held in suspension.

Entrecôte (on-tra-kote) A steak cut from the rib section.

Entrée (on-tray) (1) Main dish. (2) On a classical menu, a portioned piece of meat or game that has been boiled, braised, grilled, or pan-fried; not the main dish.

Entrée chaude (on-tray shode) A hot entrée, in the classical sense.

Entrée froide (on-tray frwahd) A cold entrée, in the classical sense.

Entremets (on-tra-may) On a classical menu, a course consisting of a sweet dish such as a pastry, pudding, or frozen dish. The term is also used more generally to refer to a side dish that is not part of the main course. In medieval times an entremets was an entertainment between courses.

Enzymes Organic substances within foods that soften or break down tissues.

Espagnole (ess-pan-yole) A brown sauce made from an enriched beef stock thickened with roux. Basic espagnole is a mother sauce for many small sauces.

Étuver (ay-too-vay) To cook a food in its own juices in a covered pot without added moisture.

Event order An order form for a one-time special event such as a banquet or reception; also called a **function sheet.**

Executive chef Manager of all aspects of food production in a large operation. An executive chef is typically a skilled cook who is also trained and experienced in production management.

Eye flow The way in which the eye naturally follows the lines of a pattern of food laid out on a platter. Good eye flow can sharpen focus and create an effect of height.

Fahrenheit (far-en-hite) **scale** (abbreviated **F**) The system used in most U.S. kitchens to measure temperature. On the Fahrenheit scale the freezing point of pure distilled water is 32° and its boiling point is 212° at standard atmospheric pressure. Compare with **Celsius scale.**

Farce (pronounced as spelled) A stuffing. **Farci** (far-see) Stuffed.

Fats and oils Characteristic components of meats, poultry, some fish, many dairy products, nuts, and a few vegetables; used as a cooking medium in frying and as ingredients in recipes, especially in baking.

Fermentation In yeast doughs, the action by which yeast breaks down the sugars in flour, releasing carbon dioxide, which leavens the dough.

Filet, fillet (fil-lay) (1) Meat: A boneless cut from the tenderloin. (2) Fish: A full-length segment removed from the bones. A fillet of a round fish is an entire side; a flatfish fillet is half a side. **To fillet** a fish is to remove the fillets from the bones.

Fine dice A cube-shaped cut $1/8''$ (3 mm) in size; brunoise.

Fin fish Fish having fins, as opposed to shellfish.

Finish-cook To bring a partially cooked food to doneness, usually just before service.

Finished sauce A completed sauce ready for service. It may be simply a seasoned basic sauce, or it may be enriched and then seasoned.

Fish stick A crosscut of a fish fillet.

Flame To add wine or liqueur to a dish and ignite. **Flambé** (flahm-bay) Flamed.

Flatfish A type of fish that is flat and compressed from side to side. It is pale on the underside and dark on the other upper side, with both eyes on the dark side. Its backbone runs down the middle of the body instead of along the top under the fins, as on a round fish. Halibut, sole, and flounder are typical flatfish.

Flavones Pigments in white vegetables: white in an acid medium, yellow in an alkaline medium.

Flavor (1) The way a food tastes, through a combination of sweet, sour, bitter, and salt tastes perceived by the tongue and the aromas perceived by the nose. (2) **To flavor** is to add an ingredient whose distinctive taste complements the predominant flavor of a dish without masking that flavor or losing its own identity. Compare with **Season.**

Flavor builder Ingredient added in cooking to enrich the flavor of the main ingredient.

Flavor building   Producing a blend of flavors to reinforce the flavor and body of a liquid.

Flavoring, flavorer   (1) An ingredient of distinctive taste added to a dish to complement the predominant flavor. (2) In baking, an ingredient usually added to provide a major flavor, such as an extract, oil, chocolate, or spice.

Fleuron (flur-on)   A small, shaped puff pastry, usually served as a garnish with fish.

Florentine   Served with or containing spinach.

Flour   A starch product milled from the kernel of a cereal grain, usually wheat; used as a thickener in soups and sauces, as a coating, and as the major body and structure in doughs and batters.

Foie gras (fwah grah—literally, fat liver)   Traditionally, the liver of specially fattened geese, usually used in the form of a meat paste, **pâté de foie gras.**

Fold   To mix a whipped ingredient lightly with another ingredient or mixture by gently turning one over and over the other with a flat implement.

Fond (fawn)   (1) Stock. In French, *fond de cuisine* (fawn da kwee-zeen—literally, base of cooking). *Fond blanc* (fawn blahnk) is veal stock. *Fond brun* (fawn brun) is brown beef stock. *Fond de poisson* (fawn da pwa-sone) is fish stock. *Fond de volaille* (fawn da vol-eye) is chicken stock. (2) Pan drippings and food bits clinging to the bottom of a pan in which food was cooked, which are incorporated during deglazing to enrich a sauce.

Fond lié (fawn lee-ay)   A brown sauce made by thickening a dark stock with cornstarch.

Food cost   Cost of the edible products purchased for production—the dollars-and-cents value of food products used by the cook.

Food-cost percentage   Percentage of food cost in relation to dollar sales in a given operation.

Forestière (forest-yair)   Served with or containing mushrooms.

Formula   A recipe, especially one used in the bakeshop.

Freezer burn   White spots having off flavors and pulpy texture, caused by dehydration through exposure to air at below-freezing temperatures.

Fricassee (frick-a-see)   A braised dish of white meat or poultry served in a blond sauce.

Frosting   See **Icing.**

Fry   To cook food in hot fat. See also **Deep-fry, Pan-fry, Sauté.**

Fumet (fue-may—literally, essence)   A flavorful stock, usually fish, used for poaching and frequently used as the body of an accompanying sauce.

Function sheet   An order form for a one-time special event, such as a banquet or reception; also called an **event order.**

Galantine (gal-un-teen)   A showy meat creation from classical cuisine, made of a special meat filling ground to a smooth paste, with a special decorative garniture, wrapped in skin and poached in stock; served chilled and sliced.

Game hen   An immature chicken five to seven weeks old weighing less than 2 pounds. A Cornish or Rock Cornish game hen is a specially bred game hen.

Garde manger (gard mon-zhay)   Station or department that produces cold foods, usually in a large kitchen doing extensive buffet and display work or one having a European tradition; equivalent to the pantry or salad department in other types of operation. **Chef garde manger:** Person in charge of cold-food production.

Garnish   To add a colorful edible accent, such as a sprig of parsley, to a finished dish entirely for eye appeal. A garnish may be eaten but that is not its purpose.

Garniture   Something edible added to a finished dish for eye appeal, flavor, and often textural contrast, such as croutons added to a bowl of soup. A garniture becomes part of the dish and is eaten with it.

Gelatin   A semisolid jellylike substance, or **gel,** used as a binding agent in salads, desserts, and cold entrées. (2) The dry powder or leaves that are dissolved to produce the gel. Powdered fruit-flavored gelatin has sugar added.

Gelatinization (ja-lat'-un-a-zay'-shun)   The reaction of starch to heat and moisture in which dry starch granules absorb liquid, swell, and become jellylike, thickening and binding a product with which they are mixed.

Genoise (zhun-wahz)   Butter sponge cake made by the foam method.

Glacé (glas-say)   Glazed.

Glaze   (1) To add a shine or gloss to the surface of a product for taste or eye appeal by basting during cooking, by coating with sauce and broiling briefly, or by coating a cold food with aspic or chaudfroid sauce. Baked products are glazed with egg wash, coatings, and icings. (2) A stock reduced to a gelatinous consistency.

Gluten   The protein substance that provides structure in baked goods. Gluten, found mainly in wheat flour, is formed when the proteins *gliadin* and *glutenin* combine in the presence of moisture.

Good grade   Third-highest USDA meat grade, indicating less fat or lower-quality fat, with coarser-textured meat fibers. Good-grade meat is less tender and juicy and often less flavorful than prime and choice meats.

Grade   A measure of the quality of a food product. For example, meat, poultry, and eggs are quality-graded by federal agents according to federal standards. Some packinghouses have established their own grades and standards.

Gram (abbreviated **g**)   The basic metric unit of weight, equal to 0.035 ounce.

Grand jus (grahn zhue)   Ordinary brown stock.

Grande marmite (grahnd mar-meet), *petite marmite* (puh-teet mar-meet)   Ordinary light stock, usually called ordinary stockpot. The difference between the two is in the size of the pot.

Grate   To reduce to fine pieces by forcing through a grater.

Gratiné (gra-tee-nay)   Glazed in the salamander or broiler.

Gravy   American term for a jus or sauce made from juices and pan drippings of the meat being served.

Grease   To coat a pan surface with fat to prevent sticking.

Green meat   Meat that has not had time to be softened by enzymatic action following the onset of rigor mortis.

Grill   To cook on a grate with heat from below.

Gueridon (gair-ee-don)   A rolling cart or table used to prepare food tableside.

Gumbo   A soup thickened with brown roux and crowded with meat or fish and vegetables, usually served with rice.

Hen   A female bird. A chicken hen, also called a fowl or stewing chicken, is mature and suitable only for stewing. A young turkey hen (five to seven months old) is suitable for roasting.

Herbs (urbs)   The leafy parts of various aromatic plants used in flavoring and flavor building.

Hold   To keep a partly or fully prepared food product at a safe temperature for a short period before its intended use at a specific time.

Hollandaise (hol-lun-daze)   Butter sauce made with an emulsion of egg yolks, clarified butter, and a flavor reduction. One of the five mother sauces.

Hors d'oeuvre (or durve)   A small appetizer, usually having a major ingredient, that is served whole and eaten with a pick or cocktail fork; served from a buffet or passed on a tray.

Hors-d'oeuvre chaud (show)   Hot hors d'oeuvre; course on a classical menu.

Hors-d'oeuvre froid (frwah)   Cold hors d'oeuvre; course on a classical menu.

House dressing   Special recipe for a salad dressing featured by the restaurant serving it.

Icing   A sweet mixture, made mostly of sugar, used for coating and filling pastries, cakes, cookies, and breads.

Implied height   An illusion of height on a plate, achieved by establishing a focal point with an eye-catching ingredient or with line patterns leading to a single point.

Jardinière   Served with root vegetables cut julienne.

Job description   A written description of everything pertinent to a given position, such as the specific duties, responsibilities, skills required, and wages or salary paid.

Julienne   (1) A small, very thin cut ⅛″ × ⅛″ × 1½–2″ (3 mm × 3 mm × 4–5 cm). (2) Food that is cut julienne.

Jus (zhue)   An unthickened accompaniment to a roast meat, consisting of the natural juices from the roast degreased, mixed with stock, and enriched by simmering with a mirepoix. See also **Au jus.**

Kilogram (kill-o-gram, abbreviated **kg**)   1000 grams, or 2.2 pounds. Sometimes shortened to kilo (kee-loh).

Knead   To manipulate dough in order to develop gluten.

Labor cost   (1) Of production: the wages and salaries that are paid to the persons who produce the food. (2) Of a product: the cost in wages to produce a single portion.

Lard   To thread strips of fat (**lardons**) through meat with a larding needle, a long, large-eyed needle designed for the purpose.

Leading sauce   See **Mother sauce.**

Leaven, leavener   Any agent that introduces air or gas into a batter or dough, causing it to rise.

Legume (leg′-yoom or lug-yoom′)   A vegetable that grows in pods, such as peas, beans, lentils.

Légume (lay-guym)   (1) French for vegetable. (2) On a classical menu, a vegetable course, usually served with the *rôti.*

Liaison (lee′-ay-zon)   A combination of egg yolks and cream (in a ratio of 1 to 2 by volume) used to give a velvety texture to soups and sauces.

Lié (lee-ay)   Bound or thickened.

Liter (lee-ter, abbreviated **L**)   The basic metric unit of volume, equal to 1.056 quarts.

Lox   Smoked Nova Scotia salmon.

Lyonnaise (lion-ez)   Any dish with a garniture of onions.

Macaroon   A small cookie made of egg white, sugar, and ground almonds.

Macedoine (mass-a-dwan)   Mixed cut vegetables or fruits, or any mixture of several foods in the same category, such as mixed seafoods.

Maître d'hôtel (met-ra doh-tel) **butter** A compound butter made with lemon juice and chopped parsley or other fresh herbs.

Make up To form a dough or batter into uniform shapes and sizes prior to baking.

Marbling Fat distributed throughout meat.

Margarine A butterlike fat made from hardened vegetable oils.

Marinade Any liquid made up for the purpose of marinating, usually containing oil, an acid, and flavor builders.

Marinate To soak a food in a flavorful liquid to add flavor or to tenderize.

Marrow (1) Tissue from the insides of bones. (2) A vegetable of the squash family.

Marzipan (mar-za-pan) Almond paste made from finely ground almonds, confectioners' sugar, and egg white, often molded into decorative shapes.

Mask To disguise by covering completely with sauce or by flavoring to hide true taste.

Master chef A master of all the culinary arts. The term applies to skill level, not job title.

Mayonnaise A flavored, seasoned emulsion of egg yolks and oil. Mayonnaise can be a finished salad dressing, a basic dressing for other salad dressings, or a mother sauce for other cold sauces.

Medallion Classical term applied to food that is cut or shaped like a medallion—flat and round or oval.

Medium (meat) Having a warm pink center.

Medium rare (meat) Having a slightly warm deep-pink or pale-red center.

Medium well (meat) Having a slightly hot and slightly pink center.

Melba toast Thinly sliced bread baked twice.

Melt To convert a product from a solid to a liquid by heating.

Menu (1) A list of the dishes to be offered for service at a meal. (2) The card on which the dishes offered for service are listed for the guest, usually with their prices.

Meringue (ma-rang') Egg white whipped until stiff with sugar, used in making desserts. Hard meringues use 2 parts sugar to 1 part white. Soft meringues are made with equal parts sugar and whites.

Metric system A system of measurement based on the decimal system.

Mignon (meen-yone) Very small. **Filet mignon** A small filet of beef.

Milliliter (mil'-a-lee-ter, abbreviated **mL**) 0.001 liter, 0.001 quart, or 0.034 fluidounce.

Mince To cut very fine.

Mirepoix (mee-ra-pwah) A standard flavor builder for stocks, soups, and sauces made up of 50 percent onions (or onions and leeks), 25 percent celery, and 25 percent carrots, usually cut concassé. A **light mirepoix** omits carrots; a **dark mirepoix** may add tomato.

Mise en place (meez on plass) Everything in its proper place; a good production setup with everything ready to go.

Mix To combine ingredients in such a way that the parts of each are evenly dispersed in the whole.

Moist-heat method Any cooking method in which heat is transferred to the product by a water-based liquid or steam. Boiling, simmering, poaching, braising, and steaming are all moist-heat methods.

Mollusks Shellfish that live inside a pair of shells, such as clams, oysters, and scallops, or under a single shell, such as abalone.

Monter au beurre (mawn-tay oh burr) To swirl butter into a hot sauce just before serving.

Mother sauce A basic sauce from which other sauces are made; also known as a **leading sauce.** The mother sauces are béchamel, velouté, espagnole, tomato sauce, and hollandaise.

Mousse A dish made with a puréed major flavor ingredient often mixed with gelatin and folded with whipped cream; often molded.

Mousseline (moos-a-leen) **sauce** Any sauce that has whipped cream folded into it.

Nap, nappé (nap-pay) To coat evenly with a sauce, usually with one stroke of the ladle.

Nonselective menu A menu that does not offer the diner a choice of foods.

Nutrition The science of nourishing the body.

Nutritional balance The providing of foods containing needed nutrients in the right proportions to fulfill the body's daily requirements.

Oil (1) A fat that is liquid at room temperature—usually a plant product. (2) **To oil** is to spread a light coat of oil on a pan or food surface.

Oil-and-vinegar dressing Any salad dressing based on a temporary oil–vinegar–water emulsion.

Omelet A beaten egg mixture cooked rapidly over heat in a primed pan; often filled or flavored and usually folded.

Onion clouté (kloo-tay) An onion stuck with cloves, used as a flavor builder.

Onion piqué (pee-kay) A flavor builder for soups and sauces made by affixing a bay leaf to a small peeled onion with a clove.

Oven-fry, ovenize   To brown in a fry pan and finish-cook in an oven; a common way of producing "fried" chicken in volume.

Palatability   The degree to which a food is edible and pleasing to the taste.

Pancake   A fried cake made from a batter of flour, water, and egg.

Pan-dressed   Market term for fish that are eviscerated and scaled or skinned; possibly also headless, tailless, definned, boned, or any combination of such states—in short, ready-to-cook, dressed for the pan.

Pan-fry   To cook food to doneness in a small to moderate amount of fat in a pan over moderate heat.

Pantry   A kitchen station where cold foods are prepared.

Papillote   (pap-ee-yote)   An envelope or bag in which a food is steamed in its own juices. Foods **en papillote** are cooked by this method.

Parboil   To simmer in liquid or fat until approximately 50 percent done.

Pare   To peel.

Parisienne   (pa-ree-zee-en)   Small round cuts made with a small ball cutter; usually applied to potatoes.

Partial cooking   Any cooking process that is stopped before the product reaches doneness. To partial-cook is to cook partway to doneness.

Partial-cook/quick-chill   A method of production in which a product (usually a vegetable) is partially cooked, then quick-chilled with ice and refrigerated until needed, then finish-cooked just before service; used for large-quantity production.

Pasta   (pahs-ta)   A starchy product made from a paste of hard flour and water; macaroni, spaghetti, and noodles are the most familiar varieties.

Pastry   A baked food, often sweet, made with a flour–fat–liquid dough.

Pastry bag   A flexible canvas or plastic funnel used to force a soft mass of food into decorative shapes through a pastry tube, or tip.

Pastry cream   (*crème pâtissière*—krem pa-tees-yair)   A stirred custard sauce thickened by eggs and starch.

Pastry shop   Production station preparing pastries and desserts, especially display items; bakery.

Pâté   (pah-tay—literally, paste)   A mixture of finely ground meats, flavored, seasoned, and baked.

Pâte à chou   (pot a shoo)   A paste of eggs, flour, and liquid used for cream puffs, éclairs, and savory preparations; also called **chou paste.**

Pâtissier   (pa-tees-yay)   Pastry cook.

Paupiette   (pope-yet)   A fish fillet or a thin slice of meat rolled into a cylinder shape around another bit of food and poached or braised.

Paysanne   (pay-zan)   (1) A cut that is a segment of a slice, 1/8 to 3/8" (3–8 mm) thick, often triangular. (2) Rustic, or in the style of the peasant.

Petits fours   (petty fours)   (1) Tiny fancy iced cakes. (2) Small rich cookies in decorative shapes.

pH   Symbol for expressing degree of acidity or alkalinity. See **Acid.**

Pie   A sweet or savory filling encased in pastry or a baked crust.

Pièce de résistance   (pyess da ray-zee-stahns)   The main dish on a classical menu, consisting of a large, elaborately presented piece of poultry, meat, or game such as a roast suckling pig or a saddle of venison.

Pilaf   (pee-lahf)   A method of cooking rice, covered, with sautéed onion and just enough stock to be completely absorbed.

Pipe   To force a mass of food through a pastry tube to make special decorations or shapes.

Piquant   (peek-unt)   Sharp-flavored, spicy.

Planked   Served on a board.

Poach   To cook food submerged in liquid at temperatures of roughly 160–180°F (70–85°C). A liquid at these temperatures has bubbles on the bottom of the pan but is undisturbed.

Poêler   (po-a-lay)   To cook with fat in a covered pot, a moist-heat method that uses steam from the food's natural juices.

Poisson   (pwah-sone)   (1) Fish (French). (2) On a classical menu, a course consisting of a small portion of fish or shellfish.

Portion control   The measurement of portions to guarantee that the quantity served is the quantity specified.

Portioning   The breaking down, or dividing up, of large quantities into specific serving quantities or portions.

Potage   (poh-tahzh'—rhymes with garage)   (1) A soup naturally thickened by a purée of its major ingredients. (2) In French, any of several different kinds of soup. (3) The soup course on a menu.

Pot roast   A large cut of meat braised whole in a pot and sliced for service.

Predominant flavor   The major flavor in a dish, determining the character of the dish.

Prep   Kitchen slang meaning to clean fresh produce; also known as **rough prep.**

Prepreparation, preprep   All the cleaning, cutting, processing, setting up, and production that is done before final preparation of food for service.

Prime   To polish a cooking surface at high heat with salt and fat or oil to overcome its porousness; to **condition,** to **season.**

Prime grade   The highest USDA quality grade for meat, indicating thick, white, brittle fat cover, fine-textured flesh, and abundant marbling.

Prime rib   A seven-rib cut of meat from the forequarter.

Printanière (pran-ton-yair)   Served with fresh spring vegetables.

Processing   An inclusive term referring to all the things done to foods in getting them ready to cook or serve, such as cleaning, cutting, mixing, breading, puréeing.

Produce (prod'-oos)   Fresh fruits and vegetables as they come from the market.

Production   That part of a food-service operation in which foods from the market are transformed into finished dishes for service.

Production schedule   An overall plan for a specific production period stating who is responsible for what products and when each product must be ready.

Production worksheet   A written work schedule for a person or department for a given production period stating all information necessary for production, such as food to be prepared, quantity needed, time needed, place needed, style of service.

Profit   The difference between costs and sales.

Profiterole (pra-fit'-a-roll)   A small, unsweetened cream puff used as a garniture.

Proof   To ferment a yeast dough a second time.

Provençale (pro-von-sahl)   In the style of Provence, usually with garlic and tomato.

Psi   Pounds per square inch, a measure of added pressure in cooking.

Puff pastry   A rolled-in stiff dough leavened by steam from butter, which produces a light, flaky pastry when baked.

Pullman (as in bread or ham)   Food packaged in the shape of a railroad car.

Punch, punch down   To deflate a yeast dough after fermentation, to expel gas, redistribute the yeast, and equalize the temperature.

Purée (pew-ray)   To mash a cooked product to a fine pulp, usually by forcing it through a sieve or putting it into a blender.

Quality control   Policies and practices for assuring consistency in meeting standards of taste, texture, appearance, nutritional value, and level of excellence for each product served.

Quantity control   Policies and practices for ensuring that food is purchased, produced, and served in the amounts needed with a minimum of waste.

Quenelle (ka-nell')   A light, delicate meat dumpling.

Quiche (keesh)   A pie with a savory custard filling.

Quick bread   An easily and quickly made bread leavened chemically or by steam; biscuits, muffins, and pancakes are examples.

Quick-chill   To lower the temperature of a just-cooked product to below 40°F (4°C) within 2 minutes.

Radiation   The transfer of heat through energy waves radiating directly from a heat source to the food, as the skin is sunburned by the sun's rays.

Raft   Clearmeat after it has coagulated in clarifying a consommé.

Ragoût (rah-goo)   A flavorful stew made of meat, fish, or poultry, poached or braised, with or without vegetables.

Ramekin (ram-a-kin)   Small   earthenware   baking dish.

Rancidity   Chemical deterioration of fats or oils characterized by stale, unpleasant taste and smell.

Rare (meat)   Cool and red in the center.

Recipe   An abbreviated set of directions for making a product, including a list of ingredients and instructions for combining them. See also **Formula, Standardized recipe.**

Reconstitute   To restore a product to its normal state, such as by adding liquid to a dried product, or reheating a sauce that has been frozen or refrigerated.

Red sauce   (1) Tomato sauce, one of the five mother sauces, thickened with tomato purée or roux. (2) A cold cocktail sauce served with shrimp and crab.

Reduce   To boil or simmer a liquid until it reaches a smaller volume through evaporation. A liquid so reduced has a greater concentration of flavor and a thicker texture.

Reduction   A product reduced in volume by boiling or simmering. In classical sauce-making, the term refers to a mixture of highly flavored ingredients that are reduced by 70 to 80 percent and added to a sauce to provide its major flavor.

Relishes   (1) Sticks or cuts of raw vegetables, pickles, and olives served as appetizers. (2) Bottled condiment mixtures such as pickle relish or chutney.

Render   To heat pieces of animal fat to separate the fat from the connective tissue.

Requisition   An in-house form used to order supplies from a storeroom or purchasing department.

Rest To let stand. A roast is rested to allow the juices to settle. Dough is rested to relax the gluten.

Risotto A creamy rice dish originating in Italy, prepared with butter and stock.

Rissolé (ris-a-lay) Browned.

Roast To cook by heated air, usually in an enclosed space such as an oven or barbecue pit, but also on a revolving spit before an open fire. Roasting nearly always refers to meats. Compare to **Bake.**

Roaster A young bird tender enough to roast but less tender than a fryer. A roaster chicken is usually three to five months old; a roaster duckling or fryer-roaster turkey is usually under 16 weeks old.

Roe Fish eggs.

Roll To pass a product through a powdery substance; to dredge.

Rolled-in dough A soft or stiff dough with fat rolled in layers with the flour–liquid mixture.

Rotate stock To put new products either behind or under existing supplies of the same product, to ensure that the oldest will be used first.

Rôti (ro-tee) (1) Roast (French). (2) On a classical menu, a course consisting of a portion of roasted meat served with a salad.

Roulade (roo-lahd) A thin slice of meat rolled around another food, as ham around asparagus.

Round fish (1) A whole fish. (2) A fish having a rounded bony structure, as a trout or salmon does, as opposed to a flatfish such as flounder.

Roux (roo) A thickening agent of fat and flour in a 1-to-1 ratio by weight, made by blending and cooking over low heat. A **white roux** is one that is cooked only until thick and foamy. A **blond roux** is one cooked until its color is blond. A **brown roux** is one cooked until it looks brown and tastes and smells nutty.

Sachet Herbs and spices tied in a piece of cheese-cloth and added to the cooking pot or pan.

Saddleback (lobster) To arrange the raw flesh on top of the shell before cooking.

Salad A dish made up of cut-up raw or cooked foods, usually accompanied by a flavorful dressing, served cold as an appetizer, main course, side dish, or separate salad course following the main course.

Salad dressing A liquid or a semiliquid served with or on a salad to give it specific flavor.

Salamander Small overhead broiler used for quick glazing or browning.

Salmonella (sal-mun-ell'-a) A family of disease-producing bacteria, the most common of the hazardous kitchen bacteria.

Sanitation Methods and practices by which bacteria capable of producing food-borne disease are eliminated or kept at harmless levels.

Sanitize To rid surfaces and utensils of bacteria by washing with a germicide.

Sauce A seasoned, usually thickened, liquid used to enhance a dish. A basic sauce is an unseasoned sauce used for making finished sauces. A finished sauce is a completed sauce ready for service. See also **Mother sauce; Small sauce; Blond, Brown, Red, Yellow,** and **White sauces.**

Saucier (so-see-ay) Sauce cook; usually responsible for preparing all dishes in which sauce is used.

Sauté (so-tay) To flip quickly in a small amount of hot fat in a pan.

Savory (1) A piquant, nonsweet flavor or dish. (2) A morsel served as a last course designed to cleanse and stimulate the palate before the port.

Scaling Using a scale to weigh ingredients or doughs and batters to be evenly divided for baking.

Scallopine Very thin slices of tender meat, often flattened by pounding; usually sautéed.

Score To mark the surface of a product with grids, a hot poker, or shallow cuts from a knife blade.

Sear To expose the surface of meat to extreme heat in a hot pan or oven to brown it before cooking at a lower temperature.

Season (1) To heighten a food's own flavor by adding seasonings; compare with **Flavor.** (2) To prime a cooking surface; see **Prime.**

Seasonings Substances that heighten the taste of a food without altering that taste or adding their own flavors—namely, salt, pepper, and fresh lemon juice.

Shelf life The length of time a food can be stored without health hazard or quality loss.

Shellfish Fish having shells, as opposed to fin fish.

Shortening A fat that is solid at room temperature; used for deep-frying and in baking as a creaming and tenderizing agent.

Shred To cut in very fine strips or pieces.

Shuck To remove the outer covering, such as shells from oysters or husks from corn.

Simmer To cook food submerged in liquid just below a boil, or to cook the liquid itself, at temperatures of 180°F (85°C) to just below the boiling point. A simmering liquid has bubbles floating up slowly from the bottom, and the surface is fairly quiet.

Simple syrup A solution of sugar in water, used to thin fondant, flavored to become a dessert syrup, or cooked through various stages from thread (230°F/

110°C) to caramel (320–340°F/160–170°C) for syrups and candy.

Skim To remove foam, scum, or fat from the surface of a stock, soup, or sauce.

Slack time Time allowed during preparation for a product to undergo a change—a frozen product to thaw, juices in cooked meats to settle, gluten in dough to relax before baking.

Slice A crosscut ⅛ to ⅜" (3–8 mm) thick. **To slice** is to cut into even slices, usually across the grain.

Slurry A flour–water mixture (equal parts by volume) used as an emergency thickener for sauces; sometimes called a **whitewash.**

Small sauce A sauce deriving from a mother sauce, made by adding flavoring and seasonings; also called a **secondary sauce.**

Smoke point The temperature at which a fat smokes, indicating that its chemical structure is breaking down and it is no longer suitable for cooking.

Smother To mask.

Sorbet (sore-bay) Sherbet; used on a classical menu as a light course separating two heavier courses.

Soubise (soo-beez) With onion purée.

Soufflé (soo-flay) A light and fluffy sweet or savory dish, made with heavy béchamel, egg yolks, and a major flavor ingredient, folded with whipped egg whites, baked; served immediately.

Soup A cooked, flavored, seasoned liquid served as a dish in itself. A **clear soup** is unthickened and usually translucent. A **naturally thickened soup** is thickened by a purée of its own ingredients (see **Potage**). A **cream soup** is thickened with a thickening agent.

Soup du jour (due joor) Soup of the day, a menu term indicating that the kind varies from day to day.

Sous-chef (soo-shef—literally, under-chef) A production supervisor reporting to an executive chef. A sous-chef is typically a skilled cook and will do some cooking as well as supervising.

Spices The dried roots, bark, and seeds of certain tropical plants, used in flavoring and flavor building.

Stagger-cook To cook in small batches as needed for service; to **batch-cook.**

Staling Deterioration of quality in baked goods through loss of moisture.

Standardized recipe A recipe developed for use in a particular operation to record the way the operation makes a given dish.

Staphylococcus (staf'-uh-luh-cock'-us), **staph** for short A type of bacteria that produces toxin in foods at temperatures of 44–115°F (7–46°C). Cooking will destroy the bacteria but not the toxin.

Static menu A menu that offers the same dishes day after day; a fixed menu. Contrast with **Cycle menu.**

Station (1) A functional area of a kitchen layout, such as a salad station or a vegetable station. (2) Any area set up with supplies and equipment in order to complete a production task; a work station.

Station head, station supervisor Person in charge of all production for a given station or department. A station head may be both supervisor and working cook.

Steak (1) Fish: A crosscut section of the body of a large pan-dressed fish. (2) Meat: A tender cut from the rib, loin, sirloin, tenderloin, round, or chuck.

Steam To cook with steam, usually in a cabinet type cooker under pressure. Steam-cooking under pressure is hotter and faster than cooking in liquid.

Steep To leave immersed in a liquid over a period of time in order to convey flavor to the liquid, as tea leaves are steeped in boiling water to make tea.

Stew A dish composed of meat, poultry, or fish simmered or braised together with other ingredients at low temperatures and served with the cooking liquid, which is usually thickened to make a sauce.

Stir-fry To cook bite-size ingredients over high heat in a small amount of oil, tossing them with utensils, until crisp-tender.

Stock A flavored liquid used in making soups, sauces, and sauce-based entrées. A **light stock** is made from bones of veal (or beef), chicken, or fish. A **dark stock,** or **brown stock,** is made from the browned bones of beef or veal or both.

Stock herbs and spices Bay leaf, cloves, parsley stems, thyme, and peppercorns, used for flavor-building in making stocks.

Store To keep a food product for future use at a safe temperature for an unspecified period of time.

Strain To remove lumps or particles from a liquid by passing it through a fine mesh of cloth or metal or both.

Stuffing A flavorful product stuffed into a cavity in a bird, fish, meat, or vegetable.

Suprême (1) A dish of cold food served embedded in ice—a suprême of fresh fruit, for example. (2) A boneless poultry breast.

Sweat To cook slowly in fat over low or moderate heat without browning, sometimes with a cover on the pan.

Sweet On a classical or English menu, a hot or cold pastry, pudding, or frozen dish.

Table d'hôte (tobbled oat—literally, table of the host) (1) A nonselective fixed-price menu served at a specific time to all guests. (2) A menu on which a price is given for a whole dinner, as opposed to a la carte pricing of each item.

Tapioca A starch made from the cassava plant, used as a thickener.

Temper To add a hot liquid little by little to a cold liquid to raise its temperature slowly.

Temperature The intensity of heat—that is, the degree of warmth or coldness, usually measured on the Fahrenheit or Celsius scale. In food preparation, applied most often to (1) internal temperature of foods as a measure of doneness, (2) temperature of a cooking medium such as air in an oven or liquid in a pot, (3) temperature of a holding or storing environment such as a freezer, refrigerator, or hot cabinet.

Tenderloin Boneless cut of muscle from the loin section of an animal.

Terrine A pâté, usually encased in fat and baked in a special earthenware dish.

Texture The quality of a product or dish perceivable by the sense of feel: its consistency, its thick–thin, smooth–coarse, tender–tough, crisp–soft qualities.

Thickening agent A substance that increases the viscosity of a liquid—that is, makes it more difficult to pour. Commonly used thickening agents are starches and gelatin.

Timbale (tim-bul) (1) A small mold. (2) A dish cooked, served, or molded in a timbale.

Tomato sauce Any red sauce made from stock thickened with tomato purée and sometimes roux.

Tournedos (toor'-na-doe) A small slice of filet of beef, 2 to 3 ounces.

Tourner (toor-nay) To turn; to shape with a knife by rotating knife and product in opposite directions. **Tourné** means having been so cut.

Toxin A poisonous substance.

Trencher Medieval substitute for the plate, usually a thick, hard slab of bread several days old.

Trichinosis (trick-a-noh'-sis) A food-borne disease caused by the parasite **trichina** (trick-eye'-na), sometimes found in uncooked or undercooked fresh pork that has not been government-inspected.

Truffle A flavorful black fungus that grows underground and is harvested by pigs, a popular (and expensive) ingredient in classical garnitures.

Truss To tie meat or poultry into a compact shape, such as tying the legs and wings of a bird close to the body for even cooking.

Try out To heat animal fat to separate usable fat from connective tissue; to render.

Turnover (1) Daily replacement of fat used in deep-frying. (2) A filled pastry in which half the crust is turned over the filling, forming a triangle.

Unity In food presentation, harmony between the shape of the plate or platter and the pattern of food arrangement.

Variable Something that is not constant or precise at all times in all places. In this text the symbol * is used in recipes to signal a variable.

Variety meats Animal organs such as liver, heart, kidneys, tongue, sweetbreads; meat mixtures such as sausage; and other processed meats such as corned beef, peppered beef, and pastrami.

Velouté (ve-loo-tay) A sauce made from a light stock and blond roux. **Chicken velouté** is made from chicken stock, **veal velouté** from veal stock, and **fish velouté** from fish stock or fumet. The veloutés are mother sauces for many small sauces.

Venison Flesh of deer.

Vichy (vee-shee) (1) Cooked in vichy water. (2) Boiled and served with butter and parsley, usually applied to carrots.

Vinaigrette (vin-a-gret) A salad dressing of vinegar and oil.

Vinegar A strongly acid liquid produced by fermentation; used in salad dressings and as a preservative. Commonly used vinegars are (1) **cider,** a brown fermented vinegar made from apple cider, having a strong apple flavor; (2) **white,** a vinegar distilled from a fermented product (usually molasses), having no color and a neutral flavor; (3) **wine,** a fermented vinegar having the flavor and color of the wine from which it was made.

Vitamins Minute organic substances in foods that enable the body to function properly.

Vol-au-vent (vo-lo-von) A large pastry shell used for serving entrées.

Volume A way of measuring quantity by the amount of space it occupies; used mainly for liquids. The most commonly used measures are gallons, quarts, and fluid-ounces; other volume measures are pints, cups, tablespoons, and teaspoons. Metric units are liters, deciliters, and milliliters.

Wedge A wedge-shaped cut of food, usually a section of a round or oval product such as an apple or lemon.

Well done (meat) Fully cooked; having a hot, moist center with no pink color remaining.

Whey (whay) The watery liquid remaining after milk protein (curd) has coagulated.

Whip   To beat with a rapid lifting motion, usually with a whip, to incorporate air into a product.

White sauce   A sauce made by thickening milk with a white roux. See **Béchamel.**

Whitewash   See **Slurry.**

Yellow sauce   Butter sauce, made by emulsifying clarified butter and egg yolks.

Yield   (1) The quantity of finished product a given recipe will produce, often expressed in number of servings of a specified size. (2) Edible portion of a raw product, usually expressed as a percentage.

Zest   Colored outer portion of a citrus fruit, containing flavorful oils.

A selection of books for reference, research, and reading pleasure

The following books are grouped according to subject. Many of them could appropriately be listed under several different heads. We have placed each one where we feel it has the most contribution to make as a supplement to this text.

Bibliography

Food science and nutrition

Bennion, Marion, *The Science of Food.* New York: Harper & Row, 1980.

Brody, Jane E., *Jane Brody's Nutrition Book.* New York: Bantam, 1981.

Food and Nutrition Board, National Academy of Sciences–National Research Council, *Recommended Dietary Allowances,* 1980.

Pennington, Jean A., and Helen Nichols Church, *Food Values of Portions Commonly Used,* 14th ed. New York: Harper & Row, 1985.

Stare, Fredrick J., and Margaret McWilliams, *Living Nutrition,* 4th ed. New York: Wiley, 1984.

USDA and U.S. Dept. of Health and Human Services, *Dietary Guidelines for Americans,* 2nd ed., 1985. This pamphlet is also known as Home and Garden Bulletin No. 232.

Sanitation

Longree, Karla, and Gertrude G. Blaker, *Sanitary Techniques in Food Service,* 2nd ed. New York: Macmillan, 1982.

NIFI, ed., *Applied Foodservice Sanitation,* 3rd ed. Dubuque, IA: Wm. C. Brown, 1985.

Technique and method

Culinary Institute of America, *The Professional Chef's Knife.* New York: Van Nostrand Reinhold, 1978.

Pépin, Jacques, *La Methode, An Illustrated Guide to the Fundamentals of Cooking.* New York: Times Books, 1979.

513

Pépin, Jacques, *La Technique, The Fundamental Techniques of Cooking—An Illustrated Guide.* New York: Times Books, 1976.

Classical cuisine
Escoffier, A., *The Escoffier Cook Book, A Guide to the Fine Art of Cookery* (American edition of the *Guide Culinaire*). New York: Crown, 1969.

Escoffier, A., *Le Guide Culinaire,* H. L. Cracknell and R. J. Kaufman, trs. New York: Smith Publications, 1980.

Escoffier, A., *Le Guide Culinaire,* H. L. Cracknell and R. J. Kaufman, trs. New York: Van Nostrand Reinhold, 1983.

Hering's Dictionary of Classical and Modern Cookery, Walter Bickel, ed., 5th rev. English ed. New York: Van Nostrand Reinhold, 1974.

Hering's Dictionary of Classical and Modern Cookery, Richard Herring, ed. New York: Radio City Book Store, 1981.

Montagné, Prosper, *The New Larousse Gastronomique: The Encyclopedia of Food, Wine, and Cooking,* Charlotte Turgeon, ed., New York: Crown, 1977.

Saulnier, Louis, *Le Repertoire de La Cuisine.* Woodbury, NY: Barron's, 1977.

Saulnier, Louis, *Le Repertoire de La Cuisine.* New York: Radio City Book Store, 1970.

History
Cosman, Madeleine P., *Fabulous Feasts: Medieval Cookery and Ceremony.* New York: George Braziller, 1977.

Hale, William Harlan, *The Horizon Cookbook and Illustrated History of Eating and Drinking Through the Ages.* New York: American Heritage, 1968.

Jones, Evan, *American Food,* 2nd ed. New York: Random House, 1981.

Tannahill, Reay, *Food in History.* New York: Stein & Day, 1974.

Cold food and buffet
St. Laurent, Georges C., Jr., and Chet Holden, *Buffets: A Guide for Professionals.* New York: Wiley, 1986.

Sonnenschmidt, Frederic H., and Jean F. Nicolas, *The Professional Chef's Art of Garde Manger,* 3rd ed. New York: Van Nostrand Reinhold, 1982.

Waldner, George K., and Klaus Mitterhauser, *The Professional Chef's Book of Buffets.* New York: Van Nostrand Reinhold, 1968.

Baking
Amendola, Joseph, *The Baker's Manual for Quantity Baking and Pastry Making,* 3rd ed. Hasbrouck Heights, NJ: Hayden, 1972.

Gisslen, Wayne, *Professional Baking.* New York: Wiley, 1985.

The New International Confectioner, 3rd rev. ed., Wilfred J. Fance, ed. New York: Van Nostrand Reinhold, 1981.

The New International Confectioner, rev. ed. New York: Radio City Book Store, 1973.

Other texts
Culinary Institute of America, *The Professional Chef,* 4th ed., Le Roi A. Folsom, ed. New York: Van Nostrand Reinhold, 1974.

Gisslen, Wayne, *Professional Cooking.* New York: Wiley, 1983.

Haines, Robert G., *Food Preparation for Hotels, Restaurants, and Cafeterias,* 2nd ed. Chicago: American Technical Society, 1973.

Knight, John B., and Lendal H. Kotschevar, *Quantity Food Production, Planning, and Management.* New York: Van Nostrand Reinhold, 1985.

Kotschevar, Lendal H., *Standards, Principles, and Techniques in Quantity Food Production,* 3rd ed. New York: Van Nostrand Reinhold, 1974.

Pauli, Eugen, *Classical Cooking the Modern Way.* New York: Van Nostrand Reinhold, 1979.

Powers, Jo Marie, *Basics of Quantity Food Production.* New York: Wiley, 1979.

West, Bessie B., et al., *Food for Fifty,* 7th ed. New York: Macmillan, 1985.

Handbooks

Cavallaro, Ann, *Careers in Food Services.* New York: Lodestar, 1981.

Kotschevar, Lendal H., *Quantity Food Purchasing,* 2nd ed. New York: Wiley, 1975.

Levie, Albert, *The Meat Handbook,* 4th ed. Westport, CT, AVI, 1979.

Meat Buyer's Guide. Tucson, AZ: National Association of Meat Purveyors, 1976.

Moyer, William C., *The Buying Guide for Fresh Fruits, Vegetables, Herbs, and Nuts,* 5th rev. ed. Fullerton, CA: Blue Goose, 1974.

Scriven, Carl, and James Stevens, *Food Equipment Facts.* New York: Wiley, 1982.

For fun and information

Child, Julia, et al., *Mastering the Art of French Cooking,* rev. ed. New York: Knopf, 1983.

Sass, Lorna J., *To the King's Taste.* New York: Metropolitan Museum of Art, 1975.

Time-Life Books, *The Good Cook: Techniques and Recipes* series.

Time-Life Books, *Foods of the World* series.

Index

Index of Recipes